Hockey Scouting Report 2001

SHERRY ROSS

GREYSTONE
BOOKS

Douglas & McIntyre Publishing Group
Vancouver / Toronto / New York

To Alice and Leonard Sunshine,
because you can never thank your parents too many times.

Greystone Books
A division of Douglas & McIntyre Ltd.
2323 Quebec Street, Suite 201
Vancouver, British Columbia V5T 4S7

Editing by Anne Rose and Kerry Banks
Cover design by Peter Cocking
Cover photograph of Pavel Bure by Jim McIsaac/Bruce Bennett Studios
Typesetting by MicroMega Designs
Printed and bound in Canada

The publisher gratefully acknowledges the support of the Canada Council for the
Arts and of the British Columbia Ministry of Tourism, Small Business and Culture.
The publisher also wishes to acknowledge the financial support of the Government of Canada
through the Book Publishing Industry Development Program (BPIDP) for its publishing
activities.

SHERRY ROSS

Yrs. of NHL service: 22
Born: Randolph, NJ
Position: press box
Height: no way
Weight: you gotta be kidding
Uniform no.: DKNJ
Shoots: straight

LAST SEASON
Ross is the hockey columnist for the *New York Daily News*.

THE FINESSE GAME
The versatile Ross began her career in 1978-79, covering the New York Rangers for the *Morristown (N.J.) Daily Record*. In addition to working as a sportswriter for the *Bergen (N.J.) Record*, *Newsday*, and the *National*, she became the NHL's first female team broadcaster in 1992, when she was hired as a colour commentator by the New Jersey Devils. In 1994, she became the first woman to call a major professional men's sports championship as the colour analyst for the NHL radio network in the Stanley Cup Finals.

As a freelance writer, Ross has contributed to *Sports Illustrated*, the *Hockey News* and *Beckett Hockey Monthly*, as well as various team programs. She is the secretary-treasurer for the Professional Hockey Writers' Association.

THE PHYSICAL GAME
Ross is still able to manage an 82-game schedule, and thanks to a jogging regime was able to enjoy 40 Bruce Springsteen concerts on the recent tour. Frequent trips to Disney World and riding her horse, Cody, help break up the rink routine.

THE INTANGIBLES
Although her hand-eye coordination may have diminished over the years, her enthusiasm for the game keeps Ross from unplugging her laptop.

ACKNOWLEDGEMENTS
As the boss said so many times on the stage this past year, "You can't get there by yourself."

I can't get here alone, either. This book annually takes the cooperation of so many men — general managers, coaches, assistants, players and scouts — who never cease to amaze me with their generous donations of time and insight. Without them, this book would not be possible. They must remain anonymous to protect their identities from their bosses, and their players, but I know who they are and they cannot be thanked enough.

It's amazing how many sultry summer days are spent on the phone with someone who exhibits a sheer love for the game. That's the point of this book. It's not just for poolies (though when I was thanked by someone during the playoffs for helping him win a pool, that was a darned good feeling), and it's not just for pros. It's for anyone who wants to gain a better understanding of what makes players tick — or, in the case of Matthew Barnaby, get ticked off.

A huge bouquet to Frank Brown, the NHL vice-president of public relations. We've had our share of headaches — not the least of which was me losing a trunkload of resource material Frank went out of his way to recoup in record time — but Frank has never failed to come through for me professionally. Many other teams provided excellent resource guides and assistance, most prominently Chris Botta of the New York Islanders, Chris Brumwell of the Vancouver Canucks, Kevin Dessart, Mike Levine and Rick Minch of the New Jersey Devils, Peter Hanlon of the Calgary Flames and John Rosasco of the New York Rangers.

As usual, I dumped all of this very late on my editors, Anne Rose and Kerry Banks, and my computer wizard Kelly Dresser. Once again they made better saves than Martin Brodeur did in Game 6 against Dallas.

My *Daily News* colleagues — John Dellapina, Ralph Vacchiano and Anthony McCarron (now a baseball guy) — made my real job fun. E. J. Hradeck, my good companion for much of the ride, was always a source of information and a needed laugh.

People often ask me if I have a favourite team, and I do. It's the E Street Band. Watching Bruce, Max Weinberg, Clarence Clemons, Steven Van Zandt, Nils Lofgren, Roy Bittan, Danny Federici and Patti Scialfa work as often as I had the fortune to is a lesson in what talent, great teamwork and a tireless work ethic can do. If only as many players in this book could dedicate themselves to the game as Bruce and the gang have done to music.

CONTENTS

POINT LEADERS

NHL Scoring Statistics 1999-2000

RANK	POS.	PLAYER	GP	G	A	PTS	+/-	PP	S	PCT
1.	R	JAROMIR JAGR	63	42	54	96	25	10	290	14.5
2.	R	PAVEL BURE	74	58	36	94	25	11	360	16.1
3.	R	MARK RECCHI	82	28	63	91	20	7	223	12.6
4.	L	PAUL KARIYA	74	42	44	86	22	11	324	13.0
5.	R	TEEMU SELANNE	79	33	52	85	6	8	236	14.0
6.	R	OWEN NOLAN	78	44	40	84	-1	18	261	16.9
7.	R	TONY AMONTE	82	43	41	84	10	11	260	16.5
8.	C	MIKE MODANO	77	38	43	81	0	11	188	20.2
9.	C	JOE SAKIC	60	28	53	81	30	5	242	11.6
10.	C	STEVE YZERMAN	78	35	44	79	28	15	234	15.0
11.	L	BRENDAN SHANAHAN	78	41	37	78	24	13	283	14.5
12.	C	JEREMY ROENICK	75	34	44	78	11	6	192	17.7
13.	L	JOHN LECLAIR	82	40	37	77	8	13	249	16.1
14.	R	VALERI BURE	82	35	40	75	-7	13	308	11.4
15.	R	PAVOL DEMITRA	71	28	47	75	34	8	241	11.6
16.	L	LUC ROBITAILLE	71	36	38	74	11	13	221	16.3
17.	C	MATS SUNDIN	73	32	41	73	16	10	184	17.4
18.	C	DOUG GILMOUR	74	25	48	73	-9	10	113	22.1
19.	C	RON FRANCIS	78	23	50	73	10	7	150	15.3
20.	D	NICKLAS LIDSTROM	81	20	53	73	19	9	218	9.2
21.	R	MILAN HEJDUK	82	36	36	72	14	13	228	15.8
22.	L	PATRIK ELIAS	72	35	37	72	16	9	183	19.1
23.	C	DOUG WEIGHT	77	21	51	72	6	3	167	12.6
24.	C	RAY WHITNEY	81	29	42	71	16	5	198	14.6
25.	C	ADAM OATES	82	15	56	71	13	5	93	16.1
26.	R	MARIUSZ CZERKAWSKI	79	35	35	70	-16	16	276	12.7
27.	C	VINCENT DAMPHOUSSE	82	21	49	70	4	3	204	10.3
28.	C	*SCOTT GOMEZ	82	19	51	70	14	7	204	9.3
29.	C	VIKTOR KOZLOV	80	17	53	70	24	6	223	7.6
30.	C	PETR SYKORA	79	25	43	68	24	5	222	11.3
31.	C	PETR NEDVED	76	24	44	68	2	6	201	11.9
32.	L	MIROSLAV SATAN	81	33	34	67	16	5	265	12.5
33.	C	VINCENT LECAVALIER	80	25	42	67	-25	6	166	15.1
34.	C	CHRIS DRURY	82	20	47	67	8	7	213	9.4
35.	R	ZIGMUND PALFFY	64	27	39	66	18	4	186	14.5
36.	C	ALEXEI KOVALEV	82	26	40	66	-3	9	254	10.2
37.	C	PIERRE TURGEON	52	26	40	66	30	8	139	18.7
38.	L	MARKUS NASLUND	82	27	38	65	-5	6	271	10.0
39.	C	ROBERT LANG	78	23	42	65	-9	13	142	16.2
40.	C	STEVE SULLIVAN	80	22	43	65	19	2	180	12.2
41.	R	THEOREN FLEURY	80	15	49	64	-4	1	246	6.1
42.	C	JAROME IGINLA	77	29	34	63	0	12	256	11.3
43.	L	STEVE THOMAS	81	26	37	63	1	9	151	17.2
44.	C	JEFF O'NEILL	80	25	38	63	-9	4	189	13.2
45.	R	GLEN MURRAY	78	29	33	62	13	10	202	14.4

GP = games played; G = goals; A = assists; PTS = points; +/- = goals-for minus goals-against while player is on ice; PP = power-play goals; S = no. of shots; PCT = percentage of goals to shots; * = rookie

RANK	POS.	PLAYER	GP	G	A	PTS	+/-	PP	S	PCT
46.	C	SERGEI FEDOROV	68	27	35	62	8	4	263	10.3
47.	C	CLIFF RONNING	82	26	36	62	-13	7	248	10.5
48.	C	ANDREW CASSELS	79	17	45	62	8	6	109	15.6
49.	D	CHRIS PRONGER	79	14	48	62	52	8	192	7.3
50.	L	JEFF FRIESEN	82	26	35	61	-2	11	191	13.6
51.	C	JOE THORNTON	81	23	37	60	-5	5	171	13.5
52.	C	ALEXEI ZHAMNOV	71	23	37	60	7	5	175	13.1
53.	C	RADEK BONK	80	23	37	60	-2	10	167	13.8
54.	C	ERIC LINDROS	55	27	32	59	11	10	187	14.4
55.	L	BRETT HULL	79	24	35	59	-21	11	223	10.8
56.	R	DANIEL ALFREDSSON	57	21	38	59	11	4	164	12.8
57.	C	MARTIN STRAKA	71	20	39	59	24	3	146	13.7
58.	C	JOZEF STUMPEL	57	17	41	58	23	3	126	13.5
59.	C	STEVE RUCCHIN	71	19	38	57	9	10	131	14.5
60.	D	ROB BLAKE	77	18	39	57	10	12	327	5.5
61.	R	MARIAN HOSSA	78	29	27	56	5	5	240	12.1
62.	R	JONAS HOGLUND	82	29	27	56	-2	9	215	13.5
63.	R	JASON ARNOTT	76	22	34	56	22	7	244	9.0
64.	C	BRYAN SMOLINSKI	79	20	36	56	2	2	160	12.5
65.	C	VACLAV PROSPAL	79	22	33	55	-2	5	204	10.8
66.	D	ERIC DESJARDINS	81	14	41	55	20	8	207	6.8
67.	D	PHIL HOUSLEY	78	11	44	55	-12	5	176	6.3
68.	L	RYAN SMYTH	82	28	26	54	-2	11	238	11.8
69.	C	MICHAEL NYLANDER	77	24	30	54	6	5	122	19.7
70.	D	SERGEI GONCHAR	73	18	36	54	26	5	181	9.9
71.	C	MARK MESSIER	66	17	37	54	-15	6	131	13.0
72.	C	MICHAL HANDZUS	81	25	28	53	19	3	166	15.1
73.	L	GARY ROBERTS	69	23	30	53	-10	12	150	15.3
74.	C	MARC SAVARD	78	22	31	53	-2	4	184	12.0
75.	C	MIKE SILLINGER	80	23	29	52	-30	8	146	15.8
76.	D	RAY BOURQUE	79	18	34	52	-2	13	260	6.9
77.	D	SANDIS OZOLINSH	82	16	36	52	17	6	210	7.6
78.	L	SHAWN MCEACHERN	69	29	22	51	2	10	219	13.2
79.	R	SHANE DOAN	81	26	25	51	6	1	221	11.8
80.	C	CURTIS BROWN	74	22	29	51	19	5	149	14.8
81.	C	DARCY TUCKER	77	21	30	51	-12	1	138	15.2
82.	L	*ALEX TANGUAY	76	17	34	51	6	5	74	23.0
83.	D	OLEG TVERDOVSKY	82	15	36	51	5	5	153	9.8
84.	C	PETER FORSBERG	49	14	37	51	9	3	105	13.3
85.	C	*MICHAEL YORK	82	26	24	50	-17	8	177	14.7
86.	L	TODD BERTUZZI	80	25	25	50	-2	4	173	14.5
87.	L	ANDREW BRUNETTE	81	23	27	50	-32	9	107	21.5
88.	R	RADEK DVORAK	81	18	32	50	5	2	157	11.5
89.	C	DAYMOND LANGKOW	82	18	32	50	1	5	222	8.1
90.	L	CHRIS SIMON	75	29	20	49	11	7	201	14.4
91.	L	MARTIN RUCINSKY	80	25	24	49	1	7	242	10.3
92.	C	CHRIS GRATTON	72	15	34	49	-23	4	202	7.4
93.	D	ROBERT SVEHLA	82	9	40	49	23	3	143	6.3
94.	R	SAMI KAPANEN	76	24	24	48	10	7	229	10.5
95.	R	PAT VERBEEK	68	22	26	48	22	7	138	15.9
96.	L	FREDRIK MODIN	80	22	26	48	-26	3	167	13.2
97.	C	*SIMON GAGNE	80	20	28	48	11	8	159	12.6
98.	R	ALEX SELIVANOV	67	27	20	47	2	10	122	22.1
99.	L	ANSON CARTER	59	22	25	47	8	4	144	15.3
100.	R	MIKE JOHNSON	80	21	26	47	6	6	132	15.9

GP = games played; G = goals; A = assists; PTS = points; +/- = goals-for minus goals-against while player is on ice; PP = power-play goals; S = no. of shots; PCT = percentage of goals to shots; * = rookie

GOAL LEADERS   ASSIST LEADERS

RANK	PLAYER	G	PLAYER	A
1.	PAVEL BURE	58	MARK RECCHI	63
2.	OWEN NOLAN	44	ADAM OATES	56
3.	TONY AMONTE	43	JAROMIR JAGR	54
4.	JAROMIR JAGR	42	JOE SAKIC	53
5.	PAUL KARIYA	42	NICKLAS LIDSTROM	53
6.	BRENDAN SHANAHAN	41	VIKTOR KOZLOV	53
7.	JOHN LECLAIR	40	TEEMU SELANNE	52
8.	MIKE MODANO	38	DOUG WEIGHT	51
9.	LUC ROBITAILLE	36	*SCOTT GOMEZ	51
10.	MILAN HEJDUK	36	RON FRANCIS	50
11.	STEVE YZERMAN	35	VINCENT DAMPHOUSSE	49
12.	VALERI BURE	35	THEOREN FLEURY	49
13.	PATRIK ELIAS	35	DOUG GILMOUR	48
14.	MARIUSZ CZERKAWSKI	35	CHRIS PRONGER	48
15.	JEREMY ROENICK	34	PAVOL DEMITRA	47
16.	TEEMU SELANNE	33	CHRIS DRURY	47
17.	MIROSLAV SATAN	33	ANDREW CASSELS	45
18.	MATS SUNDIN	32	PAUL KARIYA	44
19.	RAY WHITNEY	29	STEVE YZERMAN	44
20.	JAROME IGINLA	29	JEREMY ROENICK	44
21.	GLEN MURRAY	29	PETR NEDVED	44
22.	MARIAN HOSSA	29	PHIL HOUSLEY	44
23.	JONAS HOGLUND	29	MIKE MODANO	43
24.	SHAWN MCEACHERN	29	PETR SYKORA	43
25.	CHRIS SIMON	29	STEVE SULLIVAN	43
26.	MARK RECCHI	28	RAY WHITNEY	42
27.	JOE SAKIC	28	VINCENT LECAVALIER	42
28.	PAVOL DEMITRA	28	ROBERT LANG	42
29.	RYAN SMYTH	28	TONY AMONTE	41
30.	ZIGMUND PALFFY	27	MATS SUNDIN	41
31.	MARKUS NASLUND	27	JOZEF STUMPEL	41
32.	SERGEI FEDOROV	27	ERIC DESJARDINS	41
33.	ERIC LINDROS	27	OWEN NOLAN	40
34.	ALEX SELIVANOV	27	VALERI BURE	40
35.	ALEXEI KOVALEV	26	ALEXEI KOVALEV	40
36.	PIERRE TURGEON	26	PIERRE TURGEON	40
37.	STEVE THOMAS	26	ROBERT SVEHLA	40
38.	CLIFF RONNING	26	ZIGMUND PALFFY	39
39.	JEFF FRIESEN	26	MARTIN STRAKA	39
40.	SHANE DOAN	26	ROB BLAKE	39
41.	*MICHAEL YORK	26	LUC ROBITAILLE	38
42.	MARK PARRISH	26	MARKUS NASLUND	38
43.	SERGEI BEREZIN	26	JEFF O'NEILL	38
44.	SERGEI ZHOLTOK	26	DANIEL ALFREDSSON	38
45.	DOUG GILMOUR	25	STEVE RUCCHIN	38
46.	PETR SYKORA	25	IGOR LARIONOV	38
47.	VINCENT LECAVALIER	25	BRENDAN SHANAHAN	37
48.	JEFF O'NEILL	25	JOHN LECLAIR	37
49.	MICHAL HANDZUS	25	PATRIK ELIAS	37
50.	TODD BERTUZZI	25	STEVE THOMAS	37

P.I.M. LEADERS

RANK	PLAYER	PIM
1.	DENNY LAMBERT	219
2.	TODD SIMPSON	202
3.	TIE DOMI	198
4.	MATTHEW BARNABY	197
5.	ERIC CAIRNS	196
6.	SEAN BROWN	192
7.	IAN LAPERRIERE	185
8.	KRZYSZTOF OLIWA	184
9.	PAUL LAUS	172
10.	PETR SVOBODA	170
11.	PETER WORRELL	169
12.	BOB BOUGHNER	166
13.	DARCY TUCKER	163
14.	JEFF ODGERS	162
15.	CRAIG BERUBE	162
16.	ROB RAY	158
17.	KELLY BUCHBERGER	152
18.	RONNIE STERN	151
19.	*TYSON NASH	150
20.	DARIUS KASPARAITIS	146
21.	CHRIS SIMON	146
22.	*ANDRE ROY	145
23.	MATT JOHNSON	144
24.	RYAN VANDENBUSSCHE	143
25.	LUKE RICHARDSON	140

P-PLAY LEADERS

PLAYER	PP
OWEN NOLAN	18
MARIUSZ CZERKAWSKI	16
STEVE YZERMAN	15
VALERI BURE	13
MILAN HEJDUK	13
RAY BOURQUE	13
BRENDAN SHANAHAN	13
LUC ROBITAILLE	13
JOHN LECLAIR	13
ROBERT LANG	13
JAROME IGINLA	12
GARY ROBERTS	12
ROB BLAKE	12
PAUL KARIYA	11
TONY AMONTE	11
MIKE MODANO	11
BRETT HULL	11
RYAN SMYTH	11
BILL GUERIN	11
PAVEL BURE	11
ADAM GRAVES	11
JEFF FRIESEN	11
STEVE RUCCHIN	10
RAY FERRARO	10
DOUG GILMOUR	10

GOALIE
WIN LEADERS

RANK	PLAYER	W
1.	MARTIN BRODEUR	43
2.	ROMAN TUREK	42
3.	OLAF KOLZIG	41
4.	CURTIS JOSEPH	36
5.	ARTURS IRBE	34
6.	ED BELFOUR	32
7.	PATRICK ROY	32
8.	CHRIS OSGOOD	30
9.	GUY HEBERT	28
10.	STEVE SHIELDS	27
11.	TOMMY SALO	27
12.	FRED BRATHWAITE	25
13.	JOCELYN THIBAULT	25
14.	JOHN VANBIESBROUC	25
15.	MIKE VERNON	24
16.	*J-SEBASTIEN AUBIN	23
17.	JEFF HACKETT	23
18.	MIKE RICHTER	22
19.	RON TUGNUTT	22
20.	*BRIAN BOUCHER	20
21.	STEPHANE FISET	20
22.	*MARTIN BIRON	19
23.	MIKE DUNHAM	19
24.	PATRICK LALIME	19
25.	SEAN BURKE	19

GOALIE
G.A.A. LEADERS

PLAYER	GAA
*BRIAN BOUCHER	1.91
ROMAN TUREK	1.95
ED BELFOUR	2.10
JOSE THEODORE	2.10
JOHN VANBIESBROUC	2.20
DOMINIK HASEK	2.21
MARTIN BRODEUR	2.24
OLAF KOLZIG	2.24
PATRICK ROY	2.28
PATRICK LALIME	2.33
TOMMY SALO	2.33
MIKHAIL SHTALENKO	2.35
CHRIS OSGOOD	2.40
JEFF HACKETT	2.40
ARTURS IRBE	2.42
*MARTIN BIRON	2.42
MIKE VERNON	2.47
CURTIS JOSEPH	2.49
GUY HEBERT	2.51
RON TUGNUTT	2.52
JAMIE STORR	2.53
SEAN BURKE	2.55
STEVE SHIELDS	2.56
*J-SEBASTIEN AUBIN	2.58
TREVOR KIDD	2.63

ANAHEIM MIGHTY DUCKS

Players' Statistics 1999-2000

POS.	NO.	PLAYER	GP	G	A	PTS	+/-	PIM	PP	SH	GW	GT	S	PCT
L	9	PAUL KARIYA	74	42	44	86	22	24	11	3	3		324	13.0
R	8	TEEMU SELANNE	79	33	52	85	6	12	8		6	2	236	14.0
C	20	STEVE RUCCHIN	71	19	38	57	9	16	10		2	2	131	14.5
D	10	OLEG TVERDOVSKY	82	15	36	51	5	30	5		5		153	9.8
C	11	KIP MILLER	74	10	32	42	0	14	2		2		82	12.2
C	17	MATT CULLEN	80	13	26	39	5	24	1		1		137	9.5
D	2	FREDRIK OLAUSSON	70	15	19	34	-13	28	8		1	1	120	12.5
C	22	JORGEN JONSSON	81	12	19	31	-8	16	1	2	1		116	10.3
L	21	TED DONATO	81	11	19	30	-3	26	2		3		138	8.0
L	16	MARTY McINNIS	62	10	18	28	-4	26	2	1	2		129	7.8
R	29	*LADISLAV KOHN	77	5	16	21	-17	27	1		1	1	123	4.1
L	12	MIKE LECLERC	69	8	11	19	-15	70			2		105	7.6
R	19	JEFF NIELSEN	79	8	10	18	4	14	1				113	7.1
C	14	ANTTI AALTO	63	7	11	18	-13	26	1		1		102	6.9
D	7	PAVEL TRNKA	57	2	15	17	12	34				1	54	3.7
C	15	TONY HRKAC	67	4	9	13	-3	8	1				39	10.3
D	24	RUSLAN SALEI	71	5	5	10	3	94	1				116	4.3
D	28	NICLAS HAVELID	50	2	7	9	0	20			2		70	2.9
D	5	KEVIN HALLER	67	3	5	8	-8	61			2		50	6.0
R	33	ED WARD	52	6	1	7	-7	59		2			56	10.7
D	27	PASCAL TREPANIER	37		4	4	2	54					33	
L	32	STU GRIMSON	50	1	2	3	0	116					14	7.1
D	23	JASON MARSHALL	55		3	3	-10	88					41	
D	6	*VITALY VISHNEVSKI	31	1	1	2	0	26	1				17	5.9
G	31	GUY HEBERT	68		2	2	0	2						
L	18	*MAXIM BALMOCHNYKH	6	1	1	2	2						6	
L	8	JEREMY STEVENSON	3				-1	7					2	
R	18	*FRANK BANHAM	3				0	2					4	
G	30	DOMINIC ROUSSEL	20				0	6						

GP = games played; G = goals; A = assists; PTS = points; +/- = goals-for minus goals-against while player is on ice; PIM = penalties in minutes; PP = power-play goals; SH = shorthanded goals; GW = game-winning goals; GT = game-tying goals; S = no. of shots; PCT = percentage of goals to shots; * = rookie

MAXIM BALMOCHNYKH

Yrs. of NHL service: 0
Born: Lipetsk, Russia; Mar. 7, 1979
Position: left wing
Height: 6-1
Weight: 200
Uniform no.: 18
Shoots: left

Career statistics:

GP	G	A	TP	PIM
6	0	1	1	2

1999-2000 statistics:

GP	G	A	TP	+/-	PIM	PP	SH	GW	GT	S	PCT
6	0	1	1	+2	2	0	0	0	0	6	0.0

LAST SEASON

Will be entering first NHL season. Appeared in 40 games with Cincinnati (IHL), scoring 9-21 — 21. Missed nine games with knee injury.

THE FINESSE GAME

Anaheim has been desperately seeking a second line ever since they drafted Paul Kariya; Balmochnykh may turn out the be the missing piece of the puzzle.

Balmochnykh would give the Ducks a different look, since he is a power forward. He possesses excellent puckhandling skills and is willing and able to fight his way through traffic. He was considered a finesse player when he was drafted, but he has shown a liking for trench warfare.

An excellent skater with speed, Balmochnykh's defensive game is well along. He will need to play with finishers, though, since he is a better playmaker than shooter. His shot is only fair, but he will get his goals from a 10-foot radius of the crease. His work ethic at this point is inconsistent. He needs to bring it every night.

THE PHYSICAL GAME

Balmochnykh is tough and has a mean streak. He had 82 penalty minutes with Cincinnati and served an eight-game suspension for hitting another player over the head with his stick. He isn't huge, but he is very strong and has a fierce attitude.

THE INTANGIBLES

Balmochnykh nearly stuck with the Mighty Ducks after training camp, but a knee injury derailed him just six games in and the wise decision was made to let him go back to the minors to rehab and to acclimate himself to the pro game. He needs to mature more physically and emotionally. Some nagging injuries slowed his development last season. He also had heart surgery before he was drafted (in 1997). This kid has been through a lot.

PROJECTION

He's a copy editor's nightmare, but get used to the name: you're going to see it a lot in the Anaheim game summaries. A 20-point rookie season would mark a commendable beginning for Balmochnykh.

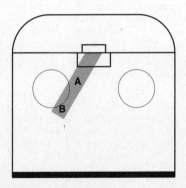

MATT CULLEN

Yrs. of NHL service: 3
Born: Virginia, Minn; Nov. 2, 1976
Position: centre
Height: 6-1
Weight: 195
Uniform no.: 11
Shoots: left

Career statistics:

GP	G	A	TP	PIM
216	30	61	91	94

1997-98 statistics:

GP	G	A	TP	+/-	PIM	PP	SH	GW	GT	S	PCT
61	6	21	27	4	23	2	0	0	0	75	8.0

1998-99 statistics:

GP	G	A	TP	+/-	PIM	PP	SH	GW	GT	S	PCT
75	11	14	25	-12	47	5	1	1	1	112	9.8

1999-2000 statistics:

GP	G	A	TP	+/-	PIM	PP	SH	GW	GT	S	PCT
80	13	26	39	+5	24	1	0	1	0	137	9.5

LAST SEASON

Career high in goals, assists and points. Missed two games due to coach's decision.

THE FINESSE GAME

Cullen again saw some playing time with Paul Kariya and Teemu Selanne, sometimes both. He has first-line potential and above-average dedication.

Cullen also has good speed and a good slap shot, and he handles the puck well in traffic and is willing to take it there. He is strong on his skates with a quick first step. He has soft hands for passing and a nice scoring touch, but he needs to shoot more. He is more of a playmaker, which will be an advantage if he continues to play with finishers like Kariya and Selanne. When his wingers are covered, he shouldn't force the pass but take the shot.

An intelligent player with good hockey vision, Cullen has improved his defensive awareness, but it is the one area where he needs to show more improvement. Think of how Steve Rucchin handles his safety-valve role when he is on the top line. He's the kind of two-way centre Cullen has to emulate.

THE PHYSICAL GAME

Cullen is strong and fast, and he has an aggressive streak to go along with his work ethic. He plays hard every shift.

THE INTANGIBLES

Cullen is valued for his character as well as his skills. He is going to get another shot at the top job in training camp, but he could be the player most affected by the arrival of German Titov, since Cullen will probably slip below Steve Rucchin on the depth chart at centre. Cullen seemed to lose some confidence down the stretch and was a healthy scratch for the Ducks' last two games.

PROJECTION

Cullen's high end would appear to be around 50 points — but only if he gets a full-time job.

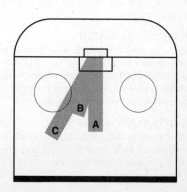

TED DONATO

Yrs. of NHL service: 8
Born: Dedham, Mass.; Apr. 28, 1969
Position: centre
Height: 5-10
Weight: 181
Uniform no.: 21
Shoots: left

Career statistics:

GP	G	A	TP	PIM
614	134	174	308	342

1996-97 statistics:

GP	G	A	TP	+/-	PIM	PP	SH	GW	GT	S	PCT
67	25	26	51	-9	37	6	2	2	0	172	14.5

1997-98 statistics:

GP	G	A	TP	+/-	PIM	PP	SH	GW	GT	S	PCT
79	16	23	39	+6	54	3	0	5	1	129	12.4

1998-99 statistics:

GP	G	A	TP	+/-	PIM	PP	SH	GW	GT	S	PCT
82	11	16	27	-8	41	3	0	0	0	106	10.4

1999-2000 statistics:

GP	G	A	TP	+/-	PIM	PP	SH	GW	GT	S	PCT
81	11	19	30	-3	26	2	0	3	0	138	8.0

LAST SEASON

Tied for third on team in game-winning goals. Missed one game due to coach's decision.

THE FINESSE GAME

Donato is a small man who is able to survive in a big man's game because of his hockey sense. He is a good power-play perfomer on the second unit. When he gets the chance, he can work down low or use a shot from the point.

He is also a strong penalty killer. He can thrive as a forward on the shorthanded unit because opponents are more concerned about getting the puck than hitting, and Donato is usually in the middle part of the ice. He gets a lot of defensive assignments but creates offense with his anticipation.

Donato is like a quarterback, very aware of what is going on around him and always communicating with his teammates so that they know what is going on, too. He has good hands and makes hard or soft passes as the occasion warrants.

THE PHYSICAL GAME

Donato is cunning and doesn't allow himself to get into situations where he's close to the boards and could get taken out. He is an elusive skater. He can be outmuscled, but he hustles for the puck and often manages to keep it alive along the boards.

THE INTANGIBLES

Donato is a veteran character player who can fill many roles. He was an unrestricted free agent after last season. He had a weak second half, with only four goals after the All-Star break.

PROJECTION

Donato's game is best suited to his being a third-line checker — in that position he could chip in 15 goals.

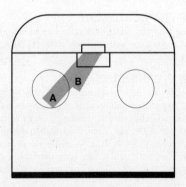

GUY HEBERT

Yrs. of NHL service: 8
Born: Troy, N.Y.; Jan. 7, 1967
Position: goaltender
Height: 5-11
Weight: 185
Uniform no.: 31
Catches: left

Career statistics:

GP	MIN	GA	SO	GAA	A	PIM
437	24939	1150	26	2.77	6	22

1996-97 statistics:

GP	MIN	GAA	W	L	T	SO	GA	S	SAPCT	PIM
67	3863	2.67	29	25	12	4	172	2133	.919	4

1997-98 statistics:

GP	MIN	GAA	W	L	T	SO	GA	S	SAPCT	PIM
46	2660	2.93	13	24	6	3	130	1339	.903	4

1998-99 statistics:

GP	MIN	GAA	W	L	T	SO	GA	S	SAPCT	PIM
69	4083	2.42	31	29	9	6	165	2114	.922	0

1999-2000 statistics:

GP	MIN	GAA	W	L	T	SO	GA	S	SAPCT	PIM
68	3976	2.51	28	31	9	4	166	1805	.908	2

LAST SEASON

Fifth among NHL goalies in minutes played. Missed two games due to neck spasms.

THE PHYSICAL GAME

Hebert lost his angles, lost his confidence and lost a lot of games the Ducks should have won last season, by allowing too many soft goals.

Hebert, who only used to occasionally lapse into the bad habit of staying too deep in his net, did so far too frequently last season. He is not a very big goalie, so he has to pay sharp attention to his angles and coming out to the top of his crease to take away as much of the net as possible. He has good reflexes and stands up well when he is on. He deadens pucks with his pads and doesn't leave big rebounds.

Hebert uses his stick effectively around the net to control rebounds and deflect passes, but he doesn't handle the puck aggressively outside his net. He doesn't have to whip the puck up-ice like Martin Brodeur, but he should be secure enough to make little passes, to avoid pressure and help his defensemen.

Hebert's lateral movement has improved. He takes away a lot of the net low and forces shooters to go high. Since he is a small goalie, shooters expect him to go down and scramble, but he stands his ground effectively.

THE MENTAL GAME

Hebert needs to work hard with a goalie coach to regain confidence in his abilities. He showed no tendency last season to bounce back from a bad game. Especially in the stretch, when the Ducks still had a glimmer of playoff hope, Hebert faltered time and again.

THE INTANGIBLES

The only player who has been with the team since the 1993 Expansion Draft, this Duck is an endangered species. Anaheim dangled Hebert in the Expansion Draft, but he has two years remaining on his original $12-million deal and no one bit. Them GM Pierre Gauthier traded for the young Jean-Sebastien Giguere. Those two moves should motivate Hebert.

PROJECTION

His teammates and coaches have lost faith in Hebert. He will have to win it back with a strong start, and a 30-win season.

PAUL KARIYA

Yrs. of NHL service: 6
Born: North Vancouver, B.C.; Oct. 16, 1974
Position: left wing
Height: 5-11
Weight: 175
Uniform no.: 9
Shoots: left

Career statistics:

GP	G	A	TP	PIM
376	210	254	464	117

1996-97 statistics:

GP	G	A	TP	+/-	PIM	PP	SH	GW	GT	S	PCT
69	44	55	99	+36	6	15	3	10	0	340	12.9

1997-98 statistics:

GP	G	A	TP	+/-	PIM	PP	SH	GW	GT	S	PCT
22	17	14	31	+12	23	3	0	2	1	103	16.5

1998-99 statistics:

GP	G	A	TP	+/-	PIM	PP	SH	GW	GT	S	PCT
82	39	62	101	+17	40	11	2	4	0	429	9.1

1999-2000 statistics:

GP	G	A	TP	+/-	PIM	PP	SH	GW	GT	S	PCT
74	42	44	86	+22	24	11	3	3	0	324	13.0

LAST SEASON

Led team in plus-minus, power-play goals and short-handed goals. Third in NHL in shots. Fourth in NHL and led team in points. Tied for fourth in NHL and led team in goals. Tied for fifth in NHL in power-play points (31). Second on team in assists. Tied for third on team in shorthanded goals. Missed one game with sore hip. Missed seven games with broken left foot.

THE FINESSE GAME

One of the best skaters in the NHL, Kariya is so smooth and fluid his movements appear effortless. He's also explosive, with a good change of direction; he can turn a defender inside out on a one-on-one rush. His speed is a weapon, since he forces defenders to play off him for fear of being burnt, and that opens the ice for his playmaking options. He combines his skating with no-look passes that are uncanny.

Teemu Selanne is the perfect linemate for him, because the Finnish Flash breaks as soon as he sees Kariya with control of the puck. Kariya puts on a burst of speed and can lift his alley-oop pass over the sticks of defenders just ahead of Selanne, for him to skate into. Kariya uses his speed defensively, too, and is quick on the backcheck to break up passes. He kills penalties by hounding the point men and pressuring them into bad passes, which he turns into scoring chances.

A magician with the puck, Kariya can make a play when it looks as if there are no possible options. He likes to use the net for protection, like his idol Wayne Gretzky, and make passes from behind the goal line. His release on his shot is excellent.

Kariya is a low-maintenance superstar. He has worked on his weaknesses, becoming stronger on the puck, less fancy in his passing and more willing to shoot. He is able to carry a team on his back.

THE PHYSICAL GAME

Kariya has powerful thighs and legs and has improved his upper body. He was able to make a successful comeback from a career-threatening concussion. He is something of a workout nut — so much so that he actually had to scale back his off-season conditioning this year. Kariya believed he had a difficult training camp and poor start last season because he pushed himself too hard in preparation.

THE INTANGIBLES

Kariya scored nearly 20 per cent of his team's goals and was the Ducks' best all-around player. Still, he suffered some criticism because he is such a quiet leader and because the Ducks failed to make the playoffs. His plus-22 was a career best.

PROJECTION

We thought 100 points was a given last year for Kariya, and if Selanne hadn't gone into a mystifying funk, it would have been. Adding German Titov as his line's centre should boost Kariya's totals.

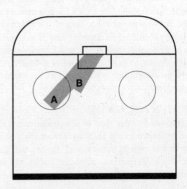

JASON MARSHALL

Yrs. of NHL service: 5
Born: Cranbrook, B.C.; Feb. 22, 1971
Position: right defense
Height: 6-2
Weight: 205
Uniform no.: 23
Shoots: right

Career statistics:

GP	G	A	TP	PIM
299	6	26	32	606

1996-97 statistics:

GP	G	A	TP	+/-	PIM	PP	SH	GW	GT	S	PCT
73	1	9	10	+6	140	0	0	0	0	34	2.9

1997-98 statistics:

GP	G	A	TP	+/-	PIM	PP	SH	GW	GT	S	PCT
72	3	6	9	-8	189	1	0	0	0	68	4.4

1998-99 statistics:

GP	G	A	TP	+/-	PIM	PP	SH	GW	GT	S	PCT
72	1	7	8	-5	142	0	0	0	0	63	1.6

1999-2000 statistics:

GP	G	A	TP	+/-	PIM	PP	SH	GW	GT	S	PCT
55	0	3	3	-10	88	0	0	0	0	41	-

PROJECTION

Marshall will be hard-pressed to get points in the double-digits, but his PIM will be close to 100 if he gets the ice time. He could be on the move to another team, but Anaheim's frequent benching of him down the stretch diminished his trade value.

LAST SEASON

Third on team in penalty minutes. Missed 27 games due to coach's decision.

THE FINESSE GAME

Marshall is big and mobile with good puck skills. He has been slow to come to hand, mostly from having to learn the mental discipline of playing his position, and odds are we've seen the best of what he has to offer.

He will never be involved much offensively. He lacks the instincts to be much of a factor from the point and his shot is only average. He is a good skater for his size.

Marshall can be his own worst enemy. If he makes a mistake he is very hard on himself. He doesn't have much confidence in his game and doesn't take well to benchings or to challenges to his job.

THE PHYSICAL GAME

Marshall is big and likes to play a physical game. He sticks up for his teammates and will take the initiative to set a physical tone. He is a hard worker and shows up most nights. He can have games where he gets a little headstrong and starts running around out of position, committing sins of commission rather than omission.

THE INTANGIBLES

Marshall can be in the mix for Anaheim since they are going to bank heavily on a couple of young kids. They will need a steady head to guide them, and if Marshall is willing to accept a support role as a mentor, he might be a number five.

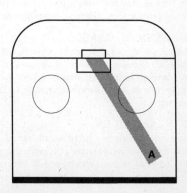

MARTY MCINNIS

Yrs. of NHL service: 8
Born: Hingham, Mass.; June 2, 1970
Position: left wing
Height: 5-11
Weight: 183
Uniform no.: 16
Shoots: right

Career statistics:

GP	G	A	TP	PIM
565	130	201	331	219

1996-97 statistics:

GP	G	A	TP	+/-	PIM	PP	SH	GW	GT	S	PCT
80	23	26	49	-8	22	5	1	4	1	182	12.6

1997-98 statistics:

GP	G	A	TP	+/-	PIM	PP	SH	GW	GT	S	PCT
75	19	25	44	+1	34	5	4	0	0	128	14.8

1998-99 statistics:

GP	G	A	TP	+/-	PIM	PP	SH	GW	GT	S	PCT
81	19	35	54	-15	42	11	1	5	0	146	13.0

1999-2000 statistics:

GP	G	A	TP	+/-	PIM	PP	SH	GW	GT	S	PCT
62	10	18	28	-4	26	2	1	2	0	129	7.8

LAST SEASON
Missed 20 games with groin strain.

THE FINESSE GAME
The versatile McInnis does a lot of the little things well. He plays positionally, is smart and reliable defensively, and turns his checking work into scoring opportunities with quick passes and his work down low. He is a very patient shooter.

McInnis isn't fast but he is deceptive, with a quick first few strides to the puck. He seems to be more aware of where the puck is than his opponents are, so while they're looking for the puck he's already heading towards it. McInnis saw some time on the first power-play unit, but that is a bit of a stretch for him.

McInnis is a good penalty killer because of his tenacity and anticipation. He reads plays well on offense and defense. Playing the off-wing opens up his shot for a quick release; he's always a shorthanded threat. He's an ideal third-line winger because he can check and provide some offensive counterpunch.

THE PHYSICAL GAME
McInnis is not big or tough, but he is sturdy and will use his body to bump and scrap for the puck. He always tries to get in the way, though he loses a lot of battles in tight to larger forwards, because he is not that strong.

THE INTANGIBLES
McInnis can be used in a lot of situations and with many different line combinations. His groin injury obviously hindered him last season, and he underwent sports hernia surgery. He should be ready for training camp, assuming the Ducks re-sign him (he was an unretsricted free agent).

PROJECTION
A healty McInnis will pot 15 to 20 goals in a second- or third-line role.

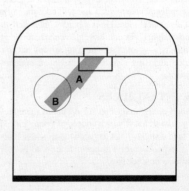

STEVE RUCCHIN

Yrs. of NHL service: 6
Born: London, Ont.; July 4, 1971
Position: centre
Height: 6-3
Weight: 210
Uniform no.: 20
Shoots: left

Career statistics:

GP	G	A	TP	PIM
398	103	197	300	110

1996-97 statistics:

GP	G	A	TP	+/-	PIM	PP	SH	GW	GT	S	PCT
79	19	48	67	+26	24	6	1	2	1	153	12.4

1997-98 statistics:

GP	G	A	TP	+/-	PIM	PP	SH	GW	GT	S	PCT
72	17	36	53	+8	13	8	1	3	0	131	13.0

1998-99 statistics:

GP	G	A	TP	+/-	PIM	PP	SH	GW	GT	S	PCT
69	23	39	62	+11	22	5	1	5	1	145	15.9

1999-2000 statistics:

GP	G	A	TP	+/-	PIM	PP	SH	GW	GT	S	PCT
71	19	38	57	+9	16	10	0	2	2	131	14.5

LAST SEASON

Led team in shooting percentage. Second on team in power-play goals. Third on team in goals, assists, points and plus-minus. Missed 11 games with infected left ankle.

THE FINESSE GAME

The arrival of German Titov is expected to lessen some of the offensive burden off of Rucchin and allow him to play as a number two centre, which is what he should have been all along. He could continue to see time with either Paul Kariya or Teemu Selanne if Craig Hartsburg decides to split up his two offensive weapons.

Rucchin can think offense more in his second-line role, since he doesn't have to focus as much on being the safety valve. He has good size and range, and sharp hockey sense, which enables him to make the most of his above-average skating, passing and shooting skills. He grinds and digs the puck off the wall, and has the vision and the passing skills to find a breaking Kariya or Selanne. He is patient and protects the puck well.

Rucchin is one of the best-kept secrets in the NHL when it comes to face-offs. He ranked second only to Adam Oates last year according to the somewhat questionable stats kept by the league, but he really is good at it. He can win a draw outright, or if he fails, tie up the opposing centre,

THE PHYSICAL GAME

Rucchin can be a real force. He's strong and balanced, willing to forecheck hard and fight for the puck along the boards and in the corners. When he wins the puck,

he's able to create a smart play with it. He has a long reach for holding off defenders and working the puck one-handed, or reaching in defensively to knock the puck away from an attacker.

He often matches up against other teams' big centres.

THE INTANGIBLES

Rucchin is more than just the water boy for Kariya and Selanne. He's one of the important, underrated leaders on the team. He had a tough time coming back from the staph infection in his ankle after January, or his point totals would have been more impressive.

PROJECTION

Rucchin will still get plenty of ice time, if maybe a bit less on the power play, and 55 to 60 points is expected.

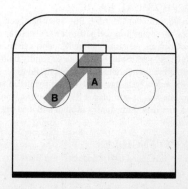

RUSLAN SALEI

Yrs. of NHL service: 4
Born: Minsk, Belarus; Nov. 2, 1974
Position: left defense
Height: 6-1
Weight: 200
Uniform no.: 24
Shoots: left

Career statistics:

GP	G	A	TP	PIM
241	12	30	42	266

1996-97 statistics:

GP	G	A	TP	+/-	PIM	PP	SH	GW	GT	S	PCT
30	0	1	1	-8	37	0	0	0	0	14	0.0

1997-98 statistics:

GP	G	A	TP	+/-	PIM	PP	SH	GW	GT	S	PCT
66	5	10	15	+7	70	1	0	0	1	104	4.8

1998-99 statistics:

GP	G	A	TP	+/-	PIM	PP	SH	GW	GT	S	PCT
74	2	14	16	+1	65	1	0	0	0	123	1.6

1999-2000 statistics:

GP	G	A	TP	+/-	PIM	PP	SH	GW	GT	S	PCT
71	5	5	10	+3	94	1	0	0	0	116	4.3

PROJECTION

Salei will get a prominent full-time rule. Assuming he can stay out of Colin Capmbell's office, he'll be a regular with low point, high PIM totals.

LAST SEASON

Second on team in penalty minutes with career high. Served 10-game suspension. Missed one game due to coach's decision.

THE FINESSE GAME

Salei is a fairly agile skater but doesn't have great breakaway speed. He skates well backwards, is mobile and is not easy to beat one-on-one.

His defensive reads are very good, and he can kill penalties. There is a possibility he could see time on a second power-play unit, because he moves the puck well and appears to have an NHL-calibre point shot. He shoots well off the pass — and it's high velocity.

Salei has become steadier and seems unfazed by the attention his controversial game brings with it. After sitting out 10 of the first 11 games of the season for shoving Mike Modano into the boards, Salei never missed a beat upon his return.

THE PHYSICAL GAME

Goon defenseman? Hardly. But Salei has been suspended three times in the past three seasons for dangerous hits, and he ranks among Modano's list of dirtiest NHL players. Salei is mature and solidly built and he initiates a lot of contact. He is not afraid to hit anyone. He has a little nasty streak that results in some cheap hits, but he can play it hard and clean, too. He will sometimes start running around and lose track of his man.

THE INTANGIBLES

Salei has advanced into the Ducks' top four.

TEEMU SELANNE

Yrs. of NHL service: 8
Born: Helsinki, Finland; July 3, 1970
Position: right wing
Height: 6-0
Weight: 200
Uniform no.: 8
Shoots: right

Career statistics:

GP	G	A	TP	PIM
564	350	383	729	197

1996-97 statistics:

GP	G	A	TP	+/-	PIM	PP	SH	GW	GT	S	PCT
78	51	58	109	+28	34	11	1	8	2	273	18.7

1997-98 statistics:

GP	G	A	TP	+/-	PIM	PP	SH	GW	GT	S	PCT
73	52	34	86	+12	30	10	1	10	3	268	19.4

1998-99 statistics:

GP	G	A	TP	+/-	PIM	PP	SH	GW	GT	S	PCT
75	47	60	107	+18	30	25	0	7	1	281	16.7

1999-2000 statistics:

GP	G	A	TP	+/-	PIM	PP	SH	GW	GT	S	PCT
79	33	52	85	+6	12	8	0	6	2	236	14.0

LAST SEASON

Led team in assists and game-winning goals. Seventh in NHL in assists. Fifth in NHL in power-play assists (23). Second on team in goals, points, shots and shooting percentage. Tied for third on team in power-play goals. Missed three games with groin injury.

THE FINESSE GAME

Selanne has Porsche turbo speed. He gets down low and then simply explodes past defensemen, even when starting from a standstill. He gets tremendous thrust from his legs and has quick feet. Acceleration, balance, change of gears, it's all there.

Everything you could ask for in a shot is there as well. He employs all varieties of attacks and is equally comfortable on either wing. He plays off Paul Kariya's puck control and exquisite lead passes. Often the two players will simply "alley oop" to the other with perfect timing, so that they receive the puck in full stride.

Selanne is constantly in motion. If his first attempt is stopped, he'll pursue the puck behind the net, make a pass and circle out again for a shot. He is almost impossible to catch and is tough to knock down because of his balance. He will set up on the off-wing on the power play and can score on the backhand. His shot is not especially hard, but it is quick and accurate.

Selanne doesn't just try to overpower with his skating, he also outwits opponents. He has tremendous hockey instincts and vision, and is as good a playmaker as a finisher. He has a reputation for being selfish with the puck, but he is more generous with Kariya and feeds him for one-timers.

THE PHYSICAL GAME

Anaheim is pretty much a one-line team, so Kariya, Selanne and — this season — German Titov have to deal with checking pressure every night. Teams set out to bump and grind Selanne from the first shift, and he has to fight his way through the junk. When the referees are slow on the whistle, he takes matters into his own hands, usually with his stick. He is one of the toughest players in the league, European or otherwise. He is big and uses his strength along the wall, but he takes a beating.

THE INTANGIBLES

Selanne falling 14 goals off his league-high total of two seasons ago is baffling. He played with Kariya most of the season (they were occasionally broken up to alleviate checking pressure), and Anaheim still didn't have a number one centre — but that was the case two years ago as well. The most astounding stat is those paltry eight power-play goals, after he scored 25 in 1998-99.

PROJECTION

With Titov added to the mix, Selanne should rebound to the 50-goal, 100-point level.

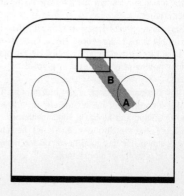

GERMAN TITOV

Yrs. of NHL service: 7
Born: Moscow, Russia; Oct. 16, 1965
Position: centre/left wing
Height: 6-1
Weight: 190
Uniform no.: 13
Shoots: left

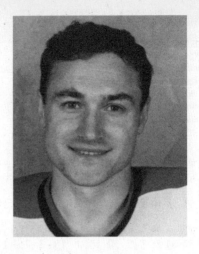

Career statistics:

GP	G	A	TP	PIM
487	135	195	330	214

1996-97 statistics:

GP	G	A	TP	+/-	PIM	PP	SH	GW	GT	S	PCT
79	22	30	52	-12	36	12	0	4	0	192	11.5

1997-98 statistics:

GP	G	A	TP	+/-	PIM	PP	SH	GW	GT	S	PCT
68	18	22	40	-1	38	6	1	2	0	133	13.5

1998-99 statistics:

GP	G	A	TP	+/-	PIM	PP	SH	GW	GT	S	PCT
72	11	45	56	+18	34	3	1	3	1	113	9.7

1999-2000 statistics:

GP	G	A	TP	+/-	PIM	PP	SH	GW	GT	S	PCT
70	17	29	46	-1	38	4	2	3	0	122	13.9

LAST SEASON

Signed by Anaheim as free agent from Edmonton, July 1, 2000. Acquired by Edmonton from Pittsburgh for Josef Beranek, Mar. 14, 2000. Tied for second on Oilers in shorthanded goals. Third on Oilers in assists and shooting percentage. Missed five games with shoulder injury.

THE FINESSE GAME

Titov constantly drives his coaches and teammates crazy. He works so hard to get himself in a great scoring position and then . . . he doesn't shoot. If the Ducks plan to use him between Teemu Selanne and Paul Kariya, this shouldn't be a problem. They can finish what Titov starts.

Titov uses a short stick and does a lot of one-handed puckhandling. This gives him good control and makes it harder for the defense to knock the puck loose without knocking him down and taking a penalty. It also gives him a quick release on his under-utilized wrister.

Titov shows great hockey sense in all zones. He is creative, but is a streaky scorer. He lacks consistency and doesn't step up on a nightly basis. He can play on the first power-play unit and is a solid two-way forward.

Titov is an agile skater, if not blazing fast. He is very quick coming off the boards and driving to the circle for a shot, and he has a good inside-out move and change of gears. Strong on his skates, he is tough to knock down. He has good hands on the draw. He kills penalties well and blocks shots.

THE PHYSICAL GAME

Titov uses his size well and is very solid. He takes a hit to make a play, blocks shots and sacrifices his body. He protects the puck in an unusual way, by getting his left leg out to kick away the stick of a defender so that he can't be sweep- or poke-checked. It's a move that requires superb balance.

THE INTANGIBLES

Titov is 35 and will have to be in great shape if he sees as much ice time as expected on Anaheim's top line.

PROJECTION

Titov should be more productive — in the 20-goal, 65-point range.

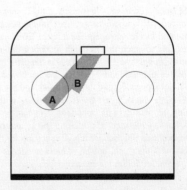

PAVEL TRNKA

Yrs. of NHL service: 3
Born: Plzen, Czech Republic; July 27, 1976
Position: left defense
Height: 6-3
Weight: 200
Uniform no.: 7
Shoots: left

Career statistics:

GP	G	A	TP	PIM
168	5	23	28	134

1997-98 statistics:

GP	G	A	TP	+/-	PIM	PP	SH	GW	GT	S	PCT
48	3	4	7	-4	40	1	0	0	1	46	6.5

1998-99 statistics:

GP	G	A	TP	+/-	PIM	PP	SH	GW	GT	S	PCT
63	0	4	4	-6	60	0	0	0	0	50	.0

1999-2000 statistics:

GP	G	A	TP	+/-	PIM	PP	SH	GW	GT	S	PCT
57	2	15	17	+12	34	0	0	0	1	54	3.7

PROJECTION

Trnka should be in the 20- to 25-point range.

LAST SEASON

Second on team in plus-minus. Career highs in goals, assists and points. Missed 10 games with sprained left ankle. Missed five games with groin strain. Missed 10 games due to coach's decision.

THE FINESSE GAME

Trnka watched an awful lot of games from the press box again last season as part of his continuing NHL education, and injuries didn't help.

He is a highly skilled player, though he will not put a lot of points on the board. He hasn't been a scorer at the minor-league level, either, which indicates it simply might not be there. He uses his finesse skills in a defensive role by making the smart first pass or skating the puck out of the zone. He lacks a shot or the puck movement from the point that would make him a more productive player. Playing with Oleg Tverdovsky may help him improve this aspect of his game.

Trnka's defensive game has improved dramatically. He challenges better and doesn't back in on top of his goalie, which was a common flaw of his. His defensive reads have improved.

THE PHYSICAL GAME

Trnka can handle a lot of ice time, when he gets it. He is a willing hitter but not a big banger. He is more of a bumper.

THE INTANGIBLES

Trnka may benefit from the retirement of Fredrik Olausson, since he lost power-play time when Olausson arrived two seasons ago, and this could be a big season for him. He took a step forward last year after a bit of a backslide the season before. He is still a project.

OLEG TVERDOVSKY

Yrs. of NHL service: 6
Born: Donetsk, Ukraine; May 18, 1976
Position: left defense
Height: 6-0
Weight: 185
Uniform no.: 10
Shoots: left

Career statistics:

GP	G	A	TP	PIM
410	49	143	192	159

1996-97 statistics:

GP	G	A	TP	+/-	PIM	PP	SH	GW	GT	S	PCT
82	10	45	55	-5	30	3	1	2	0	144	6.9

1997-98 statistics:

GP	G	A	TP	+/-	PIM	PP	SH	GW	GT	S	PCT
46	7	12	19	+1	12	4	0	1	1	83	8.4

1998-99 statistics:

GP	G	A	TP	+/-	PIM	PP	SH	GW	GT	S	PCT
82	7	18	25	+11	32	2	0	2	0	117	6.0

1999-2000 statistics:

GP	G	A	TP	+/-	PIM	PP	SH	GW	GT	S	PCT
82	15	36	51	+5	30	5	0	5	0	153	9.8

LAST SEASON

Led team defensemen in points. Second on team in game-winning goals. Third on team in shots. Career high in goals. Only Duck to appear in all 82 games; current ironman streak is 208, third longest in NHL.

THE FINESSE GAME

Tverdovsky is an impressive talent, who passes the puck well and shoots bullets. He is clearly an "offenseman," but he has worked at improving his decision-making process and is not as high-risk as he was in his first few years in the league.

He can still get lazy defensively, casually moving the puck around the wall or banging it off the glass. He prefers to grab the puck and go, or look for a streaking Paul Kariya. He's among the best in the league at the headman pass.

Tverdovsky has Brian Leetch potential. He's an explosive skater and can carry the puck at high tempo. He works the point on the power play, utilizing a nice lateral slide along the blueline, and he kills penalties. He also sees his options and makes his decisions at lightning speed.

THE PHYSICAL GAME

Some of Tverdovsky's defensive weaknesses can be attributed to the fact that he sometimes plays the puck instead of the man, or tries to poke-check without backing it up with his body. Physically, when he makes the right decision he can eliminate the man, and he looks to be improving in this area by at least tying up his man.

He loves to play and is enthusiastic and extremely competitive.

THE INTANGIBLES

The return to the Mighty Ducks, the team that gave Tverdosvky his start, was the right one. He was a terrific fit for Anaheim's top line. He is going to keep getting better.

PROJECTION

We'll live with some of Tverdovsky's defensive lapses as long as he provides those 50 to 55 points and keeps playing as hard as he does every night.

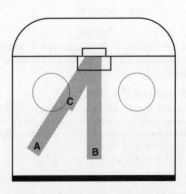

VITALY VISHNEVSKI

Yrs. of NHL service: 1
Born: Kharkov, Russia; Mar. 18, 1980
Position: left defense
Height: 6-2
Weight: 200
Uniform no.: 6
Shoots: left

Career statistics:

GP	G	A	TP	PIM
31	1	1	2	26

1999-2000 statistics:

GP	G	A	TP	+/-	PIM	PP	SH	GW	GT	S	PCT
31	1	1	2	0	26	1	0	0	0	17	5.9

LAST SEASON

First NHL season. Appeared in 31 games with Cincinnati (IHL), scoring 1-3 — 4.

THE FINESSE GAME

Vishnevski was the top-ranked non-North American player in the 1998 draft. He is an excellent skater with a long, powerful stride and good straightaway speed. He has good mobility and good balance. He has no trouble keeping pace with NHL-calibre skaters.

He has good size and strength, and plays a power game. He is a warrior around the crease and along the wall.

Vishnevski has to improve his defensive reads. He moves the puck extremely well and is poised and composed under pressure. But he doesn't have much offensive upside. He just wants to get the puck out of his zone and knock the stuffing out of anyone who tries to skate back in with it. Opponents are going to be hurried into a lot of quick decisions when they come down his side of the ice.

THE PHYSICAL GAME

Vishnevski is a solid 200 pounds and a mean hitter. He ended Ziggy Palffy's season in March with a clean but wicked check. He competes hard. He is an even better skater than Scott Stevens, so expect to see a lot of West Coast versions of those Stevens-style body bombs. He is confident in his checking ability and seeks out big hits at the blueline and in the neutral zone. He will hit anyone, regardless of name, number or salary rank. He is a bigger Darius Kasparaitis, and really gets under people's skin.

THE INTANGIBLES

This is the kid rival GMs were talking about whenever they punched in Pierre Gauthier's number on their speed dial. Gauthier needn't bother to return their messages. Vishnesvki is still a bit green, but if he doesn't start the season with the Ducks it would be a surprise. He probably wasn't quite ready to make the jump, but Gauthier wanted him to develop under his club's watchful eyes. He plays better with better players and would make a great fit with Oleg Tverdovsky.

PROJECTION

Vishnevski *and* Ruslan Salei on the same team? No one is going to be getting any easy points from Anaheim this season.

ATLANTA THRASHERS

Players' Statistics 1999-2000

POS.	NO.	PLAYER	GP	G	A	PTS	+/-	PIM	PP	SH	GW	GT	S	PCT
L	15	ANDREW BRUNETTE	81	23	27	50	-32	30	9		2	1	107	21.5
C	21	RAY FERRARO	81	19	25	44	-33	88	10		3		170	11.2
R	28	DONALD AUDETTE	63	19	24	43	2	57	1	1	4		162	11.7
D	38	YANNICK TREMBLAY	75	10	21	31	-42	22	4	1	2	1	139	7.2
C	9	HNAT DOMENICHELLI	59	11	18	29	-21	16	1		1		125	8.8
L	12	STEPHEN GUOLLA	66	10	19	29	-11	15	4			1	86	11.6
R	11	DEAN SYLVESTER	52	16	10	26	-14	24	1		2		98	16.3
C	13	*PATRIK STEFAN	72	5	20	25	-20	30	1				117	4.3
C	14	MIKE STAPLETON	62	10	12	22	-29	30	4		1		146	6.8
D	2	*PETR BUZEK	63	5	14	19	-22	41	3				90	5.6
L	29	JOHAN GARPENLOV	73	2	14	16	-30	31					79	2.5
D	8	*FRANTISEK KABERLE	51	1	15	16	-10	10		1			76	1.3
C	24	*ANDREAS KARLSSON	51	5	9	14	-17	14	1				74	6.8
R	22	SHEAN DONOVAN	51	5	7	12	-17	26	1		1		66	7.6
L	27	DENNY LAMBERT	73	5	6	11	-17	219	2				83	6.0
D	5	GORD MURPHY	58	1	10	11	-26	38					74	1.4
D	4	CHRIS TAMER	69	2	8	10	-32	91					61	3.3
D	33	MAXIM GALANOV	40	4	3	7	-12	20					47	8.5
L	39	*PER SVARTVADET	38	3	4	7	-8	6					36	8.3
L	17	MATT JOHNSON	64	2	5	7	-11	144					54	3.7
D	6	DAVID HARLOCK	44		6	6	-8	36					29	
R	25	STEVE STAIOS	27	2	3	5	-5	66					38	5.3
D	7	CHRIS MCALPINE	34	2	2	4	-8	26				1	34	5.9
D	3	*SERGEI VYSHEDKEVICH	7	1	3	4	-3	2	1				5	20.0
R	37	*HERBERT VASILJEVS	7	1		1	-3	4					2	50.0
D	36	RUMUN NDUR	27	1		1	-17	71					6	16.7
L	23	MARTIN PROCHAZKA	3		1	1	-1						5	
D	23	BRETT CLARK	14		1	1	-12	4					13	
L	26	*BRYAN ADAMS	2				-1						1	
C	9	VLADIMIR VUJTEK	3				0						2	
D	28	GEORDIE KINNEAR	4				-1	13					2	
L	22	*ERIC BERTRAND	12				-6	4					12	
G	35	*SCOTT LANGKOW	15				0							
G	30	*SCOTT FANKHOUSER	16				0	4						
G	1	DAMIAN RHODES	28				0	2						
G	34	*NORM MARACLE	32				0							

GP = games played; G = goals; A = assists; PTS = points; +/- = goals-for minus goals-against while player is on ice; PIM = penalties in minutes; PP = power-play goals; SH = shorthanded goals; GW = game-winning goals; GT = game-tying goals; S = no. of shots; PCT = percentage of goals to shots; * = rookie

DONALD AUDETTE

Yrs. of NHL service: 9
Born: Laval, Que.; Sept. 23, 1969
Position: right wing
Height: 5-8
Weight: 175
Uniform no.: 10
Shoots: right

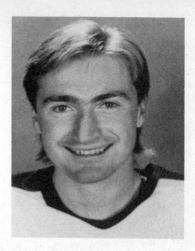

Career statistics:

GP	G	A	TP	PIM
521	201	167	368	431

1996-97 statistics:

GP	G	A	TP	+/-	PIM	PP	SH	GW	GT	S	PCT
73	28	22	50	-6	48	8	0	5	1	182	15.4

1997-98 statistics:

GP	G	A	TP	+/-	PIM	PP	SH	GW	GT	S	PCT
75	24	20	44	+10	59	10	0	5	1	198	12.1

1998-99 statistics:

GP	G	A	TP	+/-	PIM	PP	SH	GW	GT	S	PCT
49	18	18	36	+7	51	6	0	2	0	152	11.8

1999-2000 statistics:

GP	G	A	TP	+/-	PIM	PP	SH	GW	GT	S	PCT
63	19	24	43	+2	57	1	1	4	0	162	11.7

LAST SEASON

Acquired from Los Angeles with Frantisek Kaberle for Kelly Buchberger and Nelson Emerson, Mar. 13, 2000. Led team in plus-minus and game-winning goals. Second on team in shots and shooting percentage. Tied for second on team in goals. Third on team in assists and points.

THE FINESSE GAME

Audette is not very big, yet he makes his living around the net by smartly jumping in and out of the holes.

A bustling forward who barrels to the net at every opportunity, Audette is eager and feisty down low and has good hand skills. He also has keen scoring instincts, along with the quickness to make good things happen. His feet move so fast (with a choppy stride) that he doesn't look graceful, but he can really get moving and he has good balance.

A scorer first, Audette has a great top-shelf shot, which he gets away quickly and accurately. He can also make a play, but he will do this at the start of a rush. Once he is inside the offensive zone and low, he wants the puck. Considering his scoring touch, though, his selfishness can be forgiven.

Audette is at his best on the power play. He is savvy enough not to just stand around and take punishment. He times his jumps into the space between the left post and the bottom of the left circle.

THE PHYSICAL GAME

Opponents hate Audette, which he takes as a great compliment. He runs goalies, yaps and takes dives — then goes out and scores on the power play after the opposition has taken a bad penalty.

Audette will forecheck and scrap for the puck, though he isn't as diligent coming back. He's not very big, but around the net he plays like he's at least a six-footer. He keeps jabbing and working away until he is bowled over by an angry defender.

THE INTANGIBLES

Audette scored seven goals in 14 games following his trade to the Thrashers, making a very good argument for management to re-sign the restrtced free agent. Audette lacks size but not heart.

PROJECTION

Audette will get a lot of ice time and a 30-goal, 60-point season is possible.

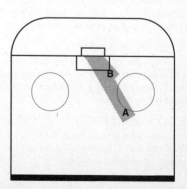

ANDREW BRUNETTE

Yrs. of NHL service: 5
Born: Sudbury, Ontario; Aug. 24, 1973
Position: left wing
Height: 6-0
Weight: 212
Uniform no.: 15
Shoots: left

Career statistics:

GP	G	A	TP	PIM
220	52	69	121	80

1996-97 statistics:

GP	G	A	TP	+/-	PIM	PP	SH	GW	GT	S	PCT
23	4	7	11	-3	12	0	0	0	0	23	17.4

1997-98 statistics:

GP	G	A	TP	+/-	PIM	PP	SH	GW	GT	S	PCT
28	11	12	23	+2	12	4	0	2	2	42	26.2

1998-99 statistics:

GP	G	A	TP	+/-	PIM	PP	SH	GW	GT	S	PCT
77	11	20	31	-10	26	7	0	1	0	65	16.9

1999-2000 statistics:

GP	G	A	TP	+/-	PIM	PP	SH	GW	GT	S	PCT
81	23	27	50	-32	30	9	0	2	1	107	21.5

PROJECTION

Brunette will continue to see prime ice time with Atlanta, as he did with Nashville and should score another 20 to 25 goals.

LAST SEASON

Led team in goals, assists and points with career highs. Led team and fourth in NHL in shooting percentage. Second on team in power- play goals.

THE FINESSE GAME

Thank god for expansion, because although Brunette is not an NHL- calibre skater, he has been able to prove that he is an NHL-calibre scorer. Brunette might best be described as Dave Andreychuk in miniature. He has excellent, soft hands for flicking in pucks out of midair, making deflections, scooping up rebounds. Brunette will not be scoring goals off the rush.

The problem with being a smaller Andreychuk is that Brunette does not have the same range the big 500-goal scorer does, and he will not be able to reach around defensemen or lean on his stick in front of the net the way that Andreychuk did in his prime.

Still, Brunette possesses a goal-scorer's mentality and should be among Atlanta's team leaders in that department. He will be an asset on the power play.

THE PHYSICAL GAME

Brunette has a power forward's build and has a little bit of an edge to him. To use an Andreychuk comparison again, he has a pretty long fuse and he has to be provoked before he'll snap.

THE INTANGIBLES

Brunette has shown he can play at the NHL level, but he will not be the star he was in the minor because of the pace of the major- league game.

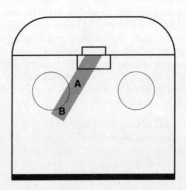

PETR BUZEK

Yrs. of NHL service: 1
Born: Jihlava, Czech.; Apr. 26, 1977
Position: left defense
Height: 6-0
Weight: 205
Uniform no.: 2
Shoots: left

Career statistics:

GP	G	A	TP	PIM
67	5	14	19	45

1997-98 statistics:

GP	G	A	TP	+/-	PIM	PP	SH	GW	GT	S	PCT
2	0	0	0	0	2	0	0	0	0	0	0.0

1998-99 statistics:

GP	G	A	TP	+/-	PIM	PP	SH	GW	GT	S	PCT
2	0	0	0	0	2	0	0	0	0	0	.0

1999-2000 statistics:

GP	G	A	TP	+/-	PIM	PP	SH	GW	GT	S	PCT
63	5	14	19	-22	41	3	0	0	0	90	5.6

LAST SEASON

First NHL season. Missed two games with dehydration. Missed six games with concussion. Missed one game with shoulder injury. Missed four games with groin injury.

THE FINESSE GAME

The first player in Thrashers history to represent the team at an NHL All-Star Game, Buzek developed with a franchise, Dallas, known for creating good defensive prospects. And Buzek is one. He is a great story, too, coming back as he has from injuries suffered in a 1995 car accident, which cost him an entire season and which understandably curtailed his development.

Buzek is a good skater, not speedy, but with good balance. He has very good hand skills. Buzek is a fine passer and playmaker. He is very unselfish. he has a good grasp of the game and can be used in all situations. He doesn't have elite offensive skills — in fact, there's no area where you could call his game great — but he does a lot of things very well.

Buzek plays equally hard and well in all zones.

THE PHYSICAL GAME

Buzek plays a tough, aggressive style but stays within the rules and boundaries.

THE INTANGIBLES

Nagging injuries and his taste of his first full NHL season caused Buzek to wear down a little in the second half. He should be better prepared for this campaign.

PROJECTION

Buzek will be a top four defenseman in Atlanta again this season with the potential to score 30 points.

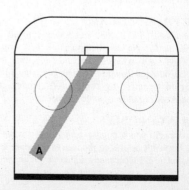

HNAT DOMENICHELLI

Yrs. of NHL service: 3
Born: Edmonton, Alberta; Feb. 17, 1976
Position: centre/left wing
Height: 6-0
Weight: 175
Uniform no.: 17
Shoots: left

Career statistics:

GP	G	A	TP	PIM
136	28	33	61	42

1996-97 statistics:

GP	G	A	TP	+/-	PIM	PP	SH	GW	GT	S	PCT
23	3	3	6	-3	9	1	0	0	0	30	10.0

1997-98 statistics:

GP	G	A	TP	+/-	PIM	PP	SH	GW	GT	S	PCT
31	9	7	16	+4	6	1	0	1	2	70	12.9

1998-99 statistics:

GP	G	A	TP	+/-	PIM	PP	SH	GW	GT	S	PCT
23	5	5	10	-4	11	3	0	0	0	45	11.1

1999-2000 statistics:

GP	G	A	TP	+/-	PIM	PP	SH	GW	GT	S	PCT
59	11	18	29	-21	16	1	0	1	0	125	8.8

PROJECTION

Domenichelli could be a 25/25 man (that's goals and points) — if he plays on one of Atlanta's top two forward lines.

LAST SEASON

Acquired from Calgary with rights to Dmitri Vlasenkov for Darryl Shannon and Jason Botterill, Feb. 11, 2000. Career highs in goals, assists and points. Appeared in 12 games with Saint John (AHL), scoring 6-7 — 13.

THE FINESSE GAME

Domenichelli's size is a big drawback. He's of average height but very, very slender and easy to knock off the puck. But he is quick enough to jump in and out of holes and he has great hands and a good shot.

His best asset is his hockey sense, and he can play centre or wing. He is a creative playmaker with good vision, but won't pass up a good shot if he has it. Domenichelli saw a lot of power-play time towards the end of last season and needs to earn his way onto the top unit this year, where he can make an impact.

He is a good skater with quickness and agility, but doesn't possess real breakaway speed.

THE PHYSICAL GAME

Domenichelli tries, but he's just not going to win one-on-one battles. He has strength more than size, but doesn't yet seem to have the appetite for battling in the high-traffic areas. Another smallish guy, Theo Fleury, excelled because he did pay the price, and Domenichelli must learn to do the same.

THE INTANGIBLES

Domenichelli was a point-a-game player in the minors. He won't be able to produce at that pace in the NHL, but he did seem happy with the trade and scored 6-9 — 15 in 27 games with the Thrashers.

SHEAN DONOVAN

Yrs. of NHL service: 5
Born: Timmins, Ont.; Jan. 22, 1975
Position: right wing
Height: 6-2
Weight: 190
Uniform no.: 12
Shoots: right

Career statistics:

GP	G	A	TP	PIM
347	42	43	85	220

1996-97 statistics:

GP	G	A	TP	+/-	PIM	PP	SH	GW	GT	S	PCT
73	9	6	15	-18	42	0	1	0	0	115	7.8

1997-98 statistics:

GP	G	A	TP	+/-	PIM	PP	SH	GW	GT	S	PCT
67	8	10	18	+6	70	0	0	0	0	81	9.9

1998-99 statistics:

GP	G	A	TP	+/-	PIM	PP	SH	GW	GT	S	PCT
68	7	12	19	+4	37	1	0	1	0	81	8.6

1999-2000 statistics:

GP	G	A	TP	+/-	PIM	PP	SH	GW	GT	S	PCT
51	5	7	12	-17	26	1	0	1	0	66	7.6

LAST SEASON

Acquired from Colorado for Rick Tabaracci, Dec. 8, 1999. Missed 20 games with broken foot. Missed three games with abdominal strain.

THE FINESSE GAME

Donovan has big-league speed, but lacks the hand skills to make the best use of it. His quickness and powerful stride allow him to shift directions with agility. And he doesn't waste energy. He knows where he is supposed to be positioned and reads plays well. He has good anticipation, which stamps him as a strong penalty killer, though he is not a shorthanded scoring threat yet because of his lack of moves on a breakaway.

Donovan may never be a great point producer because of his lack of scoring or playmaking touch. For the second straight season he showed fatal lapses in effort and, as a result, was a healthy scratch down the stretch and into the playoffs. He has a future as a third-line checking winger, but has to become more consistent. He isn't fazed by facing some of the league's better wingers, and has the skating ability to shadow almost anyone.

THE PHYSICAL GAME

Donovan is always busy making hits, and he brings a lot of energy to a game when he is in the mood. He doesn't have much of a mean streak but shows an occasional willingness to agitate. He needs to get under his opponents' skin a little more. He takes the body but doesn't punish people. He is well-conditioned and has good stamina. He doesn't get pushed off the puck easily.

THE INTANGIBLES

A player with Donovan's kind of speed can have a comfortable, 10-year NHL career, but he'll only be successful if he can add more scoring and intensity.

PROJECTION

All speed, no finish. He is a longshot to get much more than 20 points.

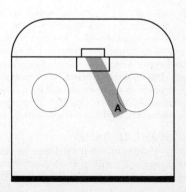

25

RAY FERRARO

Yrs. of NHL service: 16
Born: Trail, B.C.; Aug. 23, 1964
Position: centre
Height: 5-9
Weight: 193
Uniform no.: 21
Shoots: left

Career statistics:

GP	G	A	TP	PIM
1101	365	420	1079	1123

1996-97 statistics:

GP	G	A	TP	+/-	PIM	PP	SH	GW	GT	S	PCT
81	25	21	46	-22	112	11	0	2	0	152	16.4

1997-98 statistics:

GP	G	A	TP	+/-	PIM	PP	SH	GW	GT	S	PCT
40	6	9	15	-10	42	0	0	2	0	45	13.3

1998-99 statistics:

GP	G	A	TP	+/-	PIM	PP	SH	GW	GT	S	PCT
65	13	18	31	0	59	4	0	4	0	84	15.5

1999-2000 statistics:

GP	G	A	TP	+/-	PIM	PP	SH	GW	GT	S	PCT
81	19	25	44	-33	88	10	0	3	0	170	11.2

LAST SEASON

Signed as free agent, Aug. 9, 1999. Led team in power-play goals and shots. Second on team in assists, points and game-winning goals. Tied for second on team in goals. Missed one game due to coach's decision.

THE FINESSE GAME

Ferraro excels at the short game. From the bottoms of the circles in, he uses his quickness and hand skills to work little give-and-go plays through traffic.

A streaky player, when he is in the groove he plays with great concentration and hunger around the net. He is alert to not only his first, but also his second and third options, and he makes a rapid play selection. His best shot is his wrister from just off to the side of the net, which is where he likes to work on the power play. He has good coordination and timing for deflections. When his confidence is down, however, Ferraro gets into serious funks.

Ferraro's skating won't win medals. He has a choppy stride and lacks rink-long speed, but he shakes loose in a few quick steps and maintains his balance well. Handling the puck does not slow him down.

Defensively, Ferraro has improved tremendously and is no longer a liability. In fact, he's a pretty decent two-way centre, though the scales still tip in favour of his offensive ability. He has particularly improved in his defensive work down low. He's good on face-offs.

THE PHYSICAL GAME

Ferraro is on the small side but is deceptively strong. Many players aren't willing to wade into the areas where they will get crunched, and he will avoid those situations when he can. But if it's the right play, he will take the abuse and whack a few ankles.

THE INTANGIBLES

Probably because he feared no one other than NHL2Night would give him work, Ferraro signed as a free agent with the expansion Thrashers last summer, and was desperately hoping for a trade to a contender in March. When that didn't happen, Ferraro stepped into the leadership void left after Kelly Buchberger was traded and played hard for what remained in a meaningless season.

PROJECTION

More than half of his goals came on the power play, where he will continue to see ice time. Another 20-goal season is in the cards.

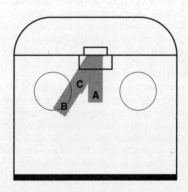

GORD MURPHY

Yrs. of NHL service: 12
Born: Willowdale, Ont.; Mar. 23, 1967
Position: right defense
Height: 6-2
Weight: 191
Uniform no.: 5
Shoots: right

Career statistics:

GP	G	A	TP	PIM
820	82	225	307	643

1996-97 statistics:

GP	G	A	TP	+/-	PIM	PP	SH	GW	GT	S	PCT
80	8	15	23	+3	51	2	0	0	0	137	5.8

1997-98 statistics:

GP	G	A	TP	+/-	PIM	PP	SH	GW	GT	S	PCT
79	6	11	17	-3	46	3	0	0	0	123	4.9

1998-99 statistics:

GP	G	A	TP	+/-	PIM	PP	SH	GW	GT	S	PCT
51	0	7	7	+4	16	0	0	0	0	56	.0

1999-2000 statistics:

GP	G	A	TP	+/-	PIM	PP	SH	GW	GT	S	PCT
58	1	10	11	-26	38	0	0	0	0	74	1.4

LAST SEASON

Missed 16 games with dislocated shoulder. Missed six games with hip injuries.

THE FINESSE GAME

Murphy has concentrated on becoming a better defensive player in recent years, and it has extended his career. He uses his finesse skills in a two-way role. A strong and agile skater, he executes tight turns and accelerates in a stride or two. He moves the puck well and then joins the play eagerly.

Murphy also carries the puck well, though he gets into trouble when he overhandles in his own zone. He usually makes a safe pass, holding on until he is just about decked and then making a nice play. He mans the point on the power play and uses a pull-and-drag shot, rather than a big slapper, giving him a very quick release. He is patient with the puck along the blueline, sliding laterally until he spots the open lane.

Murphy plays a smart positional game and makes intelligent defensive reads. He doesn't get suckered into pulling out of his position. He makes a steady, reliable partner for a more offensive-minded or inexperienced player.

THE PHYSICAL GAME

Murphy uses his finesse skills to defend. His long reach makes him an effective poke-checker, and he would rather wrap his arms around an attacker than move him out of the crease with a solid hit. He's more of a pusher than a hitter. He is responsible defensively and is used to killing penalties. He logs a lot of ice time and holds up well under the grind.

THE INTANGIBLES

Murphy is not, and will never be, a tough customer, but he has improved his positional play and can step up and provide some offensive spark. He is often asked to work as part of a top defensive pairing, which is beyond his ability, though he is likely to assume that role with the Thrashers.

PROJECTION

Murphy will be one of Atlanta's top four defensemen, and his points should be around 20.

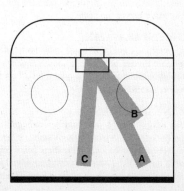

DAMIAN RHODES

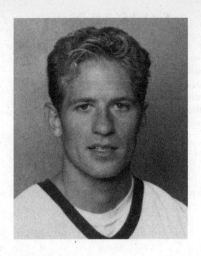

Yrs. of NHL service: 6
Born: St. Paul, MN; May 28, 1969
Position: goaltender
Height: 6-0
Weight: 190
Uniform no.: 1
Catches: left

Career statistics:

GP	MIN	GA	SO	GAA	A	PIM
256	14498	657	12	2.72	6	18

1996-97 statistics:

GP	MIN	GAA	W	L	T	SO	GA	S	SAPCT	PIM
50	2934	2.72	14	20	14	1	133	1213	.890	2

1997-98 statistics:

GP	MIN	GAA	W	L	T	SO	GA	S	SAPCT	PIM
50	2743	2.34	19	19	7	5	107	1148	.907	0

1998-99 statistics:

GP	MIN	GAA	W	L	T	SO	GA	S	SAPCT	PIM
45	2480	2.44	22	13	7	3	101	1060	.905	4

1999-2000 statistics:

GP	MIN	GAA	W	L	T	SO	GA	S	SAPCT	PIM
28	1561	3.88	5	19	3	1	101	803	.874	2

LAST SEASON

Missed 45 games with ankle sprain.

THE PHYSICAL GAME

Rhodes makes good first saves and doesn't give up bad rebounds. He either guides the pucks to the corners or deadens the puck in front of him. He is better off the less he plays the puck. Don't be fooled by the goal he "scored" in 1998-99. It was put into an empty net by Devils defenseman Lyle Odelein, and Rhodes got credit because he was the last opposition player to touch the puck. He's not Martin Brodeur, though sometimes he thinks he is, which is when he gets into real trouble.

Rhodes is technically sound. Uncontrolled rebounds allow the shooter to drive in for the second chance, but he doesn't give away many. You have to beat him; he won't beat himself.

Rhodes is a stand-up goalie who plays his angles well and is solid in his fundamentals. He gives his team a chance to win the game.

THE MENTAL GAME

Rhodes needs to have confidence in his body after his leg injuries. He can be a bit of a loose cannon, so the day-to-day burden of being a goalie on a bad team might not wear well on him.

THE INTANGIBLES

Rhodes may not be a true number one goalie — injuries prevented him from taking a stab at it last season — but he's the best the Thrashers have got. He played in the last three weeks of last season and faced a lot of shots, which will give him a taste of what to expect this season.

PROJECTION

Rhodes will be forced to win a lot of low-scoring games. He will see a lot of 40-shot nights and would do well to get 15 wins.

PATRIK STEFAN

Yrs. of NHL service: 1
Born: Pribham, Czech.; Sept. 16, 1980
Position: centre
Height: 6-1
Weight: 205
Uniform no.: 13
Shoots: left

Career statistics:

GP	G	A	TP	PIM
140	22	60	82	66

1999-2000 statistics:

GP	G	A	TP	+/-	PIM	PP	SH	GW	GT	S	PCT
72	5	20	25	-20	30	1	0	0	0	117	4.3

LAST SEASON

First NHL season. Missed three games with back spasms. Missed two games with concussion. Missed two games with flu.

THE FINESSE GAME

There is little doubt Stefan is a special talent. He is a tall skater whose stance is upright, allowing him to keep his head up to see all of the ice and all of his options. He uses a long stick for a long reach to beat defenders one-on-one in open ice. He loves to carry the puck and has drawn comparisons to Jaromir Jagr for his end-to-end ability. He didn't use his speed as well as he should have in his rookie season.

An excellent passer who can thread a puck through a crowd, he shoots well forehand and backhand and isn't shy about using his shot. He is good on draws and can run a power play.

Stefan needs to work on the defensive game. He has the hockey smarts to do so.

THE PHYSICAL GAME

Stefan is a bit lean and needs to get stronger to handle NHL checking attention.

THE INTANGIBLES

The concussion Stefan suffered two seasons ago is still a question mark, especially since he suffered another "minor" one last season.

PROJECTION

If he's sound, Stefan is ready to make an impression with the expansion Thrashers. He is the complete package. He won't have a lot of help, but he is the kind of player who can make others around him better. His offensive output will certainly rise.

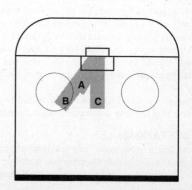

CHRIS TAMER

Yrs. of NHL service: 6
Born: Dearborn, Mich.; Nov. 17, 1970
Position: left defense
Height: 6-2
Weight: 212
Uniform no.: 4
Shoots: left

Career statistics:

GP	G	A	TP	PIM
374	11	34	45	771

1996-97 statistics:

GP	G	A	TP	+/-	PIM	PP	SH	GW	GT	S	PCT
45	2	4	6	-25	131	0	1	0	0	56	3.6

1997-98 statistics:

GP	G	A	TP	+/-	PIM	PP	SH	GW	GT	S	PCT
79	0	7	7	+4	181	0	0	0	0	55	.0

1998-99 statistics:

GP	G	A	TP	+/-	PIM	PP	SH	GW	GT	S	PCT
63	1	5	6	-14	124	0	0	1	0	48	2.1

1999-2000 statistics:

GP	G	A	TP	+/-	PIM	PP	SH	GW	GT	S	PCT
69	2	8	10	-32	91	0	0	0	0	61	3.3

LAST SEASON

Third on team in penalty minutes. Missed six games due to knee injury. Missed seven games due to coach's decision.

THE FINESSE GAME

Tamer is a conservative, stay-at-home defenseman. He has limited skating and stick skills but is smart enough to stay within his limitations and play a positional game.

He plays a poised game and learns from his mistakes. He does the little things well, chipping a puck off the boards or angling an attacker to the wall. He kill penalties, blocks shots and finishes his checks.

Tamer is smart enough when he is firing from the point to make sure his shot doesn't get blocked. He will take something off his shot, or put it wide so the forwards could attack the puck off the end boards.

THE PHYSICAL GAME

Tamer doesn't nail people, but he has some strength and will use it to push people out of the crease, and he'll battle in the corners. He doesn't have a good skating base to be a punishing open-ice hitter, but he defends himself and sticks up for his teammates. He doesn't have a serious nasty side, but is often guilty of late hits.

Tamer is a well-conditioned athlete and he can handle a lot of ice time, despite suffering from asthma.

THE INTANGIBLES

Tamer had a slow start, but was probably the Thrashers' most consistent defenseman in the second half of the season and stepped up when there were injuries. He will be in Atlanta's top four. He will never be a star, but he gives solid support and can complement a more offensive player, like Frantisek Kaberle. His point production will be low, but he is an intelligent rearguard who will only get better.

PROJECTION

Tamer won't get many points, but his PIM total will always be in triple digits.

YANNICK TREMBLAY

Yrs. of NHL service: 3
Born: Pointe-aux-Tremles, Que.; Nov. 15, 1975
Position: right defense
Height: 6-2
Weight: 200
Uniform no.: 38
Shoots: right

Career statistics:

GP	G	A	TP	PIM
153	14	32	46	44

1996-97 statistics:

GP	G	A	TP	+/-	PIM	PP	SH	GW	GT	S	PCT
5	0	0	0	-4	0	0	0	0	0	2	0.0

1997-98 statistics:

GP	G	A	TP	+/-	PIM	PP	SH	GW	GT	S	PCT
38	2	4	6	-6	6	1	0	0	0	45	4.4

1998-99 statistics:

GP	G	A	TP	+/-	PIM	PP	SH	GW	GT	S	PCT
35	2	7	9	0	16	0	0	0	0	37	5.4

1999-2000 statistics:

GP	G	A	TP	+/-	PIM	PP	SH	GW	GT	S	PCT
75	10	21	31	-42	22	4	1	2	1	139	7.2

PROJECTION

Tremblay will be in the top four defensemen for Atlanta and will see a lot of power-play time, so 35 to 40 points is a reasonable target.

LAST SEASON

Led team defensemen in points. Career highs in goals, assists and points. Tied for third on team in power-play goals. Missed two games with hip injury. Missed one game with groin injury.

THE FINESSE GAME

Tremblay is a decent skater who plays a finesse game. He has an accurate shot from the point — not hard, but he gets his shot through, which is important on the power play. He loves to shoot, too. And he handles the puck well.

Tremblay's skating style is efficient and he can handle a lot of minutes (he averaged close to 20 per game last season), but he did seem to wear down in the second half at the end of his first full NHL season.

Tremblay blocks a lot of shots and kills penalties.

THE PHYSICAL GAME

Tremblay is tall but not filled out, and he doesn't play a very physical game. He angles his man out but doesn't always finish his checks. He is rather mild-mannered.

THE INTANGIBLES

You neved know what player rescued from a team's farm system is going to step it up when he gets his shot with an expansion team. Tremblay was last season's surprise for the Thrashers. Drafted out of Toronto's system, where he was a high-scoring defenseman in the minors. Tremblay became Atlanta's best offensive defenseman.

BOSTON BRUINS

Players' Statistics 1999-2000

POS.	NO.	PLAYER	GP	G	A	PTS	+/-	PIM	PP	SH	GW	GT	S	PCT
C	6	JOE THORNTON	81	23	37	60	-5	82	5		3		171	13.5
L	33	ANSON CARTER	59	22	25	47	8	14	4		1	1	144	15.3
L	14	SERGEI SAMSONOV	77	19	26	45	-6	4	6		3		145	13.1
L	12	BRIAN ROLSTON	77	16	15	31	-12	18	5		6		206	7.8
C	41	JASON ALLISON	37	10	18	28	5	20	3		1	1	66	15.2
D	20	DARREN VAN IMPE	79	5	23	28	-19	73	4				97	5.2
R	11	P.J. AXELSSON	81	10	16	26	1	24			4		186	5.4
R	23	STEVE HEINZE	75	12	13	25	-8	36	2		2	2	145	8.3
R	26	MIKE KNUBLE	73	12	8	20	-7	26	2		2		78	15.4
C	28	*ANDRE SAVAGE	43	7	13	20	-8	10	2		1	1	70	10.0
D	18	KYLE MCLAREN	71	8	11	19	-4	67	2		3		142	5.6
C	22	MIKKO ELORANTA	50	6	12	18	-10	36	1				59	10.2
D	32	DON SWEENEY	81	1	13	14	-14	48					82	1.2
R	10	CAMERON MANN	32	8	4	12	-6	13	1			1	48	16.7
C	17	SHAWN BATES	44	5	7	12	-17	14			1		65	7.7
D	25	HAL GILL	81	3	9	12	0	51					120	2.5
R	21	*ERIC NICKULAS	20	5	6	11	-1	12	1				28	17.9
L	57	*ANTTI LAAKSONEN	27	6	3	9	3	2			1		23	26.1
D	37	MATTIAS TIMANDER	60		8	8	-11	22					39	
D	53	BRANDON SMITH	22	2	4	6	-4	10					24	8.3
D	29	MARTY MCSORLEY	27	2	3	5	2	62					24	8.3
L	48	JOE HULBIG	24	2	2	4	-8	8					15	13.3
L	16	KEN BELANGER	37	2	2	4	-4	44					20	10.0
L	51	*JAY HENDERSON	16	1	3	4	1	9					18	5.6
R	27	LANDON WILSON	40	1	3	4	-6	18					67	1.5
D	55	*JONATHAN GIRARD	23	1	2	3	-1	2					17	5.9
C	39	*JOEL PRPIC	14		3	3	-6						13	
C	61	MARQUIS MATHIEU	6	2		2	-2	4					3	
R	42	PETER FERRARO	5	1		1	-1						3	
C	46	SEAN PRONGER	11	1		1	-4	13					7	
G	47	*JOHN GRAHAME	24		1	1	0	8						
R	45	AARON DOWNEY	1				0							
D	49	*JOHNATHAN AITKEN	3				-3						2	
L	54	*JEFF ZEHR	4				-1	2					3	
D	44	*NICHOLAS BOYNTON	5				-5						6	
G	35	ROBBIE TALLAS	27				0	6						
G	34	BYRON DAFOE	41				0							

GP = games played; G = goals; A = assists; PTS = points; +/- = goals-for minus goals-against while player is on ice; PIM = penalties in minutes; PP = power-play goals; SH = shorthanded goals; GW = game-winning goals; GT = game-tying goals; S = no. of shots; PCT = percentage of goals to shots; * = rookie

JASON ALLISON

Yrs. of NHL service: 4
Born: North York, Ontario; May 29, 1975
Position: centre
Height: 6-3
Weight: 205
Uniform no.: 41
Shoots: right

Career statistics:

GP	G	A	TP	PIM
305	76	152	228	190

1996-97 statistics:

GP	G	A	TP	+/-	PIM	PP	SH	GW	GT	S	PCT
72	8	26	34	-6	34	2	0	1	0	99	8.1

1997-98 statistics:

GP	G	A	TP	+/-	PIM	PP	SH	GW	GT	S	PCT
81	33	50	83	+33	60	5	0	8	2	158	20.9

1998-99 statistics:

GP	G	A	TP	+/-	PIM	PP	SH	GW	GT	S	PCT
82	23	53	76	+5	68	5	1	3	0	158	14.6

1999-2000 statistics:

GP	G	A	TP	+/-	PIM	PP	SH	GW	GT	S	PCT
37	10	18	28	+5	20	3	0	1	1	66	15.2

LAST SEASON

Missed 45 games with injuries to left hand and right wrist, undergoing surgery to repair both injuries.

THE FINESSE GAME

When healthy, Allison is capable of completely dominating games. He is strong on the puck, skates well, has excellent vision and sure, soft hands to put passes where they need to go. He is the complete package offensively.

He also faces top checkers every shift and still excels. He makes players on his line better, and has established good chemistry with Anson Carter, in particular. Allison is night in and night out one of the best forwards on the ice.

The puck follows Allison around the rink. He has great patience, uncanny hockey sense and is one of the top-10 centres in the league when he is at the top of his game. Although his impact is predominantly on offense, he is often put on the ice to protect leads late in games, so his defense is hardly suspect.

He wants to get even better, and has worked with skating instructors in the off-season to step up his foot speed.

THE PHYSICAL GAME

Allison is not quite as strong or tough as some of the league's best power forwards, but he goes through traffic and makes plays despite the checking attention focussed on him. He is hungry to score and will pay the price to do so.

Allison plays through pain. He soldiered on for nearly half a season with an injury that eventually required surgery.

THE INTANGIBLES

If Allison's injuries are behind him, he is poised for a big season. He and Joe Thornton form a formidable one-two punch at centre. Opponents won't know which line to key their checkers on.

PROJECTION

Allison was criticized for his dedication by coach Pat Burns, which is probably why he kept trying to play despite his injury (shades of Eric Lindros and Bob Clarke). A 30-goal, 85-point season is not beyond his ability.

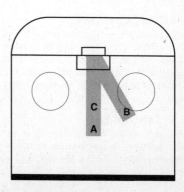

P. J. AXELSSON

Yrs. of NHL service: 3
Born: Kungalv, Sweden; Feb. 26, 1975
Position: right wing
Height: 6-1
Weight: 174
Uniform no.: 11
Shoots: left

Career statistics:

GP	G	A	TP	PIM
240	25	45	70	80

1997-98 statistics:

GP	G	A	TP	+/-	PIM	PP	SH	GW	GT	S	PCT
82	8	19	27	-14	38	2	0	1	0	144	5.6

1998-99 statistics:

GP	G	A	TP	+/-	PIM	PP	SH	GW	GT	S	PCT
77	7	10	17	-14	18	0	0	2	0	146	4.8

1999-2000 statistics:

GP	G	A	TP	+/-	PIM	PP	SH	GW	GT	S	PCT
81	10	16	26	+1	24	0	0	4	0	186	5.4

PROJECTION

Axelsson may be able to score 10 to 15 goals, but not much more than that. However, he could earn Selke Trophy recognition further up the road.

LAST SEASON

Second on team in shots and game-winning goals. Missed one game with charley horse.

THE FINESSE GAME

Axelsson is a smart player with a real head for the game. He has the skills (especially skating) that stamp him as a bona fide NHLer.

Axelsson is a role player but happily accepts that job. He is a very fast skater, yet unlike a lot of Swedes he is not strong on the puck. His hand skills are just about average, though he was a fairly decent scorer in the Swedish Elite League, and he doesn't fumble with the puck. His future in this league will be based less on his scoring than on his defensive ability. The Bruins last year asked him to carry too much of an offensive load because of injuries. That is not Axelsson's game. Killing penalties is where he excells.

Axelsson's primary asset is his work ethic. He never stops skating, never stops fighting for the puck and he loves big checking assignments against other teams' top lines.

THE PHYSICAL GAME

Axelsson is competitive, a solid checker who will finish all of his hits. He will stand up to big power forwards and won't be intimidated, despite the fact that he is the kind of tall but scrawny player that some big guys could use as a toothpick. Axelsson is not fun to play against.

THE INTANGIBLES

Axelsson is a catalyst. Slotted correctly as a regular third-line left wing, he contributes an honest 16 to 18 minutes every night. He is a low-risk, high-energy performer.

ANSON CARTER

Yrs. of NHL service: 4
Born: Toronto, Ont.; June 6, 1974
Position: centre/right wing
Height: 6-1
Weight: 175
Uniform no.: 33
Shoots: right

Career statistics:

GP	G	A	TP	PIM
230	73	75	148	76

1996-97 statistics:

GP	G	A	TP	+/-	PIM	PP	SH	GW	GT	S	PCT
38	11	7	18	-7	9	2	1	2	0	79	13.9

1997-98 statistics:

GP	G	A	TP	+/-	PIM	PP	SH	GW	GT	S	PCT
78	16	27	43	+7	31	6	0	4	0	179	8.9

1998-99 statistics:

GP	G	A	TP	+/-	PIM	PP	SH	GW	GT	S	PCT
55	24	16	40	+7	22	6	0	6	0	123	19.5

1999-2000 statistics:

GP	G	A	TP	+/-	PIM	PP	SH	GW	GT	S	PCT
59	22	25	47	+8	14	4	0	1	1	144	15.3

LAST SEASON

Led team in plus-minus and shooting percentage. Second on team in goals and points. Career high in points. Third on team in assists. Missed 23 games with shoulder injury. Missed 15 games with right wrist surgery.

THE FINESSE GAME

Carter is a deceptive skater with a long, rangy, loping stride, but he isn't a bit awkward in turns. What really sets him apart, though, is his hockey intelligence. He thinks the game well in all zones.

Carter has pushed himself hard to improve his skating and shooting, and both skills are now polished. He has graduated to playing on the top line with Jason Allison. Carter even had to fill in at centre when Allison missed half the season with injuries. Carter's production suffered as a result of being moved from his natural position and from the absence of his playmaking partner.

Carter drives to the net well. He has good balance and is hard to knock off his skates. He isn't a power forward, but he goes into the high-traffic areas and has soft hands for receiving passes and releasing a quick shot.

THE PHYSICAL GAME

A late bloomer physically, Carter still needs to add some muscle but he is not afraid to hit, not afraid to take a hit and, like Peter Forsberg, will make a preemptive hit while carrying the puck. He's not dirty or mean, just honestly tough. As one of the few blacks to make it to the NHL, you know he's mentally tough.

THE INTANGIBLES

Carter has emerged as a quiet team leader. Smart and articulate, he is captain material.

PROJECTION

Carter's ice time and prominent role in the attack mean he should hit the 30-goal mark this season.

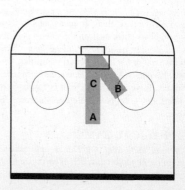

PAUL COFFEY

Yrs. of NHL service: 20
Born: Weston, Ont.; June 1, 1961
Position: right defense
Height: 6-0
Weight: 190
Uniform no.: 77
Shoots: left

Career statistics:

GP	G	A	TP	PIM
1391	396	1131	1527	1772

1996-97 statistics:

GP	G	A	TP	+/-	PIM	PP	SH	GW	GT	S	PCT
57	9	25	34	+11	38	1	1	2	0	110	8.2

1997-98 statistics:

GP	G	A	TP	+/-	PIM	PP	SH	GW	GT	S	PCT
57	2	27	29	+3	30	1	0	1	0	107	1.9

1998-99 statistics:

GP	G	A	TP	+/-	PIM	PP	SH	GW	GT	S	PCT
54	2	12	14	-7	28	1	0	0	0	87	2.3

1999-2000 statistics:

GP	G	A	TP	+/-	PIM	PP	SH	GW	GT	S	PCT
69	11	29	40	-6	40	6	0	3	1	155	7.1

LAST SEASON

Signed by Boston as free agent from Carolina, July 13, 2000. Third on Hurricanes in shots. Missed 13 games due to coach's decision.

THE FINESSE GAME

Coffey creates a lot of open ice for his teammates because he is so intimidating as a skater: he may have the most fluid, effortless skating mechanism in the game. An agile, shifty attacker with a delicious change of pace, he has terrific balance, uses his edges well, and commands a respectable amount of space from defensemen who lack the range to step up and press the issue. With the time he buys himself, Coffey sizes up the passing options and exploits them, because he handles the puck well while whirling at top speed or changing directions.

Few players are better at the long home-run pass, and Coffey has all the finesse skills of a forward when he works down low. He has tremendous vision to make a play, feather a pass or work a give-and-go. He has a whole menu of shots, from wristers to slaps. He is a world-class point man on the power play, faking slaps and sending passes low, sliding the puck over to his point partner for a one-timer, or drilling the shot himself. He prefers to attack down the right side.

Notice all we've talked about is Coffey's offensive skills. No team has Coffey on its roster for his defense.

THE PHYSICAL GAME

Coffey uses his skating to get in an opponent's way, but he isn't going to hit as much as he is going to steer an opponent to bad ice. Like a quarterback taught to throw the ball away rather than "eat" it and accept a sack, Coffey frequently will say, "Here, be my guest," with the puck, rather than persevering through contact.

Coffey will block shots when it counts, such as during the playoffs, but most of his defense is based on his anticipation in picking off passes and his skill with the puck.

THE INTANGIBLES

Coffey is a luxury item for teams now, and he didn't end up on a team that can afford the luxury. Being expected to "replace" Ray Bourque just makes Boston an even stranger fit for him. He was a good influence on young defensemen in Carolina, though, and the Bruins do have some prospects coming along that he can help.

PROJECTION

Coffey's offensive totals continue to decline, and he has slowed down a bit, but he should still be good for 40 points.

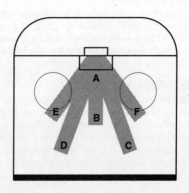

BYRON DAFOE

Yrs. of NHL service: 5
Born: Sussex, England; Feb. 25, 1971
Position: goaltender
Height: 5-11
Weight: 175
Uniform no.: 34
Catches: left

Career statistics:

GP	MIN	GA	SO	GAA	A	PIM
271	15247	693	20	2.73	5	33

1996-97 statistics:

GP	MIN	GAA	W	L	T	SO	GA	S	SAPCT	PIM
40	2162	3.11	13	17	5	0	112	1178	.905	0

1997-98 statistics:

GP	MIN	GAA	W	L	T	SO	GA	S	SAPCT	PIM
65	3693	2.24	30	25	9	6	138	1602	.914	2

1998-99 statistics:

GP	MIN	GAA	W	L	T	SO	GA	S	SAPCT	PIM
68	4001	1.99	32	23	11	10	133	1800	.926	25

1999-2000 statistics:

GP	MIN	GAA	W	L	T	SO	GA	S	SAPCT	PIM
41	2307	2.96	13	16	0	3	114	1030	.889	0

PROJECTION

Dafoe should be able to eke out 25 wins with an improved (slightly) Bruins team.

LAST SEASON

Missed 12 games in contract dispute. Missed 23 games with right knee surgery.

THE PHYSICAL GAME

Dafoe's game is technically sound and quite aggressive, sometimes overly so. He usually controls his rebounds well, but on nights when he doesn't his challenging style leaves him vulnerable on second shots. He can get a bit scrambly, as if he doesn't trust his defense. The Bruins will have a young but sound defense this year, so maybe Dafoe will relax a bit. Goalies for weaker teams tend to do too much. He plays a better game the less he tries to accomplish.

Dafoe is slightly smaller than many of today's goalies, but when he stands up and plays his angles he is able to maximize his size.

He is quite average in a lot of areas — especially stickhandling. He thinks the game well, though, and he stays alert and doesn't beat himself.

THE MENTAL GAME

Dafoe has battled to get his playing chance and he handles adversity well. He has to prove himself again now, coming off an injury-marred season.

THE INTANGIBLES

Last season, the Bruins were one of the worst offensive teams in the league, and the pressure of never knowing if he would get the goal support wore on Dafoe. He got off to a slow start because of missing training camp with a contract dispute, the knee surgery also set him back. Dafoe is in need of a big rebound season.

HAL GILL

Yrs. of NHL service: 3
Born: Concord, Mass.; Apr. 6, 1975
Position: right defense
Height: 6-7
Weight: 240
Uniform no.: 25
Shoots: left

Career statistics:

GP	G	A	TP	PIM
229	8	20	27	161

1997-98 statistics:

GP	G	A	TP	+/-	PIM	PP	SH	GW	GT	S	PCT
68	2	4	6	+4	47	0	0	0	0	56	3.6

1998-99 statistics:

GP	G	A	TP	+/-	PIM	PP	SH	GW	GT	S	PCT
80	3	7	10	-10	63	0	0	2	0	102	2.9

1999-2000 statistics:

GP	G	A	TP	+/-	PIM	PP	SH	GW	GT	S	PCT
81	3	9	12	0	51	0	0	0	0	120	2.5

LAST SEASON

Career high in assists and points. Missed one game with flu.

THE FINESSE GAME

Gill's only drawback is his skating. He has slow feet, which may keep him from becoming an elite defenseman, but every other facet of his game is Grade A.

A player who can be used in any game situation *and* when the heat is on, Gill excells. He has a huge shot from the point, though his lack of mobility along the blueline makes it a less effective scoring weapon. His puck movement is advanced. He was not much of a scorer at the college level and he won't be in the NHL, either, but his finesse skills serve him well in a defensive role. He makes the first pass on the breakout or gets the puck and moves it out of the zone.

Gill is one of the tallest players in the NHL, and he uses his reach well. Playing with Ray Bourque obviously helped his development, as it did Kyle McLaren's, although oddly Gill played better once Bourque departed for Colorado. Gill is calm with the puck and has a high panic threshold.

THE PHYSICAL GAME

Gill competes hard every night. He is not intimidated by some of the league's tough customers and is one of the few defensemen in the East who can stay on his feet after a hit by someone like New Jersey's Bobby Holik. Gill is solid and imposing, and can intimidate with his size. He is strong on the boards, strong in the corners and he clears out the front of his net. He doesn't fight. He doesn't have to. He has a pretty long fuse, but don't confuse that with a lack of bravery. Gill is a gamer. The Bruins would like to see him initiate more, but that isn't his nature.

THE INTANGIBLES

How's this for a compliment? Jaromir Jagr called Gill the toughest player he competes against. Gill gained excellent experience by playing for Team USA at the World Championships. It will only help his development. He is clearly ready to take on more responsibility.

PROJECTION

Gill became a top four defenseman with Boston last season, as we predicted, and he will stick. He is one of the best young rearguards in the league, though he doesn't get the attention he deserves because his point totals are tiny.

JONATHAN GIRARD

Yrs. of NHL service: 0
Born: Joliette, Que.; May 27, 1980
Position: right defense
Height: 5-11
Weight: 192
Uniform no.: 55
Shoots: right

Career statistics:

GP	G	A	TP	PIM
26	1	2	3	2

1998-99 statistics:

GP	G	A	TP	+/-	PIM	PP	SH	GW	GT	S	PCT
3	0	0	0	+1	0	0	0	0	0	3	0.0

1999-2000 statistics:

GP	G	A	TP	+/-	PIM	PP	SH	GW	GT	S	PCT
23	1	2	3	-1	2	0	0	0	0	17	5.9

LAST SEASON

Will be entering first NHL season. Appeared in 26 games with Moncton (QMJHL), scoring 10-12 — 35. Appeared in one game with Providence (AHL), scoring 0-1-1.

THE FINESSE GAME

Girard is a power-play specialist who may help the Bruins replace some of the firepower lost when Ray Bourque was traded to Colorado. How's that for pressure?

Girard actually didn't get to play with Boston after Bourque's departure, since by then he had been returned to junior after starting the season with the Bruins. He is small and was used as a forward at times, since his defensive-zone play still needs some honing. He is slow in his decision-making and his puck movement in his own zone. He has to learn that at the NHL level, players get on him faster and can read his intentions.

Girard has good puck skills and is a quick skater. He has the kind of lateral movement that stamp the elite point men, and a major-league slap shot. He is also creative enough not to just blast the puck, but will look to fake a defender with a slap and work the puck in deep for a one-timer by a teammate. His has very good offensive instincts. He will be fun to watch in four-on-four overtime.

THE PHYSICAL GAME

In Don Sweeney, Girard has a role model for smaller than average NHL defensemen. Sweeney plays big. Girard doesn't.

THE INTANGIBLES

Girard was very disappointed when he was sent down after starting the season with the parent club, and his mental letdown required some time for him to recover from. He will be given every shot to earn a full-time job.

PROJECTION

Assuming Girard can get some key power-play time, he could score 20 to 25 points.

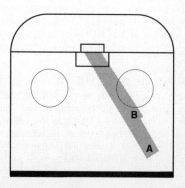

ANDREI KOVALENKO

Yrs. of NHL service: 8
Born: Balakovo, Russia; June 7, 1970
Position: right wing
Height: 5-10
Weight: 215
Uniform no.: 51
Shoots: left

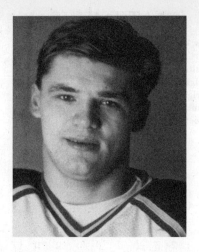

Career statistics:

GP	G	A	TP	PIM
544	157	185	342	362

1996-97 statistics:

GP	G	A	TP	+/-	PIM	PP	SH	GW	GT	S	PCT
74	32	27	59	-5	81	14	0	2	0	163	19.6

1997-98 statistics:

GP	G	A	TP	+/-	PIM	PP	SH	GW	GT	S	PCT
59	6	17	23	-14	28	1	0	2	1	89	6.7

1998-99 statistics:

GP	G	A	TP	+/-	PIM	PP	SH	GW	GT	S	PCT
74	19	21	40	-6	32	3	0	4	1	104	18.3

1999-2000 statistics:

GP	G	A	TP	+/-	PIM	PP	SH	GW	GT	S	PCT
76	15	24	39	-13	38	2	0	3	0	114	13.2

LAST SEASON

Signed as a free agent from Carolina, July 25, 2000. Missed three games with back spasms. Missed one game with knee injury. Missed two games due to coach's decision.

THE FINESSE GAME

Kovalenko has a high skill level and can play a brisk, sometimes abrasive, style. When he is on his best game, he can play on a top line and make things happen. He is woefully inconsistent, however.

Kovalenko bustles right into traffic. He is an intelligent player who doesn't panic with the puck and is a natural on the power play. He doesn't hang onto the puck long but likes to make short give-and-go plays in the offensive zone. He always keeps his wheels in motion. He is tough with the puck in corners and along the boards. He has an excellent backhand shot. He is an accurate shooter with a quick release on his wrist shot. He should shoot more, but like many Russian players he hates to take a low-percentage shot and would rather work to get into position for a better one.

Defensive work is his downfall, but he has become more conscientious and makes fewer high-risk plays.

THE PHYSICAL GAME

Kovalenko's nickname is the "Little Tank," because of his chunky build. Checks often bounce right off him because he is so solid. He can be tough around the net and in the offensive corners. He will take some punishment in front of the net on the power play, and gets a lot of goals off the rebounds.

THE INTANGIBLES

Kovalenko wears out his welcome quickly. He gets a fresh start in Boston, a team that is wed to a better work ethic than he exhibits on a nightly basis.

PROJECTION

Kovalenko has the skills to score 30 goals, but he hasn't done it since 1996-97, and even with the switch in scenery, 20 would be a surprise.

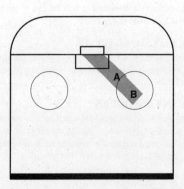

CAMERON MANN

Yrs. of NHL service: 2
Born: Thompson, Man.; Apr. 20, 1977
Position: right wing
Height: 6-0
Weight: 194
Uniform no.: 10
Shoots: right

Career statistics:

GP	G	A	TP	PIM
74	13	7	20	34

1997-98 statistics:

GP	G	A	TP	+/-	PIM	PP	SH	GW	GT	S	PCT
9	0	1	1	+1	4	0	0	0	0	6	0.0

1998-99 statistics:

GP	G	A	TP	+/-	PIM	PP	SH	GW	GT	S	PCT
33	5	2	7	0	17	1	0	1	1	42	11.9

1999-2000 statistics:

GP	G	A	TP	+/-	PIM	PP	SH	GW	GT	S	PCT
32	8	4	12	-6	13	1	0	0	1	48	16.7

LAST SEASON

Second NHL season. Missed eight games due to coach's decision. Appeared in 29 games with Providence (AHL), scoring 7-12 — 19.

THE FINESSE GAME

The Mann show is pure offense. His problem is that if he doesn't score, he doesn't do anything else to help his team win, so Mann has to produce or it's back to Providence.

He is fluid on his skates: he has speed, a quick start from a standstill and his stride is effortless. Capable of beating a player one-on-one, he concentrates his efforts in the attacking zone. He has to learn to play equally as hard in all three zones.

Mann has a good scoring touch around the net, with a hard shot. His stickhandling is above average. He would be a good fit among the team's young forwards. There won't be a lot of pressure on him behind Anson Carter, especially if Sergei Samsonov (Mann's chief rival for the second-line left-wing job) fails to come through. Mann can't carry a team but he can add to its depth. He has enough skill.

THE PHYSICAL GAME

Mann has fair size and strength but he is not a physical force. He seldom instigates, but he does not back down when challenged and he possesses a good work ethic. He has picked up his work in the corners a notch.

THE INTANGIBLES

Mann may have a latent edge to his game, but most scouts believe he is soft and won't pay the price. This could be his last chance to win a job with the Bruins.

PROJECTION

Mann has the potential to earn a spot on the top two lines with Boston. He's been able to score in the minors and could be a 20-goal scorer — if he earns a major role this season.

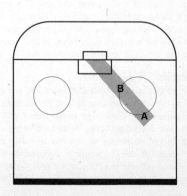

KYLE MCLAREN

Yrs. of NHL service: 5
Born: Humbolt, Sask.; June 18, 1977
Position: left defense
Height: 6-4
Weight: 210
Uniform no.: 18
Shoots: left

Career statistics:

GP	G	A	TP	PIM
321	29	70	99	298

1996-97 statistics:

GP	G	A	TP	+/-	PIM	PP	SH	GW	GT	S	PCT
58	5	9	14	-9	54	0	0	1	0	68	7.4

1997-98 statistics:

GP	G	A	TP	+/-	PIM	PP	SH	GW	GT	S	PCT
66	5	20	25	+13	56	2	0	0	0	101	5.0

1998-99 statistics:

GP	G	A	TP	+/-	PIM	PP	SH	GW	GT	S	PCT
52	6	18	24	+1	48	3	0	0	0	97	6.2

1999-2000 statistics:

GP	G	A	TP	+/-	PIM	PP	SH	GW	GT	S	PCT
71	8	11	19	-4	67	2	0	3	0	142	5.6

LAST SEASON
Third on team in penalty minutes. Career high in goals. Missed seven games with sprained thumb. Missed four games with torn knee cartilage.

THE FINESSE GAME
McLaren is big and mobile. His puckhandling ability is well above average, and he moves the puck out of the zone quickly and without panicking. He can rush with the puck or make the cautious bank off the boards to clear the zone. McLaren jumps eagerly into the play.

He can play either right or left defense, and his advanced defensive reads allow him to adapt, which is very hard to do for a young player.

McLaren is an effective penalty killer because he is fearless. He blocks shots and takes away passing lanes. He can also play on the power play, and probably will improve in this area because he plays heads-up and has a hard and accurate slap shot with a quick release. As he gains more confidence he will become more of an offensive factor, but frequently he puts the cart before the horse and goes on the attack — before he has taken care of his own end of the ice.

THE PHYSICAL GAME
McLaren is a mean, punishing hitter. He is almost scary in his fierce checking ability. He is tough and aggressive, but he doesn't go looking for fights and doesn't take foolish penalties. When he does get into a scrap, he can go toe-to-toe and has already earned some respect around the league as a player you don't want to tick off. He is strong on the puck, strong on the wall and doesn't allow loitering in front of his crease.

McLaren has a tendency to lose his edge and get too freewheeling and offensive. Every time he lapses into this bad habit, the coaching staff have to rein him in and bring him back to a simple game. He averaged more than 23 minutes of ice time last season, so he can handle a heavy workload.

THE INTANGIBLES
At 22, McLaren has the second most seniority on the team after Don Sweeney. Now that Raymond Bourque is gone, this is McLaren's defense. He underwent off-season arthroscopic surgery on his wrist and knee, which should ease some nagging problems.

PROJECTION
The less McLaren thinks about getting points the more easily he will score. He should get close to 40 points this season as he takes an important next step in his development.

SAMI PAHLSSON

Yrs. of NHL service: 0
Born: Ornskoldsvik, Sweden; Dec. 17, 1977
Position: centre
Height: 5-11
Weight: 190
Uniform no.: n.a.
Shoots: left

Career statistics: (Swedish Elite League)

GP	G	A	TP	PIM
206	48	51	99	246

LAST SEASON

Will be entering first NHL season. Acquired with
Brian Rolston and Martin Grenier for Ray Bourque
and Dave Andreychuk, Mar. 6, 2000. Appeared in 47
games with MoDo (Sweden), scoring 11-11 — 27.

THE FINESSE GAME

Pahlsson is a highly skilled centre with a hard edge.
His primary attention is on his defense, but he has
very good playmaking skills. He can turn turnovers
into points, and he churns up a lot of loose pucks with
his forechecking. He won't be scoring the goals himself, but his partners will have plenty of good chances.

Pahlsson has a solid, gritty all-around game. He is
positionally sound and he is excellent on draws. His
skating is NHL calibre. He isn't breakaway-quick, but
his anticipation will buy him a few steps every time.

THE PHYSICAL GAME

Pahlsson is average height but solid, and he plays even
bigger. He seems to have a very long reach. He digs in
the corners and is tough. Those 87 penalty minutes are
high for the Swedish Elite League.

THE INTANGIBLES

Pahlsson has a good chance to make the team in training camp, probably as a third-line centre behind Jason
Allison and Joe Thornton. He's already had a taste of
things to come: he played for Sweden in the World
Championships with P.J. Axelsson, his likely Bruins
linemate.

PROJECTION

When the Ray Bourque deal was made, Bruins fans
were lamenting, "Sami who?" They're about to find
out. He could score 10 goals in a checking role, which
might not sound like much, but he is also going to
make the Bruins a harder team to fight your way
through.

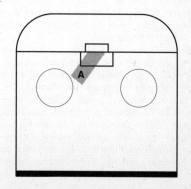

BRIAN ROLSTON

Yrs. of NHL service: 6
Born: Flint, Mich.; Feb. 21, 1973
Position: left wing
Height: 6-2
Weight: 185
Uniform no.: 14
Shoots: left

Career statistics:

GP	G	A	TP	PIM
414	94	111	205	93

1996-97 statistics:

GP	G	A	TP	+/-	PIM	PP	SH	GW	GT	S	PCT
81	18	27	45	+6	20	2	2	3	0	237	7.6

1997-98 statistics:

GP	G	A	TP	+/-	PIM	PP	SH	GW	GT	S	PCT
76	16	14	30	+7	16	0	2	1	0	185	8.6

1998-99 statistics:

GP	G	A	TP	+/-	PIM	PP	SH	GW	GT	S	PCT
82	24	33	57	+11	14	5	5	3	0	210	11.4

1999-2000 statistics:

GP	G	A	TP	+/-	PIM	PP	SH	GW	GT	S	PCT
77	16	15	31	-12	18	5	0	6	0	206	7.8

LAST SEASON

Acquired by Boston from Colorado with Sami Pahlsson, Martin Grenier, and option of first-round pick in 2000 or 2001 for Ray Bourque and Dave Andreychuk, Mar. 6, 2000. Acquired by Colorado from New Jersey with option of switching first-round draft pick in 2000 for Claude Lemieux and second-round draft choice in 2000, Nov. 3, 1999. Led Boston in shots and game-winning goals. Tied for second on Boston in power-play goals.

THE FINESSE GAME

Rolston will get into goal-scoring grooves in the season, then just as maddeningly will lurch into a slump that lasts weeks. As a shooter, he can be woefully impatient. He has a cannon from the top of the circles in with a quick release. But he tends to hurry his shots, even when he has time to wait, which results in wildly inaccurate shots. He wastes many odd-man-rush opportunities, especially shorthanded ones, by not forcing the goalie to handle the puck and denying the trailing player a chance at a rebound. Watching Rolston waste one scoring opportunity after another is an exercise in rapid-fire frustration.

Rolston's game is speed. He is a fast, powerful skater who drives to the net and loves to shoot. He passes well on his forehand and backhand, and reads breakout plays by leading his man smartly.

He is an aggressive penalty killer who deserves some Selke Trophy consideration. He uses his quick getaway stride to pull away for shorthanded breaks. He takes some pride in this role, and works diligently. Although he doesn't like it, he has been shoehorned into the role of a defensive winger. Rolston thought he could be a better producer on a more offensive team, but that didn't turn out to be the case in his stint with the Avalache, where he was 8-10 — 18 in 50 games.

He makes a highly effective shadow, as he is one of the few players with the size, skill, and smarts to match strides with a Jaromir Jagr or Pavel Bure.

THE PHYSICAL GAME

Rolston will take a hit to make a play, and has taken the next step to start initiating fights for pucks. He can be intimidated, however, and lacks true grit. His better games come against skating clubs. He is durable; in part because he keeps himself out of areas where he can get hurt.

THE INTANGIBLES

Three teams in one season is a lot of change for a player to handle — especially when one goes from one contender (New Jersey) to another (Colorado) to a clunker (Boston). Rolston showed good attitude in Beantown, where he was used a lot in all playing situations. The extremely likeable Rolston will have to deal with the mental burden of being one of the players the Bruins got in return for the godlike Ray Bourque.

PROJECTION

Rolston always looks like he is on the verge of a 30-goal season, but 20 is more his limit.

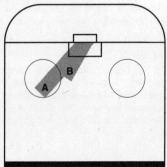

SERGEI SAMSONOV

Yrs. of NHL service: 3
Born: Moscow, Russia; Oct. 27, 1978
Position: left wing
Height: 5-8
Weight: 184
Uniform no.: 14
Shoots: left

Career statistics:

GP	G	A	TP	PIM
237	66	77	143	30

1997-98 statistics:

GP	G	A	TP	+/-	PIM	PP	SH	GW	GT	S	PCT
81	22	25	47	+9	8	7	0	3	0	159	13.8

1998-99 statistics:

GP	G	A	TP	+/-	PIM	PP	SH	GW	GT	S	PCT
79	25	26	51	-6	18	6	0	8	1	160	15.6

1999-2000 statistics:

GP	G	A	TP	+/-	PIM	PP	SH	GW	GT	S	PCT
77	19	26	45	-6	4	6	0	3	0	145	13.1

spite having his name on the Calder Trophy, he still has a lot to prove. He needs to return to the 25-goal level.

LAST SEASON

Led team in power-play goals. Second on team in assists and points. Third on team in goals and shooting percentage. Tied for third on team in game-winning goals. Missed five games with knee injury.

THE FINESSE GAME

Consistency continues to elude Samsonov. When he's on, he is an absolute treat to watch. He is an outstanding skater — the puck doesn't slow him down a hair. He performs the hockey equivalent of a between the legs dribble, putting pucks between the legs (his or the defenders') and executing cutbacks.

He has outstanding quickness and breakaway speed. He plays on his off-wing but uses all of the ice. A better scorer than playmaker, he has a quick release on his shot. He tends to be streaky.

Samsonov is too in love with his skating. His idea of a great play is to try to go the length of the ice and through all five defenders before taking a shot, as if hockey were some kind of obstacle course. If he can keep the game more simple and use his linemates better, he will have more success.

He is reliable enough defensively.

THE PHYSICAL GAME

Sturdily built, Samsonov is a little tank. He can't be scared off the play and he handles himself well in traffic and in tight spaces along the boards and corners.

THE INTANGIBLES

This could be the season that determines what kind of player Samsonov is. Being occasionally brilliant isn't good enough.

PROJECTION

Samsonov took a step backwards last season, and de-

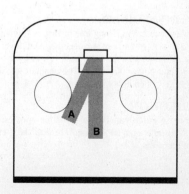

ANDRE SAVAGE

Yrs. of NHL service: 1
Born: Ottawa, Ont.; May 27, 1975
Position: centre
Height: 6-0
Weight: 195
Uniform no.: 28
Shoots: right

Career statistics:

GP	G	A	TP	PIM
49	8	13	21	10

1998-99 statistics:

GP	G	A	TP	+/-	PIM	PP	SH	GW	GT	S	PCT
6	1	0	1	+2	0	0	0	0	0	8	12.5

1999-2000 statistics:

GP	G	A	TP	+/-	PIM	PP	SH	GW	GT	S	PCT
43	7	13	20	-8	10	2	0	1	1	70	10.0

LAST SEASON

First NHL season. Appeared in 30 games with Providence (AHL), scoring 15-17 — 32. Missed four games with trapezius muscle strain. Missed three games with bruised sternum. Missed one game due to coach's decision.

THE FINESSE GAME

Savage has been a scorer at the college (Michigan Tech) and minor league levels befor getting his chance in the majors. His biggest drawback is his last of speed. Savage is not overly fast.

He is however, smart and hardworking. He is good in traffic and along the wall. His point totals will always be much heavier in assists than goals, because Savage is a playmaker first. Savage has a fine passing touch.

If only Savage had a little better foot speed, the could earn a spot on the checking line, because Savage has terrific hockey sense and works diligently at his assignments. Unless he can improve his skating, he will be a bubble player.

THE PHYSICAL GAME

Savage has average size and no mean streak to speak of.

THE INTANGIBLES

Savage is another in a long line of Bruins "lunchpail' types, players who desire elevates their skill level. He could earn time on a third or fourth line and see some second unit power play duty. The depature of Steve Heinze may open up a roster spot.

PROJECTION

Whether Savage can find a full-time spot on the Bruins roster is a question mark. If he does, he is capable of 35 points.

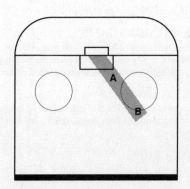

DON SWEENEY

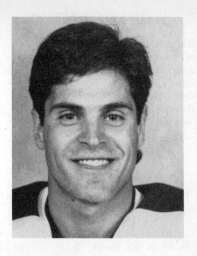

Yrs. of NHL service: 12
Born: St. Stephen, N.B.; Aug. 17, 1966
Position: left defense
Height: 5-10
Weight: 188
Uniform no.: 32
Shoots: left

Career statistics:

GP	G	A	TP	PIM
832	44	180	224	578

1996-97 statistics:

GP	G	A	TP	+/-	PIM	PP	SH	GW	GT	S	PCT
82	3	23	26	-5	39	0	0	0	0	113	2.7

1997-98 statistics:

GP	G	A	TP	+/-	PIM	PP	SH	GW	GT	S	PCT
59	1	15	16	+12	24	0	0	0	0	55	1.8

1998-99 statistics:

GP	G	A	TP	+/-	PIM	PP	SH	GW	GT	S	PCT
81	2	10	12	+14	64	0	0	0	0	79	2.5

1999-2000 statistics:

GP	G	A	TP	+/-	PIM	PP	SH	GW	GT	S	PCT
81	1	13	14	-14	48	0	0	0	0	82	1.2

LAST SEASON

Missed one game due to flu.

THE FINESSE GAME

Sweeney has found a niche for himself in the NHL. He's mobile, physical and greatly improved in the area of defensive reads. He has good hockey sense for recognizing offensive situations as well.

Although he mostly stays at home and out of trouble, he is a good enough skater to get involved in the attack and to take advantage of open ice. He is a good passer and has an adequate shot, and he has developed more confidence in his skills. He skates his way out of trouble and moves the puck well.

Sweeney is also a clever player who knows his strengths and weaknesses. Despite being a low draft pick (166th overall), he doesn't let anyone overlook him because of his effort and intelligence.

THE PHYSICAL GAME

Sweeney is built like a little human Coke machine. He is tough to play against and, while wear and tear is a factor, he never hides. He is always in the middle of physical play. He utilizes his lower-body drive and has tremendous leg power. He is also shifty enough to avoid a big hit when he sees it coming, and many a large forechecking forward has sheepishly picked himself up off the ice after Sweeney has scampered away from the boards with the puck.

The ultimate gym rat, Sweeney devotes a great deal of time to weightlifting and overall conditioning. Pound for pound, he is one of the strongest defensemen in the NHL. Of course, it won't hurt to pair him with the physical Kyle McLaren.

THE INTANGIBLES

The Bruins thought highly enough of Sweeney to outbid several other teams for his free agent services — and knowing how chintzy the Bruins are, that is indeed high praise. Sweeney is highly competitive; despite his small size, a lot of teams would welcome him on their blueline. Boston has gotten a little deeper on defense, but Sweeney remains a top-four staple. His experience will be greatly needed now that Ray Bourque is gone.

PROJECTION

Sweeney's point totals won't go much higher than 20.

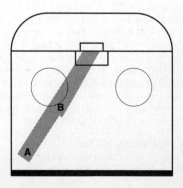

JOE THORNTON

Yrs. of NHL service: 3
Born: London, Ont.; July 2, 1979
Position: centre
Height: 6-4
Weight: 198
Uniform no.: 6
Shoots: left

Career statistics:

GP	G	A	TP	PIM
217	42	66	108	170

1997-98 statistics:

GP	G	A	TP	+/-	PIM	PP	SH	GW	GT	S	PCT
55	3	4	7	-6	19	0	0	1	0	33	9.1

1998-99 statistics:

GP	G	A	TP	+/-	PIM	PP	SH	GW	GT	S	PCT
81	16	25	41	+3	69	7	0	1	0	128	12.5

1999-2000 statistics:

GP	G	A	TP	+/-	PIM	PP	SH	GW	GT	S	PCT
81	23	37	60	-5	82	5	0	3	0	171	13.5

LAST SEASON

Led team in goals, assists, points and penalty minutes, all career highs. Second on team in shooting percentage. Tied for second on team in power-play goals. Tied for third on team in game-winning goals. Missed one game with bruised knee.

THE FINESSE GAME

So much for writing off a teenaged first-rounder as a first-year bust. All Thornton has done after a slow and careful rookie year is bring his game up to a level where he is just a year or two away from NHL stardom, and he has done it with a team that assembles its talent on the cheap and for a coach he doesn't like very much.

Thornton has all of the tools, and the toolbox — a big, strong frame. His key assets are his exceptional vision of the ice and the hand skills to make things happen.

He is so adept at finding holes and passing lanes that teammates have to be exceptionally alert when playing with him, because he will create something out of nothing. He also loves to shoot and work the boards, corners and front of the net. He needs to be prodded to keep his feet moving, though, as he often drifts into a bad habit of standing and waiting for things to happen. He needs to make things happen.

Thornton's skating could use some improvement, but it's NHL calibre. He is steadily improving his work on draws. He handled the promotion to first-line duty last season as a centre, and survived despite intense checking pressure with Jason Allison absent for half the season. He is ready for the big time.

THE PHYSICAL GAME

Thornton has a short fuse and can be goaded off his game. Opponents know it. The reason he has a team-high PIM total is that the Bruins haven't provided him with some sort of protector. Yes, Thornton can take care of himself, but who wants him in the box that much? He digs and bangs and plays with an edge, but he needs to keep his natural aggression under control.

THE INTANGIBLES

Thornton underwent off-season shoulder surgery, and if he rehabs that well, there should be nothing holding him back this season except the lack of a strong supporting cast.

PROJECTION

Considering the situation in Boston last season, Thornton did a remarkable job surpassing the 20-goal mark we had predicted for him. He should continue to gradually increase his goal and point totals, to 25 to 30 and 70 to 75, respectively.

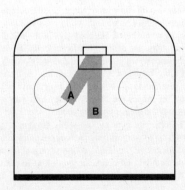

BUFFALO SABRES

Players' Statistics 1999-2000

POS	NO.	PLAYER	GP	G	A	PTS	+/-	PIM	PP	SH	GW	GT	S	PCT
C	93	DOUG GILMOUR	74	25	48	73	-9	63	10		3	1	113	22.1
L	81	MIROSLAV SATAN	81	33	34	67	16	32	5	3	5	1	265	12.5
C	37	CURTIS BROWN	74	22	29	51	19	42	5		4	1	149	14.8
C	77	CHRIS GRATTON	72	15	34	49	-23	136	4		1	1	202	7.4
C	41	STU BARNES	82	20	25	45	-3	16	8	2	2		137	14.6
C	27	MICHAEL PECA	73	20	21	41	6	67	2		3		144	13.9
R	25	VACLAV VARADA	76	10	27	37	12	62					140	7.1
R	61	*MAXIM AFINOGENOV	65	16	18	34	-4	41	2		2		128	12.5
D	5	JASON WOOLLEY	74	8	25	33	14	52	2		2		113	7.1
L	29	VLADIMIR TSYPLAKOV	63	12	20	32	23	14	1		2		76	15.8
L	8	GEOFF SANDERSON	67	13	13	26	4	22	4		3		136	9.6
R	15	DIXON WARD	71	11	9	20	1	41	1	2	2		101	10.9
D	74	JAY MCKEE	78	5	12	17	5	50	1		1		84	6.0
C	9	ERIK RASMUSSEN	67	8	6	14	1	43			2		76	10.5
D	3	JAMES PATRICK	66	5	8	13	8	22			3		40	12.5
D	44	ALEXEI ZHITNIK	74	2	11	13	-6	95	1				139	1.4
D	42	RICHARD SMEHLIK	64	2	9	11	13	50					67	3.0
D	51	*BRIAN CAMPBELL	12	1	4	5	-2	4					10	10.0
R	32	ROB RAY	69	1	3	4	0	158					17	5.9
D	4	RHETT WARRENER	61		3	3	18	89					68	
C	16	CHRIS TAYLOR	11	1	1	2	-2	2					15	6.7
L	55	*DENIS HAMEL	3	1		1	-1						3	33.3
C	12	*DOMENIC PITTIS	7	1		1	1	6					6	16.7
D	20	*JASON HOLLAND	9		1	1	0						8	
G	39	DOMINIK HASEK	35		1	1	0	12						
D	20	DOUG HOUDA	1				0	12						
D	21	MIKE HURLBUT	1				1	2					1	
L	64	DAVID MORAVEC	1				-1						2	
D	45	*DIMITRI KALININ	4				0	4					3	
L	24	PAUL KRUSE	11				-2	43					7	
D	34	*J-LUC GRAND-PIERRE	11				-1	15					10	
G	30	DWAYNE ROLOSON	14				0							
G	43	*MARTIN BIRON	41				0	6						

GP = games played; G = goals; A = assists; PTS = points; +/- = goals-for minus goals-against while player is on ice; PIM = penalties in minutes; PP = power-play goals; SH = shorthanded goals; GW = game-winning goals; GT = game-tying goals; S = no. of shots; PCT = percentage of goals to shots; * = rookie

MAXIM AFINOGENOV

Yrs. of NHL service: 1
Born: Moscow, Russia; Sept. 4, 1979
Position: right wing
Height: 5-11
Weight: 176
Uniform no.: 61
Shoots: left

Career statistics:

GP	G	A	TP	PIM
65	16	18	34	41

1999-2000 statistics:

GP	G	A	TP	+/-	PIM	PP	SH	GW	GT	S	PCT
65	16	18	34	-4	41	2	0	2	0	128	12.5

LAST SEASON

First NHL season. Tied for eighth among NHL rookies in goals and points. Appeared in 15 games with Rochester (AHL), scoring 6-12 — 18.

THE FINESSE GAME

Afinogenov is a powerful skater with explosive speed and excellent balance. He may have too much confidence in his puckhandling skills, because he likes to take the Alexei Kovalev route to the net.

Fun, maybe. Effective, no. Afinogenov needs to use his linemates better and be more of a give-and-go player. His shot isn't great. It's his intimidating speed and the quickness of his shot that gives him the offensive edge.

Afinogenov is quite similar in playing style to Boston's Sergei Samsonov, another talented but inconsistent scorer.

THE PHYSICAL GAME

Afinogenov is not very big, but on the shifts where he turns on his intensity he can't be intimidated. He plays with determination in the attacking zone and has to learn to apply that to the rest of the ice.

THE INTANGIBLES

This was Afinogenov's first year pro, and his first year in North America. That's a lot of adjusting for a 20-year-old, which he was at the start of the season. He gained playoff experience in the NHL and the minors, and that will move him forward.

PROJECTION

His production in three-quarters of a season indicates he can score 20 to 25 goals if he applies himself to stick around long enough for a full one.

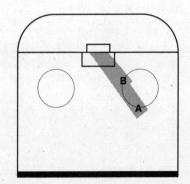

DAVE ANDREYCHUK

Yrs. of NHL service: 18
Born: Hamilton, Ont.; Sept. 29, 1963
Position: left wing
Height: 6-3
Weight: 220
Uniform no.: 23
Shoots: right

Career statistics:

GP	G	A	TP	PIM
1303	552	620	1175	892

1996-97 statistics:

GP	G	A	TP	+/-	PIM	PP	SH	GW	GT	S	PCT
82	27	34	61	+38	48	4	1	2	1	233	11.6

1997-98 statistics:

GP	G	A	TP	+/-	PIM	PP	SH	GW	GT	S	PCT
75	14	34	48	+19	26	4	0	2	0	180	7.8

1998-99 statistics:

GP	G	A	TP	+/-	PIM	PP	SH	GW	GT	S	PCT
52	15	13	28	+1	20	4	0	3	1	110	13.6

1999-2000 statistics:

GP	G	A	TP	+/-	PIM	PP	SH	GW	GT	S	PCT
77	20	16	36	-20	30	8	0	3	1	233	8.6

LAST SEASON

Signed as a free agent by Buffalo, July 13, 2000. Missed two games with knee injury.

THE FINESSE GAME

Andreychuk just can't get enough of the game, but defenders have certainly had their fill of him. The big winger uses a very stiff shaft on his long stick, enabling him to lean on it hard in front of the net. He tries to keep his blade on the ice for deflections, and by pushing his 220 pounds on the stick, he makes it almost impossible for a defender to lift it off the ice. His touch just isn't as deadly as it once was.

Andreychuk has slow feet but a cherry-picker reach, which he uses with strength and intelligence. He is a lumbering skater. He works in tight areas, though, so he only needs a big stride or two to plant himself where he wants to be. He has marvellous hand skills in traffic and is an underrated passer. He can use his stick to artfully pick pucks out of midair, to slap at rebounds or for wraparounds.

From the hash marks in, Andreychuk has long been one of the most dangerous snipers in the league. On the other four-fifths of the ice, he is a liability because of his lack of foot speed, which is now even slower.

Andreychuk needs to play with people who can get him the puck and with people who can skate, to compensate for his skating deficiencies.

THE PHYSICAL GAME

If you're looking for someone to protect his smaller teammates, or to inspire a team with his hitting, Andreychuk is not your man. He is a giant shock absorber, soaking up hits without retaliating. He has a long fuse and seldom takes a bad penalty, especially when his team is on the power play.

He's tough in his own way — in front of the opponent's net — at least. He is nearly impossible to budge, and with his long arms can control pucks. He isn't dominating, but he is physically prominent within five feet of the crease. He pays the price to score goals, but the goals aren't coming the way they used to.

THE INTANGIBLES

Andreychuk scored only one goal in 14 regular season games with the Avs after the trade, but he did net three (two on the power play) in the playoffs. He was an unrestricted free agent after the season and the Avs had no interest in re-signing him. He can still be a useful player in the right spot. He also possesses one of the best hockey brains in the business.

PROJECTION

We thought last season that Andreychuk could hit 20 goals. This could be his last shot at it.

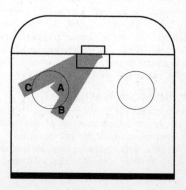

STU BARNES

Yrs. of NHL service: 9
Born: Edmonton, Alta.; Dec. 25, 1970
Position: centre
Height: 5-11
Weight: 175
Uniform no.: 41
Shoots: right

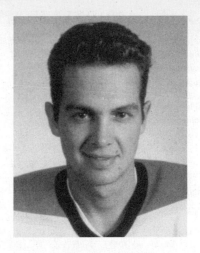

Career statistics:

GP	G	A	TP	PIM
596	161	193	354	230

1996-97 statistics:

GP	G	A	TP	+/-	PIM	PP	SH	GW	GT	S	PCT
81	19	30	49	-23	26	5	0	3	3	176	10.8

1997-98 statistics:

GP	G	A	TP	+/-	PIM	PP	SH	GW	GT	S	PCT
78	30	35	65	+15	30	15	1	5	0	196	15.3

1998-99 statistics:

GP	G	A	TP	+/-	PIM	PP	SH	GW	GT	S	PCT
81	20	16	36	-11	30	13	0	3	0	180	11.1

1999-2000 statistics:

GP	G	A	TP	+/-	PIM	PP	SH	GW	GT	S	PCT
82	20	25	45	-3	16	8	2	2	0	137	14.6

LAST SEASON

Second on team in power-play goals. Tied for second on team in shorthanded goals. Only Sabre to appear in all 82 games.

THE FINESSE GAME

It's hard to begrudge Barnes any of the success he enjoys. He pursues the puck intelligently and finishes his checks. He employs these traits at even strength, whether killing penalties or on the power play. He reads the play coming out of the zone and uses his anticipation to pick off passes. He plays with great enthusiasm. He has sharply honed puck skills and offensive instincts, which he puts to effective use on the power play. He has good quickness and can control the puck in traffic. He uses a slap shot or a wrist shot in tight.

Barnes wastes few of the quality chances that come his way. He has a quick release and is accurate with his shot. One of his favourite plays is using his right-handed shot for a one-timer on the power play.

He has a good work ethic; his effort overcomes his deficiency in size. He's clever and plays a smart small man's game. He plays all three forward positions. He tends to get into scoring slumps, but never quits working to try to snap out of them.

THE PHYSICAL GAME

Barnes is not big but he gets in the way. He brings a little bit of grit to the lineup, but what really stands out is his intensity and spirit. He can energize his team with one gutsy shift. He always keeps his feet moving and draws penalties. He gets outmuscled down low.

THE INTANGIBLES

Barnes is one of those guys who just turns it up in the playoffs. He has had two solid springs in a row. He had three goals in five games as one of Buffalo's best forwards in the first-round exit this year, and helped the Sabres get into the playoffs with a key late-season goal. The epitome of hard work, Barnes is fortunate to play in an organization where that asset is prized. He is a consummate pro.

PROJECTION

As we stated last year, realistically, 20 goals is the right target for Barnes. That's where we expect him to be again this year.

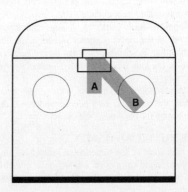

CURTIS BROWN

Yrs. of NHL service: 4
Born: Unity, Sask.; Feb. 12, 1976
Position: centre
Height: 6-0
Weight: 190
Uniform no.: 37
Shoots: left

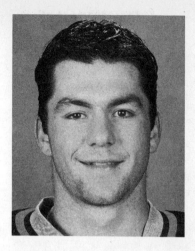

Career statistics:

GP	G	A	TP	PIM
248	55	76	131	152

1996-97 statistics:

GP	G	A	TP	+/-	PIM	PP	SH	GW	GT	S	PCT
28	4	3	7	+4	18	0	0	1	0	31	12.9

1997-98 statistics:

GP	G	A	TP	+/-	PIM	PP	SH	GW	GT	S	PCT
63	12	12	24	+11	34	1	1	2	1	91	13.2

1998-99 statistics:

GP	G	A	TP	+/-	PIM	PP	SH	GW	GT	S	PCT
78	16	31	47	+23	56	5	1	3	3	128	12.5

1999-2000 statistics:

GP	G	A	TP	+/-	PIM	PP	SH	GW	GT	S	PCT
74	22	29	51	+19	42	5	0	4	1	149	14.8

LAST SEASON

Second on team in plus-minus and shooting percentage. Third on team in goals, points and shots. Career high in goals. Tied for third on team in power-play goals. Missed six games with flu. Missed one game with concussion.

THE FINESSE GAME

Brown is a little cannonball, strong and quick on his skates and unafraid to get involved around the net. He is an excellent penalty killer, with terrific reads and anticipation, and the jump to pick off passes and turn them into shorthanded chances.

A coverted left wing, Brown makes an ideal number three centre, which is where he was moved after the arrival of Doug Gilmour and Chris Gratton. He has enough offensive skills to play on the top two lines, but his chief asset is a defensive ability. Brown will create things with his speed on the forecheck and then has the hands to make the tape-to-tape pass. He is a playmaker first.

Brown's hockey sense and defensive awareness are exceptional. He has started to gain a little of the reputation needed to be considered for the Selke Trophy.

THE PHYSICAL GAME

Brown is little but plays with a bit of swagger. He isn't really tough. He just gives the impression that he won't back off. He is abrasive and annoying.

THE INTANGIBLES

Brown continues to improve and playing with Gilmour will be a good learning experience that will only help round out his game. Brown carried the Sabres through the first half, while Peca was struggling and before the big trades, but he slumped in the second half as he wore down.

PROJECTION

Brown will get a lot of ice time again and should produce 50 points.

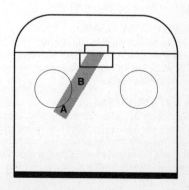

J. P. DUMONT

Yrs. of NHL service: 1
Born: Montreal, Que.; Apr. 1, 1978
Position: right wing
Height: 6-1
Weight: 187
Uniform no.: 17
Shoots: left

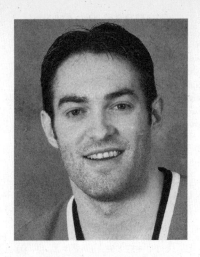

Career statistics:

GP	G	A	TP	PIM
72	19	14	33	28

1998-99 statistics:

GP	G	A	TP	+/-	PIM	PP	SH	GW	GT	S	PCT
25	9	6	15	+7	10	0	0	2	0	42	21.4

1999-2000 statistics:

GP	G	A	TP	+/-	PIM	PP	SH	GW	GT	S	PCT
47	10	8	18	-6	18	0	0	1	0	86	11.6

LAST SEASON

Acquired from Chicago with Doug Gilmour for Michal Grosek, Mar. 10, 2000. Appeared in 13 games with Rochester (AHL), scoring 7-10 — 17.

THE FINESSE GAME

Dumont has all of the weapons needed to become a scorer in the NHL. He is an instinctive shooter and playmaker, seeing his options a step ahead of everyone else. He disguises his intentions well. Because he is unselfish with the puck, defenders may expect the pass. But Dumont has an excellent wrist and slap shot so you can't allow him to cruise to the net. He is pure hands. He has shown less willingness to pay the price around the net after a head injury.

Dumont goes through and around players like the breeze, with excellent puck control. His skating is NHL calibre. He has good acceleration for short bursts or rink-long sprints. He has had to work on his conditioning and has taken power-skating lessons, so he is willing to work to improve his game. His hand-eye coordination for tip-ins and rebounds is outstanding.

As is typical with many young players, the knock on Dumont is his lack of intensity at times, but he is maturing. He is one of those rare players who finds the back of the net by any means possible.

THE PHYSICAL GAME

Dumont is tall but whippet-thin. He will need to fill out with some muscle now that he's no longer playing with boys. He has an edge to his game, which shows he may thrive in the pros.

THE INTANGIBLES

Dumont is only 22 and this is his third NHL organization. That's not a good sign. This is a watershed year for him. Dumont suffered a concussion two years ago and played a little timid after it. Chicago kept him out of games in 1998-99 in order to protect his rookie status and give him a shot at the Calder Trophy, and, in retrospect, that has backfired. The Sabres sent him to the minors to rebuild his confidence, and if he gets a chance to play with Doug Gilmour, he could give Buffalo some desperately needed offense.

PROJECTION

We were one of Dumont's biggest tubthumpers, but now we'll drop the 50-goal talk. If he can score 20 playing a full season in Buffalo his career will be back on track.

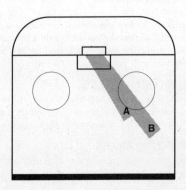

DOUG GILMOUR

Yrs. of NHL service: 17
Born: Kingston, Ont.; June 25, 1963
Position: centre
Height: 5-11
Weight: 172
Uniform no.: 93
Shoots: left

Career statistics:

GP	G	A	TP	PIM
1271	422	883	1305	1145

1996-97 statistics:

GP	G	A	TP	+/-	PIM	PP	SH	GW	GT	S	PCT
81	22	60	82	+2	68	4	1	1	1	143	15.4

1997-98 statistics:

GP	G	A	TP	+/-	PIM	PP	SH	GW	GT	S	PCT
63	13	40	53	+10	68	3	0	5	0	94	13.8

1998-99 statistics:

GP	G	A	TP	+/-	PIM	PP	SH	GW	GT	S	PCT
72	16	40	56	-16	56	7	1	4	0	110	14.5

1999-2000 statistics:

GP	G	A	TP	+/-	PIM	PP	SH	GW	GT	S	PCT
74	25	48	73	-9	63	10	0	3	1	113	22.1

LAST SEASON

Acquired from Chicago with J.P. Dumont for Michal Grosek, Mar. 10, 2000. Led Sabres in assists, points, power-play goals and shooting percentage. Second on team in goals. Missed six games with hip injury. Missed two games due to flu. Missed one game with rib injury.

THE FINESSE GAME

A creative playmaker, Gilmour has eschewed the banana blade for a nearly straight model, so he can handle the puck equally well on his forehand or backhand. He will bring people right in on top of him before he slides a little pass to a teammate, creating time and space. He is very intelligent and has great anticipation. He loves to set up from behind the net, and intimidates because he plays with such supreme confidence.

Gilmour doesn't shoot much; he's a set-up man who needs finishers around him. When he does shoot he won't use a big slapper, but instead scores from close range either as the trailer or after losing a defender with his subtle dekes and moves. He's not a smooth, gifted skater, but he is nimble and quick.

Gilmour ranks as one of the best face-off men in the NHL and routinely beats big, stronger centres on draws. In his own end he is very sound positionally. He is a defensively solid player. His awful plus-minus reflects just how bad the 'Hawks and Gilmour's injury must have been.

THE PHYSICAL GAME

Gilmour competes with passion and savvy, challenging bigger opponents. Although he's listed at 185 pounds, he plays at around 165 during the season. He is more effective at the lighter weight.

THE INTANGIBLES

The Sabres didn't get to see the best of Gilmour due to a virus that caused him to lose 12 pounds by playoff time. He is heading into his last season. He provides never-say-die leadership. He often responds with a big shift after his team has been scored upon and will ignite his teamates with an inspirational bump or goal. He will do everything he can to win a game, but the reservoir is only so deep.

PROJECTION

We said last season it would be a challenge for Gilmour to score 70 points, which he managed to do on a weak 'Hawks team. He scored 17 points in just 11 games with Buffalo, and could be a point-a-game player in his career finale.

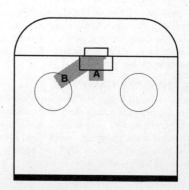

CHRIS GRATTON

Yrs. of NHL service: 7
Born: Brantford, Ont.; July 5, 1975
Position: centre
Height: 6-4
Weight: 218
Uniform no.: 77
Shoots: left

Career statistics:

GP	G	A	TP	PIM
526	112	202	314	956

1996-97 statistics:

GP	G	A	TP	+/-	PIM	PP	SH	GW	GT	S	PCT
82	30	32	62	-28	201	9	0	4	0	230	13.0

1997-98 statistics:

GP	G	A	TP	+/-	PIM	PP	SH	GW	GT	S	PCT
82	22	40	62	+11	159	5	0	2	0	182	12.1

1998-99 statistics:

GP	G	A	TP	+/-	PIM	PP	SH	GW	GT	S	PCT
78	8	26	34	-28	143	1	0	1	1	181	4.4

1999-2000 statistics:

GP	G	A	TP	+/-	PIM	PP	SH	GW	GT	S	PCT
72	15	34	49	-23	136	4	0	1	1	202	7.4

LAST SEASON

Acquired from Florida with a second-round draft choice in 2001 for Brian Holzinger, Wayne Primeau and a third-round draft choice in 2000, Mar. 10, 2000.

THE FINESSE GAME

Gratton was supposed to be a power centre, and is happier playing there than when he is on the wing, but he is clearly overmatched in the middle. One of the major reasons is his lack of foot speed, which really hurts him despite a lot of coaching in this area.

Gratton's game is meat and potatoes. He's a grinder and needs to work hard every shift, every night, to make an impact. He has a hard shot, which he needs to use more. He gets his goals from digging around the net and there's some Cam Neely in him, but he lacks the long, strong stride Neely used in traffic. He has good hand-eye coordination and can pick passes out of midair for a shot. He has a big, noisy, but not always effective slapshot.

Gratton is an unselfish playmaker. He's not the prettiest of passers, but he has some poise with the puck and he knows when to pass and when to shoot. He has shown an ability to win face-offs, and works diligently in his own end.

THE PHYSICAL GAME

Gratton is a hard-working sort who doesn't shy from contact, but he has to initiate more. If his skating improves he will be able to establish a more physical presence. He doesn't generate enough speed from leg drive to be much of a checker. He won't be an impact player in the NHL until he does.

THE INTANGIBLES

Gratton was picked up by Buffalo for help down the stretch and into the playoffs, but scored only one goal in 14 regular-season games after the trade — into an empty net, by the way — and was a huge disappointment with no goals in in the playoffs. This is a pivotal season for him.

PROJECTION

Gratton scored 30 goals in 1996-97, but it's hard to imagine him repeating that. He is likely to score in the 20-goal range, and that appears to be his top end. Enough of the promise. That's the reality.

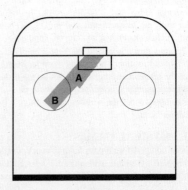

DOMINIK HASEK

Yrs. of NHL service: 9
Born: Pardubice, Czech Republic; Jan. 29, 1965
Position: goaltender
Height: 5-11
Weight: 168
Uniform no.: 39
Catches: left

Career statistics:

GP	MIN	GA	SO	GAA	A	PIM
449	25969	977	45	2.26	10	90

1996-97 statistics:

GP	MIN	GAA	W	L	T	SO	GA	S	SAPCT	PIM
67	4037	2.27	37	20	10	5	153	2177	.930	30

1997-98 statistics:

GP	MIN	GAA	W	L	T	SO	GA	S	SAPCT	PIM
72	4220	2.09	33	23	13	13	147	2149	.932	12

1998-99 statistics:

GP	MIN	GAA	W	L	T	SO	GA	S	SAPCT	PIM
64	3817	1.87	30	18	14	9	119	1877	.937	14

1999-2000 statistics:

GP	MIN	GAA	W	L	T	SO	GA	S	SAPCT	PIM
35	2066	2.21	15	11	6	3	76	937	.919	12

LAST SEASON

Missed 40 games with groin injury.

THE PHYSICAL GAME

Nobody has worse technique nor better leg reflexes than Hasek; his foot speed is simply tremendous. He wanders and flops and sprawls. But he stops the puck. Usually, what Hasek sees he stops, and to him the puck seems to be moving more slowly than it does for other goalies. He watches it come off the shooter's stick into his glove or body, and he always seems in control, even while he looks to be flopping like a trout.

Hasek is adept at directing his rebounds away from onrushing attackers. He prefers to hold pucks for face-offs — in fact, he chases into the face-off circles for them — and the Sabres have a decent corps of centres so that tactic works fine for his team. Hasek instructs his defensemen to get out of the way so he can see the puck, and they follow orders.

Hasek learned to come out of his net a little bit more but he still doesn't cut down his angles well. He also has to work on his puckhandling. He has the single most bizarre habit of any NHL goalie we've seen in recent years. In scrambles around the net he abandons his stick entirely and grabs the puck with his blocker hand. His work with the stick is brutal, which may be why he lets go of it so often. Opponents have been complaining that he just happens to drop the stick in the way of the shooter trying to get to the loose puck.

THE MENTAL GAME

On the ice, Hasek is competitive and unflappable. He is always prepared for tough saves early in a game, and has very few lapses of concentration. His excitable style doesn't bother his teammates, who have developed faith in his ability. When he dives, when he blows up at an opponent's nudge, it's all with a purpose.

THE INTANGIBLES

This will be the last hurrah for Hasek — unless he becomes the Frank Sinatra of goalies and changes his mind about retirement again. Can he still dominate? He was only human in the playoffs. It's not likely he'll want to yield many starts to Martin Biron, although it would be beneficial to Hasek to do so.

PROJECTION

Buffalo takes pride in being more than a one-man team, but Hasek is still the man who should rack up 30 wins for the Sabres, assuming his groin injury does not recur. Hasek will be 36 midway through the season. Not many goalies are that good this late.

JAY MCKEE

Yrs. of NHL service: 4
Born: Kingston, Ont.; Sept. 8, 1977
Position: left defense
Height: 6-3
Weight: 195
Uniform no.: 74
Shoots: left

Career statistics:

GP	G	A	TP	PIM
250	7	41	48	204

1996-97 statistics:

GP	G	A	TP	+/-	PIM	PP	SH	GW	GT	S	PCT
43	1	9	10	+3	35	0	0	0	0	29	3.4

1997-98 statistics:

GP	G	A	TP	+/-	PIM	PP	SH	GW	GT	S	PCT
56	1	13	14	-1	42	0	0	0	0	55	1.8

1998-99 statistics:

GP	G	A	TP	+/-	PIM	PP	SH	GW	GT	S	PCT
72	0	6	6	+20	75	0	0	0	0	57	.0

1999-2000 statistics:

GP	G	A	TP	+/-	PIM	PP	SH	GW	GT	S	PCT
78	5	12	17	+5	50	1	0	1	0	84	6.0

PROJECTION

McKee has become a regular in Buffalo's top four — he and Warrener were actually the top pairing as Alexei Zhtinik's game fell off dramatically — and still has some upside. With a little more confidence, McKee is capabale of a 20- to 25-point season.

LAST SEASON

Missed one game with flu.

THE FINESSE GAME

McKee has been studiously applying his skills to the defensive aspects of his game, to the point where his offensive game has been totally neglected. He has a future as more of a two-way defenseman if he builds off the confidence his defensive game should have provided him.

McKee is a strong skater, which powers his open-ice hits. He has good acceleration and quickness to carry the puck out of the zone. He gets involved in the attack because of his skating, but he doesn't have elite hands or playmaking skills.

He has sharp hockey sense and plays an advanced positional game for a young player. With Rhett Warrener's acquisition, McKee found a sympatico defense partner and his game picked up over the latter part of the season and into the playoffs.

THE PHYSICAL GAME

McKee has good size and is wiry and tough, if a little on the lean side. He exhibited a mean streak in junior but has been a little quieter at the pro level; he could get a little more involved.

THE INTANGIBLES

Mckee is never better than when he is paired with the fluid Rhett Warrener. McKee was minus-13 when Warrener was out of the lineup and plus-18 when Warrener was in the lineup. McKee scored four of his five goals in the last 13 games.

MICHAEL PECA

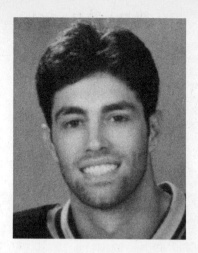

Yrs. of NHL service: 6
Born: Toronto, Ont.; March 26, 1974
Position: centre
Height: 5-11
Weight: 180
Uniform no.: 27
Shoots: right

Career statistics:

GP	G	A	TP	PIM
400	102	127	229	384

1996-97 statistics:

GP	G	A	TP	+/-	PIM	PP	SH	GW	GT	S	PCT
79	20	29	49	+26	80	5	6	4	0	137	14.6

1997-98 statistics:

GP	G	A	TP	+/-	PIM	PP	SH	GW	GT	S	PCT
61	18	22	40	+12	57	6	5	1	1	132	13.6

1998-99 statistics:

GP	G	A	TP	+/-	PIM	PP	SH	GW	GT	S	PCT
82	27	29	56	+7	81	10	0	8	1	199	13.6

1999-2000 statistics:

GP	G	A	TP	+/-	PIM	PP	SH	GW	GT	S	PCT
73	20	21	41	+6	67	2	0	3	0	144	13.9

LAST SEASON

Missed seven games with shoulder injury.

THE FINESSE GAME

Whether it was burnout from overwork in the 1999 Stanley Cup playoffs, or the pressure of a contract year bearing down on him, Peca looked like a shell of his old self for the first half of last season. Just when he started to find his game again (21 points in 26 games), he was injured just before the end of the season.

Peca is a strong, sure skater who plays every shift as if a pink slip will be waiting on the bench if he slacks off. He's good with the puck but not overly creative. He just reads offensive plays well and does a lot of the little things — especially when forechecking — that create turnovers and scoring chances. His goals come from his quickness and his effort. He challenges anyone for the puck.

Although Peca is known for his dogged defensive play, he is intelligent enough to be a useful offensive player. The Sabres skate him on their power-play unit. His hustle and attitude have earned him his NHL job, and league-wide respect. Peca thinks the game well and can be used in all situations.

Peca is at his worst offensively when he has too much time to think. He creates breakaway chances with his reads and anticipation but seldom converts. He is smart about disrupting plays and knows what to do once he gains control of the puck.

THE PHYSICAL GAME

Peca plays much bigger than his size. He's gritty and honest, and is always trying to add more weight. He has a tough time even keeping an extra five pounds on, and the Sabres have to be cautious about overplaying him, though they frequently have no choice. Although he lacks the size to match up with some of the league's bigger forwards, he is tireless in his pursuit and effort.

He's among the best open-ice hitters in the league. Peca is able to launch successful strikes against bigger players because of his timing, balance and leg strength. He will also drop the gloves and go after even the biggest foe. He is prickly and in-your-face, although opponents are less impressed with his diving skills.

THE INTANGIBLES

Peca's contract hassle with the Sabres (he's a restricted free agent) is expected to drag on through training camp and may mean a delayed start to the season for Peca.

PROJECTION

Peca should produce 50 points if he doesn't miss much of the season.

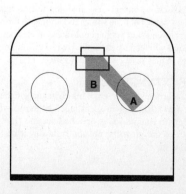

ERIK RASMUSSEN

Yrs. of NHL service: 2
Born: Minneapolis, Minn.; Mar. 28, 1977
Position: centre
Height: 6-2
Weight: 193
Uniform no.: 9
Shoots: left

Career statistics:

GP	G	A	TP	PIM
130	13	16	29	94

1997-98 statistics:

GP	G	A	TP	+/-	PIM	PP	SH	GW	GT	S	PCT
21	2	3	5	+2	14	0	0	0	0	28	7.1

1998-99 statistics:

GP	G	A	TP	+/-	PIM	PP	SH	GW	GT	S	PCT
42	3	7	10	+6	37	0	0	0	0	40	7.5

1999-2000 statistics:

GP	G	A	TP	+/-	PIM	PP	SH	GW	GT	S	PCT
67	8	6	14	+1	43	0	0	2	0	76	10.5

LAST SEASON

Missed six games with hand injury. Missed one game with back injury.

THE FINESSE GAME

Big, tough and skilled, Rasmussen is the type of forward the Sabres have been waiting for. They're still waiting, because Rasmussen doesn't bring his "A" game to the ice every night. If both he and Vaclav Varada make the commitment to flex their muscles this season, the Sabres will become a much more formidable team.

Rasmussen doesn't have great hands, but he has good ones to complement a scoring instinct and a desire to drive to the net. He usually looks to make a play first; the Sabres will try to encourage him to make better use of his wrist shot. He also has a hard slap shot.

Rasmussen is a strong skater with a long stride. He has good balance and agility and is tough to knock off his feet. He needs to learn to play a full 60 minutes and not take any shifts off.

THE PHYSICAL GAME

Rasmussen is abrasive and annoying to play against. He isn't huge, but he is strong and willing to throw his weight around and get in people's faces. He competes hard and will lead by example. He is still learning that he has to play hard every night to stick.

THE INTANGIBLES

After a strong start (seven of his eight goals in the first 28 games), Rasmussen spent much of the season on the fourth line and was benched for the final two games of the playoffs; not the right direction to be heading in.

PROJECTION

Rasmussen needs to build up his confidence and his point production (to 30 or so) or the Sabres are bound to run out of patience soon. He's still young, and still a valued prospect.

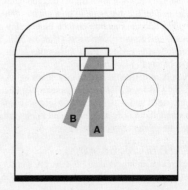

MIROSLAV SATAN

Yrs. of NHL service: 5
Born: Topolcany, Slovakia; Oct. 22, 1974
Position: left wing
Height: 6-1
Weight: 185
Uniform no.: 81
Shoots: left

Career statistics:

GP	G	A	TP	PIM
379	138	114	252	158

1996-97 statistics:

GP	G	A	TP	+/-	PIM	PP	SH	GW	GT	S	PCT
76	25	13	38	-3	26	7	0	3	0	119	21.0

1997-98 statistics:

GP	G	A	TP	+/-	PIM	PP	SH	GW	GT	S	PCT
79	22	24	46	+2	34	9	0	4	0	139	15.8

1998-99 statistics:

GP	G	A	TP	+/-	PIM	PP	SH	GW	GT	S	PCT
81	40	26	66	+24	44	13	3	6	1	208	19.2

1999-2000 statistics:

GP	G	A	TP	+/-	PIM	PP	SH	GW	GT	S	PCT
81	33	34	67	+16	32	5	3	5	1	265	12.5

LAST SEASON

Led team in goals for second consecutive season. Led team in shorthanded goals, game-winning goals and shots. Second on team in points. Tied for second on team in assists. Third on team in plus-minus. Tied for third on team in power-play goals. Missed one game due to coach's decision.

THE FINESSE GAME

Satan has terrific breakaway speed, which allows him to pull away from many defenders. He uses his skills in a strictly offensive sense. He developed as a fairly conscientious two-way player but in recent years has become more of a high-risk player.

Satan isn't shy about shooting. He keeps his head up and looks for his shooting holes, and is accurate with a wrist and snap shot. He sees his passing options and will sometimes make the play, but he is the sniper on whatever line he is playing and prefers to take the shot himself. One fault is his tendency to hold onto the puck too long.

Satan's biggest drawback is his lack of intensity, and with it, a lack of consistency. When he isn't scoring, he isn't doing much else to help his team win.

THE PHYSICAL GAME

Satan isn't huge, and being the prime checking objective on a team that isn't exactly loaded with offensive options takes its toll at crunch time. He has a wiry strength, and shouldn't be as intimidated as he appears to be.

THE INTANGIBLES

Playing with Doug Gilmour for a full season should help Satan's game. If Gilmlour could only pass along some of his famous grit. He is entering his scoring prime.

PROJECTION

Goals, goals, goals. Forget playmaking. Satan wants to score. He can net 40 now that Gilmour is on the scene.

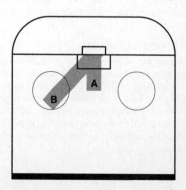

RICHARD SMEHLIK

Yrs. of NHL service: 7
Born: Ostrava, Czech Republic; Jan. 23, 1970
Position: right defense
Height: 6-3
Weight: 208
Uniform no.: 42
Shoots: left

Career statistics:

GP	G	A	TP	PIM
473	41	117	158	373

1996-97 statistics:

GP	G	A	TP	+/-	PIM	PP	SH	GW	GT	S	PCT
62	11	19	30	+19	43	2	0	1	0	100	11.0

1997-98 statistics:

GP	G	A	TP	+/-	PIM	PP	SH	GW	GT	S	PCT
72	3	17	20	+11	62	0	1	0	0	90	3.3

1998-99 statistics:

GP	G	A	TP	+/-	PIM	PP	SH	GW	GT	S	PCT
72	3	11	14	-9	44	0	0	0	0	61	4.9

1999-2000 statistics:

GP	G	A	TP	+/-	PIM	PP	SH	GW	GT	S	PCT
64	2	9	11	+13	50	0	0	0	0	67	3.0

LAST SEASON

Missed 10 games with rib injury. Missed three games with back injury.

THE FINESSE GAME

Smehlik's skating is his strong suit. He is agile with good lateral movement and very solid on his skates. Because his balance is so good, he is tough to knock down.

He thinks defense, and his impressive finesse skills are dedicated to the defensive aspect of the game. If Smehlik takes more responsibility offensively, he can respond. He has good passing skills and fair hockey vision, and he can spot and hit the breaking forward. Most of his assists will be traced back to a headman feed out of the defensive zone. He plays well at the point and has a rocket shot, but isn't clever enough with the puck to be a really effective member of the power play.

Smehlik is vulnerable to a strong forecheck. Teams are aware of this deficiency and try to work his corner.

THE PHYSICAL GAME

Smehlik can use his body well but has to be more consistent and authoritative. He has to clean up his crease better, something he doesn't do well since he's not a mean hitter. It's not in his nature to be aggressive. He prefers to use his stick to break up plays, and he does that effectively. He has a long reach and is able to intercept passes, or reach in around a defender to pry the puck loose.

THE INTANGIBLES

Smehlik is a borderline number four defenseman who works hard to maximize his skills. He struggled last season, mostly because his regular partner Alexei Zhitnik was so awful, and because of injuries.

PROJECTION

Smehlik has some decent skills, but his probable level is the 25- to 30-point range. He will continue to get plenty of ice time.

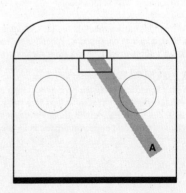

VLADIMIR TSYPLAKOV

Yrs. of NHL service: 5
Born: Moscow, Russia; Apr. 18, 1969
Position: left wing
Height: 6-0
Weight: 185
Uniform no.: 9
Shoots: left

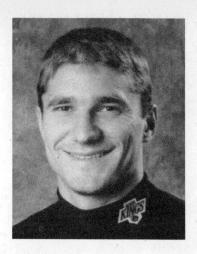

Career statistics:

GP	G	A	TP	PIM
295	62	94	156	80

1996-97 statistics:

GP	G	A	TP	+/-	PIM	PP	SH	GW	GT	S	PCT
67	16	23	39	+8	12	1	0	2	0	118	13.6

1997-98 statistics:

GP	G	A	TP	+/-	PIM	PP	SH	GW	GT	S	PCT
73	18	34	52	+15	18	2	0	1	0	113	15.9

1998-99 statistics:

GP	G	A	TP	+/-	PIM	PP	SH	GW	GT	S	PCT
69	11	12	23	-7	32	0	2	2	0	111	9.9

1999-2000 statistics:

GP	G	A	TP	+/-	PIM	PP	SH	GW	GT	S	PCT
63	12	20	32	+23	14	1	0	2	0	76	15.8

LAST SEASON
Led team in plus-minus.

THE FINESSE GAME
Tsyplakov is a highly skilled forward who likes to play an up-tempo game. He's a run-and-gun, give-and-go kind of player who'll get the puck and find the open man or jump into the holes for a pass. He has good anticipation and quick acceleration. He has very good hands and a quick release on his shot.

Tsyplakov was drafted as a 26-year-old by the Kings in 1995 to fill a specific need: scoring. He plays on the second power-play unit. He is not as effective on the power play as he should be with his shot because he shies away from the high-percentage areas, where he has to pay a price to stake out his territory. He is a perimeter player, and that minimizes his NHL-calibre skills.

THE PHYSICAL GAME
Tsyplakov dislikes physical contact and is easily intimidated. He has been through several injuries and surgeries in past seasons (shoulder, hernia, knee), which may have had an effect, but he simply just doesn't seem to have the taste for it.

THE INTANGIBLES
Tsyplakov was an unrestricted free agent last season. He fits so nicely on a line with Michael Peca and Vaclav Varada that the Sabres might rehire him, but only if the price is right.

PROJECTION
If he wins a job somewhere, Tsyplakov could be a 20-goal scorer, but he will find ice time on the top two lines almost impossible to come by.

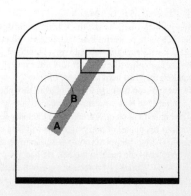

VACLAV VARADA

Yrs. of NHL service: 3
Born: Vsetin, Czech Republic; Apr. 26, 1976
Position: right wing
Height: 6-0
Weight: 200
Uniform no.: 25
Shoots: left

Career statistics:

GP	G	A	TP	PIM
181	22	57	79	140

1996-97 statistics:

GP	G	A	TP	+/-	PIM	PP	SH	GW	GT	S	PCT
5	0	0	0	0	2	0	0	0	0	2	0.0

1997-98 statistics:

GP	G	A	TP	+/-	PIM	PP	SH	GW	GT	S	PCT
27	5	6	11	0	15	0	0	1	1	27	18.5

1998-99 statistics:

GP	G	A	TP	+/-	PIM	PP	SH	GW	GT	S	PCT
72	7	24	31	+11	61	1	0	1	0	123	5.7

1999-2000 statistics:

GP	G	A	TP	+/-	PIM	PP	SH	GW	GT	S	PCT
76	10	27	37	+12	62	0	0	0	0	140	7.1

PROJECTION

Varada has a 30-goal season in his future, but that future could be three seasons away yet. Power forwards take awhile to develop, and in the meantime, an increase to 15 to 20 goals should be expected.

LAST SEASON

Missed three games with ear injury. Missed three games due to coach's decision.

THE FINESSE GAME

Varada is the closest thing the Sabres have to a power forward, but he has yet to demonstrate the kind of scoring touch that the role demands. When he is on, he plays with such intensity and reckless abandon that by the end of the game his face is cut and scraped, as if he had been attacked by crazed weasels.

Varada has excellent size and great hands. He is wonderful with the puck, a superb stickhandler. He can also make plays, though his future is as a scorer. He has a good wrist and slap shot. He needs to be an involved player and not stay on the perimeter. He has a passion for scoring and drives to the net for his best chances. He handles himself well in traffic. He is a solidly balanced skater and an effective forechecker.

THE PHYSICAL GAME

Varada is thick: thick arms, thick legs, thick thighs. He is much more powerful than he looks. He gives the Sabres some desperately needed size on the right side, but he needs to play like a power forward every night. He can be gritty and hard to play against.

He has to stop looking for the big hit, though. He took a number of bad penalties last year.

The biggest knock on Varada is his intensity level. If he brings his game up every night, he will be a budding star. There is plenty of room on this team for anyone who can put the puck in the net. He had six goals in the last 10 games, a promising sign, although he 0-fered in the playoffs.

DIXON WARD

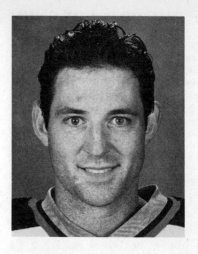

Yrs. of NHL service: 8
Born: Leduc, Alta.; Sept. 23, 1968
Position: left wing
Height: 6-0
Weight: 200
Uniform no.: 15
Shoots: right

Career statistics:

GP	G	A	TP	PIM
466	90	116	206	364

1996-97 statistics:

GP	G	A	TP	+/-	PIM	PP	SH	GW	GT	S	PCT
79	13	32	45	+17	36	1	2	4	0	93	14.0

1997-98 statistics:

GP	G	A	TP	+/-	PIM	PP	SH	GW	GT	S	PCT
71	10	13	23	+23	42	0	2	3	1	99	10.1

1998-99 statistics:

GP	G	A	TP	+/-	PIM	PP	SH	GW	GT	S	PCT
78	20	24	44	+10	44	2	1	4	1	101	19.8

1999-2000 statistics:

GP	G	A	TP	+/-	PIM	PP	SH	GW	GT	S	PCT
71	11	9	20	+1	41	1	2	2	0	101	10.9

LAST SEASON

Tied for second on team in shorthanded goals. Missed three games with neck injury. Missed seven games due to coach's decision.

THE FINESSE GAME

Ward is a powerful skater with good anticipation and he can put on a quick burst of speed. His work along the boards and in front of the net is consistent and effective. He has good hands to take advantage of whatever opportunities are created from his efforts. He has a good shot from the top of the slot and also drives to the net to follow up his shot.

Ward is alert defensively and is a good penalty killer. He isn't overly creative, but he can handle second-unit power-play shifts. He has enough hockey sense to play in almost any situation.

Ward was demoted to the fourth line last season by the Sabres.

THE PHYSICAL GAME

Ward has average size but he uses his body willingly. He plays the game with enthusiasm and finishes his checks.

THE INTANGIBLES

Ward won a $1.2 million salary arbitration from the Sabres in 1999, but little went right for him after that. An unrestricted free agent during the off-season, Ward seemed to attract tepid interest from his old team. He could be a pretty valuable role player and penalty killer for a new team.

PROJECTION

Ward is a feisty, intelligent player who could chip in 15 to 20 goals if he ends up in the right spot.

RHETT WARRENER

Yrs. of NHL service: 5
Born: Shaunavon, Sask.; Jan. 27, 1976
Position: left defense
Height: 6-1
Weight: 209
Uniform no.: 4
Shoots: left

Career statistics:

GP	G	A	TP	PIM
291	5	26	31	406

1996-97 statistics:

GP	G	A	TP	+/-	PIM	PP	SH	GW	GT	S	PCT
62	4	9	13	+20	88	1	0	1	0	58	6.9

1997-98 statistics:

GP	G	A	TP	+/-	PIM	PP	SH	GW	GT	S	PCT
79	0	4	4	-16	99	0	0	0	0	66	.0

1998-99 statistics:

GP	G	A	TP	+/-	PIM	PP	SH	GW	GT	S	PCT
61	1	7	8	+2	84	0	0	0	0	44	2.3

1999-2000 statistics:

GP	G	A	TP	+/-	PIM	PP	SH	GW	GT	S	PCT
61	0	3	3	+18	89	0	0	0	0	68	-

LAST SEASON

Missed eight games with groin injury. Missed six games with hip injury. Missed two games with ankle injury. Missed two games with shoulder injury.

THE FINESSE GAME

Warrener's game is heavily slanted to defense. He has a foundation of good hockey sense, completed by his size and firm passing touch. Warrener plays a simple game, wins a lot of the one-on-one battles and sticks within his limitations. His defensive reads are quite good for a young player. He plays his position well and moves people out from in front of the net. He blocks shots, and he can start a quick transition with a breakout pass.

Warrener might struggle a bit with his foot speed. His turns and lateral movement are okay but he lacks quickness and acceleration, which hampers him from becoming a more effective two-way defenseman.

THE PHYSICAL GAME

Warrener likes the aggressive game. Sometimes he gets a little too rambunctious and gets out of position, but that is to be expected from a young player looking to make an impact. He's a solid hitter but doesn't make the open-ice splatters. Warrener is not a self-starter. He needs someone to stay on him about his conditioning and his effort.

THE INTANGIBLES

When Warrener is paired with a stay-at-home type like Jay McKee, he gets more involved in the attack. He can be the defensive partner, too, if he is teamed with a more offensive defenseman. Injuries affected Warrener last season — not only his own, but McKee's, because Warrener doesn't seem to match up as well with any of the other Sabres blueliners.

Warrener is an underrated player, one of those types who does so many little things well that you don't notice how much you missed him until he's out of the lineup, which he was too frequently. He's a quiet leader for the Sabres.

PROJECTION

Warrener won't win any Norris Trophies, but he can be a foundation defenseman who produces 20 points a year.

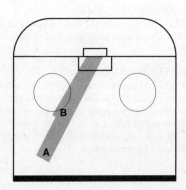

JASON WOOLLEY

Yrs. of NHL service: 8
Born: Toronto, Ont.; July 27, 1969
Position: right defense
Height: 6-1
Weight: 188
Uniform no.: 5
Shoots: left

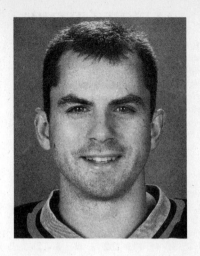

Career statistics:

GP	G	A	TP	PIM
408	44	155	199	243

1996-97 statistics:

GP	G	A	TP	+/-	PIM	PP	SH	GW	GT	S	PCT
60	6	30	36	+4	30	2	0	1	0	86	7.0

1997-98 statistics:

GP	G	A	TP	+/-	PIM	PP	SH	GW	GT	S	PCT
71	9	26	35	+8	35	3	0	2	1	129	7.0

1998-99 statistics:

GP	G	A	TP	+/-	PIM	PP	SH	GW	GT	S	PCT
80	10	33	43	+16	62	4	0	2	1	154	6.5

1999-2000 statistics:

GP	G	A	TP	+/-	PIM	PP	SH	GW	GT	S	PCT
74	8	25	33	+14	52	2	0	2	0	113	7.1

PROJECTION

Woolley needs to score in the 40-point range to make up for the other things he fails to bring to the ice.

LAST SEASON

Led team defensemen in points for second consecutive season. Missed four games with rib injury. Missed two games with flu. Missed one game with hip injury.

THE FINESSE GAME

Woolley is pretty much a one-way defenseman, but since that one way has never been at the elite level of a Paul Coffey, he was always considered something of a journeyman.

That changed last season when Woolley stepped in to make an impact on the Sabres' power play. He rushes the puck well and sets up from the point. He does not have a bullet shot but he gets it away quickly and keeps it low and on net. He has the vision to spot a man low for a pass.

Woolley is mobile but doesn't possess blazing speed. He can lug the puck or make an outlet pass.

THE PHYSICAL GAME

Woolley uses his finesse skills in his defense. He has good size but isn't an intimidating physical presence.

THE INTANGIBLES

Woolley had to settle for $950,000 after salary arbitration in 1999 and it seemed to affect his season. He has another contract hassle looming. Woolley was a restricted free agent during the off-season. His numbers weren't dazzling, but the Sabres don't have much else in the way of a power-play quarterback, unless rookie Brian Campbell is ready to move in.

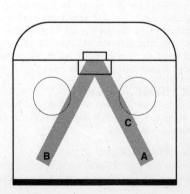

ALEXEI ZHITNIK

Yrs. of NHL service: 8
Born: Kiev, Ukraine; Oct. 10, 1972
Position: left defense
Height: 5-11
Weight: 204
Uniform no.: 44
Shoots: left

Career statistics:

GP	G	A	TP	PIM
574	65	211	276	688

1996-97 statistics:

GP	G	A	TP	+/-	PIM	PP	SH	GW	GT	S	PCT
80	7	28	35	+10	95	3	1	0	1	170	4.1

1997-98 statistics:

GP	G	A	TP	+/-	PIM	PP	SH	GW	GT	S	PCT
78	15	30	45	+19	102	2	3	3	2	191	7.9

1998-99 statistics:

GP	G	A	TP	+/-	PIM	PP	SH	GW	GT	S	PCT
81	7	26	33	-6	96	3	1	2	0	185	3.8

1999-2000 statistics:

GP	G	A	TP	+/-	PIM	PP	SH	GW	GT	S	PCT
74	2	11	13	-6	95	1	0	0	0	139	1.4

LAST SEASON

Third on team in penalty minutes. Missed six games with finger injury. Missed one game with shoulder injury. Missed one game with eye injury.

THE FINESSE GAME

Zhitnik has a bowlegged skating style that ex-coach Barry Melrose once compared to Bobby Orr's. Zhitnik is no Orr, but he was born with skates on. He has speed, acceleration and lateral mobility.

All those skills went to waste last season, especially on the offensive side. Zhitnik played defense reasonably well enough. He gets into position, takes away the passing lanes, and plays a strong transition game.

Even though Zhitnik is not an elite offensive player, his production plunged by 20 points. His goals were down by 13. On a team as low-scoring as the Sabres, that is a devastating blow.

Zhitnik needs to develop his lateral movement better, to use all of the blueline and stop his shots from getting blocked. He has a good, hard shot, and he keeps it low for deflections in front. He still likes to think about going on the attack before his own end is cleaned up, and will occasionally make the risky play.

THE PHYSICAL GAME

Zhitnik plays sensibly and doesn't take bad penalties. His lower-body strength is impressive. He can really unload on some checks.

THE INTANGIBLES

Who was this guy? Zhitnik easily deserved to be a healthy scratch half the season, but Sabres could not afford to keep him out of the lineup. How will they afford to put him back in? Zhitnik was a restricted free agent during the off-season. He will be looking for a raise, and he was no bargain last year at $2.5 million.

Zhitnik seems to have lost confidence, or interest, in playing to his skill level.

PROJECTION

Zhitnik usually gets prime ice time and should produce in the 35-point range.

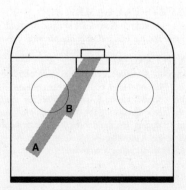

CALGARY FLAMES

Players' Statistics 1999-2000

POS.	NO.	PLAYER	GP	G	A	PTS	+/-	PIM	PP	SH	GW	GT	S	PCT
R	8	VALERI BURE	82	35	40	75	-7	50	13		6	1	308	11.4
C	12	JAROME IGINLA	77	29	34	63	0	26	12		4		256	11.3
D	6	PHIL HOUSLEY	78	11	44	55	-12	24	5		2	1	176	6.3
C	27	MARC SAVARD	78	22	31	53	-2	56	4		3	1	184	12.0
D	53	DEREK MORRIS	78	9	29	38	2	80	3		2		193	4.7
R	25	SERGEI KRIVOKRASOV	75	10	27	37	-5	44	3		2	2	159	6.3
R	62	ANDREI NAZAROV	76	10	22	32	3	78	1		1		110	9.1
C	11	JEFF SHANTZ	74	13	18	31	-13	30	6		1		112	11.6
D	2	DARRYL SHANNON	76	6	21	27	-27	87	1		1		112	5.4
C	24	JASON WIEMER	64	11	11	22	-10	120	2		3		104	10.6
C	23	CLARKE WILM	78	10	12	22	-6	67	1	3			81	12.3
L	16	CORY STILLMAN	37	12	9	21	-9	12	6		3	1	59	20.3
L	22	BILL LINDSAY	80	8	12	20	-7	86			2		147	5.4
C	15	*MARTIN ST. LOUIS	56	3	15	18	-5	22			1		73	4.1
L	21	ANDREAS JOHANSSON	40	5	10	15	-2	22	1				58	8.6
D	33	BRAD WERENKA	73	4	9	13	13	90			1		62	6.5
D	28	*ROBYN REGEHR	57	5	7	12	-2	46	2				64	7.8
D	5	TOMMY ALBELIN	41	4	6	10	-3	12	1	1	1		37	10.8
D	4	BOBBY DOLLAS	50	3	7	10	6	28	1				36	8.3
C	7	MARC BUREAU	63	3	5	8	-4	12		1			51	5.9
D	32	CALE HULSE	47	1	6	7	-11	47					41	2.4
L	38	*JEFF COWAN	13	4	1	5	2	16					26	15.4
L	17	*JASON BOTTERILL	27	1	4	5	-11	17			1		19	5.3
D	55	STEVE SMITH	20		4	4	-13	42					10	
L	37	*SERGEI VARLAMOV	7	3		3	0				1		11	27.3
C	26	*STEVE BEGIN	13	1	1	2	-3	18					3	33.3
D	3	DENIS GAUTHIER	39	1	1	2	-4	50					29	3.4
C	39	BENOIT GRATTON	10		2	2	1	10					4	
L	26	*TRAVIS BRIGLEY	17		2	2	-6	4					17	
D	29	WADE BELAK	40		2	2	-4	122					11	
D	34	STEWART MALGUNAS	4		1	1	1	2						
C	19	*OLEG SAPRYKIN	4		1	1	-4	2					2	
R	17	*CHRIS CLARK	22		1	1	-3	14					17	
C	18	STEVE DUBINSKY	23		1	1	-12	4					29	
D	32	*LEE SOROCHAN	1				0							
L	25	DAVE ROCHE	2				-1	5					3	
R	15	*RICO FATA	2				-1							
D	45	*DARREL SCOVILLE	6				1	2					1	
G	47	J GIGUERE	7				0	2						
D	36	ERIC CHARRON	21				-3	37					8	
G	31	GRANT FUHR	23				0	2						
G	40	FRED BRATHWAITE	61				0	4						

GP = games played; G = goals; A = assists; PTS = points; +/- = goals-for minus goals-against while player is on ice; PIM = penalties in minutes; PP = power-play goals; SH = shorthanded goals; GW = game-winning goals; GT = game-tying goals; S = no. of shots; PCT = percentage of goals to shots; * = rookie

VALERI BURE

Yrs. of NHL service: 5
Born: Moscow, Russia; June 13, 1974
Position: right wing
Height: 5-10
Weight: 168
Uniform no.: 8
Shoots: right

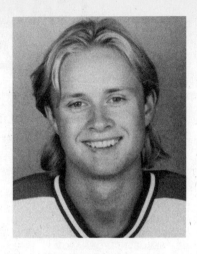

Career statistics:

GP	G	A	TP	PIM
393	112	135	247	147

1996-97 statistics:

GP	G	A	TP	+/-	PIM	PP	SH	GW	GT	S	PCT
64	14	21	35	+4	6	4	0	2	1	131	10.7

1997-98 statistics:

GP	G	A	TP	+/-	PIM	PP	SH	GW	GT	S	PCT
66	12	26	38	-5	35	2	0	2	0	179	6.7

1998-99 statistics:

GP	G	A	TP	+/-	PIM	PP	SH	GW	GT	S	PCT
80	26	27	53	0	22	7	0	4	0	260	10.0

1999-2000 statistics:

GP	G	A	TP	+/-	PIM	PP	SH	GW	GT	S	PCT
82	35	40	75	-7	50	13	0	6	1	308	11.4

LAST SEASON

Led team in goals, points, power-play goals, game-winning goals and shots. Fourth in NHL in shots. Second on team in assists. Third on team in shooting percentage. Tied for fourth in NHL in power-play goals. Tied for fifth in NHL in power-play points (31). Career highs in goals, assists and points. Only Flame to appear in all 82 games.

THE FINESSE GAME

Bure was one of the nicer success stories of last season, as the flashes of brilliance he had displayed in his earlier stint with Montreal bloomed full-force in Calgary. Although he is not as lightning-fast as big brother Pavel, Valeri does have his own distinct qualities, which might be appreciated more if he had a different last name. He has a great sense of anticipation and wants the puck every time he's on the ice. And he can make things happen, though he sometimes tries to force the action rather than let the game flow naturally. He gets carried away in his pursuit of the puck and gets caught out of position, whereas if he just showed patience the puck would come to him.

Bure works well down low on the power play, but will also switch off and drop back to the point. He shows supreme confidence in his shot and scoring ability, and is very tough to defend against one-on-one.

He has good hands to go along with his speed and seems to get a shot on goal or a scoring chance on every shift. He is smart and creative, and can make plays as well as finish.

THE PHYSICAL GAME

Bure is strong for his size and last season was more willing to pay the price. He has to keep a little grit in his game to succeed.

THE INTANGIBLES

Bure was a third-line player in Montreal who needed to be a top six forward. He earned that job and the respect of (now ex-Flames coach) Brian Sutter, who is not so easy to impress. Bure's always had the knack. He either found the right guy to push him or decided it was time to push himself. Bure has emerged as a leader on and off the ice and a star in his own right.

PROJECTION

Bure should be a consistent 30- to 35-goal scorer.

RICO FATA

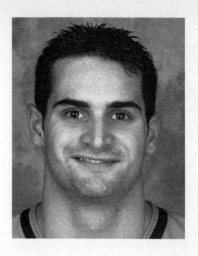

Yrs. of NHL service: 0
Born: Sault Ste. Marie, Ont.; Feb. 12, 1980
Position: centre / right wing
Height: 5-11
Weight: 202
Uniform no.: 15
Shoots: left

Career statistics:

GP	G	A	TP	PIM
22	0	1	1	4

1998-99 statistics:

GP	G	A	TP	+/-	PIM	PP	SH	GW	GT	S	PCT
20	0	1	1	0	4	0	0	0	0	13	0.0

1999-2000 statistics:

GP	G	A	TP	+/-	PIM	PP	SH	GW	GT	S	PCT
2	0	0	0	-1	0	0	0	0	0	0	-

LAST SEASON

Will be entering first NHL season. Appeared in 76 game with Saint John (AHL), scoring 29-29 — 58. Led AHL rookies in goals. Named to AHL All-Rookie Team.

THE FINESSE GAME

Fata has blazing speed, and his skating ability in junior allowed him to dominate games. He is a nifty, shifty skater with great accleration. What he has learned at the pro level is that sometimes a first effort isn't good enough, that sometimes a second or third will be required, and there will always be someone nearly as skilled as you trying to prevent you from doing your job.

Fata can make plays at high tempo. He has learned to use his outside speed and cut back to the middle at the right moment to catch the defenseman flat-footed. He has a good shot and likes to use it. Fata can intimidate with his speed, and will create a lot of turnovers on the forecheck. He is creative and has terrific hands. He can do a lot with the puck in an uptempo game.

Fata needed to learn some defensive awareness, which was one of the major reasons why he was sent to the minors instead of junior.

THE PHYSICAL GAME

Fata is average height but he has a sturdy build and is very emotional and competitive.

THE INTANGIBLES

Fata appears to have the drive to want to succeed at the NHL level. He certainly has the wheels.

PROJECTION

There are plenty of job openings on the Flames' forward lines. If Fata doesn't grab one right away, he should be there by midseason. If he scores 10 to 15 goals in his rookie year he will be off to a good start.

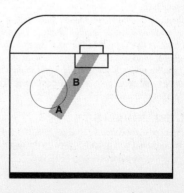

DENIS GAUTHIER

Yrs. of NHL service: 2
Born: Montreal, Que.; Oct. 1, 1976
Position: left defense
Height: 6-2
Weight: 195
Uniform no.: 3
Shoots: left

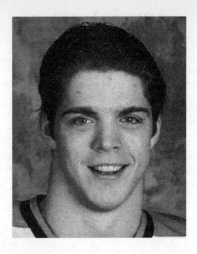

Career statistics:

GP	G	A	TP	PIM
104	4	5	9	134

1997-98 statistics:

GP	G	A	TP	+/-	PIM	PP	SH	GW	GT	S	PCT
10	0	0	0	-5	16	0	0	0	0	3	0.0

1998-99 statistics:

GP	G	A	TP	+/-	PIM	PP	SH	GW	GT	S	PCT
55	3	4	7	+3	68	0	0	0	0	40	7.5

1999-2000 statistics:

GP	G	A	TP	+/-	PIM	PP	SH	GW	GT	S	PCT
39	1	1	2	-4	50	0	0	0	0	29	3.4

LAST SEASON

Second NHL season. Missed 30 games with hip injury. Missed 11 games with shoulder injury.

THE FINESSE GAME

Gauthier is going to be one of those defensemen you have to watch every night in order to appreciate him, because he is a stay-at-home type whose numbers will never be gaudy.

A good skater, he is strong and balanced on his skates. His lower-body strength and speed power his hitting. He is capable of hitting in open ice because of his mobility.

Gauthier won't take off on many rushes. He prefers to skate the puck out of his zone or make the outlet pass or the bank off the boards.

THE PHYSICAL GAME

Gauthier is a powerful, fierce hitter. Anyone on the receiving end of a Gauthier check knows he has been rocked. He is especially good at catching people coming across the middle of the with his head down. One of his role models is Dave Manson. Another is Scott Stevens. Ouch.

Gauthier is a burr. He doesn't fight, but he is always annoying people, always sticking his nose in, and smirking like Dennis Miller while he does it. He is an agitator who always gets people worried about him, and he relishes going after other team's stars. Gauthier is in excellent physical condition. He can handle a lot of ice time.

THE INTANGIBLES

Gauthier has a good chance to stick as a fifth defenseman for now and will quickly move up the depth chart as he gains more experience.

PROJECTION

Gauthier will have minor point totals and major penalties.

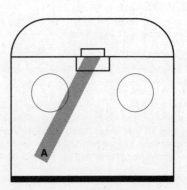

PHIL HOUSLEY

Yrs. of NHL service: 18
Born: St. Paul, Minn.; Mar. 9, 1964
Position: right defense
Height: 5-10
Weight: 185
Uniform no.: 6
Shoots: left

Career statistics:

GP	G	A	TP	PIM
1288	313	817	1130	738

1996-97 statistics:

GP	G	A	TP	+/-	PIM	PP	SH	GW	GT	S	PCT
77	11	29	40	-10	24	3	1	2	0	167	6.6

1997-98 statistics:

GP	G	A	TP	+/-	PIM	PP	SH	GW	GT	S	PCT
64	6	25	31	-10	24	4	1	0	0	116	5.2

1998-99 statistics:

GP	G	A	TP	+/-	PIM	PP	SH	GW	GT	S	PCT
79	11	43	54	+14	52	4	0	1	0	193	5.7

1999-2000 statistics:

GP	G	A	TP	+/-	PIM	PP	SH	GW	GT	S	PCT
78	11	44	55	-12	24	5	0	2	1	176	6.3

LAST SEASON

Led team in assists for second consecutive season. Led team defensemen in points for second consecutive season. Tied for fourth among NHL defensemen in points. Second in NHL in power-play assists (30). Third in NHL in power-play points (35). Third on team in points. Missed one game due to flu. Missed three games due to coach's decision.

THE FINESSE GAME

Among the best-skating defensemen in the NHL, Housley, like Paul Coffey, takes a lot of heat for his defensive shortcomings. A better team could afford to use Housley as a pure power-play specialist, but in Calgary he shoulders the full workload.

Housley's skating fuels his game. He can accelerate in a heartbeat and his edges are deep and secure, giving him the ability to avoid checks with gravity-defying moves. Everything he does is at high tempo. He intimidates with his speed and skills, forcing defenders back and opening up more ice for himself and his teammates. He can continue to be an effective offensive weapon because he has barely lost a step over the years.

Housley has an excellent grasp of the ice. On the power play he is a huge threat. His shots are low, quick and heavy, either beating the goalie outright or setting up a rebound for the forwards down deep. He also sets up low on the power play, and he isn't shy about shooting from an impossible angle that can catch a goalie napping on the short side.

Housley has great anticipation and can break up a rush by picking off a pass and turning the play into a counterattack. He is equally adept with a long headman or short cup-and-saucer pass over a defender's stick.

THE PHYSICAL GAME

Housley is not the least bit physical. He is not strong enough to shove anyone out of the zone, so his defensive play is based on his pursuit of the puck. He is likely to avoid traffic areas unless he feels he can get in and out with the puck quickly enough.

Success on a rush, even a two-on-one, against Housley is not guaranteed, since he is a good enough skater to position himself properly and break up the play with his stick.

THE INTANGIBLES

Housley has found a comfortable niche with the Flames and their core of young defensemen. Housley is entering his walk year. Could it be his last?

PROJECTION

Housley easily met (and surpassed) the 50 points we set him down for last season. At 36, he still has great wheels and is in good health, so another 50-point season is attainable.

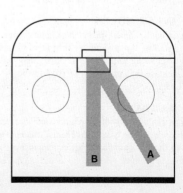

TONI LYDMAN

Yrs. of NHL service: 0
Born: Lahti, Finland; Sept. 25, 1977
Position: left defense
Height: 6-1
Weight: 183
Uniform no.: n.a.
Shoots: left

Career statistics: (Finnish Elite League)

GP	G	A	TP	PIM
224	18	39	57	201

LAST SEASON

Will be entering first NHL season. Appeared in 46 games with HIFK Helsinki, scoring 4-18 — 22.

THE FINESSE GAME

Lydman is a good skater and puckhandler who should help step up the Flames' mobility and take some of the pressure off of Phil Housley.

Lydman isn't exactly an offenseman. He is more of a two-way defenseman, more like a Tommy Albelin — who has been one of the more underrated NHL journeymen throughout his NHL career — but Lydman is more highly skilled in all respects. He is very dependable both ways. He makes a good first pass. Lydman can jump into the play and has a good shot.

Lydman is quietly competitive and seems to have the grit to compete on a nightly basis.

THE PHYSICAL GAME

Lydman isn't a rugged player but he's not afraid of the North American style. He played well enough last year to impress former Flames coach Brian Sutter, who has no tolerance for soft players. He has decent size, is strong along the wall, and is a good enough skater to surprise an opponent with an open-ice body-check, which he is not too timid to throw.

THE INTANGIBLES

Lydman had a shot to make the Flames at training camp in 1999, but a shoulder injury prevented the team from being able to assess him fairly, and by agreement he was sent back to play in the Finnish Elite League.

PROJECTION

Lydman can be a 30- to 35-point scorer in a year or two, but it would be wise to give him a season to acclimate to the pro game and expect less in his rookie year.

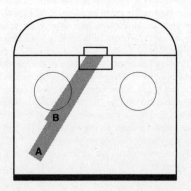

DEREK MORRIS

Yrs. of NHL service: 3
Born: Edmonton, Alberta; Aug. 24, 1978
Position: right defense
Height: 6-0
Weight: 200
Uniform no.: 53
Shoots: right

Career statistics:

GP	G	A	TP	PIM
231	25	76	101	241

1997-98 statistics:

GP	G	A	TP	+/-	PIM	PP	SH	GW	GT	S	PCT
82	9	20	29	+1	88	5	1	1	1	120	7.5

1998-99 statistics:

GP	G	A	TP	+/-	PIM	PP	SH	GW	GT	S	PCT
71	7	27	34	+4	73	3	0	2	2	150	4.7

1999-2000 statistics:

GP	G	A	TP	+/-	PIM	PP	SH	GW	GT	S	PCT
78	9	29	38	+2	80	3	0	2	0	193	4.7

LAST SEASON

Third on team in plus-minus and shots. Missed three games with concussion.

THE FINESSE GAME

Morris possesses all high-level skills, but what truly sets him apart from the other defensemen of his generation is his brain. For a young player, he has a real grasp for the technical part of the game. He is a thinker and understands hockey thoroughly. He is already a steady performer and approaching All-Star status.

Morris plays in all game situations, on the first penalty-killing unit and on the first power-play unit. He is a fan of Paul Coffey, and he possesses the kind of skating that brings to mind his role model. Morris is better defensively, however, and will become a better all-around player. He handles the puck well in an up-tempo game and may develop into the kind of defenseman who can take over a game.

Morris needs only to improve his one-on-one play and get a little stronger to continue on the path to becoming an elite defenseman. He is occasionally prone to a defensive breakdown but he learns from his mistakes.

THE PHYSICAL GAME

Morris has improved his stamina but will need to maintain a serious stength and conditioning program. He is not overly big, but he is very strong. You can't run him over and he gets a lot of power from his legs for hitting and moving people out of the front of the net.

THE INTANGIBLES

Morris is very well-liked by his teammates and coaches for his desire to learn and willingness to listen. He is a blue chipper who is going to start earning the attention he deserves. Playing with and learning from Housley will help him develop his offensive skills even more. His development at such a young age is remarkable.

PROJECTION

As Morris continues to mature he will gain confidence in his offensive game without losing anything from his defense. There is a 60-point season in his not-too-distant future.

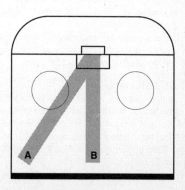

ANDREI NAZAROV

Yrs. of NHL service: 6
Born: Chelyabinsk, Russia; May 22, 1974
Position: right wing
Height: 6-5
Weight: 230
Uniform no.: 62
Shoots: right

Career statistics:

GP	G	A	TP	PIM
321	41	60	101	699

1996-97 statistics:

GP	G	A	TP	+/-	PIM	PP	SH	GW	GT	S	PCT
60	12	15	27	-4	222	1	0	1	0	116	10.3

1997-98 statistics:

GP	G	A	TP	+/-	PIM	PP	SH	GW	GT	S	PCT
54	2	2	4	-13	170	0	0	0	0	50	4.0

1998-99 statistics:

GP	G	A	TP	+/-	PIM	PP	SH	GW	GT	S	PCT
62	7	9	16	-4	73	0	0	2	1	71	9.9

1999-2000 statistics:

GP	G	A	TP	+/-	PIM	PP	SH	GW	GT	S	PCT
76	10	22	32	+3	78	1	0	1	0	110	9.1

LAST SEASON

Second on team in plus-minus. Missed six games due to coach's decision.

THE FINESSE GAME

Nazarov isn't overly creative with the puck, but with his size does he have to be? This giant has decent hand skills around the net, though he does have some trouble fishing out loose pucks from his feet in goalmouth scrambles, presumably because his head is so far from the ice it's tough to see.

The biggest improvement in Nazarov's game is in his skating. He can handle some second-line and second-unit power-play time with assurance. He is not at his best handling the puck for long and is insecure if forced to rush with it; defenders have a relatively easy time stripping it from him because the puck is so far from his feet. He plops himself in front of the net on power plays and creates a wall that is nearly impossible for the goalie to see around. Nazarov needs to play with linemates who will get him the puck. He has decent hands and can shoot.

Nazarov is smart and understands the game well. He is aware of his limitations and won't try to do too much. He has an obvious love for the game.

THE PHYSICAL GAME

Nazarov was asked by former coach Brian Sutter to cut out the stupid penalties and be more of a hockey player. Nazarov already has enough of a reputation to scare off all but the most fearless opponents. It was the lazy penalties that he had to cut back on, and for the most part, he has.

Nazarov developed a reputation in San Jose as a mean player, which was kind of an unfair stamp. He is a good, hard, physical player, but he isn't the sort who goes looking to hurt people. Nazarov seemed confused about his role for a few years but is getting more comfortable. He'll fight when he has to, and his long reach makes him tough for even some of the league's best brawlers to cope with. He will protect his teammates.

THE INTANGIBLES

Nazarov is still raw and rough. Calgary used him as a third-line winger and he was able to get some ice time.

PROJECTION

If he can earn enough minutes, Nazarov could produce 40 points.

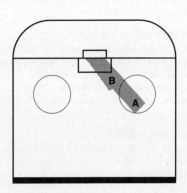

ROBYN REGEHR

Yrs. of NHL service: 1
Born: Recife, Brazil; Apr. 19, 1980
Position: left defense
Height: 6-2
Weight: 210
Uniform no.: 28
Shoots: left

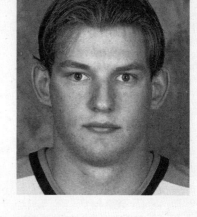

Career statistics:

GP	G	A	TP	PIM
57	5	7	12	46

1999-2000 statistics:

GP	G	A	TP	+/-	PIM	PP	SH	GW	GT	S	PCT
57	5	7	12	-2	46	2	0	0	0	64	7.8

LAST SEASON

First NHL season. Missed 11 games with concussion. Missed five games with leg injury.

THE FINESSE GAME

Regehr is a power player with a good passing touch — an exciting combination in a young defenseman.

Regehr seems to have lost none of his skating ability after suffering injuries to both of his legs. He has a good first step for such a big kid, and his skating is strong and well-balanced. He is defense-oriented, but with his heads-up passing and intelligence keys many breakouts that lead to scoring chances. He does not get involved in the rush himself. When parked on the point, he has a decent slapshot, but it is hardly his best skill.

Regehr plays at a very intense, competitive level on a nightly basis.

Regehr played in all defensive situations five-on-five and killing penalties. He did not and will not see any power-play time. Regehr is mature beyond his years and will keep getting better.

THE PHYSICAL GAME

Regehr has NHL size. He's strong but not a fighter. He won't go out and try to beat people up, but he is tough to play against because he hits. He finishes his checks and pins players to the boards. He resembles a young Rod Langway.

THE INTANGIBLES

Regehr wasn't even supposed to be on skates by December after a tragic car accident resulted in two broken legs and the death of two people. His amazing recovery made him the youngest nominee in the history of the Masterton Trophy, and a probable future winner. He is a quality person and a quality player who will be part of Calgary's lineup for the forseeable future. Regehr was the player Calgary selected off a short list from Colorado to complete the Theo Fleury trade in 1999.

PROJECTION

Regehr will never score many goals. But he will prevent a lot of them from being scored. If he gets 10 goals a season, that will be an amazing output. More importantly, Regehr has all the makings of a franchise defenseman.

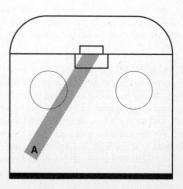

MARC SAVARD

Yrs. of NHL service: 3
Born: Ottawa, Ont.; July 17, 1977
Position: centre
Height: 5-11
Weight: 185
Uniform no.: 10
Shoots: left

Career statistics:

GP	G	A	TP	PIM
176	32	72	104	98

1997-98 statistics:

GP	G	A	TP	+/-	PIM	PP	SH	GW	GT	S	PCT
28	1	5	6	-4	4	0	0	0	0	32	3.1

1998-99 statistics:

GP	G	A	TP	+/-	PIM	PP	SH	GW	GT	S	PCT
70	9	36	45	-7	38	4	0	1	0	116	7.8

1999-2000 statistics:

GP	G	A	TP	+/-	PIM	PP	SH	GW	GT	S	PCT
78	22	31	53	-2	56	4	0	3	1	184	12.0

LAST SEASON

Led team in shooting percentage. Tied for third on team in game-winning goals. Missed two games with concussion. Missed two games due to coach's decision.

THE FINESSE GAME

Savard's size and skating will prevent him from ever playing a dominating game. He is an intelligent play-maker whose points will always be heavier in assists than goals. He doesn't have a very quick or accurate shot.

Savard really has a knack for delivering the puck to a guy who can do something dangerous with it, instead of passing just because he's tired of carrying it. He possesses good vision and instincts for the power play. A left-handed shot, he favours the attacking right-wing corner/half-boards for his "office." He will not even try one-on-one moves. He's a distributor.

Savard is not very quick off the mark and his speed is about average. He is pretty sturdy though, which makes his dives all the more comical. He is one of the most blatant actors in the game and draws a huge share of penalties. It's a wonder NHL referees have not cottoned onto his act, because he's really terrible at it.

THE PHYSICAL GAME

Savard won't touch a soul with an intentional, clean hit. He is sneaky mean, however, and if he can, he'll pay you back. He is small and is targeted by a lot of bigger guys, so that's how he has learned to defend himself. He absorbs some pretty stiff hits without being the least bit intimidated. He is actually quite strong for his size. His defensive play will be limited to stick-checking.

THE INTANGIBLES

Savard never played the game all-out every shift although former coach Brian Sutter did his best to hammer that lesson home last season, which explains the benchings. He will be a top-two centre in Calgary by default.

PROJECTION

Depending on his ice time, Savard could score from 40 to 50 points, with the emphasis on assists.

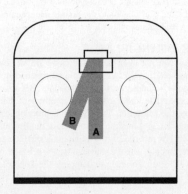

JEFF SHANTZ

Yrs. of NHL service: 7
Born: Duchess, Alta; Oct. 10, 1973
Position: centre
Height: 6-1
Weight: 185
Uniform no.: 11
Shoots: right

Career statistics:

GP	G	A	TP	PIM
455	61	115	176	225

1996-97 statistics:

GP	G	A	TP	+/-	PIM	PP	SH	GW	GT	S	PCT
69	9	21	30	+11	28	0	1	1	0	86	10.5

1997-98 statistics:

GP	G	A	TP	+/-	PIM	PP	SH	GW	GT	S	PCT
61	11	20	31	0	36	1	2	2	0	69	15.9

1998-99 statistics:

GP	G	A	TP	+/-	PIM	PP	SH	GW	GT	S	PCT
76	13	17	30	+14	44	1	1	3	0	82	15.9

1999-2000 statistics:

GP	G	A	TP	+/-	PIM	PP	SH	GW	GT	S	PCT
74	13	18	31	-13	30	6	0	1	0	112	11.6

LAST SEASON

Tied for third on team in power-play goals. Matched career high in goals. Missed eight games with rib injury.

THE FINESSE GAME

Shantz doesn't excel in many technical areas, but he possesses good hockey sense and good skills, though his game is heavily defense-oriented. Ideally, he is a number three forward (he can play centre or right wing). If injuries arise, however, he can fill in on a more offensive-minded line.

A good skater, Shantz is smooth in his turns with average quickness. He handles the puck well and sees his passing options. He won't be forced into many bad passes — he prefers to eat the puck rather than toss it away.

Shantz has a decent touch around the net but doesn't score many highlight goals. He has a heavy shot without the quick release. Most of his scoring comes from in tight off his forechecking efforts — perfect for a dump-and-chase style of attack. Shantz is very good on face-offs.

THE PHYSICAL GAME

The major question mark about Shantz was whether he was big and strong enough to prosper in the NHL, but he checks pretty hard and seems to be acquiring a taste for physical play. He doesn't have much size and will need to keep up his conditioning and strength work. He's gritty, doesn't take bad penalties and plays hard but clean.

THE INTANGIBLES

Shantz is developing into a solid two-way forward.

PROJECTION

We called for 40 points for a healthy Shantz last season. He would have made it but for the rib injury (or at least come close), and with some potential upgrades up front in Calgary, he could reach 40 easily.

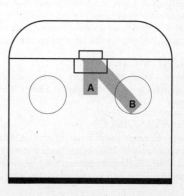

CORY STILLMAN

Yrs. of NHL service: 5
Born: Peterborough, Ont.; Dec. 20, 1970
Position: centre
Height: 6-0
Weight: 180
Uniform no.: 16
Shoots: left

Career statistics:

GP	G	A	TP	PIM
327	88	102	190	147

1996-97 statistics:

GP	G	A	TP	+/-	PIM	PP	SH	GW	GT	S	PCT
58	6	20	26	-6	14	2	0	0	0	112	5.4

1997-98 statistics:

GP	G	A	TP	+/-	PIM	PP	SH	GW	GT	S	PCT
72	27	22	49	-9	40	9	4	1	1	178	15.2

1998-99 statistics:

GP	G	A	TP	+/-	PIM	PP	SH	GW	GT	S	PCT
76	27	30	57	+7	38	9	3	5	1	175	15.4

1999-2000 statistics:

GP	G	A	TP	+/-	PIM	PP	SH	GW	GT	S	PCT
37	12	9	21	-9	12	6	0	3	1	59	20.3

LAST SEASON

Tied for third on team in power-play goals and game-winning goals. Missed 45 games with shoulder injuries and surgery.

THE FINESSE GAME

A natural centre, Stillman brings a pivot's playmaking ability to the wing. He's intelligent and has sound hockey instincts, but doesn't have that extra notch of speed an elite player at the NHL level needs. Since he's not very big (which hampers his odds of playing centre), he needs every advantage he can get.

Stillman has a good enough point shot to be used on the power play. He can beat a goalie with his shot from just inside the blueline. He has good hands and a keen understanding of the game. He possesses great patience and puckhandling skills, and is efficient in small areas. He has the potential to become an effective player if he is supported by gifted forwards.

Stillman is a goal scorer, and possesses a kind of selfishness that is intrinsic to good scorers. He wants the puck, and he wants to shoot it. He creates off the forecheck, not with his size but with his anticipation.

THE PHYSICAL GAME

Stillman is thick and sturdy enough to absorb some hard hits. He is not overly aggressive but will protect the puck.

THE INTANGIBLES

The Flames nearly gave up on Stillman but he never gave up on himself. Stillman has learned to work hard for an NHL job. He will need to rehab from his shoulder problems. He will be one of the top six Flames forwards if healthy.

PROJECTION

Stillman can be a consistent 30-goal scorer, and probably would have been last season if he hadn't had shoulder surgery.

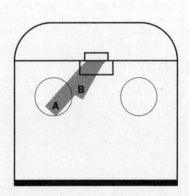

DANIEL TKACZUK

Yrs. of NHL service: 0
Born: Toronto, Ont.; June 10, 1979
Position: centre
Height: 6-0
Weight: 190
Uniform no.: n.a.
Shoots: left

Career AHL statistics:
GP	G	A	TP	PIM
80	25	41	66	56

LAST SEASON
Will be entering first NHL season. Appeared in 80 games with Saint John, scoring 25-41 — 66. Led AHL rookies in points. Named to AHL All-Rookie Team.

THE FINESSE GAME
Tkaczuk is developing into a smart two-way player. He probably doesn't have the goods to be a first-line centre in the NHL, but he could make an excellent number two.

Tkaczuk has learned to play in all game situations. He won't be a major offensive force, although he is a decent goal scorer. He will be better used as a setup man for finishing wingers, and he will be their defensive conscience as well.

Tkaczuk's skating is barely NHL calibre and it's something he will need to work on to improve his foot speed and his power skating.

Tkzacuk is strong on draws and should develop into a very effective penalty-killer.

THE PHYSICAL GAME
Tkaczuk needs to get stronger. He lacks lower body strength.

THE INTANGIBLES
Tkaczuk spent a season in the minors learning the game and looks ready to step in. The hardest lesson for him to learn is how much effort is required on a nightly basis at the pro level.

PROJECTION
Tkaczuk has seemed slow to develop, probably because he is going to be a player whose skills are more subtle. The Flames won't rush him — new GM Craig Button is from Dallas, an organization where patience is a watchword — and if Tkaczuk earns a full-time role he will be eased in with perhaps a 20-point season.

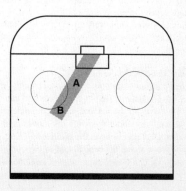

JASON WIEMER

Yrs. of NHL service: 6
Born: Kimberley, B.C.; Apr. 14, 1976
Position: left wing
Height: 6-1
Weight: 215
Uniform no.: 24
Shoots: left

Career statistics:

GP	G	A	TP	PIM
386	50	52	112	716

1996-97 statistics:

GP	G	A	TP	+/-	PIM	PP	SH	GW	GT	S	PCT
63	9	5	14	-13	134	2	0	0	0	103	8.7

1997-98 statistics:

GP	G	A	TP	+/-	PIM	PP	SH	GW	GT	S	PCT
79	12	10	22	-10	160	3	0	2	0	122	9.8

1998-99 statistics:

GP	G	A	TP	+/-	PIM	PP	SH	GW	GT	S	PCT
78	8	13	21	-12	177	1	0	1	0	128	6.3

1999-2000 statistics:

GP	G	A	TP	+/-	PIM	PP	SH	GW	GT	S	PCT
64	11	11	22	-10	120	2	0	3	0	104	10.6

LAST SEASON

Second on team in penalty minutes. Tied for third on team in game-winning goals. Missed 18 games with knee injuries.

THE FINESSE GAME

Wiemer has the build and the touch for standing in the traffic areas and picking pucks out of scrambles. He also has a touch of mean that merits him some room and time to execute. His release has improved, but he does not have an NHL-calibre shot that will make him a power forward who can post big numbers. Wiemer has to grind out his goals.

Wiemer does the dirty work in the corners, but needs to play with some skilled linemates because he doesn't have the finesse or creativity to make any pretty plays. He can finish off what someone with more vision opens up for him, however.

Wiemer's major shortcoming is his skating (though his foot speed is improving), but it is not enough of a problem to prevent him from becoming an impact player. He is very strong and well balanced for work around the net. He relies on his strength and his reach.

THE PHYSICAL GAME

Wiemer relishes body contact and will usually initiate checks to intimidate. He is very strong and can hit to hurt. He drives to the net and pushes defenders back, and he isn't shy about dropping his gloves or raising his elbows. He functions as the grinder on a line, since he will scrap along the boards and in the corners for the puck. He can complement almost any linemate.

THE INTANGIBLES

Life got a lot easier for Wiemer once coaches accepted the idea that he was not going to be the next Cam Neely. Wiemer had to learn his job and he had to be pushed, and playing him as a checking-line centre accomplished both. He was rushed into the NHL before he was ready. Some of the damage has been undone by the confidence he rebuilt in his game last season.

PROJECTION

Wiemer will probably score in the 15-goal range as he continues in his third-line role and picks up some second-unit power-play time.

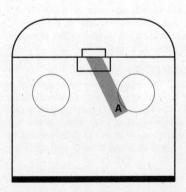

CAROLINA HURRICANES

Players' Statistics 1999-2000

POS.	NO.	PLAYER	GP	G	A	PTS	+/-	PIM	PP	SH	GW	GT	S	PCT
C	21	RON FRANCIS	78	23	50	73	10	18	7		4		150	15.3
C	92	JEFF O'NEILL	80	25	38	63	-9	72	4		7		189	13.2
L	10	GARY ROBERTS	69	23	30	53	-10	62	12		1		150	15.3
R	24	SAMI KAPANEN	76	24	24	48	10	12	7		5	2	229	10.5
D	22	SEAN HILL	62	13	31	44	3	59	8		2		150	8.7
R	18	ROBERT KRON	81	13	27	40	-4	8	2	1	3	1	134	9.7
D	77	PAUL COFFEY	69	11	29	40	-6	40	6		3	1	155	7.1
L	51	ANDREI KOVALENKO	76	15	24	39	-13	38	2		3		114	13.2
L	13	BATES BATTAGLIA	77	16	18	34	20	39	3		3		86	18.6
L	23	MARTIN GELINAS	81	14	16	30	-10	40	3				139	10.1
C	27	ROD BRIND'AMOUR	45	9	13	22	-13	26	4	1	1		87	10.3
L	28	PAUL RANHEIM	79	9	13	22	-14	6			2		98	9.2
D	2	GLEN WESLEY	78	7	15	22	-4	38	1			2	99	7.1
D	5	MAREK MALIK	57	4	10	14	13	63			1		57	7.0
R	16	*TOMMY WESTLUND	81	4	8	12	-10	19		1			67	6.0
L	20	SANDY MCCARTHY	71	6	5	11	-3	120	1				80	7.5
D	14	STEVEN HALKO	58		8	8	0	25					54	
L	17	JEFF DANIELS	69	3	4	7	-8	10				1	28	10.7
D	33	DAVE KARPA	27	1	4	5	9	52					24	4.2
D	45	*DAVID TANABE	31	4		4	-4	14	3				28	14.3
D	4	NOLAN PRATT	64	3	1	4	-22	90			1		47	6.4
C	15	*BYRON RITCHIE	26		2	2	-10	17					13	
D	7	CURTIS LESCHYSHYN	53		2	2	-19	14					31	
G	1	ARTURS IRBE	75		1	1	0	14						
R	25	*SHANE WILLIS	2				-1						1	
G	30	MARK FITZPATRICK	3				0							

GP = games played; G = goals; A = assists; PTS = points; +/- = goals-for minus goals-against while player is on ice; PIM = penalties in minutes; PP = power-play goals; SH = shorthanded goals; GW = game-winning goals; GT = game-tying goals; S = no. of shots; PCT = percentage of goals to shots; * = rookie

BATES BATTAGLIA

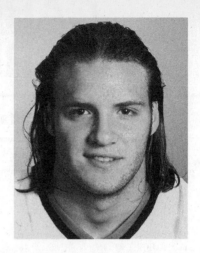

Yrs. of NHL service: 3
Born: Chicago, Illinois; Dec. 5, 1975
Position: left wing
Height: 6-2
Weight: 185
Uniform no.: 33
Shoots: left

Career statistics:

GP	G	A	TP	PIM
170	25	33	58	71

1997-98 statistics:

GP	G	A	TP	+/-	PIM	PP	SH	GW	GT	S	PCT
33	2	4	6	-1	10	0	0	1	0	21	9.5

1998-99 statistics:

GP	G	A	TP	+/-	PIM	PP	SH	GW	GT	S	PCT
60	7	11	18	+7	22	0	0	0	2	52	13.5

1999-2000 statistics:

GP	G	A	TP	+/-	PIM	PP	SH	GW	GT	S	PCT
77	16	18	34	+20	39	3	0	3	0	86	18.6

LAST SEASON

Led team in plus-minus and shooting percentage. Career highs in goals, assists and points. Missed three games with shoulder injury. Missed two games due to coach's decision.

THE FINESSE GAME

Battaglia is a good skater and is strong on the puck. He has had to drill hard to perfect most of his skills, because he is not a natural. His first strides are a bit sluggish, but he has a strong stride once he gets moving.

He goes hard to the net to create his scoring chances. He moves the puck alertly and plays smart positional hockey. He won't gamble or try to do anything fancy with the puck, which makes it easy for other grinders to play with him. He has a good head for the game, and the heart, too.

Battaglia is versatile and can play all three forward positions. He is a natural centre but will probably be used on the wing. He is skilled enough to take an occasional spin on one of the top lines with players like Ron Francis and Sami Kapanen, which is where he played early in the season, but he can't keep it up for long.

THE PHYSICAL GAME

Battaglia has good size and is willing to use it. He works hard and his enthusiasm alone will bug other players. A Chicago native, he grew up emulating Jeremy Roenick. He'll never have Roenick's scoring touch, but he'll bring the nonstop work ethic of a young Roenick every night.

THE INTANGIBLES

Battaglia has a solid, 10-year NHL future in store as a third-line forward. He'll bring energy to every shift.

He made a big jump going from college to the NHL and he is still finding his niche. He was much more relaxed and efficient in his role last season. He was a restricted free agent during the off-season.

PROJECTION

Battaglia's goal output will average 15 per season, and he will provide spark in a largely defensive role.

ROD BRIND'AMOUR

Yrs. of NHL service: 11
Born: Ottawa, Ont.; Aug. 9, 1970
Position: centre/left wing
Height: 6-1
Weight: 202
Uniform no.: 17
Shoots: left

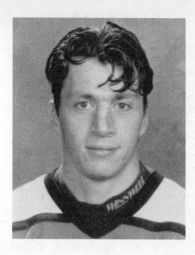

Career statistics:

GP	G	A	TP	PIM
823	282	443	725	724

1996-97 statistics:

GP	G	A	TP	+/-	PIM	PP	SH	GW	GT	S	PCT
82	27	32	59	+2	41	8	2	3	2	205	13.2

1997-98 statistics:

GP	G	A	TP	+/-	PIM	PP	SH	GW	GT	S	PCT
82	36	38	74	-2	54	10	2	8	0	205	17.6

1998-99 statistics:

GP	G	A	TP	+/-	PIM	PP	SH	GW	GT	S	PCT
82	24	50	74	+3	47	10	0	3	2	191	12.6

1999-2000 statistics:

GP	G	A	TP	+/-	PIM	PP	SH	GW	GT	S	PCT
45	9	13	22	-13	26	4	1	1	0	87	10.3

LAST SEASON

Acquired from Philadelphia with Jean-Marc Pelletier and a second-round draft choice in 2000 for Keith Primeau and a fifth-round draft choice in 2000, Jan. 13, 2000. Missed 34 games with broken foot, ending his concecutive-games played streak at 484. Missed one game with concussion.

THE FINESSE GAME

Versatility and dependability are among Brind'Amour's trademarks. He is one of the best two-way centres in the league. He wins face-offs. He checks. He has the strength and speed and stride to handle every defensive aspect of the game, the grit and desire to earn the loose pucks, the temperament and credibility to be on the ice in the last minute of a close game.

Brind'Amour may not beat many players one-on-one in open ice, but he outworks defenders along the boards and uses a quick burst of speed to drive to the net. He's a playmaker in the mucking sense, with scoring chances emerging from his commitment. He is a better player at centre than wing, though he can handle either assignment.

Brind'Amour has a long, powerful stride with a quick first step to leave a defender behind; his hand skills complement the skating assets. He drives well into a shot on the fly, and has a quick-release snap shot and a strong backhand.

When Brind'Amour does not have the puck he works ferociously to get it back. An excellent penalty killer, and the centre the Hurricanes send out if they are two men short, Brind'Amour thinks nothing of blocking shots, which is how he broke his foot.

THE PHYSICAL GAME

A king in the weight room, Brind'Amour uses his size well and is a strong skater. He can muck with the best in the corners and along the boards. He will carry the puck through traffic in front of the net and battle for position for screens and tip-ins. He is among the hardest workers on the team, even in practice, and is always striving to improve his game.

THE INTANGIBLES

After years and years of trade rumours, Brind'Amour was finally moved to Carolina. He is a coach's treasure because he can be deployed in any situation and will provide trustworthy work.

PROJECTION

Brind'Amour should score in the 30-goal range as the number one (or is it number two?) centre in Carolina.

RON FRANCIS

Yrs. of NHL service: 19
Born: Sault Ste. Marie, Ont.; Mar. 1, 1963
Position: centre
Height: 6-2
Weight: 200
Uniform no.: 21
Shoots: left

Career statistics:

GP	G	A	TP	PIM
1407	472	1087	1559	885

1996-97 statistics:

GP	G	A	TP	+/-	PIM	PP	SH	GW	GT	S	PCT
81	27	63	90	+7	20	10	1	2	0	183	14.8

1997-98 statistics:

GP	G	A	TP	+/-	PIM	PP	SH	GW	GT	S	PCT
81	25	62	87	+12	20	7	0	5	2	189	13.2

1998-99 statistics:

GP	G	A	TP	+/-	PIM	PP	SH	GW	GT	S	PCT
82	21	31	52	-2	34	8	0	2	1	133	15.8

1999-2000 statistics:

GP	G	A	TP	+/-	PIM	PP	SH	GW	GT	S	PCT
78	23	50	73	+10	18	7	0	4	0	150	15.3

LAST SEASON

Led team in assists and points. Tied for second on team in shooting percentage. Third on team in game-winning goals. Tied for third on team in goals, plus-minus and power-play goals. Missed two games with vertigo. Missed two games with back injury.

THE FINESSE GAME

Francis is a two-way centre who can still put some points on the board. Technically, he is a choppy skater who gets where he has to be with a minimum amount of style. His understanding of the game is key because he has great awareness of his positioning. He gets loads of ice time, so he has learned to pace himself to conserve energy. There are few useless bursts of speed.

Francis is Dr. Draw. On rare nights when he is struggling with an opposing centre, he'll tinker with his changes in the neutral zone, then save what he has learned for a key draw deep in either zone. Just as a great scorer never shows a goalie the same move twice in a row, Francis never uses the same technique twice in succession. He has good hand-eye coordination and uses his body well at the dot. Few players win their draws as outright as Francis does on a consistent basis.

When he focusses on a defensive role, Francis has the vision to come out of a scramble into an attacking rush. He anticipates passes, blocks shots, then springs an odd-man breakout with a smart play.

Francis doesn't have a screamingly hard shot, nor is he a flashy player. He works from the centre of the ice, between the circles, and has a quick release on a one-timer. He can kill penalties or work the point on the power play with equal effectiveness. He complements any kind of player.

THE PHYSICAL GAME

Not a big, imposing hitter, Francis will still use his body to get the job done. He will bump and grind and go into the trenches. Back on defense, he can function as a third defenseman; on offense, you will find him going into the corners or heading for the front of the net for tips and rebounds. He keeps himself in great shape.

THE INTANGIBLES

At 37, Francis was the oldest player to lead his team in scoring last season, mostly because it took until half-way through the year before the Hurricanes finally dealt Keith Primeau. Francis shouldn't have to be a number one centre anymore, but even with Rod Brind'Amour on hand, it's likely he will be asked to again.

PROJECTION

Francis bowled us over with 73 points last season (we were thinking 50). It wouldn't be a shock to see his numbers decrease by 10 points. Carolina is not a very good team.

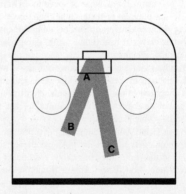

MARTIN GELINAS

Yrs. of NHL service: 11
Born: Shawinigan, Que.; June 5, 1970
Position: left wing
Height: 5-11
Weight: 195
Uniform no.: 23
Shoots: left

Career statistics:

GP	G	A	TP	PIM
744	195	192	387	474

1996-97 statistics:

GP	G	A	TP	+/-	PIM	PP	SH	GW	GT	S	PCT
74	35	33	68	+6	42	6	1	3	1	177	19.8

1997-98 statistics:

GP	G	A	TP	+/-	PIM	PP	SH	GW	GT	S	PCT
64	16	18	34	-5	40	3	2	5	0	147	10.9

1998-99 statistics:

GP	G	A	TP	+/-	PIM	PP	SH	GW	GT	S	PCT
76	13	15	28	+3	67	0	0	2	2	111	11.7

1999-2000 statistics:

GP	G	A	TP	+/-	PIM	PP	SH	GW	GT	S	PCT
81	14	16	30	-10	40	3	0	0	0	139	10.1

PROJECTION

Gelinas lacks the talent to score more than 15 goals, but that kind of production from a third-liner, combined with his energy and work ethic, make him a valuable role player.

LAST SEASON

Missed one game due to coach's decision.

THE FINESSE GAME

Gelinas plays a grinding game on the dump-and-chase. Much of his scoring is generated by his forechecking, with the majority of his goals tap-ins from about five feet out. He is strong along the boards and in front of the net. He is not a natural scorer, but he has good instincts and works hard for his chances. He is a good penalty killer.

Gelinas is ideally a third-line winger, but he can play fill-in stints on better lines in case of injuries. His hockey sense and puckhandling prevent him from blossoming in a bigger role.

Gelinas is an energetic player who provides momentum-changing shifts. He's not a goal scorer, though, and gets into trouble when he starts thinking and playing like one. He can't help a power play.

THE PHYSICAL GAME

Gelinas is a small player and seems to get himself into situations where he just gets flattened. He has very thick thighs, which power his skating and his body checks and his work in the corners. He isn't intimidated, but he does get wiped out of the play and he needs to be smarter about jumping in and out of holes, paying the price only when necessary.

THE INTANGIBLES

Gelinas is a useful role player but he has begun to become less of an impact player.

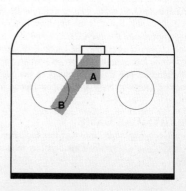

KEVIN HATCHER

Yrs. of NHL service: 15
Born: Detroit, Mich.; Sept. 9, 1966
Position: right defense
Height: 6-4
Weight: 225
Uniform no.: 4
Shoots: right

Career statistics:

GP	G	A	TP	PIM
1100	223	436	659	1356

1996-97 statistics:

GP	G	A	TP	+/-	PIM	PP	SH	GW	GT	S	PCT
80	15	39	54	+11	103	9	0	1	0	199	7.5

1997-98 statistics:

GP	G	A	TP	+/-	PIM	PP	SH	GW	GT	S	PCT
74	19	29	48	-3	66	13	1	3	1	169	11.2

1998-99 statistics:

GP	G	A	TP	+/-	PIM	PP	SH	GW	GT	S	PCT
66	11	27	38	+11	24	4	2	3	0	131	8.4

1999-2000 statistics:

GP	G	A	TP	+/-	PIM	PP	SH	GW	GT	S	PCT
74	4	19	23	-10	38	2	0	0	1	112	3.6

LAST SEASON

Signed as a free agent, July 31, 2000. Missed eight games due to coach's decision.

THE FINESSE GAME

Hatcher thinks offense all the time, usually when he shouldn't — like when he's in front of his own net. He anticipates where the puck may be going, so he gets out of position. But when you're as big as he is you shouldn't have to anticipate anything — you should just let it happen. You allow your size to take away everything so that you don't have to force it. Hatcher is not among the elite offensive defensemen for several reasons. He knows he's talented and expects the talent to do the work. He also acts like he's attached to the puck and tends to be a puck chaser.

Hatcher doesn't have a quick take-off; a smart checker will get to him quickly and force a turnover. He can finish in close offensively, but he isn't the smartest puck carrier in the world and is often better off making the short outlet pass or dumping the puck, instead of forcing a play at the blueline. He is smart about jumping into the play, though, and also clever enough to make the best play the situation dictates. He moves to the left point on the power play to open up his forehand for one-timers, although in the past few seasons he seems to have lost all confidence in his shot.

THE PHYSICAL GAME

Who wants a finesse defenseman this big? He's not very brave, and doesn't use his body as well as he should.

THE INTANGIBLES

Hatcher's stock plummeted with the Rangers. He should have been benched more than he was. Hatcher would play well every half-dozen games or so. An unrestricted free agent, the Rangers had no interest in re-signing him.

PROJECTION

Hatcher will have a hard time getting full-time employment. He has a shot at 20 points if he does.

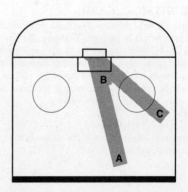

ARTURS IRBE

Yrs. of NHL service: 8
Born: Riga, Latvia; Feb. 2, 1967
Position: goaltender
Height: 5-8
Weight: 175
Uniform no.: 1
Catches: left

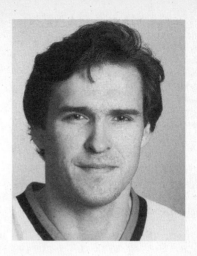

Career statistics:

GP	MIN	GA	SO	GAA	A	PIM
396	22238	1084	24	2.92	6	68

1996-97 statistics:

GP	MIN	GAA	W	L	T	SO	GA	S	SAPCT	PIM
35	1965	2.69	17	12	3	3	88	825	.825	8

1997-98 statistics:

GP	MIN	GAA	W	L	T	SO	GA	S	SAPCT	PIM
41	1999	2.73	14	11	6	2	91	982	.982	2

1998-99 statistics:

GP	MIN	GAA	W	L	T	SO	GA	S	SAPCT	PIM
62	3643	2.22	27	20	12	6	135	1753	.923	10

1999-2000 statistics:

GP	MIN	GAA	W	L	T	SO	GA	S	SAPCT	PIM
75	4345	2.42	34	28	9	5	175	1858	.906	14

LAST SEASON

Second among NHL goalies in minutes played. Third among NHL goalies in shots faced. Tied for fourth among NHL goalies in shutouts. Fifth in NHL in wins with career high. Tied for fifth among NHL goalies in penalty minutes.

THE PHYSICAL GAME

If you didn't know Irbe was a goalie, you might guess he was a gymnast — he has that kind of slender, muscular build. And if Mary Lou Retton played goal, she would probably play it as Irbe does: diving, rolling, scrambling and sticking the landing. Irbe is so flexible that when he does a split, he doesn't have to use his stick to cover what little five-hole is left. His, er, cup, is right on the ice. Teams have to try to beat him high.

Irbe is unbelievably quick. He has great confidence in his abilities and will challenge shooters by coming out well beyond his crease. He doesn't have great lateral movement, however.

Irbe needs to improve on his work outside the net. He doesn't move the puck well and gets caught while he's making decisions. He can get mixed up with his defensemen.

Irbe has trouble picking up the puck through a crowd because of his small size. He will use his stick to whack some ankles.

THE MENTAL GAME

Irbe's unusual style matches his personality. He is quite outgoing and unpredictable. It was a long stretch between number one goaltending jobs for Irbe, who is a mature competitor.

THE INTANGIBLES

Irbe is not an elite goalie nor one who will take the 'Canes to the next level, but apparently Carolina is content to make do with him for now. Because of his age, size, and especially because of his active style, Irbe needs to be limited to 60 starts a year. He had 75 last season, but we never got the chance to see how that might have affected him in the playoffs.

Irbe is good friends with Sandis Ozolinsh, whom the Hurricanes acquired in the off-season.

PROJECTION

How Irbe got 34 wins with this bunch is anybody's guess. He must be a better goalie than we previoulsy gave him credit for. He should record 28 to 30 wins.

SAMI KAPANEN

Yrs. of NHL service: 5
Born: Vantaa, Finland; June 14, 1973
Position: left wing
Height: 5-10
Weight: 170
Uniform no.: 24
Shoots: left

Career statistics:

GP	G	A	TP	PIM
318	92	112	204	46

1996-97 statistics:

GP	G	A	TP	+/-	PIM	PP	SH	GW	GT	S	PCT
45	13	12	25	+6	2	3	0	2	0	82	15.9

1997-98 statistics:

GP	G	A	TP	+/-	PIM	PP	SH	GW	GT	S	PCT
81	26	37	63	+9	16	4	0	5	0	190	13.7

1998-99 statistics:

GP	G	A	TP	+/-	PIM	PP	SH	GW	GT	S	PCT
81	24	35	59	-1	10	5	0	7	0	254	9.4

1999-2000 statistics:

GP	G	A	TP	+/-	PIM	PP	SH	GW	GT	S	PCT
76	24	24	48	+10	12	7	0	5	2	229	10.5

LAST SEASON

Led team in shots. Second on team in goals and game-winning goals. Tied for third on team in plus-minus and power-play goals. Missed four games with concussion. Missed two games with shoulder injury.

THE FINESSE GAME

Kapanen is a small, skilled forward who is always moving. He handles the puck well while in motion, though like a lot of European forwards he tends to hold the puck a tad too long. He will shoot on the fly, however, and has an NHL shot when he does release it. He has a fine wrist shot and he can score off the rush.

Kapanen has quickness, good balance, good strength, and he's smart. He makes few mistakes. He knows where to be on the ice and how to use big players as picks and screens. He sticks to the perimeter until he darts into holes. He takes care of his defensive assignments, and even though he's too small to body check, he is able to harrass opponents by lifting up a stick and swiping the puck. Kapanen is strong on the puck.

Kapanen uses a very short stick to keep the puck in close to his body. He might lose a little off his shot because of it, but he is able to create some terrific scoring chances with his passing because of his control. It also means defenders are forced to reach in for the puck.

THE PHYSICAL GAME

Kapanen plays without fear and draws a lot of penalties with his speed. He is lean without much muscle mass. He plays a spunky game and picks up the team on its quieter nights, because he sprints to the pucks and tries on every shift.

THE INTANGIBLES

Kapanen is a clone of Montreal's Saku Koivu, who gets much better press. Kapanen is Carolina's most consistent player, most dangerous player and most exciting player.

PROJECTION

With a little more depth to take some of the checking pressure off Kapanen, he could score 35 goals. Without it, his range is 25 to 30.

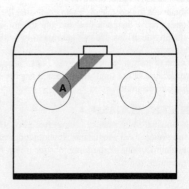

MAREK MALIK

Yrs. of NHL service: 3
Born: Ostrava, Czech.; June 24, 1975
Position: left defense
Height: 6-5
Weight: 190
Uniform no.: 5
Shoots: left

Career statistics:

GP	G	A	TP	PIM
164	7	25	32	153

1996-97 statistics:

GP	G	A	TP	+/-	PIM	PP	SH	GW	GT	S	PCT
47	1	5	6	+5	50	0	0	1	0	33	3.0

1997-98 statistics:

Did not play in NHL

1998-99 statistics:

GP	G	A	TP	+/-	PIM	PP	SH	GW	GT	S	PCT
52	2	9	11	-6	36	1	0	0	0	36	5.6

1999-2000 statistics:

GP	G	A	TP	+/-	PIM	PP	SH	GW	GT	S	PCT
57	4	10	14	+13	63	0	0	1	0	57	7.0

PROJECTION

Malik needs to win a steady job first. If he does, he could chip in 20 points.

LAST SEASON

Second on team in plus-minus. Third on team in penalty minutes. Missed 25 games due to coach's decision.

THE FINESSE GAME

Malik has very good potential because of his high skill level in all areas. He is a good skater for his towering size, though he is a straight-legged skater and not quick. He uses his range mostly as a defensive tool and is not much involved in the attack.

Malik is poised with the puck. He is a good passer and playmaker, and moves the puck out of his own end quickly. He won't try to do too much himself but will utilize his teammates well. He's big, but does a lot of little things well, which makes him a solid defensive player. He limits his offensive contributions to a shot from the point. However, he may yet develop better skills as a playmaker.

THE PHYSICAL GAME

Tall but weedy, Malik needs to fill out more to be able to handle some of the NHL's big boys one-on-one. Like Kjell Samuelsson, he takes up a lot of space with his arms and stick, and is more of an octopus-type defenseman than a solid hitter. He is strong in front of his net. He has some aggressiveness in him but needs to compete every night on a more consistent level.

THE INTANGIBLES

This could be the season for Malik. Certainly the door has been opened with the departures of Sean Hill, Paul Coffey and Curtis Leschyshyn.

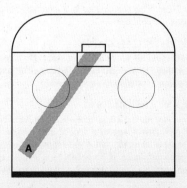

JEFF O'NEILL

Yrs. of NHL service: 5
Born: Richmond Hill, Ont.; Feb. 23, 1976
Position: centre
Height: 6-0
Weight: 190
Uniform no.: 92
Shoots: right

Career statistics:

GP	G	A	TP	PIM
366	82	108	190	285

1996-97 statistics:

GP	G	A	TP	+/-	PIM	PP	SH	GW	GT	S	PCT
72	14	16	30	-24	40	2	1	2	0	101	13.9

1997-98 statistics:

GP	G	A	TP	+/-	PIM	PP	SH	GW	GT	S	PCT
74	19	20	39	-8	67	7	1	4	1	114	16.7

1998-99 statistics:

GP	G	A	TP	+/-	PIM	PP	SH	GW	GT	S	PCT
75	16	15	31	+3	66	4	0	2	0	121	13.2

1999-2000 statistics:

GP	G	A	TP	+/-	PIM	PP	SH	GW	GT	S	PCT
80	25	38	63	-9	72	4	0	7	0	189	13.2

LAST SEASON

Led team in goals with career high. Led team in game-winning goals. Second on team in assists, points and shots. Missed two games with back spasms.

THE FINESSE GAME

To be a Pat LaFontaine — to whom O'Neill was often compared early in his career — a player needs all the tools. And except for his skating, O'Neill's intensity isn't good enough to place him among the top centres, though his skills are.

An excellent skater, with balance, speed, acceleration and quickness, he has a good sense of timing and is patient with his passes. He doesn't have a big-time release but he has a decent one-timer.

O'Neill likes to carry the puck down the left-wing boards to protect the puck, and with his speed he is able to blow by defensemen. He does not follow this move up by driving to the net. Defensively, he has to remind himself not to leave the zone before the puck does. He is often too anxious to counterattack before his team has control.

THE PHYSICAL GAME

O'Neill could always be in better shape. He is considered something of a soft player, whose effort and intensity don't come up to his skill level.

THE INTANGIBLES

O'Neill was moved to the right wing with Ron Francis after Rod Brind'Amour's arrival and looked very comfortable there. He continues to show progress, and growing confidence, in his ability to score. We questioned whether O'Neill wanted to take his game to the next level. It appears as if he is finally ready. He was a restricted free agent during the off-season.

PROJECTION

No longer satisfied to just have an NHL job, O'Neill could turn out to be something of a go-to guy after all. Expect another 25 goals and 60 points.

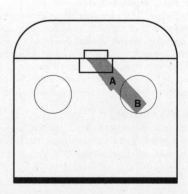

SANDIS OZOLINSH

Yrs. of NHL service: 8
Born: Riga, Latvia; Aug. 3, 1972
Position: left defense
Height: 6-1
Weight: 195
Uniform no.: 8
Shoots: left

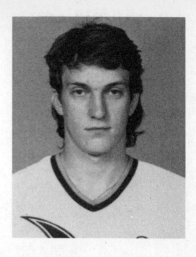

Career statistics:

GP	G	A	TP	PIM
506	115	254	369	369

1996-97 statistics:

GP	G	A	TP	+/-	PIM	PP	SH	GW	GT	S	PCT
80	23	45	68	+4	88	13	0	4	1	232	9.9

1997-98 statistics:

GP	G	A	TP	+/-	PIM	PP	SH	GW	GT	S	PCT
66	13	38	51	-12	65	9	0	2	1	135	9.6

1998-99 statistics:

GP	G	A	TP	+/-	PIM	PP	SH	GW	GT	S	PCT
39	7	25	32	+10	22	4	0	3	0	81	8.6

1999-2000 statistics:

GP	G	A	TP	+/-	PIM	PP	SH	GW	GT	S	PCT
82	16	36	52	+17	46	6	0	1	0	210	7.6

LAST SEASON

Acquired from Colorado with a second-round draft choice in 2000 for defenseman Nolan Pratt, a first-round choice in 2001, and two second-round draft choices in 2000, June 23, 2000. Tied Colorado defensemen and tied for seventh among NHL defensemen in points. Third on team in plus-minus. One of three Avs to appear in all 82 games.

THE FINESSE GAME

Ozolinsh is a pure "offenseman," but one who doesn't always recognize when it's safe to go. He sees only one traffic light, and it's stuck on green.

He likes to start things by pressing in the neutral zone, where he will gamble and try to intercept cross-ice passes. His defense partner and the forwards will always have to be alert to guard against odd-man rushes back, because he doesn't recognize when it's a good time to be aggressive or when to back off.

He will start the breakout play with his smooth skating, then spring a teammate with a crisp pass. He can pass on his forehand or backhand, which is a good thing because he is all over the ice. He will follow up the play to create an odd-man rush, trail in for a drop pass or drive to the net for a rebound.

Ozolinsh has good straightaway speed, but he can't make a lot of agile, pretty moves. Because he can't weave his way through a number of defenders, he has to power his way into open ice with the puck and drive the defenders back through intimidation. His speed often allows him to get back and help out on the odd-man rushes that he helps create.

He sometimes hangs onto the puck too long. He has a variety of shots, with his best being a one-timer from the off-side on the power play, where he slides into the backdoor on the weak side. He is not as effective when he works down low.

THE PHYSICAL GAME

Ozolinsh goes into areas of the ice where he gets hit a lot, but he is stronger than he looks. He is all business on the ice and pays the price to get the puck, but doesn't really have a taste for hitting, or the desire to keep his crease clean.

THE INTANGIBLES

Ozolinsh didn't seem particularly thrilled with the arrival of Ray Bourque. He had a terrible playoff series against Dallas, which probably sealed his departure. He will be the undisputed number one in Carolina.

PROJECTION

Four of the top five point-getters among defensemen last season played in the West. The switch to Eastern Conference play should reduce Ozolinsh's points. Add to that the fact he isn't playing with scorers like Peter Forsberg and Milan Hejduk anymore, and his numbers might shrink by 10 points.

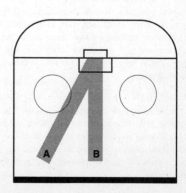

DAVID TANABE

Yrs. of NHL service: 1
Born: Minneapolis, MN; July 19, 1980
Position: right defense
Height: 6-1
Weight: 190
Uniform no.: 45
Shoots: right

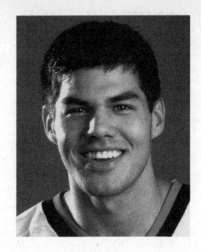

Career statistics:

GP	G	A	TP	PIM
31	4	0	4	14

1999-2000 statistics:

GP	G	A	TP	+/-	PIM	PP	SH	GW	GT	S	PCT
31	4	0	4	-4	14	3	0	0	0	28	14.3

LAST SEASON

Appeared in 32 games with Cincinnati (AHL), scoring 0-13 — 13. Missed 26 NHL games due to coach's decision.

THE FINESSE GAME

Tanabe made the game look easy when he broke in with three power-play goals in his first eight NHL games, but it fell apart very quickly for him after that and he spent most of the second half in the minors.

He is a terrific skater, who may turn into one of the best-skating defensemen of his generation. The only question is his hockey sense, because he doesn't seem to be able to make as many good things happen as he should. If he can't, he will never be the top-four defenseman the Hurricanes have him pegged as.

Tanabe can make a good first pass out of his zone or rush the puck end-to-end. He has a hard shot from the point. His defensive reads need a lot of work. Tanabe looks good on the power play, but he has to make a living at working five-on-five.

THE PHYSICAL GAME

Tanabe needs to improve his conditioning (he ran out of gas quickly) and his strength.

THE INTANGIBLES

After a hot start, the rookie defenseman tailed off and played most of the second half in the minors, although he was recalled for the final two games of the season by the parent club. He will miss Paul Coffey, who was a willing mentor for a young player with considerable offensive upside.

PROJECTION

With Sandis Ozolinsh added to the lineup, Tanabe gets another elite offenseman to play with and learn from. He showed improvement at the end of the season, and that makes us believe he will be a top four defenseman with the Hurricanes and perhaps a 30-point contributor.

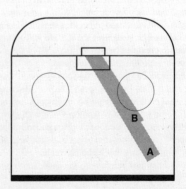

GLEN WESLEY

Yrs. of NHL service: 13
Born: Red Deer, Alta.; Oct. 2, 1968
Position: left defense
Height: 6-1
Weight: 197
Uniform no.: 20
Shoots: left

Career statistics:

GP	G	A	TP	PIM
955	113	337	450	717

1996-97 statistics:

GP	G	A	TP	+/-	PIM	PP	SH	GW	GT	S	PCT
68	6	26	32	0	40	3	1	0	0	126	4.8

1997-98 statistics:

GP	G	A	TP	+/-	PIM	PP	SH	GW	GT	S	PCT
82	6	19	25	+7	36	1	0	1	0	121	5.0

1998-99 statistics:

GP	G	A	TP	+/-	PIM	PP	SH	GW	GT	S	PCT
74	7	17	24	+14	44	0	0	2	1	112	6.3

1999-2000 statistics:

GP	G	A	TP	+/-	PIM	PP	SH	GW	GT	S	PCT
78	7	15	22	-4	38	1	0	0	2	99	7.1

LAST SEASON

Missed two games with groin injury. Missed two games with eye injury.

THE FINESSE GAME

Wesley simply isn't an offensive force, though he keeps being shoehorned into that role. He is at best a number two defenseman, and is ideally suited as a three or four. He toils in the one to two slot for Carolina because the team is so thin defensively.

Wesley is solid, but not elite. He is very good with the puck. He clicks on the power play because he knows when to jump into the holes. He has good but not great offensive instincts, which means he thinks rather than reacts when gauging when to pinch, when to rush, when to pass the puck and when to back off. He is a decent skater who is not afraid to veer into the play deep; he seldom gets trapped there. He has a good slap shot from the point and snap shot from the circle.

You could count on two hands the number of times Wesley has been beaten one-on-one during his career, and there are very few defensemen you can say that about. He makes defensive plays with confidence and is poised even when outnumbered in the rush. He has to keep his feet moving.

THE PHYSICAL GAME

Wesley is not a bone-crunching defenseman, but neither was Jacques Laperriere, and he's in the Hall of Fame. We're not suggesting that Wesley is in that class, only that you don't have to shatter glass to be a solid checker, which he is. He's not a mean hitter, but he will execute a takeout check and not let his man get back into the play.

He is also sly about running interference for his defense partner, allowing him time to move the puck and giving him confidence that he won't get hammered by a forechecker. He is also quite durable. Wesley seldom misses more than a handful of games a season.

THE INTANGIBLES

Wesley is a more relaxed player in Carolina, and is helping to break in some of the younger defensemen. He may suffer from the loss of Sean Hill and Paul Coffey.

PROJECTION

Wesley is, at best, a 30-point scorer, but 20 is more his expected output. He doesn't get nearly the amount of points he should for the ice time he receives.

CHICAGO BLACKHAWKS

Players' Statistics 1999-2000

POS.	NO.	PLAYER	GP	G	A	PTS	+/-	PIM	PP	SH	GW	GT	S	PCT
R	10	TONY AMONTE	82	43	41	84	10	48	11	5	2	1	260	16.5
C	26	STEVE SULLIVAN	80	22	43	65	19	56	2	1	6		180	12.2
C	13	ALEXEI ZHAMNOV	71	23	37	60	7	61	5		7		175	13.1
C	92	MICHAEL NYLANDER	77	24	30	54	6	30	5		2		122	19.7
L	17	MICHAL GROSEK	75	13	27	40	11	47	3		2		114	11.4
D	2	BORIS MIRONOV	58	9	28	37	-3	72	4	2	1	1	144	6.3
L	55	ERIC DAZE	59	23	13	36	-16	28	6		1	1	143	16.1
L	19	DEAN MCAMMOND	76	14	18	32	11	72	1		1		118	11.9
D	8	ANDERS ERIKSSON	73	3	25	28	4	20			1		86	3.5
D	44	BRYAN MCCABE	79	6	19	25	-8	139	2		2		119	5.0
C	11	JOSEF MARHA	81	10	12	22	-10	18	2	1	3		91	11.0
R	17	*JEAN-PIERRE DUMONT	47	10	8	18	-6	18			1		86	11.6
L	24	BOB PROBERT	69	4	11	15	10	114					38	10.5
R	34	BLAIR ATCHEYNUM	47	5	7	12	-8	6					48	10.4
D	6	KEVIN DEAN	64	3	8	11	3	36		1			47	6.4
D	4	DOUG ZMOLEK	43	2	7	9	6	60					24	8.3
D	3	BRAD BROWN	57		9	9	-1	134					15	
L	23	JEAN-YVES LEROUX	54	3	5	8	-10	43			1		36	8.3
C	20	MARK JANSSENS	36		6	6	-2	73					14	
R	16	ED OLCZYK	33	2	2	4	-8	12					33	6.1
C	12	DEREK PLANTE	33	2	2	4	-5	4	1				31	6.5
D	33	JAMIE ALLISON	59	1	3	4	-5	102					24	4.2
D	32	RADIM BICANEK	11		3	3	7	4					8	
D	5	*STEVE MCCARTHY	5	1	1	2	0	4	1				4	25.0
L	25	*KYLE CALDER	8	1	1	2	-3	2					5	20.0
R	14	RYAN VANDENBUSSCHE	52		1	1	-3	143					19	
G	31	*MARC LAMOTHE	2				0							
L	36	*CHRIS HERPERGER	9				-2	5					2	
G	29	STEVE PASSMORE	24				0	9						
G	41	JOCELYN THIBAULT	60				0	2						

GP = games played; G = goals; A = assists; PTS = points; +/- = goals-for minus goals-against while player is on ice; PIM = penalties in minutes; PP = power-play goals; SH = shorthanded goals; GW = game-winning goals; GT = game-tying goals; S = no. of shots; PCT = percentage of goals to shots; * = rookie

TONY AMONTE

Yrs. of NHL service: 9
Born: Hingham, Mass.; Aug. 2, 1970
Position: right wing
Height: 6-0
Weight: 190
Uniform no.: 10
Shoots: left

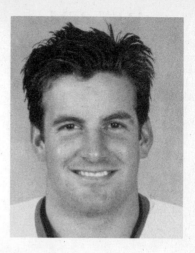

Career statistics:

GP	G	A	TP	PIM
697	290	304	594	482

1996-97 statistics:

GP	G	A	TP	+/-	PIM	PP	SH	GW	GT	S	PCT
81	41	36	77	+35	64	9	2	4	2	266	15.4

1997-98 statistics:

GP	G	A	TP	+/-	PIM	PP	SH	GW	GT	S	PCT
82	31	42	73	+21	66	7	3	5	0	296	10.5

1998-99 statistics:

GP	G	A	TP	+/-	PIM	PP	SH	GW	GT	S	PCT
82	44	31	75	0	60	14	3	8	0	256	17.2

1999-2000 statistics:

GP	G	A	TP	+/-	PIM	PP	SH	GW	GT	S	PCT
82	43	41	84	+10	48	11	5	2	1	260	16.5

LAST SEASON

Led team in goals and points for fourth consecutive season. Third in NHL in goals. Tied for sixth in NHL in points. Led team and second in NHL in shorthanded goals. Led team in power-play goals and shots. Second on team in assists and shooting percentage. Only Blackhawk to appear in all 82 games. Holds current active NHL Iron Man streak with 246 consecutive games played.

THE FINESSE GAME

Amonte is blessed with exceptional speed and acceleration. His timing is accurate and his anticipation keen. He has good balance and he can carry the puck at a pretty good clip, though he is more effective when streaking down the wing and getting the puck late. Playing on the left side leaves his forehand open for one-timers, but Amonte is equally secure on the right wing, where he played most of last season. He's been called a young Yvan Cournoyer for the way he uses his speed to drive wide around the defense to the net. His speed intimidates.

Amonte has a quick release on his wrist shot. He likes to go top shelf, just under the crossbar, and can also go to the backhand shot or a wrist shot off his back foot, like a fadeaway jumper. He is a top power-play man, since he is always working himself into open ice. He is better utilized down low on a power play than on the point. An accurate shooter, and one who takes a lot of shots, Amonte is also creative in his playmaking. He passes very well and is conscious of where his teammates are; he usually makes the best percentage play. He has confidence in his shot and wants the puck when the game is on the line.

Offensively, Amonte is a smart player away from the puck. He sets picks and creates openings for his teammates. He is an aggressive penalty killer and a shorthanded threat.

THE PHYSICAL GAME

Amonte's speed and movement keep him out of a lot of trouble zones, but he will also drive to the front of the net and take punishment there if that's the correct play. He loves to score, he loves to help his linemates score, and although he is outweighed by a lot of NHL defensemen he is seldom outworked. He's intense and is not above getting chippy and rubbing his glove in someone's face.

Amonte takes a lot of abuse and plays through the checks. He seldom takes bad retaliatory penalties. He just keeps his legs driving and draws calls with his nonstop skating.

THE INTANGIBLES

What could Amonte accomplish on a good team? He scored 17.7 percent of the Hawks' goals last season, and that is with opponents knowing he is the player they have to key on. Chicago will probably adopt a European-style game under new coach Alpo Suhonen, and Amonte should fit right in. Amonte is the heart and soul of the Hawks and is a stunning hockey bargain at $3 million (he's looking for a contract extension, but don't expect him to hold out; that's not his style).

PROJECTION

With any kind of supporting cast, Amonte would be a 50-goal, 100-point man. Unfortunately, the cavalry will not be arriving this season.

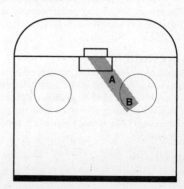

MARK BELL

Yrs. of NHL service: 0
Born: St. Paul's, Ont.; Aug. 5, 1980
Position: centre
Height: 6-3
Weight: 198
Uniform no.: n.a.
Shoots: left

Career junior statistics:

GP	G	A	TP	PIM
212	105	102	207	291

LAST SEASON

Will be entering first NHL season. Appeared in 48 games with Ottawa (OHL), scoring 34-38 — 72.

THE FINESSE GAME

Bell is all finesse. He is a terrifc puckhandler and passer, a natural point-producer who is always looking to make things happen in the offensive zone. He has a hard slap shot and a strong wrister. He has good hand-eye coordination for tipping pucks in front of the net. He also has good hockey sense, good vision, and good instincts — there is almost nothing negative about his offensive game, and it's a good bet he will be able to bring the skills that have served him in junior to the NHL level.

Bell is a smooth, fluid skater who is very strong on his skates. He can put on a good burst of speed to beat a defender wide. He uses his speed to establish an aggressive forechecking game, and he can quickly turn a turnover into a scoring chance.

His defensive game will need work, as will his proficiency on face-offs. He can be used to kill penalties.

THE PHYSICAL GAME

Bell is tall and strong and has added about 17 pounds since his draft year (1998). He suffered two concussions last season, which may understandably make him a little gun-shy when it comes to, um, getting his bell rung again.

THE INTANGIBLES

The Blackhawks haven't had an enviable draft record in recent years. Bell and Steve McCarthy will do their best to change that. Bell will be given every chance to crack the Chicago lineup. He was a little uptight in training camp in 1999 and didn't give a very good account of himself.

PROJECTION

Bell will break in with the third or fourth line but is projected as a top two centre in the near future. His injuries are a question mark, but if he is healthy he will develop into a 15-goal, 40-point player in a year or two. For his first season, 20 points would be a respectable start.

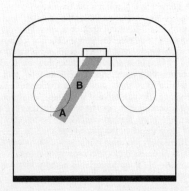

BRAD BROWN

Yrs. of NHL service: 2
Born: Baie Verte, Nfld.; Dec. 27, 1975
Position: right defense
Height: 6-4
Weight: 218
Uniform no.: 2
Shoots: right

Career statistics:

GP	G	A	TP	PIM
131	1	16	17	361

1996-97 statistics:

GP	G	A	TP	+/-	PIM	PP	SH	GW	GT	S	PCT
8	0	0	0	-1	22	0	0	0	0	1	0.0

1997-98 statistics:

Did not play in NHL

1998-99 statistics:

GP	G	A	TP	+/-	PIM	PP	SH	GW	GT	S	PCT
66	1	7	8	-4	205	0	0	0	1	26	3.8

1999-2000 statistics:

GP	G	A	TP	+/-	PIM	PP	SH	GW	GT	S	PCT
57	0	9	9	-1	134	0	0	0	0	15	-

PROJECTION

Little offensive upside. Big potential for major PIM totals.

LAST SEASON

Second NHL season. Third on team in penalty minutes. Missed four games with bruised hand. Missed 10 games with lacerated knuckle. Missed three games with sprained thumb.

THE FINESSE GAME

Brown's desire elevates a pretty modest package of skills to a degree that allows him to perform at the NHL level. He is a strong skater, though not a fast one; he will need to work on his skating for the rest of his career.

Because he doesn't move well, Brown is limited in the game situations in which he can be used. He cannot be employed on the penalty-killing unit, for example, and he has limited offensive ability, so his ice time comes only at full strength.

Brown needs to be paired with a mobile partner.

THE PHYSICAL GAME

Brown is mean and tough and plays with a lot of heart. One of his childhood idols was Marty McSorley, which gives you a pretty good idea of what Brown is about. He is a punishing hitter when someone comes into his turf. He can't make the killer open-ice hits because of his lack of mobility, but around the boards and in front of the net he is effective.

THE INTANGIBLES

Brown's lack of foot speed will prevent him from being more than a number five or six defenseman. His toughness and competitiveness will keep him in the lineup.

ERIC DAZE

Yrs. of NHL service: 5
Born: Montreal, Que.; July 2, 1975
Position: left wing
Height: 6-4
Weight: 215
Uniform no.: 55
Shoots: left

Career statistics:

GP	G	A	TP	PIM
366	129	87	216	108

1996-97 statistics:

GP	G	A	TP	+/-	PIM	PP	SH	GW	GT	S	PCT
71	22	19	41	-4	16	11	0	4	0	176	12.5

1997-98 statistics:

GP	G	A	TP	+/-	PIM	PP	SH	GW	GT	S	PCT
80	31	11	42	+4	22	10	0	7	1	216	14.4

1998-99 statistics:

GP	G	A	TP	+/-	PIM	PP	SH	GW	GT	S	PCT
72	22	20	42	-13	22	8	0	2	3	189	11.6

1999-2000 statistics:

GP	G	A	TP	+/-	PIM	PP	SH	GW	GT	S	PCT
59	23	13	36	-16	28	6	0	1	1	143	16.1

LAST SEASON

Second on team in power-play goals. Missed 16 games with herniated disc and back surgery. Missed three games with back injury. Missed one game with migraine. Missed one game with flu.

THE FINESSE GAME

Although the most impressive thing about Daze is his size, it is his skating ability that sets him apart from other lumbering big men. He isn't a speed demon, but he skates well enough to not look out of place with faster linemates.

Daze keeps his hands close together on his stick and is able to get a lot on his shot with very little backswing. He has excellent hands for shooting or scoring, and is an adept stickhandler who can draw defenders to him and then slip a pass through to a teammate. He sets screens on the power play. He has good hockey vision and an innate understanding of the game. His defensive game is woeful, as his plus-minus reflects.

Daze excells when he drives wide, protects the puck and takes it to the net. Very few defensemen can handle him when he does, but he frequently stops working and stops moving his feet. When he stands around rooted to one spot on the power play, he is useless. Although the right wing is his off-side, Daze has played it through most of his NHL career and is more comfortable there than on the left.

Daze's best weapon is his one-timer, which may be one of the most unstoppable shots in the NHL.

THE PHYSICAL GAME

Daze doesn't back down, but he doesn't show much initiative, either. He is not a prototypical power forward. There will be the occasional night when he tries to run guys over, but those games are infrequent. He doesn't have the strength or the taste for it.

Daze has a long reach — he can pass or shoot the puck even when a defenseman thinks he has him all wrapped up and under control. He must compete harder on a more consistent basis. This is the hardest lesson to hammer home with a young player, but one Daze must learn.

THE INTANGIBLES

Daze is slated to play on the top line with Tony Amonte and Alexei Zhamnov. That sounds great, but those two players don't complement Daze nor he them, and it's not likely to work.

Daze's recovery from back surgery is another issue. He could be ticketed out of Chicago if things don't fall into place for him early in the season.

PROJECTION

Daze was on pace to score 30 before his injury and surgery and that should be his target. He has the skills to be a top five goal scorer in the NHL, but he might not have the right circumstances, or the desire, to do so.

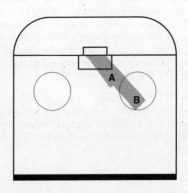

KEVIN DEAN

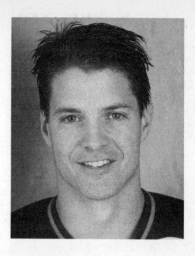

Yrs. of NHL service: 5
Born: Madison, WI; Apr. 1, 1969
Position: left defense
Height: 6-3
Weight: 205
Uniform no.: 28
Shoots: left

Career statistics:

GP	G	A	TP	PIM
245	7	36	37	104

1996-97 statistics:

GP	G	A	TP	+/-	PIM	PP	SH	GW	GT	S	PCT
28	2	4	6	+2	6	0	0	0	0	21	9.5

1997-98 statistics:

GP	G	A	TP	+/-	PIM	PP	SH	GW	GT	S	PCT
50	1	8	9	+12	12	1	0	0	0	28	3.6

1998-99 statistics:

GP	G	A	TP	+/-	PIM	PP	SH	GW	GT	S	PCT
62	1	10	11	+4	22	1	0	0	0	51	2.0

1999-2000 statistics:

GP	G	A	TP	+/-	PIM	PP	SH	GW	GT	S	PCT
64	3	8	11	+3	36	0	1	0	0	47	6.4

LAST SEASON

Acquired from Dallas with Derek Plante and a second-round draft choice in 2001 for Sylvain Cote and Dave Manson, Feb. 8, 2000. Acquired by Dallas from Atlanta for future considerations, Dec. 15, 1999. Missed five games with an irregular heartbeat. Missed 13 games due to coach's decision.

THE FINESSE GAME

Dean went from being a spare buried in the deep New Jersey system, to an expansion team, to being buried again in Dallas, and finally to Chicago. He doesn't do anything special. He is a good, solid skater, but not overly fast or agile. He has good size but isn't physical.

Dean has some hand skills, especially passing. He has tended to focus more on being a stay-at-home defenseman, but he started to push the envelope more in Chicago. He picked up 10 points in 27 games with the Hawks. He doesn't have terrific vision but he can handle second-unit power-play chores. A smart player, he understands game situations well and can be used to kill penalties.

THE PHYSICAL GAME

Dean is tall but lean, and he leans on people as opposed to hitting them. He plays hard and competes but has no tough edge to him at all.

THE INTANGIBLES

Dean is a quiet leader and was a captain in the AHL, but has never developed confidence in himself at the NHL level. He is smart and a good player to have around for younger defensemen, though he has never had a chance to establish his own game — it's tough to be a mentor when that's the case. The Hawks thought enough of Dean to sign him to a new contract during the off-season.

PROJECTION

Dean could score 15 to 20 points. He has had problems the past two seasons with an irregular heartbeat, which has to be a concern.

ANDERS ERIKSSON

Yrs. of NHL service: 3
Born: Bolinas, Sweden; Jan. 9, 1975
Position: defense
Height: 6-3
Weight: 218
Uniform no.: 8
Shoots: left

Career statistics:

GP	G	A	TP	PIM
234	12	63	75	96

1996-97 statistics:

GP	G	A	TP	+/-	PIM	PP	SH	GW	GT	S	PCT
23	0	6	6	+5	10	0	0	0	0	27	0.0

1997-98 statistics:

GP	G	A	TP	+/-	PIM	PP	SH	GW	GT	S	PCT
66	7	14	21	+21	32	1	0	2	0	91	7.7

1998-99 statistics:

GP	G	A	TP	+/-	PIM	PP	SH	GW	GT	S	PCT
72	2	18	20	+11	34	0	0	1	0	79	2.5

1999-2000 statistics:

GP	G	A	TP	+/-	PIM	PP	SH	GW	GT	S	PCT
73	3	25	28	+4	20	0	0	1	0	86	3.5

LAST SEASON

Career high in assists and points. Missed nine games due to coach's decision.

THE FINESSE GAME

Eriksson is big for an NHL defenseman, even by today's standards, but his strength lies in his mobility and puckhandling skills. He sees the ice well; his biggest asset is his ability to get the puck out of his own end fast. He is a heads-up passer who is poised with the puck. He has good hockey sense and learned the game in the powerful Detroit system.

Eriksson is improving his defensive reads and reactions. He doesn't jump into the play unless it's safe, and he won't pinch unless that is the correct play. He may err on the side of caution until he develops a little more confidence, but he has the skill level to provide some offense as a playmaker. He will probably limit his shots to the point. He has a good low shot from the point and gets it away quickly. He creates a lot of rebounds by getting his shots through, but he didn't take enough shots.

Eriksson is a very good skater with balance and agility. He doesn't have a big turning radius and he accelerates well.

THE PHYSICAL GAME

Eriksson is not a big hitter, but he is strong and he'll tie up his man along the boards and in front of the net. He does a good job of getting himself in between the attacker and the net. It's his way of neutralizing the league's bigger forwards. He will force people to try to go through him. His conditioning is very good, and he handled an average of 21 minutes a game easily.

THE INTANGIBLES

Eriksson missed training camp in a contract dispute and needed time to get up to speed, even though he was in the opening night lineup. Although he played well after being traded to Chicago at the end of the 1998-99 season, he started off this year afflicted by the "I'm not Chris Chelios" syndrome (the popular Chelios being the player he was traded for). Eriksson will be a top two defenseman in Chicago and has no excuses for a slow start. Eriksson also didn't get along well with assistant coach Trent Yawney, who was in charge of the defense. He needs to have his confidence bolstered.

PROJECTION

Eriksson can produce 35 to 40 points. He has considerable offensive upside.

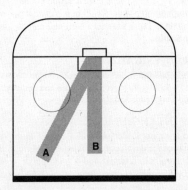

MICHAL GROSEK

Yrs. of NHL service: 6
Born: Vszkov, Czech Republic; June 1, 1975
Position: left wing
Height: 6-2
Weight: 296
Uniform no.: 18
Shoots: right

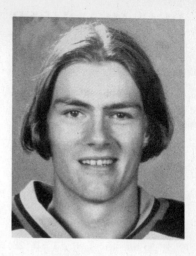

Career statistics:

GP	G	A	TP	PIM
350	67	104	171	332

1996-97 statistics:

GP	G	A	TP	+/-	PIM	PP	SH	GW	GT	S	PCT
82	15	21	36	+25	71	1	0	2	1	117	12.8

1997-98 statistics:

GP	G	A	TP	+/-	PIM	PP	SH	GW	GT	S	PCT
67	10	20	30	+9	60	2	0	1	0	114	8.8

1998-99 statistics:

GP	G	A	TP	+/-	PIM	PP	SH	GW	GT	S	PCT
76	20	30	50	+21	102	4	0	3	1	140	14.3

1999-2000 statistics:

GP	G	A	TP	+/-	PIM	PP	SH	GW	GT	S	PCT
75	13	27	40	+11	47	3	0	2	0	114	11.4

LAST SEASON

Acquired from Buffalo for Doug Gilmour and J.P. Dumont, Mar. 10, 2000. Tied for second on Chicago in plus-minus. Missed four games with groin injury.

THE FINESSE GAME

Maddeningly inconsistent, Grosek has an array of NHL-calibre skills at his disposal but doesn't always have the inclination to use them. He is still very young and has an eagerness to succeed at the NHL level. He is an excellent stickhandler, and he can be absolutely magical with the puck. He is good enough to play his off-wing (left) as well as the right. He doesn't have a great shot, but he intimidates with his speed and drives to the net. With more confidence, his release may improve.

Grosek is a bundle of talent whose first shot at an NHL job was derailed by two serious injuries. He uses his speed and size to create some room and is genuinely tough.

Defensively, Grosek's game has improved, but he doesn't have the work ethic to turn himself into a quality two-way forward.

THE PHYSICAL GAME

On his best nights, Grosek plays like a young Claude Lemieux, abrasive and a little undisciplined. But Lemieux played that way every night; Grosek only plays that way once or twice a month. He is an impact player when he takes the bit in his teeth and goes a little wild. If he could do it over the majority of the 82-game schedule, he would be a star.

THE INTANGIBLES

Grosek wore out his welcome in Buffalo, and Chicago paid an absurdly high price for him (Gilmour *and* Dumont *and* picking up $3 million of Gilmour's salary?). Grosek scored six points in 14 games after the trade. He is slotted as a top six forward in Chicago and the Hawks seem to think he can be a 25-goal scorer. We are inclined to disagree.

PROJECTION

There is no excuse for Grosek not to score 20 goals, though he could find one.

DEAN MCAMMOND

Yrs. of NHL service: 7
Born: Grand Cache, Alberta; June 15, 1973
Position: left wing
Height: 5-11
Weight: 200
Uniform no.: 37
Shoots: left

Career statistics:

GP	G	A	TP	PIM
396	76	124	200	225

1996-97 statistics:

GP	G	A	TP	+/-	PIM	PP	SH	GW	GT	S	PCT
57	12	17	29	-15	28	4	0	6	0	106	11.3

1997-98 statistics:

GP	G	A	TP	+/-	PIM	PP	SH	GW	GT	S	PCT
77	19	31	50	+9	46	8	0	3	0	28	14.8

1998-99 statistics:

GP	G	A	TP	+/-	PIM	PP	SH	GW	GT	S	PCT
77	10	20	30	+8	38	1	0	1	0	138	7.2

1999-2000 statistics:

GP	G	A	TP	+/-	PIM	PP	SH	GW	GT	S	PCT
76	14	18	32	+11	72	1	0	1	0	118	11.9

PROJECTION

McAmmond seems destined to be the kind of player who is always on the move. His top end is 20 goals, but 15 is more likely

LAST SEASON

Tied for second on team in plus-minus. Missed five games with bruised ribs.

THE FINESSE GAME

McAmmond's chief asset is his speed. He has excellent acceleration and quickness, and uses his speed to forecheck and force the play. He works the boards and the corners; he is effective in open ice as well because of his skating.

McAmmond developed as a centre, so he uses all of the ice even when he is in his regular slot on left wing. He handles the puck well in traffic and has good vision to see developing plays. He is unselfish and passes well on the forehand and backhand. He also has a nice shot in tight. He has needed some time to adjust to NHL tempo and now moves the puck more crisply. McAmmond can be a safety-valve winger for a player like Michael Nylander.

He can handle second-unit power-play time.

THE PHYSICAL GAME

McAmmond is feisty and aggressive. He isn't very big but he creates a ruckus in the offensive zone with his tenacity. He will stick his nose in just about anywhere and he can be very irritating to play against. He drives to the net with authority, often right past bigger defenders.

THE INTANGIBLES

McAmmond isn't likely to earn top six ice time among the Hawks' forwards, though he can step up in case of injuries and is a useful sort of utility forward to have on hand.

BRYAN MCCABE

Yrs. of NHL service: 5
Born: St. Catharines, Ont.; June 8, 1975
Position: left defense
Height: 6-2
Weight: 215
Uniform no.: 23
Shoots: left

Career statistics:

GP	G	A	TP	PIM
394	32	89	121	789

1996-97 statistics:

GP	G	A	TP	+/-	PIM	PP	SH	GW	GT	S	PCT
82	8	20	28	-2	165	2	1	2	0	117	6.8

1997-98 statistics:

GP	G	A	TP	+/-	PIM	PP	SH	GW	GT	S	PCT
82	4	20	24	+19	209	1	1	0	0	123	3.3

1998-99 statistics:

GP	G	A	TP	+/-	PIM	PP	SH	GW	GT	S	PCT
69	7	14	21	-11	120	1	2	0	0	98	7.1

1999-2000 statistics:

GP	G	A	TP	+/-	PIM	PP	SH	GW	GT	S	PCT
79	6	19	25	-8	139	2	0	2	0	119	5.0

LAST SEASON

Second on team in penalty minutes. Missed two games with fractured orbital bone, first games missed due to injury in five-season NHL career. Missed one game due to coach's decision.

THE FINESSE GAME

McCabe is an unorthodox skater with a bit of a hitch. He doesn't have a fluid, classic stride. He is okay going from his right to his left but suspect going from his left to his right. When he has the puck or is jumping into the play he has decent speed, but his lack of mobility defensively is one of his flaws. He is hesitant in his own zone when reading the rush and will get caught.

He also doesn't have great puck-moving skills, which is a tremendous defect for a defenseman. His passes don't go tape-to-tape. They go off the glass, or down the rink for an icing, or worse, are picked off by a defender.

McCabe has a heavy, major-league slap shot and can handle some second-unit power play because of it, but he is not very clever offensively. He kills penalties well and blocks shots.

THE PHYSICAL GAME

McCabe is willing to drop his gloves and can handle himself in a bout, though it's not a strong part of his game. He has to play with a shield after his eye injury in March. He is strong but not mean. He isn't a good enough skater to be a better body checker, but he runs around too much trying anyway. He's a young Dave Manson.

THE INTANGIBLES

McCabe has been in three organizations already and the sands of time seem to have run through his hourglass. It's time to lower expectations. McCabe is not a top four defenseman — though the Hawks out of necessity will try to keep using him in that role.

McCabe is a team player who will go to war, but doesn't have the skills to be much more. If he can take his game to another level, he needs to show it soon.

PROJECTION

McCabe can produce 25 points.

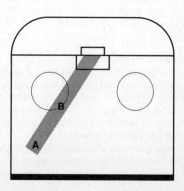

STEVE MCCARTHY

Yrs. of NHL service: 0
Born: Trail, B.C.; Feb. 3, 1981
Position: left defense
Height: 6-0
Weight: 197
Uniform no.: 5
Shoots: left

Career statistics:

GP	G	A	TP	PIM
5	1	1	2	4

1999-2000 statistics:

GP	G	A	TP	+/-	PIM	PP	SH	GW	GT	S	PCT
5	1	1	2	0	4	1	0	0	0	4	25.0

LAST SEASON

Will be entering first NHL season. Scored 13-13 — 36 in 37 games with Kootenay (WHL).

THE FINESSE GAME

A puck-savvy, swift-skating defenseman in the Scott Niedermayer/Brian Leetch mould, McCarthy should soon become a mainstay on the Chicago power play. He scored 11 of his 13 goals on the power play when he was sent back to junior, and appears to have the goods to establish his game at the NHL level.

McCarthy has major league speed, acceleration, balance and agility. He is tough to beat one-on-one. He is a tape-to-tape passer. He had a little trouble, in his brief NHL stint, with the speed of the NHL attackers and will need to learn to move the puck a little more crisply out of his own zone or make the safe bang off the boards.

McCarthy will likely be the first-unit left point man. He has a hard, accurate point shot.

THE PHYSICAL GAME

McCarthy is a little bit on the lean side. By rehabbing his shoulder, he may add some needed upper-body strength. Like Niedermayer and Leetch, he will need to add a more physical element to his game. Both of those players are better in their defensive zone than they are given credit for and use their lower body to drive through their checks. McCarthy can do the same.

THE INTANGIBLES

After starting the season with the parent club, McCarthy was returned to his junior team. It was probably the right move, since his game still has a few rough edges. He will get every chance to be one of the Hawks' top six defensemen this season, and could be a number four in the last quarter.

Veteran teammates already appreciate McCarthy for his enthusiasm and his mature demeanor. He could really use a wise and cooperative NHL defenseman to mentor him. Too bad the Hawks' don't have one. McCarthy will have to do this on his own. He could end up being thrown to the wolves too early.

One red flag: McCarthy's March shoulder surgery is rumoured to have been more serious than was originally thought and could be troublesome.

PROJECTION

Assuming he is healthy, McCarthy will only need a few seasons to start getting attention as one of the league's best offensive defensemen. A 30-point rookie season would not be a shock.

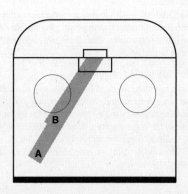

BORIS MIRONOV

Yrs. of NHL service: 8
Born: Moscow, Russia; March 21, 1972
Position: right defense
Height: 6-3
Weight: 220
Uniform no.: 3
Shoots: right

Career statistics:

GP	G	A	TP	PIM
455	58	177	235	639

1996-97 statistics:

GP	G	A	TP	+/-	PIM	PP	SH	GW	GT	S	PCT
55	6	26	32	+2	85	2	0	1	0	147	4.1

1997-98 statistics:

GP	G	A	TP	+/-	PIM	PP	SH	GW	GT	S	PCT
81	16	30	46	-8	100	10	1	1	1	203	7.9

1998-99 statistics:

GP	G	A	TP	+/-	PIM	PP	SH	GW	GT	S	PCT
75	11	38	49	+13	131	5	0	4	1	173	6.4

1999-2000 statistics:

GP	G	A	TP	+/-	PIM	PP	SH	GW	GT	S	PCT
58	9	28	37	-3	72	4	2	1	1	144	6.3

LAST SEASON

Led team defensemen in points. Second on team in shorthanded goals. Missed 16 games in contract dispute. Missed seven games with sprained left knee. Missed one game with hip pointer.

THE FINESSE GAME

Mironov has a huge slap shot and is a good puckhandler as well, so he can start a rush out of his own zone and finish things up at the other end. He has improved the release on his shot and sets things up well from the point with his passing.

Mironov has improved his defensive play to the stage where he belongs as part of a team's top defense against other teams' top lines. He uses his size well to protect the puck. He has made the game easier by allowing the play to come to him instead of trying to make too many things happen by himself.

He helps his team most with his ability to carry or pass the puck out of his own zone. Attacking teams have to back off their forecheck, because he will start his team on a breakout and jump into the play to create an odd-man rush.

THE PHYSICAL GAME

Mironov is big and mobile. He isn't a thumper, but he's strong and he eliminates people. He can and does handle a lot of minutes. He was out of shape when he agreed to terms in mid-November and didn't start playing his best hockey until the second half.

THE INTANGIBLES

Mironov is the number one defenseman in Chicago and will be asked to carry a major offensive load, especially with the expected emphasis on a European style under new coach Alpo Suhonen. The changes should suit Mironov just fine.

PROJECTION

With no contract dispute in sight, Mironov should return to the top 15 in defense scoring, and maybe even top five. He is capable of a 60-point season.

MICHAEL NYLANDER

Yrs. of NHL service: 6
Born: Stockholm, Sweden; Oct. 3, 1972
Position: centre
Height: 5-11
Weight: 190
Uniform no.: 9
Shoots: left

Career statistics:

GP	G	A	TP	PIM
386	82	166	248	150

1996-97 statistics:
Did not play in NHL

1997-98 statistics:

GP	G	A	TP	+/-	PIM	PP	SH	GW	GT	S	PCT
65	13	23	36	+10	24	0	0	2	0	117	11.1

1998-99 statistics:

GP	G	A	TP	+/-	PIM	PP	SH	GW	GT	S	PCT
33	4	10	14	-9	8	1	0	0	0	33	12.1

1999-2000 statistics:

GP	G	A	TP	+/-	PIM	PP	SH	GW	GT	S	PCT
77	24	30	54	+6	30	5	0	2	0	122	19.7

PROJECTION
Nylander is erratic and unpredictable. He is capable of a 25-goal, 60-point season, but don't bank on it.

LAST SEASON
Acquired from Tampa Bay for Bryan Muir and Reid Simpson, Nov. 12, 1999. Led team in shooting percentage. Second on team in goals with career high. Tied for third on team in power-play goals.

THE FINESSE GAME
Nylander's point production has never reflected his high skill level: he can do things with the puck that are magical. He knows all about time and space. If anything, he is guilty of hanging onto the puck too long and passing up quality shots, as he tries to force a pass to a teammate who is in a worse scoring position than Nylander is.

An open-ice player, Nylander is an excellent skater and composed with the puck. He's strictly a one-way forward. He needs to play with finishers, but also needs a safety-valve winger who is defensively alert.

THE PHYSICAL GAME
Nylander is on the small side and plays even smaller. He uses his body to protect the puck but he won't fight hard for possession.

THE INTANGIBLES
Nylander is 27 and that's a little late to still be waiting on potential when it comes to a forward. He will be the number two centre in Chicago and the Hawks will live with his defensive weaknesses if he can some up with the points. On the plus side, Nylander should flourish under Finnish coach Alpo Suhonen's expected open system.

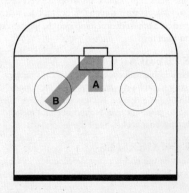

STEVE SULLIVAN

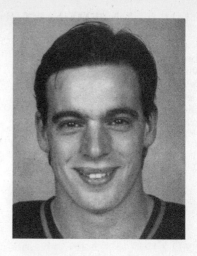

Yrs. of NHL service: 4
Born: Timmins, Ont.; July 6, 1974
Position: centre
Height: 5-9
Weight: 155
Uniform no.: 11
Shoots: right

Career statistics:

GP	G	A	TP	PIM
276	70	110	180	169

1996-97 statistics:

GP	G	A	TP	+/-	PIM	PP	SH	GW	GT	S	PCT
54	13	25	38	+14	37	3	0	3	1	108	12.0

1997-98 statistics:

GP	G	A	TP	+/-	PIM	PP	SH	GW	GT	S	PCT
63	10	18	28	-8	40	1	0	1	0	112	8.9

1998-99 statistics:

GP	G	A	TP	+/-	PIM	PP	SH	GW	GT	S	PCT
63	20	20	40	+12	28	4	0	5	0	110	18.2

1999-2000 statistics:

GP	G	A	TP	+/-	PIM	PP	SH	GW	GT	S	PCT
80	22	43	65	+19	56	2	1	6	0	180	12.2

LAST SEASON

Acquired on waivers from Toronto, Oct. 23, 1999. Led team in assists. Second on team in points and shots. Career highs in goals, assists and points. Led team in plus-minus. Second on team in game-winning goals. Missed one game with flu.

THE FINESSE GAME

One advantage to being as small as Sullivan is that you are closer to the puck than a lot of your rivals. Sullivan complicates matters by using a short stick — short even by his standards — to keep the puck in his feet. He draws penalties by protecting the puck so well; foes usually have to foul him to get it. He is able to maintain control of the puck because it is so close to his body. He wants the puck and likes to shoot. He will scrap around the net for loose pucks.

By nature a centre, Sullivan has terrific speed, hands, vision and anticipation. However, he will probably have to make his way in the NHL as a left wing, which is where the Hawks used him last season, even though that means sending him into the wars along the boards. Playing wing, he doesn't have to be down low on defensive-zone coverage.

Sullivan is quick and smart enough to get himself out of pending jams, but he does not have elite skills and has to apply himself constantly. He is strictly an offensive threat, almost a specialty player.

THE PHYSICAL GAME

You can't survive in the NHL if you are small and soft. Sullivan has to play with fire. If he gets bounced around he has to get back up, and get his stick up. His effort has to be more consistent. Last season he did a

good job of keeping his intensity level high.

THE INTANGIBLES

Sullivan was rescued from a deep Toronto system. In fact, he was a waiver-wire steal. He is a good fit in Chicago, and will be one of the team's top six forwards.

PROJECTION

Sullivan could be a 20-goal scorer again with the same kind of effort he put forth last season.

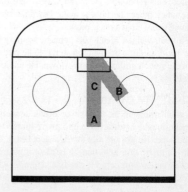

JOCELYN THIBAULT

Yrs. of NHL service: 7
Born: Montreal, Que.; Jan. 12, 1975
Position: goaltender
Height: 5-11
Weight: 170
Uniform no.: 41
Catches: left

Career statistics:

GP	MIN	GA	SO	GAA	A	PIM
327	18324	846	19	2.77	3	8

1996-97 statistics:

GP	MIN	GAA	W	L	T	SO	GA	S	SAPCT	PIM
61	3397	2.90	22	24	11	1	164	1815	.910	0

1997-98 statistics:

GP	MIN	GAA	W	L	T	SO	GA	S	SAPCT	PIM
47	2652	2.47	19	15	8	2	109	1109	.902	0

1998-99 statistics:

GP	MIN	GAA	W	L	T	SO	GA	S	SAPCT	PIM
52	3014	2.71	21	26	5	4	136	1435	.905	2

1999-2000 statistics:

GP	MIN	GAA	W	L	T	SO	GA	S	SAPCT	PIM
60	3438	2.76	25	26	7	3	158	1679	.906	2

LAST SEASON

Recorded 20 or more wins for fourth season. Missed six games with broken finger on left hand.

THE PHYSICAL GAME

Thibault is a small netminder whose technique makes him look even smaller. He is a butterfly-style goalie, but when he goes to his knees he doesn't keep his torso upright (as Patrick Roy does so splendidly), and that costs Thibault a big chunk of net.

Thibault plays deep in his net and does not challenge shooters. He relies on his reflexes, which, happily for him, happen to be excellent. He is a battler and doesn't give up on a puck, but he creates problems for himself by making the easy saves more difficult than they would be if his fundamentals were better. He has a good glove hand and quick feet, and he is a good skater with lateral mobility.

Thibault has improved his stickhandling, and how he directs his rebounds. He is not very strong on his stick, which means he fails to make key poke-checks or knock away cross-crease passes.

Thibault weighs about 160 pounds, sopping wet, so he needs a light workload (55 starts) to be effective down the stretch without wearing down. He works extremely hard.

THE MENTAL GAME

This is shaping up as a make-or-break season for Thibault, maybe his last chance to prove himself as a number one. He got off to a terrible start last season, putting himself in a hole that he tried to dig himself out of in the second half. He needs a veteran backup/confessor/coach/cheerleader in the worst way.

THE INTANGIBLES

Thibault has yet to prove he belongs among the NHL's top-level goalies. He is not going to get the chance to do so in Chicago unless the situation changes drastically.

PROJECTION

The Hawks don't figure to be a much improved team, so Thibault will probably hover around the 25-win mark again.

ALEXEI ZHAMNOV

Yrs. of NHL service: 8
Born: Moscow, Russia; Oct. 1, 1970
Position: centre
Height: 6-1
Weight: 195
Uniform no.: 26
Shoots: left

Career statistics:

GP	G	A	TP	PIM
526	187	312	499	433

1996-97 statistics:

GP	G	A	TP	+/-	PIM	PP	SH	GW	GT	S	PCT
74	20	42	62	+18	56	6	1	2	0	208	9.6

1997-98 statistics:

GP	G	A	TP	+/-	PIM	PP	SH	GW	GT	S	PCT
70	21	28	49	+16	61	6	2	3	1	193	10.9

1998-99 statistics:

GP	G	A	TP	+/-	PIM	PP	SH	GW	GT	S	PCT
76	20	41	61	-10	50	8	1	2	1	200	10.0

1999-2000 statistics:

GP	G	A	TP	+/-	PIM	PP	SH	GW	GT	S	PCT
71	23	37	60	+7	61	5	0	7	0	175	13.1

LAST SEASON

Third on team in goals, assists, points and shots. Tied for third on team in power-play goals. Missed eight games with hamstring injury. Missed three games with groin injury.

THE FINESSE GAME

If anyone is going to blossom under the expected Eurostyle of new Finnish coach Alpo Suhonen, Zhamnov is the man. Zhamnov hates to play dump-andchase.

Zhamnov's game is puck control: he can carry it at top speed or work the give-and-go. The Russian is a crafty playmaker and is not too unselfish. He has an accurate if not overpowering shot. He gets his wrist shot away quickly, and he shoots it with his feet still moving, which few players can do. As well, he can blast off the pass, or manoeuvre until he has a screen and then wrist it. He will try to score from "bad" angles. He is cool and patient with the puck, and he turns harmless-looking plays into dangerous scoring chances. On the power play, he works the left point or, if used low, can dart in and out in front of the goalie, using his soft hands for a tip.

Defensively, Zhamnov is sound and is frequently used against other teams' top forward lines. He is a dedicated backchecker and never leaves the zone too quickly.

THE PHYSICAL GAME

Zhamnov will bump to prevent a scoring chance or go for a loose puck, but body work is not his forte. The knock on Zhamnov is his lack of physical play, but he works hard and competes. He is strong and fights his

way through traffic in front of the net to get to a puck, when he wants to. He needs to do a better job of tying up the opposing centre on face-offs, since he wins few draws cleanly.

THE INTANGIBLES

The years of waiting for Zhamnov to burst into superstardom are past. But he makes a productive linemate for Tony Amonte on a very bad team. If the Hawks could find a compatible left wing or develop a solid number two line to take some of the checking pressure off...but wait, we are talking about the Blackhawks. Zhamnov just doesn't have the presence or the drive to be a true number one centre under these circumstances.

PROJECTION

Zhamnov has 100-point potential, but 70 is more realistic.

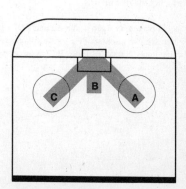

COLORADO AVALANCHE

Players' Statistics 1999-2000

POS.	NO.	PLAYER	GP	G	A	PTS	+/-	PIM	PP	SH	GW	GT	S	PCT
C	19	JOE SAKIC	60	28	53	81	30	28	5	1	5		242	11.6
R	23	MILAN HEJDUK	82	36	36	72	14	16	13		9	2	228	15.8
C	37	CHRIS DRURY	82	20	47	67	8	42	7		2		213	9.4
D	77	RAY BOURQUE	79	18	34	52	-2	26	13				260	6.9
D	8	SANDIS OZOLINSH	82	16	36	52	17	46	6		1		210	7.6
L	40	*ALEX TANGUAY	76	17	34	51	6	22	5		3	1	74	23.0
C	21	PETER FORSBERG	49	14	37	51	9	52	3		2		105	13.3
R	18	ADAM DEADMARSH	71	18	27	45	-10	106	5		4		153	11.8
L	38	DAVE ANDREYCHUK	77	20	16	36	-20	30	8		3	1	233	8.6
C	26	STEPHANE YELLE	79	8	14	22	9	28		1	1		90	8.9
L	25	SHJON PODEIN	75	11	8	19	12	29		1	3		104	10.6
L	14	DAVE REID	65	11	7	18	12	28			3		86	12.8
D	52	ADAM FOOTE	59	5	13	18	5	98	1		2		63	7.9
D	55	*MARTIN SKOULA	80	3	13	16	5	20	2				66	4.5
D	24	JON KLEMM	73	5	7	12	26	34					64	7.8
L	11	CHRIS DINGMAN	68	8	3	11	-2	132	2		1		54	14.8
D	29	ERIC MESSIER	61	3	6	9	0	24	1				28	10.7
D	7	GREG DE VRIES	69	2	7	9	-7	73					40	5.0
D	3	AARON MILLER	53	1	7	8	3	36					44	2.3
D	5	ALEXEI GUSAROV	34	2	2	4	-8	10					16	12.5
R	38	*DAN HINOTE	27	1	3	4	0	10					14	7.1
C	49	*SERGE AUBIN	15	2	1	3	1	6			1		14	14.3
R	36	JEFF ODGERS	62	1	2	3	-7	162			1		29	3.4
G	33	PATRICK ROY	63		3	3	0	10					1	
G	30	*MARC DENIS	23		2	2	0	6						
R	17	*CHRISTIAN MATTE	5		1	1	-2	4					1	
R	50	*BRIAN WILLSIE	1				0						1	
L	39	*VILLE NIEMINEN	1				0						2	
G	35	RICK TABARACCI	3				0							
D	43	*DAN SMITH	3				2							
D	44	*SAMI HELENIUS	33				-5	46					6	

GP = games played; G = goals; A = assists; PTS = points; +/- = goals-for minus goals-against while player is on ice; PIM = penalties in minutes; PP = power-play goals; SH = shorthanded goals; GW = game-winning goals; GT = game-tying goals; S = no. of shots; PCT = percentage of goals to shots; * = rookie

RAY BOURQUE

Yrs. of NHL service: 21
Born: Montreal, Que.; Dec. 28, 1960
Position: right defense
Height: 5-11
Weight: 210
Uniform no.: 77
Shoots: left

Career statistics:

GP	G	A	TP	PIM
1532	403	1117	1520	1093

1996-97 statistics:

GP	G	A	TP	+/-	PIM	PP	SH	GW	GT	S	PCT
62	19	31	50	-11	18	8	1	3	1	230	8.3

1997-98 statistics:

GP	G	A	TP	+/-	PIM	PP	SH	GW	GT	S	PCT
82	13	35	48	+2	80	9	0	3	1	264	4.9

1998-99 statistics:

GP	G	A	TP	+/-	PIM	PP	SH	GW	GT	S	PCT
81	10	47	57	-7	34	8	0	3	0	262	3.8

1999-2000 statistics:

GP	G	A	TP	+/-	PIM	PP	SH	GW	GT	S	PCT
79	18	34	52	-2	26	13	0	0	0	260	6.9

LAST SEASON

Acquired from Boston with Dave Andreychuk for Brian Rolston, Martin Grenier, Sami Pahlsson and a first-round draft choice in 2000 and 2001, Mar. 6, 2000. Tied for Avs lead and tied for fourth in NHL in power-play goals. Tied for seventh among NHL defensmen in points. Third on team in points. Second in NHL in power-play points (37). Fourth in NHL in power-play assists (24).

THE FINESSE GAME

Bourque has tremendous defensive instincts, though his offensive skills usually get the headlines. His defensive reads are almost unmatched in the NHL, and he is a superb transition player. He is not too proud to make the simple play, though, if it is the right one, instead of making a flashy play. If he is under pressure and his team is getting scrambly, he simply flips the puck over the glass for a face-off.

As a passer, Bourque can go tape-to-tape as well as anybody. He has the touch and the vision of a forward, and eagerly makes what for anyone else would be a low-percentage play, his passes and skating are so sure.

Bourque is adept at keeping the puck in the zone at the point. He is a key performer on special-team units. On the point, he has a low, heavy shot with a crisp release. And he is an excellent skater who shoots from mid-range with a handy snap shot, or in close with a wrist shot. He does not squander his scoring chances and is a precise shooter down low. He is able to go top-shelf to either corner, which few other defensemen, let alone forwards, can match.

Willing to lead a rush or jump up into the play, Bourque is a balanced skater, with speed, agility and awesome balance. It takes a bulldozer to knock him off the puck.

THE PHYSICAL GAME

Bourque is single-minded in his approach to fitness. Only twice in his 20 seasons has he failed to play more than 60 games a season (and one of those was the 1994-95 lockout year). He is no perimeter player, either. The minutes he routinely logs (25 to 28 per game) are quality, crunch-time minutes.

Bourque plays a physical game when he has to. It's amazing the punishment he has been able to absorb over the years. He is not very big by today's standards for defensemen (or forwards, for that matter). Other teams try to eliminate him physically, and he has paid a big price because of it.

THE INTANGIBLES

Bourque was so rejuvenated by his move to a contending team that instead of retiring, as had been expected, he signed a new two-year contract.

PROJECTION

Bourque on the Avs for a full season...imagine the possibilities. He could post a 60-point season at age 40.

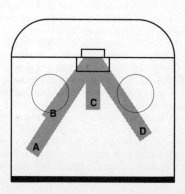

ADAM DEADMARSH

Yrs. of NHL service: 6
Born: Trail, B.C.; May 10, 1975
Position: right wing
Height: 6-0
Weight: 195
Uniform no.: 18
Shoots: right

Career statistics:

GP	G	A	TP	PIM
414	125	137	262	664

1996-97 statistics:

GP	G	A	TP	+/-	PIM	PP	SH	GW	GT	S	PCT
78	33	27	60	+8	136	10	3	4	0	198	16.7

1997-98 statistics:

GP	G	A	TP	+/-	PIM	PP	SH	GW	GT	S	PCT
73	22	21	43	0	125	10	0	6	3	187	11.8

1998-99 statistics:

GP	G	A	TP	+/-	PIM	PP	SH	GW	GT	S	PCT
66	22	27	49	-2	99	10	0	3	1	152	14.5

1999-2000 statistics:

GP	G	A	TP	+/-	PIM	PP	SH	GW	GT	S	PCT
71	18	27	45	-10	106	5	0	4	0	153	11.8

LAST SEASON

Third on team in penalty minutes and game-winning goals. Missed five games with rib injury. Missed three games with sprained knee. Missed two games with hip pointer. Missed one game with bruised toe.

THE FINESSE GAME

Deadmarsh is capable of playing in every situation. He's not as accomplished as some of the other forwards on the team, but he has a meanness and a toughness about him. He's relentless in finishing his checks. He's very strong on the puck, very strong on the boards, and he's one of the faster players in the NHL in a power package. He doesn't have the same touch around the net as Keith Tkachuk or John LeClair, but he should be a bona fide 30-goal scorer. Although better at centre than wing, he is versatile enough to handle either role.

Deadmarsh is a bigger version of Kevin Dineen. Deadmarsh is feisty and tough and can work in a checking role, but he can also score off the chances he creates with his defense and can be moved onto the top two scoring lines and not look out of place. His game is incredibly mature. He is reliable enough to be put out on the ice to protect a lead in the late minutes of a game, because he'll do what it takes to win.

Deadmarsh doesn't have to be the glamour guy, but that doesn't mean he provides unskilled labour. He has dangerous speed and quickness, and a nice scoring touch to convert the chances he creates off his forechecking. He can play centre as well as both wings, so he's versatile. He doesn't play a complex game. He's a basic up-and-down winger, a nice complement to all of the flash and dash on the Avalanche. He excells as a dedicated penalty killer.

THE PHYSICAL GAME

Deadmarsh always finishes his checks. He has a strong work ethic with honest toughness. He never backs down from a challenge and issues some of his own. He isn't a dirty player, but he will fight when challenged or stand up for his teammates.

THE INTANGIBLES

Deadmarsh has a smirk on his face all the time. Either you want to kiss it or punch it. No one knows whether that's just the way his face is, or if he's laughing at you, and that can be a real irritant when he's playing. He runs over you with that little smile and you think, "Are you serious? Are you pulling my leg?"

Colorado thought Deadmarsh underachieved last season, despite his nagging injuries. He was a restricted free agent during the off-season, and there are plenty of teams who would take him off their hands if the Avs don't feel like paying him. Deadmarsh will never be a star, but he is the kind of player who will help his team find a way to win.

PROJECTION

Deadmarsh lacks the fine touch to be an elite scorer, but he should consistently score in the 30-goal, 60-point range. He is still a well-kept secret thanks to his more flamboyant teammates.

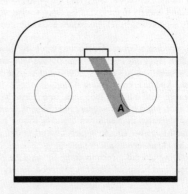

CHRIS DRURY

Yrs. of NHL service: 2
Born: Trumbull, CT; Aug. 20, 1976
Position: centre
Height: 5-10
Weight: 180
Uniform no.: 37
Shoots: right

Career statistics:

GP	G	A	TP	PIM
161	40	71	111	104

1998-99 statistics:

GP	G	A	TP	+/-	PIM	PP	SH	GW	GT	S	PCT
79	20	24	44	+9	62	6	0	3	1	138	14.5

1999-2000 statistics:

GP	G	A	TP	+/-	PIM	PP	SH	GW	GT	S	PCT
82	20	47	67	+8	42	7	0	2	0	213	9.4

LAST SEASON

Second NHL season. Second on team in assists. Third on team in points. Tied for third on team in goals. One of three Avs to appear in all 82 games.

THE FINESSE GAME

Drury has a wealth of assets, starting with his skating. He gets in on top of a goalie very quickly — and we mean right on top, because he isn't afraid of crease-crashing — and is able to control the puck while charging in. He knows where the net is and isn't afraid to get there by the shortest route possible, even though he isn't the biggest guy in the world.

Drury has quick and soft hands, and is a steady scorer. His effort is so consistent, and that's what produces his points. He already has an advanced defensive side to his game, even on nights when he isn't scoring, he is doing something to help his team win. He is a clever playmaker, but linemates can also pick up goals by following him to the net and feasting on the rebounds his efforts create.

He is capable of playing wing or centre and was used extensively at both positions, though centre is his natural position. He is a smart player who quickly grasps any concepts the coaching staff pitch him.

THE PHYSICAL GAME

Small but sturdy, Drury doesn't back down an inch and is usually the player who makes the pre-emptive hit. He sure doesn't play little. Drury plays hard and competes every shift, whether it's the first minute of the game or the last.

THE INTANGIBLES

Remarkably poised and mature, with excellent leadership skills, Drury is probably a future captain. He was a restricted free agent during the off-season. There were few young players with a better bargaining position.

PROJECTION

Drury matched his rookie goal total. We were expecting a little more and will call for 25 this time.

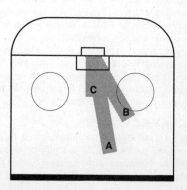

ADAM FOOTE

Yrs. of NHL service: 9
Born: Toronto, Ont.; July 10, 1971
Position: right defense
Height: 6-1
Weight: 202
Uniform no.: 52
Shoots: right

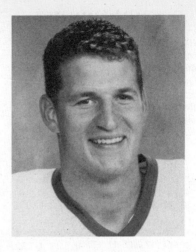

Career statistics:

GP	G	A	TP	PIM
558	28	102	130	868

1996-97 statistics:

GP	G	A	TP	+/-	PIM	PP	SH	GW	GT	S	PCT
78	2	19	21	+16	135	0	0	0	0	60	3.3

1997-98 statistics:

GP	G	A	TP	+/-	PIM	PP	SH	GW	GT	S	PCT
77	3	14	17	-3	124	0	0	1	0	64	4.7

1998-99 statistics:

GP	G	A	TP	+/-	PIM	PP	SH	GW	GT	S	PCT
64	5	16	21	+20	92	3	0	0	0	83	6.0

1999-2000 statistics:

GP	G	A	TP	+/-	PIM	PP	SH	GW	GT	S	PCT
59	5	13	18	+5	98	1	0	2	0	63	7.9

LAST SEASON

Missed seven games with shoulder injuries. Missed eight games with rib injury. Missed seven games with groin injuries.

THE FINESSE GAME

Foote is frequently overlooked because of flashier teammates like Peter Forsberg and Ray Bourque, but he is one of the most important foot soldiers (aw, we couldn't resist) on the Avalanche.

He has great foot speed and quickness. Defensively, he's strong in his coverage as a stay-at-home type, but he's not creative with the puck, probably his major deficiency. Still, all of the Avalanche defensemen are encouraged to jump into the attack and Foote eagerly does so when given the chance. He is wise in his pinches and knows when to drive to the slot, and he has a useful shot. He won't take wild chances. The Avalanche would like to wring more offensive production out of him, but at this stage of his career it is not likely to happen. Foote believes his job is to concentrate on defense, though he can handle some second-unit power-play time.

Foote usually skates the puck out of his zone and is less likely to find the man for an outlet pass. There are few defensemen in the league who can match him in getting the first few strides in and jumping out of the zone. He is an excellent penalty killer.

THE PHYSICAL GAME

Foote is big and solid and uses his body well. He plays the man and not the puck. He is highly aggressive in his defensive zone; anyone trying to get through Foote to the net will pay a price. He plays it smart and takes few bad penalties. In recent seasons, he has really stepped up his physical play and he dishes out some powerful checks. He has good lower-body strength and drives his body upwards, resulting in a heavy impact with his unfortunate target. Foote can fight when provoked and stands up for his teammates. Nagging injuries prevented him from being as big a force last season as we are accustomed to seeing.

THE INTANGIBLES

Foote is a warrior, an excellent two-way defenseman whose skills are just a notch below elite class. He is one of the more underrated blueliners around. What sets him apart is his competitiveness. He thrives on the challenge of playing against other teams' top forwards. He could be Colorado's second-most important leader, after Forsberg.

PROJECTION

Foote plays a defense-heavy game but can still score 25 to 30 points.

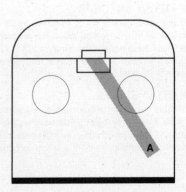

PETER FORSBERG

Yrs. of NHL service: 6
Born: Ornskoldsvik, Sweden; July 20, 1973
Position: centre
Height: 6-0
Weight: 190
Uniform no.: 21
Shoots: left

Career statistics:

GP	G	A	TP	PIM
393	142	349	491	390

1996-97 statistics:

GP	G	A	TP	+/-	PIM	PP	SH	GW	GT	S	PCT
65	28	58	86	+31	73	5	4	4	0	188	14.9

1997-98 statistics:

GP	G	A	TP	+/-	PIM	PP	SH	GW	GT	S	PCT
72	25	66	91	+6	94	7	3	7	1	202	12.4

1998-99 statistics:

GP	G	A	TP	+/-	PIM	PP	SH	GW	GT	S	PCT
78	30	67	97	+27	108	9	2	7	0	217	13.8

1999-2000 statistics:

GP	G	A	TP	+/-	PIM	PP	SH	GW	GT	S	PCT
49	14	37	51	+9	52	3	0	2	0	105	13.3

LAST SEASON

Second on team in shooting percentage. Third on team in assists. Missed 22 games with shoulder surgery. Missed seven games with concussion. Missed two games with hip pointer. Missed two games with bruised shoulder. Missed one game with separated shoulder.

THE FINESSE GAME

Injuries prevented Forsberg from having his usual stud season. This guy is used in all game situations: power play, penalty killing and four-on-four. His skill level is world class in every department.

Forsberg protects the puck as well as anybody in the league. He is so strong he can control the puck with one arm while fending off a checker, and still make an effective pass. His passing is nearly as good as teammate Joe Sakic's. He can be off-balance with his head down, digging the puck out of his skates, and he can still put a pass on a teammate's stick. The Swede seems to be thinking a play or two ahead of everyone else on the ice and has an amazing sense of every player's position.

Forsberg is a smooth skater with explosive speed (think Teemu Selanne) and can accelerate while carrying the puck. He has excellent vision of the ice and is a sublime playmaker. One of the few knocks on him is that he doesn't shoot enough. He works most effectively down between the circles with a wrist or backhand shot off the rush, and does his best work in traffic. There's a lot of Gordie Howe about him.

THE PHYSICAL GAME

Forsberg is better suited for the North American style than most Europeans — or many North Americans, for that matter. He is tough to knock down. He loves contact and dishes out more than he receives. He has a wide skating base and great balance. He can be cross-checked when he's on his backhand and still not lose control of the puck. Jaromir Jagr may be the only other player who can do that.

Forsberg has a cockiness that many great athletes carry about them like an aura; he dares people to try to intimidate him. His drive to succeed helps him handle the cheap stuff and keep going. He's got a mean streak, too: bringing his stick up into people's faces. He also takes abuse, and was a frequent target last season. He plays equally hard on any given inch of the ice. His physical game sometimes goes over the top and robs him of his offensive game, which is why rivals are so eager to engage him.

THE INTANGIBLES

Forsberg's shoulder injuries are a red flag. He had surgery on his left one during the 1999 off-season, and ended the 2000 regular season by separating his right. But he did return in the playoffs, and outplayed many of his more able-bodied teammates. The Avs may play him on the wing full-time this season.

PROJECTION

Forsberg could be the best all-around forward in the NHL. The only question mark about him this season is his constant string of injuries. Given the involved style he plays, he could miss another 20 games.

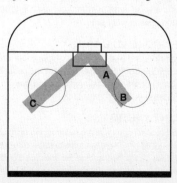

ALEXEI GUSAROV

Yrs. of NHL service: 10
Born: Leningrad, Russia; July 18, 1964
Position: left defense
Height: 6-3
Weight: 185
Uniform no.: 5
Shoots: left

Career statistics:

GP	G	A	TP	PIM
556	38	120	158	295

1996-97 statistics:

GP	G	A	TP	+/-	PIM	PP	SH	GW	GT	S	PCT
58	2	12	14	+4	28	0	0	0	0	33	6.1

1997-98 statistics:

GP	G	A	TP	+/-	PIM	PP	SH	GW	GT	S	PCT
72	4	10	14	+9	42	0	1	1	0	47	8.5

1998-99 statistics:

GP	G	A	TP	+/-	PIM	PP	SH	GW	GT	S	PCT
54	3	10	13	+12	24	1	0	0	0	28	10.7

1999-2000 statistics:

GP	G	A	TP	+/-	PIM	PP	SH	GW	GT	S	PCT
34	2	2	4	-8	10	0	0	0	0	16	12.5

LAST SEASON

Missed 18 games with broken leg. Missed 12 games with shoulder injury. Missed 10 games with broken finger. Missed four games with concussion. Missed one game with flu.

THE FINESSE GAME

Gusarov's game was once offense-heavy, but in recent years he has used his finesse skills to defensive purpose. A shifty skater with a long reach and great range, he can handle the puck on the rush or move it out of his zone. He doesn't mind gambling on offense if the ice opens up for him. Sometimes he will get overly involved in the attack and has to be reined in by coaches.

Gusarov is aggressive and confident in his skills, but he can get careless in the neutral zone and get his partner into trouble by overcommitting. He has improved his positional play but will sometimes get caught puck-watching.

He is a good penalty killer, and sees spot duty on the second power-play unit.

THE PHYSICAL GAME

Gusarov does not like the physical game. He uses his long reach and stick to fish around for the puck, rather than bump people. He's tall and lean and doesn't have the best build or base for contact.

THE INTANGIBLES

For the second consecutive season, Gusarov lost a huge chunk of playing time to injuries. No sooner did he get back in the lineup than he was out again. The Avs would like him to stay healthy enough to be part of their top four, but he is entering the final year of his contract and it would not be a surprise if Colorado moved him.

PROJECTION

Gusarov is a likely 25-point scorer, if he can stay intact.

MILAN HEJDUK

Yrs. of NHL service: 2
Born: Usti-nad-Labem, Czech.; Feb. 14, 1976
Position: right wing
Height: 5-11
Weight: 165
Uniform no.: 23
Shoots: right

Career statistics:

GP	G	A	TP	PIM
164	50	70	120	42

1998-99 statistics:

GP	G	A	TP	+/-	PIM	PP	SH	GW	GT	S	PCT
82	14	34	48	+8	26	4	0	5	0	178	7.9

1999-2000 statistics:

GP	G	A	TP	+/-	PIM	PP	SH	GW	GT	S	PCT
82	36	36	72	+14	16	13	0	9	2	228	15.8

LAST SEASON

Second NHL season. Led team in goals with career high. Tied for ninth in NHL in goals. Led team and tied for third in NHL in in game-winning goals. Led team in shooting percentage. Tied for team lead and tied for fourth in NHL in power-play goals. Second on team in points with career high. One of three Avalanche players to appear in all 82 games.

THE FINESSE GAME

So much for the sophomore jinx. Despite injury problems in Colorado, Hejduk took a big step forward from his impressive rookie season.

Hejduk has fantastic hands and is a finisher. His release is deadly quick and accurate. Most important, he is willing to pay the price around the net to score. He has excellent speed, hockey sense and vision, and he is outstanding on the power play. He has great stamina and can handle of lot of ice time.

THE PHYSICAL GAME

Hejduk is small but has a solid build; he doesn't stay out of the high-traffic areas. He suffered a broken collarbone in the 1999 playoffs but completely recovered from it last season, and wasn't a bit shy about getting physically involved again. He won't be intimidated. He plays the game with great gusto and determination.

THE INTANGIBLES

Hejduk, who spoke little English in his rookie season, was more comfortable this season, and his upbeat attitude made him popular in the Avs dressing room. On a largely veteran team, he commands a lot of respect. Like most of his teammates, he did not have a great playoffs but was less guilty than most. He was a restricted free agent during the off-season, and his performance gave him plenty of ammunition at the bargaining table.

PROJECTION

Hejduk steamrolled past our 25-goal prediction for him last season. He is now a legitimate NHL sniper; 35 goals should be the norm for him from now on.

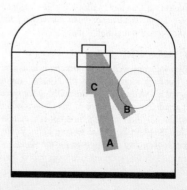

JON KLEMM

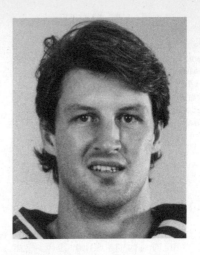

Yrs. of NHL service: 5
Born: Cranbrook, B.C.; Jan. 8, 1970
Position: right defense
Height: 6-3
Weight: 200
Uniform no.: 24
Shoots: right

Career statistics:

GP	G	A	TP	PIM
330	25	45	70	158

1996-97 statistics:

GP	G	A	TP	+/-	PIM	PP	SH	GW	GT	S	PCT
80	9	15	24	+12	37	1	2	1	0	103	8.7

1997-98 statistics:

GP	G	A	TP	+/-	PIM	PP	SH	GW	GT	S	PCT
67	6	8	14	-3	30	0	0	0	1	60	10.0

1998-99 statistics:

GP	G	A	TP	+/-	PIM	PP	SH	GW	GT	S	PCT
39	1	2	3	+4	31	0	0	0	0	28	3.6

1999-2000 statistics:

GP	G	A	TP	+/-	PIM	PP	SH	GW	GT	S	PCT
73	5	7	12	+26	34	0	0	0	0	64	7.8

LAST SEASON

Second on team in plus-minus. Missed seven games with groin injury. Missed one game with back injury.

THE FINESSE GAME

Klemm has enough finesse skills that the Avalanche can use him up front in a pinch. His defensive skills are good enough that he can be paired with a high-risk offensive defenseman, as he frequently was with Sandis Ozolinsh in the latter's Colorado tenure. Let's just say he's had a lot of experience facing two-on-ones.

Klemm is an all-purpose defenseman who does everything the team asks of him. His skating is average, but he plays within his limitations. When he's moved up front he fills the role of a grinding winger. On defense, he is as steady and low-rsik as they come, without doing anything truly special.

THE PHYSICAL GAME

Klemm doesn't go looking for hits. He eliminates his man but doesn't have the explosive drive from his legs to make powerful highlight hits.

THE INTANGIBLES

Klemm is a sportswriter's nightmare, because he's so quiet, yet he's appreciated by his coaches and teammates for his willingness to do anything for the team. He is an underrated member of the Colorado defense corps, but saw more playing time last season after the Avs lost Sylvain Lefebvre to free agency. He is a number four or five defenseman for the Avs.

PROJECTION

Klemm keeps his game conservative, but probably has a little better offensive upside than he has shown. He is capable of 20 points.

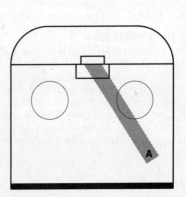

SHJON PODEIN

Yrs. of NHL service: 8
Born: Rochester, Minn.; Mar. 5, 1968
Position: left wing
Height: 6-2
Weight: 200
Uniform no.: 25
Shoots: left

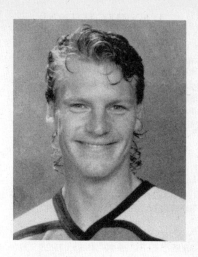

Career statistics:

GP	G	A	TP	PIM
485	57	62	119	269

1996-97 statistics:

GP	G	A	TP	+/-	PIM	PP	SH	GW	GT	S	PCT
82	14	18	32	+7	41	0	0	4	0	153	9.2

1997-98 statistics:

GP	G	A	TP	+/-	PIM	PP	SH	GW	GT	S	PCT
82	11	13	24	+8	53	1	1	2	0	126	8.7

1998-99 statistics:

GP	G	A	TP	+/-	PIM	PP	SH	GW	GT	S	PCT
55	3	6	9	-5	24	0	0	0	0	75	4.0

1999-2000 statistics:

GP	G	A	TP	+/-	PIM	PP	SH	GW	GT	S	PCT
75	11	8	19	+12	29	0	1	3	0	104	10.6

PROJECTION

In his defensive role, Podein can pop in 10 to 15 goals a season.

LAST SEASON

Missed four games with knee injury. Missed three games with fractured foot.

THE FINESSE GAME

Podein is a labourer. He works hard, loves his job and uses his size well. He started out as a centre, but he is better suited as a winger because his hands aren't great. He is happiest in a dump-and-chase game, where he can use his straightaway speed to bore in on the puck carrier.

A mucker, Podein is not a fancy scorer. He gets most of his goals from digging around the net for rebounds and loose pucks. He doesn't have particularly good hockey sense.

Podein is not an agile skater but he is sturdy for work along the boards, and he can work up a pretty good head of steam. Just don't ask him to turn.

THE PHYSICAL GAME

Podein is antagonistic, with a bit of a mean streak, and he tends to be a bit careless with his stick. He can take bad penalties because of that tendency.

THE INTANGIBLES

Podein plays well on a checking line. He is a high-energy player and penalty killer who can lift the bench with a strong shift. He has taken a long route to the NHL and will have to work to stay here. He will be on the bubble in Colorado but won't have trouble finding work elsewhere as a role player if the Avs decide to go younger at the position.

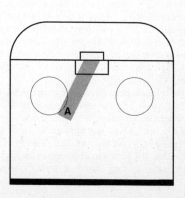

PATRICK ROY

Yrs. of NHL service: 15
Born: Quebec City, Que.; Oct. 5, 1965
Position: goaltender
Height: 6-0
Weight: 192
Uniform no.: 33
Catches: left

Career statistics:

GP	MIN	GA	SO	GAA	A	PIM
841	49108	2155	48	2.63	37	206

1996-97 statistics:

GP	MIN	GAA	W	L	T	SO	GA	S	SAPCT	PIM
62	3698	2.32	38	15	7	7	143	1861	.923	15

1997-98 statistics:

GP	MIN	GAA	W	L	T	SO	GA	S	SAPCT	PIM
65	3835	2.39	31	19	13	4	153	1825	.916	39

1998-99 statistics:

GP	MIN	GAA	W	L	T	SO	GA	S	SAPCT	PIM
61	3648	2.29	32	19	8	5	139	1673	.917	28

1999-2000 statistics:

GP	MIN	GAA	W	L	T	SO	GA	S	SAPCT	PIM
63	3704	2.28	32	21	8	2	141	1640	.914	10

LAST SEASON

Tied for second among NHL goalies in assists. Fourth consecutive season with 30 or more victories. Set NHL record with 14th season of 20 or more wins. Missed two games with groin injury. Missed one game with neck injury.

THE PHYSICAL GAME

Roy is the butterfly goalie by whom all others are judged. He tempts shooters with a gaping hole between his pads, then, when he has the guy suckered, snaps the pads closed at the last second to deny the goal. There is no one in the NHL better at this tantalizing technique.

Tall but not broad, Roy uses his body well. He plays his angles, stays at the top of his crease and squares his body to the shooter. He is able to absorb the shot and deaden it, so there are few juicy rebounds left on his doorstep.

He goes down much sooner than he did earlier in his career. The book on Roy is to try to beat him high. But usually there isn't much net there and it's a small spot for a shooter to hit. He gets into slumps when he allows wide-angle shots taken from the blueline to the top of the circle, but those lapses are seldom prolonged.

Roy comes back to the rest of the pack in his puck-handling, where he is merely average. As for his skating, he seldom moves out of his net. When he gets in trouble he moves back and forth on his knees rather than trying to regain his feet. His glove hand isn't great, either. It's good, but he prefers to use his body. If he is under a strong forecheck, he isn't shy about freezing the puck for a draw, especially since he plays with excellent face-off men in Colorado.

THE MENTAL GAME

Roy is still considered one of the best money goalies in the game. He believes it, too, which is the most important thing. Few goalies play with as much visible attitude as Roy, which can intimidate shooters.

THE INTANGIBLES

Roy's no-trade clause is up this year, but the Avs don't have anyone poised to replace him (they traded away prospect Marc Denis), so it's likely he will finish out the season with Colorado. When he is at the top of his game, Roy is still among the NHL's elite.

Roy needs four wins to become the NHL's career leader. That milestone should arrive very early in the season.

PROJECTION

Yet another 30-win season is in store. It will be his tenth.

JOE SAKIC

Yrs. of NHL service: 12
Born: Burnaby, B.C.; July 7, 1969
Position: centre
Height: 5-11
Weight: 185
Uniform no.: 19
Shoots: left

Career statistics:

GP	G	A	TP	PIM
852	403	657	1060	368

1996-97 statistics:

GP	G	A	TP	+/-	PIM	PP	SH	GW	GT	S	PCT
65	22	52	74	-10	34	10	2	5	0	261	8.4

1997-98 statistics:

GP	G	A	TP	+/-	PIM	PP	SH	GW	GT	S	PCT
64	27	36	63	0	50	12	1	2	1	254	10.6

1998-99 statistics:

GP	G	A	TP	+/-	PIM	PP	SH	GW	GT	S	PCT
73	41	55	96	+23	29	12	5	6	1	255	16.1

1999-2000 statistics:

GP	G	A	TP	+/-	PIM	PP	SH	GW	GT	S	PCT
60	28	53	81	+30	28	5	1	5	0	242	11.6

LAST SEASON

Led team and tied for eighth in NHL in points. Led team and tied for fourth in NHL in assists. Led team and tied for fourth in NHL in plus-minus. Second on team in goals, game-winning goals and shots. Missed 19 games with torn rib cartilage. Missed two games with groin injury. Missed one game with flu.

THE FINESSE GAME

Despite missing 22 games, Sakic lead the Avs in several major offensive categories and was among the league leaders in several areas as well.

He is one of the game's best playmakers. It's not a secret that he has also become one of the game's best shooters, and he isn't shy about it. How do you defend against him? Try to keep the puck far, far away.

Sakic has one of the most explosive first steps in the league. He finds and hits the holes in a hurry — even with the puck — to create his chances. He uses a stick shaft with a little "whip" in it that makes his shots more lethal. He has a terrific wrist shot and snap shot and one of the quickest releases in the game.

Sakic's most impressive gift, however, is his great patience with the puck. He will hold it until the last minute, when he has drawn the defenders to him and opened up ice, creating time and space for his linemates. This makes him a gem on the power play, where he works down low and just off the half-boards on the right wing. He can also play the point.

Sakic is a scoring threat whenever he is on the ice because he can craft a dangerous scoring chance out of a situation that looks innocent. He is lethal trailing the rush. He takes a pass in full stride without slowing, then dekes and shoots before the goalie can even flinch. He is a good face-off man, too, and if he's tied up he uses his skates to kick the puck free.

THE PHYSICAL GAME

Sakic is not a physical player, but he is stronger than he looks and, like Wayne Gretzky in his prime, spins off his checks when opponents take runs at him. He uses his body to protect the puck when he is carrying deep; you have to go through him to get it. He will try to keep going through traffic or along the boards with the puck, and often squirts free with it because he is able to maintain control and his balance. He creates turnovers with his quickness and hands, not by initiating contact.

THE INTANGIBLES

Sakic had to carry much of the load with Peter Forsberg missing nearly half the season, and he was worn down by the playoffs. He was expected to go to salary arbitration during the off-season and could become a free agent in 2001, which means he is playing for a new contract. Or the Avs could trade him before it gets to that point.

PROJECTION

Sakic would have been close to 100 points if he had stayed healthy. He is still in the elite scoring class.

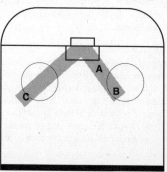

MARTIN SKOULA

Yrs. of NHL service: 1
Born: Litvinov, Czech.; Oct. 28, 1979
Position: defense
Height: 6-2
Weight: 195
Uniform no.: 55
Shoots: left

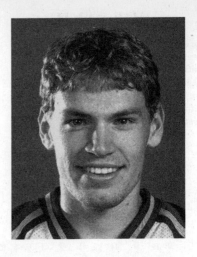

Career statistics:

GP	G	A	TP	PIM
80	3	13	16	20

1999-2000 statistics:

GP	G	A	TP	+/-	PIM	PP	SH	GW	GT	S	PCT
80	3	13	16	+5	20	2	0	0	0	66	4.5

LAST SEASON

First NHL season. Missed two games with separated shoulder.

THE FINESSE GAME

Skoula played a much more mature game than could be expected from most 20-year-old defensemen, and it was a good thing for the Avs that he did. Until Ray Bourque's arrival in March, Skoula carried a pretty heavy workload. He averaged over 18 minutes per game, which is a lot for most rookie defensemen.

Skoula excelled in his own end. He was reliable, poised with the puck, composed in his reads. He would lapse into the occasional bad habit of chasing behind the net, but seemed to respond whenever the coaching staff corrected him. His natural instincts are excellent. He reacts quickly to plays and understands game situations well.

Skoula is a wonderful skater forwards and backwards. He has a long, smooth, natural stride. He is quick and efficient. He handles the puck well and has nice hands for making or receiving passes. He has good hockey vision, and is a heads-up player. He plays a good transition game.

THE PHYSICAL GAME

Skoula is big and well-built and still growing. He isn't a mean hitter, but he registers meaningful takeouts. He proved he could handle the workload and the pace of his first pro season.

THE INTANGIBLES

Skoula could fit into the Avs' top four defensemen this season. He learned a great deal in his rookie season. He will learn a great deal more from playing a full season with Ray Bourque. Note: Calgary took Robyn Regehr instead of Skoula in the Theo Fleury deal in 1999. It will be interesting to watch both of these two young defensemen in the coming season.

PROJECTION

Skoula should move forward off his strong freshman season. He has some offensive upside, as he proved in junior, and with more confidence should move into the 25-point range.

ALEX TANGUAY

Yrs. of NHL service: 1
Born: Ste-Justine, Que.; Nov. 21, 1979
Position: centre
Height: 6-0
Weight: 180
Uniform no.: 40
Shoots: left

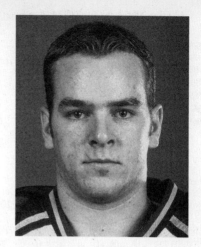

Career statistics:

GP	G	A	TP	PIM
228	118	148	265	144

1999-2000 statistics:

GP	G	A	TP	+/-	PIM	PP	SH	GW	GT	S	PCT
76	17	34	51	+6	22	5	0	3	1	74	23.0

LAST SEASON

First NHL season. Second among NHL rookies in assists. Seventh among NHL rookies in goals. Missed six games with neck strain.

THE FINESSE GAME

Tanguay was just a notch below the NHL's elite rookies last season, probably because he was a victim of numbers on a strong Colorado team. It won't take long for Tangauy to prove he is among the best in his class.

Tanguay is a strong skater with breakaway speed. He is gone in 60 seconds. Less, actually. And he does it with the puck, too. He is absolutely dynamic. He loves to have the puck but he isn't selfish and is a good playmaker.

Like any young player, Tanguay needs to develop the defensive aspect of his game, but he has pretty good awareness of his responsibility and it won't take him long to become proficient. He likes his team to rely on him and will develop into a player who can be used in all game situations.

THE PHYSICAL GAME

Tanguay isn't big but he has an aggressive side. He is highly competitive and will do what it takes to win. He is in good shape and handles a lot of minutes.

THE INTANGIBLES

Injuries gave Tanguay the opening he needed to stick with the big club last season. He needs a little more seasoning, but he had a good start and will only improve. Colorado used him on the fourth line during the playoffs, but he will be one of the team's top six forwards in the regular season.

PROJECTION

Tanguay exceeded the 15 goals we expected of him in his first full rookie season. Now we anticipate a slight upgrade to to 20-goal, 60-point realm.

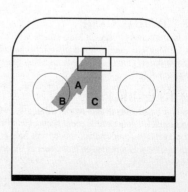

STEPHANE YELLE

Yrs. of NHL service: 5
Born: Ottawa, Ont.; May 9, 1974
Position: centre
Height: 6-1
Weight: 162
Uniform no.: 26
Shoots: left

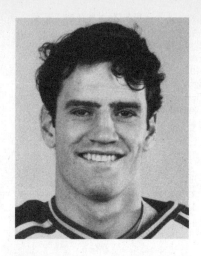

Career statistics:

GP	G	A	TP	PIM
382	45	67	112	184

1996-97 statistics:

GP	G	A	TP	+/-	PIM	PP	SH	GW	GT	S	PCT
79	9	17	26	+1	38	0	1	1	0	89	10.1

1997-98 statistics:

GP	G	A	TP	+/-	PIM	PP	SH	GW	GT	S	PCT
81	7	15	22	-10	48	0	1	0	0	93	7.5

1998-99 statistics:

GP	G	A	TP	+/-	PIM	PP	SH	GW	GT	S	PCT
72	8	7	15	-8	40	1	0	0	0	99	8.1

1999-2000 statistics:

GP	G	A	TP	+/-	PIM	PP	SH	GW	GT	S	PCT
79	8	14	22	+9	28	0	1	1	0	90	8.9

PROJECTION

Yelle's absolute top end is 15 goals, though he is more likely to score goals in single digits. His value is as a defensive forward.

LAST SEASON

Missed two games with bruised sternum. Missed one game with hip flexor.

THE FINESSE GAME

Yelle is a smart player who reads the play extremely well; it's his knowledge of the game that has made him an NHL player. His other skills are average: he's a good skater, but he sees the ice in terms of his defensive role. He's a player you want on the ice to kill penalties or to protect a lead, or sometimes just to go out and play a smart shift to settle a team down.

Yelle doesn't take many face-offs. He doesn't have the hands to get involved in the offense. He isn't even a real shorthanded threat because he doesn't have breakaway speed and will make the safe play instead of the prettier high-risk one. He kills penalties but has to be paired with a better-skating partner.

On a team of glamourous forwards, Yelle is blue collar.

THE PHYSICAL GAME

Yelle is a tall and stringy-looking athlete with toothpicks for legs. He handles himself well, because even though he doesn't look strong he finds a way to get the puck out.

THE INTANGIBLES

Yelle is a smart player and works diligently, which compensates for some of his other flaws. He's one of those players you don't notice much until he's out of the lineup. He was a restricted free agent at the end of last season.

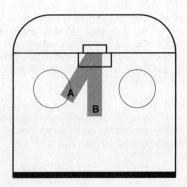

COLUMBUS
BLUE JACKETS

Expansion team — no statistics

available for the 1999-2000 season.

KEVIN DINEEN

Yrs. of NHL service: 16
Born: Quebec City, Que.; Oct. 28, 1963
Position: right wing
Height: 5-11
Weight: 190
Uniform no.: 9
Shoots: right

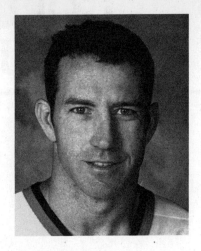

Career statistics:

GP	G	A	TP	PIM
1059	342	390	732	2029

1996-97 statistics:

GP	G	A	TP	+/-	PIM	PP	SH	GW	GT	S	PCT
78	19	29	48	-6	141	8	0	5	0	185	10.3

1997-98 statistics:

GP	G	A	TP	+/-	PIM	PP	SH	GW	GT	S	PCT
54	7	16	23	-7	105	0	0	1	0	96	7.3

1998-99 statistics:

GP	G	A	TP	+/-	PIM	PP	SH	GW	GT	S	PCT
67	8	10	18	+5	97	0	0	1	0	86	9.3

1999-2000 statistics:

GP	G	A	TP	+/-	PIM	PP	SH	GW	GT	S	PCT
67	4	8	12	+2	57	0	0	1	0	71	5.6

PROJECTION

Points will still be hard to come by (anything more than 20 would be a bonus), but Dineen will make his presence felt in other ways.

LAST SEASON

Selected by Columbus in Expansion Draft, June 23, 2000. Missed eight games with groin injuries. Missed two games with shoulder injury. Missed four games due to coach's decision.

THE FINESSE GAME

Dineen's scoring days are over, but he contributes in ways that don't show on the scoresheet. He never fails to make a handful of little plays that give his team a chance to win. He hits, kills penalties, and keeps up the grinding part of his game to the best of his 37-year-old body's ability.

Dineen is never still. His feet keep moving and pumping, and he does a good job drawing penalties. He is very scrappy in battles for the loose puck. Confident and determined, he has the hand quickness to make something happen when he forces a turnover.

Not a gifted scorer, Dineen has always had to work hard for his goals. He doesn't waste his shots and works to get into high-quality scoring positions. His game is far more defensively oriented now, and he is a good penalty killer and checking line winger.

THE PHYSICAL GAME

Dineen still sticks his nose in, even though his body (which is also afflicted with Crohn's disease) is showing a lot of wear and tear. Dineen still plays with a hard edge. He's not very big, but he uses every pound.

THE INTANGIBLES

The big-hearted Dineen, a former Masterton Trophy finalist, is a good leader to add to an inexperienced expansion team.

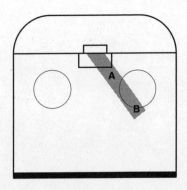

TED DRURY

Yrs. of NHL service: 7
Born: Boston, Mass.; Sept. 13, 1971
Position: centre
Height: 6-0
Weight: 185
Uniform no.: 18
Shoots: left

Career statistics:

GP	G	A	TP	PIM
413	41	52	93	367

1996-97 statistics:

GP	G	A	TP	+/-	PIM	PP	SH	GW	GT	S	PCT
73	9	9	18	-9	54	1	0	2	1	114	7.9

1997-98 statistics:

GP	G	A	TP	+/-	PIM	PP	SH	GW	GT	S	PCT
73	6	10	16	-10	82	0	1	0	0	110	5.5

1998-99 statistics:

GP	G	A	TP	+/-	PIM	PP	SH	GW	GT	S	PCT
75	5	6	11	+2	83	0	0	0	0	79	6.3

1999-2000 statistics:

GP	G	A	TP	+/-	PIM	PP	SH	GW	GT	S	PCT
66	3	2	5	-9	37	1	0	0	0	57	5.3

PROJECTION

Drury is a bubble player on a better team, but in Columbus he can fulfill a third-line checking role and score 10 to 12 goals.

LAST SEASON

Selected by Columbus from N.Y. Islanders in Expansion Draft, June 23, 2000. Acquired by Islanders from Anaheim for Tony Hrkac and Dean Malkoc, Oct. 18, 1999. Missed one game with back injury. Missed 17 games due to coach's decision.

THE FINESSE GAME

Drury is a cerebral player who is appreciated by coaches for his adaptability on the penalty kill. He sticks to the game plan. If a strong forecheck is needed, he provides it. If the team has to key on a special opponent, a Brett Hull or a Jaromir Jagr, Drury plays it the way it's drawn on the chalkboard. He can play centre or left wing.

Drury is a shifty skater with decent speed. His forte is his passing ability. He isn't much of a finisher. He is an asset on the power play because of his effort and timing in moving the puck, and he can stickhandle through traffic. He's a poor man's Craig Janney, but with better defensive instincts. He has superb hockey sense, which makes him an asset on the checking line.

THE PHYSICAL GAME

Drury is underrated by opponents, who see a rather average-sized forward and underestimate his wiry strength. He plays a determined game to stay at the NHL level.

THE INTANGIBLES

Drury still has great wheels and a good head. He will be a key role player with the expansion Blue Jackets.

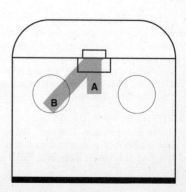

JEAN-LUC GRAND-PIERRE

Yrs. of NHL service: 1
Born: Montreal, Que.; Feb. 2, 1977
Position: right defense
Height: 6-3
Weight: 207
Uniform no.: 34
Shoots: right

Career statistics:

GP	G	A	TP	PIM
27	0	1	1	32

1998-99 statistics:

GP	G	A	TP	+/-	PIM	PP	SH	GW	GT	S	PCT
16	0	1	1	0	17	0	0	0	0	11	0.0

1999-2000 statistics:

GP	G	A	TP	+/-	PIM	PP	SH	GW	GT	S	PCT
11	0	0	0	-1	15	0	0	0	0	10	0.0

LAST SEASON

Selected by Columbus from Buffalo in Expansion Draft, June 23, 2000. Missed one game with flu. Appeared in 61 games with Rochester (AHL), scoring 5-8 — 13 with 124 penalty minutes.

THE FINESSE GAME

Grand-Pierre is big and can skate, and that's a dandy start for an NHL defense prospect. Where Grand-Pierre has come up short at the NHL level is in his hand skills and his ability to adjust to the big-league pace. He has trouble with defensive reads.

Grand-Pierre has a long, powerful stride. He has good speed and accleration for a big man. His pivots and lateral quickness is also good.

Grand-Pierre will make a determined penalty-killer. He has a long reach for picking off passes in the lanes and he blocks shots. His trouble lies in getting the puck out of the zone. He has to learn to make the quick, safe plays.

THE PHYSICAL GAME

The only thing Grand-Pierre has to learn is to pick his spots better. He's a legitimate tough guy who will stand up for his teammates. He can't afford to take dumb penalties.

THE INTANGIBLES

Grand-Pierre rode the Rochester-Buffalo shuttle for three seasons, and leaving him exposed in the expansion draft was a tough call for the Sabres. Grand-Pierre had a spunky playoffs. He is going to relish a shot at a full-time NHL job, and should be among the Blue Jackets top four defensemen.

PROJECTION

Grand-Pierre and teammate Krzysztof Oliwa will make sure the Blue Jackets won't get pushed around. Grand-Pierre is a sure bet for triple-digit PIM, but not many points.

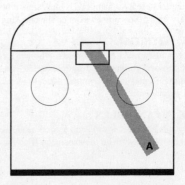

STEVE HEINZE

Yrs. of NHL service: 8
Born: Lawrence, Mass.; Jan. 30, 1970
Position: right wing
Height: 5-11
Weight: 193
Uniform no.: 23
Shoots: right

Career statistics:

GP	G	A	TP	PIM
515	131	108	239	275

1996-97 statistics:

GP	G	A	TP	+/-	PIM	PP	SH	GW	GT	S	PCT
30	17	8	25	-8	27	4	2	2	0	96	17.7

1997-98 statistics:

GP	G	A	TP	+/-	PIM	PP	SH	GW	GT	S	PCT
61	26	20	46	+8	54	9	0	6	0	160	16.3

1998-99 statistics:

GP	G	A	TP	+/-	PIM	PP	SH	GW	GT	S	PCT
73	22	18	40	+7	30	9	0	3	0	146	15.1

1999-2000 statistics:

GP	G	A	TP	+/-	PIM	PP	SH	GW	GT	S	PCT
75	12	13	25	-8	36	2	0	2	2	145	8.3

PROJECTION

With a fresh start and with an expansion team where he should get more quality ice time than he ever dreamed, Heinze has a decent shot at a 20-goal season.

LAST SEASON

Selected from Boston by Columbus in Expansion Draft, June 23, 2000. Missed six games with rib injury. Missed one game with flu.

THE FINESSE GAME

Heinze is a basic, grinding forward who skates up and down his wing. He has surprisingly good hands for a grinder, with a quick snap shot. He gets goals that go in off his legs, arms and elbows from his work in front of the net.

He's smart at trailing plays along the way and digging out loose pucks, which he either takes to the net himself or, more often, passes off.

Heinze has a good first step to the puck, which helps in his penalty killing, as he forces the puck carrier. He has a lot of confidence in his shorthanded prowess. He plays an intelligent game and is a good playmaker, with passing skills on his forehand and backhand.

THE PHYSICAL GAME

Heinze is hampered by his lack of size and strength. His probable future is as a third-line checking winger, but he doesn't have the power to line up against other teams' top forwards. He is willing to get in the way and force people to go through him. The trouble is, they usually do.

THE INTANGIBLES

Things went awry for Heinze in his hometown and he actually asked the Bruins not to protect him so that an expansion team might draft him. Goodbye Boston, hello Columbus.

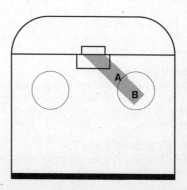

ROBERT KRON

Yrs. of NHL service: 10
Born: Brno, Czech.; Feb. 27, 1967
Position: right wing
Height: 5-11
Weight: 185
Uniform no.: 18
Shoots: left

Career statistics:

GP	G	A	TP	PIM
653	132	172	304	105

1996-97 statistics:

GP	G	A	TP	+/-	PIM	PP	SH	GW	GT	S	PCT
68	10	12	22	-18	10	2	0	4	0	182	5.5

1997-98 statistics:

GP	G	A	TP	+/-	PIM	PP	SH	GW	GT	S	PCT
81	16	20	36	-8	12	4	0	2	0	175	9.1

1998-99 statistics:

GP	G	A	TP	+/-	PIM	PP	SH	GW	GT	S	PCT
75	9	16	25	-13	10	3	1	2	0	134	6.7

1999-2000 statistics:

GP	G	A	TP	+/-	PIM	PP	SH	GW	GT	S	PCT
81	13	27	40	-4	8	2	1	3	1	134	9.7

LAST SEASON

Selected by Columbus from Carolina in Expansion Draft, June 23, 2000. Only game missed was as a healthy scratch.

THE FINESSE GAME

Kron is all promise, no finish.

On a better team, Kron is a third-line checking centre with little more than an average contribution to his team's skill level. He has good speed and can control the puck at high tempo, which gives him the ability to intimidate and drive opposing defensemen back off the blueline.

Kron thrives on open ice, whether penalty-killing or playing four-on-four. He is aware in all three zones. He can kill penalties and work on the power play as well. Defensively reliable, he can be used on the ice at any time in the game. He is a very creative player, more of a playmaker than a shooter, but he needs to shoot more because of his good hands. He tries to be too fine with his shot and misses the net frequently when he is in a prime scoring area. He likes to use a snap shot more than a slapper and will get a quick release away from 15 to 20 feet out.

THE PHYSICAL GAME

Kron is very fit, but he is a small player and doesn't play a physical style. He's not afraid and doesn't bail out of tough situations. He will need to be shored up by big forwards.

THE INTANGIBLES

Kron has trouble finding ice time on a better team, but Columbus will use him out of necessity and he'll have a job until the team gets deep enough to force him out.

PROJECTION

We didn't expect much from Kron last year, and that's what we got. Even with a full-time job in Columbus, 20 goals is his max.

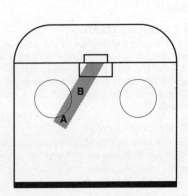

DARRYL LAPLANTE

Yrs. of NHL service: 1
Born: Calgary, Alta.; mar. 28, 1977
Position: centre
Height: 6-1
Weight: 185
Uniform no.: 21
Shoots: left

Career statistics:

GP	G	A	TP	PIM
35	0	6	6	10

1997-98 statistics:

GP	G	A	TP	+/-	PIM	PP	SH	GW	GT	S	PCT
2	0	0	0	0	0	0	0	0	0	2	0.0

1998-99 statistics:

GP	G	A	TP	+/-	PIM	PP	SH	GW	GT	S	PCT
3	0	0	0	0	0	0	0	0	0	0	0.0

1999-2000 statistics:

GP	G	A	TP	+/-	PIM	PP	SH	GW	GT	S	PCT
30	0	6	6	-2	10	0	0	0	0	19	0.0

LAST SEASON

Selected by Columbus from Detroit in Expansion Draft, June 23, 2000. Appeared in 35 games with Cincinnati (AHL), scoring 13-9-22. Missed eight games with fractured cheekbone.

THE FINESSE GAME

Got speed? Laplante was the NHL's fastest skater in the contests clocked at the teams' skills competitions last year. (Players with good wheels are always of high value in the NHL.) He actually started out as a figure skater before he turned to hockey, so footwork will not be a problem for him.

If only his hands were up to speed. Laplante is going to be one of those thrilling players who gets breakaway after breakaway but won't be burying his chances. It's unlikely he will ever be an impact scorer in the NHL. His highest minor-league total was 17 goals.

Laplante's defensive game is well advanced, and has been helped by schooling in the Detroit system. He is a natural centre who can also play either wing. He can be used to kill penalties because of his quickness. He does a decent job on face-offs.

THE PHYSICAL GAME

Laplante has good size but only fair strength. He is not particularly tough or aggressive or determined.

THE INTANGIBLES

Laplante doesn't have all the tools — if he did, he wouldn't have been exposed in the expansion draft — but speed is an important element for a first-year team. Ideally a third-line checking forward, Laplante may see time on the top two lines with the Blue Jackets.

PROJECTION

Laplante will provide a lot of excitement, but maybe only 10 goals.

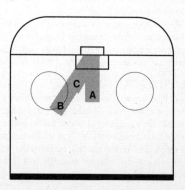

LYLE ODELEIN

Yrs. of NHL service: 10
Born: Quill Lake, Sask.; July 21, 1968
Position: right defense
Height: 5-11
Weight: 210
Uniform no.: 24
Shoots: left

Career statistics:

GP	G	A	TP	PIM
721	34	155	189	1885

1996-97 statistics:

GP	G	A	TP	+/-	PIM	PP	SH	GW	GT	S	PCT
79	3	13	16	+16	110	1	0	2	0	93	3.2

1997-98 statistics:

GP	G	A	TP	+/-	PIM	PP	SH	GW	GT	S	PCT
79	4	19	23	+11	171	1	0	0	0	76	5.3

1998-99 statistics:

GP	G	A	TP	+/-	PIM	PP	SH	GW	GT	S	PCT
70	5	26	31	+6	114	1	0	0	1	101	5.0

1999-2000 statistics:

GP	G	A	TP	+/-	PIM	PP	SH	GW	GT	S	PCT
73	2	22	24	-9	123	1	0	1	0	89	2.2

LAST SEASON

Selected by Columbus from Phoenix in Expansion Draft, June 23, 2000. Acquired by Phoenix from New Jersey for Deron Quint and a conditional draft choice in 2001, Mar. 7, 2000. Led Coyotes in penalty minutes. Missed three games with flu. Missed three games with back injury.

THE FINESSE GAME

Defense is Odelein's forte. He is very calm with the puck and able to wait until a player is on top of him, then carry the puck or find an open man. His skating is average at best, but he keeps himself out of trouble by playing a conservative game and not getting caught out of position. An attacker who comes into Odelein's piece of the ice will have to pay the price by getting through him.

Odelein's finesse skills are modest at best, but he has developed sufficient confidence to get involved in the attack if needed. He prefers to limit his contribution to shots from the point.

Odelein deserves credit for having molded himself into more than an overachieving goon. He is a physical presence despite being smaller than most NHL defensemen — and smaller than many NHL forwards.

THE PHYSICAL GAME

Odelein is a banger, a limited player who knows what his limits are, stays within them and plays effectively as a result. He's rugged and doesn't take chances. He takes the man at all times in front of the net and he plays tough. Heavy but not tall, he gives the impression of being a much bigger man. He will fight, but not very well.

Odelein can be taken off his game easily and gets caught up in yapping matches, which does his game no good.

THE INTANGIBLES

In last year's *HSR*, we said, "It would be a surprise to see him still in a New Jersey uniform in the playoffs." He wasn't. It will be even more of a surprise to see him in a Blue Jackets jersey. Columbus selected him even though Odelein was a free agent and could have signed anywhere. But Odelein wanted to join the expansion team, where he is likely to be the team captain, even though it will mean a lot of long nights. He is going to face a lot of other teams' top lines without a lot of help. His plus-minus won't be pretty.

PROJECTION

Odelein has an upbeat attitude that will help some of the younger Columbus players through a losing first season. He will give you minutes on the ice and in the box. He won't give you points, but that's not what he's here for.

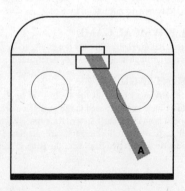

JAMIE PUSHOR

Yrs. of NHL service: 4
Born: Lethbridge, Alberta; Feb. 11, 1973
Position: right defense
Height: 6-3
Weight: 225
Uniform no.: 4
Shoots: right

Career statistics:

GP	G	A	TP	PIM
276	7	25	32	392

1996-97 statistics:

GP	G	A	TP	+/-	PIM	PP	SH	GW	GT	S	PCT
75	4	7	11	+1	129	0	0	0	0	63	6.3

1997-98 statistics:

GP	G	A	TP	+/-	PIM	PP	SH	GW	GT	S	PCT
64	2	7	9	+3	81	0	0	0	0	51	3.9

1998-99 statistics:

GP	G	A	TP	+/-	PIM	PP	SH	GW	GT	S	PCT
70	1	2	3	-20	112	0	0	0	0	75	1.3

1999-2000 statistics:

GP	G	A	TP	+/-	PIM	PP	SH	GW	GT	S	PCT
62	0	8	8	0	53	0	0	0	0	27	-

PROJECTION

Pushor won't compile points or penalty minutes, but will play a steady, stay-at-home style.

LAST SEASON

Selected by Columbus from Dallas in Expansion Draft, June 23, 2000. Career high in assists. Missed 20 games due to coach's decision.

THE FINESSE GAME

Pushor is a steady defenseman who has paid his dues. He is a good skater with average speed and accleration and above-average balance. He won't rush the puck up-ice, but he will make the smart first pass to get it out of the zone. He can get panicky and make the risky pass in front of his own goal.

Pushor reads plays well defensively. He uses his range to take away passing lanes and force attackers to the boards. He does the dirty work along the boards and in the corners. He knows his size is what got him to the NHL and it's his willingness to use his strength that will keep him there.

Pushor doesn't get involved much offensively because he lacks the hand skills and vision. He will not push his way in much beyond the blueline.

THE PHYSICAL GAME

Pushor is not overly aggressive, but he is strong on his skates and strong along the wall. He has good size and can be a solid hitter. Once in awhile he gets carried away with his checking and steps up to make risky open-ice hits in the neutral zone.

THE INTANGIBLES

Pushor was caught in a numbers game in Dallas. He would be a number six defenseman with a good club. For an expansion team, he will play in the top four.

GEOFF SANDERSON

Yrs. of NHL service: 9
Born: Hay River, N.W.T.; Feb. 1, 1972
Position: left wing
Height: 6-0
Weight: 185
Uniform no.: 80
Shoots: left

Career statistics:

GP	G	A	TP	PIM
656	225	212	437	263

1996-97 statistics:

GP	G	A	TP	+/-	PIM	PP	SH	GW	GT	S	PCT
82	36	31	67	-9	29	12	1	4	1	297	12.1

1997-98 statistics:

GP	G	A	TP	+/-	PIM	PP	SH	GW	GT	S	PCT
75	11	18	29	+1	38	2	0	2	1	197	5.6

1998-99 statistics:

GP	G	A	TP	+/-	PIM	PP	SH	GW	GT	S	PCT
75	12	18	30	+8	22	1	0	1	0	155	7.7

1999-2000 statistics:

GP	G	A	TP	+/-	PIM	PP	SH	GW	GT	S	PCT
67	13	13	26	+4	22	4	0	3	0	136	9.6

LAST SEASON

Selected by Columbus from Buffalo in Expansion Draft, June 23, 2000. Missed six games with hand injury. Missed one game with back injury.

THE FINESSE GAME

Sanderson never did make the best use of his speed, which prevented him from becoming the southpaw version of Mike Gartner in that player's prime. Still, his skating speed gives him a tremendous edge over the majority of NHL players, though it's not as big a weapon as it should be.

Sanderson has to go, go, go, and take lots of shots. When he plays that way he is far more dangerous. He can drive wide on a defenseman or open up space by forcing the defense to play back off him. He doesn't score often off the rush because he doesn't have a heavy shot. He can create chaos off the rush, though, and finish up by getting open in the slot for a pass.

He has a superb one-timer on the power play, where he likes to score on his off-wing in the deep right slot. Sanderson has become a better all-around player: he is more intelligent in his own end and his checking is more consistent. He can also kill penalties. His speed makes him a shorthanded threat.

THE PHYSICAL GAME

Sanderson has to learn and desire to fight his way through checkers. He is wiry but gets outmuscled, and although his speed keeps him clear of a lot of traffic, he has to battle when the room isn't there.

THE INTANGIBLES

Sanderson will be among the top six forwards for the expansion Blue Jackets.

PROJECTION

Sanderson was a bubble player in Buffalo. In Columbus, he can score 40 points and be a hero. Except he'll probably leave even them wanting more.

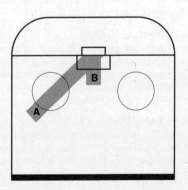

MATHIEU SCHNEIDER

Yrs. of NHL service: 11
Born: New York, N.Y.; June 12, 1969
Position: left defense
Height: 5-11
Weight: 192
Uniform no.: 25
Shoots: left

Career statistics:

GP	G	A	TP	PIM
711	115	260	375	660

1996-97 statistics:

GP	G	A	TP	+/-	PIM	PP	SH	GW	GT	S	PCT
26	5	7	12	+3	20	1	0	1	0	63	7.9

1997-98 statistics:

GP	G	A	TP	+/-	PIM	PP	SH	GW	GT	S	PCT
76	11	26	37	-12	44	4	1	1	0	181	6.1

1998-99 statistics:

GP	G	A	TP	+/-	PIM	PP	SH	GW	GT	S	PCT
75	10	24	34	-19	71	5	0	2	0	159	6.3

1999-2000 statistics:

GP	G	A	TP	+/-	PIM	PP	SH	GW	GT	S	PCT
80	10	20	30	-6	78	3	0	1	1	228	4.4

LAST SEASON

Selected by Columbus in the Expansion Draft, June 23, 2000. Led Rangers defensemen in points. Led Rangers in penalty minutes. Second on Rangers in shots. Missed two games with flu.

THE FINESSE GAME

Schneider is an excellent skater, plus he's strong. He sees the ice and moves the puck well coming out of his own end, and is capable of controlling the pace. He has developed into a good two-way defenseman with the offensive skills to get involved in the attack and to work the point on the power play. A major concern has always been his positional play, but he's learned to make fewer high-risk plays as he has gained more experience.

Strong, balanced and agile, Schneider lacks breakaway speed but is quick with his first step and changes directions smoothly. He can carry the puck but does not lead many rushes. He gets the puck out of the corner quickly. He makes good defensive decisions.

He has improved his point play, doing more with the puck than just drilling shots, though he has a tendency to get his shots blocked when he is slow on the release. He handles the puck well and looks for the passes down low. Given the green light, he is likely to get involved down low more often. He has the skating ability to recover quickly when he takes a chance.

THE PHYSICAL GAME

Schneider is a poor man's version of Chris Chelios, and plays a lot meaner than most people think. He's extremely strong on his feet. Great at making the first pass, he is not flashy, so he doesn't stand out the way a Chelios would. Like Chelios, he is prone to taking dumb penalties, often at the most inopportune moments.

Schneider's goal is to play a containment game and move the puck quickly and intelligently out of the zone. He is often matched against other teams' top scoring lines and always tries to do the job. He is best when paired with a physical defenseman. He has a tendency to hit high and gets penalties because of it.

THE INTANGIBLES

Schneider's major problem has to do with confidence. He's one of those guys you have to tell, all the time, when he's doing well, and then he'll respond. Conversely, criticism from a coach — such as the rips he often absorbed last season from John Muckler — can get Schneider into a funk. He doesn't react well to being ridden hard, even though, like all players, he needs it sometimes. Schneider's pleasantly goofy personality fools people into thinking he doesn't care. He does.

PROJECTION

Schneider's production depends heavily on where he ends up (he was an unrestricted free agent). His low end should be 30 points.

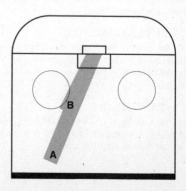

RON TUGNUTT

Yrs. of NHL service: 12
Born: Scarborough, Ont.; Oct. 22, 1967
Position: goaltender
Height: 5-11
Weight: 155
Uniform no.: 31
Catches: left

Career statistics:

GP	MIN	GA	SO	GAA	A	PIM
391	21232	1144	15	3.23	5	6

1996-97 statistics:

GP	MIN	GAA	W	L	T	SO	GA	S	SAPCT	PIM
37	1991	2.80	17	15	1	3	93	882	.895	0

1997-98 statistics:

GP	MIN	GAA	W	L	T	SO	GA	S	SAPCT	PIM
42	2236	2.25	15	14	8	3	84	882	.905	0

1998-99 statistics:

GP	MIN	GAA	W	L	T	SO	GA	S	SAPCT	PIM
43	2508	1.79	22	10	8	3	75	1005	.925	0

1999-2000 statistics:

GP	MIN	GAA	W	L	T	SO	GA	S	SAPCT	PIM
44	2435	2.54	18	12	8	4	103	1020	.899	0

PROJECTION

Tugnutt will be fortunate to reach 20 wins with this expansion team.

LAST SEASON

Signed by Minnesota as free agent from Pittsburgh, July 6, 2000. Acquired by Pittsburgh with Janne Laukkenen for Tom Barrasso, Mar. 14, 2000.

THE PHYSICAL GAME

NHL goalies don't come much smaller than Tugnutt these days. He has to come out to the top of his crease to make himself as big as possible. He is a good skater who is able to follow the play and square himself to the shooter.

Tugnutt is fine with his rebounds, but he has been playing with much better-skating teams in the past few years, and now may feel tempted to do more himself. He needs plenty of help clearing loose pucks, and won't get it.

Tugnutt has a good glove hand, though he is not an adept stickhandler. He comes out of his net well to stop hard-arounds and isn't bothered by the extra space behind the net. He communicates well with his defensemen, who like playing for him.

THE MENTAL GAME

Tugnutt has been in many situations where he wondered if he could be the number one goalie. He will be top dog in Columbus, but it's going to be a tough assignment.

THE INTANGIBLES

Tugnutt had a terrific playoffs (1.77 GAA) but wasn't able to get the Pens past the first round. It might have been his last taste of playoff hockey.

TYLER WRIGHT

Yrs. of NHL service: 5
Born: Canora, Saskatchewan; Apr. 6, 1973
Position: centre
Height: 5-11
Weight: 185
Uniform no.: 29
Shoots: right

Career statistics:

GP	G	A	TP	PIM
279	20	17	37	387

1996-97 statistics:

GP	G	A	TP	+/-	PIM	PP	SH	GW	GT	S	PCT
45	2	2	4	-7	70	0	0	2	0	30	6.7

1997-98 statistics:

GP	G	A	TP	+/-	PIM	PP	SH	GW	GT	S	PCT
82	3	4	7	-3	112	1	0	0	0	46	6.5

1998-99 statistics:

GP	G	A	TP	+/-	PIM	PP	SH	GW	GT	S	PCT
61	0	0	0	-2	90	0	0	0	0	16	0.0

1999-2000 statistics:

GP	G	A	TP	+/-	PIM	PP	SH	GW	GT	S	PCT
50	12	10	22	+4	45	0	0	1	0	68	17.6

LAST SEASON

Selected by Columbus from Pittsburgh in Expansion Draft, June 23, 2000. Career highs in goals, assists and points. Missed two games with back spasms. Missed two games with knee injury. Appeared in 25 games with Wilkes-Barre (AHL), scoring 5-15 — 20.

THE FINESSE GAME

Wright brings to mind the prototypical agitators like Keith Acton and Ken Linseman. Playing in his third-line capacity, Wright will stir things up but be on the outside of the pile after everyone else has jumped in, admiring what he started.

Wright doesn't have a lot of finish around the net. He is not a natural goal scorer. His 12 goals in just 50 games is something of a surprise. Wright started the season in the minors, where he was a very popular player and team captain. He was called up after Kevin Constantine was fired, and fit well into Herb Brooks's system. Maybe the stint will give him the confidence he needs to score 20.

He's a quick and shifty skater, and handles the puck fine, but he does not have a big-league shot. His added dimension is as a penalty killer.

THE PHYSICAL GAME

Wright is always in someone's face. He loves to try to distract other teams' top players, even from the bench. He'll get slapped around a little, because he's not much of a fighter. He's the human equivalent of a Jack Russell terrier.

THE INTANGIBLES

Wright is an enthusiastic and energetic player who adds something to a team's chemistry. He is a good leader for an expansion team and will be a fan favourite.

PROJECTION

Wright will probably see a lot of ice time with the Blue Jackets. His high end is likely 15 to 20 goals.

He began the regular season in the American Hockey League, and finished it as the Penguins' No. 3 center. Wright has developed a scoring touch to complement his feisty game, and probably won't have to worry about being sent back to the minors for a while

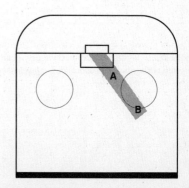

DALLAS STARS

Players' Statistics 1999-2000

POS.	NO.	PLAYER	GP	G	A	PTS	+/-	PIM	PP	SH	GW	GT	S	PCT
C	9	MIKE MODANO	77	38	43	81	0	48	11	1	8	3	188	20.2
L	16	BRETT HULL	79	24	35	59	-21	43	11		3		223	10.8
D	56	SERGEI ZUBOV	77	9	33	42	-2	18	3	1	3		179	5.0
L	15	JAMIE LANGENBRUNNER	65	18	21	39	16	68	4	2	6		153	11.8
D	3	SYLVAIN COTE	76	8	27	35	3	28	5		2		128	6.3
C	25	JOE NIEUWENDYK	48	15	19	34	-1	26	7		2		110	13.6
R	12	MIKE KEANE	81	13	21	34	9	41		4	3		85	15.3
D	5	DARRYL SYDOR	74	8	26	34	6	32	5		1		132	6.1
L	45	*BRENDEN MORROW	64	14	19	33	8	81	3		3		113	12.4
D	24	RICHARD MATVICHUK	70	4	21	25	7	42			1		73	5.5
D	2	DERIAN HATCHER	57	2	22	24	6	68					90	2.2
C	22	KIRK MULLER	47	7	15	22	-3	24	3		2		57	12.3
R	11	*BLAKE SLOAN	67	4	13	17	11	50			1		78	5.1
C	21	GUY CARBONNEAU	69	10	6	16	10	36		1	4		70	14.3
C	17	SCOTT THORNTON	65	8	6	14	-12	108	1		1		83	9.6
C	44	AARON GAVEY	41	7	6	13	0	44	1		2		39	17.9
C	36	*ROMAN LYASHENKO	58	6	6	12	-2	10			1		51	11.8
D	6	DAVE MANSON	63	1	9	10	12	62					66	1.5
C	49	*JONATHAN SIM	25	5	3	8	4	10	2		1		44	11.4
R	26	JERE LEHTINEN	17	3	5	8	1				1		29	10.3
R	29	GRANT MARSHALL	45	2	6	8	-5	38	1				43	4.7
D	4	JAMIE PUSHOR	62		8	8	0	53					27	
L	22	PAVEL PATERA	12	1	4	5	-1	4					18	5.6
L	46	JAMIE WRIGHT	23	1	4	5	4	16					15	6.7
D	18	JOEL BOUCHARD	54	1	4	5	-10	25					61	1.6
D	37	*BRAD LUKOWICH	60	3	1	4	-14	50			1		33	9.1
R	23	CHRIS MURRAY	32	2	1	3	-7	62				1	25	8.0
C	10	BRIAN SKRUDLAND	22	1	2	3	0	22					16	6.3
D	28	*RICHARD JACKMAN	22	1	2	3	-1	6	1				16	6.3
G	20	ED BELFOUR	62		3	3	0	10						
G	30	*EMMANUEL FERNANDEZ	24		2	2	0	2						
R	17	WARREN LUHNING	10		1	1	-2	13					7	
D	27	SHAWN CHAMBERS	4				-2	4					2	
R	41	KEITH ALDRIDGE	4			1							6	
L	50	*RYAN CHRISTIE	5				-1						1	
D	38	*ALAN LETANG	8				-5	2					1	

GP = games played; G = goals; A = assists; PTS = points; +/- = goals-for minus goals-against while player is on ice; PIM = penalties in minutes; PP = power-play goals; SH = shorthanded goals; GW = game-winning goals; GT = game-tying goals; S = no. of shots; PCT = percentage of goals to shots; * = rookie

ED BELFOUR

Yrs. of NHL service: 10
Born: Carman, Man.; Apr. 21, 1965
Position: goaltender
Height: 5-11
Weight: 182
Uniform no.: 20
Catches: left

Career statistics:

GP	MIN	GA	SO	GAA	A	PIM
612	35173	1446	49	2.47	18	304

1996-97 statistics:

GP	MIN	GAA	W	L	T	SO	GA	S	SAPCT	PIM
46	2723	2.89	14	24	6	2	131	1317	.900	34

1997-98 statistics:

GP	MIN	GAA	W	L	T	SO	GA	S	SAPCT	PIM
61	3581	1.88	37	12	10	9	112	1335	.916	18

1998-99 statistics:

GP	MIN	GAA	W	L	T	SO	GA	S	SAPCT	PIM
61	3536	1.99	35	15	9	5	117	1373	.915	26

1999-2000 statistics:

GP	MIN	GAA	W	L	T	SO	GA	S	SAPCT	PIM
62	3620	2.10	32	21	7	4	127	1571	.919	10

LAST SEASON

Led NHL goalies in save percentage. Tied for third among NHL goalies in goals-against average. Tied for second among NHL goalies in assists. Missed four games due to coach's decision.

THE PHYSICAL GAME

Belfour thrives on work and pressure on the ice, where he has won one Stanley Cup and brought the Stars to within a game of a second consecutive championship. His duels with Devils goalie Martin Brodeur in the last two games of the Cup finals, both decided in multiple overtime, will be remembered for many seasons to come.

Belfour's style relies more on athleticism than technique. He is always on his belly, his side, his back. He's a runner-up only to Dominik Hasek as the best goalie with the worst style in the NHL.

Belfour has great instincts and reads the play well in front of him. He plays with an inverted-V, giving the five-hole but usually taking it away from the shooter with his quick reflexes. He is very aggressive and often comes so far out of his crease that he gets tangled with his own defenders-as well as running interference on opponents. He knows he is well-padded and is not afraid to use his body, though injuries have made him less aggressive than in the past. In fact, Belfour uses his body more than his stick or glove, and that is part of his problem. He tries to make the majority of saves with his torso, making the routine saves more difficult. Fortunately, playing behind a strong team keeps his quality shots to a minimum, and on nights when he keeps the game simple, he is one of the league's best.

Belfour tends to keep his glove low. The book on him is to shoot high, but that's the case with most NHL goalies—and a lot of NHL shooters have trouble picking that spot. He sometimes gives up bad rebounds, but his defense is so good and so quick they will swoop in on the puck before the opposition gets a second or third whack.

He has a lot of confidence and an impressive ability to handle the puck, though he sometimes overdoes it. He uses his body to screen when handling the puck for a 15-foot pass, and often sets picks for his forwards.

THE MENTAL GAME

Belfour is such a battler, such a competitor. Sometimes he goes overboard, but it's easier to cool an athlete off than fire him up. His teammates believe in him fully, and he has supreme confidence, even arrogance, in his abilities. Off the ice is another issue, as he proved with an altercation with hotel security one night last season.

THE INTANGIBLES

Winning his first Cup established Belfour as one of the league's elite. Although the Stars couldn't repeat, the fault wasn't his.

PROJECTION

His teammates' injuries prevented Belfour from reaching the 35-win mark, which he should hit this season. The Stars still need to find the right backup goalie with which to spot him.

DERIAN HATCHER

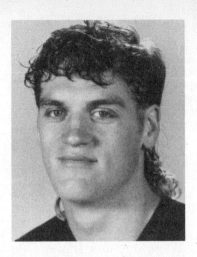

Yrs. of NHL service: 9
Born: Sterling Heights, Mich.; June 4, 1972
Position: left defense
Height: 6-5
Weight: 225
Uniform no.: 2
Shoots: left

Career statistics:

GP	G	A	TP	PIM
585	56	160	216	1110

1996-97 statistics:

GP	G	A	TP	+/-	PIM	PP	SH	GW	GT	S	PCT
63	3	19	22	+8	97	0	0	0	0	96	3.1

1997-98 statistics:

GP	G	A	TP	+/-	PIM	PP	SH	GW	GT	S	PCT
70	6	25	31	+9	132	3	0	2	0	74	8.1

1998-99 statistics:

GP	G	A	TP	+/-	PIM	PP	SH	GW	GT	S	PCT
80	9	21	30	+21	102	3	0	2	0	125	7.2

1999-2000 statistics:

GP	G	A	TP	+/-	PIM	PP	SH	GW	GT	S	PCT
57	2	22	24	+6	68	0	0	0	0	90	2.2

LAST SEASON

Tied for third on team in penalty minutes. Missed 24 games with lacerated calf muscle. Missed one game with strained Achilles tendon.

THE FINESSE GAME

Hatcher plays in all key situations and has developed confidence in his decision-making process. His skating is laboured, so he lets the play come to him. He is sturdy and well-balanced, thought the fewer strides he has to take the better.

He has very good hands for a big man, and has a good head for the game. He is fairly effective from the point on the power play — not because he has a big, booming slap shot, but because he has a good wrist shot and will get the puck on net quickly. He will join the rush eagerly once he gets into gear (his first few strides are sluggish), and he handles the puck nicely.

Hatcher plays hard in every zone, every night. His skills are just a shade below elite level but he takes steps forward every season as a leader. He is a character player, one his teammates look to for setting the tempo and seizing control of a game.

THE PHYSICAL GAME

Hatcher is a big force. He has a mean streak when provoked — just ask Devils Jason Arnott and Petr Sykora, who were victims of borderline checks in last season's Stanley Cup finals. He is a punishing hitter. But he is smart enough to realize that he's a target and opponents want to take him off his game. It's a huge detriment to the Stars when he is in the box, and not just because he is one of their key penalty killers. He plays physically every night and demands respect and

room. He's fearless. He's also a big horse and eats up all the ice time Dallas gives him, which can be 25 minutes a night. The more work he gets, the better.

THE INTANGIBLES

Hatcher will not put up big numbers, but he and Mike Modano are the cornerstones of the franchise. Hatcher is the kind of player the team looks to for consistent effort and intensity. He is a fine role model for the younger Stars, and the veterans respect him as well. He is a quiet player who wants to make a big impact.

PROJECTION

Hatcher is one of the top six defensemen in the league, though he will never have the kind of numbers that inspire Norris Trophy voters. Still, he will be a defenseman you want on your team when you have to win a clutch game. He can provide 40 points and invaluable leadership.

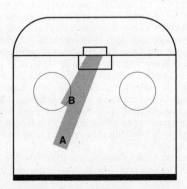

BRETT HULL

Yrs. of NHL service: 13
Born: Belleville, Ont.; Aug. 9, 1964
Position: right wing
Height: 5-10
Weight: 201
Uniform no.: 22
Shoots: right

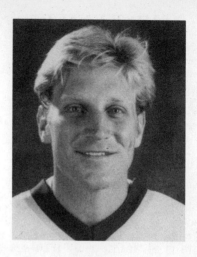

Career statistics:

GP	G	A	TP	PIM
940	610	494	1104	371

1996-97 statistics:

GP	G	A	TP	+/-	PIM	PP	SH	GW	GT	S	PCT
77	42	40	82	-9	10	12	2	6	2	302	13.9

1997-98 statistics:

GP	G	A	TP	+/-	PIM	PP	SH	GW	GT	S	PCT
66	27	45	72	-1	26	10	0	6	0	211	12.8

1998-99 statistics:

GP	G	A	TP	+/-	PIM	PP	SH	GW	GT	S	PCT
60	32	26	58	+19	30	15	0	11	0	192	16.7

1999-2000 statistics:

GP	G	A	TP	+/-	PIM	PP	SH	GW	GT	S	PCT
79	24	35	59	-21	43	11	0	3	0	223	10.8

LAST SEASON

Led team in shots. Tied for team lead in power-play goals. Second on team in goals, assists and points. Missed one game with groin injury. Missed one game with hip flexor. Missed one game with fractured nose.

THE FINESSE GAME

Signing with the Stars was the best career move Hull ever made. His 80-goal days are well behind him, but his overall game has improved enough over the past few seasons that he was not out of place on the disciplined Stars; his dedication was evident from his first shift in Dallas.

Hull plays well in all three zones but remains a shooter first. His shot is seldom blocked — he gets it away so quickly the defense doesn't have time to react — and his shots have tremendous velocity, especially his one-timers from the tops of the circles in.

Hull is always working to get himself in position for a pass but doesn't look like he's working. He sort of drifts into open ice and before a defender can react, he is firing off any kind of shot accurately. He usually moves to his off-wing on the power play. He can play the point but is a better asset down low.

Hull is an underrated playmaker who can thread a pass through traffic right onto the tape. He will find the open man because he has soft hands and good vision. When the opponent overplays him, he makes smart decisions about whether to shoot or pass.

Defensively, Hull's game has improved, but he struggled last season during Jere Lehtinen's prolonged absence, as evidenced by his team-worst plus-minus.

THE PHYSICAL GAME

Hull is compact and when he wants to hit, it's a solid check. His chronic abdominal/groin injuries, which he continues to grit his teeth and play through, make him high-risk. He is not as physically involved as he was when he was scoring goals at an absurd rate, but he will bump people.

THE INTANGIBLES

Hull might not be the prototypical team leader, but on-ice he is as competitive as any of the elite players. His presence helped keep a once uptight Dallas room loose.

PROJECTION

Hull's big-point days are over; 70 points is no longer a given.

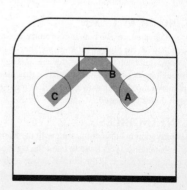

MIKE KEANE

Yrs. of NHL service: 12
Born: Winnipeg, Man.; May 28, 1967
Position: right wing
Height: 5-10
Weight: 185
Uniform no.: 12
Shoots: right

Career statistics:

GP	G	A	TP	PIM
887	129	263	402	754

1996-97 statistics:

GP	G	A	TP	+/-	PIM	PP	SH	GW	GT	S	PCT
81	10	17	27	+2	63	0	1	1	0	91	11.0

1997-98 statistics:

GP	G	A	TP	+/-	PIM	PP	SH	GW	GT	S	PCT
83	10	13	23	-12	52	2	0	1	0	128	7.8

1998-99 statistics:

GP	G	A	TP	+/-	PIM	PP	SH	GW	GT	S	PCT
81	6	23	29	-2	62	1	1	1	0	106	5.7

1999-2000 statistics:

GP	G	A	TP	+/-	PIM	PP	SH	GW	GT	S	PCT
81	13	21	34	+9	41	0	4	3	0	85	15.3

LAST SEASON

Led team in shorthanded goals. Second on team in shooting percentage. Missed one game with back injury.

THE FINESSE GAME

Keane is one of the NHL's most underrated forwards. There are few better on the boards and in the corners, and he's the perfect linemate for a finisher. If you want the puck, he'll get it. Not only will he win the battle for it, he'll make a pass and then set a pick or screen. His game is skewed more to defense, but he can still contribute with a big goal.

Keane's chief assets are his intelligence and desire. He doesn't waste energy. He's a good skater and will use his speed to forecheck or create shorthanded threats when killing penalties. He can play all three forward positions, but is most effective on the right side. He is a smart player who can be thrust into almost any playing situation — a valuable role model.

THE PHYSICAL GAME

Keane is a physical catalyst; he is constantly getting in someone's way. He always finishes his checks in all three zones, stands up for his teammates and is aggressive, though he is not a fighter. He has a ridiculously high pain threshold and has to be locked in a closet to keep him out of the lineup.

THE INTANGIBLES

As was proven in his disastrous stint with the Rangers in 1997-98, some players have to be in the right place at the right time. Keane is the kind of player who will elevate a team from good to better, but not take a mediocre (or worse) squad up a notch. Dallas is the right fit for Keane. He is never more valuable than in the playoffs. He is getting older (he's 33) but he still has an effective season or two remaining. He is treasured as much for his character as for his hard-nosed, heads-up play.

PROJECTION

As a checking forward Keane probably won't score more than 15 goals a year, but since he prevents that many, it's not a bad trade-off. If injuries hit he can step in almost anywhere but in the net.

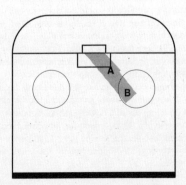

JAMIE LANGENBRUNNER

Yrs. of NHL service: 5
Born: Duluth, Minn.; July 24, 1975
Position: centre
Height: 5-11
Weight: 190
Uniform no.: 15
Shoots: right

Career statistics:

GP	G	A	TP	PIM
311	68	111	179	250

1996-97 statistics:

GP	G	A	TP	+/-	PIM	PP	SH	GW	GT	S	PCT
76	13	26	39	-2	51	3	0	3	0	112	11.6

1997-98 statistics:

GP	G	A	TP	+/-	PIM	PP	SH	GW	GT	S	PCT
81	23	29	52	+9	61	8	0	6	1	159	14.5

1998-99 statistics:

GP	G	A	TP	+/-	PIM	PP	SH	GW	GT	S	PCT
75	12	33	45	+10	62	4	0	1	0	145	8.3

1999-2000 statistics:

GP	G	A	TP	+/-	PIM	PP	SH	GW	GT	S	PCT
65	18	21	39	+16	68	4	2	6	0	153	11.8

LAST SEASON

Led team in plus-minus. Second on team in game-winning goals. Third on team in goals and penalty minutes. Missed 14 games with pinched nerve in neck. Missed one game with sprained shoulder. Missed one game with concussion.

THE FINESSE GAME

Langenbrunner has terrific hand skills. He is intelligent and poised with the puck, and can play as a centre or right wing, though his style of play makes him more suitable as a winger. He has good hockey vision and can pick his spots for shots. He is also a smart passer on either his forehand or backhand.

An average skater, Langenbrunner won't be coming in with speed and driving a shot off the wing — he's not dynamic at all. But he does have a strong short game; his offense is generated within 15 to 20 feet of the net and he has a quick release on his shot. Any deficiencies he may have are offset by his desire to compete and succeed.

Langenbrunner is a plumber, but one who is talented enough to play with the likes of Joe Nieuwendyk. Nieuwendyk's creativity has also helped Langenbrunner's awareness that a pass may come at any time, and that a scoring chance may evolve at any moment. He is an aggressive forechecker who creates turnovers for his linemates.

THE PHYSICAL GAME

Langenbrunner plays an intense game, bigger than his size allows. He will wear down physically. He competes hard in the hard areas of the ice, to either get a puck or get himself into a space to get the puck. He lacks the size to be a power forward, but he is one of the gritty types who are so annoying to play against. He won't just hang on the perimeter and won't back down — he'll even try to stir things up.

THE INTANGIBLES

Langenbrunner's knee injury in the playoffs is one of the key reasons why the Stars failed to repeat as Cup champions. He is one of the game's most significant unsung heroes, not just for his talent but for his smarts, his energy and his attitude.

PROJECTION

Injuries prevented Langenbrunner from cracking the 20-goal barrier, which appears to be his target zone.

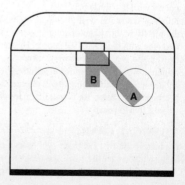

JERE LEHTINEN

Yrs. of NHL service: 5
Born: Espoo, Finland; June 24, 1973
Position: right wing
Height: 6-0
Weight: 185
Uniform no.: 26
Shoots: right

Career statistics:

GP	G	A	TP	PIM
283	68	105	173	56

1996-97 statistics:

GP	G	A	TP	+/-	PIM	PP	SH	GW	GT	S	PCT
63	16	27	43	+26	2	3	1	2	0	134	11.9

1997-98 statistics:

GP	G	A	TP	+/-	PIM	PP	SH	GW	GT	S	PCT
72	23	19	42	+19	20	7	2	6	1	201	11.4

1998-99 statistics:

GP	G	A	TP	+/-	PIM	PP	SH	GW	GT	S	PCT
74	20	32	52	+29	18	7	1	2	0	173	11.6

1999-2000 statistics:

GP	G	A	TP	+/-	PIM	PP	SH	GW	GT	S	PCT
17	3	5	8	+1	0	0	0	1	0	29	10.3

LAST SEASON

Missed 70 games with ankle injury and surgery.

THE FINESSE GAME

Lehtinen is the smartest positional player on the Stars, and the team desperately missed his Selke-quality defense and vastly underrated offense. He is remarkably hockey astute and so honest and so reliable that the other players, almost through osmosis, have to come on-board.

As much as Mike Modano did on his own in the past four seasons, much of that progress can be traced to his teaming with Lehtinen. Modano returned the favour by enhancing the Finn's latent offensive ability. Both players have become more complete because of the other, and some of their best games have come through their being linemates. It was a natural move to keep Lehtinen on the line with Modano, with Brett Hull playing the defensive safeguard role, but Lehtinen never hurts the line offensively, either. He always plays with his head up.

Lehtinen's skating is well above adequate. He's not really top flight, but he has enough quickness and balance to play with highly skilled people. He controls the puck well and is an unselfish playmaker.

Lehtinen struggles only in his finishing. He appears to have a good shot with a quick release, but at times is reluctant to shoot. He is gaining more confidence (thanks to Modano).

THE PHYSICAL GAME

Is there a loose puck that Lehtinen ever loses a battle for? He is so strong on the puck: he protects it and won't be intimidated, and he competes along the boards. He completes his checks and never stops trying.

THE INTANGIBLES

Lehtinen never asks anything of the club, never complains, just asks what he can do to become better — a coach's dream.

PROJECTION

Selke Trophy play and 20 to 25 goals: it's hard to imagine asking much more out of player. Lehtinen will deliver, assuming he makes a complete recovery from the ankle injury that made last year a complete washout.

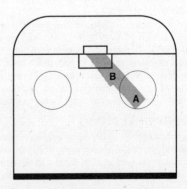

ROMAN LYASHENKO

Yrs. of NHL service: 1
Born: Murmansk, Russia; May 2, 1979
Position: centre
Height: 6-0
Weight: 188
Uniform no.: 36
Shoots: right

Career statistics:

GP	G	A	TP	PIM
58	6	6	12	10

1999-2000 statistics:

GP	G	A	TP	+/-	PIM	PP	SH	GW	GT	S	PCT
58	6	6	12	-2	10	0	0	1	0	51	11.8

LAST SEASON

First NHL season. Missed nine games with shoulder injuries. Missed two games due to coach's decision. Appeared in nine games with Milwaukee (IHL), scoring 3-2 — 5.

THE FINESSE GAME

It's telling that during Jere Lehtinen's frequent absences from the Dallas lineup last year, Lyashenko was the player often used in his place. Lyashenko is a defense-first player, as the Selke Trophy-winning Lehtinen is, but he also has the kind of offensive skills that don't make him look out of place alongside a Mike Modano.

Lyashenko is all smoothness. He has good vision and hand skills. He is progressing quickly as an NHL player, though he did not see much offensive ice time last season.

He will become a complete player who can work the power play, kill penalties, and take key face-offs. He can check the other teams' top lines and add some offensive punch. As Joe Nieuwendyk ages, Lyashenko is the player being groomed to replace him, and he'll give Dallas an impressive one-two punch up the middle.

THE PHYSICAL GAME

Lyashenko plays a solid game and takes the body well, though he is not a physical force. He fights hard for the puck and will not back down from battles along the boards.

THE INTANGIBLES

Lyashenko is the goods. He might still be a third-line player for Dallas for another season, but he's going to become very important. You can't win without players like these, and in Lehtinen and now Lyashenko, the Stars have two of them.

PROJECTION

Lyashenko has 80-point potential. The question is whether he will get enough playing time on a veteran Dallas team to scrape up those kind of points. If the Stars are ready to go younger, Lyashenko will be a key to the next generation.

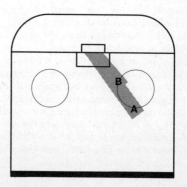

DAVE MANSON

Yrs. of NHL service: 14
Born: Prince Albert, Sask.; Jan. 27, 1967
Position: left defense
Height: 6-2
Weight: 202
Uniform no.: 22
Shoots: left

Career statistics:

GP	G	A	TP	PIM
982	98	279	377	2668

1996-97 statistics:

GP	G	A	TP	+/-	PIM	PP	SH	GW	GT	S	PCT
75	4	18	22	-26	187	2	0	0	0	175	2.3

1997-98 statistics:

GP	G	A	TP	+/-	PIM	PP	SH	GW	GT	S	PCT
81	4	30	34	+22	122	2	0	0	0	148	2.7

1998-99 statistics:

GP	G	A	TP	+/-	PIM	PP	SH	GW	GT	S	PCT
75	6	17	23	+1	155	2	0	0	0	145	4.1

1999-2000 statistics:

GP	G	A	TP	+/-	PIM	PP	SH	GW	GT	S	PCT
63	1	9	10	+12	62	0	0	0	0	66	1.5

LAST SEASON

Acquired by Dallas from Chicago with Sylvain Cote for Kevin Dean, Derek Plante and a second-round draft choice in 2001, Feb. 8, 2000. Second on Stars in plus-minus. Served two suspensions, one of three games and one of one game. Missed four games with bruised foot. Missed three games due to coach's decision.

THE FINESSE GAME

Manson is his own worst enemy. He makes mental errors that prevent him from stepping up into the ranks of the NHL's best defensemen. He makes low-percentage plays, such as skating through his own crease under a heavy forecheck. Maybe skilled Russian defensemen can get away with that; Manson can't. He can be scary in his own end when he overhandles the puck. But he is conscious of helping out his goalie, and he communicates well and clears rebounds when he keeps the game simple.

Manson will often take himself out of position with his poor defensive reads, then has to resort to using his stick to pull attackers down. Not all of his hefty PIM totals are penalties of aggression.

He is smart and effective on the power play,because he mixes up his shot with a big fake and freeze. But there isn't much that's subtle about this guy. His game is power. He doesn't have much lateral mobility so the shot is not as effective as it would be in the hands of an Al MacInnis. He is not a bad skater for a big guy, though, and he gambles down deep and is canny enough to use an accurate wrist shot when in close.

THE PHYSICAL GAME

Manson has become more disciplined, but still has a knack for taking bad penalties at the worst times. He can throw himself off his game and will lose control and run after people. He patrols the front of his net well, can hit to hurt and intimidates players into getting rid of the puck faster than they want to. They flinch from even the threat of a Manson body check.

THE INTANGIBLES

For all of his flaws, no one can fault Mansons effort. He's a trier if not a doer. And he knows his shortcomings and wants to be a better player. He plays hurt and stands up for his teammates. He is a marked man when it comes to supplementary discipline by the NHL.

PROJECTION

Manson's status is as a fifth or sixth defenseman now; whoever signs this unrestricted free agent will have to do so knowing his limitations. He will probably score 20 to 25 points. His PIM totals will be impressive, as usual.

RICHARD MATVICHUK

Yrs. of NHL service: 8
Born: Edmonton, Alta.; Feb. 5, 1973
Position: left defense
Height: 6-2
Weight: 200
Uniform no.: 24
Shoots: left

Career statistics:

GP	G	A	TP	PIM
430	23	76	99	376

1996-97 statistics:

GP	G	A	TP	+/-	PIM	PP	SH	GW	GT	S	PCT
57	5	7	12	+1	87	0	2	0	0	83	6.0

1997-98 statistics:

GP	G	A	TP	+/-	PIM	PP	SH	GW	GT	S	PCT
74	3	15	18	+7	63	0	0	0	0	71	4.2

1998-99 statistics:

GP	G	A	TP	+/-	PIM	PP	SH	GW	GT	S	PCT
64	3	9	12	+23	51	1	0	0	0	54	5.6

1999-2000 statistics:

GP	G	A	TP	+/-	PIM	PP	SH	GW	GT	S	PCT
70	4	21	25	+7	42	0	0	1	0	73	5.5

LAST SEASON

Missed seven games with knee injuries. Missed one game with sprained thumb. Missed one game with flu. Missed three games due to coach's decision.

THE FINESSE GAME

Matvichuk has found his niche as a mobile, two-way defenseman. He is a good skater with a long stride, who skates well backwards and pivots in either direction. He has started to get involved more in the attack, and is capable of that to a degree. He has the hand skills and instincts to play with the offensive players to a point, but that is not a high priority with him. He uses his hockey skills defensively. If his partner wants to go, Matvichuk will make sure to stay at home.

Matvichuk has a low, hard, accurate shot from the point. He makes smart, crisp passes and uses other players well. He can play either side defensively.

Matvichuk wants the ice time when the team needs a calm, defensive presence on the ice. He kills penalties and is one of the Stars' best shot-blockers. For one game last season he was credited with six blocked shots — when the entire Vancouver Canucks team had only eight.

THE PHYSICAL GAME

Matvichuk is aware of the importance of strength and aerobic training and wants to add even more muscle to stay competitive at the NHL level, since he was a little light by today's NHL standards. He's a hack-and-whack kind of mean guy, not a fighter. He occasionally gets into a mode where he starts fishing for the puck.

Because he plays so hard, and blocks so many shots, Matvichuk is subject to great wear and tear. He is tough, and plays through injuries.

THE INTANGIBLES

Matvichuk is part of a solid four-man corps in Dallas.

PROJECTION

Matvichuk has become a confident and capable defenseman. He may have slightly more offensive upside, though 25 to 30 points is a reliable range.

MIKE MODANO

Yrs. of NHL service: 11
Born: Livonia, Mich.; June 7, 1970
Position: centre
Height: 6-3
Weight: 200
Uniform no.: 9
Shoots: left

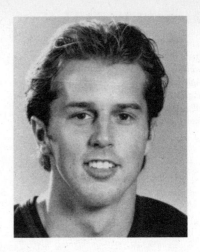

Career statistics:

GP	G	A	TP	PIM
787	349	467	786	566

1996-97 statistics:

GP	G	A	TP	+/-	PIM	PP	SH	GW	GT	S	PCT
80	35	48	83	+43	42	9	5	9	2	291	12.0

1997-98 statistics:

GP	G	A	TP	+/-	PIM	PP	SH	GW	GT	S	PCT
52	21	38	59	+25	32	7	5	2	1	191	11.0

1998-99 statistics:

GP	G	A	TP	+/-	PIM	PP	SH	GW	GT	S	PCT
77	34	47	81	+29	44	6	4	7	1	224	15.2

1999-2000 statistics:

GP	G	A	TP	+/-	PIM	PP	SH	GW	GT	S	PCT
77	38	43	81	0	48	11	1	8	3	188	20.2

LAST SEASON

Led team in goals, assists, points, game-winning goals and shooting percentage. Tied for first on team in power-play goals. Second on team in shots. Missed three games with broken nose, strained neck ligaments and concussion. Missed one game with hip flexor.

THE FINESSE GAME

Modano has world-class skills that match those of just about any player in the NHL, and he''s added a physical element in recent years to eliminate any criticism of being a soft player. When there is a lot of open ice, he's a thrilling player to watch. He has outstanding offensive instincts and great hands, and he is a smooth passer and a remarkable skater in all facets. A solid, skating defensive team like Detroit can take the neutral zone away from him, but not many teams can challenge him that way; Modano makes good use of his speed there.

Modano makes other players around him better, which is the mark of a superstar. His speed and agility with the puck leave defenders mezmerized and opens up ice for his linemates. He is the pivot for one of the best lines in the game, with Jere Lehtinen and Brett Hull. Losing Lehtinen for almost the entire season did not seem to affect Modano.

Modano has become a top penalty killer, though not quite the Selke Trophy candidate the Stars think he is. His anticipation and quick hands help him intercept passes. By going to a straighter stickblade he has improved his face-offs, and became so reliable defensively that he is thrown onto the ice in the closing minutes of a period or game.

Like Steve Yzerman, Modano learned that flirting with 100-point seasons was fun, but to become a champion one has to sacrifice some of the offensive spark to play a better all-around game. Modano has done so.

THE PHYSICAL GAME

Modano suffered an ugly injury when he was hit into the boards by Anaheim's Ruslan Salei early in the season, but thankfully the NHL did not lose this star for long. Modano plays through injuries, and in his own way he is strong and tough — maybe not aggressive and feisty, but all questions about his hockey courage have been quelled forever.

THE INTANGIBLES

Modano is a true leader, moulded by the example of teammate Joe Nieuwendyk. He has finally lived up to his potential; more great hockey can be expected.

PROJECTION

If scoring ever starts inching back upward in the NHL, Modano could return to the 90-point ranks without losing one iota of his outstanding all-around game.

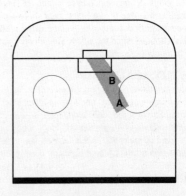

JOE NIEUWENDYK

Yrs. of NHL service: 13
Born: Oshawa, Ont.; Sept. 10, 1966
Position: centre
Height: 6-1
Weight: 195
Uniform no.: 25
Shoots: left

Career statistics:

GP	G	A	TP	PIM
883	440	417	857	479

1996-97 statistics:

GP	G	A	TP	+/-	PIM	PP	SH	GW	GT	S	PCT
66	30	21	51	-5	32	8	0	2	2	173	17.3

1997-98 statistics:

GP	G	A	TP	+/-	PIM	PP	SH	GW	GT	S	PCT
73	39	30	69	+16	30	14	0	11	0	203	19.2

1998-99 statistics:

GP	G	A	TP	+/-	PIM	PP	SH	GW	GT	S	PCT
67	28	27	55	+11	34	8	0	8	1	157	17.8

1999-2000 statistics:

GP	G	A	TP	+/-	PIM	PP	SH	GW	GT	S	PCT
48	15	19	34	-1	26	7	0	2	0	110	13.6

LAST SEASON

Third on team in power-play goals. Missed 21 games with right shoulder separation. Missed 10 games with chest contusion. Missed three games with back spasms.

THE FINESSE GAME

Hands down, Nieuwendyk has the best hands in the NHL for tipping pucks in front of the net. This skill is priceless on power plays. He has fantastic hand-eye coordination; he not only gets his blade on the puck, he acts as if he knows where he's directing it. He also has a long, powerful reach for snaring loose pucks around the crease.

Those same hand skills make Nieuwendyk one of the league's best in the face-off department (he ranked second in the NHL last season).

He is aggressive, tough and aware around the net. He can finish or make a play down low. He has the vision, poise and hand skills to make neat little passes through traffic. He's a better playmaker than finisher, but he never doubts that he will convert his chances. He has good anticipation and uses his long stick to break up passes.

One of his best moves comes on the rush, when Nieuwendyk cuts wide to the right-wing boards then pulls the puck to his forehand for a dangerous shot.

THE PHYSICAL GAME

Nieuwendyk does not initiate, but he will take punishment around the net and stand his ground. He won't be intimidated; he won't scare anyone, either. He would like to carry more weight, but consistent physical problems require him to stay on the lean side.

THE INTANGIBLES

Nieuwendyk needs to play with grinding, energy wingers to do the dirty work he is physically incapable of doing. Teammates need to be alert enough to polish off a pass that can come anytime, from anywhere. His fragility is his major drawback.

PROJECTION

Last season we predicted Nieuwendyk would have difficulty getting through a full season intact. Now that he is 34, that caveat holds truer than ever.

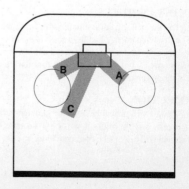

BLAKE SLOAN

Yrs. of NHL service: 1
Born: Park Ridge, IL; July 27, 1975
Position: right wing
Height: 5-10
Weight: 193
Uniform no.: 11
Shoots: right

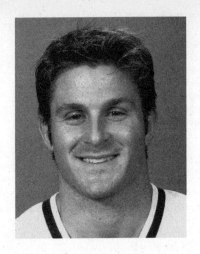

Career statistics:

GP	G	A	TP	PIM
81	4	13	17	60

1998-99 statistics:

GP	G	A	TP	+/-	PIM	PP	SH	GW	GT	S	PCT
14	0	0	0	-1	10	0	0	0	0	7	.0

1999-2000 statistics:

GP	G	A	TP	+/-	PIM	PP	SH	GW	GT	S	PCT
67	4	13	17	+11	50	0	0	1	0	78	5.1

LAST SEASON

First NHL season. Third on team in plus-minus. Missed 15 games due to fractured fibula and sprained ankle.

THE FINESSE GAME

Sloan has benefited from playing alongside veterans like Guy Carbonneau and Mike Keane. He makes safe, smart plays, the small plays that generally go unnoticed.

Sloan played in the minors as a defenseman, but because of his size and his less-than-elite skills will make his way in the NHL as a winger.

Sloan has no hands to speak of, but he finishes his checks and on the forecheck can churn up loose pucks with his effort. He is disciplined and plays within Dallas' strict system, which earned him points with the coaching staff. Sloan skates well.

THE PHYSICAL GAME

Small but solid, Sloan uses every ounce of his muscle and hustle. He was an undrafted player, and lived every minor-leaguer's dream when the Stars sought him out during their championship season to play a small role. As that role expanded, Sloan stepped up his game.

THE INTANGIBLES

Sloan has the makings of a reliable, third-line winger who can provide energy and help shut down an opponent's top line. He has to improve his defensive reads and awareness, but he has a good foundation and should move forward.

PROJECTION

Sloan's goals will probably be of the garbage variety; if he breaks double digits it will be a surprise. His plus-minus will always be commendable.

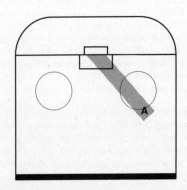

DARRYL SYDOR

Yrs. of NHL service: 8
Born: Edmonton, Alta.; May 13, 1972
Position: right defense
Height: 6-0
Weight: 195
Uniform no.: 5
Shoots: left

Career statistics:

GP	G	A	TP	PIM
623	63	226	289	471

1996-97 statistics:

GP	G	A	TP	+/-	PIM	PP	SH	GW	GT	S	PCT
82	8	40	48	+37	51	2	0	2	0	142	5.6

1997-98 statistics:

GP	G	A	TP	+/-	PIM	PP	SH	GW	GT	S	PCT
79	11	35	46	+17	51	4	1	1	0	166	6.6

1998-99 statistics:

GP	G	A	TP	+/-	PIM	PP	SH	GW	GT	S	PCT
74	14	34	48	-1	50	9	0	2	1	163	8.6

1999-2000 statistics:

GP	G	A	TP	+/-	PIM	PP	SH	GW	GT	S	PCT
74	8	26	34	+6	32	5	0	1	0	132	6.1

LAST SEASON

Missed two games with stiff neck. Missed three games with eye injury. Missed three games with groin injury.

THE FINESSE GAME

Sydor broke into the league in Los Angeles as an offensive defenseman, lost all confidence in that aspect of his game, came to Dallas, put his defensive play in order without even thinking offense, and now has a well-balanced game. Dallas asked him to be more accountable defensively, and he has emerged as a top-four defenseman on one of the league's top defensive teams.

A forward in junior until he was converted to a defenseman (by Dallas coach Ken Hitchcock), Sydor is a very strong skater with balance and agility and excellent lateral movement. He can accelerate well and changes directions easily. Not a dynamic defenseman, but better than average, he can be used up front during injury emergencies.

Sydor's offensive game can kick in at anytime. He has a fine shot from the point and can handle power-play time. He has good sense for jumping into the attack and controls the puck ably when carrying it, though he doesn't always protect it well with his body. He makes nice outlet passes and has good vision of the ice. He can rush with the puck or play dump-and-chase. In his own zone, he has developed into a safe, reliable defender.

THE PHYSICAL GAME

Sydor wants and needs to establish more of a physical presence. He is intense and has to be reined in. He has learned that sometimes going nowhere is better than trying to go everywhere. He competes hard and could still get stronger.

THE INTANGIBLES

Sydor suffered an ankle injury in the deciding game of the Stanley Cup finals that required two months of off-season rehab. It could affect his skating.

PROJECTION

It is unlikely Sydor will be an elite scoring defenseman, but 40 points from a well-rounded blueliner is an excellent season.

SHAUN VAN ALLEN

Yrs. of NHL service: 5
Born: Calgary, Alta.; Aug. 29, 1967
Position: centre
Height: 6-1
Weight: 200
Uniform no.: 22
Shoots: left

Career statistics:

GP	G	A	TP	PIM
511	55	126	181	293

1996-97 statistics:

GP	G	A	TP	+/-	PIM	PP	SH	GW	GT	S	PCT
80	11	14	25	-8	35	1	1	2	0	123	8.9

1997-98 statistics:

GP	G	A	TP	+/-	PIM	PP	SH	GW	GT	S	PCT
80	4	15	19	+4	48	0	0	0	0	104	3.8

1998-99 statistics:

GP	G	A	TP	+/-	PIM	PP	SH	GW	GT	S	PCT
79	6	11	17	+3	30	0	1	0	0	47	12.8

1999-2000 statistics:

GP	G	A	TP	+/-	PIM	PP	SH	GW	GT	S	PCT
75	9	19	28	+20	37	0	2	4	0	75	12.0

PROJECTION

Van Allen will not score more than 25 to 30 points but will provide solid defense.

LAST SEASON

Signed by Dallas from Ottawa as free agent, July 12, 2000. Led Senators in plus-minus. Tied for team lead in shorthanded goals. Tied for second on team in game-winning goals. Missed four games with abdominal strain. Missed one game with knee strain.

THE FINESSE GAME

Van Allen always posted huge numbers in the minors, but like a lot of minor-league stars he cannot transfer his scoring to the majors. The flaw in Van Allen's case is his skating, which is marginally NHL calibre — forcing him to change his strategy to that of a positional, defensive player.

When Van Allen does accomplish things offensively, such as on the power play, it's because of his smarts. He is a very good face-off man. If he controls the draw in the offensive zone he knows how to set up an attack. Van Allen also kills penalties. He seldom plays a poor game because he is aware of his limitations.

THE PHYSICAL GAME

Van Allen's solid, intelligent play is enhanced by his work ethic. He's not a banger but he will get in the way. He knows he would have been a career minor-leaguer but for this chance, and he doesn't forget what he has to do to stay in the NHL.

THE INTANGIBLES

The Stars brough Van Allen aboard as a replacement for Guy Carbonneau on the checking line. He should fit in well with a veteran Stars team in that role.

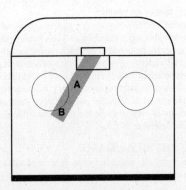

SERGEI ZUBOV

Yrs. of NHL service: 8
Born: Moscow, Russia; July 22, 1970
Position: right defense
Height: 6-1
Weight: 200
Uniform no.: 56
Shoots: right

Career statistics:

GP	G	A	TP	PIM
538	83	332	415	161

1996-97 statistics:

GP	G	A	TP	+/-	PIM	PP	SH	GW	GT	S	PCT
78	13	30	43	+19	24	1	0	3	0	133	9.8

1997-98 statistics:

GP	G	A	TP	+/-	PIM	PP	SH	GW	GT	S	PCT
73	10	47	57	+16	16	5	1	2	1	148	6.8

1998-99 statistics:

GP	G	A	TP	+/-	PIM	PP	SH	GW	GT	S	PCT
81	10	41	51	+9	20	5	0	3	0	155	6.5

1999-2000 statistics:

GP	G	A	TP	+/-	PIM	PP	SH	GW	GT	S	PCT
77	9	33	42	-2	18	3	1	3	0	179	5.0

LAST SEASON

Led team defensemen in points for third consecutive season. Third on team in assists and points. Missed five games with knee injury.

THE FINESSE GAME

Overheard on the Dallas bench, any given night: "Shoot, Zubie. Shoot! *Shoot!*" The overly patient Zubov is so close to being an elite NHL "offenseman," except for his tendency to hold the puck and look for a pass when the shot is his.

Zubov has some world-class skills. He skates with with good balance and generates power from his leg drive. He is agile in his stops and starts, even backwards. He also has a good slap shot and one-times the puck with accuracy — when he deigns to use it. He masks his intentions well, faking a shot and finding the open man with a slick pass. He's not afraid to come in deep, either. Zubov will occasionally frustrate his teammates when he slows things down with the puck on a rush or breakout while the rest of the team has already taken off like racehorses.

Zubov has strong lateral acceleration, but he is also educated enough to keep his skating stride for stride with the wing trying to beat him to the outside. So many other defensemen speed up a couple of strides then try to slow their men with stick-checks. Zubov will use his reach, superior body positioning or his agility to force the play and compel the puck carrier to make a decision. However, he doesn't always search out the right man or, when he does, he doesn't always eliminate the right man. A team has to live with that because Zubov's offensive upside is huge.

THE PHYSICAL GAME

Zubov is not physical, but he is solidly built and will take a hit to make a play. He can give a team a lot of minutes (he averaged 28:50 of ice time per game last season, second only to St. Louis' Chris Pronger) and not wear down physically.

His boyhood idol was Viacheslav Fetisov, and that role model should give you some idea of Zubov's style. He gets his body in the way with his great skating, then strips the puck when the attacker finds no path to the net. He doesn't initiate much but doesn't mind getting hit to make a play.

THE INTANGIBLES

Mentally, Zubov will still lose his focus and is capable of the most astounding giveaways. He can often atone with a terrific offensive play, but his lapses keep him from being rated among the league's best.

PROJECTION

As the Stars' top offensive defenseman, Zubov should score between 50 to 60 points this season.

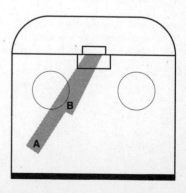

DETROIT
RED WINGS

Players' Statistics 1999-2000

POS.	NO.	PLAYER	GP	G	A	PTS	+/-	PIM	PP	SH	GW	GT	S	PCT
C	19	STEVE YZERMAN	78	35	44	79	28	34	15	2	6	1	234	15.0
L	14	BRENDAN SHANAHAN	78	41	37	78	24	105	13	1	9	1	283	14.5
D	5	NICKLAS LIDSTROM	81	20	53	73	19	18	9	4	3		218	9.2
C	91	SERGEI FEDOROV	68	27	35	62	8	22	4	4	7		263	10.3
R	15	PAT VERBEEK	68	22	26	48	22	95	7		5	1	138	15.9
C	8	IGOR LARIONOV	79	9	38	47	13	28	3		4		69	13.0
R	20	MARTIN LAPOINTE	82	16	25	41	17	121	1	1	2	1	127	12.6
D	28	STEVE DUCHESNE	79	10	31	41	12	42	1		1		154	6.5
D	55	LARRY MURPHY	81	10	30	40	4	45	7				146	6.8
L	13	VYACHESLAV KOZLOV	72	18	18	36	11	28	4		3		165	10.9
L	96	TOMAS HOLMSTROM	72	13	22	35	4	43	4		1		71	18.3
D	24	CHRIS CHELIOS	81	3	31	34	48	103					135	2.2
R	17	DOUG BROWN	51	10	8	18	8	12	1				67	14.9
R	11	MATHIEU DANDENAULT	81	6	12	18	-12	20					98	6.1
C	39	STACY ROEST	49	7	9	16	-1	12	1		1		56	12.5
L	18	KIRK MALTBY	41	6	8	14	1	24		2	1		71	8.5
R	25	DARREN MCCARTY	24	6	6	12	1	48			1		40	15.0
C	33	KRIS DRAPER	51	5	7	12	3	28			3		76	6.6
D	23	TODD GILL	54	3	6	9	-8	45			2		61	4.9
C	22	*YURI BUTSAYEV	57	5	3	8	-6	12					46	10.9
D	2	*JIRI FISCHER	52		8	8	1	45					41	
C	41	BRENT GILCHRIST	24	4	2	6	1	24					33	12.1
C	21	*DARRYL LAPLANTE	30		6	6	-2	10					19	
D	27	AARON WARD	36	1	3	4	-4	24					25	4.0
D	44	YAN GOLUBOVSKY	21	1	2	3	3	8					7	14.3
R	37	MARC RODGERS	21	1	1	2	-3	10					17	5.9
G	31	KEN WREGGET	29		1	1	0							
G	30	CHRIS OSGOOD	53		1	1	0	18						
D	3	*JESSE WALLIN	1				-2							
R	36	*B.J. YOUNG	1				0						1	
G	34	MANNY LEGACE	4				0							

GP = games played; G = goals; A = assists; PTS = points; +/- = goals-for minus goals-against while player is on ice; PIM = penalties in minutes; PP = power-play goals; SH = shorthanded goals; GW = game-winning goals; GT = game-tying goals; S = no. of shots; PCT = percentage of goals to shots; * = rookie

CHRIS CHELIOS

Yrs. of NHL service: 16
Born: Chicago, Ill.; Jan. 25, 1962
Position: right defense
Height: 6-1
Weight: 186
Uniform no.: 24
Shoots: right

Career statistics:

GP	G	A	TP	PIM
1157	168	664	832	2385

1996-97 statistics:

GP	G	A	TP	+/-	PIM	PP	SH	GW	GT	S	PCT
72	10	38	48	+16	112	2	0	2	0	194	5.2

1997-98 statistics:

GP	G	A	TP	+/-	PIM	PP	SH	GW	GT	S	PCT
81	3	39	42	-7	151	1	0	0	0	205	1.5

1998-99 statistics:

GP	G	A	TP	+/-	PIM	PP	SH	GW	GT	S	PCT
75	9	27	36	+1	93	3	1	1	1	187	4.8

1999-2000 statistics:

GP	G	A	TP	+/-	PIM	PP	SH	GW	GT	S	PCT
81	3	31	34	+48	103	0	0	0	0	135	2.2

LAST SEASON

Led team and second in NHL in plus-minus. Third on team in penalty minutes. Missed one game due to coach's decision.

THE FINESSE GAME

Whatever the team needs, Chelios will bleed to give. He can become a top offensive defenseman, pinching boldly at every opportunity. Or he can create offense off the rush, make a play through the neutral zone or quarterback the power play from the point. He has a good, low, hard slap shot. He is not afraid to skate in deep, where he can handle the puck well and use a snap shot or wrist shot with a quick release.

If defense is needed, Chelios will rule in his own zone. He is extremely confident and poised with the puck and doesn't overhandle it, though he is slowing down a step. He wants to get the puck away from his net by the most expedient means possible. He is aggressive in forcing the puck carrier to make a decision by stepping up. He also steps up in the neutral zone to break up plays with his stick.

Chelios is an instinctive player. When he is on his game, he reacts and makes plays few other defensemen can. When he struggles, which is seldom, he is back on his heels. He tries to do other people's jobs and becomes undisciplined.

Chelios has excellent anticipation and is a strong penalty killer. He's a mobile, smooth skater with good lateral movement. He is seldom beaten one-on-one, and he's even tough facing a two-on-one. In his mind, he can do anything. He usually does.

THE PHYSICAL GAME

Chelios has an absurdly high pain threshold, often playing despite injuries that would have a baseball player on the DL for a lifetime. He doesn't seem to tire, no matter how much ice time he gets, and he routinely plays 25 minutes a night and handles four-minute shifts. He is not that big but plays like an enormous defenseman. He is mean, tough and physical, strong and solid on his skates, and fearless.

THE INTANGIBLES

Chelios is no longer a top-pair defenseman at age 38. He needs to cut down his minutes (despite his ability to do so); he makes a fine number three with special teams duty added.

PROJECTION

Chelios concentrates more on defense and leaves the scoring to the fancier players, but he can still chip in with 30 points.

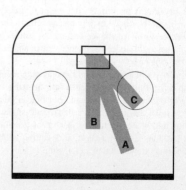

SERGEI FEDOROV

Yrs. of NHL service: 10
Born: Pskov, Russia; Dec. 13, 1969
Position: centre
Height: 6-1
Weight: 200
Uniform no.: 91
Shoots: left

Career statistics:

GP	G	A	TP	PIM
675	301	433	734	459

1996-97 statistics:

GP	G	A	TP	+/-	PIM	PP	SH	GW	GT	S	PCT
74	30	33	63	+29	30	9	2	4	0	273	11.0

1997-98 statistics:

GP	G	A	TP	+/-	PIM	PP	SH	GW	GT	S	PCT
21	6	11	17	+10	25	2	0	2	0	68	8.8

1998-99 statistics:

GP	G	A	TP	+/-	PIM	PP	SH	GW	GT	S	PCT
77	26	37	63	+9	66	6	2	3	0	224	11.6

1999-2000 statistics:

GP	G	A	TP	+/-	PIM	PP	SH	GW	GT	S	PCT
68	27	35	62	+8	22	4	4	7	0	263	10.3

LAST SEASON

Tied for team lead and for third in NHL in short-handed goals. Second on team in game-winning goals and shots. Third on team in goals. Missed six games with head injury. Missed five games with wrist injury. Missed three games with neck injury.

THE FINESSE GAME

Versatility is a Fedorov hallmark. He has played left wing, centre and even defense, and he fuels a power play and kills penalties. A tremendous package of offensive and defensive skills, he can go from checking his opponent's top centre to powering the power play from shift to shift. And his skating is nothing short of phenomenal; he can handle the puck while dazzling everyone with his blades.

Fedorov likes to gear up from his own defensive zone, using his acceleration and balance to drive wide to his right, carrying the puck on his backhand and protecting it with his body. If the defenseman lets up at all, Fedorov is by him, pulling the puck quickly to his forehand. Nor is he by any means selfish. He has 360-degree vision of the ice and makes solid, confident passes right under opponents' sticks and smack onto the tape of his teammates'.

Fedorov will swing behind the opposing net from left to right, fooling the defense into thinking he is going to continue to curl around, but he can quickly reverse with the puck on his backhand, shake his shadow and wheel around for a shot or goalmouth pass. He does it all in a flash, and skating with the puck doesn't slow him down one whit.

THE PHYSICAL GAME

When you are as gifted as Fedorov, opponents will do all they can to hit you and hurt you; when your medical history includes a concussion and a separated shoulder from such contact, you may become gun-shy. Nonetheless, although the wiry Fedorov is reluctant to absorb big hits or deliver any, he will leave the relative safety of open ice and head to the trenches when he has to.

Much of his power is generated from his strong skating. For the most part, his defense is dominated by his reads, anticipation and quickness in knocking down passes and breaking up plays. He is not much of a body checker, and he gets most of his penalties from stick and restraining fouls.

THE INTANGIBLES

Fedorov was one of the Red Wings' best performers in the postseason and the trade rumours quieted down. Still, Detroit has depleted its system a bit and he could still be trade bait.

PROJECTION

Fedorov had to cope with nagging injuries. If healthy, he's worth 70 to 80 points.

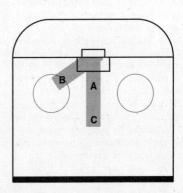

JIRI FISCHER

Yrs. of NHL service: 1
Born: Horovice, Czech.; July 31, 1980
Position: left defense
Height: 6-5
Weight: 210
Uniform no.: 2
Shoots: left

Career statistics:

GP	G	A	TP	PIM
52	0	8	8	45

1999-2000 statistics:

GP	G	A	TP	+/-	PIM	PP	SH	GW	GT	S	PCT
52	0	8	8	+1	45	0	0	0	0	41	0.0

LAST SEASON

First NHL season. Appeared in seven games with Cincinnati (AHL), scoring 0-2 — 2.

THE FINESSE GAME

For such a tall skater, Fischer doesn't look a bit gangly; he is strong on his skates and has a long stride. It doesn't take him too long to get into stride, either. He is well coordinated and agile in his turns.

Fischer has a low panic point and is confident with the puck; he is a good passer with soft hands for giving or receiving. He has some faith in his ability to skate the puck out and is willing to get involved in the rush, though he can be expected to focus on the defensive part of the game as he continues to break in.

Fischer will get some second-unit power play and penalty-killing stints. His reach makes him a natural shorthanded threat, since he takes up a lot of ice. He has a decent point shot , though his release isn't quick. One-on-one he is tough to best, because a skater has to go a long way to get around him.

THE PHYSICAL GAME

Fischer is very tall but not heavy. He needs to develop more muscle for the battles along the wall and in front of the net. He can use his long reach to wrap up and neutralize an attacker. He has a latent mean streak; opponents will quickly learn not to take liberties with him.

THE INTANGIBLES

Fischer was only 19 last year, still struggling with the pro game and the lifestyle change. He will feel more acclimated in this year's training camp and will be given every chance to become a regular. Detroit never rushes its prospects, but they are eager for this young defenseman to arrive.

PROJECTION

Fischer's not likely to make a big offensive impact.

TOMAS HOLMSTROM

Yrs. of NHL service: 4
Born: Pitea, Sweden; Jan 23, 1973
Position: left wing
Height: 6-0
Weight: 210
Uniform no.: 96
Shoots: left

Career statistics:

GP	G	A	TP	PIM
258	37	63	100	177

1996-97 statistics:

GP	G	A	TP	+/-	PIM	PP	SH	GW	GT	S	PCT
47	6	3	9	-10	33	3	0	0	0	53	11.3

1997-98 statistics:

GP	G	A	TP	+/-	PIM	PP	SH	GW	GT	S	PCT
66	7	14	21	+21	32	1	0	2	0	91	7.7

1998-99 statistics:

GP	G	A	TP	+/-	PIM	PP	SH	GW	GT	S	PCT
82	13	21	34	-11	69	5	0	4	0	100	13.0

1999-2000 statistics:

GP	G	A	TP	+/-	PIM	PP	SH	GW	GT	S	PCT
72	13	22	35	+4	43	4	0	1	0	71	18.3

LAST SEASON

Missed five games with sprained knee. Missed one game with wrist injury.

THE FINESSE GAME

Holmstrom has a toothless grin and a gutsy game. He plays in the hard five feet outside the crease, sometimes inside it, and drives goalies wild. He is Sweden's answer to Dino Ciccarelli.

With the desire and work ethic of every low draft pick to ever make it to the NHL (257th in 1994), Holmstrom is a rough-cut stone. That makes him even more important, because he provides an element of grit along the wall and in front of the net.

This Swede has style, too, and can score in the clutch. He has an excellent close-range shot; it was just a matter of time before he learned to use it. He is also a smart passer.

The change in the man-in-the-crease rule is a boon to Holmstrom's game, since that is the high-toll area where he makes his living. He is a power-play mainstay because of his ability to screen and distract defensemen.

THE PHYSICAL GAME

Stocky and strong on his skates, Holmstrom can take a bloody pounding and get right back in the trenches to position himself for a pass. What is most impressive is how he is able to provoke the attacks without getting penalized himself. He rarely takes a bad penalty. The fact that he bounces back with a jack-o'-lantern smile is especially infuriating to opponents.

THE INTANGIBLES

Holmstrom is always better in the playoffs (three goals in nine games) than in the regular season. He may suffer most from the loss of Igor Larionov to free agency.

PROJECTION

Holmstrom disappointed in the regular season. He should be a 20-goal scorer. But he comes alive in April and May.

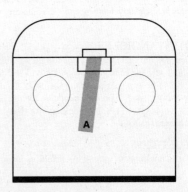

VYACHESLAV KOZLOV

Yrs. of NHL service: 7
Born: Voskresensk, Russia; May 3, 1972
Position: centre/left wing
Height: 5-10
Weight: 180
Uniform no.: 13
Shoots: left

Career statistics:

GP	G	A	TP	PIM
535	182	195	377	346

1996-97 statistics:

GP	G	A	TP	+/-	PIM	PP	SH	GW	GT	S	PCT
75	23	22	45	+21	46	3	0	6	0	211	10.9

1997-98 statistics:

GP	G	A	TP	+/-	PIM	PP	SH	GW	GT	S	PCT
80	25	27	52	+14	46	6	0	1	0	221	11.3

1998-99 statistics:

GP	G	A	TP	+/-	PIM	PP	SH	GW	GT	S	PCT
79	29	29	58	+10	45	6	1	4	2	209	13.9

1999-2000 statistics:

GP	G	A	TP	+/-	PIM	PP	SH	GW	GT	S	PCT
72	18	18	36	+11	28	4	0	3	0	165	10.9

LAST SEASON

Missed seven games with ankle injuries. Missed three games with concussion.

THE FINESSE GAME

Kozlov has a very quick getaway step that allows him to jump into holes and openings. His darting style makes it impossible for defenders to chase him and easy for them to lose him.

Offensively, he can play as freewheeling as the team wants. He seems to materialize at the right place at the right time, much like Brett Hull in his prime. He can split the defense if it plays him too close, or drive the defense back with his speed and use the open ice to find a teammate. He has great control of the puck at high speed and plays an excellent transition game. Unlike many Russian players, he does not have to be coaxed into shooting, and he has a quick release — generally to the top corners of the net.

That said, there are also times when Kozlov can be frustrating to watch. He will hold the puck past the point when he either should make a play with it or make a pass. He then either loses control of it or takes himself to lesser ice. The reasonable speculation is that by holding the puck he is buying time for teammates to break into open ice; other times, he simply appears incapable of making a decision about what to do or he is trying to make the perfect play instead of a good enough play more quickly.

THE PHYSICAL GAME

Just as a defender comes to hit him, Kozlov gets rid of the puck. Usually it goes to a teammate, sometimes it simply goes up for grabs. It would be easy to infer

Kozlov is like a quarterback who gets rid of the ball rather than getting sacked. More likely, he's taking the hit to create space for someone else by allowing the defender to take himself — and Kozlov — out of the play. Kozlov is not tall but he is solidly built. He's got a little mean streak.

THE INTANGIBLES

Kozlov underproduced again, and trade rumours inevitably followed. He is a restricted free agent and the Red Wings will probably move him during the off-season if his price is too high. He was a healthy scratch for one game in the playoffs, never a good sign.

PROJECTION

Kozlov had some nagging injuries — he was out twice with the ankle problems — and failed to achieve the 25 to 30 goals that should be the norm for him. If healthy, he should be in the 25-goal class again.

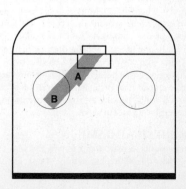

MARTIN LAPOINTE

Yrs. of NHL service: 7
Born: Ville Ste. Pierre, Que.; Sept. 12, 1973
Position: right wing
Height: 5-11
Weight: 200
Uniform no.: 20
Shoots: right

Career statistics:

GP	G	A	TP	PIM
470	81	92	173	761

1996-97 statistics:

GP	G	A	TP	+/-	PIM	PP	SH	GW	GT	S	PCT
78	16	17	33	-14	167	5	1	1	0	149	10.7

1997-98 statistics:

GP	G	A	TP	+/-	PIM	PP	SH	GW	GT	S	PCT
79	15	19	34	0	106	4	0	3	2	154	9.7

1998-99 statistics:

GP	G	A	TP	+/-	PIM	PP	SH	GW	GT	S	PCT
77	16	13	29	+7	141	7	1	4	0	153	10.5

1999-2000 statistics:

GP	G	A	TP	+/-	PIM	PP	SH	GW	GT	S	PCT
82	16	25	41	+17	121	1	1	2	1	127	12.6

LAST SEASON

Led team in penalty minutes for second consecutive season. Only Red Wing to appear in all 82 games.

THE FINESSE GAME

The reason Lapointe's name pops up so often in trade rumours is that most teams covet a big strong forward with an edge. Everything about Lapointe's game stems more from what is between his ribs than what is between his ears. It all comes from the heart: the competitiveness, the drive that sends him to the net in the straightest line possible. If a defenseman or opposing forward — or goalie — happens to get knocked down in the process, that's their problem.

Lapointe's goals and assists result more from his acceleration than his speed. He doesn't have breakaway speed, but his eagerness, his intensity and his willingness to compete make him seem faster than he actually is. He doesn't have a great shot, though he has a nice, quick release and uses a wrist or snap shot as opposed to a big windup. Most of his goals are scored in the hard areas around the crease. He screens goalies, tips shots and works for loose pucks.

Equally important, Lapointe does not let a stick-check slow him down. He'll pull a checker along like a boat tugging a water-skier. He'll steam into the play to create an odd-man rush, and he creates lots of options with a nice passing touch that prevents goalies from overplaying him to shoot.

THE PHYSICAL GAME

Lapointe wants to play, wants to win and won't take an easy way out, which means a lot of opponents end up flat on the ice. He hits them all, big or small, and hits hard. He is low but wide, with a broad upper body and solid centre of gravity that powers his physical game. He can be a menace in the corners and a force in front of the net.

THE INTANGIBLES

Lapointe drives opponents crazy, then backs up his activity with big goals. He has become a clutch playoff performer in many ways. There is a snarl in Lapointe's game, however, a fire that always seems close to the fuse. He takes a good share of over-emotional penalties. He wakes things up, and never lets opponents take the easy way out. He never lets himself take the easy way, either. He came to the team as a big-time scorer in the Quebec League and dedicated himself to learning how to check. His approach is summarized in his statement, "I'd rather change my role and have the team win instead of being a one-man show."

PROJECTION

Lapointe's regular-season goal totals are likely to stay around 15 to 20 goals. His value goes way up in the postseason.

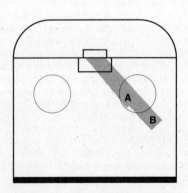

NICKLAS LIDSTROM

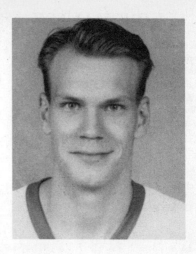

Yrs. of NHL service: 9
Born: Vasteras, Sweden; Apr. 28, 1970
Position: left defense
Height: 6-2
Weight: 185
Uniform no.: 5
Shoots: left

Career statistics:

GP	G	A	TP	PIM
693	121	375	496	182

1996-97 statistics:

GP	G	A	TP	+/-	PIM	PP	SH	GW	GT	S	PCT
79	15	42	57	+11	30	8	0	1	0	214	7.0

1997-98 statistics:

GP	G	A	TP	+/-	PIM	PP	SH	GW	GT	S	PCT
80	17	42	59	+22	18	7	1	1	1	205	8.3

1998-99 statistics:

GP	G	A	TP	+/-	PIM	PP	SH	GW	GT	S	PCT
81	14	43	57	+14	14	6	2	3	0	205	6.8

1999-2000 statistics:

GP	G	A	TP	+/-	PIM	PP	SH	GW	GT	S	PCT
81	20	53	73	+19	18	9	4	3	0	218	9.2

LAST SEASON

Finalist for 2000 Norris and Lady Byng Trophies. Named to 2000 NHL First All-Star Team. Led team defensemen in points for second consecutive season. Led NHL defensemen and third on team in points. Led team and tied for fourth in NHL in assists. Tied for team lead and tied for third in NHL in shorthanded goals. Third on team in power-play goals. Missed one game due to coach's decision.

THE FINESSE GAME

Lidstrom is an excellent skater with good vision of the ice. He prefers to look for the breakout pass, rather than carry the puck, and he has a superb point shot that stays low and accurate. His work at the point on the power play has improved significantly. His rink management is solid, his decision-making is better and his passing — especially to set up one-timers — is tape-to-tape. Lidstrom is also confident about moving down low to poach for goals.

Defensively, he uses exceptional anticipation to position himself perfectly, and has improved his reads. He is almost impossible to beat one-on-one, and sometimes even two-on-one, in open ice. He neatly breaks up passes with a quick stick. He kills penalties and willingly blocks shots. He also plays either side — an underrated asset — and is dependable in the closing minutes of a tight period or game.

Lidstrom has added enough muscle to become a wiry, strong athlete who can handle an astounding amount of quality ice time. He wastes little energy — he averaged 28 minutes of ice time per game last season — and his innate talent maximizes his stamina.

THE PHYSICAL GAME

Lidstrom truly perseveres. He does not take the body much and depends on his wits more than hard hits. But on the other side of the puck, he has little fear of contact and will accept a hit to make a play. It is a tribute to his style that he can play with quiet toughness and still be a Lady Byng candidate. This is how the game is meant to be played.

Although not a physical player, Lidstrom plays smart. With body positioning and stick positioning, he leaves opposing puck carriers no place to go and no alternative to giving up the puck — usually to him. He finds a way to tie up the opponent's stick. He has stepped up his physical play. He's not a punishing hitter, but puck carriers are wary of him because he makes them pay a price. He won't be intimidated; many teams have tried and failed with that tactic.

THE INTANGIBLES

Lidstrom has matured into the best two-way defenseman in the NHL. Because he is not as physical as Chris Pronger, Lidstrom lost out on the Norris last season (St. Louis' phenomenal season also helped Pronger's cause).

PROJECTION

At age 30, Lidstrom had his best season — and one of the best by any NHL defenseman — last year. He is a safe bet for 60 points.

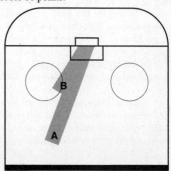

KIRK MALTBY

Yrs. of NHL service: 7
Born: Guelph, Ont.; Dec. 22, 1972
Position: right wing
Height: 6-0
Weight: 180
Uniform no.: 18
Shoots: right

Career statistics:

GP	G	A	TP	PIM
395	53	45	98	412

1996-97 statistics:

GP	G	A	TP	+/-	PIM	PP	SH	GW	GT	S	PCT
66	3	5	8	+3	75	0	0	0	0	62	4.8

1997-98 statistics:

GP	G	A	TP	+/-	PIM	PP	SH	GW	GT	S	PCT
65	14	9	23	+11	89	2	1	3	0	106	13.2

1998-99 statistics:

GP	G	A	TP	+/-	PIM	PP	SH	GW	GT	S	PCT
53	8	6	14	-6	34	0	1	2	0	76	10.5

1999-2000 statistics:

GP	G	A	TP	+/-	PIM	PP	SH	GW	GT	S	PCT
41	6	8	14	+1	24	0	2	1	0	71	8.5

LAST SEASON
Missed 41 games with hernia surgery.

THE FINESSE GAME
Maltby's skating helps keep him in position defensively; he seldom is caught up-ice. He plays well without the puck, understands the game and is coachable. He kills penalties effectively and blocks shots.

Maltby isn't overly creative, but he works tirelessly along the boards and in the corners to keep the puck alive. He has an average wrist and snap shot, yet has enough moves to be a threat when his team in shorthanded. Most of his goals are of the opportunistic type; he jumps on loose pucks and creates turnovers with his forechecking.

Astute hockey sense stamps Maltby as a two-way winger. He plays a key role for the Red Wings on the Grind Line as a fourth-line energy guy.

THE PHYSICAL GAME
There are few nights when you don't notice that Maltby is on the ice. He has good speed and he just loves to flatten people with clean, hard hits. He is not very big, but he is solid and won't back down from a challenge. He draws more than his fair share of penalties, either by forcing opponents to pull him down or by aggravating them enough that they take a whack at him.

Maltby's power emanates from his lower-body drive. He is strong and balanced and will punish with his hits. His work ethic and conditioning are strong. He wants to win the races to loose pucks.

THE INTANGIBLES
Maltby's surgery obviously derailed his season, and he was a healthy scratch for one playoff game. He's still a valued role player for the Red Wings.

PROJECTION
A healthy Maltby will do the job defensively, add energy and produce 12 to 15 goals.

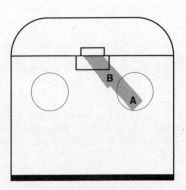

DARREN MCCARTY

Yrs. of NHL service: 7
Born: Burnaby, B.C.; April, 1972
Position: right wing
Height: 6-1
Weight: 210
Uniform no.: 25
Shoots: right

Career statistics:

GP	G	A	TP	PIM
393	83	123	206	866

1996-97 statistics:

GP	G	A	TP	+/-	PIM	PP	SH	GW	GT	S	PCT
68	19	30	49	+14	126	5	0	6	1	171	11.1

1997-98 statistics:

GP	G	A	TP	+/-	PIM	PP	SH	GW	GT	S	PCT
71	15	22	37	0	157	5	1	2	0	166	9.0

1998-99 statistics:

GP	G	A	TP	+/-	PIM	PP	SH	GW	GT	S	PCT
69	14	26	40	+10	108	6	0	1	1	140	10.0

1999-2000 statistics:

GP	G	A	TP	+/-	PIM	PP	SH	GW	GT	S	PCT
24	6	6	12	+1	48	0	0	1	0	40	15.0

LAST SEASON

Missed 39 games with groin injury. Missed 19 games with leg injury.

THE FINESSE GAME

McCarty has an awkward stride and his first few steps are rather slow, but he is strong on his skates and when he reaches top speed his acceleration is serviceable. He has decent finishing skills to go with a physical aspect. His balance is underrated. He absorbs (or delivers) hard hits from some of the biggest skaters in the league, but hardly ever staggers.

McCarty has the ability to execute the consummate pro's perfecta: the poise to follow a great play with a good one. He can deke a defender with an inside-outside move, then go backhand-forehand to finish the play with a huge goal — providing a huge boost to his team while utterly deflating the opposition.

McCarty has decent hands and will score the majority of his goals in tight. He is not terribly creative but stays with a basic power game and is solid on the forecheck. Six of his 14 goals came on the power play.

THE PHYSICAL GAME

Mean, big, strong, tough and fearless. All the ingedients are there, along with the desire to throw his body at any player or puck he can reach. If a game is off to a quiet start, look for McCarty to wake everyone up. He forechecks and backchecks fiercely, and tries to go through players, not just to them.

McCarty is not a great fighter but he is willing. He's intelligent in picking his spots. His teammates know he is always there to back them up, which is why McCarty gets to play with some of Detroit's skilled players when he's not on the Grind Line.

THE INTANGIBLES

With injuries and the death of his father, McCarty suffered through an extremely difficult season. He played with huge heart in the playoffs and was one of the club's best forwards. He is a true leader. The Red Wings are a smaller team in many ways when he is out of the lineup.

PROJECTION

If McCarty can get through a healthy season, he should score 20 goals and 50 points.

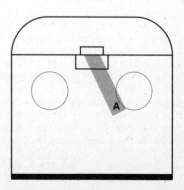

LARRY MURPHY

Yrs. of NHL service: 20
Born: Scarborough, Ont.; Mar. 8, 1961
Position: right defense
Height: 6-2
Weight: 210
Uniform no.: 55
Shoots: right

Career statistics:

GP	G	A	TP	PIM
1558	285	904	1195	1072

1996-97 statistics:

GP	G	A	TP	+/-	PIM	PP	SH	GW	GT	S	PCT
81	9	36	45	+3	20	5	0	1	1	158	5.7

1997-98 statistics:

GP	G	A	TP	+/-	PIM	PP	SH	GW	GT	S	PCT
82	11	41	52	+35	37	2	1	2	0	129	8.5

1998-99 statistics:

GP	G	A	TP	+/-	PIM	PP	SH	GW	GT	S	PCT
80	10	42	52	+21	42	5	1	2	0	168	6.0

1999-2000 statistics:

GP	G	A	TP	+/-	PIM	PP	SH	GW	GT	S	PCT
81	10	30	40	+4	45	7	0	0	0	146	6.8

LAST SEASON
Missed one game due to coach's decision.

THE FINESSE GAME
Murphy has never been a great skater. He actually has a rather choppy stride, but he has some agility and more quickness than speed. Partnering with Nicklas Lidstrom has helped hide that flaw.

He can read the ice, and will either rush the puck out of his zone under pressure or make the nice first pass that gives his team the jump on opponents. When he snares the puck, his first impulse is to make a quick pass then sprint up-ice and join the breakout.

Murphy is smart and poised, the perfect guy to collect the puck behind his goal line and start the rush up-ice on the power play. He has a fairly high panic point with the puck, and often will hold it until the last moment before passing.

Although he has been known to give away the puck, Murphy generally will not force bad passes up the middle and almost always picks the safest passing option. His pinches are well-timed, and he has the reach to prevent a lot of pucks from getting by him at the point. He has the good sense, and balance, to drop to one knee and get his body in front of any clearing attempts he is trying to block at the point, thus fewer pucks get past him.

Murphy's shot selection is intelligent. He loves to shoot but he won't fire blindly. He uses a low wrist shot rather than a big slap to keep the puck on net. He reads plays well and seldom seems to be floundering on the ice.

THE PHYSICAL GAME
Murphy does not like to play a physical game. He will bump his man in front but doesn't make strong take-outs. He prefers to position his body and force the shooter to make a play while he himself goes for the puck or stick. In his quiet way, Murphy is a tough customer.

THE INTANGIBLES
Murphy has a lot of hockey mileage on him. He has played more games than any other defenseman in NHL history.

PROJECTION
Murphy might be the quietest 1,000-point scorer in NHL annals. Although it appears he is just about done, Detroit opted to re-sign him. He could still score 25 to 30 points.

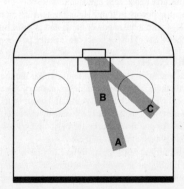

CHRIS OSGOOD

Yrs. of NHL service: 7
Born: Peace River, Alta.; Nov. 26, 1972
Position: goaltender
Height: 5-10
Weight: 175
Uniform no.: 30
Catches: left

Career statistics:

GP	MIN	GA	SO	GAA	A	PIM
337	19641	773	29	2.36	8	71

1996-97 statistics:

GP	MIN	GAA	W	L	T	SO	GA	S	SAPCT	PIM
47	2769	2.30	23	13	9	6	106	1175	.910	6

1997-98 statistics:

GP	MIN	GAA	W	L	T	SO	GA	S	SAPCT	PIM
64	3807	2.21	33	20	11	6	140	1605	.913	31

1998-99 statistics:

GP	MIN	GAA	W	L	T	SO	GA	S	SAPCT	PIM
63	3691	2.42	34	25	4	3	149	1654	.910	8

1999-2000 statistics:

GP	MIN	GAA	W	L	T	SO	GA	S	SAPCT	PIM
53	3148	2.40	30	14	8	6	126	1349	.907	18

LAST SEASON

Tied for second among NHL goalies in shutouts. Third among NHL goalies in penalty minutes. Missed 15 games with hand injury.

THE PHYSICAL GAME

Osgood is a small goalie, but by challenging shooters he makes himself look bigger in the net. He plays his angles well and has quick feet. His reflexes are excellent for close shots and he stays on his skates and doesn't flop. He has a superb glove — he's tough to beat high. His problems arise when he loses his concentration and his angles, and fails to square himself to the shooter.

He controls his rebounds well and doesn't have to scramble for too many second or third shots. His lateral movement is very good.

Osgood can handle the puck; in fact, he has scored a goal. He also uses his stick effectively to poke pucks off attackers' sticks around the net. He's no Martin Brodeur, however, and he tends to get overambitious.

THE MENTAL GAME

Osgood has been allowed to settle into his role as a number one goalie, which made him more comfortable last season. He doesn't get a lot of credit, but he doesn't lose games for his team.

THE INTANGIBLES

Osgood has played on two Cup winners but there are still a lot of other goalies we'd pick ahead of him if we needed to win a big one. He did have a terrific playoffs (1.97 GAA); Detroit's ouster was not his fault. Osgood may face some higher percentage shots if the

Red Wings break in some younger defensemen, as expected, this season.

PROJECTION

By all means, make him a high pool pick, since he's good for 30 wins.

BRENDAN SHANAHAN

Yrs. of NHL service: 13
Born: Mimico, Ont.; Jan. 23, 1969
Position: left wing
Height: 6-3
Weight: 218
Uniform no.: 14
Shoots: right

Career statistics:

GP	G	A	TP	PIM
947	435	444	879	1854

1996-97 statistics:

GP	G	A	TP	+/-	PIM	PP	SH	GW	GT	S	PCT
81	47	41	88	+32	131	20	3	7	2	336	14.0

1997-98 statistics:

GP	G	A	TP	+/-	PIM	PP	SH	GW	GT	S	PCT
75	28	29	57	+6	154	15	1	9	1	266	10.5

1998-99 statistics:

GP	G	A	TP	+/-	PIM	PP	SH	GW	GT	S	PCT
81	31	27	58	+2	123	5	0	5	0	288	10.8

1999-2000 statistics:

GP	G	A	TP	+/-	PIM	PP	SH	GW	GT	S	PCT
78	41	37	78	+24	105	13	1	9	1	283	14.5

LAST SEASON

Named to NHL First All-Star Team. Led team in game-winning goals for fourth consecutive season. Tied for third in NHL in game-winning goals. Led team and sixth in NHL in goals. Second on team and tied for fourth in NHL in power-play goals. Led team in shots. Second on team in points and penalty minutes. Third on team in shooting percentage.

THE FINESSE GAME

Skating is one of Shanahan's few flaws. He isn't quick, isn't agile, and he often looks awkward with the puck. Most of the time he's better off making the hit that frees the puck, then passing it to a teammate and breaking to a spot, because he can score from anywhere.

A wonderful package of grit, skills and smarts. On the power play, he is one of the best at staying just off the crease, waiting for a shot to come from the point, then timing his arrival at the front of the net for the moving screen, the tip or the rebound. He can get a lot on his shot even when the puck is near his feet, because of a short backswing and strong wrists.

Shanahan has wonderfully soft hands for nifty goalmouth passes, and he has a hard, accurate shot with a quick release, which he never tires of using. He loves the one-time shot and is a good enough athlete to bury it — even if the pass he receives isn't perfect.

THE PHYSICAL GAME

The dilemma for rival teams: If you play Shanahan aggressively, it brings out the best in him. If you lay off and give him room, he will kill you with his skills. Shanahan spent his formative NHL years establishing his reputation by dropping his gloves with anybody who challenged him, but he has gotten smarter without losing his tough edge.

He takes or makes a hit to create a play. He's willing to eat glass to make a pass, but would rather strike the first blow. He does that by using his strength to fight through checks to get himself in position to score. He sees the puck, goes and gets it and puts it towards the front of the net.

THE INTANGIBLES

Despite clashes with coach Scotty Bowman over the years, Shanahan eschewed free agency to re-up with the Red Wings at four years, $26 million. He is a leader, a gamer who revels in pressure situations. Teammates thrive on his intensity. With all due respect to Steve Yzerman, Shanahan is the behind-the-scenes captain of the Red Wings.

Other than his willingness to hit or to scrap, no aspect of his game is elite. But Shanahan is there when you need him to make a play that will win for you, to say the right thing in the dressing room or to orchestrate the Stanley Cup handoff. And he's always there for the fans; Shanahan is one of the NHL's most popular players. He didn't have a very good playoffs, though.

PROJECTION

The move to left wing helped Shanahan exceed the 60 points we had him pegged for last season. He should be good for another 70.

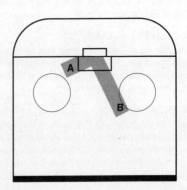

PAT VERBEEK

Yrs. of NHL service: 17
Born: Sarnia, Ont.; May 24, 1964
Position: right wing
Height: 5-9
Weight: 192
Uniform no.: 16
Shoots: right

Career statistics:

GP	G	A	TP	PIM
1293	500	513	1013	2760

1996-97 statistics:

GP	G	A	TP	+/-	PIM	PP	SH	GW	GT	S	PCT
81	17	36	53	+3	128	5	0	4	0	172	9.9

1997-98 statistics:

GP	G	A	TP	+/-	PIM	PP	SH	GW	GT	S	PCT
82	31	26	57	+15	170	9	0	8	1	190	16.3

1998-99 statistics:

GP	G	A	TP	+/-	PIM	PP	SH	GW	GT	S	PCT
78	17	17	34	+11	133	8	0	2	1	134	12.7

1999-2000 statistics:

GP	G	A	TP	+/-	PIM	PP	SH	GW	GT	S	PCT
68	22	26	48	+22	95	7	0	5	1	138	15.9

LAST SEASON

Signed as free agent, Nov. 10, 1999. Led team in shooting percentage.

THE FINESSE GAME

Verbeek has a choppy stride, so much of his best work is done in small spaces rather than in open ice. He is very strong on his skates and he likes to go into traffic zones. Larger players think they can hit him, but he's so chunky, with a low centre of gravity, that he's nearly impossible to bowl over. He's very good at carrying the puck along the boards but is no stickhandler in open ice. He has no better than fair speed.

Verbeek plays low on the power play. He wastes few quality scoring chances, though, and most of his shots come from in tight. Nothing brings out his competitive edge more than some serious crashing around the crease, most of which he initiates. When Verbeek goes into scoring slumps, he becomes frustrated and starts cheating on his defensive responsibilities and his game proceeds to fall apart.

His hands are quick enough to surprise with a backhand shot. He feels the puck on his stick and looks for openings in the net instead of scrapping with his head down and taking poor shots. He is also effective coming in late and drilling the shot.

THE PHYSICAL GAME

Verbeek is among the best in the league at drawing penalties. He can cleverly hold the opponent's stick and fling himself to the ice as if he were the injured party, and it's an effective tactic. He also draws calls honestly with his hard work by driving to the net and forcing the defender to slow him down by any means possible.

Verbeek is tough, rugged and strong, with a nasty disposition that he can tame without losing his ferocious edge. He takes more than his share of bad penalties.

THE INTANGIBLES

Verbeek was a canny pickup for the Red Wings and made a nice fit with Steve Yzerman and Brendan Shanahan. Verbeek's best years may be behind him, but he scored a pro-rated 30 goals. He slowed down in the second half, which could be a comination of age (36) and missing training camp.

PROJECTION

Verbeek was rejuvenated by signing with Detroit, but he didn't have a strong finish or playoffs (one goal in nine games). He should be good for another 25 goals, maybe for one last time.

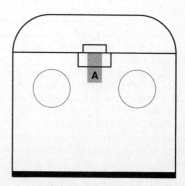

STEVE YZERMAN

Yrs. of NHL service: 17
Born: Cranbrook, B.C.; May 9, 1965
Position: centre
Height: 5-11
Weight: 185
Uniform no.: 19
Shoots: right

Career statistics:

GP	G	A	TP	PIM
1256	633	935	1562	816

1996-97 statistics:

GP	G	A	TP	+/-	PIM	PP	SH	GW	GT	S	PCT
81	22	63	85	+22	78	8	0	3	0	232	9.5

1997-98 statistics:

GP	G	A	TP	+/-	PIM	PP	SH	GW	GT	S	PCT
75	24	45	69	+3	46	6	2	0	2	188	12.8

1998-99 statistics:

GP	G	A	TP	+/-	PIM	PP	SH	GW	GT	S	PCT
80	29	45	74	+8	42	13	2	4	0	231	12.6

1999-2000 statistics:

GP	G	A	TP	+/-	PIM	PP	SH	GW	GT	S	PCT
78	35	44	79	+28	34	15	2	6	1	234	15.0

LAST SEASON

Won 2000 Selke Trophy. Named to 2000 NHL First All-Star Team. Led team and 10th in NHL in points. Led team and third in NHL in power-play goals. Second on team in goals, assists, plus-minus and shooting percentage. Third on team in game-winning goals and shots. Missed four games with knee injury.

THE FINESSE GAME

From 100-point scorer to the league's best defensive forward. How many other players have made such a complete style transition?

Instead of scoring 100 points, Yzerman now scores 70 or 80 *and* keeps the opponent from scoring 20 or 30. He is one of the three most complete forwards in the NHL, with Peter Forsberg and Mike Modano.

A sensational skater, Yzerman zigs and zags all over the ice, spending very little time in the centre. He has great balance and quick feet, and is adroit at kicking the puck up onto his blade for a shot in one, seamless motion. He's also strong for an average-sized forward. He protects the puck well with his body and has the arm strength for wraparound shots and off-balance shots through traffic.

Yzerman prefers to stickhandle down the right side of the ice. In addition to using his body to shield the puck, he uses the boards to protect it. If a defender starts reaching in with his stick he usually ends up pulling Yzerman down for a penalty.

He has steadily improved his work on draws. He is a great penalty killer because of his speed and anticipation.

THE PHYSICAL GAME

Yzerman sacrifices his body willingly in the right circumstances and thinks nothing of diving to block a shot. He pays the price along the boards and around the net, and he's deceptively strong and durable.

Yzerman knows he isn't big enough to be an intimidating hitter, but he gets his body and stick in the way and at least makes the puck carrier change direction abruptly. He simply does not give up on a play, and he plays all 200 feet of the rink.

THE INTANGIBLES

Yzerman is one of the game's great quiet captains, a leader by example who says and does all the right things. His lapses during the season are few, and he seldom experiences a prolonged scoring slump. Considering how much ice time he gets and how active a skater he is, this is a tribute to his devotion to conditioning and mental preparation. He has always seemed mature beyond his years, even when he broke into the NHL at age 18.

PROJECTION

Yzerman will again score in the 70-point range. He is a model of consistency.

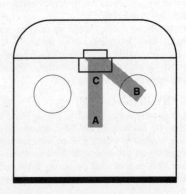

EDMONTON OILERS

Players' Statistics 1999-2000

POS.	NO.	PLAYER	GP	G	A	PTS	+/-	PIM	PP	SH	GW	GT	S	PCT
C	39	DOUG WEIGHT	77	21	51	72	6	54	3	1	4		167	12.6
L	94	RYAN SMYTH	82	28	26	54	-2	58	11		4	1	238	11.8
R	29	ALEX SELIVANOV	67	27	20	47	2	46	10		5		122	22.1
R	9	BILL GUERIN	70	24	22	46	4	123	11		2		188	12.8
L	13	GERMAN TITOV	70	17	29	46	-1	38	4	2	3		122	13.9
D	22	ROMAN HAMRLIK	80	8	37	45	1	68	5			1	180	4.4
L	26	TODD MARCHANT	82	17	23	40	7	70		1		2	170	10.0
D	5	TOM POTI	76	9	26	35	8	65	2	1	1		125	7.2
D	44	JANNE NIINIMAA	81	8	25	33	14	89	2	2			133	6.0
R	25	MIKE GRIER	65	9	22	31	9	68		3	2		115	7.8
L	18	ETHAN MOREAU	73	17	10	27	8	62	1		3		106	16.0
C	19	BOYD DEVEREAUX	76	8	19	27	7	20		1	2	1	108	7.4
C	34	JIM DOWD	69	5	18	23	10	45	2		1	1	103	4.9
R	27	GEORGES LARAQUE	76	8	8	16	5	123					56	14.3
L	17	REM MURRAY	44	9	5	14	-2	8	2		3		65	13.8
D	21	JASON SMITH	80	3	11	14	16	60			1		96	3.1
D	23	SEAN BROWN	72	4	8	12	1	192			2		36	11.1
D	55	IGOR ULANOV	57	1	8	9	-14	86					39	2.6
L	37	DANIEL CLEARY	17	3	2	5	-1	8			1		18	16.7
C	15	CHAD KILGER	40	3	2	5	-6	18					32	9.4
D	14	BERT ROBERTSSON	52		4	4	-3	34					31	
C	47	*PAUL COMRIE	15	1	2	3	-2	4					11	9.1
D	2	BRETT HAUER	5		2	2	-2	2					8	
G	35	TOMMY SALO	70		1	1	0	8						
G	1	*MIKE MINARD	1				0							
L	12	MICHEL PICARD	2				0	2					2	
L	33	*DAN LACOUTURE	5				0	10					2	
R	10	KEVIN BROWN	7				0						5	
G	30	BILL RANFORD	16				0	2						

GP = games played; G = goals; A = assists; PTS = points; +/- = goals-for minus goals-against while player is on ice; PIM = penalties in minutes; PP = power-play goals; SH = shorthanded goals; GW = game-winning goals; GT = game-tying goals; S = no. of shots; PCT = percentage of goals to shots; * = rookie

ERIC BREWER

Yrs. of NHL service: 2
Born: Vernon, B.C.; Apr. 17, 1979
Position: left defense
Height: 6-3
Weight: 195
Uniform no.: 4
Shoots: left

Career statistics:

GP	G	A	TP	PIM
89	5	8	13	52

1998-99 statistics:

GP	G	A	TP	+/-	PIM	PP	SH	GW	GT	S	PCT
63	5	6	11	-14	32	2	0	0	0	63	7.9

1999-2000 statistics:

GP	G	A	TP	+/-	PIM	PP	SH	GW	GT	S	PCT
26	0	2	2	-11	20	0	0	0	0	30	-

LAST SEASON

Second NHL season. Acquired from N.Y. Islanders with Josh Green and a second-round draft pick in 2000 for Roman Hamrlik. Missed six games with fractured toe. Appeared in 24 games with Lowell (AHL), scoring 2-2 — 4.

THE FINESSE GAME

An enigma, Brewer never seemed to return to the high level of play and promise he displayed as a rookie.

Brewer needs more time and confidence to develop into more of an offensive force. He has a little cockiness to him that shows an innate awareness of his skill level. It will get him in trouble sometimes, but it will also encourage him to try some of the high-risk moves that only elite players make. Brewer can make them.

Brewer can be used in all game situations. He can control games, the way Scott Niedermayer does with the Devils. He has the skating and puck control to dominate. He's an excellent skater with quick acceleration and lateral movement.

THE PHYSICAL GAME

Brewer is very strong in the defensive zone. He has good size — he will fill out more as he matures — and he likes to hit. He's smart in his own end.

THE INTANGIBLES

Brewer's work ethic came into question last season and led to his departure from the Islanders. His skating ability and taste for the offensive style of play should make him a nice fit in Edmonton. He is a laid-back kid by nature, so coaches need to learn how to coax a better effort out of him on a nightly basis.

PROJECTION

Brewer will eventually be a 50-point defenseman, and maybe more, but 25 points would be a great bounce-back season for him.

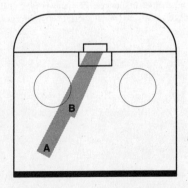

JOSH GREEN

Yrs. of NHL service: 2
Born: Camrose, Alta.; Nov. 16, 1977
Position: left wing
Height: 6-4
Weight: 212
Uniform no.: 21
Shoots: left

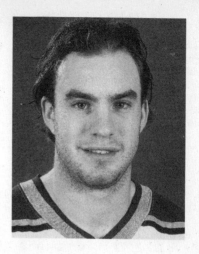

Career statistics:

GP	G	A	TP	PIM
76	13	17	30	49

1998-99 statistics:

GP	G	A	TP	+/-	PIM	PP	SH	GW	GT	S	PCT
27	1	3	4	-5	8	1	0	0	0	35	2.9

1999-2000 statistics:

GP	G	A	TP	+/-	PIM	PP	SH	GW	GT	S	PCT
49	12	14	26	-7	41	2	0	3	0	109	11.0

LAST SEASON

Acquired from N.Y. Islanders with Eric Brewer and a second-round draft choice in 2000 for Roman Hamrlik, June 24, 2000. Missed nine games with shoulder injury. Missed three games due to coach's decision. Appeared in 17 games with Lowell (AHL), scoring 6-2 — 8.

THE FINESSE GAME

Green could become an Adam Graves-type player. He is a good skater with average hands, but he's very smart with the puck and he knows what to do with it in key areas. His feet are just a little bit slow off the mark, but he has decent speed once he gets moving. He is strong on his skates and he can get a lot better if he works at his skating. He is not a plodder.

Green is a good passer and playmaker. Since his hands aren't great, he will need to dig for his goals around the net, the way Graves does every night. Green is a fairly advanced two-way player for his age (he'll turn 22 during the season).

THE PHYSICAL GAME

Green is a big, strong kid. Because his finesse skills are above average, he sometimes falls into the lazy habit of taking the easy way out and not playing the price physically. He can't afford to do that, because he has a bright future as a power forward if he keeps desire and grit in his game.

THE INTANGIBLES

Green has a chronic shoulder problem that casts a shadow over his potential.

PROJECTION

Power forwards take time to develop. Sooner or later, Green is going to be a 30-goal scorer at the NHL level. If he gets to play with Doug Weight in Edmonton, it could be sooner.

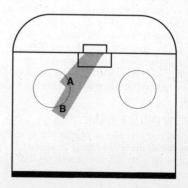

MIKE GRIER

Yrs. of NHL service: 4
Born: Detroit, Mich.; Jan. 5, 1975
Position: right wing
Height: 6-1
Weight: 232
Uniform no.: 25
Shoots: right

Career statistics:

GP	G	A	TP	PIM
292	53	69	122	240

1996-97 statistics:

GP	G	A	TP	+/-	PIM	PP	SH	GW	GT	S	PCT
79	15	17	32	+7	45	4	0	2	0	89	16.9

1997-98 statistics:

GP	G	A	TP	+/-	PIM	PP	SH	GW	GT	S	PCT
66	9	6	15	-3	73	1	0	1	0	90	10.0

1998-99 statistics:

GP	G	A	TP	+/-	PIM	PP	SH	GW	GT	S	PCT
82	20	24	44	+5	54	3	2	1	0	143	14.0

1999-2000 statistics:

GP	G	A	TP	+/-	PIM	PP	SH	GW	GT	S	PCT
65	9	22	31	+9	68	0	3	2	0	115	7.8

LAST SEASON

Led team in shorthanded goals. Missed 12 games with surgery to repair torn triceps muscle. Missed four games with bone chip in right clavicle. Missed one game due to contract dispute.

THE FINESSE GAME

Grier is a hockey player in a football player's body — an aggressive forechecker who bores in on the unfortunate puck carrier with all the intensity of a lineman blitzing a quarterback. But Grier doesn't waste energy. He is intelligent about when to come in full-tilt or when to back off a bit and pick off a hasty pass. He frightens a lot of people into mistakes, and the savvier he gets at reading their reactions, the better he'll be.

Grier definitely believes that the most direct route to the net is the best path to choose. He won't hesitate to bull his way through two defensemen to get there.

The knock on Grier has always been his skating, but it's getting much better. He has a slow first couple of strides, but he then gets into gear and is strong and balanced with fair agility. He scores his goals like Adam Deadmarsh does, by driving to the net after loose pucks. Grier was a scorer at the collegiate level and has decent hands. Since he always keeps his legs pumping, he draws a good share of penalties. He is also a sound penalty killer and a shorthanded scoring threat.

THE PHYSICAL GAME

Grier can't be too bulky or he won't be agile enough for his pursuit. He isn't a fighter. It takes a lot to provoke him. He's just an honest, tough, physical winger.

THE INTANGIBLES

Grier has dealt admirably with racism in his sport, and accepts the responsibility of being a role model for younger athletes. He made an amazing jump from college to the pros and keeps getting better. His attitude and work ethic are unassailable. He is the unsung hero of the Oilers. He has also shown good progress since his surgery and would have been able to play in the later rounds of the playoffs if Edmonton had gotten that far. He was a restricted free agent during the off-season.

PROJECTION

Although not a natural goal scorer, Grier gets enough time and plays with enough desire to get 15 to 20.

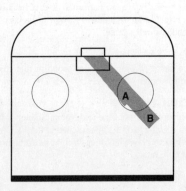

BILL GUERIN

Yrs. of NHL service: 8
Born: Wilbraham, Mass.; Nov. 9, 1970
Position: right wing
Height: 6-2
Weight: 200
Uniform no.: 9
Shoots: right

Career statistics:

GP	G	A	TP	PIM
570	175	178	353	805

1996-97 statistics:

GP	G	A	TP	+/-	PIM	PP	SH	GW	GT	S	PCT
82	29	18	47	-2	95	7	0	9	0	177	16.4

1997-98 statistics:

GP	G	A	TP	+/-	PIM	PP	SH	GW	GT	S	PCT
59	18	21	39	+1	93	9	0	4	0	178	10.1

1998-99 statistics:

GP	G	A	TP	+/-	PIM	PP	SH	GW	GT	S	PCT
80	30	34	64	+7	133	13	0	2	1	261	11.5

1999-2000 statistics:

GP	G	A	TP	+/-	PIM	PP	SH	GW	GT	S	PCT
70	24	22	46	+4	123	11	0	2	0	188	12.8

LAST SEASON

Tied for team lead in power-play goals. Second on team in shots. Tied for second on team in penalty minutes. Third on team in goals. Missed 11 games in contract dispute. Missed one game due to caoch's decision.

THE FINESSE GAME

Guerin has a terrifying slap shot, a wicked screamer that he unleashes off the wing in full flight. But like a young pitcher who lives off his fastball, he must master the change-up. There are times when a snap or wrist shot is the better choice, especially when he is set up for a one-timer, but instead of putting the puck on net, he fires a wild shot off the glass.

What he must do is keep driving to the net instead of curling around and looking to make a pass. Guerin becomes ineffective when he stops playing like a power forward and dances on the perimeter, playing an east-west instead of north-south game. His speed and power are potent weapons. But he needs to drive down the right wing and force the defense back with his speed. When he backs off and takes the easier route to the off-wing, his scoring chances decrease drastically in quality.

Hockey sense and creativity are lagging a tad behind his other attributes, but Guerin is a conscientious player and those qualities should develop. He is aware defensively and has worked hard at that part of the game, though he will still lose his checking assignments and start running around in the defensive zone.

THE PHYSICAL GAME

The more physical the game is, the more Guerin gets involved. He is big, strong and tough in every sense of the word, and, frankly, is useless when he plays otherwise.

The kind of game Guerin is going to have can usually be judged in the first few shifts. He can play it clean or mean, with big body checks or the drop of a glove. He will move to the puck carrier and battle for control until he gets it, and he's hard to knock off his skates.

In front of the net, Guerin digs hard. He works to establish position and has the hand skills to make something happen when the puck gets to his stick. He is in great shape and can routinely handle 20 minutes a night.

THE INTANGIBLES

Guerin suffered through a couple of notable slumps. He scored only one goal in his first 11 games after signing a new two-year contract in November, and in the second half of the season went through a 14-game drought. With his contract up after this season, he is likely to be trade bait.

PROJECTION

Guerin is good for 30 to 35 goals. He's been through contract hassles before, so playing this one out shouldn't faze him.

TODD MARCHANT

Yrs. of NHL service: 6
Born: Buffalo, N.Y.; Aug. 12, 1973
Position: centre
Height: 5-10
Weight: 175
Uniform no.: 26
Shoots: left

Career statistics:

GP	G	A	TP	PIM
449	91	119	210	350

1996-97 statistics:

GP	G	A	TP	+/-	PIM	PP	SH	GW	GT	S	PCT
79	14	19	33	+11	44	0	4	3	0	202	6.9

1997-98 statistics:

GP	G	A	TP	+/-	PIM	PP	SH	GW	GT	S	PCT
76	14	21	35	+9	71	2	1	3	0	194	7.2

1998-99 statistics:

GP	G	A	TP	+/-	PIM	PP	SH	GW	GT	S	PCT
82	14	22	36	+3	65	3	1	2	0	183	7.7

1999-2000 statistics:

GP	G	A	TP	+/-	PIM	PP	SH	GW	GT	S	PCT
82	17	23	40	+7	70	0	1	0	2	170	10.0

LAST SEASON

One of two Oilers to appear in all 82 games. Career highs in assists and points.

THE FINESSE GAME

A speed merchant, Marchant is a strong one-on-one player with zippy outside speed. His quick hand skills keep pace with his feet, and he is particularly adept at tempting the defender with the puck, then dragging it through the victim's legs. He then continues to the net for his scoring chances.

Marchant is opportunistic, and, with his pace, reminds scouts of a young Theo Fleury. However, he has a long way to go to match Fleury's scoring touch. He will never be an elite scorer, because he doesn't have the hands.

Marchant is smart, sees the ice well and is a solid playmaker as well as shooter. He is no puck hog. He is an excellent penalty killer and a shorthanded threat because of his speed.

THE PHYSICAL GAME

His teammates have nicknamed him "Mighty Mouse," as Marchant is fearless in the face of bigger, supposedly tougher, opposition. He hurls his body at larger foes. He is really irritating to play against, because a big lug like Derian Hatcher looks foolish trying to chase down and swat a little bitty guy like Marchant. And Hatcher looked downright villainous giving Marchant a concussion in the playoffs.

Marchant is average size but his grit makes him look bigger. He sacrifices his body, but you wonder how long his body will last under the stress he puts it through. He is well-conditioned and can handle a lot

of ice time. The mental toughness is there, too. He will take a hit to make a play but has to get smarter about picking his spots in order to survive. Edmonton is a very mobile team and Marchant's lack of size is not as much of a detriment as it could be on other teams.

THE INTANGIBLES

Marchant was a restricted free agent during the off-season. He is a key component of Edmonton's run-and-gun team.

PROJECTION

Marchant is a role player with a big heart. His top end is 20 goals, and that would be a career year.

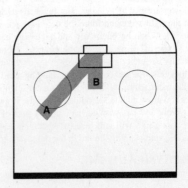

ETHAN MOREAU

Yrs. of NHL service: 4
Born: Huntsville, Ont.; Sept. 22, 1975
Position: left wing
Height: 6-2
Weight: 205
Uniform no.: 18
Shoots: left

Career statistics:

GP	G	A	TP	PIM
297	51	47	98	354

1996-97 statistics:

GP	G	A	TP	+/-	PIM	PP	SH	GW	GT	S	PCT
82	15	16	31	+13	123	0	0	1	1	114	13.2

1997-98 statistics:

GP	G	A	TP	+/-	PIM	PP	SH	GW	GT	S	PCT
54	9	9	18	0	73	2	0	0	0	87	10.3

1998-99 statistics:

GP	G	A	TP	+/-	PIM	PP	SH	GW	GT	S	PCT
80	10	11	21	-3	92	0	0	2	0	96	10.4

1999-2000 statistics:

GP	G	A	TP	+/-	PIM	PP	SH	GW	GT	S	PCT
73	17	10	27	+8	62	1	0	3	0	106	16.0

LAST SEASON

Missed eight games with rib injury. Missed one game with flu.

THE FINESSE GAME

Moreau is an intelligent, safe player with good hockey sense. He can also play centre, though his future is clearly at left wing. He is not a natural scorer but has to work for his goals; his scoring touch improves with effort. Funny how that works.

Moreau has a long reach and uses a long stick, which allow him to get his strong wrist shots away around a defenseman who may think he has Moreau tied up. Defensively, he's on his way because he has an understanding of positional play. He's a budding power forward who goes to the net hard. Moreau worked will with the spunky Todd Marchant on Edmonton's third line.

THE PHYSICAL GAME

Moreau has good size and strength and is starting to develop more of a presence. He finishes his checks, especially around the net. There may be a latent aggressive streak that will emerge with more ice time and confidence. He works hard, is strong in the corners and will take a hit to make a play.

THE INTANGIBLES

Moreau suffered through six shoulder dislocations during the season and finally had surgery during the summer to correct the problem. He continued to play a gritty game and showed drive around the net, despite the injuries. Former coach Craig Hartsburg compared Moreau to a young Bob Gainey, both for his playing style and budding leadership ability.

Moreau is very well-liked and he has some good leadership qualities.

PROJECTION

We've been high on Moreau for awhile and were pleased to see him flirt with the 20 goals we predicted for him last season. If he makes a successful comeback from his shoulder surgery, he should take the next step towards becoming a prominent power forward, with 25 goals.

JANNE NIINIMAA

Yrs. of NHL service: 4
Born: Raahe, Finland; May 22, 1975
Position: right defense
Height: 6-1
Weight: 196
Uniform no.: 24
Shoots: left

Career statistics:

GP	G	A	TP	PIM
316	20	128	148	297

1996-97 statistics:

GP	G	A	TP	+/-	PIM	PP	SH	GW	GT	S	PCT
77	4	40	44	+12	58	1	0	2	0	141	2.8

1997-98 statistics:

GP	G	A	TP	+/-	PIM	PP	SH	GW	GT	S	PCT
77	4	39	43	+13	62	3	0	1	0	134	3.0

1998-99 statistics:

GP	G	A	TP	+/-	PIM	PP	SH	GW	GT	S	PCT
81	4	24	28	+7	88	2	0	1	0	142	2.8

1999-2000 statistics:

GP	G	A	TP	+/-	PIM	PP	SH	GW	GT	S	PCT
81	8	25	33	+14	89	2	2	0	0	133	6.0

LAST SEASON

Second on team in plus-minus. Tied for second on team in shorthanded goals. Missed one game due to coach's decision.

THE FINESSE GAME

Niinimaa is a dynamic player with elite skills. He is a gambler at heart, and will make high-risk plays that cost his team defensively, but will also pay off with great offensive plays. A left-handed shot who plays the right side, he has excellent skating and puckhandling skills, which allow him to handle the amount of body shifting necessary to open his body to the rink and keep the forehand available as often as possible.

A nimble, agile player, Niinimaa sets his feet wide apart for outstanding drive, power and balance, and uses a long stride and long reach to win races to the puck. He can turn the corners at near top speed and doesn't have to slow down when carrying the puck. When the opportunity to jump into the play presents itself he is gone in a vapour trail.

Like Paul Kariya, Niinimaa does a great job of "framing" his stick and giving his teammate a passing target. He keeps the blade on the ice and available, his body position saying, "Put it here, so I can do something with it."

Having stepped into the league at age 21, a middle-aged rookie, Niinimaa learned that he could create just as much offensive danger by merely flipping a puck towards the net instead of taking the full-windup slap shot every time. Although his one-timers can be blistering, he doesn't always shoot to score; sometimes, he shoots to create a rebound or possible deflection.

THE PHYSICAL GAME

Niinimaa plays a fairly physical game, though he is not aggressive. He bumps and jolts, and makes opponents pay a price for every inch of important ice gained. He seems to relish one-on-one battles. He wants the puck and does whatever is necessary to win control of it.

THE INTANGIBLES

Trading this guy for Dan McGillis was just another one of Flyers GM Bob Clarke's boneheaded decisions. He was the Oilers' best defenseman in the playoffs.

PROJECTION

Niinimaa is going to play a lot, is going to get power-play time and is going to score 35 points.

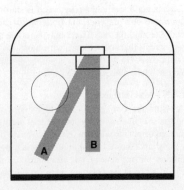

TOM POTI

Yrs. of NHL service: 2
Born: Worcester, Mass.; Mar. 22, 1977
Position: defense
Height: 6-2
Weight: 185
Uniform no.: 5
Shoots: left

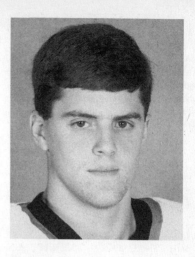

Career statistics:

GP	G	A	TP	PIM
149	14	42	56	107

1998-99 statistics:

GP	G	A	TP	+/-	PIM	PP	SH	GW	GT	S	PCT
73	5	16	21	+10	42	2	0	3	0	94	5.3

1999-2000 statistics:

GP	G	A	TP	+/-	PIM	PP	SH	GW	GT	S	PCT
76	9	26	35	+8	65	2	1	1	0	125	7.2

LAST SEASON

Second NHL season. Career highs in goals, assists and points. Missed two games with neck injury. Missed two games with ankle injuries. Missed one game with bruised thumb.

THE FINESSE GAME

Poti is a good offensive defenseman who could be on his way to being an outstanding one. He is an excellent skater, whose playing style fits in well with this fast Oilers team that embraces a European style of play.

Poti is a fine puckhandler and passer. He has been compared to Paul Coffey for his vision and his ability to spring teammates with headman passes. He has a long way to go to match Coffey's offensive reputation, but he didn't show many negative signs, either. He carries the puck with speed and disguises his intentions.

Poti uses a low shot from the point that isn't a rocket, so teammates can take advantage of it for tip-ins.

He needs to work on his defense to become a better all-around player. He is intelligent and should keep learning.

THE PHYSICAL GAME

Poti has decent size but doesn't use it well. He is still adding some muscle and needs to throw his weight around a bit more and add some grit to his game. He prefers to use his stick instead of his body to do the defensive work. He has to deal with a medical condition, a severe food allergy, which forces him to play strict attention to his nutrition and condition. His effortless skating style helps him handle a lot of minutes (he averaged just over 24 minutes), but he did seem to tail off last season from overwork.

THE INTANGIBLES

Poti is an outstanding rushing defenseman who is going to keep getting better.

PROJECTION

Poti is a blue-chip rearguard who should score in the 40-point range as he gains more confidence and gets more ice time.

TOMMY SALO

Yrs. of NHL service: 5
Born: Surahammar, Sweden; Feb. 1, 1971
Position: goaltender
Height: 5-11
Weight: 173
Uniform no.: 35
Catches: left

Career statistics:

GP	MIN	GA	SO	GAA	A	PIM
270	15432	677	21	2.63	4	55

1996-97 statistics:

GP	MIN	GAA	W	L	T	SO	GA	S	SAPCT	PIM
58	3208	2.82	20	27	7	5	151	1576	.904	4

1997-98 statistics:

GP	MIN	GAA	W	L	T	SO	GA	S	SAPCT	PIM
62	3461	2.64	23	29	5	4	152	1617	.906	31

1998-99 statistics:

GP	MIN	GAA	W	L	T	SO	GA	S	SAPCT	PIM
51	3018	2.62	17	26	7	5	132	1368	.904	12

1999-2000 statistics:

GP	MIN	GAA	W	L	T	SO	GA	S	SAPCT	PIM
70	4164	2.33	27	28	3	2	162	1875	.914	8

LAST SEASON

Fourth among NHL goalies in games and minutes played. Second among NHL goalies in shots against. Career highs in games played, minutes played and wins.

THE PHYSICAL GAME

Salo has improved at coming out to the top of his crease and beyond to challenge shooters, and it has made him a much more effective goalie, because he looks so much larger in the net. When the action is in tight, he is excellent on low shots. He has adjusted to playing with traffic, which is one of the biggest adjustments for European goalies. He has quick feet but is not a great skater; he needs to improve his lateral movement. He does have a problem with being bumped. He is out of the paint a lot and referees were lenient about goalie interference for most of last season, so Salo had to fight his own battles.

Salo has a bad habit of not holding his stick at a proper angle. When he gets into this slump he might as well not bother playing with a stick at all. He has a quick glove and tends to try and catch everything instead of using other parts of his body. Since he doesn't use his stick well, he will try to cover up on every loose puck for face-offs. Better stickhandling work would elevate his game a notch.

Salo's reflexes are outstanding.

THE MENTAL GAME

The big knock on Salo was always his lack of concentration. He seemed to let in a bad goal or two at the worst times, but he's gotten over that hump and his effort is far more consistent. Salo has great confidence in his abilities.

THE INTANGIBLES

Salo has continually improved season by season and he got some much-deserved recognition by playing in the NHL All-Star game. He seems unfazed by playing behind a wide-open offense and understands he will get a lot of work every night.

PROJECTION

Salo is among the middle of the pack of NHL goalies, but fits in well with the Oilers. If he gets 60 to 70 starts again he should manage 25 to 28 wins, again.

ALEXANDER SELIVANOV

Yrs. of NHL service: 6
Born: Moscow, Russia; March 23, 1971
Position: right wing
Height: 6-0
Weight: 208
Uniform no.: 29
Shoots: left

Career statistics:

GP	G	A	TP	PIM
400	113	103	216	341

1996-97 statistics:

GP	G	A	TP	+/-	PIM	PP	SH	GW	GT	S	PCT
69	15	18	33	-3	61	3	0	4	0	187	8.0

1997-98 statistics:

GP	G	A	TP	+/-	PIM	PP	SH	GW	GT	S	PCT
70	16	19	35	-38	85	4	0	3	1	206	7.8

1998-99 statistics:

GP	G	A	TP	+/-	PIM	PP	SH	GW	GT	S	PCT
72	14	19	33	-8	42	2	0	1	0	177	7.9

1999-2000 statistics:

GP	G	A	TP	+/-	PIM	PP	SH	GW	GT	S	PCT
67	27	20	47	+2	46	10	0	5	0	122	22.1

LAST SEASON

Led team and second in NHL in shooting percentage. Led team in game-winning goals. Second on team in goals. Third on team in points and power-play goals. Missed 15 games due to coach's decision.

THE FINESSE GAME

Selivanov is very clever with the puck. He can beat people one-on-one with his speed and puckhandling, but seldom uses his teammates as well as he should, or he would be even more productive. He loves to score, and he works to get himself in position for a quality shot. He needs to play with a creative centre who will get the puck to him, because he can finish.

Selivanov tends to take very long shifts, which drives his coaches crazy, and can be quite selfish. He is strong on the puck. He has some defensive lapses.

Selivanov has an excellent release on his shot, and is one of the many NHL players who could get called for a penalty for an illegal stick on a nightly basis. He's a left-hand shot who plays right wing. Playing with a straighter stick would help him receive passes and handle the puck on his backhand and finish better, but he likes that big curve.

THE PHYSICAL GAME

Selivanov is wiry but he is not terribly strong or aggressive. He is not intimidated. However, he will probably need at least one bodyguard on his line. He is quick and smart enough to stay out of trouble.

THE INTANGIBLES

Edmonton failed to make Selivanov a qualifying offer during the off-season, making him an unrestricted free agent. It's not as if 27-goal scorers grow on trees, but there has to be a reason for those healthy scratches. Selivanov failed to score a single point in the playoffs.

PROJECTION

There is still more upside to his game because of his tremendous creativity, but Selivanov's lack of determination will keep him around the 20-goal mark.

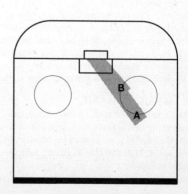

JASON SMITH

Yrs. of NHL service: 7
Born: Calgary, Alta.; Nov. 2, 1973
Position: right defense
Height: 6-3
Weight: 205
Uniform no.: 21
Shoots: right

Career statistics:

GP	G	A	TP	PIM
418	12	44	56	394

1996-97 statistics:

GP	G	A	TP	+/-	PIM	PP	SH	GW	GT	S	PCT
78	1	7	8	-12	54	0	0	0	0	74	1.4

1997-98 statistics:

GP	G	A	TP	+/-	PIM	PP	SH	GW	GT	S	PCT
81	3	13	16	-5	100	0	0	0	0	97	3.1

1998-99 statistics:

GP	G	A	TP	+/-	PIM	PP	SH	GW	GT	S	PCT
72	3	12	15	-9	51	0	0	0	0	68	4.4

1999-2000 statistics:

GP	G	A	TP	+/-	PIM	PP	SH	GW	GT	S	PCT
80	3	11	14	+16	60	0	0	1	0	96	3.1

LAST SEASON

Led team in plus-minus. Missed one game with bruised shoulder. Missed one game due to coach's decision.

THE FINESSE GAME

Smith has a low-key personality and will never be the kind of defenseman who can control a game. He can, however, keep a game from getting out of hand with his cool work in the defensive zone. He has improved his defensive reads greatly — playing a season for Kevin Lowe had a major impact — and was better at moving the puck. Smith was very consistent last season.

Smith has gained confidence and has more poise and presence. He sacrifices his body to make hits and block shots, and was the Oilers' leader in both of those categories. He doesn't give himself enough credit. He is the kind of player who needs to have the coaches give him a pat on the back.

Smith won't make anyone forget Brian Leetch. He has a fairly heavy shot but it has little movement on it. He's not very creative offensively and he doesn't gamble. However, he can kill penalties, though he'll get into trouble against a team that cycles well down low. He needs to improve his puckhandling skills.

THE PHYSICAL GAME

Smith is a solid hitter with a latent mean streak; his takeouts are effective along the boards and in front of the net. He's not as good in open ice because his mobility is not exceptional. He has a fairly long fuse but is a capable fighter.

Smith is very fit and can handle 22 to 25 minutes a game.

THE INTANGIBLES

Smith is emerging as a quiet leader. He's a little insecure but wants to learn and will work hard to improve. He is very coachable, quietly confident and has good leadership ability. He will work best paired with an offensive defenseman. Janne Niinimaa was his frequent partner last season and the duo was very effective, usually facing other teams' top lines.

PROJECTION

Smith is evolving into a reliable crunch-time player, but his numbers will never be gaudy.

RYAN SMYTH

Yrs. of NHL service: 5
Born: Banff, Alta.; Feb. 21, 1976
Position: left wing
Height: 6-1
Weight: 195
Uniform no.: 94
Shoots: left

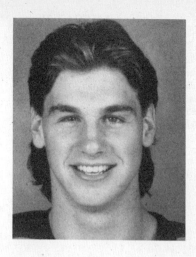

Career statistics:

GP	G	A	TP	PIM
351	102	88	190	268

1996-97 statistics:

GP	G	A	TP	+/-	PIM	PP	SH	GW	GT	S	PCT
82	39	22	61	-7	76	20	0	4	0	265	14.7

1997-98 statistics:

GP	G	A	TP	+/-	PIM	PP	SH	GW	GT	S	PCT
65	20	13	33	-24	44	10	0	2	2	205	9.8

1998-99 statistics:

GP	G	A	TP	+/-	PIM	PP	SH	GW	GT	S	PCT
71	13	18	31	0	62	6	0	2	2	161	8.1

1999-2000 statistics:

GP	G	A	TP	+/-	PIM	PP	SH	GW	GT	S	PCT
82	28	26	54	-2	58	11	0	4	1	238	11.8

LAST SEASON

Led team in goals and shots. Tied for team in lead in power-play goals. Second on team in points. Tied for second on team in game-winning goals. One of two Oilers to appear in all 82 games.

THE FINESSE GAME

Smyth was slow to recover from a knee injury he suffered in 1997-98. Now he is all the way back, playing with his fearless, confident, drive-to-the-net style.

Smyth is not a great, fluid skater, so he has to keep his feet moving. He does, with great energy that lifts his bench, his fans, and gets him behind the opponent's defense.

Smyth possesses little subtlety. Most of his goals come from the hash marks in, and probably half of them aren't the result of his shots, but tip-ins and body bounces. That's an art in itself, because Smyth has a knack for timing his moves to the net, along with a shooter's release. He has a long reach for getting to rebounds and is strong on his stick for deflections. He gets himself in the right place and is always aware of where the pass or the point shot is coming from. He has an advantage because his instincts and his reaction time are usually quicker than anyone else's.

Smyth is at a disadvantage when he is forced to shoot or make a play because he doesn't have a quick release. When he carries the puck, he doesn't have much sense of what to do with it.

THE PHYSICAL GAME

Smyth isn't built like a power forward, but when he is playing with confidence he sure tries to play like one. Smyth is one of the best forwards in the league along the wall. He uses his feet well to keep the puck alive. He is a pesky net crasher and can be an irritating presence. He doesn't throw bombs, but he is a willing thrasher along the boards and gets good leg drive for solid hits. He's not a fighter, yet he won't back down.

THE INTANGIBLES

Smyth is versatile and can go from the first power-play unit to the third line to protect a lead late in a game. He is physically fit again, and his enthusiasm is contagious. Smyth was an unrestricted free agent during the off-season.

PROJECTION

Assuming he doesn't have a protracted contract duel with the Oilers, and assuming his favourite centre Doug Weight is back, Smyth should be good for around 30 goals.

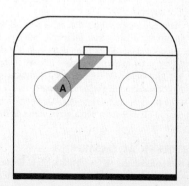

DOUG WEIGHT

Yrs. of NHL service: 9
Born: Warren, Mich.; Jan. 21, 1971
Position: centre
Height: 5-11
Weight: 191
Uniform no.: 39
Shoots: left

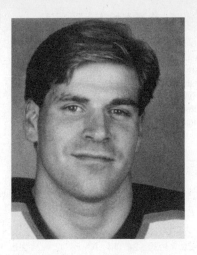

Career statistics:

GP	G	A	TP	PIM
624	155	393	557	514

1996-97 statistics:

GP	G	A	TP	+/-	PIM	PP	SH	GW	GT	S	PCT
80	21	61	82	+1	80	4	0	2	0	235	8.9

1997-98 statistics:

GP	G	A	TP	+/-	PIM	PP	SH	GW	GT	S	PCT
79	26	44	70	+1	69	9	0	4	0	205	12.7

1998-99 statistics:

GP	G	A	TP	+/-	PIM	PP	SH	GW	GT	S	PCT
43	6	31	37	-8	12	1	0	0	1	79	7.6

1999-2000 statistics:

GP	G	A	TP	+/-	PIM	PP	SH	GW	GT	S	PCT
77	21	51	72	+6	54	3	1	4	0	167	12.6

LAST SEASON

Led team in assists and points. Tied for second on team in game-winning goals. Missed five games with cracked ribs.

THE FINESSE GAME

Playmaking is Weight's strong suit. He has good vision and passes well to either side. His hands are soft and sure. When he utilizes his shot he has quick and accurate wrist and snap shots. He handles the puck well in traffic, is strong on the puck and creates a lot of scoring chances. Weight is an outstanding one-on-one player, but doesn't have to challenge all the time. He will trail the play down the right wing (his preferred side) and jump into the attack late.

Weight won't win many foot races, but he keeps his legs pumping and he often surprises people on the rush, who think they had him contained only to see him push his way past. He frequently draws penalties. He has decent quickness, good balance and a fair change of direction.

Weight has improved his defensive play slightly; he is an offensive Doug Risebrough. A late bloomer, he has succeeded on a weak team in the role of a number one centre, though a number two role would probably suit him better. Weight's point production is amazingly consistent. He seldom slumps.

On the power play, Weight does his best work off the right wing half-boards. He always seems to find a passing seam.

THE PHYSICAL GAME

Weight is inconsistent in his physical play. He shows flashes of grit but doesn't it to the ice every night, maybe because he gets banged up so easily. Still, he is built like a fire hydrant, and on the nights he's on he hits with enthusiasm, finishing every check. He initiates and annoys.

He's also a bit of a trash talker, yapping and playing with a great deal of spirit. He has worked on his strength and conditioning and can handle a lot of ice time. He is strong on his skates and hard to knock off the puck. Weight played hurt in the playoffs, with bad ribs.

THE INTANGIBLES

Weight makes a nice partner for Ryan Smyth, who last season always seemed to be in perfect scoring position, with his stick down for a Weight pass. Weight was a restricted free agent during the off-season and could be tough for the cash-strapped Oilers to re-sign.

PROJECTION

Weight's production should be around 50 assists (which he has achieved four times in his career) and 80 points.

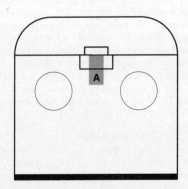

FLORIDA PANTHERS

Players' Statistics 1999-2000

POS.	NO.	PLAYER	GP	G	A	PTS	+/-	PIM	PP	SH	GW	GT	S	PCT
R	10	PAVEL BURE	74	58	36	94	25	16	11	2	14		360	16.1
C	14	RAY WHITNEY	81	29	42	71	16	35	5		3	2	198	14.6
C	25	VIKTOR KOZLOV	80	17	53	70	24	16	6		2		223	7.6
C	16	MIKE SILLINGER	80	23	29	52	-30	102	8	3	2		146	15.8
D	24	ROBERT SVEHLA	82	9	40	49	23	64	3		1		143	6.3
R	27	SCOTT MELLANBY	77	18	28	46	14	126	6		2	1	134	13.4
R	21	MARK PARRISH	81	26	18	44	1	39	6		3		152	17.1
D	28	JAROSLAV SPACEK	82	10	26	36	7	53	4		1		111	9.0
C	44	ROB NIEDERMAYER	81	10	23	33	-5	46	1		4		135	7.4
D	4	BRET HEDICAN	76	6	19	25	4	68	2		1		58	10.3
L	13	OLEG KVASHA	78	5	20	25	3	34	2				110	4.5
C	9	LEN BARRIE	60	9	14	23	9	62					61	14.8
R	26	RAY SHEPPARD	47	10	10	20	-4	4	5		2		74	13.5
D	7	MIKE WILSON	60	4	16	20	10	35			2		65	6.2
L	18	CAMERON STEWART	65	9	7	16	-2	30			3		52	17.3
D	3	PAUL LAUS	77	3	8	11	-1	172					44	6.8
L	8	PETER WORRELL	48	3	6	9	-7	169	2		1		45	6.7
D	2	LANCE PITLICK	62	3	5	8	7	44			1		26	11.5
D	22	TODD SIMPSON	82	1	6	7	5	202					50	2.0
D	5	*FILIP KUBA	13	1	5	6	-3	2	1		1		16	6.3
R	16	*IVAN NOVOSELTSEV	14	2	1	3	-3	8	2				8	25.0
L	12	ALEX HICKS	8	1	2	3	3	4					6	16.7
D	6	*DAN BOYLE	13		3	3	-2	4					9	
G	30	MIKHAIL SHTALENKOV	30		3	3	0	4						
G	29	MIKE VERNON	49		3	3	0	2						
L	48	*MARCUS NILSON	9		2	2	2	2					6	
D	45	*BRAD FERENCE	13		2	2	2	46					10	
G	32	RICH SHULMISTRA	1				0							
L	48	*DAVE DUERDEN	2				0						1	
C	47	CRAIG FERGUSON	3				-2						2	
C	40	*ERIC BOGUNIECKI	4				-1	2					5	
C	23	CHRIS WELLS	13				-5	14					5	
D	15	*JOHN JAKOPIN	17				-2	26					1	
G	37	TREVOR KIDD	28				0							

GP = games played; G = goals; A = assists; PTS = points; +/- = goals-for minus goals-against while player is on ice; PIM = penalties in minutes; PP = power-play goals; SH = shorthanded goals; GW = game-winning goals; GT = game-tying goals; S = no. of shots; PCT = percentage of goals to shots; * = rookie

PAVEL BURE

Yrs. of NHL service: 9
Born: Moscow, Russia; Mar. 31, 1971
Position: right wing
Height: 5-10
Weight: 189
Uniform no.: 10
Shoots: left

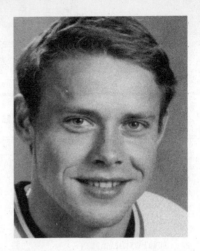

Career statistics:

GP	G	A	TP	PIM
513	325	263	588	348

1996-97 statistics:

GP	G	A	TP	+/-	PIM	PP	SH	GW	GT	S	PCT
63	23	32	55	-14	40	4	1	2	0	265	8.7

1997-98 statistics:

GP	G	A	TP	+/-	PIM	PP	SH	GW	GT	S	PCT
82	51	39	90	+5	48	13	6	4	1	329	15.5

1998-99 statistics:

GP	G	A	TP	+/-	PIM	PP	SH	GW	GT	S	PCT
11	13	3	16	+3	4	5	1	0	1	44	29.5

1999-2000 statistics:

GP	G	A	TP	+/-	PIM	PP	SH	GW	GT	S	PCT
74	58	36	94	+25	16	11	2	14	0	360	16.1

LAST SEASON

Finalist for 2000 Hart Trophy. Won 2000 Rocket Richard Trophy for leading NHL in goals. Led team and second in NHL in points. Led team in game-winning goals and shots. Led team in plus-minus, power-play goals and game-winning goals. Second on team in shooting percentage and shorthanded goals. Missed three games with broken finger. Missed five games with groin injury.

THE FINESSE GAME

Bure logs so much ice time (he led all NHL forwards with more than 25 minutes per game last season) that he needs not one, but two centres. But the Panthers couldn't even find him one good fit. They are hoping that free-agent Igor Larionov, and Olli Jokinen, acquired in the Roberto Luongo deal, will be good companions. Bure needs to play with linemates who move the puck to him quickly. Let him do the work.

Goalies never know when Bure's shot is going to come. He keeps his legs churning and the shot is on net before the keeper knows it. He does not telegraph his shot by breaking stride, and it's an awesome sight. He has great balance and agility, and he moves equally well both with the puck and without it. Bure is always lurking and looking for the headman pass.

The Russian Rocket's quickness — and his control of the puck at supersonic speed — means anything is possible. He intimidates with his skating, driving back defenders who must play off him or risk being deked out of their skates at the blueline. He opens up tremendous ice for his teammates and will leave a drop pass or, more often, try to do it himself.

Bure doesn't do much defensively. He prefers to hang out at centre ice, and when he is going through a slump he doesn't do the other little things that can make a player useful until the scoring starts to kick in again. He is a shorthanded threat because of his speed and anticipation. He is one of the best breakaway scorers in the league. His explosive skating comes from his thick, powerful thighs, which look like a speed skater's.

THE PHYSICAL GAME

Bure has a little nasty edge to him, and will make solid hits for the puck, though he doesn't apply himself as enthusiastically in a defensive role. He has to play a reckless game to drive to the net and score goals. He takes a lot of punishment getting there and that's what makes him vulnerable to injuries, though he was quite durable last season; his knee problems appear to be a thing of the past.

THE INTANGIBLES

Bure had an uninspiring playoff round against the Devils, and the Panthers obviously need to shore up their talent to prevent the same thing happening again in the postseason.

PROJECTION

We called for 50 goals for the Russian Rocket last season and he might have broken 60 if he hadn't hit a couple of nagging injuries. Fifty-eight goals today are worth far more than the 60 Bure scored a few years ago with Vancouver. If any NHL player can be worth $9 million, Bure is it.

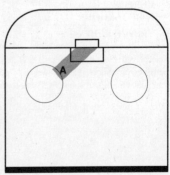

BRET HEDICAN

Yrs. of NHL service: 8
Born: St. Paul, Minn.; Aug. 10, 1970
Position: left defense
Height: 6-2
Weight: 195
Uniform no.: 4
Shoots: left

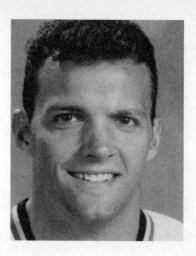

Career statistics:

GP	G	A	TP	PIM
518	27	130	157	439

1996-97 statistics:

GP	G	A	TP	+/-	PIM	PP	SH	GW	GT	S	PCT
67	4	15	19	-3	51	2	0	1	0	93	4.3

1997-98 statistics:

GP	G	A	TP	+/-	PIM	PP	SH	GW	GT	S	PCT
71	3	24	27	+3	79	1	0	0	1	84	3.6

1998-99 statistics:

GP	G	A	TP	+/-	PIM	PP	SH	GW	GT	S	PCT
67	5	18	23	+5	51	0	2	1	1	90	5.6

1999-2000 statistics:

GP	G	A	TP	+/-	PIM	PP	SH	GW	GT	S	PCT
76	6	19	25	+4	68	2	0	1	0	58	10.3

LAST SEASON

Missed two games with shoulder injury. Missed three games due to suspension. Missed one game due to coach's decision.

THE FINESSE GAME

Hedican is among the best-skating defensemen in the NHL. He has a nice, deep knee bend and his fluid stride provides good acceleration; each stride eats up lots of ice. His steady balance allows him to go down to one knee and use his stick to challenge passes from the corners. He uses quickness, range and reach to make a confident stand at the blueline.

Hedican happily uses his speed with the puck to drive down the wing and create trouble in the offensive zone. He also varies the attack. He seems to prefer the left-wing boards, but will also take the right-wing route to try to make plays off the backhand.

He is a good enough stickhandler to try one-on-one moves. He is eager to jump into the play. He will never be a great point getter or playmaker because he doesn't think the game well enough, but he tries to help his team on the attack. He is a better player in the playoffs, when he doesn't think as much and lets his natural instincts rule.

Hedican knows that if an attacker beats him, he will be able to keep up with him and steer him to bad ice. He is the perfect guy to pick up the puck behind the net and get it to the redline and start the half-court game. He doesn't always just put his head down and go, either. He will move up the middle and look for a pass to a breaking wing, though he was guilty of some giveaways at the most inopportune times last season.

THE PHYSICAL GAME

Hedican has decent size but not a great deal of strength or toughness. He won't bulldoze in front of the net, but prefers to tie people up and go for the puck. He is more of a stick-checker than a body checker, though he will sometimes knock a player off the puck at the blueline, control it and make a smart first pass. His preference is to use body positioning to nullify an opponent rather than initiate hard body contact.

THE INTANGIBLES

Hedican has steady skills to complement a more offensive player like Robert Svehla, and he is a capable top two or three defenseman, but the Panthers were reportedly looking to move him at the trade deadline and he could be changing teams again soon.

PROJECTION

Hedican is developing into a solid two-way defenseman and can be expected to improve sharply over the next few seasons as he gains confidence and experience. He hasn't taken the next step yet, and still has offensive upside. He should score around 35 points.

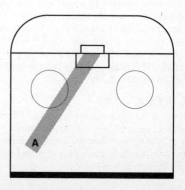

OLLI JOKINEN

Yrs. of NHL service: 2
Born: Kuopio, Finland; Dec. 5, 1978
Position: centre
Height: 6-2
Weight: 198
Uniform no.: 12
Shoots: left

Career statistics:

GP	G	A	TP	PIM
156	20	22	42	130

1998-99 statistics:

GP	G	A	TP	+/-	PIM	PP	SH	GW	GT	S	PCT
66	9	12	21	-10	44	3	1	1	0	87	10.3

1999-2000 statistics:

GP	G	A	TP	+/-	PIM	PP	SH	GW	GT	S	PCT
82	11	10	21	0	80	1	2	3	0	138	8.0

LAST SEASON

Second NHL season. Acquired from N.Y. Islanders with Roberto Luongo for Oleg Kvasha and Mark Parrish, June 23, 2000. Second on Islanders in shots. Tied for second on team in plus-minus and game-winning goals. Only Islander to appear in all 82 games.

THE FINESSE GAME

Jokinen is an offensive-minded player with terrific hockey sense. He has performed well on the world stage, usually against older players, and he makes things happen with his creativity and up-tempo skills. He has an added dollop of power in his game, which improves his upside.

Jokinen has played some wing but he is better at centre and was used in that capacity by the Islanders. He is a better playmaker than scorer. He has excellent vision and a wonderful sense of timing with his passes. He is probably too unselfish and will need to develop a shot he has confidence in, because he has the ability to.

He has a good head for the game and good vision.

THE PHYSICAL GAME

Jokinen was not very consistent in his efforts last season. The Isles thought he played too soft, which helped pave his way out. When he chooses to play hard, he uses his solid build and won't be intimidated. He has a slighty nasty side that he needs to let loose more often. He can be chippy and annoying to play against. He didn't seem to turn his game up until trade rumours surfaced in March.

THE INTANGIBLES

Three teams in three seasons could be a little unsettling for a young player, but Jokinen seems to be happy to have escaped from the Island. He is an ideal number two, which is where he will probably fit in behind Viktor Kozlov in Florida.

PROJECTION

Jokinen is just about guaranteed a top six role, and if he can develop chemistry with a finisher, 40 points is a conservative estimate. His totals will be much heavier on assists.

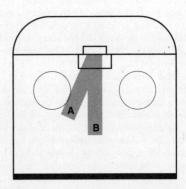

VIKTOR KOZLOV

Yrs. of NHL service: 5
Born: Togliatti, Russia; Feb. 14, 1975
Position: right wing
Height: 6-5
Weight: 225
Uniform no.: 25
Shoots: right

Career statistics:

GP	G	A	TP	PIM
365	74	139	213	104

1996-97 statistics:

GP	G	A	TP	+/-	PIM	PP	SH	GW	GT	S	PCT
78	16	25	41	-16	40	4	0	4	0	184	8.7

1997-98 statistics:

GP	G	A	TP	+/-	PIM	PP	SH	GW	GT	S	PCT
64	17	13	30	-3	16	5	2	0	0	165	10.3

1998-99 statistics:

GP	G	A	TP	+/-	PIM	PP	SH	GW	GT	S	PCT
65	16	35	51	+13	24	5	1	1	0	209	7.7

1999-2000 statistics:

GP	G	A	TP	+/-	PIM	PP	SH	GW	GT	S	PCT
80	17	53	70	+24	16	6	0	2	0	223	7.6

LAST SEASON

Led team in assists with career high. Tied for fourth in NHL in assists. Second on team in plus-minus and shots. Third on team in points with career high. Tied for third on team in power-play goals. Missed two games with shoulder injury.

THE FINESSE GAME

Kozlov is a beautiful skater for his size. He has the moves of a 150-pounder, with quickness and agility. He held his own with the fleet Pavel Bure as a linemate last season, but playing on a line with power wingers would probably suit his game better (too bad the Panthers don't have any).

Kozlov has learned to come off the boards much quicker. As a huge right-handed shooter attacking the left side, he has a move that — dare we say it — makes him look like Mario Lemieux. He can undress a defender with his stickhandling and create a scoring chance down low. He has a keen sense of timing and pace. He can also play either centre or wing. He loves to shoot, and he shoots hard. He has an accurate wrist shot with a quick release.

He won't float and he has defensive principles. He won't hang at the redline, but he is an attentive backchecker. With deceptively quick acceleration for a player of his size, he excells at the transition game.

Kozlov needs to learn to protect the puck better by keeping it closer to his feet. He often makes it too easy for a defender to strip the puck.

THE PHYSICAL GAME

Kozlov's physique makes him sturdy in contact, and when he goes down on a hook or a hold, nine times out of 10 it's a dive.

Although he has a long reach, Kozlov doesn't care to play the body defensively, though offensively he will work with the puck to get in front of the net and into scoring position. He handles the puck well in traffic. He has added some muscle but it would help to add more, since he is likely to be Florida's number one centre.

THE INTANGIBLES

If Kozlov can centre the second line with some finishers, Florida will have the depth it needs to avoid another playoff disaster like its first-round sweep at the hands of the Devils.

PROJECTION

Last season we told you Kozlov would play with Bure and post career numbers in the 70- to 80-point range. As they say in Florida, bingo! Now Kozlov may have to adjust to new linemates. His production could suffer a bit if he isn't with Bure, but 60 points is still attainable.

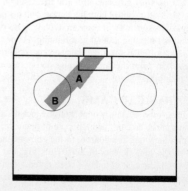

PAUL LAUS

Yrs. of NHL service: 7
Born: Beamsville, Ont.; Sept. 26, 1970
Position: right defense
Height: 6-1
Weight: 216
Uniform no.: 3
Shoots: right

Career statistics:

GP	G	A	TP	PIM
460	9	53	62	1479

1996-97 statistics:

GP	G	A	TP	+/-	PIM	PP	SH	GW	GT	S	PCT
77	0	12	12	+13	313	0	0	0	0	63	0.0

1997-98 statistics:

GP	G	A	TP	+/-	PIM	PP	SH	GW	GT	S	PCT
77	0	11	11	-5	293	0	0	0	0	64	.0

1998-99 statistics:

GP	G	A	TP	+/-	PIM	PP	SH	GW	GT	S	PCT
75	1	9	10	-1	218	0	0	0	0	54	1.9

1999-2000 statistics:

GP	G	A	TP	+/-	PIM	PP	SH	GW	GT	S	PCT
77	3	8	11	-1	172	0	0	0	0	44	6.8

LAST SEASON

Second on team in penalty minutes. Matched career high in goals. Missed five games with fractured hand.

THE FINESSE GAME

People don't like to play against a club that has Laus on its side. He is a legitimate tough guy, but one who has worked at the other aspects of his game to become a more useful player. The Panthers were so in need of size up front that they converted him to a right wing, which is where he played most of the season.

Laus has borderline NHL skating speed. He is powerful and well-balanced for battles along the boards and in the corners. He seems to know his limitations and doesn't try to overextend himself. Since he doesn't cover a lot of ice, he needs to be paired with a mobile partner. Of course, he also is afforded plenty of room since only the brave venture into his territory, and that buys him some time.

Laus uses his size and strength effectively at all times. He has to control both his temper and his playing style. His success will come from playing his position and not running around headhunting. He doesn't have much offensive instinct, but he gets some room to take shots from the point because no one wants to come near him.

THE PHYSICAL GAME

Laus hits. Anyone. At any opportunity. Since his skating isn't great, he can't catch people in open ice, but he's murder along the boards, in the corners and in front of the net. He hits to hurt. He's big, but not scary-sized like a lot of today's NHL defensemen. He is, however, powerful and mean, and he stands up for his teammates.

THE INTANGIBLES

Laus has worked hard to become more than a mere goon, and it's paid off. He is a perfectly serviceable fifth or sixth defenseman, or fourth-line right wing. He makes his teammates braver and, if his skills keep improving as they have been over the past three seasons, that will keep him on the ice. Peter Worrell's development has taken some of the heat off Laus to fight every night. He will be a bubble player.

PROJECTION

If you're in a goon pool, Laus is a pretty sure bet for 200 PIM. Those three goals are a bonus.

ROBERTO LUONGO

Yrs. of NHL service: 0
Born: Montreal, Que.; Apr. 4, 1979
Position: goaltender
Height: 6-3
Weight: 175
Uniform no.: 1
Catches: left

Career statistics:

GP	MIN	GA	SO	GAA	A	PIM
24	1292	70	1	3.25	0	0

1999-2000 statistics:

GP	MIN	GAA	W	L	T	SO	GA	S	SAPCT	PIM
24	1292	3.25	7	14	1	1	70	730	.904	0

LAST SEASON

Will be entering first NHL season. Appeared in 26 games with Lowell (AHL), with a 10-12-4 record and 2.93 goals-against average.

THE PHYSICAL GAME

Luongo is very tall and plays a butterfly style that completely takes way the top part of the net from shooters. So they try to go five-hole. Guess what? Luongo has really, really big pads (he will keep the NHL's measuring guys busy), fast legs and good flexibility.

Luongo has a tendency to try to use his feet too much to kick out the puck, and he can leave some bad rebounds. Improved confidence in using his stick and controlling the puck for his defensemen will be a help. Luongo doesn't have to be Martin Brodeur. He just need to give his defense a chance to play the puck.

Luongo's one glaring weakness is his lack of lateral movement. He needs to concentrate on improving his footwork, because it won't take NHL shooters very long to figure out how to jerk him from post to post. Luongo has to avoid staying deep in his net. He is a terrific athlete.

THE MENTAL GAME

Luungo had a tough season last year. He started in the minors, won his NHL debut in November...and it all seemed to go downhill from there. He was outplayed by Kevin Weekes and ended up back in the minors. Luongo had a tough time shaking off bad goals. One soft one would usually be followed by another.

Luongo is very likable and has a great deal of presence and poise. There will be a lot of pressure on him to perform in Florida.

THE INTANGIBLES

Luongo went from being the Islanders' goalie of the future to the Panthers' goalie now. Florida does have a veteran fall-back guy in Trevor Kidd. It's unlikely Kidd will accept much of a mentor's role, but at least Luongo has Bill Smith around for some moral support.

PROJECTION

The Panthers believe they have found their franchise goalie. If he gets 55 to 60 starts, Luongo should get 20 to 25 wins.

SCOTT MELLANBY

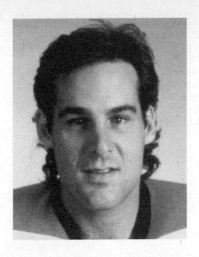

Yrs. of NHL service: 14
Born: Montreal, Que,; June 11, 1966
Position: right wing
Height: 6-1
Weight: 199
Uniform no.: 27
Shoots: right

Career statistics:

GP	G	A	TP	PIM
1016	274	346	620	1945

1996-97 statistics:

GP	G	A	TP	+/-	PIM	PP	SH	GW	GT	S	PCT
82	27	29	56	+7	170	9	1	4	0	221	12.2

1997-98 statistics:

GP	G	A	TP	+/-	PIM	PP	SH	GW	GT	S	PCT
79	15	24	39	-14	127	6	0	1	0	188	8.0

1998-99 statistics:

GP	G	A	TP	+/-	PIM	PP	SH	GW	GT	S	PCT
67	18	27	45	+5	85	4	0	3	3	136	13.2

1999-2000 statistics:

GP	G	A	TP	+/-	PIM	PP	SH	GW	GT	S	PCT
77	18	28	46	+14	126	6	0	2	1	134	13.4

LAST SEASON

Tied for third on team in power-play goals. Missed three games with concussion. Missed one game with flu. Missed one game due to coach's decision.

THE FINESSE GAME

Not having a great deal of speed or agility, Mellanby generates most of his effectiveness in tight spaces, where he can use his size. On the power play, where he lost some time due to the arrival of Pavel Bure, he sets up below the hash marks for a one-timer. He works for screens and tips. He doesn't have many moves but he can capitalize on a loose puck with some good hands in tight. Goals don't come naturally to him, however, but he's determined and pays the price in front of the net.

Mellanby has developed a quicker release and more confidence in his shot, but still needs to shoot more, since he is quite accurate with his shot.

He has become more of a two-way player in recent years, though he no longer sees many penalty-killing shifts. He is not much of a shorthanded threat. He lacks the speed and scoring instincts to convert turnovers into dangerous chances.

THE PHYSICAL GAME

Mellanby forechecks aggressively, using his body well to hit and force mistakes in the attacking zone. He engages in one-on-one battles in tight areas and tries to win his share. He is also willing to mix it up and take penalties of aggression. He seldom misses an opportunity to rub his glove in an opponent's face.

He's very strong along the boards and uses his feet when battling for the puck.

THE INTANGIBLES

Mellanby is the Panthers' captain, but management considers him a little too laid-back for the job. His ice time will continue to decline, and yet the Panthers don't have a lot of forwards with grit. He is in his walk year, which affects different players in different ways. Either he will be trying to prove himself worthy of a new contract on the free-agent market, or his uncertain future will make him nervous. He could be a rent-a-player down the stretch for a playoff team with a more traditional style than Florida's.

PROJECTION

Mellanby has been a steady 15- to 20-goal scorer the past few seasons. Those numbers are his absolute top end now.

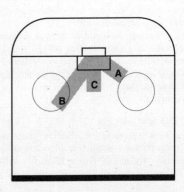

ROB NIEDERMAYER

Yrs. of NHL service: 7
Born: Cassiar, B.C.; Dec. 28, 1974
Position: centre
Height: 6-2
Weight: 201
Uniform no.: 44
Shoots: left

Career statistics:

GP	G	A	TP	PIM
606	89	145	234	385

1996-97 statistics:

GP	G	A	TP	+/-	PIM	PP	SH	GW	GT	S	PCT
60	14	24	38	+4	54	3	0	2	0	136	10.3

1997-98 statistics:

GP	G	A	TP	+/-	PIM	PP	SH	GW	GT	S	PCT
33	8	7	15	-9	41	5	0	2	0	64	12.5

1998-99 statistics:

GP	G	A	TP	+/-	PIM	PP	SH	GW	GT	S	PCT
82	18	33	51	-13	50	6	1	3	2	142	12.7

1999-2000 statistics:

GP	G	A	TP	+/-	PIM	PP	SH	GW	GT	S	PCT
81	10	23	33	-5	46	1	0	4	0	135	7.4

LAST SEASON

Missed one game with head injury.

THE FINESSE GAME

Little went right for Niedermayer last season, except that he was able to stay healthy. He wasn't a good fit with star winger Pavel Bure, and the Panthers didn't seem to know what else to do with him.

He is an excellent skater, better even than older brother Scott. Big and strong, Niedermayer has the speed to stay with some of the league's best power centres, but he doesn't play a power game.

He is a strong passer and an unselfish player, probably too unselfish. He controls the puck well at tempo and can beat a defender one-on-one. He has started to finish better and play with much more authority.

Niedermayer is excellent on face-offs and takes many of the Panthers' key draws, even when he is shifted to left wing. He works on the second-unit power play.

THE PHYSICAL GAME

Although not overly physical, Niedermayer has good size. He is an intelligent player and doesn't hurt his team by taking bad penalties. The Panthers would actually prefer to see more attitude. He has lost confidence over the past few seasons, mostly due to injuries.

THE INTANGIBLES

Don't underestimate the aftereffects of the concussion suffered by Niedermayer in 1997-98. He hasn't been the same player since. Still a great skater, he is hesistant and slow to react. He was a restricted free agent during the off-season, without much bargaining power. Sadly, he is another budding NHL star whose career appears to have been derailed by a serious head injury.

PROJECTION

Niedermayer's offensive totals are dropping alarmingly for so young a player. The Panthers have just about given up hope that he will ever be a 25-goal scorer again, and we are ready to agree. He has become more valuable for his defensive abilities.

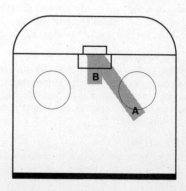

IVAN NOVOSELTSEV

Yrs. of NHL service: 1
Born: Golitsino, USSR; Jan. 23, 1979
Position: left wing
Height: 6-1
Weight: 183
Uniform no.: 16
Shoots: left

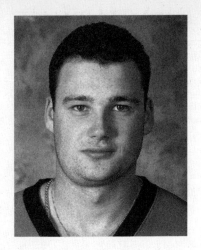

Career statistics:

GP	G	A	TP	PIM
135	85	62	147	94

1999-2000 statistics:

GP	G	A	TP	+/-	PIM	PP	SH	GW	GT	S	PCT
14	2	1	3	-3	8	2	0	0	0	8	25.0

LAST SEASON

Will be entering first NHL season. Appeared in 47 games with Louisville (AHL), scoring 14-21 — 35.

THE FINESSE GAME

This kid is already being called the "Pocket Rocket," not for Henri Richard, but for being a smaller version of legendary Maurice "Rocket" Richard. There are some who think Novoseltsev might someday claim the goal-scoring trophy that is named for Richard.

Novoseltsev is a left-handed shot who plays the right wing. This opens up his forehand for one-timers. He plays a reckless style and is always looking for the net. He also has blinding speed and the ability to pick up the puck behind his own net and go end-to-end. He intimidates with his speed, driving defensemen back on their heels before he cuts inside or outside. His wrist shot is his favourite weapon.

The usual red flag attached to Novoseltsev is his lack of defensive awareness. He can also be a bit selfish with the puck and doesn't always use his teammates well. He was coached to concentrate on his defensive duties last season in the minors, and took an important first step towards becoming a better two-way forward.

THE PHYSICAL GAME

Novoseltsev doesn't get overly involved in physical play. For one thing, you can't hit what you can't catch. He will drive to the crease for a scoring chance.

THE INTANGIBLES

Novoseltsev's development was hindered by some nagging back and groin injuries in the minors. He scored four goals in a single game for Louisville, and the Panthers are pretty optimistic he will stick with the big squad this season.

PROJECTION

Florida is trying to stay cautious, but there is a lot of buzz about this kid. Don't be surprised if he shows up as Pavel Bure's left wing. He could score 20 to 25 goals in his first full NHL season.

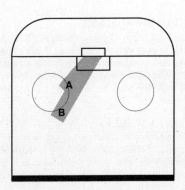

MIKE SILLINGER

Yrs. of NHL service: 8
Born: Regina, Sask.; June 29, 1971
Position: centre
Height: 5-10
Weight: 200
Uniform no.: 26
Shoots: right

Career statistics:

GP	G	A	TP	PIM
530	99	148	247	285

1996-97 statistics:

GP	G	A	TP	+/-	PIM	PP	SH	GW	GT	S	PCT
78	17	20	37	-3	25	3	3	2	0	112	15.2

1997-98 statistics:

GP	G	A	TP	+/-	PIM	PP	SH	GW	GT	S	PCT
75	21	20	41	-11	50	2	4	1	0	96	21.9

1998-99 statistics:

GP	G	A	TP	+/-	PIM	PP	SH	GW	GT	S	PCT
79	8	5	13	-29	36	0	2	0	0	92	8.7

1999-2000 statistics:

GP	G	A	TP	+/-	PIM	PP	SH	GW	GT	S	PCT
80	23	29	52	-30	102	8	3	2	0	146	15.8

LAST SEASON

Acquired from Tampa Bay for Ryan Johnson and Dwayne Hay, Mar. 14, 2000. Led Panthers in short-handed goals. Second on team in power-play goals. Third on team in shooting percentage. Career highs in goals, assists and points.

THE FINESSE GAME

One of the drawbacks to this veteran's career is his size, but Sillinger is not without his assets. He is a clever player with a knack for positioning himself in the attacking zone. And he has a good shot with a quick release.

Sillinger is an energetic skater with speed and balance. His one-step acceleration is good. He plays well in traffic, using his sturdy form to protect the puck, and he has sharp hand-eye coordination. He is a smart penalty killer and a shorthanded threat, as well as an ace on faceoffs.

Sillinger kicked around a number of organizations (Detroit, Anaheim, Vancouver, Philadelphia, Tampa Bay) and has always had a hard time finding his niche.

THE PHYSICAL GAME

Sillinger is small but burly. He is tough to budge from in front of the net because of his low centre of gravity. He is not feisty or aggressive. He keeps himself in good condition and over the past few seasons has missed very few games due to injuries.

THE INTANGIBLES

Sillinger is a special-teams specialist. He kills penalties, is a shorthanded threat, works the open ice on the power play, and can fill in (short-term) on the top two lines in a pinch. He is a grinder, a role player and a leader by example. He was an astute late-season pickup by GM Bryan Murray.

PROJECTION

Sillinger was given quality ice time and exceeded our expectations. Can he surpass 20 again? Seeing as how he popped in four goals in just 13 games with the Panthers, yes.

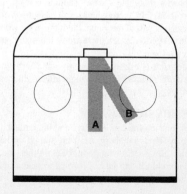

TODD SIMPSON

Yrs. of NHL service: 4
Born: Edmonton, Alta.; May 28, 1973
Position: left defense
Height: 6-3
Weight: 215
Uniform no.: 27
Shoots: left

Career statistics:

GP	G	A	TP	PIM
296	5	32	36	702

1996-97 statistics:

GP	G	A	TP	+/-	PIM	PP	SH	GW	GT	S	PCT
82	1	13	14	-14	208	0	0	1	0	85	1.2

1997-98 statistics:

GP	G	A	TP	+/-	PIM	PP	SH	GW	GT	S	PCT
53	1	5	6	-10	109	0	0	1	0	51	2.0

1998-99 statistics:

GP	G	A	TP	+/-	PIM	PP	SH	GW	GT	S	PCT
73	2	8	10	+18	151	0	0	0	0	52	3.8

1999-2000 statistics:

GP	G	A	TP	+/-	PIM	PP	SH	GW	GT	S	PCT
82	1	6	7	+5	202	0	0	0	0	50	2.0

LAST SEASON

Acquired from Calgary for Bill Lindsay, Sept. 30, 1999. Led team in penalty minutes. One of three Panthers to appear in all 82 games.

THE FINESSE GAME

Simpson is a poor man's Mark Tinordi. He is a defensive defenseman, one who made his initial reputation by fighting, just as Tinordi did. But Simpson has also worked his tail off to become a solid pro.

Although he still has a lot to learn, he is coachable and will play intelligent position defense, making attackers pay the price for coming into his area of the ice. His stickhandling and shooting skills are average. His skating is just about NHL level and could stand some improvement.

What sets Simpson apart (besides his size), though, is his determination. He won't give up on a play in any zone. He kills penalties on the first unit and blocks shots. He's smart enough to make some plays offensively, though he doesn't have much confidence in that part of the game. Put it this way: when he decides to go to the net, there aren't too many people who can stop him.

Simpson is highly competitive and will go out against other teams' top lines night after night, despite a gap in skills.

THE PHYSICAL GAME

Simpson is unafraid of big guys and big names. If he has to hit Peter Forsberg, he'll hit him. If he has to drop his gloves against a goon, he'll do that, too. He loves a good tilt, but he has learned to take a quality player with him on most nights.

THE INTANGIBLES

Simpson is leadership material, a player who fights for his teammates on the ice and goes out of his way to make them feel a part of the Panthers off the ice. He's a tremendous heart-and-soul player, a team guy and a tough guy. On a team sorely deficient in grit, Simpson is invaluable.

PROJECTION

Simpson's value can't be measured in points; it's unlikely he'll ever score more than 20.

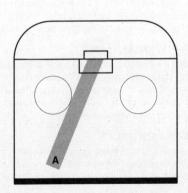

JAROSLAV SPACEK

Yrs. of NHL service: 2
Born: Rokycany, Czech.; Feb. 11, 1974
Position: left defense
Height: 5-11
Weight: 198
Uniform no.: 8
Shoots: left

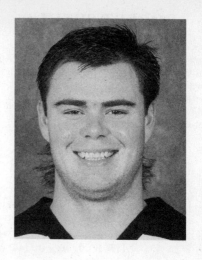

Career statistics:

GP	G	A	TP	PIM
145	13	38	51	81

1998-99 statistics:

GP	G	A	TP	+/-	PIM	PP	SH	GW	GT	S	PCT
63	3	12	15	+15	28	2	1	0	0	92	3.3

1999-2000 statistics:

GP	G	A	TP	+/-	PIM	PP	SH	GW	GT	S	PCT
82	10	26	36	+7	53	4	0	1	0	111	9.0

LAST SEASON

Second NHL season. Career high in goals, assists and points. One of three Panthers to appear in all 82 games.

THE FINESSE GAME

Spacek is an agile skater. He is good one-on-one and even defending against a two-on-one. He moves the puck very well and has some offensive upside.

Spacek uses his finesse skills in a defensive manner, positioning himself intelligently and anticipating plays. He kills penalties, and can handle some second-unit power play chores.

Spacek broke into the league as an older rookie and was able to make a quick transition to the North American style of play. But Florida frequently asks him to perform as number two defenseman, and on his best nights, he is really only a number one.

THE PHYSICAL GAME

Strength-wise, Spacek loses a lot of battles along the boards and in front of the net. He doesn't have much affinity for physical play.

THE INTANGIBLES

Spacek needs to get more battle-tough, especially with the Panthers being such a finesse-first team that is easily intimated at crunch time. He doesn't have to be fearsome. The Panthers just can't afford to have him play scared, and sometimes it looks as if he is.

PROJECTION

We predicted an improved Panthers power play would boost Spacek's totals into the 35-point range. That appears to be his top end, and another season in that range would be a success.

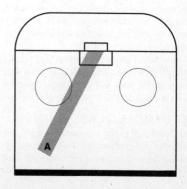

ROBERT SVEHLA

Yrs. of NHL service: 5
Born: Martin, Slovakia; Jan. 2, 1969
Position: right defense
Height: 6-1
Weight: 190
Uniform no.: 24
Shoots: right

Career statistics:

GP	G	A	TP	PIM
409	48	185	233	440

1996-97 statistics:

GP	G	A	TP	+/-	PIM	PP	SH	GW	GT	S	PCT
82	13	32	45	+2	86	5	0	3	0	159	8.2

1997-98 statistics:

GP	G	A	TP	+/-	PIM	PP	SH	GW	GT	S	PCT
79	9	34	43	-3	113	3	0	0	0	144	6.3

1998-99 statistics:

GP	G	A	TP	+/-	PIM	PP	SH	GW	GT	S	PCT
80	8	29	37	-13	83	4	0	0	1	157	5.1

1999-2000 statistics:

GP	G	A	TP	+/-	PIM	PP	SH	GW	GT	S	PCT
82	9	40	49	+23	64	3	0	1	0	143	6.3

LAST SEASON

Led team defensemen in points for fourth consecutive season. Tenth among NHL defensemen in points. Second on team in assists. Third on team in plus-minus. One of three Panthers to appear in all 82 games.

THE FINESSE GAME

Svehla is among the best in the NHL at the lost art of the sweep-check. If he does lose control of the puck, and an attacker has a step or two on him on a break-away, he has the poise to dive and use his stick to knock the puck away without touching the man's skates.

He is a terrific skater. No one, not even Jaromir Jagr, can beat Svehla wide, because he skates well backwards and laterally. He plays a quick transition. He is among the best NHL defensemen one-on-one in open ice. He pinches aggressively and intelligently and makes high-risk plays . . . unfortunately for the Panthers, he gambles too often in his own zone. Svehla also has the uncanny knack of making a change at the worst time. But by then, he is off the ice, so his plus-minus doesn't suffer.

Svehla works on the first power play, moving to the left point. He uses a long wrist shot from the point to make sure the puck will get through on net. When he kills penalties, he makes safe plays off the boards.

THE PHYSICAL GAME

Svehla is not that strong or naturally aggressive, but he competes. He gets into the thick of things by battling along the wall and in the corners for the puck. He is not a huge checker, but he pins his man and doesn't allow him back into the play. He is in peak condition and needs little recovery time between shifts, so he can handle a lot of ice time.

THE INTANGIBLES

Svehla rebounded from an erratic 1998-99 season to become far more reliable defensively. He regained confidence in his offensive game as well. He still needs to maintain his focus and intensity on a nightly basis. He had a sluggish second half after brisk start, and a very quiet playoffs. If the Panthers add a veteran puck-carrying defenseman, some of the burden will be shifted off him.

PROJECTION

Welcome back, Svehla. He should be capable of 50 points this season.

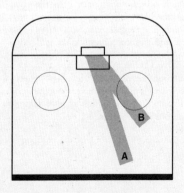

RAY WHITNEY

Yrs. of NHL service: 8
Born: Fort Saskatchewan, Alberta; May 8, 1972
Position: left wing/centre
Height: 5-10
Weight: 175
Uniform no.: 14
Shoots: right

Career statistics:

GP	G	A	TP	PIM
439	136	185	321	133

1996-97 statistics:

GP	G	A	TP	+/-	PIM	PP	SH	GW	GT	S	PCT
12	0	2	2	-6	4	0	0	0	0	24	0.0

1997-98 statistics:

GP	G	A	TP	+/-	PIM	PP	SH	GW	GT	S	PCT
77	33	32	65	+9	28	12	0	2	0	175	18.9

1998-99 statistics:

GP	G	A	TP	+/-	PIM	PP	SH	GW	GT	S	PCT
81	26	38	64	-3	18	7	0	6	1	193	13.5

1999-2000 statistics:

GP	G	A	TP	+/-	PIM	PP	SH	GW	GT	S	PCT
81	29	42	71	+16	35	5	0	3	2	198	14.6

LAST SEASON

Second on team in goals and points. Tied for second on team in game-winning goals. Third on team in assists and shots. Career high in points. Missed one game with groin injury.

THE FINESSE GAME

Whitney is not a fast skater, but he is shifty in tight quarters and that makes him very tough to check. He likes to cut to the middle of the ice and use his forehand. He is dangerous every shift.

Savvy and determined, Whitney compensates for his lack of speed with a keen sense of anticipation. He jumps into the right spot simply by knowing before his checker does that it's the right place to be. That makes him appear quicker than he really is.

Whitney is poised in traffic and well-balanced on his feet. He has exceptionally good hands for passing or shooting. He can lift a backhand shot when he is practically on top of the goalie. And he has a deceptive shot because he does not telegraph whether he is going to pass or shoot.

Whitney needs to play with a grinder on his wing because he can't win the battles on the boards.

THE PHYSICAL GAME

Whitney is small, but he plays a wily game. A centre of his ability needs to be protected with a tough winger and defenseman, but Whitney brings so much to the game that a team can make room for him. He is remarkably durable for his size.

THE INTANGIBLES

Whitney continued to overachieve for the third consecutive season. He was among the (many) Panthers to have a disappointing playoffs. He was a restricted free agent during the off-season and earned a salary bump.

PROJECTION

Whitney has the ability to be a consistent 25-goal scorer in the right circumstances, which he has found on a skilled Florida team.

LOS ANGELES KINGS

Players' Statistics 1999-2000

POS.	NO.	PLAYER	GP	G	A	PTS	+/-	PIM	PP	SH	GW	GT	S	PCT
L	20	LUC ROBITAILLE	71	36	38	74	11	68	13		7		221	16.3
R	33	ZIGMUND PALFFY	64	27	39	66	18	32	4		3	1	186	14.5
R	27	GLEN MURRAY	78	29	33	62	13	60	10	1	2	1	202	14.4
C	15	JOZEF STUMPEL	57	17	41	58	23	10	3		7	1	126	13.5
D	4	ROB BLAKE	77	18	39	57	10	112	12		5		327	5.5
C	21	BRYAN SMOLINSKI	79	20	36	56	2	48	2			2	160	12.5
R	17	NELSON EMERSON	63	15	20	35	-23	47	4			1	196	7.7
D	3	GARRY GALLEY	70	9	21	30	9	52	2		1		96	9.4
L	23	CRAIG JOHNSON	76	9	14	23	-10	28	1		1		106	8.5
C	11	JASON BLAKE	64	5	18	23	4	26			1		131	3.8
C	22	IAN LAPERRIERE	79	9	13	22	-14	185			1		87	10.3
R	9	KELLY BUCHBERGER	81	7	13	20	-36	152					76	9.2
R	12	MARKO TUOMAINEN	63	9	8	17	-12	80	2	1	1		74	12.2
D	8	*JERE KARALAHTI	48	6	10	16	3	18	4		1		69	8.7
D	5	AKI BERG	70	3	13	16	-1	45					70	4.3
D	6	SEAN O'DONNELL	80	2	12	14	4	114			1		51	3.9
D	14	MATTIAS NORSTROM	82	1	13	14	22	66					62	1.6
R	29	*BRAD CHARTRAND	50	6	6	12	4	17		1	3		51	11.8
C	19	BOB CORKUM	45	5	6	11	0	14					45	11.1
D	44	JAROSLAV MODRY	26	5	4	9	-2	18	5		1	1	32	15.6
L	42	DAN BYLSMA	64	3	6	9	-2	55	1				43	7.0
L	7	STEVE MCKENNA	46	5	5	3	125					14		
G	35	STEPHANE FISET	47	2	2	0	4							
C	37	JASON PODOLLAN	1	1	1	0	2					2		
G	1	JAMIE STORR	42	1	1	0	4							
L	28	BILL HUARD	1			0	2							
D	43	PHILIPPE BOUCHER	1			0						3		
D	54	*JAN NEMECEK	1			0								
C	28	*STEVEN REINPRECHT	1			0	2							
R	55	PAVEL ROSA	3			-1						1		
G	34	MARCEL COUSINEAU	5			0								

GP = games played; G = goals; A = assists; PTS = points; +/- = goals-for minus goals-against while player is on ice; PIM = penalties in minutes; PP = power-play goals; SH = shorthanded goals; GW = game-winning goals; GT = game-tying goals; S = no. of shots; PCT = percentage of goals to shots; * = rookie

AKI-PETTERI BERG

Yrs. of NHL service: 4
Born: Turku, Finland; July 28, 1977
Position: left defense
Height: 6-3
Weight: 198
Uniform no.: 5
Shoots: left

Career statistics:

GP	G	A	TP	PIM
234	5	34	39	159

1996-97 statistics:

GP	G	A	TP	+/-	PIM	PP	SH	GW	GT	S	PCT
41	2	6	8	-9	24	2	0	0	0	65	3.1

1997-98 statistics:

GP	G	A	TP	+/-	PIM	PP	SH	GW	GT	S	PCT
72	0	8	8	+3	61	0	0	0	0	58	0.0

1998-99 statistics:

Did not play in NHL

1999-2000 statistics:

GP	G	A	TP	+/-	PIM	PP	SH	GW	GT	S	PCT
70	3	13	16	-1	45	0	0	0	0	70	4.3

LAST SEASON

Missed two games with concussion. Missed two games with rib injury. Missed one game with flu. Missed seven games due to coach's decision.

THE FINESSE GAME

Berg returned to the NHL last season after playing in Finland for a year because of a contract impasse.

Berg has a pleasing combination of offensive and defensive skills. His skating is top-notch. He has a powerful stride with great mobility and balance. And he gets terrific drive from perfect leg extension and deep knee bends.

He sees the ice well and has excellent passing skills. He can also rush with the puck, but he prefers to make a pass and then join the play. He has more offensive upside and could develop into a solid two-way defenseman.

THE PHYSICAL GAME

Berg loves to hit. He's big and strong, and has the mobility to lay down some serious open-ice checks. His punishing checks have had some scouts comparing him to Scott Stevens. Berg plays hard and finishes his checks.

THE INTANGIBLES

Berg was rushed in the NHL at age 18 on a bad Kings team and the damage has to be undone. The Kings have him pegged as their number three defenseman this season. He needs to take a big step up.

PROJECTION

Berg can score 20 points and needs to play a little meaner than he did last season.

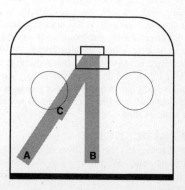

ROB BLAKE

Yrs. of NHL service: 10
Born: Simcoe, Ont.; Dec. 10, 1969
Position: right defense
Height: 6-3
Weight: 215
Uniform no.: 4
Shoots: right

Career statistics:

GP	G	A	TP	PIM
608	121	259	380	982

1996-97 statistics:

GP	G	A	TP	+/-	PIM	PP	SH	GW	GT	S	PCT
62	8	23	31	-28	82	4	0	1	0	169	4.7

1997-98 statistics:

GP	G	A	TP	+/-	PIM	PP	SH	GW	GT	S	PCT
81	23	27	50	-3	94	11	0	4	0	261	8.8

1998-99 statistics:

GP	G	A	TP	+/-	PIM	PP	SH	GW	GT	S	PCT
62	12	23	35	-7	128	5	1	2	0	216	5.6

1999-2000 statistics:

GP	G	A	TP	+/-	PIM	PP	SH	GW	GT	S	PCT
77	18	39	57	+10	112	12	0	5	0	327	5.5

LAST SEASON

Finalist for 2000 Norris Trophy. Led team defensemen in points for second consecutive season. Third among NHL defensemen in points. Led team and second in NHL in shots. Second on team in power-play goals. Third on team in game-winning goals. Missed three games with bruised knee. Missed two games with groin strain.

THE FINESSE GAME

Lower-body strength is the key to Blake's open-ice hitting, along with, of course, his skating. He is a powerful skater, quick and agile, with good balance. He steps up and challenges at the blueline, and has great anticipation. He's also quite bold, forcing turnovers at the blueline with his body positioning and quick stickwork. He is brave but not brash in his decision making.

Blake has finesse skills that make an impact in any zone of the ice. He works the point on the power play and has a good, low shot, which he rifles off the pass. He has quality hand skills and is not afraid to skip in deep to try to make something happen. He is confident about attempting to force the play deep in the offensive zone, and has sharp enough passing skills to use a backhand pass across the goalmouth.

Blake rarely goes a game without getting at least one shot on goal, and was credited with 11 in a single game against Calgary.

THE PHYSICAL GAME

Blake is among the hardest hitters in the league. He has a nasty streak and will bring up his gloves and stick them into the face of an opponent when he thinks the referee isn't watching. He can dominate with his physical play — when he does, he opens up a lot of ice for himself and his teammates. Along with partner Mattias Norstrom, Blake see the major checking duties against other teams' top lines.

THE INTANGIBLES

Blake responded strongly after an injury-plagued 1998-99 season. He will have to handle a lot of ice time again this season, as the Kings lost Sean O'Donnell in the expansion draft and they're thin at the position.

PROJECTION

One of the league's elite defenders, a healthy Blake belongs in the 55- to 60-point range.

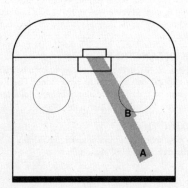

KELLY BUCHBERGER

Yrs. of NHL service: 11
Born: Langenburg, Sask.; Dec. 2, 1966
Position: left wing
Height: 6-2
Weight: 200
Uniform no.: 16
Shoots: left

Career statistics:

GP	G	A	TP	PIM
876	89	171	250	1899

1996-97 statistics:

GP	G	A	TP	+/-	PIM	PP	SH	GW	GT	S	PCT
81	8	30	38	+4	159	0	0	3	0	78	10.3

1997-98 statistics:

GP	G	A	TP	+/-	PIM	PP	SH	GW	GT	S	PCT
82	6	17	23	-10	122	1	1	1	0	86	7.0

1998-99 statistics:

GP	G	A	TP	+/-	PIM	PP	SH	GW	GT	S	PCT
52	4	4	8	-6	68	0	2	1	0	29	13.8

1999-2000 statistics:

GP	G	A	TP	+/-	PIM	PP	SH	GW	GT	S	PCT
81	7	13	20	-36	152	0	0	0	0	76	9.2

LAST SEASON

Acquired from Atlanta with Nelson Emerson for Donald Audette and Frantisek Kaberle, Mar. 13, 2000. Scored first goal in Thrashers history.

THE FINESSE GAME

What's not to like? Buchberger is an ideal third-line player. Night in and night out, he faces other teams' top forwards and does a terrific shadow job, harassing without taking bad penalties.

Buchberger works hard and provides a consistent effort. He will grind, go to the net, kill penalties — all of the grunt work. He can finish off some plays now and then, but that is not his objective. The biggest change in Buchberger is that he has developed a degree of confidence in his finesse moves and is now willing to try something that looks too difficult for a "defensive" player. Sometimes it works, sometimes it doesn't, but he can surprise opponents.

Buchberger has some straight-ahead speed and will go to the net and muck, but this kind of player needs some luck to get goals. He has earned a great deal of respect for his work ethic. He doesn't quit. He has notched five playoff-overtime goals simply because he's a gamer.

THE PHYSICAL GAME

Buchberger is a legitimately tough customer. Honest and gritty, he won't get knocked around and is a solid hitter who likes the physical part of the game. He is a very disciplined player. He's also very determined. He keeps his legs moving constantly, and a player who lets up on this winger will be sorry, because Buchberger will keep plugging with the puck or go to

the net.

THE INTANGIBLES

Even at 33, Buchberger can be a valuable role player for a team looking for someone to teach its players how to reach the next level. He was a leader and Cup winner in Edmonton and was a good pickup for the Kings.

PROJECTION

Point totals in this case are minimal and meaningless. Buchberger could score 10 points *and* be a candidate for team MVP.

NELSON EMERSON

Yrs. of NHL service: 9
Born: Hamilton, Ont.; Aug. 17, 1967
Position: centre/left wing
Height: 5-11
Weight: 175
Uniform no.: 7
Shoots: right

Career statistics:

GP	G	A	TP	PIM
652	179	280	459	496

1996-97 statistics:

GP	G	A	TP	+/-	PIM	PP	SH	GW	GT	S	PCT
66	9	29	38	-21	34	2	1	2	0	194	4.6

1997-98 statistics:

GP	G	A	TP	+/-	PIM	PP	SH	GW	GT	S	PCT
81	21	24	45	-17	50	6	0	4	1	203	10.3

1998-99 statistics:

GP	G	A	TP	+/-	PIM	PP	SH	GW	GT	S	PCT
65	13	24	37	+8	51	3	0	1	2	188	6.9

1999-2000 statistics:

GP	G	A	TP	+/-	PIM	PP	SH	GW	GT	S	PCT
63	15	20	35	-23	47	4	0	0	1	196	7.7

LAST SEASON

Acquired from Atlanta with Kelly Buchberger for Donald Audette and Frantisek Kaberle, Mar. 13, 2000. Missed eight games with fractured finger.

THE FINESSE GAME

On the power play, which has become his specialty, Emerson can either play the point or work down low. He has an excellent point shot: keeping it low, on target and tippable. He is clever with the puck and doesn't always fire from the point, but works it to the middle of the blueline, and he uses screens well. When he carries in one-on-one against a defender, especially on a shorthanded rush, he always manages to use the defenseman to screen the goalie.

Emerson works well down low at even strength. He is mature and creative, with a terrific short game. He has quick hands for passing or snapping off a shot. He likes to work from behind the net, tempting the defense to chase him behind the cage. Speed and puck control are the essence of his game.

Emerson has nice quickness and balance, and he darts in and out of traffic in front of the net. He's too small to do any physical damage, which is why he needs to play with physical linemates. He can use his speed to drive wide on a defenseman, who will think he has Emerson angled off only to watch him blast past.

THE PHYSICAL GAME

Emerson has good skating balance, and that will give him a little edge to knock a bigger player off-stride once in awhile. He works hard defensively but has to play a smart, small man's game to avoid getting pasted.

THE INTANGIBLES

As a power-play specialist, Emerson will continually find himself on the bubble. The Kings didn't get to see much of him before he got hurt.

PROJECTION

Emerson's career and his point totals are on the wane. His top end is 40 points.

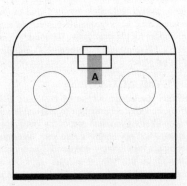

GARRY GALLEY

Yrs. of NHL service: 16
Born: Montreal, Que., Apr. 16, 1963
Position: left defense
Height: 6-0
Weight: 204
Uniform no.: 3
Shoots: left

Career statistics:

GP	G	A	TP	PIM
1093	119	461	580	1159

1996-97 statistics:

GP	G	A	TP	+/-	PIM	PP	SH	GW	GT	S	PCT
71	4	34	38	+10	102	1	1	1	0	84	4.8

1997-98 statistics:

GP	G	A	TP	+/-	PIM	PP	SH	GW	GT	S	PCT
74	9	28	37	-5	63	7	0	0	0	128	7.0

1998-99 statistics:

GP	G	A	TP	+/-	PIM	PP	SH	GW	GT	S	PCT
60	4	12	16	-9	30	3	0	0	0	77	5.2

1999-2000 statistics:

GP	G	A	TP	+/-	PIM	PP	SH	GW	GT	S	PCT
70	9	21	30	+9	52	2	0	1	0	96	9.4

PROJECTION

The days of Galley's best numbers are over, but he can score in the 25- to 30-point range in the right spot. He is 37 now and declining.

LAST SEASON

Missed nine games with post-concussion syndrome.

THE FINESSE GAME

Galley is a puck mover. He follows the play and jumps into the attack. He has decent speed, though he has lost a step. He is mobile and has a good shot that he can get away on the fly. He will pinch aggressively.

Galley works well on the power play. His lateral movement allows him to slide away from the point to the middle of the blueline, and he keeps his shots low. He is a smart player and his experience shows. He helps any younger player he is teamed with because of his poise and communication.

Galley uses his finesse ability defensively by playing well positionally, and by using his stick for poke-checks. He has become a fairly reliable two-way defenseman.

THE PHYSICAL GAME

Galley has added a physical element to his game over the past few seasons, but he is not and will never be a big hitter. He will take his man but not always take him out, and more physical forwards take advantage of him. He gets in the way, though, and does not back down. But there are times when he is simply overpowered. He also gets a little chippy now and then, just to keep people guessing.

THE INTANGIBLES

Galley became an unrestricted free agent after the season and might not be back with the Kings, though they tried to sign him at a reduced price.

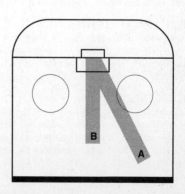

CRAIG JOHNSON

Yrs. of NHL service: 5
Born: St. Paul, Minnesota; Mar. 8, 1972
Position: left wing/centre
Height: 6-2
Weight: 198
Uniform no.: 23
Shoots: left

Career statistics:

GP	G	A	TP	PIM
325	53	64	117	170

1996-97 statistics:

GP	G	A	TP	+/-	PIM	PP	SH	GW	GT	S	PCT
31	4	3	7	-7	26	1	0	0	0	30	13.3

1997-98 statistics:

GP	G	A	TP	+/-	PIM	PP	SH	GW	GT	S	PCT
74	17	21	38	+9	42	6	0	2	0	125	13.6

1998-99 statistics:

GP	G	A	TP	+/-	PIM	PP	SH	GW	GT	S	PCT
69	7	12	19	-12	32	2	0	2	0	94	7.4

1999-2000 statistics:

GP	G	A	TP	+/-	PIM	PP	SH	GW	GT	S	PCT
76	9	14	23	-10	28	1	0	1	0	106	8.5

PROJECTION

Johnson's speed will always win him a second chance, but he has to produce in the 40-point range to keep his job as a regular.

LAST SEASON

Missed six games due to coach's decision.

THE FINESSE GAME

Johnson is a quick skater who uses his speed to gain a jump in the neutral zone. He will take a pass in full stride and take the puck to the net. He can also use his speed to create off the forecheck. He doesn't have great hands, so he needs to get rid of the puck quickly to a more talented teammate, or get the puck late for a shot.

Although Johnson has played some centre, he is better suited as a left-winger. The Kings frequently use him on the off-wing. He is not a natural scorer and has to work hard for everything he gets. He isn't quite skilled enough to be a top six forward on a better team.

Johnson is fairly alert defensively and brings a level of enthusiasm to the game that is appreciated by coaches. He is a poor man's Paul Ranheim.

THE PHYSICAL GAME

Johnson doesn't have much taste for body work. He prefers to intimidate with his speed. He is a good size, but plays smaller. He needs to gain some strength and assertiveness.

THE INTANGIBLES

Johnson doesn't have a great deal of upside and it's tough sometimes to find a role for him, but he adds speed and energy to a lineup. The benchings indicate how dissatisfied the coaches were with his nightly efforts.

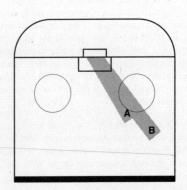

IAN LAPERRIERE

Yrs. of NHL service: 6
Born: Montreal, Que.; Jan. 19, 1974
Position: centre
Height: 6-1
Weight: 195
Uniform no.: 22
Shoots: right

Career statistics:

GP	G	A	TP	PIM
399	45	78	123	796

1996-97 statistics:

GP	G	A	TP	+/-	PIM	PP	SH	GW	GT	S	PCT
62	8	15	23	-25	102	0	1	2	0	84	9.5

1997-98 statistics:

GP	G	A	TP	+/-	PIM	PP	SH	GW	GT	S	PCT
77	6	15	21	0	131	0	1	1	0	74	8.1

1998-99 statistics:

GP	G	A	TP	+/-	PIM	PP	SH	GW	GT	S	PCT
72	3	10	13	-5	138	0	0	1	0	62	4.8

1999-2000 statistics:

GP	G	A	TP	+/-	PIM	PP	SH	GW	GT	S	PCT
79	9	13	22	-14	185	0	0	1	0	87	10.3

LAST SEASON

Led team in penalty minutes with career high. Missed three games with knee injury.

THE FINESSE GAME

The knock on Laperriere earlier in his career was his skating, but he has improved tremendously in that department. Although he'll never be a speed demon, he doesn't look out of place at the NHL level. He always tries to take the extra stride when he is backchecking so he can make a clean check, instead of taking the easy way out and committing a lazy hooking foul. He wins his share of races for the loose puck.

Laperriere grew up watching Guy Carbonneau in Montreal, and he studied well. Laperriere knows how to win a draw between his feet. He uses his stick and his body to make sure the opposing centre doesn't get the puck. He gets his bottom hand way down on the stick and tries to win draws on his backhand. He gets very low to the ice on draws. He works hard on every shift.

Laperriere is ever willing to use the backhand, either for shots or to get the puck deep. He is reliable defensively. He doesn't think the game very well, however, and his offensive reads are brutal.

THE PHYSICAL GAME

Laperriere is an obnoxious player in the Bob Bassen mold. He really battles for the puck. Although small-ish, he has absolutely no fear of playing in the "circle" that extends from the lower inside of the face-off circles to behind the net. He will pay any price. He's a momentum changer. He thrives on being the first man in on the forecheck. Laperriere has suffered some seri-

ous head injuries but remains a soldier undaunted.

He shows a ton of heart. If the Kings fall out of the playoff race, he would make an excellent deadline-time acquisition for a Cup hopeful. If they continue to improve and contend, he will be a key chemistry guy.

THE INTANGIBLES

Laperriere adds true grit to the lineup despite his small size, which is his major weakness. His nightly effort puts a lot of bigger guys to shame. He lost any bad habits the hard way by playing for a hard-nosed coach (Mike Keenan) early in his career. He is one of L.A.'s most consistent forwards.

PROJECTION

Laperriere is best suited as a third- or fourth-line centre. His skills are limited, but what he does he does well. His top range appears to be 30 points.

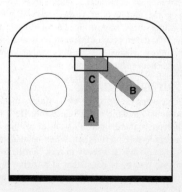

GLEN MURRAY

Yrs. of NHL service: 8
Born: Halifax, N.S.; Nov. 1, 1972
Position: right wing
Height: 6-2
Weight: 220
Uniform no.: 27
Shoots: right

Career statistics:

GP	G	A	TP	PIM
514	133	128	261	341

1996-97 statistics:

GP	G	A	TP	+/-	PIM	PP	SH	GW	GT	S	PCT
77	16	14	30	-21	32	3	0	1	0	153	10.5

1997-98 statistics:

GP	G	A	TP	+/-	PIM	PP	SH	GW	GT	S	PCT
81	29	31	60	+6	54	7	3	7	0	193	15.0

1998-99 statistics:

GP	G	A	TP	+/-	PIM	PP	SH	GW	GT	S	PCT
61	16	15	31	-14	36	3	3	3	0	173	9.2

1999-2000 statistics:

GP	G	A	TP	+/-	PIM	PP	SH	GW	GT	S	PCT
78	29	33	62	+13	60	10	1	2	1	202	14.4

LAST SEASON

Second on team in goals, matching career high. Third on team in points, power-play goals, shots and shooting percentage. Career high in points. Missed three games with chest contusion. Missed one game with lower leg contusion.

THE FINESSE GAME

Murray is a lumbering skater who needs a good old dump-and-chase game, on a line with a playmaker who can get him the puck and set him up in the slot. Fortunately, although he lost favourite centre Jozef Stumpel to newcomer Ziggy Palffy, Murray meshed with Bryan Smolinski, his former Pittsburgh teammate.

Murray is at his best on the right side, jamming in his forehand shots. He has good size and a top short game. He also has a quick release and, like a lot of great goal scorers, he just plain shoots. He doesn't even have to look at the net because he feels where the shot is going, and he protects the puck well with his body. Murray has also developed a wickedly fast slap shot and has developed confidence in this weapon. He is now more consistently using his speed and strength to get in better scoring position.

THE PHYSICAL GAME

On nights when he's playing well, Murray is leaning on people and making his presence felt. He'll bang, but on some nights he doesn't want to pay the price and prefers to rely on his shot. When he sleepwalks, he's useless. When he's ready to rock 'n roll, he's effective. He was more consistent at bringing his top game every night, though Murray will never be the

Cam Neely clone people envisioned. Still, he has made strides to becoming a solid power forward.

THE INTANGIBLES

Murray has become the number two right-winger in L.A. behind Palffy. He still gets his quality ice time, especially on the power play, and can escape some of the checking attention the top line attracts. He seems to have recovered well from a serious knee injury two years ago.

PROJECTION

Murray is now an automatic for 25 to 30 goals. At 28, he still has some prime scoring years ahead.

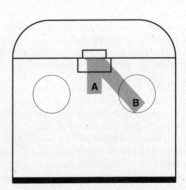

MATTIAS NORSTROM

Yrs. of NHL service: 5
Born: Mora, Sweden; Jan. 2, 1972
Position: left defense
Height: 6-1
Weight: 205
Uniform no.: 14
Shoots: left

Career statistics:

GP	G	A	TP	PIM
367	7	57	64	324

1996-97 statistics:

GP	G	A	TP	+/-	PIM	PP	SH	GW	GT	S	PCT
80	1	21	22	-4	84	0	0	0	0	106	0.9

1997-98 statistics:

GP	G	A	TP	+/-	PIM	PP	SH	GW	GT	S	PCT
73	1	12	13	+14	90	0	0	0	0	61	1.6

1998-99 statistics:

GP	G	A	TP	+/-	PIM	PP	SH	GW	GT	S	PCT
78	2	5	7	-10	36	0	1	0	0	61	3.3

1999-2000 statistics:

GP	G	A	TP	+/-	PIM	PP	SH	GW	GT	S	PCT
82	1	13	14	+22	66	0	0	0	0	62	1.6

LAST SEASON

Second on team in plus-minus. Only King to appear in all 82 games.

THE FINESSE GAME

Norstrom has attained a fairly high level of play on a team that needs him desperately and uses him extensively. He's a good skater, though he is still working on his pivots and turns. He does have straight-ahead speed, to a degree, thanks to a long stride. Along the boards he delivers strong hits. In open ice he has more misses.

Norstrom's foot skills outdistance his hand skills. He can make a decent pass but mostly he'll keep things simple with the puck — smacking it around the boards if he gets into trouble, rather than trying to make a play.

For so large a player, Norstrom uses a surprisingly short stick that cuts down on his reach defensively and limits some of his offensive options. However, he feels his responsibility is to break down the play, rather than create it. He will pinch down the boards occasionally, but only to drive the puck deeper, not to take the puck and make a play. And he won't jump into the play on offense until he has more confidence with his puck skills.

THE PHYSICAL GAME

Norstrom is hard-nosed; when he hits, you feel it. And he is willing to do what it takes to help his team win. He is solidly built and likes to throw big, loud hits. If he doesn't hit, he's not going to be around long because his talent is not going to carry him, and his hockey sense (especially his defensive reads) needs

much improvement. He sacrifices his body by blocking shots.

He knows what he's good at. Norstrom has tremendously powerful legs and is strong on his skates. He has confidence in his power game and has developed a great enthusiasm for physical play.

THE INTANGIBLES

Norstrom is a hard-working athlete who loves to practise, a player acquired more for his character than for his abilities, which are average. He is a defensive-style defenseman who will give his coach what's asked for, but won't try to do things that will put the puck, or the team, in trouble. He is Rob Blake's steady partner against other teams' top lines.

PROJECTION

Norstrom will continue to get a large chunk of ice time, but his offensive skills limit him to 15 to 20 points at best.

ZIGMUND PALFFY

Yrs. of NHL service: 6
Born: Skalica, Slovakia; May 5, 1972
Position: left wing
Height: 5-10
Weight: 183
Uniform no.: 16
Shoots: left

Career statistics:

GP	G	A	TP	PIM
395	195	202	397	205

1996-97 statistics:

GP	G	A	TP	+/-	PIM	PP	SH	GW	GT	S	PCT
80	48	42	90	+21	43	6	4	6	1	292	16.4

1997-98 statistics:

GP	G	A	TP	+/-	PIM	PP	SH	GW	GT	S	PCT
82	45	42	87	-2	34	17	2	5	1	277	16.2

1998-99 statistics:

GP	G	A	TP	+/-	PIM	PP	SH	GW	GT	S	PCT
50	22	28	50	-6	34	5	2	1	0	168	13.1

1999-2000 statistics:

GP	G	A	TP	+/-	PIM	PP	SH	GW	GT	S	PCT
64	27	39	66	+18	32	4	0	3	1	186	14.5

LAST SEASON

Second on team in points and shooting percentage. Tied for second on team in assists. Third on team in goals and plus-minus. Missed 12 games with sprained right shoulder. Missed five games with back spasms. Missed one game due to coach's decision.

THE FINESSE GAME

Palffy has elite, intellectual instincts with the puck and great vision. He has the confidence — the arrogance — to try moves that only world-class players can execute.

He has deceptive quickness. An elusive skater with a quick first step, he is shifty, and can handle the puck while dancing across the ice. He won't burn around people, but when there's an opening he can get to it in a hurry. Sometimes a defender will let up on him for a fraction of a second, when he does, Palffy has gained a full stride. His anticipation is what sets him apart.

Palffy has excellent hands for passing or shooting. Early in his career he would look to make a play before shooting, but he has since become a bona fide sniper. He is an aggressive penalty killer, always looking for the shorthanded break.

THE PHYSICAL GAME

Palffy has a little bit of an edge to him. He's got the magic ingredient that sets the superior smaller players apart from the little guys who can't make the grade. He's not exactly a physical specimen, either. One player said of Palffy, "He's as unathletic a superstar as you'll ever find."

Decidedly on the small side, Palffy can't afford to get into any battles in tight areas where he'll get

crunched. He can jump in and out of holes and pick his spots, and he often plays with great spirit. He never puts himself in a position to get bowled over but he has become less of a perimeter player and is more willing to take the direct route to the net, which has paid off in more quality scoring chances. He's not really a soft player, but he won't go into the corner if he's going to get massacred, though he's not against hacking an opponent He wants the puck.

THE INTANGIBLES

Palffy, a point-a-game player in the regular season, never got a real chance to prove what he could do in his first-ever playoff appearance, because he was hampered by his shoulder injury (he did score two goals in four games).

PROJECTION

Palffy can score 50 goals, and loves playing with disher and best pal Jozef Stumpel in L.A. If both Palffy and Stumpel had stayed healthy last season, those 50 goals would have already happened.

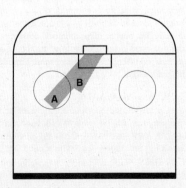

LUC ROBITAILLE

Yrs. of NHL service: 14
Born: Montreal, Que.; Feb. 17, 1966
Position: left wing
Height: 6-1
Weight: 195
Uniform no.: 20
Shoots: left

Career statistics:

GP	G	A	TP	PIM
1042	553	597	1150	915

1996-97 statistics:

GP	G	A	TP	+/-	PIM	PP	SH	GW	GT	S	PCT
69	24	24	48	+16	48	5	0	4	0	200	12.0

1997-98 statistics:

GP	G	A	TP	+/-	PIM	PP	SH	GW	GT	S	PCT
57	16	24	40	+5	66	5	0	7	0	130	12.3

1998-99 statistics:

GP	G	A	TP	+/-	PIM	PP	SH	GW	GT	S	PCT
82	39	35	74	-1	54	11	0	7	0	292	13.4

1999-2000 statistics:

GP	G	A	TP	+/-	PIM	PP	SH	GW	GT	S	PCT
71	36	38	74	+11	68	13	0	7	0	221	16.3

LAST SEASON

Led team in goals, points, power-play goals and shooting percentage. Tied for fourth in NHL in power-play goals. Tied for team lead in game-winning goals. Second on team in shots. Appeared in 1,000th career NHL game. Missed 10 games with fractured left foot. Missed one game due to coach's decision.

THE FINESSE GAME

Robitaille gets the most done when he determines one course of action and follows through on it, because he simply does not have the quickness of hand, foot or mind to do multiple tasks. Slow on his feet to begin with, his problems are magnified by questionable balance. It doesn't take much to knock him off his feet.

Carrying the puck slows Robitaille even more because it requires him to read a defense and identify a passing option. He is far better served by getting the puck, moving the puck and moving his feet to the holes. He benefited from playing with playmaker Jozef Stumpel, an excellent passer, most of last season.

Tracking those deficiencies makes you appreciate how much Robitaille wants to score goals. He has become one of the game's great scorers because of his goal-scoring instincts and fabulous shot. When he works to an opening in the front of the net and shoots off the pass he can be devastatingly effective: the shot is accurate and the release too quick for defensemen to block. Robitaille might not win many skills contests, but somehow the puck ends up in the net a majority of the time.

THE PHYSICAL GAME

Although he's considered a finesse player, the physical aspect is an under-noticed part of Robitaille's game. He's among the first to avenge any cheap shot against one of his teammates. He isn't a fighter but his sense of team is significant.

Robitaille goes to the grungy parts of the ice; he mucks for the puck. He also pays a physical price, absorbing a fair amount of hits because he isn't quick enough to get out of the way. And, because he does not think or act quickly, he gets whacked while making up his mind. Still, Robitaille has such great upper-body strength that a defender will think he has him wrapped up, only to see the puck in the net after Robitaille has somehow gotten his hands free.

THE INTANGIBLES

Robitaille had another impressive season and was one of the few positive forces for the Kings in their post-season sweep by Detroit.

PROJECTION

Robitaille got off to a hot start and would have reached the 40-goal mark we set for him if he hadn't been sidelined by an injury. We'll put the heat on him for another 40.

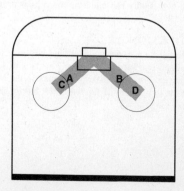

PAVEL ROSA

Yrs. of NHL service: 2
Born: Most, Czech.; June 7, 1977
Position: right wing
Height: 6-0
Weight: 195
Uniform no.: 55
Shoots: right

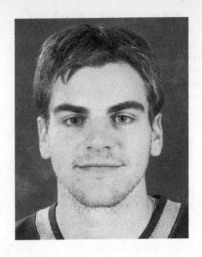

Career statistics:

GP	G	A	TP	PIM
32	4	12	16	6

1998-99 statistics:

GP	G	A	TP	+/-	PIM	PP	SH	GW	GT	S	PCT
29	4	12	16	0	6	0	0	0	0	61	6.6

1999-2000 statistics:

GP	G	A	TP	+/-	PIM	PP	SH	GW	GT	S	PCT
3	0	0	0	-1	0	0	0	0	0	1	-

LAST SEASON

Appeared in 69 games with Long Beach (IHL), scoring 22-28 — 50.

THE FINESSE GAME

Rosa's skating is the greatest hindrance to his achieving success at the NHL level. It is more than adequate for the minors — and the juniors, where he was a sniper in the Quebec League — but he will have to work hard to improve it in order to score in the bigs.

He has very nice hands and a good scoring touch around the net. Once he gets a little bigger he will be more of a factor in the trenches.

Even though Rosa was playing a short distance away in the minors, the Kings only bothered to recall him for three games.

THE PHYSICAL GAME

Rosa is on the weedy side, and needs to be more muscular to compete with the big boys in the NHL.

THE INTANGIBLES

At 23, Rosa may be entering his last-chance season, at least with the Kings. He has battled injury problems over the past few seasons, especially a concussion that seems to have really set him back, and the Kings' patience will finally run out if he has a poor training camp.

PROJECTION

The Kings want to get younger, and will give Rosa every chance to succeed. It's likely his lack of speed will prevent him from making his mark in the NHL. He needs to play on the top two lines, but he has to earn the job.

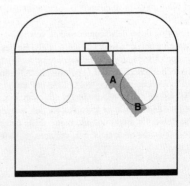

BRYAN SMOLINSKI

Yrs. of NHL service: 7
Born: Toledo, Ohio; Dec. 27, 1971
Position: centre/right wing
Height: 6-1
Weight: 200
Uniform no.: 20
Shoots: right

Career statistics:

GP	G	A	TP	PIM
523	151	194	345	342

1996-97 statistics:

GP	G	A	TP	+/-	PIM	PP	SH	GW	GT	S	PCT
64	28	28	56	+8	25	9	0	1	1	183	15.3

1997-98 statistics:

GP	G	A	TP	+/-	PIM	PP	SH	GW	GT	S	PCT
81	13	30	43	-16	34	3	0	4	0	203	6.4

1998-99 statistics:

GP	G	A	TP	+/-	PIM	PP	SH	GW	GT	S	PCT
82	16	24	40	-7	49	7	0	3	0	223	7.2

1999-2000 statistics:

GP	G	A	TP	+/-	PIM	PP	SH	GW	GT	S	PCT
79	20	36	56	+2	48	2	0	0	2	160	12.5

LAST SEASON

Scored 20 or more goals for fourth time in career. Missed three games with torn knee ligaments.

THE FINESSE GAME

Smolinski is the number two centre behind Jozef Stumpel in L.A. He has been shuffled from centre to wing during his career, but works much better in the middle, where he makes good use of the open ice. It didn't hurt that he established good chemistry with right wing Glen Murray.

Smolinski has a quick release and an accurate shot, and, on nights when he brings his "A" game, he works to get himself into quality shooting areas. Confidence is a big factor; he has a history of being a streaky/slumpy player. When he is in a slump, he turns into Mr. Perimeter.

Smolinski's skating is adequate, but it could improve with some lower-body work. He has good balance and lateral movement but he is not quick. He has a railroad-track skating base.

Smolinski has the smarts to be an asset on both specialty teams, and he has really stepped up as a penalty killer. He has good defensive awareness — his play away from the puck is sound. He is good in tight with the puck.

THE PHYSICAL GAME

Smolinski has a thick, blocky build, and he can be a solid hitter. He doesn't have much of an aggressive nature on a nightly basis, but it shows up sporadically, and on those nights he is at his most effective.

THE INTANGIBLES

Smolinski has a lot going for him physically, but he's rather easy-going and needs a fire lit under him from time to time. Teams get frustrated with him because of his lack of drive and intensity. He is not a crunch-time player.

PROJECTION

Last season we said, "Don't expect much more than 20 goals," which turned out to be Smolinski's total exactly. It's his top end.

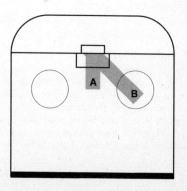

JAMIE STORR

Yrs. of NHL service: 3
Born: Brampton, Ont.; Dec. 28, 1975
Position: goaltender
Height: 6-0
Weight: 170
Uniform no.: 1
Catches: left

Career statistics:

GP	MIN	GA	SO	GAA	A	PIM
102	5441	228	7	2.51	2	10

1996-97 statistics:

GP	MIN	GAA	W	L	T	SO	GA	S	SAPCT	PIM
5	265	2.49	2	1	1	0	11	147	.925	0

1997-98 statistics:

GP	MIN	GAA	W	L	T	SO	GA	S	SAPCT	PIM
17	920	2.22	9	5	1	2	34	482	.929	0

1998-99 statistics:

GP	MIN	GAA	W	L	T	SO	GA	S	SAPCT	PIM
28	1525	2.40	12	12	2	4	61	724	.916	6

1999-2000 statistics:

GP	MIN	GAA	W	L	T	SO	GA	S	SAPCT	PIM
42	2206	2.53	18	15	5	1	93	1008	.908	4

PROJECTION
Storr should get 50 to 55 starts and 28 to 30 wins.

LAST SEASON
Career highs in games and wins. Missed 10 games with postconcussion syndrome. Missed two games with groin injury.

THE PHYSICAL GAME
Technically, Storr is pretty sound for a young player. He plays his angles well. And he's a stand-up goalie who challenges shooters and forces them to make the first move, rather than scrambling and relying on his reflexes.

Although Storr is somewhat lean, his technique doesn't take much out of him physically, much in the style of a young Kirk McLean. When he has to scramble, he can. He has good reflexes for his size and can be in a position for a second shot

Storr has a quick glove hand. He is adequate with his stick but needs to improve his work out of his net. He is indecisive and mixes up his defensemen.

THE MENTAL GAME
Easily the weakest part of Storr's game is stored in his head. He has trouble with his concentration.

THE INTANGIBLES
Storr and Stephane Fiset split the goaltending duties last season, although Fiset took over as the number one in the playoffs. Storr had been the top goalie until his mid-season injury (which he continued to play through for three games before being placed on injured reserve) while Fiset was out with a hand injury. He will have to prove himself to win the top job.

JOZEF STUMPEL

Yrs. of NHL service: 7
Born: Nitra, Slovakia; June 20, 1972
Position: centre/right wing
Height: 6-1
Weight: 208
Uniform no.: 15
Shoots: right

Career statistics:

GP	G	A	TP	PIM
472	105	242	347	127

1996-97 statistics:

GP	G	A	TP	+/-	PIM	PP	SH	GW	GT	S	PCT
78	21	55	76	-22	14	6	0	1	0	168	12.5

1997-98 statistics:

GP	G	A	TP	+/-	PIM	PP	SH	GW	GT	S	PCT
77	21	58	79	+17	53	4	0	2	1	162	13.0

1998-99 statistics:

GP	G	A	TP	+/-	PIM	PP	SH	GW	GT	S	PCT
64	13	21	34	-18	10	1	0	1	0	131	9.9

1999-2000 statistics:

GP	G	A	TP	+/-	PIM	PP	SH	GW	GT	S	PCT
57	17	41	58	+23	10	3	0	7	1	126	13.5

PROJECTION

Stumpel has missed close to 20 games with injuries, for each of the past two seasons. If he stays healthy, he's an 80-point, 55-assist man.

LAST SEASON

Led team in assists and plus-minus. Tied for team lead in game-winning goals. Missed 18 games with sports hernia. Missed seven games with left knee contusion.

THE FINESSE GAME

The arrival of Ziggy Palffy put Stumpel in a position where he was destined to succeed. Stumpel is a setup man, Palffy a finisher. Both come from the Slovakian hockey system and are great pals, and their styles mesh perfectly.

Stumpel has good hand skills, which allow him to compensate for his skating, up to a point. He also has a deft scoring touch and is a passer with a good short game. He is very patient. He uses his feet well to keep the puck alive, kick it up onto his stick or keep it in the attacking zone.

He also has keen hockey sense. But he does not shoot nearly enough, and that isn't likely to change at this point in his career.

THE PHYSICAL GAME

Stumpel is quite powerfully built, but he doesn't play to his size. He can be intimidated, and teams go after him early. Opponents know how crucial Stumpel is to the Kings' attack, and that Stumpel will take a hit to make a play in the offensive zone. He goes into the corners and bumps and protects the puck with his body, but when the action gets really fierce he backs off.

THE INTANGIBLES

Stumpel plays with two outstanding finishers in Palffy and Luc Robitaille, and is a point-a-game player.

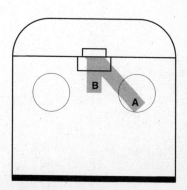

MINNESOTA WILD

Expansion team — no statistics

available for the 1999-2000 season.

EMMANUEL FERNANDEZ

Yrs. of NHL service: 1
Born: Etobicoke, Ont.; Aug. 27, 1974
Position: goaltender
Height: 6-0
Weight: 185
Uniform no.: 30
Catches: left

Career statistics:

GP	MIN	GA	SO	GAA	A	PIM
33	1790	74	1	2.48	2	2

1997-98 statistics:

GP	MIN	GAA	W	L	T	SO	GA	S	SAPCT	PIM
2	69	1.74	1	0	0	0	2	35	.943	0

1998-99 statistics:

GP	MIN	GAA	W	L	T	SO	GA	S	SAPCT	PIM
1	60	2.00	0	1	0	0	2	29	.931	0

1999-2000 statistics:

GP	MIN	GAA	W	L	T	SO	GA	S	SAPCT	PIM
24	1353	2.13	11	8	3	1	48	603	.920	2

He'll do well to get 10 victories.

LAST SEASON

Selected by Minnesota from Dallas in Expansion Draft, June 23, 2000.

THE PHYSICAL GAME

Fernandez plays an athletic, scrambling style that may actually be a good fit with an expansion club, where the top two defense pair would be number six and seven on a better team. Fernandez will have to do a lot of the work himself.

He has uncanny flexibility and quick reactions. His lateral movement is exceptional. Fernandez is one of the best goalies in the league at pushing off to get across from post to post.

Fernandez has kind of a quirky personality, but he worked hard in his backup role to Ed Belfour in Dallas to earn the respect of his teammates who might not have been otherwise eager to follow him into battle.

THE MENTAL GAME

Fernandez was a number one goalie in the minors, but will find the job much different in the NHL. One positive sign is that during Belfour's off-ice troubles in Dallas, Fernandez stepped in to play five straight. He seemed rattled at the pressure first, but went 3-1-1, winning the last three starts and allowing 14 goals in the five games.

THE INTANGIBLES

Although Jamie McLennan is three years older and has more experience, Fernandez is our pick to emerge as the number one netminder for the Wild. And it's got nothing to do with the fact that coach Jacques Lemaire is his uncle.

PROJECTION

Wins are hard to come by for any expansion goalie.

AARON GAVEY

Yrs. of NHL service: 5
Born: Sudbury, Ont.; Feb. 22, 1974
Position: centre
Height: 6-2
Weight: 200
Uniform no.: 44
Shoots: left

Career statistics:

GP	G	A	TP	PIM
204	25	24	49	180

1996-97 statistics:

GP	G	A	TP	+/-	PIM	PP	SH	GW	GT	S	PCT
57	8	11	19	-12	46	3	0	1	0	62	12.9

1997-98 statistics:

GP	G	A	TP	+/-	PIM	PP	SH	GW	GT	S	PCT
26	2	3	5	-5	24	0	0	1	0	27	7.4

1998-99 statistics:

GP	G	A	TP	+/-	PIM	PP	SH	GW	GT	S	PCT
7	0	0	0	-1	10	0	0	0	0	4	0.0

1999-2000 statistics:

GP	G	A	TP	+/-	PIM	PP	SH	GW	GT	S	PCT
41	7	6	13	0	44	1	0	2	0	39	17.9

LAST SEASON

Missed one game with knee injury. Appeared in 28 games with Kalamazoo (IHL), scoring 14-15 — 29.

THE FINESSE GAME

Gavey is a poor man's Ian Laperriere. He is a two-way centre who plays intelligent defense and has some offensive ability. His major drawback is his lack of foot speed, but he has worked very hard to turn himself into a decent player.

Everything Gavey does is rough around the edges. His main strength is on face-offs. He can be relied upon to battle for key draws in the defensive zone.

Gavey has a very good shot, a strong wrist or snap. He reads plays well and is very intelligent.

THE PHYSICAL GAME

Gavey has filled out to NHL size, and is strong for battles along the wall and on face-offs. He brings energy to every shift. He is always running into people, and running over people.

THE INTANGIBLES

Gavey has been through two three organizations — in Tampa Bay, Calgary and Dallas — without making much of an impression, but he is a useful enough player because he tries hard and brings a lot of energy to every shift. He makes it tougher for the opponent to get a point off his team, and that will make him a welcome addition to an expansion franchise.

PROJECTION

Gavey will probably win a spot on one of the top two lines in Minnesota. He has never hit double digits in goals before. This should be a first, though much more than 15 goals would be a long shot.

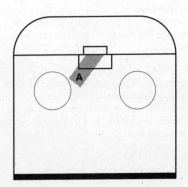

DARBY HENDRICKSON

Yrs. of NHL service: 5
Born: Richfield, Minn.; Aug. 28, 1972
Position: centre
Height: 6-0
Weight: 195
Uniform no.: 14
Shoots: left

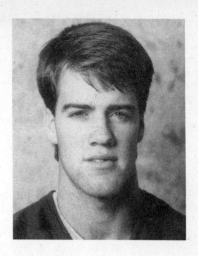

Career statistics:

GP	G	A	TP	PIM
316	35	30	65	264

1996-97 statistics:

GP	G	A	TP	+/-	PIM	PP	SH	GW	GT	S	PCT
64	11	6	17	-20	47	0	1	0	2	105	10.5

1997-98 statistics:

GP	G	A	TP	+/-	PIM	PP	SH	GW	GT	S	PCT
80	8	4	12	-20	67	0	0	0	0	115	7.0

1998-99 statistics:

GP	G	A	TP	+/-	PIM	PP	SH	GW	GT	S	PCT
62	4	5	9	-19	52	1	0	0	0	70	5.7

1999-2000 statistics:

GP	G	A	TP	+/-	PIM	PP	SH	GW	GT	S	PCT
40	5	4	9	-3	14	0	1	1	0	39	12.8

LAST SEASON

Selected by Minnesota from Vancouver in Expansion Draft, June 23, 2000. Appeared in 20 games with Syracuse (AHL), scoring 5-8 — 13. Missed four games with ankle injury. Missed 12 games due to coach's decision.

THE FINESSE GAME

Hendrickson works hard and gives an honest effort that maximizes his modest skills. He is an in-between forward, since he isn't big enough to play an effective power game, but his skills aren't elite enough for him to be considered a pure finesse playmaker.

Hendrickson is a two-way forward with better-than-average skills for a checking role. He is a good, quick skater in small areas. He is clever with the puck and will look to make a pass rather than shoot.

He is defensively alert, and with increased ice time could develop into a more confident all-around player. He's young and still learning the game. He can play any forward position, which is a plus.

THE PHYSICAL GAME

Hendrickson has a feisty side, and isn't afraid to get involved with some of the league's tougher players (like Keith Tkachuk), if not the heavyweights. He is learning to play in-your-face hockey, which will get him more ice time.

THE INTANGIBLES

Not many veterans get excited about being taken by an expansion team, but Hendrickson was a high school star in his native Minnesota and did not figure in the Canucks' plans. He is an honest third-line centre or winger on his best night, though he will be asked to carry more on an offensive load for the Wild. He is Jacques Lemaire's kind of player.

PROJECTION

Hendrickson could produce 30 points, since he will be handed a big chunk of ice time.

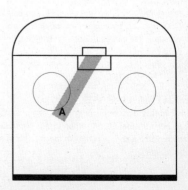

SERGEI KRIVOKRASOV

Yrs. of NHL service: 6
Born: Angarsk, Russia; Apr. 15, 1974
Position: right wing
Height: 5-11
Weight: 185
Uniform no.: 25
Shoots: left

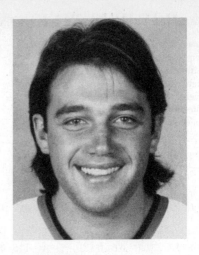

Career statistics:

GP	G	A	TP	PIM
370	77	91	168	232

1996-97 statistics:

GP	G	A	TP	+/-	PIM	PP	SH	GW	GT	S	PCT
67	13	11	24	-1	42	2	0	3	0	104	12.5

1997-98 statistics:

GP	G	A	TP	+/-	PIM	PP	SH	GW	GT	S	PCT
58	10	13	23	-1	33	1	0	2	0	127	7.9

1998-99 statistics:

GP	G	A	TP	+/-	PIM	PP	SH	GW	GT	S	PCT
70	25	23	48	-5	42	10	0	6	1	208	12.0

1999-2000 statistics:

GP	G	A	TP	+/-	PIM	PP	SH	GW	GT	S	PCT
75	10	27	37	-5	44	3	0	2	2	159	6.3

LAST SEASON

Selected by Minnesota from Calgary in Expansion Draft, June 23, 2000. Acquired by Calgary from Nashville for Cale Hulse and a third-round draft choice in 2001, Mar. 14, 2000.

THE FINESSE GAME

Krivokrasov is Russian for "exasperating." He is highly skilled but he has never been consistent. Minnesota becomes his fourth team in three seasons.

Krivokrasov controls the puck well and reads offensive plays. He will shoot or pass and has good timing in both areas. He draws defenders and opens up ice for a teammate, before dishing off and heading to the net himself for a give-and-go. Sometimes he overhandles the puck, gets too fancy and doesn't shoot when he should. He can score some phenomenal one-on-one goals, but he is tough to play with because he doesn't use his linemates well.

Krivokrasov's skating needs to get a hair quicker. He is strong and will drive to the net. He scores a lot of goals from in tight. He has improved defensively but still has lapses. He can be utterly electrifying, yet he's not a great finisher.

Krivokrasov is a threat on every shift — both ways.

THE PHYSICAL GAME

On most nights, Krivokrasov is not a physical player and can be intimidated, but other nights he breathes competitive fire and is a force on the ice. He is very strong and stocky.

THE INTANGIBLES

Krivokrasov has major-league talents but never seems to be able to bring his "A" game to the ice every night. He can be a game breaker or a heartbreaker. He gets a little leeway in playing for a new team like the Blue Jackets.

PROJECTION

Krivokrasov's top end is 20 goals, and he will need to kick his game back into full gear to do so.

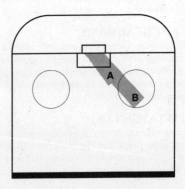

CURTIS LESCHYSHYN

Yrs. of NHL service: 12
Born: Thompson, Man.; Sept. 21, 1969
Position: left defense
Height: 6-1
Weight: 205
Uniform no.: 7
Shoots: left

Career statistics:

GP	G	A	TP	PIM
784	41	137	178	650

1996-97 statistics:

GP	G	A	TP	+/-	PIM	PP	SH	GW	GT	S	PCT
77	4	18	22	-18	38	1	1	1	0	102	3.9

1997-98 statistics:

GP	G	A	TP	+/-	PIM	PP	SH	GW	GT	S	PCT
73	2	10	12	-2	45	1	0	1	0	53	3.8

1998-99 statistics:

GP	G	A	TP	+/-	PIM	PP	SH	GW	GT	S	PCT
65	2	7	9	-1	50	0	0	0	0	35	5.7

1999-2000 statistics:

GP	G	A	TP	+/-	PIM	PP	SH	GW	GT	S	PCT
53	0	2	2	-19	14	0	0	0	0	31	-

PROJECTION

Leschyshyn will barely reach double digits in points.

LAST SEASON

Selected by Minnesota from Carolina in Expansion Draft. Missed 29 games with groin injury.

THE FINESSE GAME

Leschyshyn has average skills for a defensive defenseman. He has very slow feet, though he is balanced and strong in a containment game. His passes are soft, but he has a rather low panic point and will try to lug it out himself — not the best option given his limited skills.

Leschyshyn has a nice point shot. It's low and accurate and he gets it away quickly, but it's not elite enough to warrant any significant power-play time. He knows the importance of getting the shot on target, though. He'd rather take a little velocity off the puck to make sure his aim is true.

Leschyshyn is not overly creative and has become more defense-oriented in the past season. His reads are excellent.

THE PHYSICAL GAME

Leschyshyn is aerobically fit. He provides consistency and strong defensive-zone coverage, though he's rather passive and doesn't use his size well. But he does make efficient take-outs to eliminate his man, and doesn't run around the ice trying to pound people. He competes harder in some games than others.

THE INTANGIBLES

Leschyshyn has missed 41 games over the last two seasons with groin problems. At this stage in his career, he is barely a number six defenseman on a good team, but Minnesota will use him more extensively.

STEVE MCKENNA

Yrs. of NHL service: 3
Born: Toronto, Ont.; Aug. 21, 1973
Position: left wing
Height: 6-8
Weight: 247
Uniform no.: 7
Shoots: left

Career statistics:

GP	G	A	TP	PIM
137	5	9	14	348

1996-97 statistics:

GP	G	A	TP	+/-	PIM	PP	SH	GW	GT	S	PCT
9	0	0	0	+1	37	0	0	0	0	6	0.0

1997-98 statistics:

GP	G	A	TP	+/-	PIM	PP	SH	GW	GT	S	PCT
62	4	4	8	-9	150	1	0	0	1	42	9.5

1998-99 statistics:

GP	G	A	TP	+/-	PIM	PP	SH	GW	GT	S	PCT
20	1	0	1	-3	36	0	0	0	0	12	8.3

1999-2000 statistics:

GP	G	A	TP	+/-	PIM	PP	SH	GW	GT	S	PCT
46	0	5	5	+3	125	0	0	0	0	14	0.0

LAST SEASON

Selected by Minnesota from Los Angeles in Expansion Draft, June 23, 2000. Third on Kings in penalty minutes. Missed six games with retinal tear in left eye. Missed 30 games due to coach's decision.

THE FINESSE GAME

McKenna is all rough edges, but it has been a long-term project is for this lifetime defenseman to be converted into a mostly physical left wing. McKenna sticks his nose in and plays hard.

McKenna played mainly on the fourth line at even strength, although he saw the occasional shift with better players, who play a little bolder with him around.

McKenna's skating is a drawback, but he has good lower-body strength and works hard. He's been progressing steadily and has a solid work ethic. His game isn't pretty but he thinks the game pretty well. He just needs his feet and hands to react quickly enough at the NHL level. When he has the time, he knows what to do with the puck and can make a play.

McKenna has good leadership qualities and was a captain in college. He is a heart-and-soul player.

THE PHYSICAL GAME

McKenna is as tough as he is tall. He has a long reach. He will take on anybody, and, most often, he'll win. He's a serious pugilist who always sticks up for his teammates. He's a hard 247 pounds, and has a mean streak for punishing hits. Be afraid. Be very afraid.

THE INTANGIBLES

At least the Wild won't have to worry about anyone pushing them around if McKenna is in the lineup. His problem will be staying there. Coach Jacques Lemaire loves tough guys who have some skill, so he will give McKenna every chance.

PROJECTION

McKenna could develop into a Bob Probert-type player. In a best-case scenario, he'll score 15 goals by scaring people away and getting enough room and time to bang in loose pucks.

JEFF NIELSEN

Yrs. of NHL service: 3
Born: Grand Rapids, MN; Sept. 20, 1971
Position: right wing
Height: 6-0
Weight: 200
Uniform no.: 19
Shoots: left

Career statistics:

GP	G	A	TP	PIM
193	17	19	36	66

1996-97 statistics:

GP	G	A	TP	+/-	PIM	PP	SH	GW	GT	S	PCT
2	0	0	0	-1	2	0	0	0	0	1	0.0

1997-98 statistics:

GP	G	A	TP	+/-	PIM	PP	SH	GW	GT	S	PCT
32	4	5	9	-1	16	0	0	0	0	36	11.1

1998-99 statistics:

GP	G	A	TP	+/-	PIM	PP	SH	GW	GT	S	PCT
80	5	4	9	-12	34	0	0	2	0	94	5.3

1999-2000 statistics:

GP	G	A	TP	+/-	PIM	PP	SH	GW	GT	S	PCT
79	8	10	18	+4	14	1	0	0	0	113	7.1

PROJECTION

Nielsen should be a much better scorer for the number of games and the ice time he plays. He will see more special-teams play, by default, and could bulk up his point totals a bit with some power-play goals and assists. Don't expect a big bump, though.

LAST SEASON

Selected from Anaheim by Minnesota in Expansion Draft, June 23, 2000. Career highs in goals, assists and points. Missed one game due to injury. Missed two games due to coach's decision.

THE FINESSE GAME

Nielsen can skate, can use his great shot and can be physical. The question remains, on how many nights will he make use of his best assets? Considering how much ice time Nielsen saw last season, he should have produced more than eight goals, even by accident. He has good straightaway speed.

Although he skates well enough to earn shifts as a third-line checker, which lessens the pressure on him to score goals, even checking forwards these days are expected to chip in 10 to 15 goals.

The missing ingredients in Nielsen's game are hockey sense and the consistency to stay physically involved. On nights when he plays with more energy, he gets himself in position to score but doesn't finish well.

THE PHYSICAL GAME

Nielsen has to reach down and play to his size every night. The nights when he hits and gets involved are his best nights. If only they came along more often.

THE INTANGIBLES

Nielsen has all the tools to be a better player than he is; he needs to mature in his approach to the job. Moving to an expansion team will earn Nielsen more ice time, but he didn't show much with the Ducks, who weren't exactly a league powerhouse.

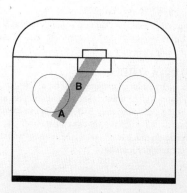

SEAN O'DONNELL

Yrs. of NHL service: 5
Born: Ottawa, Ont.; Oct. 13, 1971
Position: left defense
Height: 6-2
Weight: 225
Uniform no.: 6
Shoots: left

Career statistics:

GP	G	A	TP	PIM
381	12	59	71	799

1996-97 statistics:

GP	G	A	TP	+/-	PIM	PP	SH	GW	GT	S	PCT
55	5	12	17	-13	144	2	0	0	0	68	7.4

1997-98 statistics:

GP	G	A	TP	+/-	PIM	PP	SH	GW	GT	S	PCT
80	2	15	17	+7	179	0	0	1	0	71	2.8

1998-99 statistics:

GP	G	A	TP	+/-	PIM	PP	SH	GW	GT	S	PCT
80	1	13	14	+1	186	0	0	0	0	64	1.6

1999-2000 statistics:

GP	G	A	TP	+/-	PIM	PP	SH	GW	GT	S	PCT
80	2	12	14	+4	114	0	0	1	0	51	3.9

PROJECTION

O'Donnell cut down on his penalties last season but they will probably rise this year back to the 200 level.

LAST SEASON

Selected by Minnesota from Los Angeles in Expansion Draft, June 23, 2000. Missed two games due to coach's decision.

THE FINESSE GAME

O'Donnell has worked hard to rise above being a one-dimensional player, but his skating holds him back. He is not very good laterally and that results in his being beaten wide. He tries to line up someone and misses, because he doesn't have the quickness to get there.

O'Donnell has some offensive upside because he is alert and tries so hard, but he is really at his best when he can play a stay-at-home style. He makes a suitable partner for a high-risk defenseman. His hand skills are average at best.

O'Donnell has to improve his defensive reads. He has become a decent shot-blocker.

THE PHYSICAL GAME

O'Donnell is fearless. He is a legitimate tough guy who fights anybody. He hits hard. He uses his stick. He's a nasty customer.

THE INTANGIBLES

O'Donnell will be an original wild man. Los Angeles had a tough call to make when making players available in the draft, and they lost a gamble in exposing O'Donnell. While he is a serviceable number six, asking him to do much more, which Minnesota will do, is apt to prove problematic.

SCOTT PELLERIN

Yrs. of NHL service: 7
Born: Shediac, N.B.; Jan. 9, 1970
Position: right wing
Height: 5-11
Weight: 195
Uniform no.: 33
Shoots: left

Career statistics:

GP	G	A	TP	PIM
346	56	79	135	230

1996-97 statistics:

GP	G	A	TP	+/-	PIM	PP	SH	GW	GT	S	PCT
54	8	10	18	+12	35	0	2	2	0	76	10.5

1997-98 statistics:

GP	G	A	TP	+/-	PIM	PP	SH	GW	GT	S	PCT
80	8	21	29	+14	62	1	1	0	0	96	8.3

1998-99 statistics:

GP	G	A	TP	+/-	PIM	PP	SH	GW	GT	S	PCT
80	20	21	41	+1	42	0	5	4	0	138	14.5

1999-2000 statistics:

GP	G	A	TP	+/-	PIM	PP	SH	GW	GT	S	PCT
80	8	15	23	+8	48	0	2	2	0	120	6.7

PROJECTION

Pellerin sees prime checking time against other teams' top lines. His scoring output has dropped off since the 20 goals he had two seasons ago. Now he will be scoring just over 20 points.

LAST SEASON

Selected by Minnesota from St. Louis in Expansion Draft, June 23, 2000. Missed two games due to coach's decision.

THE FINESSE GAME

Pellerin was a Hobey Baker Award winner as the top U.S. collegiate player with the University of Maine in 1992, and shares the traits most often associated with those so honoured: quickness, intelligence and decent hand skills.

Pellerin handles most of the first-unit penalty-killing responsibilities. He can fill in short-term on one of the top two lines, but that's really asking for more than he can handle.

Pellerin is a heart-and-soul guy who gives you everything he has. Offensively, his biggest asset is his playmaking ability. He was a scorer at the college and minor-league levels and has a fairly good touch with the puck, though his shot isn't quick enough by NHL standards.

THE PHYSICAL GAME

Pellerin is small but stocky, and size is never an issue with him. He plays the same way all the time against opponents both large and small. He's feisty and won't be intimidated. He is a sturdy skater who is hard to knock off his feet. He can handle a lot of ice time. He usually ends up with the most hits in a game, and since his line usually plays against the other team's stars, that is a significant stat.

THE INTANGIBLES

Pellerin gives an honest effort every night.

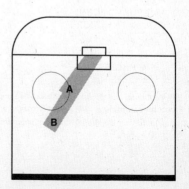

MONTREAL CANADIENS

Players' Statistics 1999-2000

POS.	NO.	PLAYER	GP	G	A	PTS	+/-	PIM	PP	SH	GW	GT	S	PCT
L	26	MARTIN RUCINSKY	80	25	24	49	1	70	7	1	4	1	242	10.3
R	15	DAINIUS ZUBRUS	73	14	28	42	-1	54	3		1		139	10.1
C	34	SERGEI ZHOLTOK	68	26	12	38	2	28	9		7	1	163	16.0
D	43	PATRICE BRISEBOIS	54	10	25	35	-1	18	5		2	2	88	11.4
C	47	TREVOR LINDEN	50	13	17	30	-3	34	4		3		87	14.9
L	49	BRIAN SAVAGE	38	17	12	29	-4	19	6	1	5		107	15.9
L	17	BENOIT BRUNET	50	14	15	29	3	13	6	1	2		103	13.6
D	22	ERIC WEINRICH	77	4	25	29	4	39	2				120	3.3
L	27	SHAYNE CORSON	70	8	20	28	-2	115	2		1		121	6.6
R	32	OLEG PETROV	44	2	24	26	10	8	1			1	96	2.1
R	23	TURNER STEVENSON	64	8	13	21	-1	61			2		94	8.5
C	31	SAKU KOIVU	24	3	18	21	7	14	1			1	53	5.7
D	28	KARL DYKHUIS	72	7	13	20	-5	46	3	1			69	10.1
C	63	CRAIG DARBY	76	7	10	17	-14	14		1	2		90	7.8
D	52	CRAIG RIVET	61	3	14	17	11	76			1	1	71	4.2
D	51	*FRANCIS BOUILLON	74	3	13	16	-7	38	2		1		76	3.9
C	37	PATRICK POULIN	82	10	5	15	-15	17		1	2		82	12.2
D	44	SHELDON SOURAY	71	3	8	11	1	114					113	2.7
L	47	JUHA LIND	47	4	6	10	-3	10					42	9.5
C	40	JESSE BELANGER	16	3	6	9	2	2					21	14.3
R	27	JIM CUMMINS	47	3	5	8	-5	92					33	9.1
D	24	CHRISTIAN LAFLAMME	65		7	7	-9	40					24	
C	30	*ARRON ASHAM	33	4	2	6	-7	24		1	1		29	13.8
D	31	SCOTT LACHANCE	57		6	6	-4	22					41	
R	60	*JASON WARD	32	2	1	3	-1	10	1				24	8.3
D	41	*MILOSLAV GUREN	24	1	2	3	-5	12	1				20	5.0
C	37	*MIKE RIBEIRO	19	1	1	2	-6	2	1				18	5.6
D	37	BARRY RICHTER	23		2	2	-5	8					13	
C	31	*MATT HIGGINS	25		2	2	-6	4					9	
C	47	TRENT MCCLEARY	12	1		1	2	4					4	25.0
L	47	DAVE MORISSETTE	1			0		5						
D	52	*STEPHANE ROBIDAS	1			0								
L	30	ANDREI BASHKIROV	2			0								
G	41	ERIC FICHAUD	9			0		2						
G	60	JOSE THEODORE	30			0								
G	31	JEFF HACKETT	56			0		4						

GP = games played; G = goals; A = assists; PTS = points; +/- = goals-for minus goals-against while player is on ice; PIM = penalties in minutes; PP = power-play goals; SH = shorthanded goals; GW = game-winning goals; GT = game-tying goals; S = no. of shots; PCT = percentage of goals to shots; * = rookie

ARRON ASHAM

Yrs. of NHL service: 1
Born: Portage La Prairie, Man.; Apr. 13, 1978
Position: right wing
Height: 5-11
Weight: 194
Uniform no.: 30
Shoots: right

Career statistics:

GP	G	A	TP	PIM
40	4	2	6	24

1998-99 statistics:

GP	G	A	TP	+/-	PIM	PP	SH	GW	GT	S	PCT
7	0	0	0	-4	0	0	0	0	0	5	.0

1999-2000 statistics:

GP	G	A	TP	+/-	PIM	PP	SH	GW	GT	S	PCT
33	4	2	6	-7	24	0	1	1	0	29	13.8

LAST SEASON

First NHL season. Appeared in 13 games with Quebec (AHL), scoring 4-5 — 9. Missed 23 games with abdominal injury. Missed one game with flu. Missed one game with back injury.

THE FINESSE GAME

Asham is a gritty forward who makes space for himself by his willingness to play a fierce game. He isn't big, but he is always willing to fight and lets his opponents know it. He has good hands for either scrapping or scoring.

Although he is listed on the roster as a centre, Asham played right wing — and wing is the right place for him. He doesn't see the ice well and isn't a good passer. His job is to disturb the defensemen into making mistakes and making a beeline for the net for rebounds and screens. He is strong along the boards.

Asham would have figured more prominently in the Canadiens' plans last season if it hadn't been for his injury. He has terrific hockey sense and the skating speed to compete at the NHL level. He is usually in the right place at the right time. He was below the radar on the Canadiens' prospects watch, but his determination has moved him past more highly regarded players.

THE PHYSICAL GAME

Asham doesn't just throw himself about wildly: he knows when to hit and when to take the edge off. He plays a smart forechecking game and doesn't go around headhunting. Experience is only going to make him a more dangerous and more valuable role player.

THE INTANGIBLES

Asham reminds some onlookers of ex-Canadien Mike Keane. He was inspired by playing with Shayne Corson, whose combination of toughness and scoring touch make him the perfect role model for Asham.

Asham lacks Corson's size, but is undeterred by the disadvantage in any given matchup.

PROJECTION

If he has recovered from his abdominal injury, Asham could start having an impact on the Canadiens' roster. They need more plucky, sturdy fellows like him, and if he scores 15 to 20 goals on top of that, his sophomore season won't be jinxed.

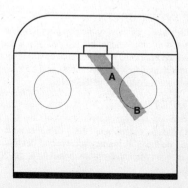

FRANCIS BOUILLON

Yrs. of NHL service: 1
Born: New York, NY; Oct. 17, 1976
Position: left defense
Height: 5-8
Weight: 189
Uniform no.: 51
Shoots: left

Career statistics:

GP	G	A	TP	PIM
74	3	13	16	38

1999-2000 statistics:

GP	G	A	TP	+/-	PIM	PP	SH	GW	GT	S	PCT
74	3	13	16	-7	38	2	0	1	0	76	3.9

LAST SEASON

First NHL season. Missed eight games due to coach's decision.

THE FINESSE GAME

Bouillon is very strong for his size. Although much smaller than today's average NHL defenseman, he understands how to play the defensive game and minimize some of the drawbacks his physique presents. He is an excellent skater, and has the ability not to get beat off the rush, whether he is facing a three-on-three or a three-on-two. He is very good in isolation situations.

Offensively, Bouillon could become a poor man's Brian Rafalski. He eagerly jumps into the attack and has some good offensive instincts. He is smart and alert and handles the puck well.

Defensively, Bouillon's biggest woe is his lack of reach. He has trouble eliminating people within a six-to-eight-foot range of the goal.

THE PHYSICAL GAME

Again, Bouillon's lack of size will always work against him, but he competes hard. He is feisty and will sometimes bring his stick up to equalize a matchup, though he was much more disciplined in the NHL last season than he was in the minors.

THE INTANGIBLES

Bouillon made the most of the opportunities that were presented to him, despite his injuries. He was overlooked and undrafted due to his lack of size (Montreal signed him as a free agent in 1998), and he knows he has to work hard to stick in the NHL.

PROJECTION

Bouillon has a lengthy career ahead of him as a Don Sweeney-type defenseman. He will never be a star, but can be a useful journeyman-type of defenseman. He has some offensive upside, possibly in the 20- to 25-point range.

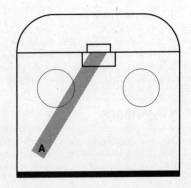

PATRICE BRISEBOIS

Yrs. of NHL service: 9
Born: Montreal, Que.; Jan. 27, 1971
Position: right defense
Height: 6-1
Weight: 188
Uniform no.: 43
Shoots: right

Career statistics:

GP	G	A	TP	PIM
499	52	161	213	365

1996-97 statistics:

GP	G	A	TP	+/-	PIM	PP	SH	GW	GT	S	PCT
49	2	13	15	-7	24	0	0	1	0	72	2.8

1997-98 statistics:

GP	G	A	TP	+/-	PIM	PP	SH	GW	GT	S	PCT
79	10	27	37	+16	67	5	0	1	0	125	8.0

1998-99 statistics:

GP	G	A	TP	+/-	PIM	PP	SH	GW	GT	S	PCT
54	3	9	12	-8	28	1	0	1	0	90	3.3

1999-2000 statistics:

GP	G	A	TP	+/-	PIM	PP	SH	GW	GT	S	PCT
54	10	25	35	-1	18	5	0	2	2	88	11.4

LAST SEASON

Led team defensemen in points. Tied for second on team in assists. Career high in goals. Missed 27 games with back injury.

THE FINESSE GAME

Brisebois has some nice skills, but he doesn't have the hockey sense to combine them in a complete package so he can be an elite-level defenseman. He has a decent first step to the puck, plus a good stride with some quickness, though he won't rush end-to-end. He carries the puck with authority but will usually take one or two strides and look for a pass, or else make the safe dump out of the zone. He steps up in the neutral zone to slow an opponent's rush.

Brisebois plays the point well enough to be on the first power-play unit, but doesn't have the rink vision and lateral movement that marks truly successful point men. He has a good point shot, though, with a sharp release, and he keeps it low and on target. He doesn't often venture to the circles on offense — when he does he has the passing skills and the shot to make something happen. And grant him this, he is *always* trying to make something good happen.

Brisebois has improved his positional play, but he often starts running around as if he is looking for someone to belt. He winds up hitting no one, while his partner is left outnumbered in front of the net. He is a good outlet passer and is getting steadier under pressure.

THE PHYSICAL GAME

Brisebois has continued to pay the price physically. Although not a punishing hitter, he is strong and will make his take-outs. He doesn't have much of a mean streak so he has to dedicate himself to taking the body (that wasn't always easy last season, given his recurring back and shoulder injuries).

THE INTANGIBLES

Brisebois has worked hard to develop better defensive presence and has become a legitimate number-three defenseman. As a French-Canadian rearguard in Montreal, he is under the microscope, and he has matured to handle a difficult situation with increased poise. Given his and the team's injuries last season, he had a remarkable year.

PROJECTION

Brisebois exceeded our expectations last season, but, with his tendency toward injury, the 40-point range is likely his top end.

BENOIT BRUNET

Yrs. of NHL service: 8
Born: Pointe-Claire, Que.; Aug. 24, 1968
Position: left wing
Height: 5-11
Weight: 195
Uniform no.: 17
Shoots: left

Career statistics:

GP	G	A	TP	PIM
443	89	136	225	205

1996-97 statistics:

GP	G	A	TP	+/-	PIM	PP	SH	GW	GT	S	PCT
39	10	13	23	+6	14	2	0	2	1	63	15.9

1997-98 statistics:

GP	G	A	TP	+/-	PIM	PP	SH	GW	GT	S	PCT
68	12	20	32	+11	61	1	2	2	1	87	13.8

1998-99 statistics:

GP	G	A	TP	+/-	PIM	PP	SH	GW	GT	S	PCT
60	14	17	31	-1	31	4	2	0	0	115	12.2

1999-2000 statistics:

GP	G	A	TP	+/-	PIM	PP	SH	GW	GT	S	PCT
50	14	15	29	+3	13	6	1	2	0	103	13.6

LAST SEASON

Tied for third on team in power-play goals. Missed 29 games with back injury. Missed three games with facial injury.

THE FINESSE GAME

One of the NHL's best-kept secrets, Brunet is one of the top defensive forwards in the league. He is virtually anonymous, despite playing in high-profile Montreal, where his quiet, efficient role as a checking winger on the third line so often goes unappreciated. Developing into a top penalty killer, he is strong on his skates and he forechecks tenaciously. He has a high skill level, too. When needed, he can move all the way to the top line to fill in during an emergency — heaven knows the Canadiens had enough of those last season.

When Brunet does choose to do anything offensively, he cuts to the net and uses a confident, strong touch in deep. He is always hustling back on defense, though, and seldom makes any high-risk plays deep in his own zone. He takes few chances and seems to come up with big points. Although he is a checking-line player, his skills and intelligence are a powerful combination. He is the best breakaway player on the team.

Brunet's hands aren't great, or he would be able to create more scoring off his forecheck. His goals come from hard work, not pretty finesse plays, and his game is heavily defense oriented. He would be somebody's dream come true at playoff time.

THE PHYSICAL GAME

Brunet isn't big, and he is overmatched when he plays against many of the league's top lines. His strength is his positional play. He takes fewer steps than other players to accomplish the same chore. Not a big hitter, he will tie up an opponent's stick and play smothering defense. He tends to be injury prone, which is the biggest negative on his resume. He works hard along the boards and in all the high-traffic areas, which is a contributing factor to his injuries.

THE INTANGIBLES

Brunet is one of the last of a dying breed, a true-bleu Montrealer who is proud to pull on the famous sweater. He is also a tremendous internal leader. He has a strong work ethic and comes to play every night. He is like a good referee. On his best nights you seldom notice him. And he seldom has any off nights.

PROJECTION

Brunet is a hard worker and an elite penalty killer who will notch 15 to 20 goals in his checking role, if healthy.

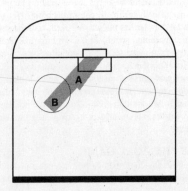

KARL DYKHUIS

Yrs. of NHL service: 7
Born: Sept-Iles, Que.; July 8, 1972
Position: right defense
Height: 6-3
Weight: 205
Uniform no.: 14
Shoots: left

Career statistics:

GP	G	A	TP	PIM
423	28	71	99	383

1996-97 statistics:

GP	G	A	TP	+/-	PIM	PP	SH	GW	GT	S	PCT
62	4	15	19	+7	35	2	0	1	0	101	4.0

1997-98 statistics:

GP	G	A	TP	+/-	PIM	PP	SH	GW	GT	S	PCT
78	5	9	14	-8	110	0	1	0	0	91	5.5

1998-99 statistics:

GP	G	A	TP	+/-	PIM	PP	SH	GW	GT	S	PCT
78	4	5	9	-23	50	1	0	0	0	88	4.5

1999-2000 statistics:

GP	G	A	TP	+/-	PIM	PP	SH	GW	GT	S	PCT
72	7	13	20	-5	46	3	1	0	0	69	10.1

LAST SEASON

Missed five games with groin injury. Missed one game with knee injury.

THE FINESSE GAME

Dykhuis has learned the importance of keeping his feet moving, because it helps him stay up with the play. His game edges towards the offensive side, but he also uses his finesse skills well in his own end. He keeps the passes short, accurate and crisp, and banks the puck off the boards or glass if that's the only option available to clear the zone.

He is a natural for penalty killing and four-on-four play because he has fine mobility and quickness, with a quick shift of gears that allows him to get up the ice in a hurry. Smart, with good hands for passing or drilling shots from the point, Dykhuis also leans towards conservatism; he won't venture down low unless the decision to pinch is a sound one.

THE PHYSICAL GAME

Although tall and rangy, Dykhuis isn't a heavyweight. But he goes out of his way to screen off opposing forecheckers and to buy time for his partner. There are times, on a regular basis, when his physical aspect is almost non-existent. He is strong and makes solid contact on those occasions when he does hit, though. He's also such a good skater that he can break up a play, dig out the loose puck and be off in just a stride or two to start an odd-man rush. He also uses his reach to break up plays.

THE INTANGIBLES

Dykhuis was a reliable part of a Montreal defense corps that is just starting to come together. With Eric Weinrich and Patrice Brisebois, he provides veteran help for such developing players as Craig Rivet and Sheldon Souray.

PROJECTION

Dykhuis will not score many points (15 to 20), even if he continues in a full-time role.

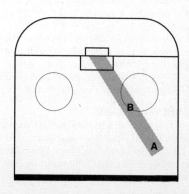

JEFF HACKETT

Yrs. of NHL service: 10
Born: London, Ont.; June 1, 1968
Position: goaltender
Height: 6-1
Weight: 180
Uniform no.: 31
Catches: left

Career statistics:

GP	MIN	GA	SO	GAA	A	PIM
403	22726	1106	22	2.92	7	56

1996-97 statistics:

GP	MIN	GAA	W	L	T	SO	GA	S	SAPCT	PIM
41	2473	2.16	19	18	4	2	89	1212	.927	6

1997-98 statistics:

GP	MIN	GAA	W	L	T	SO	GA	S	SAPCT	PIM
58	3441	2.20	21	25	11	8	126	1520	.917	8

1998-99 statistics:

GP	MIN	GAA	W	L	T	SO	GA	S	SAPCT	PIM
53	3091	2.27	24	20	9	5	117	1360	.914	6

1999-2000 statistics:

GP	MIN	GAA	W	L	T	SO	GA	S	SAPCT	PIM
56	3301	2.40	23	25	7	3	132	1543	.914	4

LAST SEASON

Missed one game with shoulder injury.

THE PHYSICAL GAME

Hackett is a student of goaltending; his technique could provide a textbook for any young student of the game. His positional play is strong: he knows when to challenge a shooter at the top of the crease and he plays his angles well and doesn't give the shooter much room.

Hackett is one of the hardest-working players on the team — if anything, he works too hard and has to be urged to conserve his energy, since he's an active goalie and isn't the most robust guy in the world. Fortunately, he makes the game easier on himself by actually stopping the puck. He allows few rebounds, so he rarely has to scramble. During the off-season, he attends camps and works to hone his skills.

Hackett has quick reflexes for bang-bang plays around the net. His glove is a great asset. He can play conservative, holding the puck for a draw to cool off the action.

Hackett's stickhandling has improved slightly over the years, but still remains the weakest aspect of his game. He is sometimes guilty of trying to do too much. He is much better off letting his defensemen handle the puck and staying out of their way.

THE MENTAL GAME

Hackett thrives on being the number one goalie. He can handle a lot of minutes and isn't fazed when facing a high number of shots. It's been awhile since he played for a contender, though it's hardly his fault. He has the character of a winner.

THE INTANGIBLES

Hackett is very popular with his teammates and was the clear-cut Canadiens MVP last season. If goalies could be captains he would be one for the Canadiens. He is tough, gritty — the kind of goalie his teammates love to play for. He is one of the league's best-kept goaltending secrets. It would be great to see what he could do for a playoff contender.

PROJECTION

Last season we predicted 25 wins for Hackett, despite the fact he was playing for Montreal. He nearly made it, an amazing feat that he should duplicate this year. Tack on 10 wins if he gets traded to a better team.

SAKU KOIVU

Yrs. of NHL service: 5
Born: Turku, Finland; Nov. 23, 1974
Position: centre
Height: 5-9
Weight: 175
Uniform no.: 11
Shoots: left

Career statistics:

GP	G	A	TP	PIM
290	68	155	223	178

1996-97 statistics:

GP	G	A	TP	+/-	PIM	PP	SH	GW	GT	S	PCT
50	17	39	56	+7	38	5	0	3	0	135	12.6

1997-98 statistics:

GP	G	A	TP	+/-	PIM	PP	SH	GW	GT	S	PCT
69	14	43	57	+8	48	2	2	3	0	145	9.7

1998-99 statistics:

GP	G	A	TP	+/-	PIM	PP	SH	GW	GT	S	PCT
65	14	30	44	-7	38	4	2	0	0	145	9.7

1999-2000 statistics:

GP	G	A	TP	+/-	PIM	PP	SH	GW	GT	S	PCT
24	3	18	21	+7	14	1	0	0	1	53	5.7

LAST SEASON

Third on team in plus-minus. Missed 45 games with shoulder injury. Missed 13 games with knee injury.

THE FINESSE GAME

A highly skilled, versatile player, Koivu brings brilliance and excitement to every shift. Considered one of the world's best playmakers, he makes things happen with his speed and intimidates by driving the defense back, then uses the room to create scoring chances.

He has great hands and can handle the puck at a fast pace. He stickhandles through traffic and reads plays well. He is intelligent and involved. Not a pure goal scorer, he needs to distribute the puck more to be a more effective centre.

Koivu has a variety of shots. Like many Europeans, he has a slick backhand for shooting or passing. He also has a strong wrist shot and is deadly accurate. The feisty Finn draws a lot of checking attention — teams facing the Canadiens simply load up against him — and he fights his way through most of it, but he is small enough to get worn down.

At the top of his game, he is one of the most dazzling players in the league.

THE PHYSICAL GAME

The lone knock on Koivu is his lack of size. He loves to play a physical game, but he just can't. He takes a beating, gets shoved around and occasionally broken. He plays through pain, but the Habs need to keep him from getting so damaged. He won't be intimidated, though, and uses his stick as an equalizer.

THE INTANGIBLES

In just over a year, Koivu had major surgeries on his wrist, shoulder and knee. None of this bodes well for his chances of getting through an entire season intact. It's gotten so that Koivu gets hurt in practice even when no one touches him.

Gritty and determined, he is well-respected by his teammates and is a probable future captain of the Canadiens, but he needs to be able to stay in the lineup.

PROJECTION

If he stays physically intact, and if Montreal increases its size up front a little bit, there is no reason why Koivu can't be a 25-goal, 60-assist man next season.

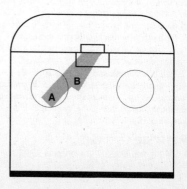

TREVOR LINDEN

Yrs. of NHL service: 12
Born: Medicine Hat, Alta.; Apr. 11, 1970
Position: centre/right wing
Height: 6-4
Weight: 210
Uniform no.: 32
Shoots: right

Career statistics:

GP	G	A	TP	PIM
859	288	374	662	668

1996-97 statistics:

GP	G	A	TP	+/-	PIM	PP	SH	GW	GT	S	PCT
49	9	31	40	+5	27	2	2	2	0	84	10.7

1997-98 statistics:

GP	G	A	TP	+/-	PIM	PP	SH	GW	GT	S	PCT
67	17	21	38	-14	82	5	2	2	0	133	12.8

1998-99 statistics:

GP	G	A	TP	+/-	PIM	PP	SH	GW	GT	S	PCT
82	18	29	47	-14	32	8	1	1	0	167	10.8

1999-2000 statistics:

GP	G	A	TP	+/-	PIM	PP	SH	GW	GT	S	PCT
50	13	17	30	-3	34	4	0	3	0	87	14.9

LAST SEASON

Third on team in shooting percentage. Missed 20 games with ankle injury. Missed 12 games with rib injury.

THE FINESSE GAME

Linden is a good player during the regular season who lifts his game a notch in the playoffs or other big games. But in the last few seasons with the Canucks, Islanders and Canadiens, he has had few opportunities to shine in the postseason. That and a series of serious injuries have caused his stock to decline.

Linden would be more effective as a winger than a centre. However, because of his size and the team's continuing lack of depth at the position, the Canadiens are likely to keep him in the middle to match up against some of the East's big centres, so he is pretty much stuck. Not a graceful skater, at times he looks awkward, and he's not as strong on his skates as a player of his size should be. Despite his heavy feet his agil'ty is satisfactory, but he lacks first-step quickness and doesn't have the all-out speed to pull away from a checker. He has a big turning radius.

Linden has improved his release, but it is not quick. He has a long reach, although unlike, say, Dave Andreychuks (who is built along similar lines), his short game is not as effective as it should be.

Linden is unselfish and makes quick, safe passing decisions that help his team break smartly up the ice, often creating odd-man rushes. He has improved tremendously in his defensive coverage. He is very good on face-offs.

THE PHYSICAL GAME

Linden is big but doesn't always play tough, and so doesn't make good use of his size. He will attack the blueline and draw the attention of both defensemen, but will pull up rather than try to muscle through and earn a holding penalty. There are people he should nullify who still seem able to get away from him. He does not skate through the physical challenges along the boards. When he plays big, he is a big, big player.

If only he would keep his feet moving, Linden would be so much more commanding. Instead, he can be angled off the play fairly easily because he will not battle for better ice.

When Linden is throwing his weight around, he drives to the net and drags a defender or two with him, opening up a lot of ice for his teammates. He creates havoc in front of the net on the power play, planting himself for sreens and deflections. When the puck is at the side boards, he's smart enough to move up higher, between the circles, forcing the penalty killers to make a decision. If the defenseman on that side steps up to cover him, space will open behind the defenseman; if a forward collapses to cover him, a point shot will open up.

THE INTANGIBLES

Linden is very likable and is a team leader.

PROJECTION

Linden will get his 20 to 25 goals and 50 to 60 points on a regular basis, if he stays healthy. Playing with yet another bad team for yet another season has to wear on him.

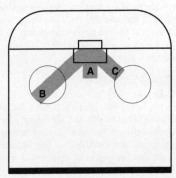

CRAIG RIVET

Yrs. of NHL service: 4
Born: North Bay, Ont.; Sept. 13, 1974
Position: right defense
Height: 6-2
Weight: 197
Uniform no.: 52
Shoots: right

Career statistics:

GP	G	A	TP	PIM
247	6	33	39	348

1996-97 statistics:

GP	G	A	TP	+/-	PIM	PP	SH	GW	GT	S	PCT
35	0	4	4	+7	24	0	0	0	0	24	0.0

1997-98 statistics:

GP	G	A	TP	+/-	PIM	PP	SH	GW	GT	S	PCT
61	0	2	2	-3	93	0	0	0	0	26	0.0

1998-99 statistics:

GP	G	A	TP	+/-	PIM	PP	SH	GW	GT	S	PCT
66	2	8	10	-3	66	0	0	0	0	39	5.1

1999-2000 statistics:

GP	G	A	TP	+/-	PIM	PP	SH	GW	GT	S	PCT
61	3	14	17	+11	76	0	0	1	1	71	4.2

LAST SEASON

Led team in plus-minus. Third on team in penalty minutes. Missed nine games with fractured cheekbone. Missed eight games with groin injury. Missed two games with virus.

THE FINESSE GAME

Rivet became part of the Canadiens' top pairing with Eric Weinrich in the absence (through injujry and later trade) of Vladimir Malakhov. There is little that Rivet does not do well.

Rivet's primary asset is his hockey sense. It has been slow to develop at the NHL level, but gradually Rivet has become an extremely reliable player in his own zone. He is a willing shot-blocker. He is an efficient skater. He passes well and moves the puck quickly out of his zone with low-risk plays.

Rivet's offensive upside is high. He has been concentrating on the defensive end of the game more, but he has the skating ability, the hands, and the shot to get involved more in the attack. He is a smart offensive player. He could become a poor man's Ray Bourque. Rivet should see continued power-play time.

Rivet also kills penalties well. The PK was one of the few areas where Montreal had any success last year, and Rivet was a part of that. Rivet competes hard and is a natural leader.

THE PHYSICAL GAME

The physical part of the game comes naturally to Rivet. He is a willing hitter, not necessarily mean, but he takes his man out with authority. He has good size and knows how to use it. Rivet is strong on his skates and finishes his checks. Not many opposing forwards look forward to coming into his corner. Rivet has added meaningful muscle in the past few seasons.

THE INTANGIBLES

This should be Rivet's best NHL season. He has developed a level of physical maturity and the intelligence to go along with it. While he will never be an elite defenseman, he could be a number two on anyone's team except for the league's top three or four teams now, and he might not be far from that rank soon. He is a sleeper to keep an eye on.

PROJECTION

Rivet is coming into his own. He is the first Canadien that opposing GMs ask about when they call looking for a trade, which should give some idea of how Rivet's stock has risen in the past season. He can contribute more offensively, possibly in the 25- to 30-point range.

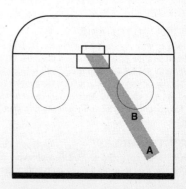

MARTIN RUCINSKY

Yrs. of NHL service: 8
Born: Most, Czech Republic; March 11, 1971
Position: left wing
Height: 6-0
Weight: 198
Uniform no.: 26
Shoots: left

Career statistics:

GP	G	A	TP	PIM
542	151	206	357	459

1996-97 statistics:

GP	G	A	TP	+/-	PIM	PP	SH	GW	GT	S	PCT
70	28	27	55	+1	62	6	3	3	1	172	16.3

1997-98 statistics:

GP	G	A	TP	+/-	PIM	PP	SH	GW	GT	S	PCT
78	21	32	53	+13	84	5	3	3	0	192	10.9

1998-99 statistics:

GP	G	A	TP	+/-	PIM	PP	SH	GW	GT	S	PCT
73	17	17	34	-25	50	5	0	1	0	180	9.4

1999-2000 statistics:

GP	G	A	TP	+/-	PIM	PP	SH	GW	GT	S	PCT
80	25	24	49	+1	70	7	1	4	1	242	10.3

LAST SEASON

Led team in points and shots. Second on team in goals and power-play goals. Third on team in game-winning goals and penalty minutes. Missed one game with concussion. Missed one game with back injury.

THE FINESSE GAME

One of the few Montreal forwards to get through the season without some major catastrophe befalling him, Rucinsky responded to the extra ice time with his best offensive season. The Czech winger is very quick, with hand skills to match at high tempo. He is most dangerous off the rush, where he can use his speed to intimidate the defense and then use the room they give him to fire his shot.

His flaw is that he is not overly patient. He has nice little moves and can beat people one-on-one. He loves to shoot, though, unlike many European players, and his shot is lethal.

Rucinsky always gives the impression that there is a lot more left in the tank.

THE PHYSICAL GAME

Rucinsky is wiry but isn't a big banger. He will takes hits to protect the puck and make a play, but he does not drive to the net through traffic and seldom initiates. He can be intimidated, and that is a problem on a team that lacks depth, like Montreal, because it is very easy for opponents to key on Rucinsky and shut him down.

THE INTANGIBLES

Rucinsky does not compete hard enough every night to make him that valuable a commodity, often getting by on his skills, but he is desperately needed to be more consistent in Montreal.

PROJECTION

In last year's *HSR* we predicted, "He'll score 50 unsatisfying points," never daring to think that total would end up leading the team in scoring. He has shown nothing to make us change that opinion.

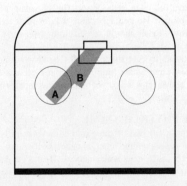

BRIAN SAVAGE

Yrs. of NHL service: 6
Born: Sudbury, Ontario; Feb. 24, 1971
Position: centre/left wing
Height: 6-1
Weight: 190
Uniform no.: 49
Shoots: left

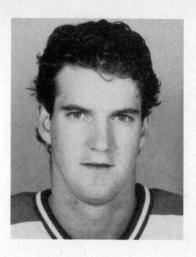

Career statistics:

GP	G	A	TP	PIM
352	120	91	211	169

1996-97 statistics:

GP	G	A	TP	+/-	PIM	PP	SH	GW	GT	S	PCT
81	23	37	60	-14	39	5	0	2	0	219	10.5

1997-98 statistics:

GP	G	A	TP	+/-	PIM	PP	SH	GW	GT	S	PCT
64	26	17	43	+11	36	8	0	7	2	152	17.1

1998-99 statistics:

GP	G	A	TP	+/-	PIM	PP	SH	GW	GT	S	PCT
54	16	10	26	-14	20	5	0	4	1	124	12.9

1999-2000 statistics:

GP	G	A	TP	+/-	PIM	PP	SH	GW	GT	S	PCT
38	17	12	29	-4	19	6	1	5	0	107	15.9

LAST SEASON

Second on team in game-winning goals and shooting percentage. Third on team in goals. Tied for third on team in power-play goals. Missed 44 games with fractured verebrae in neck.

THE FINESSE GAME

Savage missed more than half the season with an injury that nearly cost him his career, and his life. That he was able to return at all — let alone return and be an effective player — is a testament to his courage.

Savage has tremendous outside speed and a lethal shot. He has the goods to be a 40-goal scorer, and was on a pace to be just that but for the serious neck injury he suffered. He lacks the creativity and vision for playing centre (he suffers from a bit of tunnel vision), but his experience as a centre helps him as a left wing. He has a quick release and is accurate with his shot. He feasts from the hash marks in and seldom passes up a shot to make a play. He needs to play with a centre to get him the puck (Saku Koivu fits the bill, if he can stay in one piece).

Savage is a streaky scorer and he doesn't bring much to the game when he isn't scoring. Rather than working harder through the dry spells, he lets the slumps slow him down. Then it becomes a vicious circle, where it's hard for him to get ice time to break out of it.

Savage has quick hands for picking up the puck and for working on face-offs. He's a good skater. Defensively, he remains a liability, mostly because of his inconsistent effort.

THE PHYSICAL GAME

Savage doesn't use his body well and can be intimidated when playing a team that does. He is strong on his skates and he has decent size. He needs to compete more. Maybe playing with Trevor Linden will do the trick, though he doesn't seem like the answer.

THE INTANGIBLES

Savage was in the process of putting together the pieces of his game and was among the NHL's top 20 scorers before he was hurt. After the injury, he came back to score five goals in 17 games for a team that was going nowhere. He paid a huge price to get back in the game; this season could be his payoff.

PROJECTION

A sleeper pick, this born-again Savage could top the 30-goal mark.

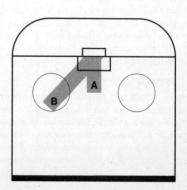

SHELDON SOURAY

Yrs. of NHL service: 3
Born: Elk Point, Alberta; July 7, 1976
Position: right defense
Height: 6-4
Weight: 235
Uniform no.: 2
Shoots: left

Career statistics:

GP	G	A	TP	PIM
201	7	22	29	309

1997-98 statistics:

GP	G	A	TP	+/-	PIM	PP	SH	GW	GT	S	PCT
60	3	7	10	+18	85	0	0	1	0	74	4.0

1998-99 statistics:

GP	G	A	TP	+/-	PIM	PP	SH	GW	GT	S	PCT
70	1	7	8	+5	110	0	0	0	0	101	1.0

1999-2000 statistics:

GP	G	A	TP	+/-	PIM	PP	SH	GW	GT	S	PCT
71	3	8	11	+1	114	0	0	0	0	113	2.7

LAST SEASON

Acquired from New Jersey with Josh DeWolf and a second-round draft pick in 2001 for Vladimir Malakhov, Mar. 1, 2000. Second on Canadiens in penalty minutes.

THE FINESSE GAME

Souray has worked hard on his skating, but still needs improvement in his turns and lateral movement. He has good straightaway speed once he gets going. He is very strong on his skates for corner and board work, which he relishes.

Since leaving the conservative New Jersey system for the more freewheeling Montreal system, Souray plays a riskier game. It could have a big payoff in his offensive contributions, but he isn't a good enough skater to recover from his mistakes; he has to be wiser about his decisions when he pinches or forces the play in the attacking zone. He can't play too staid a game, though, since he can get involved in the rush. He has a heavy slap shot and he loves to unleash it. He is likely to see some tail-end power-play time. It's not likely he will become a top-notch point man.

Souray blocks shots and plays a fairly sound positional game, though he will get rattled in his coverage now and then and start running around. Experience and confidence are the only things lacking in his game, and they should come with increased ice time.

THE PHYSICAL GAME

Souray is an imposing physical specimen and an all-around athlete. He is a little too hair-trigger in coming to the aid of his teammates, but that beats the opposite reaction. He is a good fighter and excells in a physical game. He has a major-league mean streak, and he gives a rather small Montreal team some important physical presence.

THE INTANGIBLES

Yet another of the defensive studs the Devils seem to develop at every turn, Souray was in danger of being buried in the deep New Jersey system but will have a chance to become one of the top four defensemen in Montreal. Although he hated to leave a team that was bound for playoff glory, he was happy with the chance to gain more playing time and responsibility in Montreal. This will be a key season in his development.

PROJECTION

Souray could score 20 points in a full-time role.

ERIC WEINRICH

Yrs. of NHL service: 10
Born: Roanoke, Va.; Dec. 19, 1966
Position: right defense
Height: 6-1
Weight: 210
Uniform no.: 22
Shoots: left

Career statistics:

GP	G	A	TP	PIM
759	52	225	277	619

1996-97 statistics:

GP	G	A	TP	+/-	PIM	PP	SH	GW	GT	S	PCT
81	7	25	32	+19	62	1	0	0	1	115	6.1

1997-98 statistics:

GP	G	A	TP	+/-	PIM	PP	SH	GW	GT	S	PCT
82	2	21	23	+10	106	0	0	0	0	85	2.4

1998-99 statistics:

GP	G	A	TP	+/-	PIM	PP	SH	GW	GT	S	PCT
80	7	15	22	-25	89	4	0	1	1	119	5.9

1999-2000 statistics:

GP	G	A	TP	+/-	PIM	PP	SH	GW	GT	S	PCT
77	4	25	29	+4	39	2	0	0	0	120	3.3

LAST SEASON

Tied for second on team in assists. Missed five games with fractured foot.

THE FINESSE GAME

This fine "Wein" gets better with age. Even though at this stage of his career he is best suited as a number three or four defenseman, in Montreal, he serves as a top two and handles the ice time and responsibility with poise.

Weinrich's skating is above average. He accelerates quickly and has good straightaway speed, though he doesn't have great balance for pivots or superior leg drive for power. He has improved his skating but he is not sturdy on his feet. He jumps into the rush, still, he needs to get his shots through from the point.

He is strong on the puck: shooting and passing hard. He receives quality power-play time in Montreal and has a low, accurate shot that he gets away quickly. He will not gamble down low, but will sometimes sneak into the top of the circle for a one-timer. His offensive reads are far keener than his defensive reads. His composure with the puck in all zones has improved with experience. He is an outstanding penalty killer and shot-blocker (which is how he broke his foot).

Weinrich plays better with an offensive-minded partner. He is more useful when he is the support player who can move the puck up and shift into the play.

THE PHYSICAL GAME

A good one-on-one defender, Weinrich has reached an age where he needs to watch his minutes, though he held up well last season despite averaging more than 25 minutes per game. Although not a soft player, he is not a mean, either, a criticism that dogged him early in his career. But he will fight, even though it's not in his nature, and won't get pushed around. He stands up for his teammates. His experience playing with Chris Chelios in Chicago taught him to battle hard, and Weinrich has incorporated that into his game.

THE INTANGIBLES

Weinrich has taken on more responsibility and become a better player. He provides some quiet leadership and is an inspiration, but at 34 might not have that much left in the tank. Still, you have to wonder why both Columbus and Minnesota passed on him in the expansion draft, since he is the perfect kind of player to help younger defensemen along.

PROJECTION

Weinrich should again score in the 25- to 30-point range.

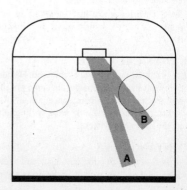

SERGEI ZHOLTOK

Yrs. of NHL service: 4
Born: Riga, Latvia; Feb. 12, 1972
Position: centre
Height: 6-0
Weight: 187
Uniform no.: 34
Shoots: right

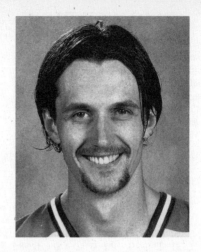

Career statistics:

GP	G	A	TP	PIM
298	57	58	115	71

1996-97 statistics:

GP	G	A	TP	+/-	PIM	PP	SH	GW	GT	S	PCT
57	12	16	28	+2	19	5	0	0	0	96	12.5

1997-98 statistics:

GP	G	A	TP	+/-	PIM	PP	SH	GW	GT	S	PCT
78	10	13	23	-7	16	7	0	1	0	127	7.9

1998-99 statistics:

GP	G	A	TP	+/-	PIM	PP	SH	GW	GT	S	PCT
70	7	15	22	-12	6	2	0	3	0	102	6.9

1999-2000 statistics:

GP	G	A	TP	+/-	PIM	PP	SH	GW	GT	S	PCT
68	26	12	38	+2	28	9	0	7	1	163	16.0

LAST SEASON

Led team in goals, power-play goals, game-winning goals and shooting percentage. Career high in goals and points. Second on team in shots. Third on team in points. Missed 11 games with chest/collarbone injury. Missed one game with cheekbone injury. Appeared in one game with Quebec (AHL), scoring 0-1-1.

THE FINESSE GAME

Zholtok has finally put it all together. Now can he keep it there?

One of the league's genuine surprises last season after years of kicking around with Boston, Ottawa and in the minors, Zholtok enjoyed his best season ever while playing on a line with crafty, skilled forwards Oleg Petrov and Dainius Zubrus. Zholtok is a pure finisher. He gets himself into position, and wants the puck for a one-timer or a wirst shot. He works to get himself into high-quality scoring areas and has a very accurate shot with a quick release.

Those qualities make him outstanding on the power play. Zholtok won't waste many scoring chances.

THE PHYSICAL GAME

Zholtok is kind of rangy but not very solid. He doesn't play a very physical game, but he has some grit in him and won't back down. His confidence is at an all-time high and that makes him a little more willing to fight through the hacks and whacks.

THE INTANGIBLES

Zholtok is extremely popular with his teammates and is a leader on the ice as well as in the dressing room.

He was one of the few highlights in an otherwise forgettable Montreal season. Now he needs to maintain his high level of play that he has shown he is capable of.

PROJECTION

Once you set the bar at 25-plus goals, the heat is on to do it again. Unless the Canadiens are again hit with an astounding rash of injuries, Zholtok should be in that range.

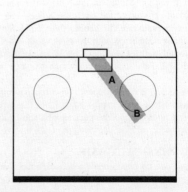

DAINIUS ZUBRUS

Yrs. of NHL service: 4
Born: Elektrani, Lithuania; June 16, 1978
Position: right wing
Height: 6-3
Weight: 215
Uniform no.: 9
Shoots: left

Career statistics:

GP	G	A	TP	PIM
290	36	76	112	147

1996-97 statistics:

GP	G	A	TP	+/-	PIM	PP	SH	GW	GT	S	PCT
68	8	13	21	+3	22	1	0	2	0	71	11.3

1997-98 statistics:

GP	G	A	TP	+/-	PIM	PP	SH	GW	GT	S	PCT
69	8	25	33	+29	42	1	0	5	0	101	7.9

1998-99 statistics:

GP	G	A	TP	+/-	PIM	PP	SH	GW	GT	S	PCT
80	6	10	16	-8	29	0	1	1	0	80	7.5

1999-2000 statistics:

GP	G	A	TP	+/-	PIM	PP	SH	GW	GT	S	PCT
73	14	28	42	-1	54	3	0	1	0	139	10.1

LAST SEASON

Led team in assists. Second on team in points. Third on team in shots. Career-high in goals. Missed six games with concussion. Missed two games with back injury. Missed one game with hip flexor.

THE FINESSE GAME

Zubrus has the ability to be a big-time offensive threat. He plays the game in a North-South direction, goal line to goal line, rather than in the East-West fashion favoured by most imports. He is helped in this regard by a long stride that covers lots of ground. His puck control is quite impressive, as though the puck is on a very short rope that is nailed to his stick. His great ability is to control the puck down low and create scoring chances for himself and his teammates. But he is not a natural goal scorer.

Splendid acceleration is a key component of Zubrus's game. He is both confident in his skating and competent enough to burst between defensemen to take the most direct path to the net. He also features enough power and balance to control a sweep behind the net, pull in front and roof a backhand shot under the crossbar from close range.

Zubrus uses his edges well and is tough to knock off the puck. He is quite willing to zoom in off the wing, use his body to shield the puck from a defender and make something happen.

The soft touch in his hands and the quick release of his shot complement the power in his legs. He can make a deft pass or a slick move, and can set up a goal or score one with roughly equal skill.

Zubrus still has a way to go to become a complete player. He is very poor in his own zone and in the neutral zone, with and without the puck.

THE PHYSICAL GAME

Zubrus will fight his own battles. He uses his size to advantage, finishes checks with authority and outmuscles as many people as he can muster. He's gritty in the corners and along the boards, and is adept at using his feet to control the puck if his upper body is tied up. He is a very strong one-on-one player.

THE INTANGIBLES

The next step in Zubrus's development is to take a more mature approach to the game. He tends to be rather self-involved and has to improve his work ethic. He needs constant attention from the coaching staff because he is not a self-starter.

PROJECTION

Zubrus could wear out his welcome in Montreal without an attitude adjustment. Tremendous skills, though, which could make him worth the effort. He has the ability, if not the desire, to be a 25-goal scorer.

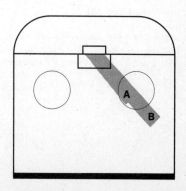

NASHVILLE PREDATORS

Players' Statistics 1999-2000

POS.	NO.	PLAYER	GP	G	A	PTS	+/-	PIM	PP	SH	GW	GT	S	PCT
C	7	CLIFF RONNING	82	26	36	62	-13	34	7		2		248	10.5
R	10	PATRIC KJELLBERG	82	23	23	46	-11	14	9		3		129	17.8
C	22	GREG JOHNSON	82	11	33	44	-15	40	2		1		133	8.3
D	44	KIMMO TIMONEN	51	8	25	33	-5	26	2	1	2		97	8.2
R	43	VITALI YACHMENEV	68	16	16	32	5	12	1	1	3		120	13.3
D	15	DRAKE BEREHOWSKY	79	12	20	32	-4	87	5		1		102	11.8
C	11	*DAVID LEGWAND	71	13	15	28	-6	30	4		2		111	11.7
R	24	SCOTT WALKER	69	7	21	28	-16	90		1		1	98	7.1
L	16	VILLE PELTONEN	79	6	22	28	-1	22	2		2		125	4.8
C	12	ROBERT VALICEVIC	80	14	11	25	-11	21	2	1	3		113	12.4
C	27	*RANDY ROBITAILLE	69	11	14	25	-13	10	2		1		113	9.7
C	71	SEBASTIEN BORDELEAU	60	10	13	23	-12	30		2	1	1	127	7.9
R	21	TOM FITZGERALD	82	13	9	22	-18	66		3	1		119	10.9
D	23	BILL HOULDER	71	3	14	17	-9	26	2		1		89	3.4
D	8	CRAIG MILLAR	57	3	11	14	-6	28			1		50	6.0
D	3	*KARLIS SKRASTINS	59	5	6	11	-7	20	1		2		51	9.8
L	36	NIKLAS ANDERSSON	24	3	8	11	-3	8	1				31	9.7
R	18	MARK MOWERS	41	4	5	9	0	10					50	8.0
D	41	*RICHARD LINTNER	33	1	5	6	-6	22					58	1.7
D	2	DAN KECZMER	24		5	5	-2	28					21	
R	40	*DAVID GOSSELIN	10	2	1	3	-4	6					14	14.3
C	9	DARREN TURCOTTE	9		1	1	0	4					13	
G	29	TOMAS VOKOUN	33		1	1	0	8						
D	20	YEVGENY NAMESTNIKOV	2				0	2					3	
D	38	*ALEXANDRE BOIKOV	2				0	2					1	
D	26	*ANDY BERENZWEIG	2				-1						3	
L	39	*MARIAN CISAR	3				-2	4					2	
R	26	PHILIP CROWE	4				0	10					1	
D	5	JAN VOPAT	6				1	6					3	
D	33	*MARC MORO	8				-3	40					3	
L	17	PATRICK COTE	21				-7	70					8	
G	1	MIKE DUNHAM	52				0	6						

GP = games played; G = goals; A = assists; PTS = points; +/- = goals-for minus goals-against while player is on ice; PIM = penalties in minutes; PP = power-play goals; SH = shorthanded goals; GW = game-winning goals; GT = game-tying goals; S = no. of shots; PCT = percentage of goals to shots; * = rookie

DRAKE BEREHOWSKY

Yrs. of NHL service: 7
Born: Toronto, Ontario; Jan. 3, 1972
Position: right defense
Height: 6-2
Weight: 212
Uniform no.: 15
Shoots: right

Career statistics:

GP	G	A	TP	PIM
348	21	67	88	573

1996-97 statistics:
Did not play in NHL

1997-98 statistics:

GP	G	A	TP	+/-	PIM	PP	SH	GW	GT	S	PCT
67	1	6	7	+1	169	1	0	1	0	58	1.7

1998-99 statistics:

GP	G	A	TP	+/-	PIM	PP	SH	GW	GT	S	PCT
74	2	15	17	-9	140	0	0	0	0	79	2.5

1999-2000 statistics:

GP	G	A	TP	+/-	PIM	PP	SH	GW	GT	S	PCT
79	12	20	32	-4	87	5	0	1	0	102	11.8

LAST SEASON

Second on team in penalty minutes. Third on team in power-play goals. Missed one game with sore knee. Missed one game with strained neck.

THE FINESSE GAME

Expansion rescues some players from the NHL's junk drawer, and Berehowsky was salvaged by the Predators. His career nearly ended by a knee injury, he had to fight his way back into the league by playing in such places as San Antonio.

Berehowsky's foot speed is not great, but he has good hands for a big guy. He gets significant power-play time by default, and logs a lot of ice time.

He would probably be a fifth or sixth defenseman on most teams; in Nashvile he is a top four. He does the best he can even though he is pressed into tough assignments for his skill level.

THE PHYSICAL GAME

Berehowsky is strong and tough and loves to mix it up. He plays with a lot of confidence and fire.

THE INTANGIBLES

Berehowsky drew more attention for his dating (attractive country singers) than his skating. Off-ice he has a good time, but he is serious about the game. He gets to the rink early and prepares himself well. He nearly lost his NHL career, which is why he appreciates it more than many young players. He is a good character player who has persevered.

PROJECTION

Berehowksy may lose ice time as the Predators improve on defense, but as there is no immediate threat of that occurring, he should be in the 25-point scoring range and 100-PIM neighbourhood.

SEBASTIEN BORDELEAU

Yrs. of NHL service: 4
Born: Vancouver, B.C.; Feb. 15, 1975
Position: centre
Height: 5-11
Weight: 188
Uniform no.: 71
Shoots: right

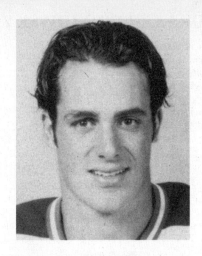

Career statistics:

GP	G	A	TP	PIM
217	34	54	88	94

1996-97 statistics:

GP	G	A	TP	+/-	PIM	PP	SH	GW	GT	S	PCT
28	2	9	11	-3	2	0	0	0	0	27	7.4

1997-98 statistics:

GP	G	A	TP	+/-	PIM	PP	SH	GW	GT	S	PCT
53	6	8	14	+5	36	2	1	0	1	55	10.9

1998-99 statistics:

GP	G	A	TP	+/-	PIM	PP	SH	GW	GT	S	PCT
72	16	24	40	-14	26	1	2	3	0	168	9.5

1999-2000 statistics:

GP	G	A	TP	+/-	PIM	PP	SH	GW	GT	S	PCT
60	10	13	23	-12	30	0	2	1	1	127	7.9

LAST SEASON

Second on team in shorthanded goals. Missed seven games with neck surgery. Missed 11 games with separated shoulder.

THE FINESSE GAME

Considering the severity of his life-threatening neck injury, it was astonishing that Bordeleau was playing last season, let alone playing and contributing.

Bordeleau has quickness and mobility. He is quick to the puck and smart around the net. He reads plays well and has good anticipation, though he doesn't have great hands. He has a pretty big shot, which he has gained more confidence in, but he usually looks to make plays first.

Bordeleau has good two-way potential and can work both special teams. He is an excellent penalty killer — a mini Guy Carbonneau. He might also earn some time on the power play in the future, but right now he is a valuable role player. He is among the best in the league in face-offs.

Bordeleau's effort is what sets him apart. He is a very determined player.

THE PHYSICAL GAME

Bordeleau is a small guy, but he is feisty and abrasive and gets in people's way. He will use his body but won't be a big hitter, for size reasons. He didn't seem any less brave after the comeback.

THE INTANGIBLES

Bordeleau missed the start of training camp recovering from surgery and a shoulder injury suffered in November. He finished the season well and was possibly the team's best all-around player in the final two months.

PROJECTION

Bordeleau can be a steady 15- to 20-goal scorer at the NHL level in a third-line role and provide some grit on a nightly basis.

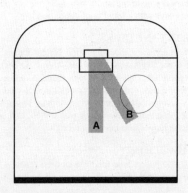

MIKE DUNHAM

Yrs. of NHL service: 4
Born: Johnson City, N.Y.; June 1, 1972
Position: goaltender
Height: 6-3
Weight: 195
Uniform no.: 1
Catches: left

Career statistics:

GP	MIN	GA	SO	GAA	A	PIM
137	7335	345	4	2.82	1	12

1996-97 statistics:

GP	MIN	GAA	W	L	T	SO	GA	S	SAPCT	PIM
26	1013	2.55	8	7	1	2	43	456	.906	2

1997-98 statistics:

GP	MIN	GAA	W	L	T	SO	GA	S	SAPCT	PIM
15	773	2.25	5	5	3	1	29	332	.913	0

1998-99 statistics:

GP	MIN	GAA	W	L	T	SO	GA	S	SAPCT	PIM
44	2472	3.08	16	23	3	1	127	1387	.908	4

1999-2000 statistics:

GP	MIN	GAA	W	L	T	SO	GA	S	SAPCT	PIM
52	3077	2.85	19	27	6	0	146	1584	.908	6

LAST SEASON

Missed six games with sprained thumb. Missed one game with flu.

THE PHYSICAL GAME

Dunham is built well for the stand-up style he favours. He injects some butterfly elements, but for the most part makes the best use of his size by staying upright and letting the puck hit him. He has to stay on his feet or his knees since he does not have great reflexes for close-in scrambles.

Dunham handles the puck fairly well. He is no Martin Brodeur, but he has obviously learned a great deal from being Brodeur's teammate for two years in New Jersey, and he helps out his defense by moving the puck. He also uses his stick well to break up passes around the crease.

Dunham has some streaks of inconsistency but he is coping well with the number one role and he gives his young team a chance to win every night by not allowing very many soft goals. That is saying something for a recent expansion team. It's tough to evaluate, but Dunham could be among the league's top 15 goaltenders.

THE MENTAL GAME

Dunham can be highly critical of his teammates, which doesn't sit too well with a team that doesn't win many games. It's obvious that Dunham is competitive and wants to win, but he has to be a little more compassionate with the people around him and try not to be such a perfectionist.

At least Dunham's nagging groin injuries appear to be a thing of the past. But during the off-season

Dunham injured his hand carrying a computer and while it was not fractured, he had to wear a cast for several weeks. Dunham appears to have the mentality to be a number one goalie, but constant losing may fray his nerves.

PROJECTION

Dunham stayed healthy enough to approach the 20-win mark we set for him last season. With two more expansion teams to beat up on, or at least be competitive with, he just might get 25.

TOM FITZGERALD

Yrs. of NHL service: 12
Born: Melrose, Mass.; Aug. 28, 1968
Position: right wing/centre
Height: 6-1
Weight: 191
Uniform no.: 21
Shoots: right

Career statistics:

GP	G	A	TP	PIM
731	107	140	237	517

1996-97 statistics:

GP	G	A	TP	+/-	PIM	PP	SH	GW	GT	S	PCT
71	10	14	24	+7	64	0	2	1	1	135	7.4

1997-98 statistics:

GP	G	A	TP	+/-	PIM	PP	SH	GW	GT	S	PCT
80	12	6	18	-4	79	0	2	1	0	119	10.1

1998-99 statistics:

GP	G	A	TP	+/-	PIM	PP	SH	GW	GT	S	PCT
80	13	19	32	-18	48	0	0	1	0	180	7.2

1999-2000 statistics:

GP	G	A	TP	+/-	PIM	PP	SH	GW	GT	S	PCT
82	13	9	22	-18	66	0	3	1	0	119	10.9

LAST SEASON

Led team in shorthanded goals. Third on team in penalty minutes. One of four Predators to appear in all 82 games.

THE FINESSE GAME

Fitzgerald is a good penalty killer but has elevated his game another step above the average third-liner by becoming a reliable crunch-time player, at least for a newer team.

He is quick and uses his outside speed to take the puck to the net. He is also less shy about using his shot, perhaps because he is working to get himself into better shooting situations. He doesn't have the fastest release and the goalie can usually adjust in time despite Fitzgerald's speed. He isn't very creative. His chances come off earnest work around the net.

Fitzgerald is versatile and he can play both centre and right wing. He makes a better winger than centre. He is only average on draws. His hands aren't very quick and he seems to be at a disadvantage against bigger centres.

THE PHYSICAL GAME

Fitzgerald is gritty and strong. He has fairly good size and he uses it along the boards and in front of the net. Although he's a pesky checker who gets people teed off, his own discipline keeps him from taking many cheap penalties. He gives his team some bang and pop and finishes his checks. He isn't huge, but he's among the best open-ice hitters in the league.

Fitzgerald is an iron man. He is durable and handles a lot of ice time. He plays through pain.

THE INTANGIBLES

Fitzgerald has grown into his role as a team leader and a spokesman for the game in an area of the U.S. that is new to the sport. He is the kind of reliable player who could draw a lot of attention from contending teams at the trade deadline.

PROJECTION

Fitzgerald will contribute 15 to 20 goals in a checking role, but lacks the finishing touch to do much more.

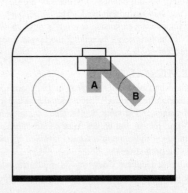

BILL HOULDER

Yrs. of NHL service: 13
Born: Thunder Bay, Ont.; Mar. 11, 1967
Position: left defense
Height: 6-3
Weight: 211
Uniform no.: 2
Shoots: left

Career statistics:

GP	G	A	TP	PIM
601	53	167	220	284

1996-97 statistics:

GP	G	A	TP	+/-	PIM	PP	SH	GW	GT	S	PCT
79	4	21	25	+16	30	0	0	2	0	116	3.4

1997-98 statistics:

GP	G	A	TP	+/-	PIM	PP	SH	GW	GT	S	PCT
82	7	25	32	+13	48	4	0	2	0	102	6.9

1998-99 statistics:

GP	G	A	TP	+/-	PIM	PP	SH	GW	GT	S	PCT
76	9	23	32	+8	40	7	0	5	0	115	7.8

1999-2000 statistics:

GP	G	A	TP	+/-	PIM	PP	SH	GW	GT	S	PCT
71	3	14	17	-9	26	2	0	1	0	89	3.4

LAST SEASON

Missed 11 games with concussion.

THE FINESSE GAME

Houlder has a big shot, but otherwise his overall skills are average. Although he struggles as a skater, especially with his turns, he has a decent first step to the puck and is strong on his skates.

A cerebral player, Houlder makes smart options with his passes and does not like to carry the puck. He prefers to dish off to a teammate or chip the puck out along the wall, rather than try to carry it past a checker.

He works well on the penalty kill despite his lack of foot speed. When in danger, he just gets the puck out. Nothing fancy; he is not a risktaker. His attack is mostly limited to point shots, though he will get brave once in awhile and gamble to the top of the circle. Most of his goals come from 60 feet out with some traffic in front. He can play on the second power play, though that is not his forte.

THE PHYSICAL GAME

Houlder is a gentle giant. There is always the expectation with bigger players that they will make monster hits, but we have the feeling that a lot of them were big as youngsters and were told by their parents not to go around picking on smaller kids. Houlder is definitely among the big guys who don't hit to hurt. If he did get involved he would be a dominating defenseman, but that's not about to happen at this stage of his career.

Still, Houlder will take out his man with quiet efficiency. He has to angle the attacker to the boards because of his lack of agility. He is vulnerable to outside speed when he doesn't close off the lane.

THE INTANGIBLES

On a young team like Nashville, a journeyman defender like Houlder, who can mentor some of the inexperienced defensemen along, is invaluable. He would be a number six defenseman anywhere else. He's a number four here.

PROJECTION

Houlder will provide solid defense and 20 points.

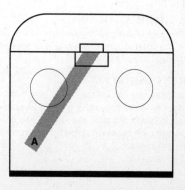

GREG JOHNSON

Yrs. of NHL service: 5
Born: Thunder Bay, Ontario; Mar. 16, 1971
Position: centre
Height: 5-10
Weight: 185
Uniform no.: 22
Shoots: left

Career statistics:

GP	G	A	TP	PIM
433	79	146	225	174

1996-97 statistics:

GP	G	A	TP	+/-	PIM	PP	SH	GW	GT	S	PCT
32	7	9	16	-13	14	1	0	0	0	52	13.5

1997-98 statistics:

GP	G	A	TP	+/-	PIM	PP	SH	GW	GT	S	PCT
74	12	22	34	-2	40	4	0	3	0	89	13.5

1998-99 statistics:

GP	G	A	TP	+/-	PIM	PP	SH	GW	GT	S	PCT
68	16	34	50	-8	24	2	3	0	0	120	13.3

1999-2000 statistics:

GP	G	A	TP	+/-	PIM	PP	SH	GW	GT	S	PCT
82	11	33	44	-15	40	2	0	1	0	133	8.3

PROJECTION

With Johnson's speed and decent hands, he should be a 20-goal scorer. History says he isn't likely to score much more than 15. But if you want assists, he's your man in Nashville.

LAST SEASON

Second on team in assists and shots. Third on team in points. One of four Predators to appear in all 82 games.

THE FINESSE GAME

Like Cliff Ronning, Johnson is a player who took full advantage of the ice time given to him by playing for an expansion team.

He can be used in may playing situations thanks to his speed, which is explosive. A small centre, he has fine finesse skills. He's also a smart and creative passer, though he doesn't shoot enough, especially given the amount of ice time he receives. When he chooses, he has an accurate wrist shot. He isn't a hard player but he competes well.

Johnson can play four-on-four, kill penalties and work on the power play. He would help himself if he took a page out of Ronning's book and shot more frequently.

THE PHYSICAL GAME

Johnson is small and gets bounced around a lot. Being one of the faster skaters in the league at least allows him to avoid some trouble.

THE INTANGIBLES

Johnson has now battled the "small man" criticism that dogs so many players by proving he is durable enough to handle ice time over the course of a full NHL season. He became a restricted free agent at the end of last season.

PATRIC KJELLBERG

Yrs. of NHL service: 2
Born: Falun, Sweden; June 17, 1969
Position: left wing
Height: 6-2
Weight: 196
Uniform no.: 10
Shoots: left

Career statistics:

GP	G	A	TP	PIM
160	34	43	77	40

1998-99 statistics:

GP	G	A	TP	+/-	PIM	PP	SH	GW	GT	S	PCT
71	11	20	31	-13	24	2	0	2	0	103	10.7

1999-2000 statistics:

GP	G	A	TP	+/-	PIM	PP	SH	GW	GT	S	PCT
82	23	23	46	-11	14	9	0	3	0	129	17.8

LAST SEASON

Led team in power-play goals and shooting percentage. Tied for team lead in game-winning goals. Second on team in goals and points. Third on team in shots. One of four Predators to appear in all 82 games.

THE FINESSE GAME

Kjellberg is a big, strong skater, but not a swift one. He is good along the wall and in the corners. He is a bigger Andreas Dackell.

Most of Kjellberg's goals come from in and around the crease. He's not flashy. He makes smart plays, though, and you really have to pay attention to notice the little things he does well. He's not a big offensive threat, but he has the finesse skills to play alongside two of the better Predators forwards, Cliff Ronning and David Legwand, on the top line.

Kjellberg isn't quick, but he is smart enough to not get burned often defensively.

THE PHYSICAL GAME

Kjellberg likes to get involved around the net. He will dig in for rebounds and garbage goals. Most of his goals come from five to 10 feet out, in the dirty areas. He'll take a beating to get open. He has a very low flash point and doesn't take bad penalties. He just takes the punishment.

THE INTANGIBLES

Kjellberg is hardly spectacular in any areas, but to earn ice time on a new team you just have to make the most of your modest skills with effort and intelligence, and Kjellberg does that. He will suffer a declining role once the Predators upgrade their talent, but he is in no immediate danger of that.

PROJECTION

We said in last year's *HSR* that Kjellberg could score 15 to 20 goals if he achieved a level of consistency. He did, he has, and he should do so again.

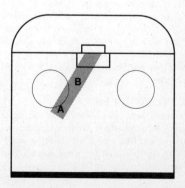

DAVID LEGWAND

Yrs. of NHL service: 1
Born: Detroit, Mich.; Aug. 17, 1980
Position: centre
Height: 6-1 1/2
Weight: 175
Uniform no.: 11
Shoots: left

Career statistics:

GP	G	A	TP	PIM
72	13	15	28	30

1998-99 statistics:

GP	G	A	TP	+/-	PIM	PP	SH	GW	GT	S	PCT
1	0	0	0	0	0	0	0	0	0	2	.0

1999-2000 statistics:

GP	G	A	TP	+/-	PIM	PP	SH	GW	GT	S	PCT
71	13	15	28	-6	30	4	0	2	0	111	11.7

LAST SEASON

First NHL season. Missed 11 games with broken bone in foot.

THE FINESSE GAME

Drafted just after Vincent Lecavalier in 1998, Legwand will be linked with Tampa Bay's centre for the first few years of his career, but the parallels just aren't there because they are two very different kinds of players. In fact, move Legwand to left wing and they would probably make very nice linemates.

Legwand is more of a shooter, possibly the best shooter available in the 1998 draft. He handles the puck well in traffic and shoots well in stride. He wants the puck when the game is on the line, because he has that goal scorer's mentality that the team is better off when the puck is on his stick rather than anyone else's. He isn't totally unselfish and is a good passer, but his first option will always be to take the shot. Legwand is very strong on the puck. He just has to find his shot and utilize his outside speed better.

Legwand is an absolutely dynamic skater. He has progressed more quickly than the Predators had dared hope.

THE PHYSICAL GAME

Legwand has been compared to Mike Modano, but physically and mentally, he is years away from being a Modano-type of player. Legwand is still boyish in build and needs to get a lot stronger to be able to compete in the NHL. He has a strong lower body and must develop the upper body to go along with it to win more battles.

THE INTANGIBLES

Expectations were raised when Legwand stepped in and stepped up last season. He ended the season playing on the top line with Cliff Ronning and Patric Kjellberg on the wings. Legwand doesn't have any elite-level help to draw on.

PROJECTION

Unless he is clobbered by the sophomore jinx, Legwand should score 35 to 40 points in a first-line role.

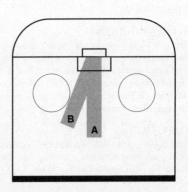

CLIFF RONNING

Yrs. of NHL service: 13
Born: Vancouver, B.C.; Oct. 1, 1965
Position: centre
Height: 5-8
Weight: 170
Uniform no.: 7
Shoots: left

Career statistics:

GP	G	A	TP	PIM
856	242	439	681	367

1996-97 statistics:

GP	G	A	TP	+/-	PIM	PP	SH	GW	GT	S	PCT
69	19	32	51	-9	26	8	0	2	0	171	11.1

1997-98 statistics:

GP	G	A	TP	+/-	PIM	PP	SH	GW	GT	S	PCT
80	11	44	55	+5	36	3	0	0	1	197	5.6

1998-99 statistics:

GP	G	A	TP	+/-	PIM	PP	SH	GW	GT	S	PCT
79	20	40	60	-3	42	10	0	4	0	257	7.8

1999-2000 statistics:

GP	G	A	TP	+/-	PIM	PP	SH	GW	GT	S	PCT
82	26	36	62	-13	34	7	0	2	0	248	10.5

LAST SEASON

Led team in assists, points and shots for second consecutive season. Led team in goals. Second on team in power-play goals. One of four Predators to appear in all 82 games.

THE FINESSE GAME

Ronning's forte is not scoring goals but creating chances for his wingers. He lets bigger linemates attract defenders so that he can dipsy-doodle with the puck. He's quick, shifty and smart (he has to be smart, otherwise he'll be flattened along the boards like an advertisement).

Ronning likes to work from behind the net, using the cage as a shield and daring defenders to chase him. Much of his game is a dare. He is a tempting target, and even smaller-sized defensemen fantasize about smashing him to the ice, but he keeps himself out of trouble by dancing in and out of openings and finding free teammates. He also works well off the halfboards on the power play.

A quick thinker and unpredictable, Ronning can curl off the wall into the slot, pass to the corners or the point and jump to the net, or beat a defender wide at the top of the circle and feed a teammate coming into the play late. He's not afraid of going into traffic. And as good a passer and playmaker as he is, Ronning isn't shy about pulling the trigger.

Ronning puts a lot of little dekes into a compact area and opens up the ice with his bursts of speed and his fakes. Unless the defense can force him along the wall and contain him, he's all over the ice trying to make things happen. He has not yet lost a step in his skating.

THE PHYSICAL GAME

No one asks jockeys to tackle running backs. Ronning is built for speed and deception. He is smart enough to avoid getting crunched and talented enough to compensate for his lack of strength. He has skills and a huge heart and competes hard every night.

Ronning is so small that usually the best he can do is tug at an opponent like a pesky little brother. He gets involved with his stick, hooking at a puck carrier's arm and worrying at the puck in a player's skates. He keeps the puck in *his* skates when he protects it, so that a checker will often have to pull Ronning down to get at the puck, which creates a power play. He is pretty durable for a small guy, and pays great attention to his physical fitness.

THE INTANGIBLES

Nashville could easily move Ronning to a team where he could be an important role player, but he is far more valuable to a new franchise that is trying to become competitive. Instead of sulking, Ronning has made the most of the opportunity and has had a positive impact on the team.

PROJECTION

Ronning has been terrifically consistent, with two consecutive seasons of 60 or more points, heavier on the assists than the goals. As Nashville's projected number one centre, he can be expected to repeat those numbers.

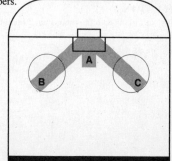

KARLIS SKRASTINS

Yrs. of NHL service: 1
Born: Riga, Latvia; July 9, 1974
Position: left defense
Height: 6-1
Weight: 196
Uniform no.: 3
Shoots: left

Career statistics:

GP	G	A	TP	PIM
61	5	7	12	20

1998-99 statistics:

GP	G	A	TP	+/-	PIM	PP	SH	GW	GT	S	PCT
2	0	1	1	0	0	0	0	0	0	0	0.0

1999-2000 statistics:

GP	G	A	TP	+/-	PIM	PP	SH	GW	GT	S	PCT
59	5	6	11	-7	20	1	0	2	0	51	9.8

LAST SEASON

First NHL season. Appeared in 19 games with Milwaukee (IHL), scoring 3-8 — 11.

THE FINESSE GAME

Skrastins has a nice future as a steady, stay-at-home defenseman. He is a good penalty killer and worked on the Predators' top unit. He blocks a lot of shots and plays a sound positional game.

He is strong, mobile, and has decent hockey sense. His offensive upside is minimal, though he handles the puck well and is poised. He concentrates on the defensive aspects of his game.

On a better team, Skrastins would be on the third pairing, but he gets assignments on a top pair with Nashville and seems to relish the challenge.

THE PHYSICAL GAME

Skrastins is a horse. He plays a lot of minutes against other teams' top players, and does so aggressively.

THE INTANGIBLES

Skrastins will be one of Nashville's top four defensemen next season. He started the season in the minors but was a regular key player late in the year. The coaches love his energy and attitude, and he has progressed faster than expected.

PROJECTION

Skrastins isn't likely to score more than 20 points.

KIMMO TIMONEN

Yrs. of NHL service: 2
Born: Kuopio, Finland; Mar. 18, 1975
Position: left defense
Height: 5-9
Weight: 180
Uniform no.: 44
Shoots: left

Career statistics:

GP	G	A	TP	PIM
101	12	33	45	56

1998-99 statistics:

GP	G	A	TP	+/-	PIM	PP	SH	GW	GT	S	PCT
50	4	8	12	-4	30	1	0	0	0	75	5.3

1999-2000 statistics:

GP	G	A	TP	+/-	PIM	PP	SH	GW	GT	S	PCT
51	8	25	33	-5	26	2	1	2	0	97	8.2

LAST SEASON

Second NHL season. Led team defensemen in points. Third on team in assists. Missed 15 games with broken wrist. Missed 12 games with broken ankle. Missed four games with abdominal strain.

THE FINESSE GAME

Timonen is the closest thing the Predators have to an offensive defenseman — consider that he lead the "D" in scoring despite missing one-quarter of the season with injuries. He has good quickness and adds a lot of skill to the Nashville backline, which doesn't have much in that department. He is not a defensive liability, and has worked to improve the defensive aspects of his game.

Timonen has to produce points because he does not bring enough to the ice in other ways. He has competed for Finland in the World Championships, so he has good ability in all offensive areas. He is not elite class, but he moves the puck and sees the ice well. He gets first-unit power-play time, but Nashville's power play ranked 25th out of 28 teams.

THE PHYSICAL GAME

Timonen is on the small side and is not very strong. He isn't going to get bigger, so he has to try to get stronger.

THE INTANGIBLES

Timonen will have a job with Nashville and be in a position to get a lot of ice time in key offensive situations, unless his game backslides dramatically. The Finn would have represented the Predators in the NHL All-Star game, which would have meant some nice recognition for him, but he was injured and couldn't play. He was a restricted free agent during the off-season.

PROJECTION

Timonen scored 33 points in only three-quarters of a season, which would presage an upgrade to the 40-point range, if he can stay healthy.

SCOTT WALKER

Yrs. of NHL service: 5
Born: Montreal, Que.; July 19, 1973
Position: right wing
Height: 5-10
Weight: 189
Uniform no.: 24
Shoots: right

Career statistics:

GP	G	A	TP	PIM
337	32	80	112	659

1996-97 statistics:

GP	G	A	TP	+/-	PIM	PP	SH	GW	GT	S	PCT
64	3	15	18	+2	132	0	0	0	0	55	5.5

1997-98 statistics:

GP	G	A	TP	+/-	PIM	PP	SH	GW	GT	S	PCT
59	3	10	13	-8	164	0	1	1	0	40	7.5

1998-99 statistics:

GP	G	A	TP	+/-	PIM	PP	SH	GW	GT	S	PCT
71	15	25	40	0	103	0	1	2	0	96	15.6

1999-2000 statistics:

GP	G	A	TP	+/-	PIM	PP	SH	GW	GT	S	PCT
69	7	21	28	-16	90	0	1	0	1	98	7.1

PROJECTION

Walker didn't quite match the splash (15 goals) he made in his first year in Nashville. Ten goals appears to be the norm for him, but if he can contribute 30 points in a checker's role, that's not shabby for a player of his type.

LAST SEASON

Led team in penalty minutes. Missed 10 games with concussion.

THE FINESSE GAME

Walker played defense in junior, but when he started his pro career in Vancouver's system he was switched to right wing, because of his size. He can still be dropped back on defense in an emergency. He is actually versatile enough to play all three forward positions, too. No one's asked him to try goal yet.

Walker has very good speed. He is an excellent penalty killer. He grinds and gets his nose in and doesn't quit on the puck. He played right wing on the checking line but, along with Ville Peltonen and Sebastian Bordeleau, was contributing his share of points.

He doesn't have great hands, but he works hard for his scoring chances and creates off the forecheck. He gets involved in traffic.

THE PHYSICAL GAME

Walker plays a feisty game. Instead of just stirring things up, he has concentrated on being more of a hockey player, so his penalty minutes have dropped. He can be a pain to play against. He has to be more consistent in his effort to stick on the top three lines. He is courageous and gritty, and he fights.

THE INTANGIBLES

Walker is a role player who can add energy and flexibility to a lineup. He has to maintain his consistency and focus to keep his job, as Nashville upgrades its talent.

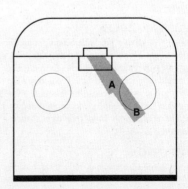

VITALI YACHMENEV

Yrs. of NHL service: 5
Born: Chelyabinsk, Russia; Jan. 8, 1975
Position: right wing
Height: 5-9
Weight: 180
Uniform no.: 43
Shoots: left

Career statistics:

GP	G	A	TP	PIM
272	52	83	135	52

1996-97 statistics:

GP	G	A	TP	+/-	PIM	PP	SH	GW	GT	S	PCT
65	10	22	32	-9	10	2	0	2	1	97	10.3

1997-98 statistics:

GP	G	A	TP	+/-	PIM	PP	SH	GW	GT	S	PCT
4	0	1	1	+1	4	0	0	0	0	4	0.0

1998-99 statistics:

GP	G	A	TP	+/-	PIM	PP	SH	GW	GT	S	PCT
55	7	10	17	-10	10	0	1	2	0	83	8.4

1999-2000 statistics:

GP	G	A	TP	+/-	PIM	PP	SH	GW	GT	S	PCT
68	16	16	32	+5	12	1	1	3	0	120	13.3

PROJECTION

We predicted 15 goals last season for Yachemenev, and he earned them despite missing 14 games with injuries. He could squeeze out 20, but that's his absolute top end.

LAST SEASON

Led team in plus-minus. Tied for team lead in game-winning goals. Second on team in shooting percentage. Third on team in goals. Missed 10 games with sprained wrist. Missed four games with concussion.

THE FINESSE GAME

In his rookie year with Los Angeles, Yachmenev played on a line with Wayne Gretzky. It was probably the best and the worst thing to happen to the young player. So much was expected of him so soon, and once he no longer had Gretzky alongside him, Yachmenev's stock plummeted.

Still, he has landed on his skates in Nashville. His shot is what got him to the NHL. He has a sniper's touch and he has to score, because he doesn't bring much else to the table. He has a tendency to hang onto the puck too long. He has some quickness but no real speed.

Yachmenev is an intelligent player with good hockey sense who can be used to kill penalties. He is a left-handed shot who plays the right wing; defensively he makes the right play on the wall. He is reliable no matter where he plays. He reminds people of Andres Dackell.

THE PHYSICAL GAME

Yachmenev isn't very big, but he is strong on his skates and solidly built. He protects the puck well and is strong along the wall.

THE INTANGIBLES

Yachmenev has become a favourite with fans and the coaching staff in Nashville for bringing a level of intelligence and energy to the ice every night.

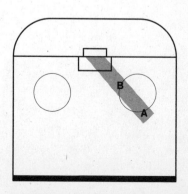

NEW JERSEY DEVILS

Players' Statistics 1999-2000

POS.	NO.	PLAYER	GP	G	A	PTS	+/-	PIM	PP	SH	GW	GT	S	PCT
L	26	PATRIK ELIAS	72	35	37	72	16	58	9		9	1	183	19.1
C	23	*SCOTT GOMEZ	82	19	51	70	14	78	7		1	2	204	9.3
C	17	PETR SYKORA	79	25	43	68	24	26	5	1	4		222	11.3
R	25	JASON ARNOTT	76	22	34	56	22	51	7		4		244	9.0
R	22	CLAUDE LEMIEUX	83	20	27	47	-3	90	7		3		257	7.8
C	16	BOBBY HOLIK	79	23	23	46	7	106	7		4	1	257	8.9
R	89	ALEXANDER MOGILNY	59	24	20	44	3	20	5	1	1	2	161	14.9
R	21	RANDY MCKAY	67	16	23	39	8	80	3		4		116	13.8
D	27	SCOTT NIEDERMAYER	71	7	31	38	19	48	1				109	6.4
D	28	*BRIAN RAFALSKI	75	5	27	32	21	28	1		1		128	3.9
D	4	SCOTT STEVENS	78	8	21	29	30	103		1	1		133	6.0
C	12	SERGEI NEMCHINOV	53	10	16	26	1	18		1	1		55	18.2
L	11	*JOHN MADDEN	74	16	9	25	7	6		6	3		115	13.9
C	18	SERGEI BRYLIN	64	9	11	20	0	20	1		1		84	10.7
L	29	KRZYSZTOF OLIWA	69	6	10	16	-2	184	1		2		61	9.8
L	20	JAY PANDOLFO	71	7	8	15	0	4					86	8.1
D	2	DERON QUINT	54	4	7	11	-2	24			1		94	4.3
D	3	KEN DANEYKO	78		6	6	13	98					74	
D	7	VLADIMIR MALAKHOV	24	1	4	5	1	23	1		1		18	5.6
G	30	MARTIN BRODEUR	72	1	4	5	0	16			1		1	100.0
D	6	BRAD BOMBARDIR	32	3	1	4	-6	6					24	12.5
D	5	*COLIN WHITE	21	2	1	3	3	40			1		29	6.9
D	2	KEN SUTTON	6		2	2	2	2					10	
C	15	STEVE KELLY	1				0							
D	24	*WILLIE MITCHELL	2				1						2	
G	31	CHRIS TERRERI	12				0	2						

GP = games played; G = goals; A = assists; PTS = points; +/- = goals-for minus goals-against while player is on ice; PIM = penalties in minutes; PP = power-play goals; SH = shorthanded goals; GW = game-winning goals; GT = game-tying goals; S = no. of shots; PCT = percentage of goals to shots; * = rookie

JASON ARNOTT

Yrs. of NHL service: 7
Born: Collingwood, Ont.; Oct. 11, 1974
Position: centre/right wing
Height: 6-3
Weight: 220
Uniform no.: 25
Shoots: right

Career statistics:

GP	G	A	TP	PIM
471	154	210	364	583

1996-97 statistics:

GP	G	A	TP	+/-	PIM	PP	SH	GW	GT	S	PCT
67	19	38	57	-21	92	10	1	2	1	248	7.7

1997-98 statistics:

GP	G	A	TP	+/-	PIM	PP	SH	GW	GT	S	PCT
70	10	23	33	-24	99	4	0	2	0	199	5.0

1998-99 statistics:

GP	G	A	TP	+/-	PIM	PP	SH	GW	GT	S	PCT
74	27	27	54	+10	79	8	0	3	1	200	13.5

1999-2000 statistics:

GP	G	A	TP	+/-	PIM	PP	SH	GW	GT	S	PCT
76	22	34	56	+22	51	7	0	4	0	244	9.0

LAST SEASON

Tied for second on team in power-play goals and game-winning goals. Third on team in shots. Missed three games with facial injury. Missed two games with flu. Missed one game with rib injury.

THE FINESSE GAME

What took the Devils so long? When they first acquired Arnott from Edmonton for Bill Guerin, in January of 1998, Arnott stuggled for nearly a year as they tried to make a right wing out of him. In 1999, they finally hit on the magic formula: Arnott as the centre for Petr Sykora and Patrik Elias.

For a player of his size, Arnott has tremendous skills. As a skater he has speed, balance, a long stride, plus agility in turning to either side. He has also added muscle to his frame, without losing any edge in his skating. He has one of the hardest shots on the team, but be doesn't always play as a power forward; or at least he didn't until last season. When he bangs and initiates, he is far more effective. Arnott's problem is that he is so skilled for a big guy that some nights he likes to take the easy way out.

Arnott is a decent passer, though he is better getting the puck late and deep. His timing with passes is fine, as he holds onto the puck until a teammate is in the open. He has become an effective weapon on the point on the power play, where his big cannon is put to use. He also smartly switches off with Sykora on the half-boards.

THE PHYSICAL GAME

Arnott has shown he is willing to pay a physical price. He has a taste for the game again — the same zest he showed in his rookie season with Edmonton — and has matured physically and emotionally. He plays mean. He plays hurt. Taking a cue from captain Scott Stevens, he has applied himself in the weight room and taken better care of himself off-ice. The payoff was a near-MVP performance in the playoffs, in which he scored the Cup-winning goal in overtime.

THE INTANGIBLES

After being booed out of Edmonton, Arnott loves the game again, and his linemates deserve a lot of the credit for reviving a career that was in premature decline. But give Arnott credit, too. The Devils stuck with him, encouraging him by making him an alternate captain, but the ultimate decision to be a player was his.

PROJECTION

Easily a 25-goal, 60-point man, with upside.

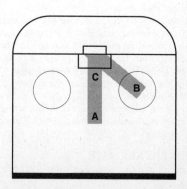

MARTIN BRODEUR

Yrs. of NHL service: 7
Born: Montreal, Que.; May 6, 1972
Position: goaltender
Height: 6-1
Weight: 205
Uniform no.: 30
Catches: left

Career statistics:

GP	MIN	GA	SO	GAA	A	PIM
447	25938	950	42	2.20	18	48

1996-97 statistics:

GP	MIN	GAA	W	L	T	SO	GA	S	SAPCT	PIM
67	3838	1.88	37	14	13	10	120	1633	.927	8

1997-98 statistics:

GP	MIN	GAA	W	L	T	SO	GA	S	SAPCT	PIM
70	4128	1.89	43	17	8	10	130	1569	.917	10

1998-99 statistics:

GP	MIN	GAA	W	L	T	SO	GA	S	SAPCT	PIM
70	4239	2.29	39	21	10	4	162	1728	.906	4

1999-2000 statistics:

GP	MIN	GAA	W	L	T	SO	GA	S	SAPCT	PIM
72	4312	2.24	43	20	8	6	161	1797	.910	16

LAST SEASON

Led NHL goalies in wins for third consecutive season. Led NHL goalies in assists (4). Tied for second among NHL goalies in shutouts. Third among NHL goalies in minutes played. Fourth among NHL goalies in PIM. Fifth goalie in NHL history to record 30 or more wins for five consecutive seasons.

THE PHYSICAL GAME

Brodeur makes the most of his generous size. He stands upright in the net and squares himself so well to the shooter that he looks enormous. He has become one of the game's best at using his stick around the net. He breaks up passes and will make a quick jab to knock the puck off an opponent's stick.

Opponents want to get Brodeur's feet moving — wraparound plays, rebounds, anything involving his skates exposes his weaknesses. Because of his puck control, he prevents a lot of scrambles and minimizes his flaws. When he falls into bad streaks, it is usually because of his footwork.

Brodeur has improved his play out of the net, so much so that if the league ever legislates against goalies handling the puck it will have to be known as the Brodeur Rule. He has to guard against cockiness, though. He gets carried away with clearing shots through the middle of the ice, but the majority of the time he handles the puck intelligently and is effective on the penalty kill sending the puck up-ice, acting as a third defenseman and thoroughly frustrating the opponents' power play.

THE MENTAL GAME

Bad games and bad goals don't rattle Brodeur for long. Although he has a tendency to show his frustration on-ice, he also bounces back quickly with strong efforts. He concentrates and doesn't lose his intensity throughout a game. Teammates love playing in front of him because of the confidence he exudes — even through the layers of padding and the mask. When he is on, his glove saves are snappy and he bounces on his feet with flair.

Teammates love to play for him because Brodeur is rarely critical, publicly or privately, of any mistakes made before the puck gets to him. He could stand to play a little less, but thrives on the work; the Devils generally let him dictate his own schedule.

THE INTANGIBLES

Winning Game 6 of the finals in double overtime against Dallas went a long way toward restoring some of the luster Brodeur's reputation lost in the years following the 1995 Cup win. He lost a triple overtime game in a duel with Ed Belfour in Game 5, so there was doubt he could handle the pressure in the clincher, but he did and nearly stole the Conn Smythe from teammate Scott Stevens in the process.

PROJECTION

We predicted another 35 wins for Brodeur last season, which he exceeded by seven. It's a good habit; no need to break it.

KEN DANEYKO

Yrs. of NHL service: 16
Born: Windsor, Ont.; Apr. 17, 1964
Position: left defense
Height: 6-0
Weight: 210
Uniform no.: 3
Shoots: left

Career statistics:

GP	G	A	TP	PIM
1070	34	125	159	2336

1996-97 statistics:

GP	G	A	TP	+/-	PIM	PP	SH	GW	GT	S	PCT
77	2	7	9	+24	70	0	0	0	1	63	3.2

1997-98 statistics:

GP	G	A	TP	+/-	PIM	PP	SH	GW	GT	S	PCT
37	0	1	1	+3	57	0	0	0	0	18	.0

1998-99 statistics:

GP	G	A	TP	+/-	PIM	PP	SH	GW	GT	S	PCT
82	2	9	11	+27	63	0	0	0	0	63	3.2

1999-2000 statistics:

GP	G	A	TP	+/-	PIM	PP	SH	GW	GT	S	PCT
78	0	6	6	+13	98	0	0	0	0	74	-

LAST SEASON

Appeared in 1,000th career NHL game. Missed one game due to knee injury. Missed three games due to coach's decision.

THE FINESSE GAME

Break down Daneyko's game — average skater, average passer, below-average shooter — and he looks like someone who would have trouble getting ice time. But Daneyko's edge is his competitive drive: he will do *anything* to win a hockey game. Add to that his strength and sound hockey sense, and the result is a powerful defensive defenseman who has been coveted by other teams for many years.

Despite his slow footwork, Daneyko has evolved into one of his team's top penalty killers. He is a good shot-blocker, though he could still use some improvement. When he goes down and fails to block a shot, he does little more than screen his goalie with his burly body.

A Daneyko rush is a rare thing. He's smart enough to recognize his limitations and he seldom joins the play or gets involved deep in the attacking zone. His offensive involvement is usually limited to a smart, safe breakout pass.

At this stage of his career, Daneyko has to be paired with a mobile partner. Only by playing alongside Scott Stevens does he stay in the top four.

THE PHYSICAL GAME

Daneyko is powerful, with great upper- and lower-body strength. His legs give him drive when he's moving opposing forwards out from around the net. He is a punishing hitter; when he makes a take-out the opponent *stays* out of the play. He is smart enough not to get beaten by superior skaters and will force an attacker to the perimeter. He has cut down on his bad penalties. Emotions still sometimes get the better of him, but he will usually get his two or five minutes' worth.

Daneyko is a formidable fighter, a player few are willing to tangle with. That means he now has to prove himself less frequently. If somebody wants a scrap, though, he's willing and extremely able, and he stands up for his teammates.

THE INTANGIBLES

Daneyko is a classic throwback to an era when guys dragged themselves onto the ice and played on fractured ankles. Despite his age, however, he is in exceptional shape. He truly takes the game of hockey to heart.

PROJECTION

Daneyko is 36 now and on the verge of becoming less of a full-time player. He has survived challenges from the young studs before, and with the Devils losing out on prospect Mike Van Ryn, Daneyko may have bought himself another season.

PATRIK ELIAS

Yrs. of NHL service: 3
Born: Trebic, Czech Republic; Apr. 13, 1976
Position: left wing
Height: 6-0
Weight: 195
Uniform no.: 26
Shoots: left

Career statistics:

GP	G	A	TP	PIM
238	72	92	164	122

1996-97 statistics:

GP	G	A	TP	+/-	PIM	PP	SH	GW	GT	S	PCT
17	2	3	5	-4	28	0	0	0	0	23	8.6

1997-98 statistics:

GP	G	A	TP	+/-	PIM	PP	SH	GW	GT	S	PCT
74	18	19	37	+19	28	5	0	6	1	147	12.2

1998-99 statistics:

GP	G	A	TP	+/-	PIM	PP	SH	GW	GT	S	PCT
74	17	33	50	+19	34	3	0	2	0	157	10.8

1999-2000 statistics:

GP	G	A	TP	+/-	PIM	PP	SH	GW	GT	S	PCT
72	35	37	72	+16	58	9	0	9	1	183	19.1

LAST SEASON

Third NHL season. Led team in goals, points, power-play goals, game-winning goals and shooting percentage. Career-high in goals, assists and points. Led team in points for first time in career. Missed nine games due to contract dispute. Missed one game due to coach's decision.

THE FINESSE GAME

The best line in the NHL? Arguably, it's Elias and mates Jason Arnott and Petr Sykora, whose skills and chemistry paid off with a championship in New Jersey.

Elias brings a centre's creativity and playmaking sensibility to the wing. His primary assets are his skating and powerful shot, which he can let rip on the fly. The less Elias thinks, the better. Once he starts to feel comfortable in his role he will let the game come to him naturally. He is not quite a power forward, though he is strong enough to muscle his way into traffic areas for scoring chances. He has an excellent release on his wrist shot.

Elias falls into slumps where he fails to get shots away on net. This is either a by-product of his tendency to look for a pass first, or a lapse in his confidence. His line does tend to start playing fancy, but when they knuckle down they are as thrilling a line as any to watch.

Elias can work on both special teams. He is reliable defensively, enjoys killing penalties and is a threat to create scoring chances off shorthanded rushes.

THE PHYSICAL GAME

Elias has good upper-body strength for work along the boards and good lowe-body strength for skating speed and balance. He is tough to knock off his skates and plays with controlled aggression. He doesn't take many bad penalties, but will bring his stick up or take a swing if he believes he is being taken advantage of. Elias can't be intimidated. A lot of teams tried during the playoffs, but Elias never backed down and frequently initiated. He is as quietly tough a forward as you can find in the NHL.

THE INTANGIBLES

Elias finally attained a level of consistency, with his lapses fewer and shorter, and emerged as one of the Devils' best forwards in the regular season and the playoffs. Will anyone ever forget seeing Elias bring Sykora's jersey onto the ice in Dallas after Sykora had been hospitalized by a Derian Hatcher hit?

PROJECTION

Despite a slow start after a contract dispute, Elias buried his disappointment over the outcome of the negotiations by burying the puck. He's joined the elite class now. A 40-goal season looms in his future.

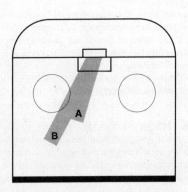

SCOTT GOMEZ

Yrs. of NHL service: 1
Born: Anchorage, AK; Dec. 23, 1979
Position: centre
Height: 5-11
Weight: 200
Uniform no.: 23
Shoots: left

Career statistics:

GP	G	A	TP	PIM
82	19	51	70	78

1999-2000 statistics:

GP	G	A	TP	+/-	PIM	PP	SH	GW	GT	S	PCT
82	19	51	70	+14	78	7	0	1	2	204	9.3

LAST SEASON

First NHL season. Won 2000 Calder Trophy. Named to NHL All-Rookie Team. Led NHL rookies and team in assists. Led NHL rookies and second on team in points. Tied for second on team and third among NHL rookies in power-play goals. Led NHL rookies in shots. One of only three NHL rookies to score a hat trick. Only Devil to appear in all 82 games.

THE FINESSE GAME

Gomez's ability to use the space behind the net to shield himself from defenders and set up plays is almost Wayne Gretzky-like. He has terrific vision and patience with the puck, and can thread a pass through what seems like the eye of a needle to find a teammate. Anyone playing with Gomez *has* to be alert, because he is adept at finding seams that others don't even know exist.

He has a very good wrist shot, not a heavy one, but accurate. You might think with his goals-to-assists ratio that Gomez doesn't shoot enough, but he isn't shy about letting it go. He is just not as gifted a goal-scorer as he is a passer. However, he makes excellent use of the extra room on a power play, and served on the Devils' second unit last season. The Devils often used him as a winger, but he isn't as good along the boards as he is in the middle of the ice.

Gomez is not a gifted skater; he needs to be constantly reminded to keep his feet moving and to not glide. He is strong on his skates, though, tough to knock off his feet and willing to work in the dirty areas for pucks. He lacks outside speed but can put on a short burst to get a jump on the defense. (He needs to work on his defense and his face-offs.)

THE PHYSICAL GAME

As easy-going as Gomez is off-ice, he is just as competitive on it. It's no surprise that one of the players he used as his mentor on the Devils was Claude Lemieux. Not a bad role model. Like Lemieux, Gomez can be chippy and chirpy. He is irritating to play against. He won't back down from a scuffle and isn't shy about starting one. He is solid and durable.

THE INTANGIBLES

More than a charming Cinderella story — Mexican-Columbian kid from Alaska makes NHL — Gomez is a player. He took the chance afforded him when Brendan Morrison and Patrik Elias were late reporting to the Devils due to contract disputes, and made it impossible for the team to send him back to the minors. He still has some rough edges, but his raw talent and desire to succeed are in evidence.

PROJECTION

Gomez suffered the inevitable post All-Star slump, but redeemed himself after being publicly challenged by coach Larry Robinson in the playoffs. His rookie numbers will be tough to match, but he should be in the 60-point range.

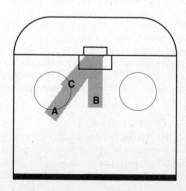

BOBBY HOLIK

Yrs. of NHL service: 10
Born: Jihlava, Czech Republic; Jan. 1, 1971
Position: centre
Height: 6-3
Weight: 220
Uniform no.: 16
Shoots: right

Career statistics:

GP	G	A	TP	PIM
717	200	247	447	760

1996-97 statistics:

GP	G	A	TP	+/-	PIM	PP	SH	GW	GT	S	PCT
82	23	39	62	+24	54	5	0	6	0	192	12.0

1997-98 statistics:

GP	G	A	TP	+/-	PIM	PP	SH	GW	GT	S	PCT
82	29	36	65	+23	100	8	0	8	1	238	12.2

1998-99 statistics:

GP	G	A	TP	+/-	PIM	PP	SH	GW	GT	S	PCT
78	27	37	64	+16	119	5	0	8	0	253	10.7

1999-2000 statistics:

GP	G	A	TP	+/-	PIM	PP	SH	GW	GT	S	PCT
79	23	23	46	+7	106	7	0	4	1	257	8.9

LAST SEASON

Tied for team lead in shots. Tied for second on team in game-winning goals and power-play goals. Second on team in penalty minutes. Missed three games with suspension.

THE FINESSE GAME

Holik is limited as a creative playmaker, because he lacks vision. He plays a fairly straightforward power game and needs to play with wingers who do the same. He does not play well when forced to carry the puck. His best formula is to dump-and-chase, cycle and create off the forecheck.

Holik has a terrific shot, a bullet drive that he gets away quickly from a rush down the left side. He also has great hands for working in tight, in traffic and off the backhand. On the backhand (at which Europeans are so much more adept than North Americans), Holik uses his bulk to obscure the vision of his defenders, protecting the puck and masking his intentions. He has a fair wrist shot.

He's a powerful skater with good balance, but lacks jump and agility. Once he starts churning, though, Holik can get up a good head of steam. He is more responsible defensively. In the playoffs last season, he frequently functioned as something of a checking centre against opponents who had physical first lines.

THE PHYSICAL GAME

Holik is just plain big. And mean. He's a serious hitter who can hurt and who applies his bone-jarring body checks at the appropriate times. He takes some bad penalties, and can be easily frustrated when he feels he is being hooked and held and the opposition isn't penalized.

THE INTANGIBLES

Although Holik's playoff numbers were low, the Devils asked him to fulfill a different role in battling against players like Keith Primeau and Mats Sundin, and he is developing into a two-way centre.

PROJECTION

Whether Holik is comfortable with the new job the Devils have created for him over the long haul is a question mark. He has never cracked the 30-goal barrier. Another season with 25 could be in the making.

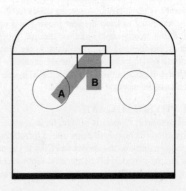

CLAUDE LEMIEUX

Yrs. of NHL service: 16
Born: Buckingham, Que.; July 16, 1965
Position: right wing
Height: 6-1
Weight: 215
Uniform no.: 22
Shoots: right

Career statistics:

GP	G	A	TP	PIM
1003	345	353	698	1584

1996-97 statistics:

GP	G	A	TP	+/-	PIM	PP	SH	GW	GT	S	PCT
45	11	17	28	-4	43	5	0	4	0	168	6.5

1997-98 statistics:

GP	G	A	TP	+/-	PIM	PP	SH	GW	GT	S	PCT
78	26	27	53	-7	115	11	1	1	1	261	10.0

1998-99 statistics:

GP	G	A	TP	+/-	PIM	PP	SH	GW	GT	S	PCT
82	27	24	51	0	102	11	0	8	1	292	9.2

1999-2000 statistics:

GP	G	A	TP	+/-	PIM	PP	SH	GW	GT	S	PCT
83	20	27	47	-3	90	7	0	3	0	257	7.8

LAST SEASON

Acquired from Colorado with Colorado's second-round draft pick in 2000 for Brian Rolston and the Devils' option to switch first-round draft choices in 2001. Tied for team lead in shots. Tied for second on team in power-play goals.

THE FINESSE GAME

Lemieux is a shooter, a disturber, a force. He loves the puck, wants the puck, needs the puck and is sometimes obsessed with the puck. When he is struggling, that selfishness hurts the team. But when he gets into his groove everyone is happy to stand back and let him roll.

When Lemieux is on, he rocks the house. He has a hard slap shot and shoots well off the fly. He is not afraid to jam the front of the net for tips and screens and will battle for loose pucks. He has great hands for close-in shots. But There are fewer nights like that now for Lemieux, who turned 35 during the off-season, so he has wisely concentrated on other areas. The Devils relied upon him almost solely as a checking winger. He is defensively responsible and can kill penalties. He can also take face-offs, since he will work hard to tie up the opposing man on the draw.

What hasn't changed about Lemieux is that his value increases once the regular season ends.

THE PHYSICAL GAME

Lemieux is strong, with good skating balance and great upper-body and arm strength. He is very tough along the boards and in traffic in front of the net, out-duelling many bigger opponents because of his fierce desire. Because he is always whining and yapping, the abuse he takes is often ignored, but it's not unusual to find him with welts across his arms and cuts on his face. The satisfaction comes from knowing that his opponent usually looks even worse.

Of course, Lemieux also infuriates opponents by goading them into dropping their gloves — he then turtles. He will gleefully inform you that he's a lover, not a fighter.

THE INTANGIBLES

Lemieux played out his walk year by winning his fourth Stanley Cup. There was no better way to boost his free-agency value. If he doesn't re-sign with the Devils, he could be the missing piece of the puzzle for another team that is close to the top.

PROJECTION

Lemieux will probably score 20 goals during the regular season; he is one of the great playoff performers of his generation. He has never played on a team that missed the playoffs, and that isn't a coincidence.

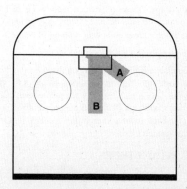

JOHN MADDEN

Yrs. of NHL service: 1
Born: Barrie, Ont.; May 4, 1975
Position: centre
Height: 5-11
Weight: 195
Uniform no.: 11
Shoots: left

Career statistics:

GP	G	A	TP	PIM
78	16	10	26	6

1998-99 statistics:

GP	G	A	TP	+/-	PIM	PP	SH	GW	GT	S	PCT
4	0	1	1	-2	0	0	0	0	0	4	0.0

1999-2000 statistics:

GP	G	A	TP	+/-	PIM	PP	SH	GW	GT	S	PCT
74	16	9	25	+7	6	0	6	3	0	115	13.9

LAST SEASON

First NHL season. Led NHL in shorthanded goals. Second on team in shooting percentage. Missed seven games due to coach's decision. Missed one game due to personal reasons.

THE FINESSE GAME

Madden strikes terror into the hearts of opponents' point men. He is so keen in his pursuit of the puck, so savvy at reading a player's intention and so quick with his first few strides once he forces a turnove, that Madden is a constant shorthanded scoring threat. Some teams even refuse to play forwards on the point against the Devils because of Madden's prowess at forcing the play. That is a huge compliment to the Devils rookie.

Madden's acceleration is awesome. He is built like a sprinter, and gets out of the blocks to gain a shorthanded breakaway or create a two-on-one. He has decent hands (not great ones, or he never would have been ignored in college). He uses his speed to drive a defenseman back or force a goalie to be less aggressive against him.

Madden has good hockey sense and vision. He is an unselfish player, a good passer, too, but not necessarily a clever playmaker. His quick hands serve him well on draws. Above all, he is tenacious. He lacks the size to stack up against other teams' power forwards, but he always gives an honest account of himself.

THE PHYSICAL GAME

Madden is solidly built, sturdy on his skates and willing to wade into high-traffic areas. He pays the price in all the dirty areas, taking a heap of abuse, but his plays are clean (his PIM total looks like a misprint). He came back from a knee injury to help the Devils win the Stanley Cup.

THE INTANGIBLES

Whatever the Devils' scouts are being paid, it's not enough. While watching Brendan Morrison, then a Devils prospect playing at the University of Michigan, the Devils were attracted to his teammate, Madden, and they signed the defensive-minded centre to a free-agent contract. Madden was simply one of the most valuable Devils through all of last season, and especially in the playoffs. He's cocky and confident, with the ability to back up the attitude.

PROJECTION

It takes a special player to deserve Selke Trophy consideration in a rookie's first NHL season. And if the award didn't rely so heavily on years of reputation, Madden could easily have been a finalist. He will make it soon.

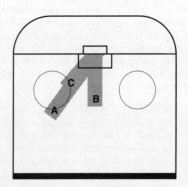

RANDY MCKAY

Yrs. of NHL service: 11
Born: Montreal, Que.; Jan. 25, 1967
Position: right wing
Height: 6-1
Weight: 205
Uniform no.: 21
Shoots: right

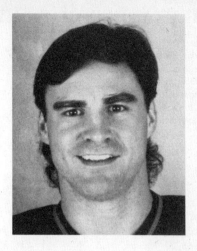

Career statistics:

GP	G	A	TP	PIM
711	126	157	283	1537

1996-97 statistics:

GP	G	A	TP	+/-	PIM	PP	SH	GW	GT	S	PCT
77	9	18	27	+15	109	0	0	2	0	92	9.8

1997-98 statistics:

GP	G	A	TP	+/-	PIM	PP	SH	GW	GT	S	PCT
74	24	24	48	+30	86	8	0	5	0	141	17.0

1998-99 statistics:

GP	G	A	TP	+/-	PIM	PP	SH	GW	GT	S	PCT
70	17	20	37	+10	143	3	0	5	0	136	12.5

1999-2000 statistics:

GP	G	A	TP	+/-	PIM	PP	SH	GW	GT	S	PCT
67	16	23	39	+8	80	3	0	4	0	116	13.8

LAST SEASON

Tied for second on team in game-winning goals. Missed seven games with ankle injury. Missed four games with hip flexor. Missed one game due to general soreness. Missed three games with suspension.

THE FINESSE GAME

There is never a lack of effort on McKay's part. His reputation earns him extra ice and extra time, and he makes use of both. He is one of those rare tough guys who has enough skills to make himself a useful player in other areas, including the power play. And he has the ability to beat a defender one on-one by setting his skates wide, dangling the puck, then drawing it through the defenseman's legs and blowing past him for a shot. His offense dropped off sharply last season, however, and McKay needs to regain some kind of touch or be relegated to the fourth line.

McKay is alert enough to find a linemate with a pass. He doesn't have great hockey vision, but he doesn't keep his eyes glued to the puck, either. Still, most of his points come from driving to the net.

The problem for McKay comes in the assessments of him as an overachieving fourth-liner, which is how he made his name, or weighing him as the second-line winger on the team. He doesn't have the scoring touch to be a top-six forward.

THE PHYSICAL GAME

McKay has become so valuable to the Devils in his new role that he rarely drops his gloves. Even though he is an absolutely ferocious fighter, don't expect to see him duking it out anymore. His penalty minutes were a career-low for a full NHL season. That doesn't

mean McKay is any less intense, however. He is astoundingly strong on his skates, tough to knock down and nearly impossible to knock out. His problems arise when he plays too fancy and thinks about being a goal scorer instead of working for his chances.

THE INTANGIBLES

McKay's reputation and his status among his teammates (who voted him as the players' player last season) keep him from slipping below the radar, but the signs point to his skills beginning a decline. He could have his ice time threatened. Injuries didn't help his cause last season.

PROJECTION

McKay can put up another 20 to 25 goals if he can continue to earn the ice time; nobody works harder for it.

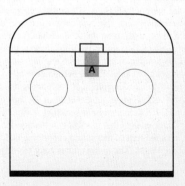

ALEXANDER MOGILNY

Yrs. of NHL service: 11
Born: Khabarovsk, Russia; Feb. 18, 1969
Position: right wing
Height: 5-11
Weight: 187
Uniform no.: 89
Shoots: left

Career statistics:

GP	G	A	TP	PIM
705	353	405	758	351

1996-97 statistics:

GP	G	A	TP	+/-	PIM	PP	SH	GW	GT	S	PCT
76	31	42	73	+9	18	7	1	4	1	174	17.8

1997-98 statistics:

GP	G	A	TP	+/-	PIM	PP	SH	GW	GT	S	PCT
51	18	27	45	-6	36	5	4	1	1	118	15.3

1998-99 statistics:

GP	G	A	TP	+/-	PIM	PP	SH	GW	GT	S	PCT
59	14	31	45	0	58	3	2	1	1	110	12.7

1999-2000 statistics:

GP	G	A	TP	+/-	PIM	PP	SH	GW	GT	S	PCT
59	24	20	44	+3	20	5	1	1	2	161	14.9

LAST SEASON

Acquired from Vancouver for Brendan Morrison and Denis Pederson, Mar. 14, 2000. Second on team in shooting percentage. Missed eight games with back injury. Missed six games with pelvis injury. Missed eight games with shoulder injury.

THE FINESSE GAME

Mogilny's biggest problems continue to be nconsistency and motivation. He has so many wondrous skills, but most of the time he just doesn't seem interested, even in the heat of a Stanley Cup drive (as he was with the Devils last season). What a waste.

Skating is the basis of Mogilny's game. He has a burst of speed from a standstill and hits his top speed in just a few strides. When he streaks down the ice there is a good chance you'll see something new, something you didn't expect. He is unbelievably quick.

Mogilny's anticipation sets him apart from players who are merely fast. He won't skate deeply into his own defensive zone. He waits for a turnover and a chance to get a jump on the defenseman, with a preferred move to the outside. He's not afraid to go inside either, so a defenseman intent on angling him to the boards could just as easily get burned inside.

Mogilny can beat you in so many ways. He has a powerful and accurate wrist shot from the tops of the circles in. He shoots without breaking stride. He can work a give-and-go that is a thing of beauty. He one-times with the best of them. And everything is done at racehorse speed. The game comes easy to Mogilny. Maybe that's the problem.

THE PHYSICAL GAME

Mogilny doesn't work as hard as he should; there always seems to be something left in the tank. There are nights when he is invisible on the ice — unpardonable for a player of his ability and importance.

Mogilny intimidates with his speed but will also add a physical element. He has great upper-body strength and will drive through a defender to the net.

THE INTANGIBLES

Mogilny's value on the free-agent market probably doubled by adding his name to the Stanley Cup last season.

PROJECTION

Mogilny should easily hit the 30-goal range again. He is capable of more.

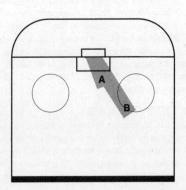

SCOTT NIEDERMAYER

Yrs. of NHL service: 8
Born: Edmonton, Alta.; Aug. 31, 1973
Position: right defense
Height: 6-0
Weight: 200
Uniform no.: 27
Shoots: left

Career statistics:

GP	G	A	TP	PIM
597	70	245	315	320

1996-97 statistics:

GP	G	A	TP	+/-	PIM	PP	SH	GW	GT	S	PCT
81	5	30	35	-4	64	3	0	3	0	159	3.1

1997-98 statistics:

GP	G	A	TP	+/-	PIM	PP	SH	GW	GT	S	PCT
81	14	43	57	+5	27	11	0	1	0	175	8.0

1998-99 statistics:

GP	G	A	TP	+/-	PIM	PP	SH	GW	GT	S	PCT
72	11	35	46	+16	26	1	1	3	0	161	6.8

1999-2000 statistics:

GP	G	A	TP	+/-	PIM	PP	SH	GW	GT	S	PCT
71	7	31	38	+19	48	1	0	0	0	109	6.4

LAST SEASON

Led team defensemen in scoring for fifth consecutive season. Third on team in plus-minus. Missed nine regular-season games and one playoff game due to suspension. Missed one game with hip flexor. Missed one game due to illness.

THE FINESSE GAME

Niedermayer is poised on that border that separates the truly elite offensive defensemen (Sandis Ozolinsh, Al MacInnis) from the wannabes, and we're not so sure he is going to make it across.

Niedermayer carries the puck well on the rush. The 27-year-old is an exceptional skater, one of the best-skating defensemen in the NHL. He has it all: speed, balance, agility, mobility, lateral movement and strength. Plus he has unbelievable edge for turns and eluding pursuers. That said, Niedermayer doesn't seem to have the vision the great ones have, or the snaky lateral movement that makes a point shot so dangerous. The missing component may be more mental than physical. He has nights when he is "on," and he is spectacular (those nights tend to come against high-profile teams, or in the playoffs, when he is more interested in his surroundings). But he takes a lot of nights off, when the challenge fails to excite him.

Niedermayer is a far better defensive player than many of the other top scorers at his position. Even when he makes a commitment mistake in the offensive zone, he can get back so quickly his partner is seldom outnumbered.

THE PHYSICAL GAME

An underrated body checker because of the focus on the glitzier parts of his game, Niedermayer has continued to improve his strength and is a willing, if not vicious, hitter. Peter Worrell might disagree with that, having been the recipient of a stick across the helmet in retaliation for a hit, for which Niedermayer served a 10-game suspension.

Niedermayer's skating ability helps him tremendously, giving more impetus to his open-ice checks. He makes rub-outs along the wall. He would rather be in open ice but will pay the price in the trenches. He knows the defensive game well. He has a quiet toughness and won't be intimidated, as he proved last year when he played his best hockey in the playoffs.

THE INTANGIBLES

Niedermayer is a restricted free agent; his last two negotiations with the Devils did not go smoothly. Even with new ownership, GM Lou Lamoriello is likely to play hardball with Niedermayer again, and he could miss the start of the season.

PROJECTION

Niedermayer continues to mature into an excellent all-around defenseman, but he will not be among the league's leading defenseman scorers. His range is around 40 points.

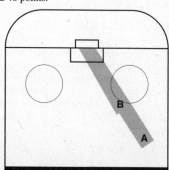

BRIAN RAFALSKI

Yrs. of NHL service: 1
Born: Dearborn, MI; Sept. 28, 1973
Position: right defense
Height: 5-11
Weight: 200
Uniform no.: 28
Shoots: right

Career statistics:

GP	G	A	TP	PIM
75	5	27	32	28

1999-2000 statistics:

GP	G	A	TP	+/-	PIM	PP	SH	GW	GT	S	PCT
75	5	27	32	+21	28	1	0	1	0	128	3.9

LAST SEASON

Signed as a free agent, June 18, 1999. First NHL season. Named to NHL All-Rookie Team. Missed five games with rib injury. Missed one game with flu.

THE FINESSE GAME

Rafalski is an excellent skater. He's not quite in the class of teammate Scott Niedermayer, but he is darned close, and he allows the Devils the luxury of placing one smooth-skating, puckhandling defenseman with a physical partner. In Rafalski's case, that was captain Scott Stevens, and Stevens benefited as much from Rafalski's presence as Rafalski did in playing alongside one of the league's premier defensive defensemen.

Rafalski's greatest asset is his ability to get the puck out of the zone. It sounds so simple, but watch other teams' defenses struggle with clearing the puck and you'll appreciate what Rafalski can do by skating the puck out of danger, making a smart pass or just banging it off the boards. He doesn't look for the highlight play. He makes the smart one, which usually turns into a highlight.

He has the speed and the hands to get involved in the attack, and does so willingly. Knowing he has Stevens as a backup, Rafalski is confident when he pinches or joins the rush. He has a good shot from the point and sees significant power-play time.

THE PHYSICAL GAME

The downside to being Stevens's partner is that teams want to stay away from the right wing on the attack (Stevens plays left defense) and will overload on the left side, meaning Rafalski had to fight more than his share of physical battles. He is small and makes the best use of his finesse skills in a defensive mode, but he will also get his body in the way. He is durable and strong on his skates.

THE INTANGIBLES

Overlooked because of his size, Rafalski played in Europe after college to make his name in Finland, where he was unearthed by the Devils as a free agent. What a find. He stepped in as an older rookie but seldom looked like a first-year player. He is intelligent, poised and utterly unflappable. His panic point is miniscule. Along with Stevens, he routinely handled matchups against other teams' best forwards and never blinked.

PROJECTION

Expectations will be high after Rafalski's impressive debut. He can build off of that into a 40-point season.

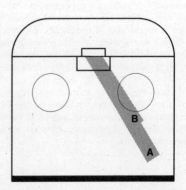

SCOTT STEVENS

Yrs. of NHL service: 18
Born: Kitchener, Ont.; Apr. 1, 1964
Position: left defense
Height: 6-2
Weight: 210
Uniform no.: 4
Shoots: left

Career statistics:

GP	G	A	TP	PIM
1353	179	649	828	2561

1996-97 statistics:

GP	G	A	TP	+/-	PIM	PP	SH	GW	GT	S	PCT
79	5	19	24	+26	70	0	0	1	0	166	3.0

1997-98 statistics:

GP	G	A	TP	+/-	PIM	PP	SH	GW	GT	S	PCT
80	4	22	26	+19	80	1	0	1	0	94	4.3

1998-99 statistics:

GP	G	A	TP	+/-	PIM	PP	SH	GW	GT	S	PCT
75	5	22	27	+29	64	0	0	1	0	111	4.5

1999-2000 statistics:

GP	G	A	TP	+/-	PIM	PP	SH	GW	GT	S	PCT
78	8	21	29	+30	103	0	1	1	0	133	6.0

LAST SEASON

Won 2000 Conn Smythe Trophy. Led team in plus-minus for second consecutive season. Tied for fourth in NHL in plus-minus. Missed three games with flu. Missed one game due to coach's decision.

THE FINESSE GAME

Stevens has never won a Norris Trophy, but his performance for the Stanley Cup-winning Devils last season proved how underrated and valuable a commodity he has been throughout his NHL career.

A very good skater, Stevens is secure and strong, capable both forwards and backwards and with good lateral mobility. He has a tendency to overhandle the puck in the defensive zone, though. Instead of quickly banging the puck off the boards to clear the zone, it seems to take him an unusual amount of time to get the puck teed up, and it's often kept in by the attacking team. Stevens then digs in twice as hard to win the puck back, but he often creates more work for himself.

Stevens has a tremendous work ethic that more than makes up for some of his shortcomings (most of those are sins of commission rather than omission). He is a bear on penalty killing because he just won't quit, and a fearless shot-blocker. Stevens occasionally gets suckered into chasing the puck carrier behind the net at inopportune moments.

Opponents used to delight in goading a young, immature Stevens into taking bad penalties. The tactic can still be effective, but only occasionally. Stevens is a smart player who recognizes the challenges presented to him every night and rarely fails to meet them. He works best paired with a mobile partner.

Brian Rafalski, an older rookie, was an immediate fit with him last season and could add years to Stevens's career if they stay together.

THE PHYSICAL GAME

One of the most punishing open-ice hitters in the NHL, Stevens has the skating ability to line up the puck carrier, and the size and strength to explode on impact. His hit on Eric Lindros in the playoffs will be talked about for years, and not only because it may have ended the concussion-afflicted centre's career. It was simply a hit of astonishing power, a body bomb.

Stevens is also effective in small spaces. He shovels most opponents out from in front of the net and crunches them along the boards. He prides himself on his conditioning and can handle a lot of minutes.

THE INTANGIBLES

Stevens' leadership, once called into question, was established by leading the Devils to a second Stanley Cup. He isn't a rah-rah, speechmaking kind of guy, but leads by example. He bloomed again with the return of coach Larry Robinson, with whom he forms a mutual admiration society.

PROJECTION

Forget the point totals. Just focus on the goals that don't end up in the Devils' net on Stevens's watch.

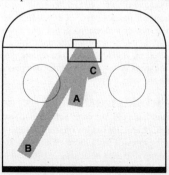

TURNER STEVENSON

Yrs. of NHL service: 6
Born: Prince George, B.C.; May 18, 1972
Position: right wing
Height: 6-3
Weight: 215
Uniform no.: 23
Shoots: right

Career statistics:

GP	G	A	TP	PIM
385	45	66	111	611

1996-97 statistics:

GP	G	A	TP	+/-	PIM	PP	SH	GW	GT	S	PCT
65	8	13	21	-14	97	1	0	0	0	76	10.5

1997-98 statistics:

GP	G	A	TP	+/-	PIM	PP	SH	GW	GT	S	PCT
63	4	6	10	-8	110	1	0	0	0	43	9.3

1998-99 statistics:

GP	G	A	TP	+/-	PIM	PP	SH	GW	GT	S	PCT
69	10	17	27	+6	88	0	0	2	1	102	9.8

1999-2000 statistics:

GP	G	A	TP	+/-	PIM	PP	SH	GW	GT	S	PCT
64	8	13	21	-1	61	0	0	2	0	94	8.5

LAST SEASON

Selected from Montreal by Columbus in Expansion Draft, June 23, 2000. Traded to New Jersey as part of future considerations for Krzysztof Oliwa, June 23, 2000. Missed 17 games with back injury. Missed one game with virus.

THE FINESSE GAME

Stevenson has slow hand speed to go along with his slow foot speed — hardly a lethal combination in the NHL, except to his own hopes of earning a job as an NHL regular. Effort is never an issue, because Stevenson would love to be more of a contributor. He doesn't shoot enough and has to take the puck to the net with more authority. He is strong along the offensive boards, especially below the goal line. When he gets into a situation, he always makes the opposition player pay the price.

Stevenson's main flaw is his lack of foot speed, though he is a fair skater for his size. He has a good, long stride and is balanced and agile.

Stevenson has a variety of shots and uses all of them with power and accuracy, but his release needs improvement. He will follow the puck to the net and not give up on shots. He is also a decent passer and possesses some vision and creativity. He plays a short power game.

THE PHYSICAL GAME

Stevenson isn't tall but he is solidly built and thick through his trunk. He can lay on some serious hits. It's too bad he doesn't have more of a mean streak. He seems to have no idea what kind of physical presence he could add to the team. His back injury also pre-vented him from doing more body work last season.

THE INTANGIBLES

A poor man's Randy McKay, Stevenson adds quiet toughness and leadership when he is healthy enough to contribute. But his back injury makes him an iffy prospect. He lacks McKay's hands, but he can give a team an honest eight to 12 minutes a night. He should inherit the fourth-line role vacated by Oliwa's departure to Columbus.

PROJECTION

Stevenson is a role player who can contribute some energy shifts, but his top end is 12 to 15 goals.

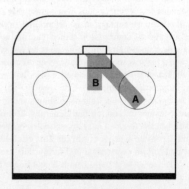

PETR SYKORA

Yrs. of NHL service: 5
Born: Plzen, Czech Republic; Nov. 19, 1976
Position: centre
Height: 5-11
Weight: 185
Uniform no.: 17
Shoots: left

Career statistics:

GP	G	A	TP	PIM
221	60	89	149	84

1996-97 statistics:

GP	G	A	TP	+/-	PIM	PP	SH	GW	GT	S	PCT
19	1	2	3	-8	4	0	0	0	0	26	3.8

1997-98 statistics:

GP	G	A	TP	+/-	PIM	PP	SH	GW	GT	S	PCT
58	16	20	36	0	22	3	1	4	0	130	12.3

1998-99 statistics:

GP	G	A	TP	+/-	PIM	PP	SH	GW	GT	S	PCT
2	0	0	0	-1	0	0	0	0	0	2	.0

1999-2000 statistics:

GP	G	A	TP	+/-	PIM	PP	SH	GW	GT	S	PCT
79	25	43	68	+24	26	5	1	4	0	222	11.3

LAST SEASON

Second on team in goals, assists and plus-minus. Tied for second on team in game-winning goals. Third on team in assists. Tied career-high in assists. Missed three games with flu.

THE FINESSE GAME

Sykora has excellent hands in tight, for passing or shooting. He defies the usual European stereotype of the reluctant shooter, because he's a goal scorer, though he does tend to pass up a low-percentage shot to work for a better one. His wrist shot is excellent. He also has adequate snap and slap shots. He is one of the Devils' better power-play specialists.

There are only a few things Sykora doesn't do well technically, but what really sets him apart is his intelligence. Playing against men as a 17-year-old in the IHL in 1994-95 obviously spurred his development, and taught him how to survive as a smaller player in the mean NHL.

He is a fine skater, with a fluid stride, and he accelerates in a few steps. He is quick on a straightaway, with or without the puck, and is also agile in his turns. He picks his way through traffic well, and would rather try to outfox a defender and take the shortest path to the net than drive wide.

Sykora sees the ice well and is a heads-up passer with a great touch. He needs to improve on his face-offs. His defensive play has improved, though he blew a few key assignments at crucial points last season. He can be used to kill penalties because of his ability to read the play and his quickness, though the Devils seldom used him in this role last season.

THE PHYSICAL GAME

One of the most sickening sights in the game last year was Sykora being flattened with a high hit by Derian Hatcher in what turned out to be the deciding game of the Stanley Cup finals. But don't expect Sykora to be intimidated. He'll battle for the puck behind or in front of the net, but he is simply not a big, or mean, player. He is strong for his size and his skating provides him with good balance. His work ethic is strong.

THE INTANGIBLES

Meshing wonderfully with longtime friend Patrik Elias and centre Jason Arnott, Sykora has joined the ranks of the elite forwards in the league with his playoff performance. He is a more consistent player now, still a little moody and prone to the occasional slump, but his lapses are shorter and less severe. Working with a sports psychologist who is also a friend has done wonders for his game.

PROJECTION

Sykora belongs in the ranks of the 70-point scorers now.

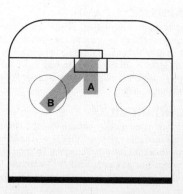

COLIN WHITE

Yrs. of NHL service: 0
Born: New Glasgow, N.S.; Dec. 12, 1977
Position: left defense
Height: 6-3
Weight: 215
Uniform no.: 5
Shoots: left

Career statistics:

GP	G	A	TP	PIM
21	2	1	3	40

1999-2000 statistics:

GP	G	A	TP	+/-	PIM	PP	SH	GW	GT	S	PCT
21	2	1	3	+3	40	0	0	1	0	29	6.9

LAST SEASON

First NHL season. Appeared in 52 games with Albany (AHL), scoring 5-21 — 26. Missed three games with neck injury. Missed two games with knee injury.

THE FINESSE GAME

White isn't a very fast skater, but he has a long stride and is balanced. He has learned to play within his limits, which tends to keep him out of trouble. He knows he can't go chasing better skaters around and has learned to let the play come to him. This patience has been rewarded.

White is a fearsome bodychecker. He has excellent size, which he uses to his full advantage. He is not agile enough to throw open-ice body bombs like teammate Scott Stevens, but along the wall and in front of the net he is punishing. He blocks shots, and was used by the Devils on some penalty kills when their regulars needed a break.

White is a good passer who moves the puck quickly. He does not make many low-percentage plays. He has obviously been well-schooled in the Devils' system and uses the boards and his partner well.

White has a decent shot from the point and may get the tail-end of some power plays.

THE PHYSICAL GAME

An able and willing fighter, White actually needed time in the minors to learn to keep his head. He is quick to jump to the aid of a teammate, quick to initiate and quick with his fists. He had 265 PIM with Albany in 1998-99, his second pro season. White absolutely loves to hit.

THE INTANGIBLES

White developed quickly enough that the Devils felt confident in trading veteran Lyle Odelein and Sheldon Souray to set up for their Cup run. Despite playing with a high-risk partner in Vladimir Malakhov, White gave the Devils quality minutes during the playoffs and was often given priority assignments late in games. White has now played for a Memorial Cup team (with Hull) and a Stanley Cup winner. White counts Dave Manson and Wendel Clark as his idols, and plays with the toughness and the mean streak those two athletes possess. A restricted free agent at the end of the season, White did nothing to hurt his bargaining position.

PROJECTION

White will be one of the Devils' top five this season, with a chance to take over Ken Daneyko's role as number four later this season or next year. He will technically be a rookie this year, and could merit consideration for the All-Rookie team, if voters give defensive defensemen a good look. His point totals will be low; his PIM will be high.

NEW YORK ISLANDERS

Players' Statistics 1999-2000

POS.	NO.	PLAYER	GP	G	A	PTS	+/-	PIM	PP	SH	GW	GT	S	PCT
R	21	MARIUSZ CZERKAWSKI	79	35	35	70	-16	34	16		4	1	276	12.7
R	15	BRAD ISBISTER	64	22	20	42	-18	100	9		1	1	135	16.3
C	18	*TIM CONNOLLY	81	14	20	34	-25	44	2	1	1	1	114	12.3
C	13	CLAUDE LAPOINTE	76	15	16	31	-22	60	2	1	3		129	11.6
C	38	DAVE SCATCHARD	65	12	18	30	-3	117		1	1		128	9.4
L	25	JOSH GREEN	49	12	14	26	-7	41	2		3		109	11.0
D	29	KENNY JONSSON	65	1	24	25	-15	32	1				84	1.2
C	62	OLLI JOKINEN	82	11	10	21	0	80	1	2	3		138	8.0
R	1	BILL MUCKALT	45	8	11	19	11	21	1		1	1	79	10.1
R	6	JAMIE HEWARD	54	6	11	17	-9	26	2		1		92	6.5
D	20	JAMIE RIVERS	75	1	16	17	-4	84	1				95	1.1
C	13	MATS LINDGREN	43	9	7	16	0	24	1		1		68	13.2
L	12	MIKE WATT	45	5	6	11	-8	17	1				49	10.2
C	37	*DMITRI NABOKOV	26	4	7	11	-8	16					40	10.0
D	3	ZDENO CHARA	65	2	9	11	-27	57			1	1	47	4.3
D	33	ERIC CAIRNS	67	2	7	9	-5	196					55	3.6
D	41	*RAYMOND GIROUX	14	9	9	9	0	10					24	
D	34	*MATHIEU BIRON	60	4	4	8	-13	38	2		2		70	5.7
L	43	MIKAEL ANDERSSON	55	2	6	8	-3	4	1				57	3.5
C	24	JOHAN DAVIDSSON	19	3	4	7	0	2			1		29	10.3
C	28	*JASON KROG	17	2	4	6	-1	6	1				22	9.1
R	44	MARK LAWRENCE	29	1	5	6	-13	26				1	33	3.0
C	17	TED DRURY	66	3	2	5	-9	37	1				57	5.3
R	14	CHRIS FERRARO	11	1	3	4	1	8					15	6.7
R	8	STEVE WEBB	65	1	3	4	-4	103					27	3.7
R	16	VLADIMIR ORSZAGH	11	2	1	3	1	4					16	12.5
D	58	ARIS BRIMANIS	18	2	1	3	-5	6	2				16	12.5
D	36	*EVGENY KOROLEV	17	1	2	3	-10	8					7	14.3
D	56	IAN HERBERS	43		3	3	-6	47					14	
L	39	*SEAN HAGGERTY	5	1	1	2	3	4					2	50.0
D	55	*VLAD CHEBATURKIN	17	1	1	2	-3	8					9	11.1
D	34	ERIC BREWER	26		2	2	-11	20					30	
L	24	SCOTT PEARSON	2		1	1	1						5	
D	17	DALLAS EAKINS	2		1	1	3	2					4	
D	7	*RAY SCHULTZ	9		1	1	1	30					2	
G	80	KEVIN WEEKES	56		1	1	0						1	
C	16	DANIEL LACROIX	1				-1							
R	32	*PETR MIKA	3				-1						1	
G	17	WADE FLAHERTY	4				0							
G	35	*STEPHEN VALIQUETTE	6				0							
G	1	*ROBERTO LUONGO	24				0							

GP = games played; G = goals; A = assists; PTS = points; +/- = goals-for minus goals-against while player is on ice; PIM = penalties in minutes; PP = power-play goals; SH = shorthanded goals; GW = game-winning goals; GT = game-tying goals; S = no. of shots; PCT = percentage of goals to shots; * = rookie

MATHIEU BIRON

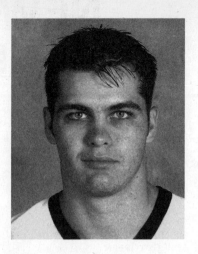

Yrs. of NHL service: 1
Born: Lac-St. Charles, Que.; Aug. 29, 1980
Position: right defense
Height: 6-6
Weight: 212
Uniform no.: 34
Shoots: right

Career statistics:

GP	G	A	TP	PIM
60	4	4	8	38

1999-2000 statistics:

GP	G	A	TP	+/-	PIM	PP	SH	GW	GT	S	PCT
60	4	4	8	-13	38	2	0	2	0	70	5.7

LAST SEASON

First NHL season. Missed nine games due to coach's decision.

THE FINESSE GAME

Biron has all of the skills desired in a young NHL defenseman. He skates well for a big guy. He has a long, smooth stride with good acceleration, and he's tight in his turns.

He has an excellent shot. He has a nice touch with the puck for passing or shooting, but has to improve his speed in moving the puck, yet not be hasty. He was guilty of some ghastly giveaways last season. He was a scorer at the junior level and should develop more poise and confidence with the puck. He could be involved on the Isles' second power-play unit.

Biron started last season well, then seemed to hit a stretch where he got in trouble every time he was on the ice.

THE PHYSICAL GAME

Biron had more confidence in his game as he was used more by coach Butch Goring in the last two months of the season. He picked up his hitting and saw his ice time increase. He is well-balanced and hard to knock off his feet. He has to initiate more, but he is very at home when the hitting picks up. He needs to develop more lower-body strength to pack a bigger wallop in his checks.

THE INTANGIBLES

Biron was probably force-fed a little too much before he was capable of handling an NHL job. Getting sent to play for Canada at the World Juniors — where he was the only player from Team Canada named to the all-tournament team — helped patch up some of the dings on his confidence. His taste of the NHL should help him win a battle for a job as a number five or six defenseman this season, and having experienced defensemen like Roman Hamrlik and Kevin Haller in camp can only help.

Biron has a good attitude that doesn't seem to have been permanently scarred by some of his struggles last season.

PROJECTION

Big defensemen take longer to graduate. Biron will be worth the wait. He needs to learn defense first, but he has good offensive upside and could score in the 20-point range.

ERIC CAIRNS

Yrs. of NHL service: 4
Born: Oakville, Ont.; June 27, 1974
Position: defense
Height: 6-5
Weight: 225
Uniform no.: 33
Shoots: left

Career statistics:

GP	G	A	TP	PIM
155	2	14	16	458

1996-97 statistics:

GP	G	A	TP	+/-	PIM	PP	SH	GW	GT	S	PCT
40	0	1	1	-7	147	0	0	0	0	17	0.0

1997-98 statistics:

GP	G	A	TP	+/-	PIM	PP	SH	GW	GT	S	PCT
39	0	3	3	-3	92	0	0	0	0	17	.0

1998-99 statistics:

GP	G	A	TP	+/-	PIM	PP	SH	GW	GT	S	PCT
9	0	3	3	+1	23	0	0	0	0	2	.0

1999-2000 statistics:

GP	G	A	TP	+/-	PIM	PP	SH	GW	GT	S	PCT
67	2	7	9	-5	196	0	0	0	0	55	3.6

LAST SEASON

Led team and fifth in NHL in penalty minutes with career high. Missed four games due to suspension. Missed four games due to coach's decision. Missed one game with upper back strain. Appeared in four games with Providence (AHL), scoring 1-1 — 2.

THE FINESSE GAME

It is natural to think a player as big as Cairns would be clumsy, but he has some smarts with the puck and enough skill to skate the puck out of the defensive zone. Occasionally, he can beat a forechecker, but Cairns knows better than to make a habit of that. He doesn't have great foot speed and can get caught flat-footed.

With the puck, Cairns favours backhand moves that allow him to use his body to shield the puck from defenders. He is content to get the puck deep in the zone and let the forwards do the offensive work, but his point shot is accurate when he elects to use it. Out of his own zone, he makes an accurate outlet pass.

Although not a great skater, Cairns turns pretty smoothly and makes up for any shortcomings on speed by using his size and reach. He may look like someone who can be beaten easily to the outside, but he generally does a nice job of angling a puck carrier to less dangerous ice. Cairns works every off-season to improve his footwork.

THE PHYSICAL GAME

Cairns is a willing fighter and seems to like playing policeman if any opponent starts taking liberties with his teammates. He likes the big hits and mean rubouts, but does a pretty good job of avoiding the cheap hooking and holding penalties big defensemen always seem to get against smaller, quicker forwards. He has become a legitimate NHL fighter and one who doesn't need to prove himself anymore at every challenge. He took on all of the league's most fearsome fighters, including Tie Domi, Peter Worrell and Sandy McCarthy.

THE INTANGIBLES

Cairns moved out of his comfort zone and worked to earn a shot with the Isles. He will be a number five or six defenseman for them this season.

PROJECTION

Cairns will never be a star and he isn't going to score much, but he has made himself a decent NHL prospect. He's still a project — it's going to take lots of extra work before and after practice — but size, strength and reach, sensibly packaged and deployed, are a commodity in the NHL. If he plays his cards right he can have a good career as a dependable stay-at-home, and as a partner for the offensive guy who's going to be up-ice all night.

ZDENO CHARA

Yrs. of NHL service: 3
Born: Trencin, Czech Republic; Mar. 18, 1977
Position: right defense
Height: 6-9
Weight: 255
Uniform no.: 3
Shoots: left

Career statistics:

GP	G	A	TP	PIM
149	4	16	20	190

1997-98 statistics:

GP	G	A	TP	+/-	PIM	PP	SH	GW	GT	S	PCT
25	0	1	1	+1	50	0	0	0	0	10	0.0

1998-99 statistics:

GP	G	A	TP	+/-	PIM	PP	SH	GW	GT	S	PCT
59	2	6	8	-8	83	0	1	0	0	56	3.6

1999-2000 statistics:

GP	G	A	TP	+/-	PIM	PP	SH	GW	GT	S	PCT
65	2	9	11	-27	57	0	0	1	1	47	4.3

LAST SEASON

Missed 16 games with shoulder injury. Missed one game with flu.

THE FINESSE GAME

For a player of his height, Chara is very well-coordinated. He has to get a half-step quicker to be in a better position for his checks, though. If he is out of position at all his hits are sure to be called high sticks and elbows, for the simple reason that he is so much taller than everyone else — their faces just happen to be in the wrong place. By keeping his hands down and his feet moving, Chara can avoid taking those needless penalties. He was much better at this at the end of last season.

He moves the puck well but he has a tendency to admire his passes, like a baseball player waiting to break into a slow home-run jog around the bases. This leaves him open to hits when he is off-balance.

With his long arms and long stick, Chara can be a bigger, tougher version of Kjell Samuelsson. He needs to improve his puck control and adjust to the NHL pace, but he is well on his way.

THE PHYSICAL GAME

Chara is solid, with a good centre of gravity that is rare to find in a player of his altitude. Players simply bounce off him. He goes through phases when he loses his edge, though. When he starts getting those high-sticking calls he has a tendency to back down for awhile. He doesn't mind a good scrap, and he has a long reach. He has handled assignments against other teams' top lines. He loves to hit, and he was among the leaders not only on the Islanders but in the NHL in that department last season.

THE INTANGIBLES

Chara is very hard on himself. He is often his own worst enemy. He has a great reputation as a gamer, and as a kid who is coachable and willing to work to improve his game. At six foot nine, he is the tallest defenseman in NHL history. Chara was an unrestricted free agent during the off-season.

PROJECTION

Chara could become a number four defenseman with the Isles. He was much steadier last season and now gains a couple of new mentors in Roman Hamrlik and Kevin Haller. Chara will never be an offensive force.

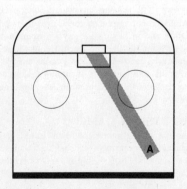

TIM CONNOLLY

Yrs. of NHL service: 1
Born: Baldwinsville, NY; May 7, 1980
Position: centre
Height: 6-0
Weight: 186
Uniform no.: 18
Shoots: right

Career statistics:

GP	G	A	TP	PIM
81	14	20	34	44

1999-2000 statistics:

GP	G	A	TP	+/-	PIM	PP	SH	GW	GT	S	PCT
81	14	20	34	-25	44	2	1	1	1	114	12.3

LAST SEASON

First NHL season. Third on team in points and shooting percentage. Tied for third in goals. Tied for eighth among NHL rookies in points. Missed one game due to coach's decision.

THE FINESSE GAME

Connolly has reminded some scouts of Steve Yzerman because of his ability to make plays at a very high tempo.

He sometimes overhandles the puck, probably a carryover from when he was able to dominate games at the junior level. Once he sheds that habit, he will be far more effective. He is an exceptional one-on-one player. He works the give-and-go well.

For a 19-year-old, Connolly has great confidence in his abilities. He is creative and not afraid to try new moves. A quick and agile skater with a low centre of gravity, he maintains his control of the puck through traffic. He has a drive to succeed and to score.

Connolly will become a mainstay on both the power play and the penalty-killing units. He is smart and his anticipation is exceptional.

THE PHYSICAL GAME

Connolly needs to spend time in the weight room — he's still growing, too, so some natural maturing will helps. He is pretty strong for his size already. Connolly has a bit of an attitude, which hasn't exactly endeared him to some veteran officials. He might not get the benefit of some penalty calls.

THE INTANGIBLES

Likely to be the number two centre behind Oleg Kvasha at the start of the season, Connolly could end up as the number one.

PROJECTION

A sophomore slump is unlikely. Connolly just needs a little better supporting cast to get into the 50-point ranks in his second NHL season.

He has it in him to be a bona fide star. A summer of weight training and natural growth will help. There is the concern of a sophomore slump, but he's mentally mature for a teenager. It's a sure bet to buy a No. 18 jersey on Long Island.

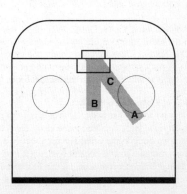

MARIUSZ CZERKAWSKI

Yrs. of NHL service: 6
Born: Radomsko, Poland; Apr. 13, 1972
Position: right wing
Height: 6-0
Weight: 195
Uniform no.: 25
Shoots: left

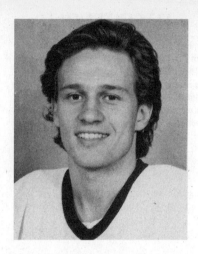

Career statistics:

GP	G	A	TP	PIM
422	125	124	249	136

1996-97 statistics:

GP	G	A	TP	+/-	PIM	PP	SH	GW	GT	S	PCT
76	26	21	47	0	16	4	0	3	0	182	14.3

1997-98 statistics:

GP	G	A	TP	+/-	PIM	PP	SH	GW	GT	S	PCT
68	12	13	25	+11	23	2	0	1	0	136	8.8

1998-99 statistics:

GP	G	A	TP	+/-	PIM	PP	SH	GW	GT	S	PCT
78	21	17	38	-10	14	4	0	1	2	205	10.2

1999-2000 statistics:

GP	G	A	TP	+/-	PIM	PP	SH	GW	GT	S	PCT
79	35	35	70	-16	34	16	0	4	1	276	12.7

LAST SEASON

Led team in goals, assists and points, all career highs. Led team and second in NHL in power-play goals. Led team in shots and game-winning goals. Second on team in shooting percentage. Missed three games with strained oblique muscle.

THE FINESSE GAME

Far from sulking after the depature of his favourite linemate, Ziggy Palffy, Czerkawski took over as the Isles' leading scorer and finally fulfilled the promise his skills had long hinted at.

Czerkawski is superb in open ice, with great one-on-one moves and a phenomenal shot. He likes to use all of the ice, and will cut across the middle or to the right side to make the play. He is a shifty skater, not one with great straightaway speed, but he puts the slip on a defender with a lateral move and is off. Last year, Czerkawski stopped being so unselfish and was much more aggressive in using his shots and in his driving to the net.

A quick wrist shot is Czerkawski's best weapon. With the extra room on the power play he is at his best. He has soft hands for passes and good vision. He needs to play with someone who will get him the puck, since he will not go into the corners for it.

THE PHYSICAL GAME

Czerkawski has to get better at protecting the puck and perform at least a willing game along the boards. He uses his body in the offensive zone, but in a perfunctory manner, and he doesn't like to get involved too much in the defensive zone. He can be intimidated physically. He is quick enough to peel back and help

out with backchecking, since he is very smart at anticipating passes, but he will rarely knock anyone off the puck.

THE INTANGIBLES

Czerkawski is the most skilled forward on the Islanders. Through a tough season, he was their go-to guy and took a big step forward in his development.

PROJECTION

Czerkawski answered the bell. His output of 35 goals last season is exactly what we said he could if he took the puck to the net with more determination. He did. A great season was the payoff. Now that he knows he can do it, he can do it again.

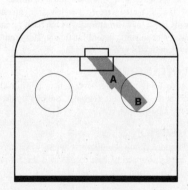

RADEK DVORAK

Yrs. of NHL service: 5
Born: Tabor, Czech Republic; Mar. 9, 1977
Position: left wing
Height: 6-2
Weight: 187
Uniform no.: 19
Shoots: left

Career statistics:

GP	G	A	TP	PIM
380	80	115	195	128

1996-97 statistics:

GP	G	A	TP	+/-	PIM	PP	SH	GW	GT	S	PCT
76	18	21	39	-2	30	2	0	1	0	139	12.9

1997-98 statistics:

GP	G	A	TP	+/-	PIM	PP	SH	GW	GT	S	PCT
64	12	24	36	-1	33	2	3	0	1	112	10.7

1998-99 statistics:

GP	G	A	TP	+/-	PIM	PP	SH	GW	GT	S	PCT
82	19	24	43	+7	29	0	4	0	0	182	10.4

1999-2000 statistics:

GP	G	A	TP	+/-	PIM	PP	SH	GW	GT	S	PCT
81	18	32	50	+5	16	2	1	1	0	157	11.5

LAST SEASON

Acquired from Florida for Todd Harvey and a fourth-round draft pick in 2001, Dec. 20, 1999. Led team in plus-minus. Third on team in assists. Tied for third on team in points.

THE FINESSE GAME

Dvorak has exceptional speed. He might be one of the five fastest skaters in the Eastern Conference. He bursts down the wing and will mix up the defense by sometimes driving wide and sometimes cutting through the middle. He takes the puck with him at a high tempo and creates off the rush.

Dvorak's hands are average, which is always going to limit him scoring-wise. He can't always complete what he creates with his speed. He should definitely take more shots — 200 should be routine for a player of his quickness. He is a heads-up passer but needs to be more of a finisher.

Dvorak has become a more complete player by adding defensive awareness to his game. He is very conscientious. He is a fine penalty killer.

THE PHYSICAL GAME

Dvorak has very strong legs, which power his explosive skating, and he's not a bit intimidated by North American play.

THE INTANGIBLES

Dvorak is a terrific fit with Jan Hlavac and Petr Nedved — his Rangers Czech-mates with whom he clicked almost immediately — than he is with anyone else on the team. He is really a second- or third-line winger, but with those two he looks like a first-line forward on some nights.

PROJECTION

Dvorak's speed will always tease teams into thinking they can get a little more out of him scoring-wise, but odds are we have seen about his top limit and 20-goal is his calling.

KEVIN HALLER

Yrs. of NHL service: 10
Born: Trochu, Alberta; Dec. 5, 1970
Position: left defense
Height: 6-2
Weight: 192
Uniform no.: 5
Shoots: left

Career statistics:

GP	G	A	TP	PIM
611	40	92	132	849

1996-97 statistics:

GP	G	A	TP	+/-	PIM	PP	SH	GW	GT	S	PCT
62	2	11	13	-12	85	0	0	0	0	77	2.6

1997-98 statistics:

GP	G	A	TP	+/-	PIM	PP	SH	GW	GT	S	PCT
65	3	5	8	-5	94	0	0	0	0	67	4.5

1998-99 statistics:

GP	G	A	TP	+/-	PIM	PP	SH	GW	GT	S	PCT
82	1	6	7	-1	122	0	0	0	0	64	1.6

1999-2000 statistics:

GP	G	A	TP	+/-	PIM	PP	SH	GW	GT	S	PCT
67	3	5	8	-8	61	0	0	2	0	50	6.0

LAST SEASON

Signed as free agent with N.Y. Islanders, July 3, 2000. Missed 12 games with Anaheim with left knee sprain. Missed one game with arthroscopic surgery on right knee. Missed two games due to coach's decision.

THE FINESSE GAME

Haller is a gazelle on skates, with an amazingly light and quick first few strides. He makes skating look effortless and he likes to carry the puck — though he doesn't get involved much offensively once he is inside the offensive zone. In fact, he usually gets rid of the puck once he hits the redline.

Haller has a decent shot from the point. He keeps it low and it tends to get through traffic. He is also a fair passer. He can lead a rush by skating the puck out of his own zone or he will make a heads-up breakout pass.

Haller has worked hard at improving his defensive reads. He has concentrated so much on defense that he thinks little about getting involved in the attack. He doesn't have great hockey smarts, however, which may be the most limiting factor in his development.

THE PHYSICAL GAME

Haller is tough and, frequently, mean. He'll stick the top players, and he won't back down from anyone. He isn't huge but he plays a pretty big game, and he has an edge that a lot of defensemen don't have. Haller plays a lot like Darius Kasparaitis, but Haller is bigger and stronger. He gets in people's faces, and does it without taking a lot of dumb penalties.

THE INTANGIBLES

Haller will mean a nice upgrade to the Islanders defense. He is best suited as a number four or five, and if the Isles don't ask too much of him, he will provide a steady game and help bring along younger players like Mathieu Biron. He is a nice complement to finesse players. Haller is only 29 and has some quality hockey years left, though he did have troublesome knees last season.

PROJECTION

Haller was an attractive free agent signing and should do well in his return to the East (he played in Montreal, Buffalo, Hartford, and Philadelphia). His point totals will barely scrape into the double digits.

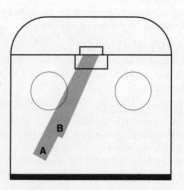

ROMAN HAMRLIK

Yrs. of NHL service: 8
Born: Gottwaldov, Czech Republic; Apr. 12, 1974
Position: left defense
Height: 6-2
Weight: 202
Uniform no.: 22
Shoots: left

Career statistics:

GP	G	A	TP	PIM
573	74	214	288	660

1996-97 statistics:

GP	G	A	TP	+/-	PIM	PP	SH	GW	GT	S	PCT
79	12	28	40	-29	57	6	0	0	1	238	5.0

1997-98 statistics:

GP	G	A	TP	+/-	PIM	PP	SH	GW	GT	S	PCT
78	9	32	41	-15	70	5	1	3	0	198	4.5

1998-99 statistics:

GP	G	A	TP	+/-	PIM	PP	SH	GW	GT	S	PCT
75	8	24	32	+9	70	3	0	0	0	172	4.7

1999-2000 statistics:

GP	G	A	TP	+/-	PIM	PP	SH	GW	GT	S	PCT
80	8	37	45	+1	68	5	0	0	1	180	4.4

LAST SEASON

Acquired from Edmonton for Eric Brewer, Josh Green amd a second-round draft pick in 2000, June 24, 2000. Led Oilers defensemen in points. Second on team in assists. Third on team in shots. Missed two games with bruised finger.

THE FINESSE GAME

Hamrlik is better defensively than some people think, and not as good offensively as some other people think. He has turned into a solid two-way defenseman whose game doesn't have many valleys, or peaks.

Hamrlik can handle marathon ice time and has the desire to dominate a game. He has all the tools. He is a fast, strong skater — forwards and backwards.

He is a mobile defenseman with a solid shot and good passing skills, but Hamrlik is not creative. But he knows how to outsmart and not just overpower attackers. He loves to get involved offensively, despite not having elite skills. He has an excellent shot with a quick release. He could be smarter about taking some velocity off his shot in order to get a less blockable shot through.

Hamrlik has learned to make less risky plays in his own zone. He makes a great first pass out of the zone. Defensively, he runs into problems when he is trying to move the puck out of his zone and when he is forced to handle the puck on his backhand, but that is about the only way the opposition can cope with him.

THE PHYSICAL GAME

Hamrlik is aggressive and likes physical play, though he is not a huge, splashy hitter. He is in great shape and routinely plays 25 or more minutes a night — he led the Oilers in ice time last season.

THE INTANGIBLES

Hamrlik has matured into a reliable defenseman. He was happy in Edmonton and not thrilled with the trade that sent him to the Islanders. Playing a season under exdefenseman Kevin Lowe really helped his game.

PROJECTION

Hamrlik should be a 10-goal, 30-point scorer.

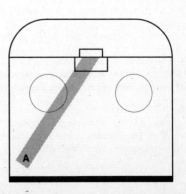

BRAD ISBISTER

Yrs. of NHL service: 3
Born: Edmonton, Alberta; May 7, 1977
Position: right wing
Height: 6-3
Weight: 222
Uniform no.: 16
Shoots: right

Career statistics:

GP	G	A	TP	PIM
162	35	32	67	248

1997-98 statistics:

GP	G	A	TP	+/-	PIM	PP	SH	GW	GT	S	PCT
66	9	8	17	+4	104	1	0	1	0	115	7.8

1998-99 statistics:

GP	G	A	TP	+/-	PIM	PP	SH	GW	GT	S	PCT
32	4	4	8	+1	46	0	0	2	0	48	8.3

1999-2000 statistics:

GP	G	A	TP	+/-	PIM	PP	SH	GW	GT	S	PCT
64	22	20	42	-18	100	9	0	1	1	135	16.3

LAST SEASON

Led team in shooting percentage. Second on team in goals, points and power-play goals. Third on team in penalty minutes and shots. Tied for third on team in goals. Career highs in goals, assists and points. Missed 18 games with sprained ankle.

THE FINESSE GAME

Isbister is not a creative sort, but fits in well in a strong forechecking scheme because he plays up and down his left wing. He is a solid skater with straightaway speed and quickness. He has excellent acceleration from the blueline in, and he cuts to the net.

Isbister's hand skills are a shade below average. He is a decent passer when he has a little time, but, unlike more creative players, tends not to see more than one option. His goals will come from driving to the net.

With better hands and a quicker shot, Isbister could be a power forward in the making. He certainly tries to play like one.

THE PHYSICAL GAME

Isbister is strong, able to fend off a defender with one arm and keep going. He protects the puck well. He is an enthusiastic forechecker and likes to be the first man in. He will take or make a hit to make a play happen. He has an aggressive nature and will aggravate a lot of players by making them eat glass. He has to be more consistent in his effort on a nightly basis.

THE INTANGIBLES

Isbister was a restricted free agent during the off-season. If the Islanders can fit him into their budget, he will be among their top six forwards.

PROJECTION

Isbister moved forward a little more quickly than we expected. If he hadn't been injured, he would have scored between 25 and 30 goals, which sounds like a worthy target for him this season.

KENNY JONSSON

Yrs. of NHL service: 6
Born: Angelholm, Sweden; Oct. 6, 1974
Position: left defense
Height: 6-3
Weight: 195
Uniform no.: 29
Shoots: left

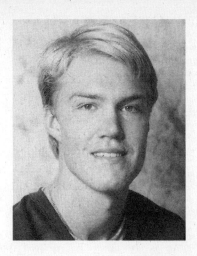

Career statistics:

GP	G	A	TP	PIM
395	32	119	151	196

1996-97 statistics:

GP	G	A	TP	+/-	PIM	PP	SH	GW	GT	S	PCT
81	3	18	21	+10	24	1	0	0	0	92	3.3

1997-98 statistics:

GP	G	A	TP	+/-	PIM	PP	SH	GW	GT	S	PCT
81	14	26	40	-2	58	6	0	2	0	108	13.0

1998-99 statistics:

GP	G	A	TP	+/-	PIM	PP	SH	GW	GT	S	PCT
63	8	18	26	-18	34	6	0	0	0	91	8.8

1999-2000 statistics:

GP	G	A	TP	+/-	PIM	PP	SH	GW	GT	S	PCT
65	1	24	25	-15	32	1	0	0	0	84	1.2

LAST SEASON

Led team defensemen in points for second consecutive season. Second on team in assists. Missed seven games with concussion. Missed five games with headaches. Missed four games with virus. Missed one game with sprained wrist.

THE FINESSE GAME

At his best, Jonsson is probably one of the top eight defensemen in the league, but no one knows it. He reads the ice and passes the puck very well. He's not overly creative, nor is he a risk taker. He makes a very good first pass out of the zone, but he will also bank it off the boards if that is the safer play. He doesn't shoot for the home run pass on every shift, but he will recognize the headman play when it's there.

Jonsson suffered from injuries, a depleted Islanders team, and what looked like general depression and was hardly his old self last season.

Jonsson moves the puck up and plays his position. He always makes sure he has somebody beaten before he makes a pass. He can be used in almost every game situation. He kills penalties, works the point on the power play, plays four-on-four and can be used in the late stages of a period or a game to protect a lead. He's reliable and coachable.

Jonsson is a talented skater, big and mobile, yet he tends to leave himself open after passes and gets nailed.

THE PHYSICAL GAME

Jonsson is smart and plays with an edge. The knock on him earlier in his career was that he was a bit soft and didn't like to play through traffic, but that has changed. He competes hard every night and in the hard areas of the ice. He could stand to improve his off-season conditioning a little, especially considering all the minutes he gets.

THE INTANGIBLES

Adding Roman Hamrlik and Kevin Haller to the lineup will lift some of the defensive load off of Jonsson. He is due for a big bounce-back season. Jonsson was a restricted free agent during the off-season. His concussion and the migraine headaches that hit him late in the season are a concern. The Isles nearly had him dealt to Florida before the trade deadline, and if there is a contract impasse, he could be moved.

PROJECTION

Jonsson can score in the 40-point range and provide a solid all-around game and quiet leadership.

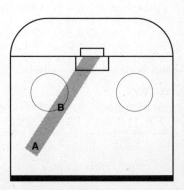

OLEG KVASHA

Yrs. of NHL service: 2
Born: Moscow, Russia; July 26, 1978
Position: left wing
Height: 6-5
Weight: 205
Uniform no.: 16
Shoots: left

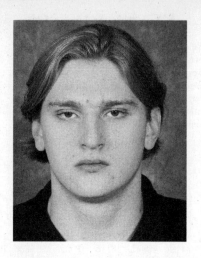

Career statistics:

GP	G	A	TP	PIM
146	17	33	50	79

1998-99 statistics:

GP	G	A	TP	+/-	PIM	PP	SH	GW	GT	S	PCT
68	12	13	25	+5	45	4	0	2	1	138	8.7

1999-2000 statistics:

GP	G	A	TP	+/-	PIM	PP	SH	GW	GT	S	PCT
78	5	20	25	+3	34	2	0	0	0	110	4.5

LAST SEASON

Acquired from Florida with Mark Parrish for Roberto Luongo and Olli Jokinen, June 24, 2000. Second NHL season. Missed two games with sprained knee.

THE FINESSE GAME

Kvasha has tremendous speed and great hands. He can make a lot of things happen with the puck in full stride. He can also play centre, and he brings a centre's vision to the left wing. He has terrific hockey sense and vision. He anticipates well and sees holes a split second before they open.

Kvasha could use his shot more. He has an excellent wrist shot that is his best weapon. No one with his size and playing time should register a puny 110 shots in 78 games.

Kvasha was a major disappointment last season, despite getting playing time with Pavel Bure.

THE PHYSICAL GAME

Kvasha is strong, has good size and will drive to the net. He is not above crashing the goalie. But he can be intimidated.

THE INTANGIBLES

Islanders GM Mike Milbury fell in love with Kvasha's size and used his major bargaining chip, the young goalie Luongo, to get him. Milbury envisions Kvasha playing a gritty, gutsy game against some of the Isles' more physical Eastern rivals. Perhaps he was out of town during the Devils' playoff sweep of the Panthers, in which Kvasha was invisible.

PROJECTION

Kvasha is still young, still learning, and will be on the top line with the Islanders. He needs to regain the form of his rookie season to post the 20 goals he is capable of.

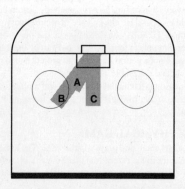

CLAUDE LAPOINTE

Yrs. of NHL service: 9
Born: Lachine, Que.; Oct. 11, 1968
Position: centre
Height: 5-9
Weight: 181
Uniform no.: 13
Shoots: left

Career statistics:

GP	G	A	TP	PIM
597	96	132	228	537

1996-97 statistics:

GP	G	A	TP	+/-	PIM	PP	SH	GW	GT	S	PCT
73	13	5	18	-11	49	0	3	3	1	80	16.3

1997-98 statistics:

GP	G	A	TP	+/-	PIM	PP	SH	GW	GT	S	PCT
78	10	10	20	-9	47	0	1	3	0	82	12.2

1998-99 statistics:

GP	G	A	TP	+/-	PIM	PP	SH	GW	GT	S	PCT
82	14	23	37	-19	62	2	2	1	0	134	10.4

1999-2000 statistics:

GP	G	A	TP	+/-	PIM	PP	SH	GW	GT	S	PCT
76	15	16	31	-22	60	2	1	3	0	129	11.6

LAST SEASON

Tied for second on team in game-winning goals. Third on team in goals. Missed two games with sprained knee. Missed two games with flu. Missed one game with sore foot. Missed one game with facial lacerations.

THE FINESSE GAME

Lapointe is so quick and smart that he gets a breakaway every other game, but he doesn't have the hands to finish off his chances. He is heady and aggressive. As a low draft pick (234th overall in 1988), he has always had to fight for respect. His effort is what has kept him around this long.

Lapointe is one of those useful veteran forwards who will always find a spot in a lineup because of his intelligence, yet he'll always be worried about his job because he doesn't do anything special.

He drives to the front of the net, knowing that that's where good things happen. He has good acceleration and quickness with the puck, plus decent hand skills to make things work down low. He isn't blessed with great vision, but he doesn't take unnecessary chances, either, and can be used in clutch situations.

Lapointe was used as a checking-line winger, where he can make use of his speed, but he might be used as a third-line centre this season. He is a very effective penalty killer.

THE PHYSICAL GAME

Lapointe is small but solidly built. He uses his low centre of gravity and good balance to bump people much bigger than he is; he surprises some by knocking them off the puck. He doesn't quit and is dogged in the corners and in front of the net. He is gritty and hardworking.

THE INTANGIBLES

Lapointe is used as a checker, an energy guy, a penalty killer and on face-offs. He doesn't score many goals but the ones he does score tend to be big. He is an excellent team man. He wore down midway through the season because he was overused, but he bounced back late in the year.

PROJECTION

Lapointe is a useful role-playing centre who can get 15 goals and contribute 15 hard minutes every night.

MATS LINDGREN

Yrs. of NHL service: 4
Born: Skelleftea, Sweden; Oct. 1, 1974
Position: left wing
Height: 6-2
Weight: 200
Uniform no.: 10
Shoots: left

Career statistics:

GP	G	A	TP	PIM
254	43	49	92	102

1996-97 statistics:

GP	G	A	TP	+/-	PIM	PP	SH	GW	GT	S	PCT
69	11	14	25	-7	12	2	3	1	0	71	15.5

1997-98 statistics:

GP	G	A	TP	+/-	PIM	PP	SH	GW	GT	S	PCT
82	13	13	26	0	42	1	3	3	0	131	9.9

1998-99 statistics:

GP	G	A	TP	+/-	PIM	PP	SH	GW	GT	S	PCT
60	10	15	25	+6	24	3	1	1	0	83	12.0

1999-2000 statistics:

GP	G	A	TP	+/-	PIM	PP	SH	GW	GT	S	PCT
43	9	7	16	0	24	1	0	1	0	68	13.2

a slightly improving cast around him, this could be the season Lindgren lets his offensive light shine.

LAST SEASON
Tied for second on team in plus-minus. Missed 39 games with shoulder surgery.

THE FINESSE GAME
Lindgren has a reputation primarily as a defensive player, but he was an offensive player in Sweden and has a real future as a solid two-way centre. He is a fine skater with balance, agility and quickness. He is especially clever in tight, moving the puck at the right moment and knowing when to shoot and when to pass. He has very good puckhandling skills and can do many clever things with the puck.

Lindgren also kills penalties and is a shorthanded threat. He needs to gain more confidence in his shot, though, because it could be a more dangerous weapon. He has a wrister with a lot on it. With his size, hands and vision, he is a poor man's Mats Sundin.

Lindgren has terrific hockey sense, and plays well in all zones.

THE PHYSICAL GAME
Lindgren is solidly built and capable of playing a power game. He'll never dominate physically, but he will battle for the puck in high-traffic areas.

THE INTANGIBLES
If Lindgren can stay healthy, he could see more time alongside Mariusz Czerkawski, with whom he has been able to click in the short stretches when they played together.

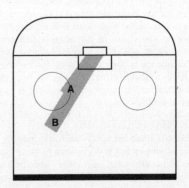

PROJECTION
Lindgren has a 20-goal, 50-point season in him. With

BILL MUCKALT

Yrs. of NHL service: 2
Born: Surrey, B.C.; July 15, 1974
Position: right wing
Height: 6-0
Weight: 190
Uniform no.: 17
Shoots: right

Career statistics:

GP	G	A	TP	PIM
118	24	31	55	119

1998-99 statistics:

GP	G	A	TP	+/-	PIM	PP	SH	GW	GT	S	PCT
73	16	20	36	-9	98	4	2	1	0	119	13.4

1999-2000 statistics:

GP	G	A	TP	+/-	PIM	PP	SH	GW	GT	S	PCT
45	8	11	19	+11	21	1	0	1	1	79	10.1

LAST SEASON

Second NHL season. Acquired from Vancouver with Kevin Weekes and Dave Scatchard for Felix Potvin and two draft choices, Dec. 19, 1999. Led team in plus-minus. Missed 40 games with shoulder dislocation and surgery.

THE FINESSE GAME

Muckalt has all the skills: good skating, good speed and a good touch around the net. He is a natural goal scorer. His best asset is his hockey sense. He understands the game and has good vision. He has grit and determination around the net, and is a character player on and off the ice.

He is a late bloomer who shot up the depth chart in Vancouver thanks to his skating (which is NHL calibre), his shot and his passing ability.

THE PHYSICAL GAME

Muckalt is of average size, but he is fairly strong and willing to do the work along the boards.

THE INTANGIBLES

Muckalt has had two odd first seasons. He was a leading candidate for rookie of the year in Vancouver until a coaching change from Mike Keenan to Marc Crawford led to a disappointing second half. He got off to a slow start after the trade to the Isles, then was starting to come around when he suffered a season-ending injury. The Isles like his skills and his leadership ability and plan to make him a top six forward.

PROJECTION

Muckalt scored 19 points in half a season, which makes 40 — or maybe more — a certainty if he stays healthy for a full year.

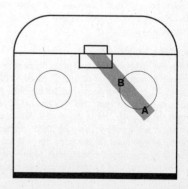

MARK PARRISH

Yrs. of NHL service: 2
Born: Edina, MN; Feb. 2, 1977
Position: left wing
Height: 6-0
Weight: 185
Uniform no.: 21
Shoots: right

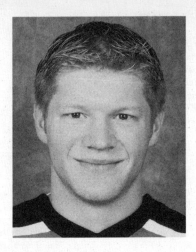

Career statistics:

GP	G	A	TP	PIM
154	50	31	81	64

1998-99 statistics:

GP	G	A	TP	+/-	PIM	PP	SH	GW	GT	S	PCT
73	24	13	37	-6	25	5	0	5	1	129	18.6

1999-2000 statistics:

GP	G	A	TP	+/-	PIM	PP	SH	GW	GT	S	PCT
81	26	18	44	+1	39	6	0	3	0	152	17.1

LAST SEASON

Acquired from Florida with Oleg Kvasha for Roberto Luongo and Olli Jokinen, June 24, 2000. Second NHL season. Led Panthers in shooting percentage. Tied for second in team in game-winning goals. Tied for third on team in power-play goals. Missed one game with back strain.

THE FINESSE GAME

What sophomore jinx? Parrish merely improved his goals, assists and points over his impressive rookie season and stamped himself as a legitimate NHL finisher.

He has excellent outside speed and reads. He was able to beat a mobile defender like Brian Leetch for a goal last season. Parrish is a goal scorer by skill and by nature. He goes to the net hard because he knows he has to score to stay in the lineup.

Parrish has terrific hands and a great shot. He will get a lot of first-unit power-play time. He does some of his best work around the front of the net. He loves to score.

THE PHYSICAL GAME

Parrish doesn't have great size but he doesn't avoid the high-traffic areas. His speed is his best weapon. He held up better over the full season last year than he did in his rookie year, which is part of the learning experience.

THE INTANGIBLES

Parrish is the real goods. He will probably be the number two right wing behind Mariusz Czerkawski on his new team. He might not be too thrilled by going from a Cup contender to a team that will have to claw its way into the playoffs. He is developing into a quiet leader and character player, so with the right attitude, he can be a huge asset for the Isles. He will have to take some of the heat for being one of the players coming back in the deal for the popular Luongo, even though it wasn't his doing.

PROJECTION

We expected Parrish to top the 25-goal mark last season, and he did. It could be more difficult this year with a weaker supporting cast and so many new elements coming into play, but Parrish is good for at least 20, and that's lowball. He is capable of scoring 30, but the circumstances might not be right for him in his first year on Long Island.

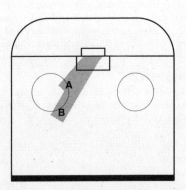

DAVE SCATCHARD

Yrs. of NHL service: 3
Born: Hinton, Alberta; Feb. 20, 1976
Position: centre
Height: 6-2
Weight: 220
Uniform no.: 38
Shoots: right

Career statistics:

GP	G	A	TP	PIM
223	38	42	80	422

1997-98 statistics:

GP	G	A	TP	+/-	PIM	PP	SH	GW	GT	S	PCT
76	13	11	24	-4	165	0	0	1	1	85	15.3

1998-99 statistics:

GP	G	A	TP	+/-	PIM	PP	SH	GW	GT	S	PCT
82	13	13	26	-12	140	0	2	2	0	130	10.0

1999-2000 statistics:

GP	G	A	TP	+/-	PIM	PP	SH	GW	GT	S	PCT
65	12	18	30	-3	117	0	1	1	0	128	9.4

LAST SEASON

Acquired from Vancouver with Bill Muckalt and Kevin Weekes for Felix Potvin and two draft choices, Dec. 19, 1999. Second on team in penalty minutes. Missed eight games with concussion.

THE FINESSE GAME

Scatchard can play a third-line centre's role and brings a little offensive touch to the job. He has a long reach and uses it well around the net as well as defensively. He is not creative, but produces most of his scoring chances by taking the puck to the net. His goals come from effort. He needs to take more shots. He does not have an NHL release.

Scatchard is an admirer of teammate Mark Messier, with whom he played in Vancouver, and their games have some similarities, though Scatchard will never become the dominating force Messier was. Scatchard can play centre or either wing. He is developing into a sound two-way forward.

Scatchard is a good skater with a quick first step. He also has decent hands. He likes to forecheck and churn up turnovers.

THE PHYSICAL GAME

Scatchard needs to build more upper-body strength. He likes to play an aggressive game. He will take a hit to make a play and he protects the puck well. He will also get involved, but he needs a little more muscle to back up the game he is willing to play.

THE INTANGIBLES

Scatchard made it to the NHL ahead of more highly regarded prospects on his effort, and he will have to keep his work ethic up to stick. He will probably never be more than a third-line player, but he can be effective in that role. His concussion ended his season, so it's difficult to know how the injury might affect him.

PROJECTION

Scatchard can rack up 15 goals and 150 PIM with regular playing time.

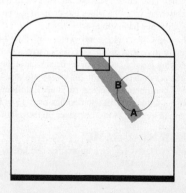

JOHN VANBIESBROUCK

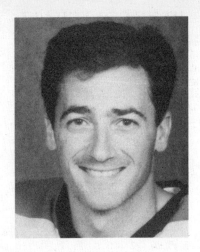

Yrs. of NHL service: 16
Born: Detroit, Mich.; Sept. 4, 1963
Position: goaltender
Height: 5-8
Weight: 176
Uniform no.: 34
Catches: left

Career statistics:

GP	MIN	GA	SO	GAA	A	PIM
829	47545	2367	38	2.99	32	298

1996-97 statistics:

GP	MIN	GAA	W	L	T	SO	GA	S	SAPCT	PIM
57	3347	2.29	27	19	10	2	128	1582	.919	8

1997-98 statistics:

GP	MIN	GAA	W	L	T	SO	GA	S	SAPCT	PIM
60	3451	2.87	18	29	11	4	165	1638	.899	6

1998-99 statistics:

GP	MIN	GAA	W	L	T	SO	GA	S	SAPCT	PIM
62	3712	2.18	27	18	15	6	135	1380	.902	12

1999-2000 statistics:

GP	MIN	GAA	W	L	T	SO	GA	S	SAPCT	PIM
50	2950	2.20	25	15	9	3	108	1143	.906	6

LAST SEASON

Acquired from N.Y. Islanders for a fourth-round draft choice in 2001, July 25, 2000. Fifth among NHL goalies in goals-against average.

THE PHYSICAL GAME

There are few goalies who play a better positional game than Vanbiesbrouck. He doesn't make wild, diving saves, because he doesn't have to. He blends a strong technical game with good reflexes, anticipation and confidence. He isn't very big, so he plays his angles and squares himself to the shooter to take away as much of the net as possible. He makes himself look like a much bigger goalie. He is very aggressive, forcing the shooter to make the first move.

Vanbiesbrouck plays a butterfly-style that takes away a lot of low shots and he has a quick glove hand, so most shooters try to go high stick-side on him, but that's a hard corner to pick. He reads wraparound plays well and seldom gets beaten. He gets into occasional trouble when he plays too deep in his net and holds his glove hand too low.

Vanbiesbrouck is a good skater with fine lateral motion. Active with his stick, he uses it to poke-check, guide rebounds, break up passes or whack at any ankles camping out too close to his crease. He won't surrender a centimetre of his ice. He is also confident out of his net with the puck, sometimes overly so. He'll get burned by trying to force passes up the middle.

THE MENTAL GAME

Vanbiesbrouck is highly competitive and keeps himself in superb condition. He has already lost his job to one rookie senastion — Brian Boucher — in Philadelphia. If it happens on Long Island, it won't faze him, but he's still prepared to be a number one goalie and likes the return to the New York area (he started his career with the Rangers).

THE INTANGIBLES

Yes, yes, we know...Rick DiPietro. Heard all about him. But whether the Isles start off the season with DiPietro as their number one and he falters, or if they work him in gradually, it will be the veteran Vanbiesbrouck who handles the brunt of the goaltending chores for the Isles.

PROJECTION

Vanbiesbrouck's days as an elite goalie may be over, but at least he won't beat himself too often — in the regular season, anyway. The team in front of him will struggle, and if he loses playing time to the kid, 20 wins may be the best he can do.

NEW YORK RANGERS

Players' Statistics 1999-2000

POS.	NO.	PLAYER	GP	G	A	PTS	+/-	PIM	PP	SH	GW	GT	S	PCT
C	93	PETR NEDVED	76	24	44	68	2	40	6	2	4		201	11.9
R	14	THEOREN FLEURY	80	15	49	64	-4	68	1		1		246	6.1
C	18	*MICHAEL YORK	82	26	24	50	-17	18	8		4	2	177	14.7
R	20	RADEK DVORAK	81	18	32	50	5	16	2	1	1		157	11.5
L	27	*JAN HLAVAC	67	19	23	42	3	16	6		2		134	14.2
R	15	JOHN MACLEAN	77	18	24	42	-2	52	6	2	3		158	11.4
L	9	ADAM GRAVES	77	23	17	40	-15	14	11		4		194	11.9
L	13	VALERI KAMENSKY	58	13	19	32	-13	24	3		1		88	14.8
D	21	MATHIEU SCHNEIDER	80	10	20	30	-6	78	3		1	1	228	4.4
R	12	ALEXANDRE DAIGLE	58	8	18	26	-5	23	1		1	1	52	15.4
D	2	BRIAN LEETCH	50	7	19	26	-16	20	3		2	1	124	5.6
R	16	ROB DIMAIO	62	6	19	25	-9	50					111	5.4
D	4	KEVIN HATCHER	74	4	19	23	-10	38	2			1	112	3.6
D	3	*KIM JOHNSSON	76	6	15	21	-13	46	1		1		101	5.9
C	26	TIM TAYLOR	76	9	11	20	-4	72			2	1	79	11.4
D	45	STEPHANE QUINTAL	75	2	14	16	-10	77			1		102	2.0
L	28	ERIC LACROIX	70	4	8	12	-12	24			1		46	8.7
D	24	SYLVAIN LEFEBVRE	82	2	10	12	-13	43				1	67	3.0
L	21	KEVIN STEVENS	38	3	5	8	-7	43	1				44	6.8
D	47	RICHARD PILON	54		6	6	-2	70					16	
L	36	JOHAN WITEHALL	9	1	1	2	0	2					6	16.7
R	22	JASON DAWE	3		1	1	0	2					8	
D	16	JASON DOIG	7		1	1	-2	22					3	
C	21	P.J. STOCK	11		1	1	1	11					2	
L	28	DARREN LANGDON	21		1	1	-2	26					13	
G	30	KIRK MCLEAN	22		1	1	0	2						
C	26	DEREK ARMSTRONG	1			0							1	
G	31	JEAN LABBE	1			0								
D	36	TERRY VIRTUE	1				-2						2	
L	39	DANIEL GONEAU	1				-1						3	
D	36	*ALEXEI VASILJEV	1				-1	2						
D	45	*DALE PURINTON	1				-1	7					1	
G	33	MILAN HNILICKA	2				0							
R	38	CHRISTOPHER KENADY	2				-1						1	
C	15	MANNY MALHOTRA	27				-6	4					18	
G	45	MIKE RICHTER	61				0	4						

GP = games played; G = goals; A = assists; PTS = points; +/- = goals-for minus goals-against while player is on ice; PIM = penalties in minutes; PP = power-play goals; SH = shorthanded goals; GW = game-winning goals; GT = game-tying goals; S = no. of shots; PCT = percentage of goals to shots; * = rookie

PAVEL BRENDL

Yrs. of NHL service: 0
Born: Opocno, Czech Rep.; Mar. 23, 1981
Position: right wing
Height: 6-0
Weight: 204
Uniform no.: n.a.
Shoots: right

Career junior statistics:

GP	G	A	TP	PIM
124	132	113	245	134

1999-2000 statistics:
Did not play in NHL.

LAST SEASON
Appeared in 61 games with Calgary (WHL), scoring 59-52 — 111.

THE FINESSE GAME
When you start throwing the name "Mike Bossy" around while trying to describe a 19-year-old's playing style, you know you are dealing with something special. Brendl could be that kind of player.

Certainly the Rangers thought so, since they traded two players (Niklas Sundstrom and Dan Cloutier) to Tampa Bay in order to move up in the 1999 draft and take Brendl. It is said that three things happen when Brendl shoots the puck: he misses the net, he hits the goalie, or he scores. In other words, the goalie is virtually helpless to make a save, so accurate and heavy are Brendl's wrist and slap shots.

The only potential drawback is the question of whether Brendl's skating is NHL calibre. He is strong and balanced on his skates, but until he is tested at the top level his foot speed is suspect. Brendl also isn't the most accomplished defensive player, but then again, neither was Bossy.

THE PHYSICAL GAME
Brendl has excellent size and the desire to take the puck to the net in traffic. He is poised under fire and can shoot or make a play in a throng of defenders; most checkers at the junior level bounced off him.

Brendl is extremely lax in his conditioning. He is accustomed to being able to turn his game on for one shift and be a hero in junior. That is not going to happen in the NHL. Brendl started working out last season with a strength and conditioning coach.

THE INTANGIBLES
Brendl does not want to go back to junior this year. He faces a battle in training camp because of so many highly paid veterans ahead of him on the depth chart, and the Rangers may be reluctant — in the wake of the Manny Malhotra fiasco of the past two seasons —
to keep a young player around who doesn't get much playing time. If he pushes himself hard in camp, he could stick, but he is going to have to be impressive. Brendl is a very young 19 who needs to learn the professional part of the game.

PROJECTION
Brendl has the special ability to score goals and win games. The Rangers could use that, if he's ready. Brendl could see fourth-line and spot power-play duty to start the season.

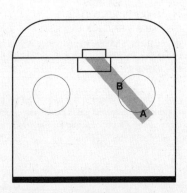

THEOREN FLEURY

Yrs. of NHL service: 12
Born: Oxbow, Sask.; June 29, 1968
Position: right wing/centre
Height: 5-6
Weight: 160
Uniform no.: 14
Shoots: right

Career statistics:

GP	G	A	TP	PIM
886	389	529	918	1558

1996-97 statistics:

GP	G	A	TP	+/-	PIM	PP	SH	GW	GT	S	PCT
81	29	38	67	-12	104	9	2	3	3	336	8.6

1997-98 statistics:

GP	G	A	TP	+/-	PIM	PP	SH	GW	GT	S	PCT
82	27	51	78	0	197	3	2	4	1	282	9.6

1998-99 statistics:

GP	G	A	TP	+/-	PIM	PP	SH	GW	GT	S	PCT
75	40	53	93	+26	86	8	3	5	2	301	13.3

1999-2000 statistics:

GP	G	A	TP	+/-	PIM	PP	SH	GW	GT	S	PCT
80	15	49	64	-4	68	1	0	1	0	246	6.1

LAST SEASON

Led team in assists and shots. Second on team in points. Missed one game with back spasms. Missed one game with knee injury.

THE FINESSE GAME

What happened to Fleury last season? The Garden fans who saw him at his best when he visited their building once a season with the Calgary Flames did not see the same Fleury on a nightly basis last season. The reasons were muitlple: lack of a big complementary centre, his initial reluctance to play in the East and plain old bad luck.

One thing Fleury continued to do consistently was shoot the puck, but not accurately. He hit a number of posts and crossbars and broke as many sticks in frustration over goalie saves as he scored goals.

Fleury's skating ability, which has always served him well as a small player in keeping him out of danger zones, worked against him with teammates who never seemed to know where he was going to be. Especially on the power play, Fleury never seemed to be in the right place at the right time. Only one power-play goal, when he played on the first unit all season?

Fleury always has his legs churning, and he draws penalties by driving to the net. He has a strong wrist shot that he can get away from almost anywhere. He can score even if he is pulled to his knees.

He is an effective penalty killer, blocking shots and getting the puck out along the boards. And he is poised and cool with the puck under attack, holding it until he finds an opening instead of just firing blindly. His hand quickness makes him effective on draws, and he takes offensive-zone draws.

THE PHYSICAL GAME

Fleury can take a hit and not get knocked down because he is so solid and has a low centre of gravity. He uses his stick liberally and will take a lot of penalties sticking up for himself and his teammates. The abuse over a long season tends to wear him down, yet Fleury is remarkably durable.

THE INTANGIBLES

The pressure of a four-year, $28-million deal — his salary was mentioned after almost every Rangers loss, which is to say, frequently — wore on Fleury.

PROJECTION

Considering the Rangers' investment in Fleury, and new GM Glen Sather's familiarity with him from the old Battle of Alberta days, you have to figure that the club will make finding him a suitable centre a priority. We have to believe last year was an aberration. If anyone is due for a bounce-back season, this is the guy.

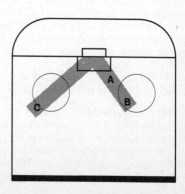

ADAM GRAVES

Yrs. of NHL service: 12
Born: Toronto, Ont.; Apr. 12, 1968
Position: left wing
Height: 6-0
Weight: 205
Uniform no.: 9
Shoots: left

Career statistics:

GP	G	A	TP	PIM
907	293	248	541	1375

1996-97 statistics:

GP	G	A	TP	+/-	PIM	PP	SH	GW	GT	S	PCT
82	33	28	61	+10	66	10	4	3	5	269	12.3

1997-98 statistics:

GP	G	A	TP	+/-	PIM	PP	SH	GW	GT	S	PCT
72	23	12	35	-30	41	10	0	2	1	226	10.2

1998-99 statistics:

GP	G	A	TP	+/-	PIM	PP	SH	GW	GT	S	PCT
82	38	15	53	-12	47	14	2	7	0	239	15.9

1999-2000 statistics:

GP	G	A	TP	+/-	PIM	PP	SH	GW	GT	S	PCT
77	23	17	40	-15	14	11	0	4	0	194	11.9

LAST SEASON

Finalist for 2000 Masterton Trophy. Led team in power-play goals. Tied for team lead in game-winning goals. Third on team in goals. Missed five games due to personal reasons.

THE FINESSE GAME

Graves is a short-game player who scores a whopping percentage of his goals off deflections, rebounds and slam dunks. A shot from the top of the circle is a long-distance effort for him. He favours the wrist shot; his rarely used slap shot barely exists. He is much better when working on instinct because, when he has time to make plays, he will outthink himself.

Although not very fast in open ice and something of an awkward skater, Graves's balance and strength are good and he can get a few quick steps on a rival. He is smart with the puck. He protects it with his body and is strong enough to fend off a checker with one arm and shovel the puck to a linemate with the other. He needs to play on a line with scorers, because he is a grinder first, a scorer second. He will drive to the net to screen the goalie and dig for rebounds, so he needs to play with someone who shoots to make the most of his efforts.

Graves is a former centre who can step in on draws. He is an intelligent penalty killer.

THE PHYSICAL GAME

Graves has worked hard to overcome a back injury that threatened his career. He has confidence in his body's ability to respond the way he wants, and this is reflected in his tough play. Despite all the dismal nights he had to endure as a Ranger last season,

Graves never shirked.

THE INTANGIBLES

Graves dealt with the unimaginable loss of one of his twin sons, born prematurely, by trying to make sure the tragedy distracted his teammates as little as possible. Graves is a natural leader who shows up in the grandest fashion on those nights when the rest of his teammates fail to. Those nights when the points aren't coming, Graves never hurts his club and finds other ways to contribute. A frequent winner of "Players' Player" awards, such is the respect he has earned. Off the ice, the absurdly modest Graves is one of the genuine good guys.

PROJECTION

In the right circumstances, Graves could score 30 goals.

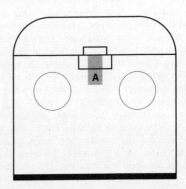

JAN HLAVAC

Yrs. of NHL service: 1
Born: Prague, Czech.; Sept. 20, 1976
Position: left wing
Height: 6-0
Weight: 185
Uniform no.: 27
Shoots: left

Career statistics:

GP	G	A	TP	PIM
67	19	23	42	16

1999-2000 statistics:

GP	G	A	TP	+/-	PIM	PP	SH	GW	GT	S	PCT
67	19	23	42	+3	16	6	0	2	0	134	14.2

LAST SEASON

First NHL season. Second on team in plus-minus. Third on team in shooting percentage. Tied for third on team in power-play goals. Missed two games due to hip flexor. Missed on game with bruised foot. Missed nine games due to coach's decision. Appeared in three games with Hartford (AHL), scoring 0-1-1.

THE FINESSE GAME

Hlavac has scoring talent and deceptive speed. He has been a top-level scorer in the Czech League. With any sort of confidence and if he gets enough power-play time, he could establish that same kind of scoring presence in the NHL.

He is a good stickhandler who can move the puck at a high tempo. He has good anticipation and accleration. He is occasionally guilty of overhandling the puck, and he usually looks for centre Petr Nedved instead of taking it to the net himself. Hlavac has a good scoring touch and needs to shoot more.

Hlavac forechecks intelligently and creates plays off the turnovers. He is very good passer and playmaker and has good defensive awareness.

THE PHYSICAL GAME

Hlavac is strong on his skates, even though he isn't very big. He has a quiet toughness to him.

THE INTANGIBLES

Hlavac was a frequently benched, part-time forward until Radek Dvorak's arrival in December led to the creation of the Czech-mate line with Nedved. Then all the pieces clicked into place.

PROJECTION

Hlavac has offensive upside which should surface in a year or two. If the Rangers develop a little help up front to take some of the checking heat off this line, Hlavac could move into the 30-goal range. Motivation is an issue. He could just as easily score 10 if he's not in the mood.

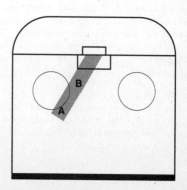

KIM JOHNSSON

Yrs. of NHL service: 1
Born: Malmo, Sweden; Mar. 16, 1976
Position: left defense
Height: 6-1
Weight: 175
Uniform no.: 3
Shoots: left

Career statistics:

GP	G	A	TP	PIM
76	6	15	21	46

1999-2000 statistics:

GP	G	A	TP	+/-	PIM	PP	SH	GW	GT	S	PCT
76	6	15	21	-13	46	1	0	1	0	101	5.9

LAST SEASON

First NHL season.Missed one game with lacerated eyelid. Missed five games due to coach's decision.

THE FINESSE GAME

Johnsson is mobile. He is quick to get to the puck and quick to move it. When he is playing with confidence, he eagerly joins the rush.

Johnsson works the point on the second power-play unit. He has a good shot from the point. It is not overpowering, but he releases it quickly and he keeps it low and on net. He is not afraid to venture into the circles because he knows his skating can help him recover. He has a little cockiness in his game that makes him try some plays creatively.

Johnsson is quite reliable defensively. He plays his position well and makes smart defensive reads. He has a long reach for making sweep and poke checks and tying up an opponent's stick.

THE PHYSICAL GAME

Johnsson has average size for an NHL defenseman. He is not very physical or aggressive. Johnsson needs to get stronger. His lack of strength around his net is a drawback.

THE INTANGIBLES

Johnsson was arguably the Rangers' best defenseman for the first half of last season. His play dropped off in the second half, probbaly due to a combination of the travel, the schedule and the general malaise around the team, which must have been difficult for a young player to handle.

PROJECTION

Johnsson has a lot of important ingredients for a young defenseman and could be in the Rangers' top four. He should improve to 30 to 35 points.

VALERI KAMENSKY

Yrs. of NHL service: 8
Born: Voskresensk, Russia; April 18, 1966
Position: left wing
Height: 6-2
Weight: 198
Uniform no.: 13
Shoots: right

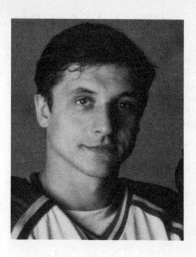

Career statistics:

GP	G	A	TP	PIM
518	179	267	446	327

1996-97 statistics:

GP	G	A	TP	+/-	PIM	PP	SH	GW	GT	S	PCT
68	28	38	66	+5	38	8	0	4	1	165	17.0

1997-98 statistics:

GP	G	A	TP	+/-	PIM	PP	SH	GW	GT	S	PCT
75	26	40	66	-2	60	8	0	4	0	173	15.0

1998-99 statistics:

GP	G	A	TP	+/-	PIM	PP	SH	GW	GT	S	PCT
65	14	30	44	+1	28	2	0	2	0	123	11.4

1999-2000 statistics:

GP	G	A	TP	+/-	PIM	PP	SH	GW	GT	S	PCT
58	13	19	32	-13	24	3	0	1	0	88	14.8

LAST SEASON

Led team in shooting percentage. Missed 23 games with fractured right forearm. Missed one game with ankle contusion.

THE FINESSE GAME

Kamensky is primarily a one-way forward. A gifted skater with speed and quickness, he is as dangerous without the puck as he is with it because of his sense for open ice. He's also as effective in four-on-four situations as he is as an outstanding transition player. His passes are flat and on the money, with just the right velocity; the recipient does not have to slow down but can collect the puck in stride.

Kamensky has quick hands and a good release on his wrist shot. He gets a lot of power-play time and excells at getting open in the left slot; he just rips his one-timer. Given his amount of ice time with the extra man, however, Kamensky should produce more on the power play than he has in recent seasons. He will continue to get prime power-play time with the Rangers.

Kamensky has to score, because he does little else to contribute to a team's victory.

THE PHYSICAL GAME

Kamensky has in the past been willing to take abuse and keep playing. But either his pain threshold has dropped or the troublesome forearm injury at the start of last season made him gun-shy, because Kamensky was so far on the Rangers' perimeter he was often in Brooklyn.

THE INTANGIBLES

A bigger disappointment than Theo Fleury, if that's possible, Kamensky was one of the NHL's poster boys for teams staying fiscally responsible. The Rangers let him dangle in the expansion draft, with no interest from the new teams. Wise of them. Kamensky owes the Rangers — big time. Motivation is a huge question mark. Always an outstanding playoff performer, he has to help the Rangers get there first.

PROJECTION

Too volatile a player to pick for your team, real or imagined.

BRIAN LEETCH

Yrs. of NHL service: 12
Born: Corpus Christi, Tex.; Mar. 3, 1968
Position: left defense
Height: 5-11
Weight: 190
Uniform no.: 2
Shoots: left

Career statistics:

GP	G	A	TP	PIM
857	194	597	781	419

1996-97 statistics:

GP	G	A	TP	+/-	PIM	PP	SH	GW	GT	S	PCT
82	20	58	78	+31	40	9	0	2	0	256	7.8

1997-98 statistics:

GP	G	A	TP	+/-	PIM	PP	SH	GW	GT	S	PCT
76	17	33	50	-36	32	11	0	2	2	230	7.4

1998-99 statistics:

GP	G	A	TP	+/-	PIM	PP	SH	GW	GT	S	PCT
82	13	42	55	-7	42	4	0	1	0	184	7.1

1999-2000 statistics:

GP	G	A	TP	+/-	PIM	PP	SH	GW	GT	S	PCT
50	7	19	26	-16	20	3	0	2	1	124	5.6

LAST SEASON

Missed 32 games with broken right forearm.

THE FINESSE GAME

Leetch is a premier passer who sees the ice clearly, identifies the optimum passing option on the move and hits his target with a forehand or backhand pass. He is terrific at picking passes out of the air and keeping attempted clearing passes from getting by him at the point.

He has a fine first step that sends him towards top speed almost instantly. He can be posted at the point, then see an opportunity to jump into the play down low and bolt into action. His anticipation is superb. He seems to be thinking about five seconds ahead of everyone else on the ice. He instantly starts a transition from defense to offense, and always seems to make the correct decision to pass or skate with the puck.

Leetch has a remarkable knack for getting his point shot through traffic and to the net. He even uses his eyes to fake. He is adept at looking and/or moving in one direction, then passing the opposite way.

Leetch smartly jumps into holes to make the most of an odd-man rush, and he is more than quick enough to hop back on defense if the puck goes the other way. He has astounding lateral movement, leaving forwards completely out of room when it looked like there was open ice to get past him. He uses this as a weapon on offense to open up space for his teammates.

Leetch has a range of shots. He'll use a slapper from the point, usually through a screen because it won't overpower any NHL goalie, but he'll also use a wrist shot from the circle. He is gifted with the one-

on-one moves that help him wriggle in front for 10-footers on the forehand or backhand, and he has worked on one-timers from close to the net.

THE PHYSICAL GAME

Leetch initiates contact and doesn't hesitate to make plays in the face of being hit. Although not strong enough, or mean enough to manhandle people, he still gets physically involved. He competes for the puck and is a first-rate penalty killer. He sacrifices his body to block shots, which is how he broke his arm last season.

Leetch cuts off the ice, gives the skater nowhere to go, strips the puck or steals a pass, then starts the transition game. He'll then follow the rush and may finish off the play with a goal. He works best when paired with a stay-at-home partner with a mean streak.

THE INTANGIBLES

Leetch has plummeted from the ranks of the league's elite defensemen, despite his elite skills. That may be more a reflection on the talent drop-off surrounding him, but Leetch has to shoulder his share of the burden, too.

PROJECTION

Leetch needs to return to the ranks of the 50-point scorers. Now he's given up the burden of the team captaincy to Mark Messier, he may be able to do it.

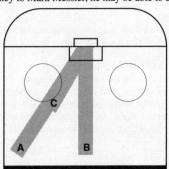

SYLVAIN LEFEBVRE

Yrs. of NHL service: 11
Born: Richmond, Que.; Oct. 14, 1967
Position: right defense
Height: 6-2
Weight: 205
Uniform no.: 2
Shoots: left

Career statistics:

GP	G	A	TP	PIM
798	28	134	162	586

1996-97 statistics:

GP	G	A	TP	+/-	PIM	PP	SH	GW	GT	S	PCT
71	2	11	13	+12	30	1	0	0	0	77	2.6

1997-98 statistics:

GP	G	A	TP	+/-	PIM	PP	SH	GW	GT	S	PCT
81	0	10	10	+2	48	0	0	0	0	66	.0

1998-99 statistics:

GP	G	A	TP	+/-	PIM	PP	SH	GW	GT	S	PCT
76	2	18	20	+18	48	0	0	0	0	64	3.1

1999-2000 statistics:

GP	G	A	TP	+/-	PIM	PP	SH	GW	GT	S	PCT
82	2	10	12	-13	43	0	0	0	1	67	3.0

LAST SEASON

One of two Rangers to appear in all 82 games.

THE FINESSE GAME

Lefebvre is a good argument for instituting an NHL award for best defensive defensemen (as opposed to the Norris Trophy, which in recent years has gone to offensive defensemen). If there was such a piece of hardware, Lefebvre would have been a finalist through much of his career, if not a winner. He's one of the best at one-on-one coverage. He's always in position and always square with his man. He reads the play well and makes good outlet passes from his own end.

Lefebvre plays his position the way any coach would try to teach it to a youngster. Safe and dependable, he makes the first pass and then forgets about the puck. He couldn't be any less interested in the attack. If he has the puck at the offensive blueline and doesn't have a lane, he just throws it into the corner. His game is defense first, and he is very basic and consistent in his limited role. He does it all playing against the other teams' top lines on a nightly basis.

Lefebvre actually has below-average skills in speed and puckhandling, but by playing within his limits and within the system he is ultrareliable.

THE PHYSICAL GAME

Tough without being a punishing hitter, Lefebvre patrols and controls the front of his net and plays a hard-nosed style. He plays a containment game.

THE INTANGIBLES

Lefebrve is a quiet leader, well respected by teammates and opponents. Age is catching up with him, but intelligence makes up for a lost step here and there. He was one of the few free agent moves the Rangers made last season that wasn't a catastrophe. He was their most reliable defenseman.

PROJECTION

Lefebvre prevents points, he doesn't score them.

JOHN MACLEAN

Yrs. of NHL service: 16
Born: Oshawa, Ont.; Nov. 20, 1964
Position: right wing
Height: 6-0
Weight: 200
Uniform no.: 15
Shoots: right

Career statistics:

GP	G	A	TP	PIM
1098	389	412	801	1262

1996-97 statistics:

GP	G	A	TP	+/-	PIM	PP	SH	GW	GT	S	PCT
80	29	25	54	+11	49	5	0	6	0	254	11.4

1997-98 statistics:

GP	G	A	TP	+/-	PIM	PP	SH	GW	GT	S	PCT
77	16	27	43	-6	42	6	0	3	1	213	7.5

1998-99 statistics:

GP	G	A	TP	+/-	PIM	PP	SH	GW	GT	S	PCT
82	28	27	55	+5	46	11	1	2	0	231	12.1

1999-2000 statistics:

GP	G	A	TP	+/-	PIM	PP	SH	GW	GT	S	PCT
77	18	24	42	-2	52	6	2	3	0	158	11.4

LAST SEASON

Tied for team lead in shorthanded goals. Tied for third on team in power-play goals. Missed four games with eye injury. Missed one game due to coach's decision.

THE FINESSE GAME

MacLean still thinks of himself as a goal scorer, but he is such a good defensive forward that he can be used in a checking role, and provide offense on the counter-attack. He lacks the speed to be an effective shadow against the league's faster forwards, but he is an intelligent player positionally and harasses puck carriers into clumsy passes with his forechecking. He pressures the points when killing penalties. And he has great anticipation for picking passes out of lanes that he fools the opposition into thinking are open. He is more than half a step slow now, though, and really has to rely on his smarts to beat someone else to the puck.

There is no such thing as an impossible angle for MacLean. He will shoot anytime, from anywhere on the ice, and will usually put the puck on net or out into traffic in front of the crease — where there is always a chance the puck will hit someone or something and go skittering into the net. So what if all of his scoring chances are no longer the brilliant highlight shots that characterized his presurgery (1991) career? His pure goal-scoring instincts still make him a threat.

Slow in open ice but strong along the boards and in the corners, MacLean chugs and churns and draws restraining fouls. He also indulges in a bit of diving. Somehow, he gets to where he has to go, but his wheels are average on his best night.

THE PHYSICAL GAME

MacLean uses a wide-based skating stance and is tough to budge from the front of the net. He will take a lot of abuse to get the job done in traffic, and will not be intimidated. He has cut down on his retaliatory penalties, but won't take much garbage before snapping. Despite his problems with his knee, he is remarkably durable. He is extremely competitive and fights down to the last second of a game.

THE INTANGIBLES

Should the Rangers actually play any of their younger prospects, MacLean is an ideal guy to have around. He's a veteran with a solid NHL reputation, but he also goes out of his way to make kids feel part of a team. They could also learn a thing or two from his work ethic and savvy. The Rangers left him unprotected in the expansion draft. It's questionable if he's part of their plans.

PROJECTION

MacLean's big-number days are over as he has become more of a role-playing forward, but he can still kick in 15 to 20 goals a season.

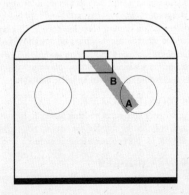

VLADIMIR MALAKHOV

Yrs. of NHL service: 8
Born: Sverdlovsk, Russia; Aug. 30, 1968
Position: right defense
Height: 6-3
Weight: 220
Uniform no.: 38
Shoots: left

Career statistics:

GP	G	A	TP	PIM
466	70	201	271	477

1996-97 statistics:

GP	G	A	TP	+/-	PIM	PP	SH	GW	GT	S	PCT
65	10	20	30	+3	43	5	0	1	0	177	5.6

1997-98 statistics:

GP	G	A	TP	+/-	PIM	PP	SH	GW	GT	S	PCT
74	13	31	44	+16	70	8	0	2	0	166	7.8

1998-99 statistics:

GP	G	A	TP	+/-	PIM	PP	SH	GW	GT	S	PCT
62	13	21	34	-7	77	8	0	3	0	143	9.1

1999-2000 statistics:

GP	G	A	TP	+/-	PIM	PP	SH	GW	GT	S	PCT
24	1	4	5	+1	23	1	0	1	0	18	5.6

LAST SEASON

Acquired by New Jersey from Montreal for Sheldon Souray and Josh DeWolf, Mar. 1, 2000. Missed 55 games due to knee injury.

THE FINESSE GAME

Malakhov has elite pro skills and an amateur attitude. (We don't mean to insult hardworking amateurs, we're just trying to make a point.) He continues to be one of the most enigmatic defensemen in the game.

He has an absolute bullet of a shot — maybe the hardest shot in the league — which no one talks about. He rifles off a one-timer or shoots on the fly, and has outstanding offensive instincts for both shooting and playmaking. He moves the puck and jumps into the play, but lacks vision, lateral movement and confidence.

Malakhov is so talented he never looks like he's trying hard. Most nights he's not. He seems discouraged at times when things aren't going smoothly. If he tries a few plays early in a game that don't work, you might as well put him on the bench for the rest of the night. If he has a few good shifts early, especially offensively, odds are he'll be one of the three stars.

Defensively, Malakhov is in love with the poke-check, and uses his long reach to cut down passing lanes. Positionally, though, he will frequently give up on the play and leave his defense partner to his own devices.

Malakhov can be used on both special teams. He is a mobile skater, with good agility and balance. He has a huge stride, which he developed playing bandy — a Russian game similar to hockey that is played on an ice surface the size of a soccer field. He has a good point shot.

THE PHYSICAL GAME

Malakhov could be a major physical force because of his size and strength, but he has a very low pain threshold; he really doesn't have the taste for the physical game. Every once in awhile, he does get the urge, and when he does, he is a solid checker because of his size and skating ability.

THE INTANGIBLES

Maybe that bunny hill story that got him run out of Montreal wasn't quite true, but Malakhov's dedication to the game is nonetheless questionable. It's a shame, too, because with his world-class skills, the Russian should be a Norris Trophy winner. He has never put the whole package together; until he does he will remain the number one tease in the NHL. By playing for a Cup winner, he was able to bring his price tag back up, though, and he will be a highly sought-after free agent despite his flaws.

PROJECTION

A healthy Malakhov will get his 30 to 40 points without being anywhere near the impact player he could and should be.

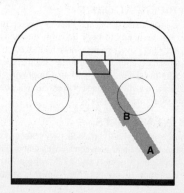

MANNY MALHOTRA

Yrs. of NHL service: 2
Born: Mississauga, Ont.; May 18, 1980
Position: centre
Height: 6-1 1/2
Weight: 210
Uniform no.: 6
Shoots: left

Career statistics:

GP	G	A	TP	PIM
100	8	8	16	17

1998-99 statistics:

GP	G	A	TP	+/-	PIM	PP	SH	GW	GT	S	PCT
73	8	8	16	-2	13	1	0	2	0	61	13.1

1999-2000 statistics:

GP	G	A	TP	+/-	PIM	PP	SH	GW	GT	S	PCT
27	0	0	0	-6	4	0	0	0	0	18	-

LAST SEASON

Second NHL season. Missed four games with sprained left ankle. Missed 22 games due to coach's decision. Appeared in five games with Guelph (OHL), scoring 2-2 — 4. Appeared in 12 games with Hartford (AHL), scoring 1-5 — 6.

THE FINESSE GAME

Malhotra is a versatile player who may turn into a young Rod Brind'Amour, able to check, work on the power play, play centre, play wing, give a team a lead or protect it. Malhotra brings so many things to a team.

Malhotra is a two-way centre. He will never be a big-time scorer, because his shot is not an awesome weapon, but by working to get in position and dig for short-range chances he will get his share. Malhotra also has a terrific first step and reads offensive plays well. He gets more than his fair share of breakaways. He has to read plays better defensively. He has a very young game.

Malhotra's play is fuelled by his will and determination. Few recent young players have been so highly ranked in terms of character. He understands the game well and is highly coachable.

THE PHYSICAL GAME

Malhotra is big and strong and likes to play a physical game, but he needs to bulk up a bit more to play against the big boys, against whom he looked coltish. He has been described as an ultimate team player and a kid who thrives on hard work and improving himself. He's a low-maintenance player. He will not take a night, or a shift, off.

THE INTANGIBLES

Malhotra has basically wasted two seasons while caught in a tug-of-war between a coach who wouldn't play him (John Muckler) and a GM who refused to send him back to juniors (Neil Smith). Malhotra didn't help himself by moping when he was assigned to the Canadian world junior team, or to Guelph or Hartford. He was unhappy and let everyone know it.

Smith and Muckler have been fired. Malhotra needs to start the season in the minors, since it's unlikely he will get much ice time on the Rangers now that Mark Messier has returned. Malhotra has to lose some of his wide-eyed, golly-gee-whiz demeanour. While endearing, it's annoying to his teammates. He's a man now, battling for a man's job, and he has to act the part.

PROJECTION

Muckler dismissively called Malhotra nothing better than a third-line player in last year's training camp. Couched in better terms, that's accurate. But what Malhotra should become is an excellent third-line centre. He's going to be an important player on a winning team for a long time.

MARK MESSIER

Yrs. of NHL service: 21
Born: Edmonton, Alta.; Jan. 18, 1961
Position: centre
Height: 6-1
Weight: 205
Uniform no.: 11
Shoots: left

Career statistics:

GP	G	A	TP	PIM
1479	627	1087	1714	1717

1996-97 statistics:

GP	G	A	TP	+/-	PIM	PP	SH	GW	GT	S	PCT
71	36	48	84	+12	88	7	5	9	1	227	15.9

1997-98 statistics:

GP	G	A	TP	+/-	PIM	PP	SH	GW	GT	S	PCT
82	22	38	60	-10	58	8	2	2	0	139	15.8

1998-99 statistics:

GP	G	A	TP	+/-	PIM	PP	SH	GW	GT	S	PCT
59	13	35	48	-12	33	4	2	2	0	97	13.4

1999-2000 statistics:

GP	G	A	TP	+/-	PIM	PP	SH	GW	GT	S	PCT
66	17	37	54	-15	30	6	0	4	0	131	13.0

LAST SEASON

Signed as free agent with NY Rangers, July 13, 2000. Tied for Canucks lead in game-winning goals. Tied for second on Canucks in power-play goals. Third on team in assists, points and shots. Tied for third on team in goals. Missed 15 games with knee injury.

THE FINESSE GAME

Messier has always been better at making the utmost use of his teammates, rather than trying one-on-one moves. His hallmark is his bottomless determination to win, which prevents his more skilled but less brave cohorts from faltering. He just drags them right to the front lines with him.

Messier is strong on his skates: he changes directions, pivots, bursts into open ice and, when his game is at its strongest, does it all with or without the puck. He still has tremendous acceleration and a powerful burst of straightaway speed, which is tailor-made for killing penalties and scoring shorthanded goals — even if he cheats into the neutral zone, looking for a breakaway pass, too often.

Messier's shot of choice is a wrister off the back ("wrong") foot from the right-wing circle, which is where he always seems to gravitate. It's a trademark, and it still fools many a goalie. He also makes as much use of the backhand, for passing and shooting, as any other North American player in the league. He will weave to the right-wing circle, fake a pass to the centre, get the goalie to cheat away from the post, then flip a backhand under the crossbar. He shoots from almost anywhere and is unpredictable in his shot selection when the back-foot wrist is not available.

THE PHYSICAL GAME

The Messier mean streak is legendary, but less frequently evident. He is a master of the preemptive strike, the elbows or stick held teeth-high when a checker is coming towards him.

THE INTANGIBLES

Messier's strength is founded now on his reputation, and he has returned to the team where his status is near that of a god. The Rangers want him more for his ability to wring the best out of his teammates, who were an underachieveing bunch in his three-year absence. There are few better big-game players in NHL history than Messier, but the past is the past.

PROJECTION

Age and injuries — Messier will turn 40 in January — will probably sideline him for about a quarter of the season. Messier could still be a point-a-game player when he's in the lineup and should be good for about 60 points.

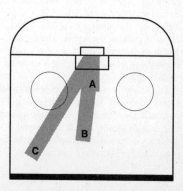

PETR NEDVED

Yrs. of NHL service: 9
Born: Liberec, Czech Republic; Dec. 9, 1971
Position: centre
Height: 6-3
Weight: 195
Uniform no.: 93
Shoots: left

Career statistics:

GP	G	A	TP	PIM
573	202	250	452	410

1996-97 statistics:

GP	G	A	TP	+/-	PIM	PP	SH	GW	GT	S	PCT
74	33	38	71	-2	66	12	3	4	0	189	17.5

1997-98 statistics:

Did not play in NHL

1998-99 statistics:

GP	G	A	TP	+/-	PIM	PP	SH	GW	GT	S	PCT
56	20	27	47	-6	50	9	1	3	0	153	13.1

1999-2000 statistics:

GP	G	A	TP	+/-	PIM	PP	SH	GW	GT	S	PCT
76	24	44	68	+2	40	6	2	4	0	201	11.9

LAST SEASON

Led team in points. Tied for team lead in game-winning and shorthanded goals. Second on team in goals and assists. Third on team in shots. Tied for third on team in power-play goals. Missed four games with groin injury. Missed two games with bruised ribs.

THE FINESSE GAME

Sometimes the right linemates make all the difference. Nedved came alive in midseason after the Rangers acquired Radek Dvorak, then put him on a line with Nedved and Jan Hlavac. The three Czech forwards were far better together than when apart, able to read and feed off one another. The problem with all three is that they don't shoot enough. It's usually a case of overpassing to the player who ends up being in the worst scoring position, and Nedved is one of the chief offenders. But, tall but slightly built, he is good at handling the puck in traffic or in open ice at tempo. He sees the ice well and has a creative mind.

Nedved makes use of the time and space. He may have the best wrist shot in the NHL, with a hair-trigger release and radar-like accuracy. He likes to go high on the glove side, picking the corner. The Rangers tried using him as a power-play quarterback at times, but he lacks a heavy shot from the point and is better up front on the half-boards.

Good on attacking-zone draws, Nedved knows his way around a face-off. He has good hand quickness and cheats well. On offensive-zone draws, he turns his body so that he's almost facing the boards. That is about it for his defensive contribution, though he can kill penalties because of his quickness and anticipation.

THE PHYSICAL GAME

The knock on Nedved early in his career was his inconsistency and his distaste for the physical aspect of the game, but he has filled out and grown up in every sense of the word. He competes hard and isn't deterred when facing some of the league's top forwards. His problem is that, as a number one centre by default in New York, he took a major beating on a nightly basis. Although willing to play through pain, his body could not always respond. He handled a lot of minutes and would benefit from a decreased workload.

THE INTANGIBLES

One wonders what kind of impact Mark Messier's return to the Rangers will have on Nedved? It was supposedly Messier who wanted Nedved out of New York a few years ago, because Messier was unhappy with Nedved's devotion and work ethic.

PROJECTION

Nedved needs to develop some chemistry with a pure shooter (Pavel Brendl?), in order for his passing skills to pay off. An 80-point season is possible if his line stays intact.

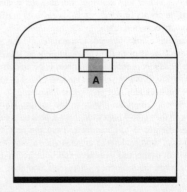

RICHARD PILON

Yrs. of NHL service: 12
Born: Saskatoon, Sask.; Apr. 30, 1968
Position: left defense
Height: 6-0
Weight: 205
Uniform no.: 2
Shoots: left

Career statistics:

GP	G	A	TP	PIM
554	6	57	63	1561

1996-97 statistics:

GP	G	A	TP	+/-	PIM	PP	SH	GW	GT	S	PCT
52	1	4	5	+4	179	0	0	0		0	17	5.9

1997-98 statistics:

GP	G	A	TP	+/-	PIM	PP	SH	GW	GT	S	PCT
76	0	7	7	+1	291	0	0	0	0	37	0.0

1998-99 statistics:

GP	G	A	TP	+/-	PIM	PP	SH	GW	GT	S	PCT
52	0	4	4	-8	88	0	0	0	0	27	.0

1999-2000 statistics:

GP	G	A	TP	+/-	PIM	PP	SH	GW	GT	S	PCT
54	0	6	6	-2	70	0	0	0	0	16	-

LAST SEASON
Acquired from N. Y. Islanders on waivers, Dec. 1, 1999. Missed 14 games with shoulder injuries.

THE FINESSE GAME
Pilon is power. He takes command of his own end of the ice and is a very steady defensive rearguard. He is not remotely involved in offense. His career scoring totals look like a month's work for Sandis Ozolinsh.

But unlike Ozolinsh, Pilon's main concern is getting the puck out of his own zone safely. He will make a conservative chip off the glass rather than gamble on a pass up the middle. He is a much better passer than he is given credit for, but he won't waste time looking for the high-risk play. He is a heavy-footed skater. His offensive input is limited to a so-so shot from the point.

Pilon is a very determined penalty killer and blocks shots willingly.

THE PHYSICAL GAME
Pilon is a fierce, mean hitter. He usually hits high instead of low, and he can topple players. He can also fight, but the impulse is curtailed because of the visor he is forced to wear (an eye injury he received years ago nearly ended his career). He can snap, which makes opponents wary of him.

What Pilon is not is a possible spokesman for Bally's. He needs to step up his conditioning to earn a regular role for new coach Ron Low.

THE INTANGIBLES
The Rangers are severely lacking in the team toughness department. Pilon can be part of that as a number five or six defenseman.

PROJECTION
Pilon scores a goal once every other year, so he's overdue. A better bet is 200-plus penalty minutes, if he can remain intact.

STEPHANE QUINTAL

Yrs. of NHL service: 12
Born: Boucherville, Que.; Oct. 22, 1968
Position: right defense
Height: 6-3
Weight: 225
Uniform no.: 5
Shoots: right

Career statistics:

GP	G	A	TP	PIM
950	48	142	190	1021

1996-97 statistics:

GP	G	A	TP	+/-	PIM	PP	SH	GW	GT	S	PCT
71	7	15	22	+1	100	1	0	0	0	139	5.0

1997-98 statistics:

GP	G	A	TP	+/-	PIM	PP	SH	GW	GT	S	PCT
71	6	10	16	+13	97	0	0	0	0	88	6.8

1998-99 statistics:

GP	G	A	TP	+/-	PIM	PP	SH	GW	GT	S	PCT
82	8	19	27	-23	84	1	1	4	0	159	5.0

1999-2000 statistics:

GP	G	A	TP	+/-	PIM	PP	SH	GW	GT	S	PCT
75	2	14	16	-10	77	0	0	1	0	102	2.0

LAST SEASON

Second on team in penalty minutes. Missed four games due to team suspension. Missed one game due to coach's decision. Missed one game with concussion. Missed one game with neck spasms.

THE FINESSE GAME

Quintal's game is limited by his lumbering skating. He has some nice touches, including a decent point shot, and a good head and hands for passing, but his best moves have to be executed at a virtual standstill. He needs to be paired with a quick skater or his shifts will be spent solely in the defensive zone.

Fortunately, Quintal is aware of his flaws. He plays a smart positional game and doesn't get involved in low-percentage plays in the offensive zone. He won't step up in the neutral zone to risk an interception but will fall back into a defensive mode. He takes up a lot of ice with his body and stick, and when he doesn't overcommit, he reduces the space available to a puck carrier. Quintal should not carry the puck. He tends to get a little panicky under pressure.

Although he can exist as an NHL regular in the five-on-five mode, Quintal is a risky proposition for any specialty-team play.

THE PHYSICAL GAME

Strong on his skates, Quintal thrives on contact and works hard along the boards and in front of the net. He hits hard without taking penalties and is a tough and willing fighter if he has to do it. He has the strength to clear the crease and is a good skater for his size.

THE INTANGIBLES

The Rangers suspended Quintal, one of their many overpriced free agents, for telling a French-language newspaper in Montreal that he wanted to be traded back to the Canadiens. If the Rangers have Quintal in their future plans at all, it will help him that his former Montreal partner, Vladimir Malakhov, has been signed for the upcoming season. Quintal was an ill fit with every Ranger he played with last season, especially Brian Leetch.

PROJECTION

Quintal can score 20 to 25 points and he is a serviceable, second-pairing defenseman if he is paired with a mobile partner. Otherwise, he tries to do too much and ends up accomplishing nothing.

MIKE RICHTER

Yrs. of NHL service: 10
Born: Abingdon, Pa.; Sept. 22, 1966
Position: goaltender
Height: 5-11
Weight: 185
Uniform no.: 35
Catches: left

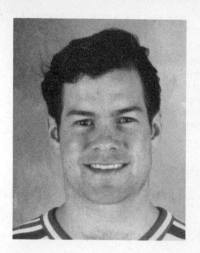

Career statistics:

GP	MIN	GA	SO	GAA	A	PIM
553	31659	1505	22	2.85	8	30

1996-97 statistics:

GP	MIN	GAA	W	L	T	SO	GA	S	SAPCT	PIM
61	3598	2.68	33	22	6	4	161	1945	.917	4

1997-98 statistics:

GP	MIN	GAA	W	L	T	SO	GA	S	SAPCT	PIM
72	4143	2.66	21	31	15	0	184	1888	.903	2

1998-99 statistics:

GP	MIN	GAA	W	L	T	SO	GA	S	SAPCT	PIM
68	3878	2.63	27	30	8	4	170	1898	.910	0

1999-2000 statistics:

GP	MIN	GAA	W	L	T	SO	GA	S	SAPCT	PIM
61	3622	2.87	22	31	8	0	173	1815	.905	4

LAST SEASON

Fifth among NHL goalies in shots faced. Missed five games with back injury. Missed nine games with knee injury.

THE PHYSICAL GAME

The Rangers should consider putting a collar around Richter's neck and an invisible fence around the perimeter of his crease. He is a stickhandling nightmare: puck exchanges with his defensemen are often laughable and, at times, life-threatening, because Richter simply cannot decide whether to leave the puck behind the net or try a cute little pass to help the cause. The results are usually calamitous. Either there is a turnover for an easy goal or some defenseman, trying to find Richter's pass in his feet, gets creamed from behind by a forechecker. Richter would be far better off just staying in the paint.

Richter uses his stick for poke-checks in one-on-one battles, but still doesn't use it enough as a pass-blocking tool. Too often, he concedes the pass across the crease and relies on his lateral movement to make a quick save he wouldn't have to make at all if he merely prevented the puck from reaching the shooter.

Nonetheless, Richter is agile, flexible and athletic, and boasts exceptional post-to-post quickness. Quick reflexes allow him to reach second-chance shots off rebounds or one-timers off odd-man rushes.

He rarely gets beat to the low corners. Shooters beat him high on the glove side or on slam-dunks to the weak side after he has overplayed an angle. He gets a whopping percentage of the first shots. While he catches more pucks now, and holds onto them more, he still leaves some juicy rebounds.

THE MENTAL GAME

Richter may be the most patient one-on-one goalie in the NHL. Confident and fluid, he simply lets himself make whatever save is necessary. If that results in him losing his stick and at least one of his gloves, no problem. When he trusts his instincts and just flows, he is the NHL's best package of concentration, reflexes and puckstopping skill in clutch situations.

Eceptional at finding the puck through traffic, Richter is able to make stops on close-range shots off passes from behind the net. Similarly, when the puck is moving from point to point, he stays focussed, stays crouched, sees the puck and stays with it. He tends to lose his concentration on long shots, and gets beaten every now and then by a ridiculous goal.

THE INTANGIBLES

Richter injured his knee during the skills competition at the All-Star game and played anyway. Well, no one said goalies were smart. He continued to play hurt the second half of the season until finally undergoing knee surgery at the end of the year. While his dedication is admirable, playing while wounded did little to help the Rangers' meagre chances of winning a given game.

PROJECTION

The Rangers were able to keep Kirk McLean as a backup, and should use him to give Richter some more time off. Richter doesn't play well when his job is threatened, and McLean isn't a threatening presence. Just keep him out of the All-Star game.

MICHAEL YORK

Yrs. of NHL service: 1
Born: Pontiac, MI; Jan. 3, 1978
Position: centre
Height: 5-9
Weight: 179
Uniform no.: 18
Shoots: right

Career statistics:

GP	G	A	TP	PIM
82	26	24	50	18

1999-2000 statistics:

GP	G	A	TP	+/-	PIM	PP	SH	GW	GT	S	PCT
82	26	24	50	-17	18	8	0	4	2	177	14.7

LAST SEASON

Finalist for 2000 Calder Trophy. First NHL season. Led team in goals and first among NHL rookies in goals. Tied for first among NHL rookies and second on team in power-play goals. Second among NHL rookies in shots. Third among NHL rookies and tied for third on team in points. Second on team and fourth among NHL rookies in shooting percentage. Sixth among NHL rookies in assists. One of two Rangers to appear in all 82 games.

THE FINESSE GAME

York's goal-scoring last season was a surprise. York's reputation in college (Michigan State) was that of a playmaker, but York proved equally proficient and clever with his shotmaking. York lacks an overpowering shot, but he is patient with the puck and has a nice touch on an accurate wrist shot, which he releases quickly.

York's size is a drawback, but he is very smart and uses the ice in the middle of the ice well. The reason the Rangers traded Marc Savard, a similar style of player, was because of York's development, and York is a better defensive player than Savard.

York is good on draws. He is very smart, and that's what is going to keep him around the NHL for a long time.

THE PHYSICAL GAME

York is small but durable. He staggered a few times during the season, but never really wore down to the point where he ever hurt the team by staying in the lineup. He's driven and competitive, with a quiet confidence. He won't be intimidated.

THE INTANGIBLES

York is extremely versatile — he can handle wing or centre, and play more of a defensive role than he did last year. He works very hard to get out of slumps.

PROJECTION

Mark Messier's expected arrival and Petr Nedved's role as the number two centre will probably bump York down to a third-line role with some power-play duty.

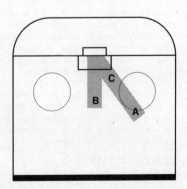

OTTAWA SENATORS

Players' Statistics 1999-2000

POS.	NO.	PLAYER	GP	G	A	PTS	+/-	PIM	PP	SH	GW	GT	S	PCT
C	14	RADEK BONK	80	23	37	60	-2	53	10		5	1	167	13.8
R	11	DANIEL ALFREDSSON	57	21	38	59	11	28	4	2			164	12.8
R	18	MARIAN HOSSA	78	29	27	56	5	32	5		4		240	12.1
C	13	VACLAV PROSPAL	79	22	33	55	-2	40	5		4		204	10.8
L	15	SHAWN MCEACHERN	69	29	22	51	2	24	10		4	1	219	13.2
C	39	JOE JUNEAU	65	13	24	37	3	22	2		2		126	10.3
D	6	WADE REDDEN	81	10	26	36	-1	49	3		2	1	163	6.1
R	10	ANDREAS DACKELL	82	10	25	35	5	18			1	1	99	10.1
D	33	JASON YORK	79	8	22	30	-3	60	1		1		159	5.0
L	20	MAGNUS ARVEDSON	47	15	13	28	4	36	1	1	4	1	91	16.5
C	22	SHAUN VAN ALLEN	75	9	19	28	20	37		2	4		75	12.0
D	3	PATRICK TRAVERSE	66	6	17	23	17	21	1				73	8.2
L	7	ROB ZAMUNER	57	9	12	21	-6	32		1			103	8.7
D	4	CHRIS PHILLIPS	65	5	14	19	12	39			1		96	5.2
D	29	IGOR KRAVCHUK	64	6	12	18	-5	20	5		1		126	4.8
D	5	SAMI SALO	37	6	8	14	6	2	3		1		85	7.1
R	9	KEVIN DINEEN	67	4	8	12	2	57			1		71	5.6
C	12	*MIKE FISHER	32	4	5	9	-6	15			1		49	8.2
R	26	*ANDRE ROY	73	4	3	7	3	145			1		39	10.3
L	56	*PETR SCHASTLIVY	13	2	5	7	4	2	1		1		22	9.1
L	17	COLIN FORBES	53	2	5	7	-5	30					57	3.5
D	2	GRANT LEDYARD	40	2	4	6	-3	8			1		42	4.8
C	21	KEVIN MILLER	9	3	2	5	1	2	1		2		11	27.3
L	23	YVES SARAULT	11		2	2	-3	7					13	
G	30	MICHAEL FOUNTAIN	1					0						
D	52	*DAVID VAN DRUNEN	1					0						
D	59	*ERICH GOLDMANN	1					0						
G	1	*JANI HURME	1					0						
C	25	VIACHESLAV BUTSAYEV	5				-4						2	
D	44	*KAREL RACHUNEK	6				0	2					3	
D	24	JOHN GRUDEN	9				0	4					3	
C	38	*JOHN EMMONS	10				-2	6					3	
G	35	TOM BARRASSO	25				0	6						
G	40	PATRICK LALIME	38				0	4						

GP = games played; G = goals; A = assists; PTS = points; +/- = goals-for minus goals-against while player is on ice; PIM = penalties in minutes; PP = power-play goals; SH = shorthanded goals; GW = game-winning goals; GT = game-tying goals; S = no. of shots; PCT = percentage of goals to shots; * = rookie

DANIEL ALFREDSSON

Yrs. of NHL service: 5
Born: Grums, Sweden; Dec. 11, 1972
Position: right wing
Height: 5-11
Weight: 187
Uniform no.: 11
Shoots: right

Career statistics:

GP	G	A	TP	PIM
328	99	170	269	118

1996-97 statistics:

GP	G	A	TP	+/-	PIM	PP	SH	GW	GT	S	PCT
76	24	47	71	+5	30	11	1	1	2	247	9.7

1997-98 statistics:

GP	G	A	TP	+/-	PIM	PP	SH	GW	GT	S	PCT
55	17	28	45	+7	18	7	0	7	0	149	11.4

1998-99 statistics:

GP	G	A	TP	+/-	PIM	PP	SH	GW	GT	S	PCT
58	11	22	33	+8	14	3	0	5	0	163	6.7

1999-2000 statistics:

GP	G	A	TP	+/-	PIM	PP	SH	GW	GT	S	PCT
57	21	38	59	+11	28	4	2	0	0	164	12.8

LAST SEASON

Led team in assists. Tied for team lead in shorthanded goals. Second on team in points. Missed 20 games with knee injury. Missed one game with foot injury. Missed three games with sprained knee. Missed one game due to coach's decision.

THE FINESSE GAME

Alfredsson has a big-time NHL shot, and he has returned to the big-time form he flashed in his rookie season.

His release is hair-trigger. He also has a solid work ethic; he didn't make it to the NHL on cruise control. Alfredsson has to work for his space, and he does. One of the reasons why he is so good on the power play is because of his work in open ice. He has excellent vision and hands. He can be quiet an entire game and then kill a team with two shots.

Alfredsson likes to play a puck control game and needs to work with other forwards who will distribute the puck, such as Vinny Prospal. Alfredsson is well schooled in the defensive aspects of the game, and he works diligently along the wall. He is a constant shorthanded threat when killing penalties because of his speed and anticipation. There are few better players in the league one-on-one or on the breakaway (he scored on his only penalty shot attempt of the season).

THE PHYSICAL GAME

Alfredsson has a very thick and powerful lower body to fuel his skating. He is fearless and takes a lot of abuse to get into the high-scoring areas. He will skate up the wall and cut to the middle of the ice. He might get nailed by the off-side defenseman, but on the next rush he will try it again. He won't be scared off, and on the next chance he may get the shot away and in.

Alfredsson's major problem is his fragility. Like Montreal's Saku Koivu, he is showing himself to be vulnerable to major dings that knock him out for a third of the season. In the past three years, he has averaged only 57 games played.

THE INTANGIBLES

In Alexei Yashin's absence, Alfredsson was given the captaincy and this is his team, not Yashin's, now. Even in the unlikely event of Yashin's return to the Senators, Alfredsson is the alpha male. Teammates respect him for his work ethic and he is a leader by example.

PROJECTION

Alfredsson is a point-a-game player. The only concern is how many games he will be able to appear in.

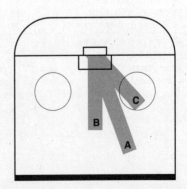

MAGNUS ARVEDSON

Yrs. of NHL service: 3
Born: Karlstad, Sweden; Nov. 25, 1971
Position: left wing
Height: 6-2
Weight: 198
Uniform no.: 20
Shoots: left

Career statistics:

GP	G	A	TP	PIM
188	47	54	101	122

1997-98 statistics:

GP	G	A	TP	+/-	PIM	PP	SH	GW	GT	S	PCT
61	11	15	26	+2	36	0	1	0	1	90	12.2

1998-99 statistics:

GP	G	A	TP	+/-	PIM	PP	SH	GW	GT	S	PCT
80	21	26	47	+33	50	0	4	6	0	136	15.4

1999-2000 statistics:

GP	G	A	TP	+/-	PIM	PP	SH	GW	GT	S	PCT
47	15	13	28	+4	36	1	1	4	1	91	16.5

LAST SEASON

Led team in shooting percentage. Tied for second on team in game-winning goals. Missed one game with thigh contusion. Missed 34 games with bowel surgery.

THE FINESSE GAME

Arvedson has great speed and is strong on the puck. He was not much of a scorer in Sweden but he has a good shot — unfortunately, like many Europeans, he doesn't use it enough. He is unselfish and will usually look to set up a teammate. He is an accurate shooter when he does fire.

Arvedson has a lot of offensive upside. He is good and smart enough to play on one of the top two lines, and was doing so last season before he ran into an open door at the bench in Philadelphia and suffered an injury severe enough to require the removal of part of his bowel.

He is good enough defensively that he was a Selke Trophy candidate in only his second NHL season. He kills penalties and can be used as a checking centre, though he could just as easily be a Jere Lehtinen-style two-way winger.

THE PHYSICAL GAME

Arvedson is big and strong and able to handle the rigours of an NHL schedule. He can handle a checking assignment to cover the top players, kill penalties and contribute offensively.

THE INTANGIBLES

Arvedson returned from his surgery to score two goals in the remaining two games of the season, but, understandably, did not have an impressive playoffs.

PROJECTION

Arvedson could score 20 goals if he continues to see the ice time he did last year, and if he's healthy. He suffered from back problems a year ago, and after the surgery last season, his health forecast is a little iffy. The Senators need him full-time.

TOM BARRASSO

Yrs. of NHL service: 17
Born: Boston, Mass.; Mar. 31, 1965
Position: goaltender
Height: 6-3
Weight: 211
Uniform no.: 35
Catches: right

Career statistics:

GP	MIN	GA	SO	GAA	A	PIM
715	40890	2230	34	3.27	48	429

1996-97 statistics:

GP	MIN	GAA	W	L	T	SO	GA	S	SAPCT	PIM
5	270	5.78	0	5	0	0	26	186	.860	0

1997-98 statistics:

GP	MIN	GAA	W	L	T	SO	GA	S	SAPCT	PIM
63	3542	2.07	31	14	13	7	122	1556	.922	14

1998-99 statistics:

GP	MIN	GAA	W	L	T	SO	GA	S	SAPCT	PIM
43	2306	2.55	19	16	3	4	98	993	.901	20

1999-2000 statistics:

GP	MIN	GAA	W	L	T	SO	GA	S	SAPCT	PIM
7	418	3.16	3	4	0	0	22	182	.879	0

LAST SEASON

Acquired from Pittsburgh for Janne Laukkenen and Ron Tugnutt, Mar. 14, 2000. Missed three games with finger injury. Missed 11 games with back injury. Missed two games with groin injury. Missed 17 games with knee injury.

THE PHYSICAL GAME

One of the most impressive things about Barrasso is that, although he is often on his knees, he is almost never on his side. He might be the best in the league at recovering from going down and will be back on his skates with his glove in position for the next shot.

Barrasso loves to handle the puck: he's like a third defenseman in both his willingness to leave the crease and in his ability to pass. He holds the NHL record for career assists by a goaltender (48). He's a good skater, able to get to and control a lot of pucks that most goalies wouldn't dare try to reach. Most of the time he uses the boards for his passes, rather than making a risky play up the middle, but every so often he is vulnerable to the interception.

Because of Barrasso's range, teams have to adapt their attack. Hard dump-ins won't work, because he stops them behind the net and zips the puck right back out for an alert counterattack by his teammates. Since he comes out around the post to his right better than his left, teams have to aim soft dumps to his left, making him more hesitant about making the play and giving the forecheckers time to get in on him. His lone weakness appears to be shots low on the glove side.

THE MENTAL GAME

Barrasso is still one of the game's most intense com-petitors. He has battled through injuries and personal crises through the past few seasons and has lost little of his edge. He will whack guys in the ankle or get his body in the way for a subtle interference play.

THE INTANGIBLES

Barrasso did not endear himself to the public by un-apologetically using an expletive during a live post-game TV interview late last year. He doesn't care. All that matters to Barrasso is his own little goalie world. Even though Ottawa made it known they would try to re-sign the free agent during the off-season, Barrasso cleared out his locker before the traditional "break-up day" meeting after the playoffs and never bothered to bid his short-term teammates farewell.

PROJECTION

Expansion could create a last chance for Barrasso to be a number one goalie somewhere. He has started to break down physically.

RADEK BONK

Yrs. of NHL service: 6
Born: Krnov, Czech Republic; Jan. 9, 1976
Position: centre
Height: 6-3
Weight: 215
Uniform no.: 14
Shoots: left

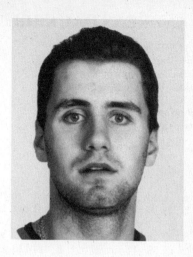

Career statistics:

GP	G	A	TP	PIM
397	70	102	172	195

1996-97 statistics:

GP	G	A	TP	+/-	PIM	PP	SH	GW	GT	S	PCT
53	5	13	18	-4	14	0	1	0	1	82	6.1

1997-98 statistics:

GP	G	A	TP	+/-	PIM	PP	SH	GW	GT	S	PCT
65	7	9	16	-13	16	1	0	0	0	93	7.5

1998-99 statistics:

GP	G	A	TP	+/-	PIM	PP	SH	GW	GT	S	PCT
81	16	16	32	+15	48	0	1	6	0	110	14.5

1999-2000 statistics:

GP	G	A	TP	+/-	PIM	PP	SH	GW	GT	S	PCT
80	23	37	60	-2	53	10	0	5	1	167	13.8

LAST SEASON

Led team in points and game-winning goals. Tied for team lead in power-play goals. Second on team in assists and shooting percentage. Third on team in goals and penalty minutes. Career highs in goals, assists and points. Missed two games with flu.

THE FINESSE GAME

The season-long holdout by Alexei Yashin left Bonk as the number one centre in Ottawa by default. Considering the flaws in his game — his lack of foot speed being the biggest thing holding him back — Bonk did a competent job. He is fine when he gets a good head of speed up but he doesn't explode in his first two strides (the way Joe Sakic does, for example). Bonk can't utilize his skills when he can't accelerate away from stick-checks. His skating is the primary reason why he has not been able to be an impact scorer in the NHL as he was in the minors, and why he has never lived up to the expectations of being the third player drafted overall (in 1994).

Bonk is a puck magnet; the puck always seems to end up on his stick in the slot. He scores the majority of his goals from work in tight, getting his stick free. He has a heavy shot but doesn't have a quick release. He is a smart and creative passer and plays well in advance of his years, with a great deal of poise.

Defensively, Bonk keeps improving. He performed frequently as a third-line centre. He is decent on face-offs, and can be used to kill penalties because of his anticipation. He is a poor man's Bobby Holik when he plays with a little edge.

THE PHYSICAL GAME

Although Bonk has good size, he does not show signs of becoming a power forward. He is aggressive only in pursuit of the puck. He goes into the corners and wins many one-on-one battles because of his strength and hand skills. He can lose his cool and will take the occasional bad penalty.

THE INTANGIBLES

Bonk has somehow survived in the organization, thanks largely to coach Jacques Martin's faith in him. But for the third straight postseason, Bonk failed to register a point in the playoffs — not exactly a sign of a crunch-time performer.

PROJECTION

We said in last year's *HSR* that "Bonk's absolute top end is 20 goals." He exceeded that by three, thanks to the huge chunks of playing time he received, as well as the support of linemates Marina Hossa and Magnus Arvedson. Under any other circumstances, he would not be a first-line forward.

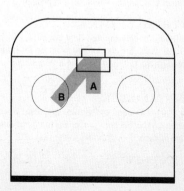

ANDREAS DACKELL

Yrs. of NHL service: 4
Born: Gavle, Sweden; Dec. 29, 1972
Position: right wing
Height: 5-10
Weight: 191
Uniform no.: 10
Shoots: right

Career statistics:

GP	G	A	TP	PIM
320	52	97	149	80

1996-97 statistics:

GP	G	A	TP	+/-	PIM	PP	SH	GW	GT	S	PCT
79	12	19	31	-6	8	2	0	3	0	79	15.2

1997-98 statistics:

GP	G	A	TP	+/-	PIM	PP	SH	GW	GT	S	PCT
82	15	18	33	-11	24	3	2	2	1	130	11.5

1998-99 statistics:

GP	G	A	TP	+/-	PIM	PP	SH	GW	GT	S	PCT
77	15	35	50	+9	30	6	0	3	0	107	14.0

1999-2000 statistics:

GP	G	A	TP	+/-	PIM	PP	SH	GW	GT	S	PCT
82	10	25	35	+5	18	0	0	1	1	99	10.1

LAST SEASON

Only Senator to appear in all 82 games.

THE FINESSE GAME

Dackell has good hockey sense and is sound defensively. He does a lot of subtle things well. Tapes of his game could be used to illustrate hustling on backchecks to knock the puck away from an attacker, attacking in the neutral zone without committing yourself, playing strong along the wall and keeping your man out of the play. Dackell is a last-minute man, one of the guys put on the ice in the final minute of a period or game to protect a lead. He kills penalties and protects the puck well.

He has a decent, accurate shot that he could utilize more. He seems to score timely goals, though he endured two lengthy scoring droughts (one of 26 games and one of 15 games). He doesn't have blazing speed but works hard to be where he's supposed to be. He's very smart and hard to knock off the puck.

THE PHYSICAL GAME

Dackell isn't overly big and he's not a banger, however, he'll make his checks and wont be intimidated. He could be the toughest 30-PIM-a-year player in the NHL.

THE INTANGIBLES

Much of what Dackell contributes to a team is subtle, but he is a valuable role player on the Senators. He was one of their better players in the playoffs.

PROJECTION

Dackell can handle a second-line role as a safety-valve winger, but because of his lack of scoring touch, he is better suited as a third-line checking forward who can provide a steady 15 goals a season.

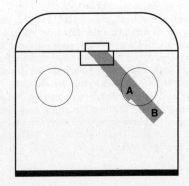

MIKE FISHER

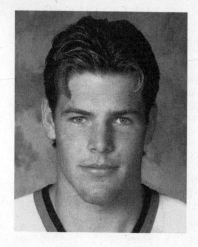

Yrs. of NHL service: 1
Born: Peterborough, Ont.; June 5, 1980
Position: centre
Height: 6-0
Weight: 180
Uniform no.: 12
Shoots: right

Career statistics:

GP	G	A	TP	PIM
32	4	5	9	15

1999-2000 statistics:

GP	G	A	TP	+/-	PIM	PP	SH	GW	GT	S	PCT
32	4	5	9	-6	15	0	0	1	0	49	8.2

LAST SEASON

First NHL season. Missed 45 games with knee injury and reconstructive surgery. Missed three games with hip pointer.

THE FINESSE GAME

None of Fisher's skills are elite, but he had a very good all-around game for such an inexperienced player.

He is a good skater. He puts his speed and agility to work on a smart forechecking game, and he is well-balanced and shifty on his feet. He possesses good instincts and intelligence. And he reads plays well in all zones.

Fisher has potential to develop into a keen penalty killer because of his speed and anticipation. His chief offensive asset is that of a playmaker. He plays a good puck control game and creates time and space for his linemates with his patience with the puck. He has a deft passing touch. He doesn't have a great shot. His scoring chances come from his desire and his willingness to drive to the front of the net.

THE PHYSICAL GAME

Amid a finesse-laden lineup in Ottawa, Fisher stood out because of his willingness to play a physical game — he wins most of his battles for loose pucks. He has decent size but is still growing. And he is very competitive and will sacrifice his body to make a play.

THE INTANGIBLES

Fisher made the most of the opportunity provided by Alexei Yashin's absence. He could become a two-way, number two centre in Ottawa unless the team adds a more experience centre.

PROJECTION

Fisher will get every chance to earn a full-time role with the Sens after making a good impression last season. He will probably need a month or two at the start of the season to get going after coming back from his knee surgery. If he plays a regular role, expect a slow start and a solid finish — 40 points would not surprise us.

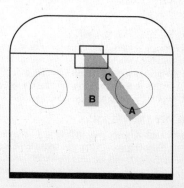

MARIAN HOSSA

Yrs. of NHL service: 2
Born: Stara Lubovna, Slovakia; Jan. 12, 1979
Position: left wing
Height: 6-1
Weight: 185
Uniform no.: 18
Shoots: left

Career statistics:

GP	G	A	TP	PIM
138	44	42	86	69

1997-98 statistics:

GP	G	A	TP	+/-	PIM	PP	SH	GW	GT	S	PCT
7	0	1	1	-1	0	0	0	0	0	10	0.0

1998-99 statistics:

GP	G	A	TP	+/-	PIM	PP	SH	GW	GT	S	PCT
60	15	15	30	+18	37	1	0	2	2	124	12.1

1999-2000 statistics:

GP	G	A	TP	+/-	PIM	PP	SH	GW	GT	S	PCT
78	29	27	56	+5	32	5	0	4	0	240	12.1

LAST SEASON

Second NHL season. Tied for team lead in goals and shots. Tied for second on team in game-winning goals. Third on team in points. Tied for third on team in power-play goals. Missed two games with bruised left wrist. Missed one game with virus. Missed one game with concussion.

THE FINESSE GAME There isn't one player in Hossa's age group who has a better offensive game. He is a pure goal scorer, with excellent hands and the kind of instincts that cannot be taught or drilled into a player. He is nothing short of brilliant on the attack, and destined to be a great, great scorer. His ability to finish is far advanced for only a second-year NHLer.

Hossa is a swift and mobile skater, always dangerous one-on-one. There are some similarities between him and fellow Slovak, Ziggy Palffy. Hossa works hard in the offensive zone, but needs to work on his defensive game and his play without the puck. He also needs to be more consistent in his effort.

Hossa works well down low, and has keen hockey sense and excellent vision. He also has size and skating ability. This guy is the complete offensive package.

THE PHYSICAL GAME

Hossa made a remarkable comeback following major reconstructive knee surgery. He seemed to have no lack of confidence in his rebuilt knee. He uses his size well — better in the offensive zone than the rest of the ice. He isn't shy about physical play at all.

THE INTANGIBLES

Hossa scored only one goal in his last 17 regular season and playoff games. That was because he was affected so deeply by his careless high stick, which may have ended the career of Toronto's Bryan Berard (eye injury). Hossa received some counselling after the event. The lone question mark to his remarkable development is how long the incident will continue to haunt him.

PROJECTION

If you are looking for a future NHL goal-scoring leader, look no further. All Hossa needs is a little more seasoning and a bona fide number one centre. Add five goals to his total next season, and five more the next... and maybe more if the Sens can move Alexei Yashin and get the right pivotman in return.

SHAWN MCEACHERN

Yrs. of NHL service: 8
Born: Waltham, Mass.; Feb. 28, 1969
Position: centre/left wing
Height: 5-11
Weight: 195
Uniform no.: 15
Shoots: left

Career statistics:

GP	G	A	TP	PIM
593	180	192	372	266

1996-97 statistics:

GP	G	A	TP	+/-	PIM	PP	SH	GW	GT	S	PCT
65	11	20	31	-5	18	0	1	2	0	150	7.3

1997-98 statistics:

GP	G	A	TP	+/-	PIM	PP	SH	GW	GT	S	PCT
81	24	24	48	+1	42	8	2	4	2	229	10.5

1998-99 statistics:

GP	G	A	TP	+/-	PIM	PP	SH	GW	GT	S	PCT
77	31	25	56	+8	46	7	0	4	1	223	13.9

1999-2000 statistics:

GP	G	A	TP	+/-	PIM	PP	SH	GW	GT	S	PCT
69	29	22	51	+2	24	10	0	4	1	219	13.2

LAST SEASON

Tied for team lead in goals and power-play goals. Second on team in shots. Tied for second on team in game-winning goals. Third on team in shooting percentage. Missed eight games with fractured left thumb. Missed four games with bruised left clavicle. Missed one game with stomach virus.

Second on team in goals, points and shots. Tied for second on team in power-play goals. Missed four games with groin injury. Missed one game with wrist injury.

THE FINESSE GAME

McEachern suffers from serious tunnel vision, which negates some of the advantage his speed brings to the lineup. He skates with his head down, looking at the ice instead of the play around him. He is strong and fast, with straightaway speed, but he tends to expend his energy almost carelessly and has to take short shifts.

McEachern's skating is what keeps him employed among the top six forwards. He can shift speeds and direction smoothly without losing control of the puck. He can play both left wing and centre, but is better on the wing because he doesn't use his linemates as well as a centre should. An accurate shooter with a hard wrister, he has a quick release on his slap shot, which he likes to let go after using his outside speed. He is strong on face-offs and is a smart penalty killer who pressures the puck carrier.

McEachern was expected to suffer from the season-long absence of Alexei Yashin. Instead, McEachern redoubled his intensity. Many of his goals result from beating the defenders to loose pucks around the net. He has decent hands in tight.

THE PHYSICAL GAME

Generally an open-ice player, McEachern will also pursue the puck with some diligence in the attacking zone. But he is light, and although he can sometimes build up momentum with his speed for a solid bump, he loses most of the close-in battles for the puck. He's a yapper; many nights he can distract opponents, who want to rip his head off.

McEachern has some quiet grit. He soldiered on through the playoffs even though his fractured thumb was not completely healed.

THE INTANGIBLES

McEachern is a versatile player who can fill a lot of roles with his speed. He isn't a true first-line winger, but he'll fill that role with the Senators until someone takes his job away.

PROJECTION

As long as McEachern continues to earn prime ice time, he can score 30 goals and 60 points.

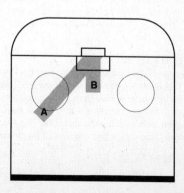

CHRIS PHILLIPS

Yrs. of NHL service: 3
Born: Fort McMurray, Alta.; Mar. 9, 1978
Position: left defense
Height: 6-2
Weight: 200
Uniform no.: 4
Shoots: left

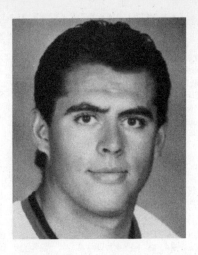

Career statistics:

GP	G	A	TP	PIM
171	13	28	41	109

1997-98 statistics:

GP	G	A	TP	+/-	PIM	PP	SH	GW	GT	S	PCT
72	5	11	16	+2	38	2	0	2	0	107	4.7

1998-99 statistics:

GP	G	A	TP	+/-	PIM	PP	SH	GW	GT	S	PCT
34	3	3	6	-5	32	2	0	0	0	51	5.9

1999-2000 statistics:

GP	G	A	TP	+/-	PIM	PP	SH	GW	GT	S	PCT
65	5	14	19	+12	39	0	0	1	0	96	5.2

LAST SEASON

Missed 17 games with ankle surgery.

THE FINESSE GAME

Phillips is a very good skater for his size. He has all of the attributes (decent speed, lateral mobility, balance and agility), and he skates well backwards and has a small turning radius. Carrying the puck doesn't slow him down much. He is skilled enough to be used up front, which the Senators have done frequently over the past two seasons.

However, moving Phillips from defense to left wing and back to defense has hampered his development. He seemed to be on a Scott Stevens track, and was confused by the switching. Now, he is now not comfortable in either position. He has trouble making defensive reads, and needs more experience playing that position full time.

He will never post Ray Bourque numbers, but Phillips can handle Bourque-like ice time. He has a feel for the offensive part of the game. He joins the attack intelligently and has a hard shot from the point, as well as a good wrist shot when he goes in deep. He is not a great skater: he has a short stride and is not fluid. He doesn't move the puck well, and lacks vision.

THE PHYSICAL GAME

Phillips is solidly built and there are very few question marks about his honest brand of toughness. He likes to hit, and he's mobile enough to catch a defender and drive with his legs to pack a wallop in his checks. He is plagued with troublesome ankles (he had a second surgery last season), which has slowed his progress.

THE INTANGIBLES

Phillips is starting to fall between the cracks. From being touted as a sure-fire defense prospect in Ottawa, there is now a question as to whether he will be able to take the next step and add some much-needed offense to his game. Ottawa needs to stick him back on defense and leave him there to find out what they've got, or trade him and let him develop in a fresh setting.

PROJECTION

This will be another wait-and-see season for Phillips. If he can stay healthy, he can provide 30 points.

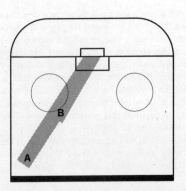

VACLAV PROSPAL

Yrs. of NHL service: 3
Born: Ceske-Budejvice, Czech Republic; Feb. 17, 1975
Position: centre
Height: 6-2
Weight: 185
Uniform no.: 13
Shoots: left

Career statistics:

GP	G	A	TP	PIM
232	43	88	131	123

1996-97 statistics:

GP	G	A	TP	+/-	PIM	PP	SH	GW	GT	S	PCT
18	5	10	15	+3	4	4	0	0	0	35	14.3

1997-98 statistics:

GP	G	A	TP	+/-	PIM	PP	SH	GW	GT	S	PCT
56	6	19	25	-11	21	4	0	0	0	88	6.8

1998-99 statistics:

GP	G	A	TP	+/-	PIM	PP	SH	GW	GT	S	PCT
79	10	26	36	+8	58	2	0	3	0	114	8.8

1999-2000 statistics:

GP	G	A	TP	+/-	PIM	PP	SH	GW	GT	S	PCT
79	22	33	55	-2	40	5	0	4	0	204	10.8

LAST SEASON

Tied for second on team in game-winning goals. Third on team in assists and shots. Tied for third on team in power-play goals. Missed three games due to coach's decision.

THE FINESSE GAME

Prospal has a power-play weapon, and it's not an overpowering shot, but his ability to thread the puck through penalty killers to an open man.

He loves to score (his wrist shot and one-timers are accurate) and make plays. He had to learn to play without the puck, and he's succeeded. His defensive game has also improved. He thinks the game well and is an unselfish player, which makes him a natural fit with Daniel Alfredsson.

The only rap on Prospal is his skating ability, but it's NHL calibre and his view of the ice and his hockey sense compensate for any lack of pure speed.

THE PHYSICAL GAME

Prospal is tall but lean and needs a little more muscle for one-on-one battles. Right now he gives the impression of being a little smaller than he is, but he's an eager player who will get involved. However, he doesn't always do this on a nightly basis and he gets benched (as he did for three games in December) because of it.

THE INTANGIBLES

Prospal worked nicely with Alfredsson, and if the two can remain linemates they'll be an effective duo for the Senators. Ottawa would like to upgrade at centre (assuming Alexei Yashin is moved); Prospal would be one of the vulnerable players if that happens. He was at odds with coach Jacques Martin after his December benching, and the Senators tried to move him then.

PROJECTION

Prospal finally stepped up to the 20-goal, 50-point level we had been waiting for him to attain. That's all, folks. Because of his skating, don't expect much more than what he produced last season.

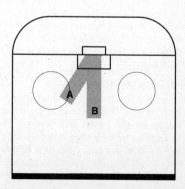

WADE REDDEN

Yrs. of NHL service: 4
Born: Lloydminster, Sask.; June 12, 1977
Position: left defense
Height: 6-2
Weight: 193
Uniform no.: 6
Shoots: left

Career statistics:

GP	G	A	TP	PIM
315	32	85	117	171

1996-97 statistics:

GP	G	A	TP	+/-	PIM	PP	SH	GW	GT	S	PCT
82	6	24	30	+1	41	2	0	1	0	102	5.9

1997-98 statistics:

GP	G	A	TP	+/-	PIM	PP	SH	GW	GT	S	PCT
80	8	14	22	+17	27	3	0	2	0	103	7.8

1998-99 statistics:

GP	G	A	TP	+/-	PIM	PP	SH	GW	GT	S	PCT
72	8	21	29	+7	54	3	0	1	1	127	6.3

1999-2000 statistics:

GP	G	A	TP	+/-	PIM	PP	SH	GW	GT	S	PCT
81	10	26	36	-1	49	3	0	2	1	163	6.1

LAST SEASON

Led team defensemen in points with career high. Missed one game due to stomach virus.

THE FINESSE GAME

Redden has tried to pattern his game after Ray Bourque, and the young defenseman does have a few things in common with the Boston great. He is a good skater who can change gears swiftly and smoothly, and his superb rink vision enables him to get involved in his team's attack. He has a high skill level. His shot is hard and accurate and he is a patient and precise passer; his ability to move the puck is one of his best assets.

Redden plays older than his years and has a good grasp of the game; tested at higher and higher levels of competition he has elevated his game. His poise is exceptional.

Redden's work habits and attitude are thoroughly professional. He is a player who is willing to learn in order to improve his game. Injuries to the defense corps wore him down late in the season, mentally more than physically, and he missed the playoffs due to a fractured foot. He consistently plays against other teams' top lines.

THE PHYSICAL GAME

Redden is not a big hitter, but he finishes his checks and stands up well. What he lacks in aggressiveness he makes up for with his competitive nature. He can handle a lot of ice time. He plays an economical game without a lot of wasted effort, and he is durable and can skate all night long. He would move up a step if he dished it out instead of just taking it. Redden has a very long fuse.

THE INTANGIBLES

Redden has a laid-back nature, but he raises his game when something is on the line.

PROJECTION

In last year's *HSR* we predicted that Redden could produce 35 to 40 points and not lose anything from his defensive game. He did just that and should repeat.

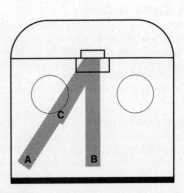

ANDRE ROY

Yrs. of NHL service: 1
Born: Port Chester, NY; Feb. 8, 1975
Position: left wing
Height: 6-3
Weight: 202
Uniform no.: 26
Shoots: left

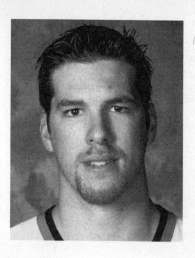

Career statistics:

GP	G	A	TP	PIM
86	4	5	9	157

1996-97 statistics:

GP	G	A	TP	+/-	PIM	PP	SH	GW	GT	S	PCT
10	0	2	2	-5	12	0	0	0	0	12	0.0

1999-2000 statistics:

GP	G	A	TP	+/-	PIM	PP	SH	GW	GT	S	PCT
73	4	3	7	+3	145	0	0	1	0	39	10.3

LAST SEASON

First NHL season. Led team and NHL rookies in penalty minutes. Missed three games due to suspension. Missed one game with knee injury. Missed five games due to coach's decision.

THE FINESSE GAME

The NHL no longer has a place for a pure goon, and Roy has sufficient skills to earn ice time as a fourth-line energy guy to complement his enforcer role. He is a decent skater with a better than average shot, for a player of his limitations. That makes him more than a one-dimensional player.

Roy averages around six or seven minutes a game, but he will give his team quality minutes. He protects his teammates well and will continue to learn to cut down on bad penalties.

If he were a better skater, Roy could be a more effective banger and forechecker. Most of Roy's best battles are fought along the wall, where he can gain a strength advantage.

THE PHYSICAL GAME

Roy is an intimidating physical specimen and a big hitter. He isn't a legitimate heavyweight, but he is a willing fighter. He has learned to pick his spots better. He knows when retaliation is in order, or when he can spark his team, or when he has to send a message. He usually won't fight just for the sake of it.

THE INTANGIBLES

Roy banged around the minors and in Boston's system for four years before getting his first full-time job with the Senators last year. Ottawa liked him enough to give him a new two-year deal at the end of last season. He has paid his dues to get here and we don't expect Roy to become complacent. He was one of Ottawa's most effective players in the postseason in his limited role, waking up the team on his line with Shaun Van Allen and Colin Forbes.

PROJECTION

Ottawa is in need of some beef up front and Roy provides it, along with the occasional point. He could double his production from last year, which would signal a big step forward for a player of this type.

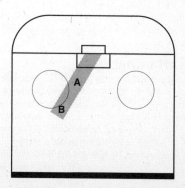

SAMI SALO

Yrs. of NHL service: 2
Born: Turku, Finland; Sept. 2, 1974
Position: right defense
Height: 6-3
Weight: 190
Uniform no.: 5
Shoots: right

Career statistics:

GP	G	A	TP	PIM
98	13	20	33	26

1998-99 statistics:

GP	G	A	TP	+/-	PIM	PP	SH	GW	GT	S	PCT
61	7	12	19	+20	24	2	0	1	0	106	6.6

1999-2000 statistics:

GP	G	A	TP	+/-	PIM	PP	SH	GW	GT	S	PCT
37	6	8	14	+6	2	3	0	1	0	85	7.1

LAST SEASON

Second NHL season. Missed 43 games with fractured left wrist. Missed one game with sprained right knee. Missed one game with bruised chest. Missed one game due to coach's decision.

THE FINESSE GAME

Salo is highly skilled. He has very quick feet and good mobility, which, combined with his long reach, make him hard to beat one-on-one. He also possesses one of the hardest shots in the NHL. He likes to get involved offensively, and steps up into the play alertly. He really started showing off his offensive upside last season, as he became more comfortable at the NHL level. He will eventually develop into a regular on the point on the first power-play unit.

Salo has good hands for passing or receiving the puck, and he makes a crisp first pass out of the zone. He has a good head for the game, calm with the puck under pressure. He reads plays well and moves the puck without mistakes. He is the epitome of a low-risk defenseman, a classic crunch-time defenseman for protecting a lead.

Salo has quickly established himself as a top four defenseman on a solid team.

THE PHYSICAL GAME

Salo won't punish anyone. He is more of a positional defenseman who will ride guys out. He has good size but is not physical.

THE INTANGIBLES

Salo really wanted to play in the NHL, even taking a pay cut just to get a shot with Ottawa two years ago. What a payoff. Despite serious injuries last season, he displayed in his half-year that he has taken the next step. He is playing in relative obscurity in Ottawa, but don't be surprised if you notice Salo every time he plays in your town. He is that solid. He broke into the lead as an older rookie and made a rapid adjustment.

PROJECTION

A healthy Salo will flirt with the 40-point mark this season.

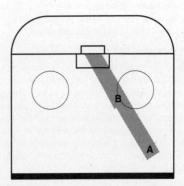

PETR SCHASTLIVY

Yrs. of NHL service: 0
Born: Yaroslav, Russia; Apr. 18, 1979
Position: left wing
Height: 6-1
Weight: 204
Uniform no.: 56
Shoots: left

Career statistics:

GP	G	A	TP	PIM
13	2	5	7	2

1999-2000 statistics:

GP	G	A	TP	+/-	PIM	PP	SH	GW	GT	S	PCT
13	2	5	7	+4	2	1	0	1	0	22	9.1

LAST SEASON

Will be entering first full NHL season. Appeared in 46 games with Grand Rapids (IHL), scoring 16-12 — 28.

THE FINESSE GAME

In his brief NHL stint last season, Schastlivy demonstrated he has the chance to give Ottawa the finishing kick from the left side that Marian Hossa does from the right.

He will be as prolific a scorer as Hossa. Highly skilled, a season of learning the language and the pro life in the minors will give this Russian forward a good foundation for the start of the season. He had a terrific training camp in 1999, but Ottawa made the wise move to send him down to allow him to break in more gradually.

Schastlivy is a creative player. He is unpredictable and doesn't telegraph his moves, which will make it hard for defenders. His speed drives the defense back, and he knows how to make use of the time and space his moves create.

Schlastlivy might never be a star, but he has the kind of skating ability and the shot to become a 10-year player. He plays a puck control game, but nothing excites him quite so much as scoring goals. You can see the light in his eyes before the red light goes on.

THE PHYSICAL GAME

Schastlivy has decent size and doesn't seem to shy away from North American play, but he is not an aggressive player. He pays the price around the net.

THE INTANGIBLES

Few teams scout Europe and Russia as well as the Senators. Schastlivy could have made a bigger splash last season, but for a shoulder injury that knocked him out of 16 games while he was still in the minors with Grand Rapids. He was the 101st pick overall in 1998, and should be ready to step into a full-time role with the Sens next season.

PROJECTION

Ottawa's forward lines are still a muddle because of the Alexei Yashin situation, but Schastlivy should be ready to step into the number two role on the left side. A 30-point rookie season is not out of the question.

ALEXEI YASHIN

Yrs. of NHL service: 6
Born: Sverdlovsk, Russia; Nov. 5, 1973
Position: centre
Height: 6-3
Weight: 215
Uniform no.: 19
Shoots: right

Career statistics:

GP	G	A	TP	PIM
422	178	225	403	203

1996-97 statistics:

GP	G	A	TP	+/-	PIM	PP	SH	GW	GT	S	PCT
82	35	40	75	-7	44	10	0	5	1	291	12.0

1997-98 statistics:

GP	G	A	TP	+/-	PIM	PP	SH	GW	GT	S	PCT
82	33	39	72	+6	24	5	0	6	0	291	11.3

1998-99 statistics:

GP	G	A	TP	+/-	PIM	PP	SH	GW	GT	S	PCT
82	44	50	94	+16	54	19	0	5	1	337	13.1

1999-2000 statistics:

Missed NHL season.

LAST SEASON

Missed entire season in contract holdout.

THE FINESSE GAME

Yashin isn't a flashy skater, but he has drawn comparisons to Ron Francis with his quiet effectiveness, and he is spectacular at times. He doesn't go all-out every shift, though, and on those occasions it looks like he's either pacing himself or he's fatigued. Because it looks as if he isn't trying, when things go poorly for him people assume he's loafing. His protracted contract battles of the past have also made the critics quick to attack. Still, Yashin had nearly an MVP season last year, and he was more consistent in his effort on a nightly basis.

Yashin's skills are world class — on par with those of any other player of his generation. He has great hands and size. As he stickhandles in on the rush, he can put the puck through the legs of two or three defenders enroute to the net. He has to learn, though, that he can go directly to the net and not wait for the defense to come to him, so that he can dazzle by using their legs as croquet wickets.

Last year, Yashin unleashed his powerful shot with more certainty and regularity; the results said it all. He doesn't have pure breakaway speed, but he is powerful and balanced, though he doesn't utilize his teammates well. He wants the puck a lot and has to play with unselfish linemates.

THE PHYSICAL GAME

Yashin is big and rangy and he protects the puck well. He has stepped up his desire to play through checks, and pays the price in traffic. He is also smart and skilled enough to avoid unnecessary wallops.

THE INTANGIBLES

Assuming the Ottawa Senators finally give in and trade their contract headache, Yashin will return to the NHL this season. But questions remain. How much will a year off (in which he played in Europe) hurt him? And how will he be received by his new teammates, who have to be leery of his devotion to winning when year after year his bottom line seems to be his checking account?

PROJECTION

With the right team, in the right frame of mind, and with the right salary, of course, Yashin could be in for an 80-point season if he starts the year in someone's training camp.

JASON YORK

Yrs. of NHL service: 7
Born: Ottawa, Ont.; May 20, 1970
Position: right defense
Height: 6-2
Weight: 195
Uniform no.: 33
Shoots: right

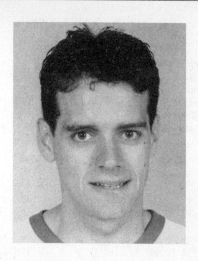

Career statistics:

GP	G	A	TP	PIM
419	24	116	140	341

1996-97 statistics:

GP	G	A	TP	+/-	PIM	PP	SH	GW	GT	S	PCT
75	4	17	21	-8	67	1	0	0	0	121	3.3

1997-98 statistics:

GP	G	A	TP	+/-	PIM	PP	SH	GW	GT	S	PCT
73	3	13	16	+8	62	0	0	0	0	109	2.8

1998-99 statistics:

GP	G	A	TP	+/-	PIM	PP	SH	GW	GT	S	PCT
79	4	31	35	+17	48	2	0	0	1	177	2.3

1999-2000 statistics:

GP	G	A	TP	+/-	PIM	PP	SH	GW	GT	S	PCT
79	8	22	30	-3	60	1	0	1	0	159	5.0

LAST SEASON

Missed three games with groin injury. Career high in goals.

THE FINESSE GAME

York is just entering his defensive prime. He is a smart, all-around defenseman, who concentrated on learning the defensive part of the game first at the NHL level. Now the offensive ability he showed in the minors is coming into play as well.

York's finesse skills are fine. He is a good skater with a hard point shot, and he can handle the point on the second power-play unit — though he isn't quite good enough to step up to the first five. He's a fine penalty killer. He reads plays well (his offensive reads are far superior to his defensive reads) and has the skating ability to spring some shorthanded chances. He can be used in any game situation.

York continues to be the Senators' best all-around defenseman and makes a solid pairing with Wade Redden. They usually face other teams' top lines.

THE PHYSICAL GAME

York has made the conscious decision to add a physical element to his game. He plays with some zip now. He is not a big checker but employs positional play to angle attackers to the boards, using his stick to sweep-check or poke pucks. Once he gains control of the puck, he moves it quickly with no panicky mistakes. He doesn't have a polished defensive game but he does work hard.

THE INTANGIBLES

York has shown gradual, steady improvement in his game over the past two seasons. While he will never be an elite NHL defenseman, he is a reliable blueliner who could fit into the top four on almost anyone's team. He does a lot of little things well and his energy and enthusiasm for the game are apparent.

PROJECTION

York moved into the 30-point ranks and maintained a solid defensive base. He can do it again.

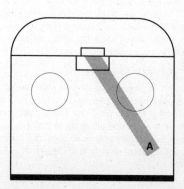

ROB ZAMUNER

Yrs. of NHL service: 8
Born: Oakville, Ont.; Sept. 17, 1969
Position: left wing
Height: 6-2
Weight: 202
Uniform no.: 7
Shoots: left

Career statistics:

GP	G	A	TP	PIM
541	94	130	224	357

1996-97 statistics:

GP	G	A	TP	+/-	PIM	PP	SH	GW	GT	S	PCT
82	17	33	50	+3	56	0	4	3	0	216	7.9

1997-98 statistics:

GP	G	A	TP	+/-	PIM	PP	SH	GW	GT	S	PCT
77	14	12	26	-31	41	0	3	4	1	126	11.1

1998-99 statistics:

GP	G	A	TP	+/-	PIM	PP	SH	GW	GT	S	PCT
58	8	11	19	-15	24	1	1	2	0	89	9.0

1999-2000 statistics:

GP	G	A	TP	+/-	PIM	PP	SH	GW	GT	S	PCT
57	9	12	21	-6	32	0	1	0	0	103	8.7

LAST SEASON

Missed 20 games with sprained left knee. Missed five games with groin injury.

THE FINESSE GAME

Zamuner finally got the chance to prove what he could do with a good team last season, only to run into injury problems and a season disrupted by the Alexei Yashin controversy.

He doesn't have great speed, but he compensates for it in other ways, including all-out effort. A complementary player, he is a grinder who can also handle the puck, and he has some hand skills. Lacking speed, he plays well positionally and takes away the attacker's angles to the net. He doesn't skate as well as many of today's third-line checking wingers, but he is smart enough.

Zamuner was a sniper at the minor-league level, but has not been able to make the same impact in the NHL. He has a decent touch for scoring or passing, but it's average at best. He is a shorthanded threat because of his anticipation and work ethic, and he easily turns penalty-killing shifts into shorthanded counterattacks. He has a knack for scoring key goals.

THE PHYSICAL GAME

Zamuner had problems in the past with fitness, until he realized what a big edge he could have with better conditioning. He has good size and he uses it effectively; he is pesky and annoying to play against. On many nights he will be the most physically active forward, adding a real spark with his effort.

THE INTANGIBLES

Zamuner was considered a disappointment in Ottawa last season and will be looking to redeem himself. He adds some much needed grit to a rather dainty lineup.

PROJECTION

Zamuner has become a checking winger who can provide a steady 15 goals a season.

PHILADELPHIA FLYERS

Players' Statistics 1999-2000

POS.	NO.	PLAYER	GP	G	A	PTS	+/-	PIM	PP	SH	GW	GT	S	PCT
R	8	MARK RECCHI	82	28	63	91	20	50	7	1	5	1	223	12.6
L	10	JOHN LECLAIR	82	40	37	77	8	36	13		7	2	249	16.1
C	88	ERIC LINDROS	55	27	32	59	11	83	10	1	2	1	187	14.4
D	37	ERIC DESJARDINS	81	14	41	55	20	32	8		4	1	207	6.8
C	18	DAYMOND LANGKOW	82	18	32	50	1	56	5		7		222	8.1
C	12	*SIMON GAGNE	80	20	28	48	11	22	8	1	4		159	12.6
R	92	RICK TOCCHET	80	15	20	35	-1	90	4		1	1	130	11.5
R	26	VALERI ZELEPUKIN	77	11	21	32	-3	55	2		3	1	125	8.8
R	20	KEITH JONES	57	9	16	25	8	82	1				92	9.8
L	29	GINO ODJICK	59	8	11	19	-5	100			4		115	7.0
D	3	DANIEL MCGILLIS	68	4	14	18	16	55	3		1		128	3.1
C	25	KEITH PRIMEAU	23	7	10	17	10	31	1		1		51	13.7
R	11	JODY HULL	67	10	3	13	8	4		2	2		63	15.9
D	6	CHRIS THERIEN	80	4	9	13	11	66	1		1		126	3.2
L	32	CRAIG BERUBE	77	4	8	12	3	162					63	6.3
C	28	KENT MANDERVILLE	69	1	7	8	-6	16			1		62	1.6
D	43	*ANDY DELMORE	27	2	5	7	-1	8			1		55	3.6
D	22	LUKE RICHARDSON	74	2	5	7	14	140			1		50	4.0
D	2	ADAM BURT	67	1	6	7	-2	45			1		49	2.0
C	15	PETER WHITE	21	1	5	6	1	6					24	4.2
R	9	MARK GREIG	11	3	2	5	0	6			1		14	21.4
D	55	ULF SAMUELSSON	49	1	2	3	8	58			1		17	5.9
D	44	*MARK EATON	27	1	1	2	1	8			1		25	4.0
D	24	ZARLEY ZALAPSKI	12		2	2	0	6					6	
C	23	TODD WHITE	4	1		1	-1						4	25.0
G	33	*BRIAN BOUCHER	35		1	1	0	4						
G	34	JOHN VANBIESBROUCK	50		1	1	0	6						
C	38	STEVE WASHBURN	1				0						1	
R	14	MIKE MANELUK	1				0	4					2	
D	39	*JEFF LANK	2				0	2						

GP = games played; G = goals; A = assists; PTS = points; +/- = goals-for minus goals-against while player is on ice; PIM = penalties in minutes; PP = power-play goals; SH = shorthanded goals; GW = game-winning goals; GT = game-tying goals; S = no. of shots; PCT = percentage of goals to shots; * = rookie

BRIAN BOUCHER

Yrs. of NHL service: 1
Born: Woonsocket, RI; Jan. 2, 1977
Position: goaltender
Height: 6-1
Weight: 190
Uniform no.: 33
Catches: left

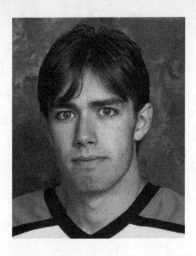

Career statistics:

GP	MIN	GA	SO	GAA	A	PIM
33	2038	65	4	1.91	1	4

1999-2000 statistics:

GP	MIN	GAA	W	L	T	SO	GA	S	SAPCT	PIM
35	2038	1.91	20	10	3	4	65	790	.918	4

LAST SEASON

First NHL season. Named to NHL All-Rookie Team. Led NHL goalies in goals-against average. Fourth among NHL goalies in save percentage. First rookie goalie since 1950-51 to appear in at least 25 games and have GAA under 2.00. Appeared in one game with Philadelphia (AHL), recording 0-0-1 record and 2.77 GAA.

THE PHYSICAL GAME

The Flyers drafted a goalie in the first round for the first time in their history in 1995, and much of the reason was because Boucher reminded them so much of longtime Flyers workhorse Ron Hextall.

Boucher is tall like Hextall, but more agile. He has very good reflexes. He skates well out his net to control pucks, although he does not handle the puck as well as Hextall did. Boucher is something of a hybrid butterfly/standup goalie. He tends to go down a little too quickly and stays back too deep in his net. When he becomes more confident at the NHL level, positions himself better, and challenges shooters more, he will appear even bigger in the nets.

Boucher does a good job of keeping his torso upright when he drops to his knees. He has a good glove and uses his blocker to angle shots into the corner. He makes good use of his stick for breaking up passes around the front of his net.

THE MENTAL GAME

After winning that five-overtime game against Pittsburgh in the playoffs, who can doubt that Boucher is mentally ready for the pressure of a full-time job? The only difference will be Boucher learning to pace himself over a full season, as opposed to the role a goalie can get on for a two-month playoff run.

Boucher has a world of confidence in his abilities. The Flyers had enough confidence in him to trade away veteran John Vanbiesbrouck during the off-season.

THE INTANGIBLES

Boucher has shown steady growth every time he has stepped up in class. His lone setback was a knee injury in his first pro season (1997-98), but the Flyers have taken their time with him and the payoff is imminent.

Boucher's game does have some flaws. If he is is willing to work to correct them, he has a bright future as an NHL goaltending star. If he doesn't, this could be the remake of the Jim Carey story. Fortunately, Boucher seems to have the drive to succeed.

PROJECTION

Boucher faces his first full season as the Flyers number one goalie. He is behind a solid crew that developed respect for him in the playoffs. He should win half of his starts — 30 to 35 wins is a safe bet.

ANDY DELMORE

Yrs. of NHL service: 1
Born: LaSalle, Ont.; Dec. 26, 1976
Position: right defense
Height: 6-1
Weight: 192
Uniform no.: 43
Shoots: right

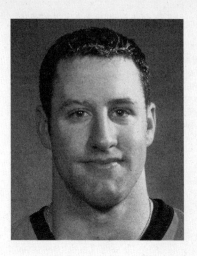

Career statistics:

GP	G	A	TP	PIM
29	2	6	8	8

1998-99 statistics:

GP	G	A	TP	+/-	PIM	PP	SH	GW	GT	S	PCT
2	0	1	1	-1	0	0	0	0	0	2	0.0

1999-2000 statistics:

GP	G	A	TP	+/-	PIM	PP	SH	GW	GT	S	PCT
27	2	5	7	-1	8	0	0	1	0	55	3.6

LAST SEASON

First NHL season. Appeared in 39 games with Philadelphia (AHL), scoring 12-14 — 26. Missed nine games with sprained right knee. Missed two games due to coach's decision.

THE FINESSE GAME

Delmore, who was undrafted and signed as a free agent with the Flyers in 1997, is an excellent skater with a hard shot. That might be good enough to keep him in the league as a forward, but Delmore is a defenseman. And his defensive reads are barely adequate. He needs a lot of work on his defensive game and to be paired with a reliable, stay-at-home defenseman who can almost act as an on-ice coach. Delmore has potential, but he is a project.

Last season, the Flyers refused to put him on the ice (except for power plays) in the later stages of tight games because he is a defensive liability. But high risks can mean high rewards; he will use his blazing speed to rush the puck when other more sensible defensemen wouldn't. If it pays off with a goal, then Delmore is a hero. If not, he's a minus.

Delmore has a hard, accurate shot with a quick release, and is totally unafraid to gamble in deep.

THE PHYSICAL GAME

Delmore has average NHL size for a defenseman but is not in any way physical. He needs to be willing to use his body to at least tie up an opposing forward. He will block shots.

THE INTANGIBLES

Scoring those five splashy playoff goals raised the bar for Delmore, who may find expectations of his role as an "offenseman" too lofty to fulfill. Coaches love his attitude and enthusiasm as much as they hate those defensive gaffes.

PROJECTION

Delmore's defensive shortcomings may make it tough for him to land a top four role. Speed is in short supply on the Flyers' blueline, which works to his advantage. He will definitely get some power-play time, probably enough to boost him to the 25-point level on such a high-powered team.

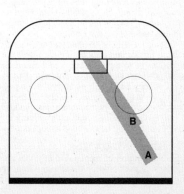

ERIC DESJARDINS

Yrs. of NHL service: 12
Born: Rouyn, Que.; June 14, 1969
Position: right defense
Height: 6-1
Weight: 200
Uniform no.: 37
Shoots: right

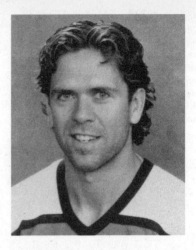

Career statistics:

GP	G	A	TP	PIM
827	102	333	435	564

1996-97 statistics:

GP	G	A	TP	+/-	PIM	PP	SH	GW	GT	S	PCT
82	12	34	46	+25	50	5	1	1	0	183	6.6

1997-98 statistics:

GP	G	A	TP	+/-	PIM	PP	SH	GW	GT	S	PCT
77	6	27	33	+11	36	2	1	0	0	150	4.0

1998-99 statistics:

GP	G	A	TP	+/-	PIM	PP	SH	GW	GT	S	PCT
68	15	36	51	+18	38	6	0	2	0	190	7.9

1999-2000 statistics:

GP	G	A	TP	+/-	PIM	PP	SH	GW	GT	S	PCT
81	14	41	55	+20	32	8	0	4	1	207	6.8

LAST SEASON

Led team defensemen in points for sixth consecutive season. Tied for fourth among NHL defensemen in points. Tied for team lead in plus-minus. Second on team in assists. Tied for third on team in power-play goals. Missed one game due to mouth injury.

THE FINESSE GAME

Desjardins is a number-two defenseman who, for the past several seasons, has been forced to play as a number one while the Flyers continued to make changes everywhere in their lineup but where it was most needed.

He has the puckhandling skills and poise to beat the first forechecker *and* carry the puck out of the defensive zone. He makes accurate breakout passes and has enough savvy to keep the play simple, gain the redline and dump the puck deep in attacking ice if no other option is available. He makes the smart, safe play all the time.

Stable and capable enough to handle power-play duty, Desjardins is wise enough to realize only the ultra-elite overpower NHL goalies with point shots. Although he has a strong one-timer, his slap shot is not always accurate. He is much more dangerous offensively when he uses his wrist shot, or simply flips deflectable pucks toward the net.

A fine skater with light, agile feet and a small turning radius, Desjardins goes up-ice well with the play, keeping the gap to the forwards small and remaining in good position to revert to defense if there is a turnover. A long reach helps him challenge puck carriers to make plays more quickly, change their minds or shoot from a lower-percentage angle. He keeps his stick active while killing penalties, sweeping it on the ice to contest passing lanes and intercept pucks.

THE PHYSICAL GAME

A solid combination of mental and physical strength, Desjardins is particularly effective when penalty killing in front of the net. He immobilizes the opponent's stick first, then ties up the body — which separates him from the huge percentage of defensemen who are satisfied to do one or the other but not both. He plays a hard game more than a punishing one, but uses his strength in more subtle ways to gain position in front of both goals. On offense, he will venture to the corners from time to time and will beat his check to the front of the net after winning a battle for the puck.

Desjardins is quietly tough, but he is not big enough to survive the ice time he is consistently given and tends to wear down, especially in the playoffs.

THE INTANGIBLES

When the controversial decision was made to strip Eric Lindros of his captaincy, and give the "C" to Desjardins, he became the ultimate company man. It was a popular choice, as his teammates like and respect him and were fed up with the Lindros sideshow.

A quiet leader on-ice and in the dressing room, Desjardins wants it more than you do, unless you prove different. He patrols the front of his net like a Doberman, but plays a clean, controlled game and rarely takes stupid penalties. He always seems to be where he is most needed, does not panic and does not fight. He is steady and professional and easy to underappreciate.

PROJECTION

Desjardins scores consistently in the 40- to 50-point range. He isn't a dominating defenseman, which preempts any of that Norris Trophy chatter, but he gives a lot of steady minutes.

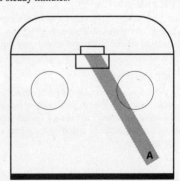

SIMON GAGNE

Yrs. of NHL service: 1
Born: Ste. Foy, Que.; Feb. 29, 1980
Position: centre
Height: 6-0
Weight: 185
Uniform no.: 12
Shoots: left

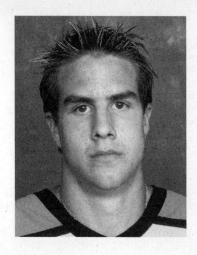

Career statistics:

GP	G	A	TP	PIM
80	20	28	48	22

1999-2000 statistics:

GP	G	A	TP	+/-	PIM	PP	SH	GW	GT	S	PCT
80	20	28	48	+11	22	8	1	4	0	159	12.6

LAST SEASON

First NHL season. Tied for first among NHL rookies in power-play goals. Second among NHL rookies in goals. Third among NHL rookies in assists. Fourth among NHL rookies in points. Tied for third on team in power-play goals and shooting percentage. Missed two games due to stomach virus.

THE FINESSE GAME

Gagne is one of those effortless skaters who can be as effective in the closing shifts of the game, when his team is desperate for a goal, as he is in the opening minutes. He doesn't seem to tire. Sleek and fluid, with seamless changes of direction and pace, he can carry the puck without slowing one whit. He plays a strong puck control game, and is one of those puck magnets. He always seems to be involved in the play with the puck.

Gagne is an unselfish player, and works best when teamed with pure finishers. He can score on his own, too, and is a natural goal scorer with an excellent wirst shot. He is outstanding on the power play. He always has his head up and senses his best options.

Gagne needs work on his face-offs. His defensive game is not bad but needs improvement, as might be expected for a player with only one year of pro experience.

THE PHYSICAL GAME

Gagne will get his body in the way but he is not a physical player. He has some problems when the Flyers are facing a team that is big and strong up the middle. In those games, the Flyers usually move him to the wing. He needs to tackle the weight room.

THE INTANGIBLES

There are many scouts who believe that, in the long run, Gagne will prove to be the best forward out of last year's strong rookie crop.

PROJECTION

Assuming the Eric Lindros era has indeed come to an end in Philadelphia, Gagne can be expected to inherit the number two centre's role behind Keith Primeau, and he should move forward off of his impressive rookie totals. A 55-point season would be a big step up.

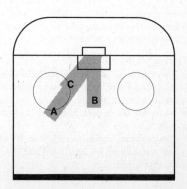

KEITH JONES

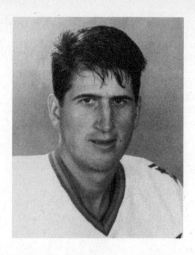

Yrs. of NHL service: 8
Born: Brantford, Ont.; Nov. 8, 1968
Position: right wing
Height: 6-2
Weight: 200
Uniform no.: 20
Shoots: left

Career statistics:

GP	G	A	TP	PIM
480	117	144	258	761

1996-97 statistics:

GP	G	A	TP	+/-	PIM	PP	SH	GW	GT	S	PCT
78	25	23	48	+3	118	14	1	7	0	170	14.7

1997-98 statistics:

GP	G	A	TP	+/-	PIM	PP	SH	GW	GT	S	PCT
23	3	7	10	-4	22	1	0	2	0	31	9.7

1998-99 statistics:

GP	G	A	TP	+/-	PIM	PP	SH	GW	GT	S	PCT
78	20	33	53	+23	98	3	0	3	0	135	14.8

1999-2000 statistics:

GP	G	A	TP	+/-	PIM	PP	SH	GW	GT	S	PCT
57	9	16	25	+8	82	1	0	0	0	92	9.8

LAST SEASON

Missed 25 games due to knee surgery.

THE FINESSE GAME

Jones missed the start of the season with knee surgery and rehab, then never found his rhythm to fit back into a Flyers team that was ruptured at the start of the season, repaired at the end, and fractured again in the postseason.

Jones doesn't have the greatest hands in the world and he'll never be confused with John LeClair, but he has a good shot. Most of his power-play goals came from within 10 feet of the net. He's a spark plug. He likes to make things happen by driving to the front of the net, taking a defenseman with him. His skating is adequate, and he uses quick bursts of speed to power himself to and through the traffic areas.

An eager finisher who plays well at both ends of the ice, Jones keeps the game simple and does his job. He isn't very creative, but his efforts churn up loose pucks for teammates smart enough to trail in his wake. He is the antithesis of a natural scorer, because everything he accomplishes is through effort.

THE PHYSICAL GAME

Jones is energetic and uses his size well. He is tough and willing to pay a physical price; the Flyers could use a couple of more like him. He isn't the biggest player on the ice, but there are nights when you come away thinking he is.

He finishes every check in every zone. He sometimes runs around a bit but he is becoming more responsible defensively.

THE INTANGIBLES

Jones was one of the few friends Eric Lindros had on the team, and it may have resulted in the Flyers leaving him unprotected in the expansion draft. They could also have been gambling that no one would take him because of his salary, but with all that was going on, on and off the ice in Flyerland, it sure looked like a message was being sent.

PROJECTION

Jones should return to 20-goal status — players usually need a season to recuperate from major knee surgery — and it's highly likely he will be doing it with a team other than the Flyers.

DAYMOND LANGKOW

Yrs. of NHL service: 4
Born: Edmonton, Alberta; Sept. 27, 1976
Position: centre
Height: 5-11
Weight: 175
Uniform no.: 18
Shoots: left

Career statistics:

GP	G	A	TP	PIM
311	55	79	134	192

1996-97 statistics:

GP	G	A	TP	+/-	PIM	PP	SH	GW	GT	S	PCT
79	15	13	28	-1	35	3	1	1	1	170	8.8

1997-98 statistics:

GP	G	A	TP	+/-	PIM	PP	SH	GW	GT	S	PCT
68	8	14	22	-9	62	2	0	1	0	156	5.1

1998-99 statistics:

GP	G	A	TP	+/-	PIM	PP	SH	GW	GT	S	PCT
78	14	19	33	-8	39	4	1	2	0	149	9.4

1999-2000 statistics:

GP	G	A	TP	+/-	PIM	PP	SH	GW	GT	S	PCT
82	18	32	50	+1	56	5	0	7	0	222	8.1

LAST SEASON

Tied for team lead in game-winning goals. Third on team in shots. One of three Flyers to appear in all 82 games.

THE FINESSE GAME

Considered a throw-in when the Flyers reacquired Mikael Renberg in 1998, Langkow has emerged as the steal of the deal.

His primary drawback is his size. Small men can succeed in the NHL, however, and it appears Langkow could be one of them, especially on a good-sized Flyers team. He has terrific hockey sense, which is probably his chief asset, to go along with his stick-handling ability and shot. He is a fine passer with good vision, and he is patient with the puck. He is not shy about shooting and possesses an effective wrist shot and slap shot.

Langkow has good speed, spies his options quickly and works hard. He knows what's going to happen before it does, which is the mark of an elite playmaker. He will harass opponents on the forecheck and create turnovers. He could become a solid two-way forward. His defensive awareness is above average.

THE PHYSICAL GAME

Langkow is a spunky, fast, in-your-face kind of player. He has some sandpaper in his game, which gives him an edge ove' small forwards who rely only on their finesse skills. He doesn't mind aggravating people, and he'll throw punches at far bigger men. He won't be intimidated, either, and does his scoring in the trenches despite getting hit. He has a high pain threshold.

THE INTANGIBLES

Langkow shows all the signs of being one of those indespensible forwards that other teams dislike playing against. He finally has found a niche with the Flyers, and if he works hard to keep it he will continue to get his share of ice time.

PROJECTION

Langkow was often forced to step up and play in the top six, and he can survive that for a stretch, but his future is as a third-line checking forward and second-unit power-play forward. He will have a long career in that role and should average 20 goals a season consistently.

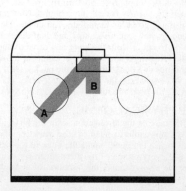

JOHN LECLAIR

Yrs. of NHL service: 9
Born: St. Albans, Vermont; July 5, 1969
Position: left wing
Height: 6-3
Weight: 226
Uniform no.: 10
Shoots: left

Career statistics:

GP	G	A	TP	PIM
665	309	445	615	321

1996-97 statistics:

GP	G	A	TP	+/-	PIM	PP	SH	GW	GT	S	PCT
82	50	47	97	+44	58	10	0	5	2	324	15.4

1997-98 statistics:

GP	G	A	TP	+/-	PIM	PP	SH	GW	GT	S	PCT
82	51	36	87	+30	32	16	0	9	1	303	16.8

1998-99 statistics:

GP	G	A	TP	+/-	PIM	PP	SH	GW	GT	S	PCT
76	43	47	90	+36	30	16	0	7	3	246	17.5

1999-2000 statistics:

GP	G	A	TP	+/-	PIM	PP	SH	GW	GT	S	PCT
82	40	37	77	+8	36	13	0	7	2	249	16.1

LAST SEASON

Led team in goals for second consecutive season. Seventh in NHL in goals. Fifth consecutive season with 40 or more goals. Led team and tied for fifth in NHL in power-play goals. Led team in shots and shooting percentage. Second on team in points. Third on team in assists. One of three Flyers to appear in all 82 games.

THE FINESSE GAME

You rarely find a player who shoots as often as LeClair does and who has such a high shooting percentage. Most snipers waste a lot of shots, and high-percentage shooters are most selective. LeClair combines the two by working to get into the highest quality scoring areas and using a terrific shot with a quick release.

A team can defend against LeClair all night long, then lose position on him once and the puck is in the net. He knows his job is to score goals and he doesn't let up — from the opening whistle to the final second of the game.

He is big enough to post up in front and drive through the melees for all the rebounds, deflections and garbage goals his teammates can create. He also has enough power in his skating and confidence in his strength to cut in from the wing and drive to the net, but the left wing's attributes as a scorer far outweigh his abilities as a puckhandler. If the puck were a football, you could imagine him putting it under his arm, lowering his head and ramming it across the goal line.

THE PHYSICAL GAME

LeClair may be the strongest man in the NHL and is nearly impossible to push off the puck legally. He wants to win the puck, wants the puck in the net and will use every ounce of his strength to try to put it there. He always draws the attention of at least one defender, but accepts his role willingly. Because of a long reach and a big body, LeClair finds a way to place himself between the puck and the defender. Those times when he has a defender under each arm behind the net, he will happily kick the puck to the front.

The frequent disappointment is that LeClair puts so much into winning the puck behind the goal line but doesn't really have the deft touch to make a smooth relay to someone who might be driving to the net. His passing skills are dubious, his puckhandling skills erratic. Teams try to neutralize him by forcing him to carry the puck and make plays.

For all his size and positioning, LeClair isn't a true power forward. He lacks the meanness around the net that a Mark Messier, for example, had in his prime. LeClair is more like Dave Andreychuk. You can hack and whack him, but as his low PIM totals suggest, he rarely fights back.

THE INTANGIBLES

LeClair failed to score a goal against the Devils in a playoff series that the Flyers couldn't close out after holding a 3-1 edge in games. It's going to haunt him all season, and his response to that letdown could manifest itself in a big season.

PROJECTION

The expected departure of Eric Lindros should not affect LeClair, who seemed to team quite happily with either Mark Recchi or Keith Primeau in No. 88's absence. Expect another 40-plus season of goals.

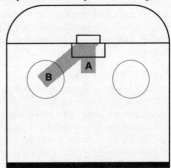

ERIC LINDROS

Yrs. of NHL service: 8
Born: London, Ont.; Feb. 28, 1973
Position: centre
Height: 6-4
Weight: 236
Uniform no.: 88
Shoots: right

Career statistics:

GP	G	A	TP	PIM
486	290	369	659	946

1996-97 statistics:

GP	G	A	TP	+/-	PIM	PP	SH	GW	GT	S	PCT
52	32	47	79	+31	136	9	0	7	2	198	16.2

1997-98 statistics:

GP	G	A	TP	+/-	PIM	PP	SH	GW	GT	S	PCT
63	30	41	71	+14	134	10	1	4	0	202	14.9

1998-99 statistics:

GP	G	A	TP	+/-	PIM	PP	SH	GW	GT	S	PCT
71	40	53	93	+35	120	10	1	2	3	242	16.5

1999-2000 statistics:

GP	G	A	TP	+/-	PIM	PP	SH	GW	GT	S	PCT
55	27	32	59	+11	83	10	1	2	1	187	14.4

LAST SEASON

Second on team in power-play goals and shooting percentage. Third on team in goals and points. Missed 14 games with postconcussion syndrome. Missed five games with concussion. Missed five games with back spasms. Missed two games with bruised left hand.

THE FINESSE GAME

A healthy Lindros can bore straight ahead, freight-train you with the puck and drive to the net. There are times, though, when opponents so completely prepare themselves for his brute power that they are stunned when, instead of plowing through them, he puts the puck through their feet, steps around them then regains it.

Lindros has the balance and soft hands to control the puck in extremely tight quarters and make those nimble moves at the high speed he reaches quickly. That said, it remains more his nature to muscle the puck to a teammate or to the front of the net, and to let his strength do most of the work — because strength remains the watchword of his game.

To offset the torque his arms can generate, the stick Lindros uses has an extremely firm shaft with only a slight curve to the blade. That helps on face-offs, adds velocity to his wrist and snap shots, and makes his backhand shot a significant weapon, both for its speed and its accuracy to the upper corners from close range.

Of course, the caveat to all of the above is that Lindros is seldom healthy, and might never again be at the top of his powers.

THE PHYSICAL GAME

Scott Stevens' devastating check on Lindros in Game 7 of the Eastern Conference finals could well have spelled the end of Lindros's career. He showed great pluck, if not intelligence, by coming back for two playoff games, but it's hard to picture Lindros ever being a physical force again after what he has gone through in the past several seasons.

THE INTANGIBLES

The Flyers retained Lindros's rights at the end of the 2000 season, but with all of the baggage — the Lindros family criticizing the team's medical staff, GM Bob Clarke essentially calling Lindros a mama's (and papa's) boy in public, and being stripped of his captaincy — Lindros either has to get out of Philadelphia or get out of hockey entirely.

PROJECTION

Even if Lindros gets a fresh start with another team, it's likely he will take off the start of the season to ascertain whether he is healthy enough to continue as an NHL player. This could be a sad, ugly premature ending for a star player.

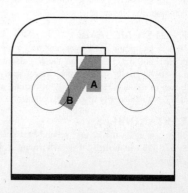

DANIEL MCGILLIS

Yrs. of NHL service: 4
Born: Hawkesbury, Ont.; July 1, 1972
Position: left defense
Height: 6-2
Weight: 220
Uniform no.: 3
Shoots: left

Career statistics:

GP	G	A	TP	PIM
299	29	87	116	277

1996-97 statistics:

GP	G	A	TP	+/-	PIM	PP	SH	GW	GT	S	PCT
73	6	16	22	+2	52	2	1	2	0	139	4.3

1997-98 statistics:

GP	G	A	TP	+/-	PIM	PP	SH	GW	GT	S	PCT
80	11	20	31	-21	109	6	0	3	1	137	8.0

1998-99 statistics:

GP	G	A	TP	+/-	PIM	PP	SH	GW	GT	S	PCT
78	8	37	45	+16	61	6	0	4	0	164	4.9

1999-2000 statistics:

GP	G	A	TP	+/-	PIM	PP	SH	GW	GT	S	PCT
68	4	14	18	+16	55	3	0	1	0	128	3.1

PROJECTION

McGillis needs to improve his point totals to overcome his defensive shortcomings, or improve his defense, because his points totals aren't flashy enough to mask his deficiencies.

LAST SEASON

Third on team in plus-minus. Missed 10 games with groin injury. Missed four games with fractured foot.

THE FINESSE GAME

The problem with not having players in the right slots is that other players are then asked to step into roles they can't quite carry off, and that has been McGillis' woe in Philadelphia. He is asked to overachieve as a number three, and often a number two, defenseman, and with no true number one on the Flyers he can't pull it off every night. Don't blame McGillis.

McGillis was an offensive defenseman in college, and he is still struggling with the defensive part of his game. His scoring skills are not elite class — he'll never be an "offenseman" — but he can provide point production with an edge.

Not a quick skater, McGillis is strong and agile enough for his size. He uses his finesse skills in a defensive role — sweep checks, poke checks — but needs to improve his reads.

THE PHYSICAL GAME

McGillis steps up and challenges, and he's a big, big hitter. He's not afraid to go after the st's also developed a very sly, nasty streak. Even two referees can't catch him in the act. He is quickly becoming a disliked, and not necessarily respected, opponent.

THE INTANGIBLES

McGillis was again the Flyers' second-best defenseman last season behind the all-purpose Eric Desjardins.

KEITH PRIMEAU

Yrs. of NHL service: 10
Born: Toronto, Ont.; Nov. 24, 1971
Position: centre
Height: 6-4
Weight: 210
Uniform no.: 55
Shoots: left

Career statistics:

GP	G	A	TP	PIM
620	186	239	423	1158

1996-97 statistics:

GP	G	A	TP	+/-	PIM	PP	SH	GW	GT	S	PCT
75	26	25	51	-3	161	6	3	2	2	169	15.4

1997-98 statistics:

GP	G	A	TP	+/-	PIM	PP	SH	GW	GT	S	PCT
81	26	37	63	+19	110	7	3	2	0	180	14.4

1998-99 statistics:

GP	G	A	TP	+/-	PIM	PP	SH	GW	GT	S	PCT
78	30	32	62	+8	75	9	1	5	1	178	16.9

1999-2000 statistics:

GP	G	A	TP	+/-	PIM	PP	SH	GW	GT	S	PCT
23	7	10	17	+10	31	1	0	1	0	51	13.7

LAST SEASON

Acquired from Carolina with a fifth-round pick in 2000 for Rod Brind'Amour, Jean-Marc Pelletier and a second-round pick in 2000, Jan. 23, 2000. Missed 12 games with rib injury. Missed 47 games in contract dispute.

THE FINESSE GAME

Although Primeau would probably make a better left wing, with the almost-certain departure of Eric Lindros in Philadelphia, he is by default the Flyers' number one centre. He is'effective there, because of his size and skating, but he doesn't have the good playmaking skills, vision or sense to make the most of the centre-ice position. He doesn't have the puck on his stick much, nor does he use his wingers well or establish much chemistry.

Primeau's assets — his strength, his speed, his work along the boards — would serve him much better as a winger. There is less contact in the middle, and he limits himself by thinking more like a scorer than a power forward.

Primeau has a huge stride with a long reach. A left-hand shot, he will steam down the right side, slide the puck to his backhand, get his feet wide apart for balance, then shield the puck with his body and use his left arm to fend off the defenseman before shovelling the puck to the front of the net. He's clever enough to accept the puck at top speed and, instead of wondering what to do with it, make a move.

Primeau has worked hard at all aspects of his game and can be used in almost any role, including penalty killing and four-on-four play. His face-off work has improved dramatically. He wants to be the go-to guy and has earned that right.

THE PHYSICAL GAME

It's not that Primeau doesn't like to hit, because he does. When he plays with a little bit of an edge he can dominate for a period or an entire game. He has a fiery temper and can lose control. Emotion is a desirable quality, but he has become too valuable a player to spend too much time in the penalty box. He can't be overly tame, though. He needs to wig out once in awhile to scare people.

It used to be that if Primeau had contact with someone, he would be the one to fall. Now, he has improved his posture and balance, and can knock some pretty big men on their cans. Primeau suffered a concussion during the playoffs, and although he returned quickly from the injury, it obviously took its toll.

THE INTANGIBLES

As a left-handed shot, Primeau needs to be paired with a suitable right wing; Mark Recchi could prove to be the man. Over the course of a full season, Primeau will be able to hit his stride, but the Flyers need to find a strong number-two centre to alleviate some of the checking pressure, which was Primeau's problem in Carolina.

PROJECTION

A full season with the Flyers should see Primeau reaching the 80-point range.

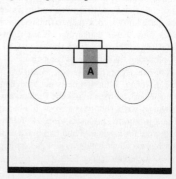

MARK RECCHI

Yrs. of NHL service: 11
Born: Kamloops, B.C.; Feb. 1, 1968
Position: right wing
Height: 5-10
Weight: 180
Uniform no.: 11
Shoots: left

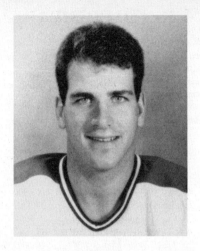

Career statistics:

GP	G	A	TP	PIM
863	361	572	933	619

1996-97 statistics:

GP	G	A	TP	+/-	PIM	PP	SH	GW	GT	S	PCT
82	34	46	80	-1	58	7	2	3	0	202	16.8

1997-98 statistics:

GP	G	A	TP	+/-	PIM	PP	SH	GW	GT	S	PCT
82	32	42	74	+11	51	9	1	6	0	216	14.8

1998-99 statistics:

GP	G	A	TP	+/-	PIM	PP	SH	GW	GT	S	PCT
71	16	37	53	-7	34	3	0	2	0	171	9.4

1999-2000 statistics:

GP	G	A	TP	+/-	PIM	PP	SH	GW	GT	S	PCT
82	28	63	91	+20	50	7	1	5	1	223	12.6

LAST SEASON

Led NHL in assists. Third in league and led team in points. Led NHL in power-play assists (32) and points (39). Tied for team lead in plus-minus. Second on team in goals and shots. Third on team in game-winning goals. Tied for third on team in shooting percentage. One of three Flyers to appear in all 82 games.

THE FINESSE GAME

Easily the Flyers' MVP, Recchi enjoyed a strong rebound season after the one in 1998-99, which was marred by a rare streak of injuries and illness for the onetime ironman. Whatever the Flyers asked of him, Recchi delivered, whether it was playing wing or centre, but where he came through biggest was on the power play.

Recchi, a little package with a lot of firepower, is one of the top small players in the game and certainly one of the most productive. He's a feisty and relentless worker in the offensive zone. He busts into open ice, finding the holes almost before they open, and excells at the give-and-go. His vision and patience with the puck make him the ideal man to find in open ice on the power play. He is dangerous off the right-wing half-boards with his unerring ability to find John LeClair parked at the left side of the crease.

Recchi can score, too. He has a dangerous shot from the off-wing. Although he is not as dynamic as Maurice Richard, he likes to use the Richard cut-back while rifling a wrist shot back across. It's heavy, it's on net and it requires no backswing. He follows his shot to the net for a rebound and can make a play as well. He has excellent hands, vision and anticipation for any scoring opportunity.

Recchi has worked hard to improve his defensive play. He kills penalties well because he hounds the point men aggressively and knocks the puck out of the zone. Then he heads off on a breakaway or forces the defender to pull him down.

He isn't a pretty skater but he always keeps his feet moving. While other players are coasting, Recchi's blades are in motion, and he draws penalties. He is ready to spring into any play. He resembles a puck magnet because he is always going where the puck is. He protects the puck well, keeping it close to his feet.

THE PHYSICAL GAME

Recchi gets chopped at because he doesn't hang around the perimeter. He accepts the punishment to get the job done. He is a solid player with a low centre of gravity, and he is tough to knock off the puck.

THE INTANGIBLES Recchi has become a more unselfish player. The benefit is that defenders have a tougher time playing him — will he shoot or make a play? — and he makes the players around him better. His strong work ethic just continues to intensify.

PROJECTION

In last year's *HSR,* we predicted Recchi could return to the 100-point ranks. He fell just short and should be taking aim at that mark again. If your pool includes power-play stats, Recchi is your man.

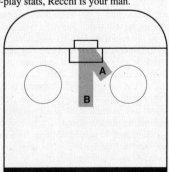

338

LUKE RICHARDSON

Yrs. of NHL service: 13
Born: Ottawa, Ont.; Mar. 26, 1969
Position: left defense
Height: 6-4
Weight: 210
Uniform no.: 22
Shoots: left

Career statistics:

GP	G	A	TP	PIM
947	28	115	143	1571

1996-97 statistics:

GP	G	A	TP	+/-	PIM	PP	SH	GW	GT	S	PCT
82	1	11	12	+9	91	0	0	0	0	67	1.5

1997-98 statistics:

GP	G	A	TP	+/-	PIM	PP	SH	GW	GT	S	PCT
81	2	3	5	+7	139	2	0	0	0	57	3.5

1998-99 statistics:

GP	G	A	TP	+/-	PIM	PP	SH	GW	GT	S	PCT
78	0	6	6	-3	106	0	0	0	0	49	.0

1999-2000 statistics:

GP	G	A	TP	+/-	PIM	PP	SH	GW	GT	S	PCT
74	2	5	7	+14	140	0	0	1	0	50	4.0

LAST SEASON

Second on team in penalty minutes. Missed five games with bruised clavicle. Missed two games with suspension. Missed one game due to coach's decision.

THE FINESSE GAME

Richardson can sometimes play solid defense, but he is more often indecisive. When to step up at the blueline, when to back off: you can see the thought process at work in his head, and so can the attacker.

Richardson is a good skater with lateral mobility and balance, but not much speed. To a degree, he overcomes some of his skating flaws by simply taking up as much space as he can with his size. He can't carry the puck and doesn't jump up into the rush well. He seldom uses his point shot, which is merely adequate.

Defensively, Richardson doesn't know when to stay in front of his net and when to challenge in the corners. Despite his 11 years in the league, the necessary improvement hasn't always shown. At least Richardson has become less of a headhunter and doesn't run around looking for the big hit.

THE PHYSICAL GAME

Richardson is the kind of player you hate to play against but love to have on your side. He hits to hurt and is an imposing presence on the ice. He scares people. When he checks he separates the puck carrier from the puck and doesn't let the man get back into play. When he is on the ice his teammates play a bit bigger and braver. He plays hurt.

THE INTANGIBLES

Richardson's abilities are limited, and his attitude had him looking for a trade at the end of the 1998-99 season. But something caused Richardson (the lack of interest from other clubs?) to stop sulking, and he became a serviceable player who saw steady work.

PROJECTION

Richardson's role is as a physical stay-at-home defender; his point totals will remain low (10 to 15 points).

CHRIS THERIEN

Yrs. of NHL service: 6
Born: Ottawa, Ont.; Dec. 14, 1971
Position: left defense
Height: 6-4
Weight: 230
Uniform no.: 6
Shoots: left

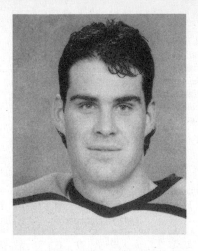

Career statistics:

GP	G	A	TP	PIM
433	21	89	110	385

1996-97 statistics:

GP	G	A	TP	+/-	PIM	PP	SH	GW	GT	S	PCT
71	2	22	24	+26	64	0	0	0	0	107	1.9

1997-98 statistics:

GP	G	A	TP	+/-	PIM	PP	SH	GW	GT	S	PCT
78	3	16	19	+5	80	1	0	1	0	102	2.9

1998-99 statistics:

GP	G	A	TP	+/-	PIM	PP	SH	GW	GT	S	PCT
74	3	15	18	+16	48	1	0	0	0	115	2.6

1999-2000 statistics:

GP	G	A	TP	+/-	PIM	PP	SH	GW	GT	S	PCT
80	4	9	13	+11	66	1	0	1	0	126	3.2

LAST SEASON

Missed one game due to personal reasons. Missed one game due to coach's decision.

THE FINESSE GAME

Although not particularly quick, Therien is a fluid skater for his size and has improving offensive instincts. He handles the puck well and looks to move it as his first option, but he can skate it out of the defensive zone and make a crisp pass while in motion. If that option is not available, he keeps it simple and bangs the puck off the boards.

Good balance allows Therien to maximize his size when, rather than use the typical big-man play and slide on the ice, he takes a stride, drops to one knee and keeps his stick flat on the ice — making himself a larger and wider obstacle.

Therien doesn't have much lateral speed, but he is a strong, straight-ahead skater who can get up the ice in a hurry. He also has enough offensive sense that he can play the point on the power play.

THE PHYSICAL GAME

Therien uses his reach to good advantage. He can dominate physically and has started punishing opposing forwards in front of the net in penalty-killing situations. Extremely alert away from the puck, he dedicates himself to gaining body position and making sure his man doesn't get it.

Therien knows big defensemen can be penalty magnets, but he keeps much of his game within the rules. He keeps the elbows down, and plays an effective, clean physical game. When he hits along the boards or battles in the corners, he tends to lower his body position and use his weight to smear an opponent along the boards. (Other big defensemen are too upright in those situations or try to use their arms to pin opponents, which isn't as effective.) Therien makes his heft and bulk work for him.

THE INTANGIBLES

Therien is a top-four defenseman in Philadelphia and handles a lot of ice time, but he will never be a dominating rearguard. He needs to play with a mobile defenseman. He is a bit exposed when he doesn't get to play with a partner like Eric Desjardins. Therien needs to be motivated at times.

PROJECTION

Therien's offensive instincts do not translate into points, because he usually takes only one or two shots per game. Nonetheless, he plays fairly mistake-free hockey and has channelled his enthusiasm into dogged, effective play, making him a key contributor. He is a fairly typical journeyman.

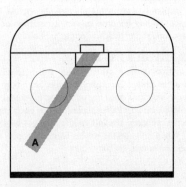

RICK TOCCHET

Yrs. of NHL service: 16
Born: Scarborough, Ont.; Apr. 9, 1964
Position: right wing
Height: 6-0
Weight: 205
Uniform no.: 92
Shoots: right

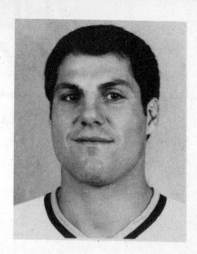

Career statistics:

GP	G	A	TP	PIM
1070	426	686	912	2863

1996-97 statistics:

GP	G	A	TP	+/-	PIM	PP	SH	GW	GT	S	PCT
53	21	19	40	-3	98	4	0	2	1	157	13.4

1997-98 statistics:

GP	G	A	TP	+/-	PIM	PP	SH	GW	GT	S	PCT
68	26	19	45	+1	157	8	0	6	0	161	16.1

1998-99 statistics:

GP	G	A	TP	+/-	PIM	PP	SH	GW	GT	S	PCT
81	26	30	56	+5	147	6	1	5	0	178	14.6

1999-2000 statistics:

GP	G	A	TP	+/-	PIM	PP	SH	GW	GT	S	PCT
80	15	20	35	-1	90	4	0	1	1	130	11.5

LAST SEASON

Acquired by Philadelphia from Phoenix for Mikael Renberg, Mar. 8, 2000. Missed two games with flu. Played in 1,000th career NHL game.

THE FINESSE GAME

Tocchet has worked hard to make the most of the finesse skills he possesses, and that makes everything loom larger. His skating is powerful, though he does not have great mobility or breakaway speed. He is explosive in short bursts and is most effective in small areas. He works extremely well down low and in traffic. He drives to the front of the net and into the corners for the puck.

Tocchet's shooting skills are better than his passing skills. He has limited vision of the ice for making a creative play but is a master at the bang-bang play. He'll smack in rebounds and deflections and set screens as defenders try to knock him down. He does his best work on the goalie's front porch.

Because of his strong, accurate wrist shot, Tocchet gets most of his goals from close range, though he can also fire a one-timer from the tops of the circles. He'll rarely waste a shot from the blueline. He is a good give-and-go player because his quickness allows him to jump into the holes. Because he lacks stickhandling prowess, he beats few people one-on-one.

THE PHYSICAL GAME

There is no hiding from Tocchet. He is a tough hitter and he frequently gets his stick and elbows up. He has long had a history of letting his emotions get the better of him, and although he has matured somewhat, he is acutely aware of his position as one of the few tough, physical forwards on a team of finesse players. Tocchet knows he must play rugged to be effective and he can do that cleanly, but he will also get everyone's attention by bending the rules. With more judicious use of his ice time — he is no longer a front-line player — Tocchet can be very effective.

THE INTANGIBLES

Tocchet's work ethic is inspiring. He is always one of the last players off the ice, has he is usually working on puckhandling drills. Before games, he is one of the first to the rink and is riding the bike; after games, he is lifting weights. He started his career as a goon but has remade himself into a solid NHLer. He was healthy again last season, and as long as he can stay on his feet he'll be an impact player. He is a positive role model to have on hand to teach younger players the importance of a work ethic.

PROJECTION

Tocchet's days as a 30-goal scorer are over. He can still get 15 goals in a role in which his physical play is more important than his production. An unrestricted free agent, he could rejoin the Coyotes.

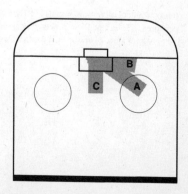

PHOENIX COYOTES

Players' Statistics 1999-2000

POS.	NO.	PLAYER	GP	G	A	PTS	+/-	PIM	PP	SH	GW	GT	S	PCT
C	97	JEREMY ROENICK	75	34	44	78	11	102	6	3	12	1	192	17.7
R	19	SHANE DOAN	81	26	25	51	6	66	1	1	4		221	11.8
C	39	TRAVIS GREEN	78	25	21	46	-4	45	6		2	1	157	15.9
L	17	GREG ADAMS	69	19	27	46	-1	14	5				129	14.7
R	11	DALLAS DRAKE	79	15	30	45	11	62		2	5		127	11.8
L	7	KEITH TKACHUK	50	22	21	43	7	82	5	1	1		183	12.0
D	27	TEPPO NUMMINEN	79	8	34	42	21	16	2		2		126	6.3
D	21	JYRKI LUMME	74	8	32	40	9	44	4		3		142	5.6
C	10	*TREVOR LETOWSKI	82	19	20	39	2	20	3	4	3		125	15.2
R	20	MIKAEL RENBERG	72	10	25	35	-1	32	3		1		122	8.2
C	36	JUHA YLONEN	76	6	23	29	-6	12		1	1		82	7.3
L	18	MIKA ALATALO	82	10	17	27	-3	36	1		1		107	9.3
D	3	KEITH CARNEY	82	4	20	24	11	87			1		73	5.5
D	4	LYLE ODELEIN	73	2	22	24	-9	123	1		1		89	2.2
L	26	MIKE SULLIVAN	79	5	10	15	-4	10		2	1		59	8.5
C	12	BENOIT HOGUE	27	3	10	13	-1	10					39	7.7
D	23	CHRIS JOSEPH	47	2	9	11	-8	6	1				86	2.3
D	24	STAN NECKAR	66	2	8	10	1	36					34	5.9
L	29	LOUIE DEBRUSK	61	4	3	7	1	78					24	16.7
D	33	J.J. DAIGNEAULT	53	1	6	7	-17	22					44	2.3
D	15	*RADOSLAV SUCHY	60		6	6	2	16					36	
C	8	DANIEL BRIERE	13	1	1	2	0					1	9	11.1
R	20	DAVID OLIVER	9	1		1	0	2	1				6	16.7
L	62	*JEAN-GUY TRUDEL	1				-1							
C	64	*WYATT SMITH	2				-2							
L	70	*KEVIN SAWYER	3				1	12						
C	14	*TAVIS HANSEN	5				0						2	
G	42	*ROBERT ESCHE	8				0	4					1	
G	31	BOB ESSENSA	30				0							
G	1	SEAN BURKE	42				0	12						

GP = games played; G = goals; A = assists; PTS = points; +/- = goals-for minus goals-against while player is on ice; PIM = penalties in minutes; PP = power-play goals; SH = shorthanded goals; GW = game-winning goals; GT = game-tying goals; S = no. of shots; PCT = percentage of goals to shots; * = rookie

GREG ADAMS

Yrs. of NHL service: 16
Born: Nelson, B.C.; Aug. 1, 1963
Position: left wing
Height: 6-3
Weight: 195
Uniform no.: 17
Shoots: left

Career statistics:

GP	G	A	TP	PIM
996	344	376	720	316

1996-97 statistics:

GP	G	A	TP	+/-	PIM	PP	SH	GW	GT	S	PCT
50	21	15	36	+27	2	5	0	4	1	113	18.6

1997-98 statistics:

GP	G	A	TP	+/-	PIM	PP	SH	GW	GT	S	PCT
49	14	18	32	+11	20	7	0	1	0	75	18.7

1998-99 statistics:

GP	G	A	TP	+/-	PIM	PP	SH	GW	GT	S	PCT
75	19	24	43	-1	26	5	0	3	0	176	10.8

1999-2000 statistics:

GP	G	A	TP	+/-	PIM	PP	SH	GW	GT	S	PCT
69	19	27	46	-1	14	5	0	0	0	129	14.7

LAST SEASON

Third on team in power-play goals. Tied for third on team in points. Missed 11 games with sinus surgery.

THE FINESSE GAME

Adams is faster than he looks. He has a long, almost lazy stride, but he covers a lot of ground quickly and with an apparent lack of effort.

He can shoot a hard slap shot on the fly off the wing, but most of his goals come from within five feet of the net. He drives fearlessly to the goal and likes to arrive by the most expedient route possible. If that means crashing through defensemen, then so be it. Adams has good, shifty moves in deep and is an unselfish player. He played a lot of centre early in his career and is nearly as good a playmaker as a finisher. He has excellent hands for redirections and rebounds.

One of Adams's best scoring moves is a high backhand in tight. He always has his head up and is looking for the holes; one of the few knocks on him is that he doesn't shoot enough. He has worked hard at improving his defensive awareness and has become a reliable player. He reads his defensemen's pinches well and is always back to cover up at the point.

THE PHYSICAL GAME

Adams has a light frame and always plays hard, which is why he is so vulnerable to injury. He is nearly always wearing an ice pack or getting medical attention for a nick or bruise, if not a broken bone or nerve damage. Although he enjoyed a fairly healthy season last year, Adams has become increasingly fragile, but keeps coming back. For someone who spends as much time getting whacked in the high-traffic areas, he has a remarkably long fuse. He remains calm and determined, and seldom takes bad retaliatory penalties.

THE INTANGIBLES

The problem with Adams is that he is often hurt, and usually with a serious injury. He can accomplish so much when he is in the lineup, but you can never count on a full season. He is an extremely popular player with his teammates and the fans. You keep waiting for Adams to fade, but he keeps coming back with a serviceable season. Adams was an unrestricted free agent during the off-season and could be on the move again.

PROJECTION

Adams will probably miss about 15 to 20 games, for one medical reason or another, but will still find a way to score 45 or 50 points.

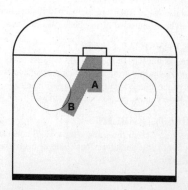

DANIEL BRIERE

Yrs. of NHL service: 2
Born: Gatineau, Quebec; Oct. 6, 1977
Position: centre
Height: 5-9
Weight: 160
Uniform no.: 8
Shoots: left

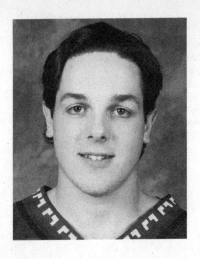

Career statistics:

GP	G	A	TP	PIM
77	9	15	24	30

1997-98 statistics:

GP	G	A	TP	+/-	PIM	PP	SH	GW	GT	S	PCT
5	1	0	1	+1	2	0	0	0	0	4	25.0

1998-99 statistics:

GP	G	A	TP	+/-	PIM	PP	SH	GW	GT	S	PCT
64	8	14	22	-3	30	2	0	2	0	90	8.9

1999-2000 statistics:

GP	G	A	TP	+/-	PIM	PP	SH	GW	GT	S	PCT
13	1	1	2	0	0	0	0	0	1	9	11.1

LAST SEASON

Second NHL season. Appeared in 58 games with Springfield (AHL), scoring 29-42 — 71.

THE FINESSE GAME

Briere is an exciting young player whose only drawback is his lack of size. Fortunately for him, the Coyotes have some good-sized wingers to use up front with him, and with a player of Briere's talent, room can be made for a smaller player — but Briere has to earn it.

He has a great release on an accurate shot, but Briere's chief asset is as a playmaker. He will be dynamite on the power play, with the extra space allowing him the extra half-second of time to make a play. He uses his time and space wisely. He has a great passing touch with the puck, plus terrific hockey sense and vision. He knows how to play this game.

Briere is an excellent, shifty skater, which serves him well in the offensive zone since players will be forced to restrain him rather than hit him. If the crackdown on restraining fouls continues into the new season, Briere will be a dynamic force. Defensively, he has to use his skating and his hand skills to survive. He will be outmuscled in any physical matchups.

THE PHYSICAL GAME

Briere has not played in the NHL with the feisty side he has shown in the minors, which could have been a result of the injury. He needs to play with an edge, like Theo Fleury in his prime.

THE INTANGIBLES

Briere didn't seem the same after a 1998 concussion (courtesy of Ruslan Salei). This could be his make-or-break season.

PROJECTION

Most of his points will be assists, not goals, and we would rather wait a season to see how he develops. But it wouldn't be a surprise to see Briere score 45 to 50 points this season if he wins a job.

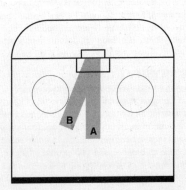

KEITH CARNEY

Yrs. of NHL service: 8
Born: Providence, R.I.; Feb. 3, 1970
Position: left defense
Height: 6-2
Weight: 205
Uniform no.: 3
Shoots: left

Career statistics:

GP	G	A	TP	PIM
506	25	96	121	519

1996-97 statistics:

GP	G	A	TP	+/-	PIM	PP	SH	GW	GT	S	PCT
81	3	15	18	+26	62	0	0	1	0	77	3.9

1997-98 statistics:

GP	G	A	TP	+/-	PIM	PP	SH	GW	GT	S	PCT
80	3	19	22	-2	91	1	1	0	0	71	4.2

1998-99 statistics:

GP	G	A	TP	+/-	PIM	PP	SH	GW	GT	S	PCT
82	2	14	16	+15	62	0	2	0	0	62	3.2

1999-2000 statistics:

GP	G	A	TP	+/-	PIM	PP	SH	GW	GT	S	PCT
82	4	20	24	+11	87	0	0	1	0	73	5.5

LAST SEASON

Tied for second on team in plus-minus. Third on team in penalty minutes. Career highs in assists and points. One of three Coyotes to appear in all 82 games.

THE FINESSE GAME

Carney was considered an offensive defenseman when he first tried to break into the NHL, but he lacked the elite skills to succeed on that style alone. He has turned his finesse skills to his defensive advantage and emphasizes play in his own zone, though he is capable of contributing some offense.

Carney is quick and agile and he positions himself well defensively. He is a smart power-play point man who works on the second unit on the right side. He is among the NHL's better penalty killers, and he has good hockey sense and great anticipation. He reads the play well, is a fine skater and moves the puck smoothly and quickly out of the zone. He is a very good shot-blocker.

Carney compliments an offensive partner well, and has successfully partnered Teppo Numminen. He is not strictly stay-at-home, though. He picks his spots wisely.

THE PHYSICAL GAME

Carney is not a hitter but he will get in the way of people; instead of punishing; he ties up his man effectively. A well-conditioned athlete, he is an honest worker who is about the last one off the ice in practice. He does tend to take bad penalties.

THE INTANGIBLES

Carney is a number four or five defenseman being used as a number two or three in Phoenix, so he can't be criticized when he falls short of the mark. He is quiet and steady, but 21 minutes of ice time a night against other teams' top lines is a tall order, and he will wear down again late in the season if he is used that way.

PROJECTION

His focus on defense will again limit Carney's total to around 20 points.

SHANE DOAN

Yrs. of NHL service: 5
Born: Halkirk, Alberta; Oct. 10, 1976
Position: right wing
Height: 6-1
Weight: 215
Uniform no.: 19
Shoots: right

Career statistics:

GP	G	A	TP	PIM
330	48	65	113	305

1996-97 statistics:

GP	G	A	TP	+/-	PIM	PP	SH	GW	GT	S	PCT
63	4	8	12	-3	49	0	0	0	0	100	4.0

1997-98 statistics:

GP	G	A	TP	+/-	PIM	PP	SH	GW	GT	S	PCT
33	5	6	11	-3	35	0	0	3	0	42	11.9

1998-99 statistics:

GP	G	A	TP	+/-	PIM	PP	SH	GW	GT	S	PCT
79	6	16	22	-5	54	0	0	0	0	156	3.8

1999-2000 statistics:

GP	G	A	TP	+/-	PIM	PP	SH	GW	GT	S	PCT
81	26	25	51	+6	66	1	1	4	0	221	11.8

LAST SEASON

Led team in shots. Second on team in goals and points. Career highs in goals, assists and points. Third on team in game-winning goals. Missed one game due to coach's decision.

THE FINESSE GAME

Doan's game is speed. He is fast and strong, and forechecks aggressively and intelligently along the wall and in the corners. He intimidates with his skating because he gets in on a defenseman fast. Once he gains control of the puck he finds the open man in front of the net. He isn't overly creative, but will thrive on the dump-and-chase play, where he can just skate on his wing and race for the puck.

Doan has an acceptable wrist and slap shot and last season finally decided to try it out on NHL goalies. What a surprise! That scoring touch he had in junior never left. He has stopped thinking purely like a checker and drives to the net instead of turning away from the play.

Playing with Jeremy Roenick, Doan saw power-play time and was given plenty of responsibility to score. He is an excellent penalty-killer and added a huge dimension to his game when he started scoring. Doan had more goals and points last year than in his previous four seasons combined.

THE PHYSICAL GAME

Doan is strong and a very good body checker. He seems to have a mean streak lurking under his exterior. He will lay some hard hits on people. He plays with a little edge but doesn't take many bad penalties.

THE INTANGIBLES

Doan took the big step forward last season, making good on the promising offensive upside that was lurking beneath his conservaive surface to become the Coyotes' top right wing. Not many forwards score 25 goals and play as well defensively and physically as Doan. He is well-respected by teammates and coaches and could be the next captain of the Coyotes.

PROJECTION

Doan can develop into a Jere Lehtinen type of forward who can score 25 goals a season.

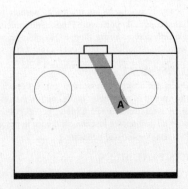

JOE JUNEAU

Yrs. of NHL service: 8
Born: Pont-Rouge, Que.; Jan. 5, 1968
Position: centre/left wing
Height: 6-0
Weight: 195
Uniform no.: 90
Shoots: right

Career statistics:

GP	G	A	TP	PIM
547	127	287	466	194

1996-97 statistics:

GP	G	A	TP	+/-	PIM	PP	SH	GW	GT	S	PCT
58	15	27	42	-11	8	9	1	3	0	124	12.1

1997-98 statistics:

GP	G	A	TP	+/-	PIM	PP	SH	GW	GT	S	PCT
56	9	22	31	-8	26	4	1	1	0	87	10.3

1998-99 statistics:

GP	G	A	TP	+/-	PIM	PP	SH	GW	GT	S	PCT
72	15	28	43	-4	22	2	1	3	0	150	10.0

1999-2000 statistics:

GP	G	A	TP	+/-	PIM	PP	SH	GW	GT	S	PCT
65	13	24	37	+3	22	2	0	2	0	126	10.3

LAST SEASON

Drafted by Minnesota from Ottawa in Expansion Draft, June 23, 2000. Acquired by Phoenix from Minnesota for rights to Rickard Wallin, June 23, 2000. Missed seven games with recurring hip flexor injury.

THE FINESSE GAME

A natural centre, even when playing in the middle, Juneau gravitates to the left wing and generates most of his scoring chances from there. He varies his play selection. He will take the puck to the net on one rush, then pull up at the top of the circle and hit the trailer late on the next rush.

Although the circles are his office, Juneau is not exclusively a perimeter player. He will go into traffic, and is bigger than he looks on-ice. His quick feet and light hands make him seem smaller, because he is so crafty with the puck.

Laterally, Juneau is among the best skaters in the NHL. He has an extra gear that allows him to pull away from people. He does not have breakaway speed, but he has great anticipation and gets the jump on a defender with his first few steps.

Juneau doesn't shoot the puck enough and gets a little intimidated when there is a scramble for a loose puck in front of the net. He is not always willing to sacrifice his body that way. He shoots a tad prematurely. When he could wait and have the goalie down and out, he unloads quickly, because he hears footsteps. His best shot is a one-timer from the left circle.

Juneau is fine on draws and kills penalties.

THE PHYSICAL GAME

Juneau has improved his toughness and willingness to take a hit to make a play — probably dressing-room osmosis — but he is still something of a featherweight. You can almost see him psych himself up to make or take a hit. It doesn't come naturally to him.

THE INTANGIBLES

Juneau played last season with Ottawa, and despite the vacancy at centre, didn't shine. He is clearly a support player now, which is what Phoenix will be asking of him.

PROJECTION

Juneau had a better-than-average (for him) playoffs, which is probably what attracted the Coyotes. He can provide special teams help and contribute 40 points, mostly assists.

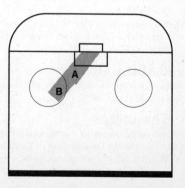

NIKOLAI KHABIBULIN

Yrs. of NHL service: 5
Born: Sverdlovsk, Russia; Jan. 13, 1973
Position: goaltender
Height: 6-1
Weight: 176
Uniform no.: 35
Catches: left

Career statistics:

GP	MIN	GA	SO	GAA	A	PIM
284	16027	735	21	2.75	6	62

1996-97 statistics:

GP	MIN	GAA	W	L	T	SO	GA	S	SAPCT	PIM
72	4091	2.83	30	33	6	7	193	2094	.908	16

1997-98 statistics:

GP	MIN	GAA	W	L	T	SO	GA	S	SAPCT	PIM
70	4026	2.74	30	28	10	4	184	1835	.900	22

1998-99 statistics:

GP	MIN	GAA	W	L	T	SO	GA	S	SAPCT	PIM
63	3657	2.13	32	23	7	8	130	1681	.923	8

1999-2000 statistics:

Missed NHL season.

PROJECTION

As long as he is back in shape and is limited to around 60 starts, he should post 25 to 28 wins.

LAST SEASON

Missed NHL season in contract dispute. Appeared in 33 games with Long Beach (IHL), posting a 21-11-1 record with 1.83 GAA and five shutouts.

THE PHYSICAL GAME

Khabibulin is a butterfly-style goalie who positions himself like a shortstop. He gets down low and always gets his body behind the shot, and he stays on his feet and moves with the shooter. He may perform the best split-save in the league: it's stunningly graceful and athletic, and his legs look about five feet long. He leaves only the tiniest five-hole because he also gets the paddle of his stick down low across the front of the crease. Shooters have to go upstairs on him, but he doesn't give away a lot of net high.

Khabibulin is solid in his fundamentals. He plays well out on the top of his crease, which is unusual for Russian goalies, who tend to stay deep in their net. He is aggressive but patient at the same time, and waits for the shooter to commit first. He still has room to improve his puckhandling.

Khabibulin needs to have his minutes watched closely. He tends to break down sharply with too much activity.

THE MENTAL GAME

Khabibulin is able to maintain a strong attitude despite a lack of offensive support.

THE INTANGIBLES

Missing an entire season in a contract dispute was more damaging to the Coyotes than to Khabibulin's career. Phoenix is expected to re-sign him for the season.

TREVOR LETOWSKI

Yrs. of NHL service: 1
Born: Thunder Bay, Ont.; Apr. 5, 1977
Position: centre
Height: 5-10
Weight: 173
Uniform no.: 10
Shoots: right

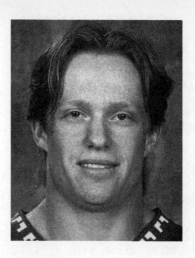

Career statistics:

GP	G	A	TP	PIM
96	21	22	43	22

1998-99 statistics:

GP	G	A	TP	+/-	PIM	PP	SH	GW	GT	S	PCT
14	2	2	4	+1	2	0	0	0	0	8	25.0

1999-2000 statistics:

GP	G	A	TP	+/-	PIM	PP	SH	GW	GT	S	PCT
82	19	20	39	+2	20	3	4	3	0	125	15.2

LAST SEASON

First NHL season. Led team and tied for third in NHL in shorthanded goals. Tied for third among NHL rookies in goals. Third on team and third among NHL rookies in shooting percentage. Sixth among NHL rookies in points. One of three Coyotes to appear in all 82 games.

THE FINESSE GAME

Letowski is a shorthanded specialist. In addition to his four shorthanded goals, he assisted on three more shorties. He wasn't too shabby on a second power-play unit or at even strength, either.

Letowski is a small centre with good quickness. He devoted himself to the defensive aspects of the game even as a junior, which probably accounts for his low draft position (174th overall in 1996), though he did have seasons of 99 and 108 points after his draft year. After paying his dues in the minors, he has turned into one of those nifty little forwards who could find an NHL job with any team.

Letowksi has good anticipation and makes excellent reads in his forechecking. He pressures the points on the power play to harry them into making bad passes, which he can then convert into shorthanded scoring chances. He is an opportunistic scorer with soft hands and a good, patient shot. He is average on face-offs.

THE PHYSICAL GAME

Letowkski has a big heart in a small frame. He is very competitive and not shy about going after the puck in the corners, though he lacks the strength for one-on-one battles. He is Jeremy Roenick's Mini-Me.

THE INTANGIBLES

One of the overlooked freshman stars of last year, Letowski played with the poise of a much more experienced player. He is a restricted free agent, but one of the players worth spending money on.

PROJECTION

Letowski ended the year as Phoenix' number two centre, and appears to have a lock on the job for this season. He should make the next step to the 45- to 50-point range.

JYRKI LUMME

Yrs. of NHL service: 12
Born: Tampere, Finland; July 16, 1966
Position: right defense
Height: 6-1
Weight: 205
Uniform no.: 20
Shoots: left

Career statistics:

GP	G	A	TP	PIM
788	100	313	413	508

1996-97 statistics:

GP	G	A	TP	+/-	PIM	PP	SH	GW	GT	S	PCT
66	11	24	35	+8	32	5	0	2	0	107	10.3

1997-98 statistics:

GP	G	A	TP	+/-	PIM	PP	SH	GW	GT	S	PCT
74	9	21	30	-25	34	4	0	1	1	117	7.7

1998-99 statistics:

GP	G	A	TP	+/-	PIM	PP	SH	GW	GT	S	PCT
60	7	21	28	+5	34	1	0	4	0	121	5.8

1999-2000 statistics:

GP	G	A	TP	+/-	PIM	PP	SH	GW	GT	S	PCT
74	8	32	40	+9	44	4	0	3	0	142	5.6

LAST SEASON

Third on team in assists. Missed four games with bruised hand. Missed three games with bruised shoulder.

THE FINESSE GAME

Lumme is one of the better-kept secrets in the NHL. He is an accomplished puck carrier who can rush the puck out of danger and make a smart first pass to start the attack. He likes to gamble a bit offensively, but he has the skating ability to be able to wheel back into a defensive mode.

Lumme's point shot isn't overpowering, but he keeps it low and on net and times it well. He is a smart point man. He has very good hands and is adept at keeping the puck in. He also uses his lateral mobility to slide along the blueline into the centre to quarterback the power play. He will also glide to the top of the circle for a shot. He can control a game and make everyone play at his pace.

Defensively, Lumme uses his hand skills for sweep- and poke-checks. He will challenge at the blueline to try to knock the puck free. He is tough to beat one-on-one, and always comes out of the corner with the puck. He uses his feet well along the boards to keep the puck alive, and he's a strong penalty killer because of his range and anticipation.

THE PHYSICAL GAME

Lumme is all finesse. He will take a hit to protect the puck or make a play, but he won't throw himself at anybody. Other teams like to key on Lumme, because if he gets hit often and hard enough, he can be taken out of a game early.

THE INTANGIBLES

Although the Finn is not a number one defenseman, because his all-around skills aren't good enough, he's just a cut below the NHL's best rearguards. He has improved defensively, but his key value remains his open-ice play and his involvement in the attack. He makes the job easy for his partner.

PROJECTION

Lumme didn't quite make the 60-point comeback season we predicted for him. It didn't help that the team wasn't very good up front. With no immediate upgrade in sight, we'll scale back our expectations to 45 to 50 points.

BRAD MAY

Yrs. of NHL service: 9
Born: Toronto, Ont.; Nov. 29, 1971
Position: left wing
Height: 6-1
Weight: 210
Uniform no.: 9
Shoots: left

Career statistics:

GP	G	A	TP	PIM
577	91	110	201	1556

1996-97 statistics:

GP	G	A	TP	+/-	PIM	PP	SH	GW	GT	S	PCT
42	3	4	7	-8	106	1	0	1	0	75	4.0

1997-98 statistics:

GP	G	A	TP	+/-	PIM	PP	SH	GW	GT	S	PCT
63	13	10	23	+2	154	4	0	2	0	97	13.4

1998-99 statistics:

GP	G	A	TP	+/-	PIM	PP	SH	GW	GT	S	PCT
66	6	11	17	-14	102	1	0	1	0	91	6.6

1999-2000 statistics:

GP	G	A	TP	+/-	PIM	PP	SH	GW	GT	S	PCT
59	9	7	16	-2	90	0	0	3	0	66	13.6

There's a reason why May was cheaper.

PROJECTION

Injuries were again a factor for May's poor production, but not an alibi. He won't do much beyond 10 to 15 goals, even thought he will get top six playing time in Phoenix.

LAST SEASON

Acquired from Vancouver for future considerations, June 24, 2000. Third on Canucks in penalty minutes. Tied for third on Canucks in game-winning goals. Missed 13 games with knee injury.

THE FINESSE GAME

May is better off trying to make the safe play instead of the big play, as more often than not, the safe play leads to the big play. He has more than brute strength on his side and possesses nice passing skills, but he's not a very smart player and doesn't think the game well at all.

He is not much of a finisher, and it's starting to look like he never will be. He needs to feel relaxed and confident. He is certainly not a natural scorer; his goals come off his hard work around the net. He is a patient shooter and uses the defenseman well as a screen.

May does have sound defensive instincts. He is not a very fast or agile skater so he has to be conscious of keeping his position. He won't be able to race back to cover for an error in judgement.

THE PHYSICAL GAME

May is strong along the boards and in front of the net. A well-conditioned athlete, he has good balance and leg drive and is difficult to knock off his feet. He takes a hit to make a play and protects the puck well. He plays through pain.

THE INTANGIBLES

Phoenix signed May as a cheaper replacement for Dallas Drake (lost to St. Louis in free agency).

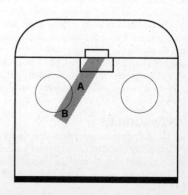

STANISLAV NECKAR

Yrs. of NHL service: 5
Born: Ceske Budejovice, Czech Republic; Dec. 22, 1975
Position: left defense
Height: 6-1
Weight: 196
Uniform no.: 24
Shoots: left

Career statistics:

GP	G	A	TP	PIM
261	8	22	30	160

1995-96 statistics:

GP	G	A	TP	+/-	PIM	PP	SH	GW	GT	S	PCT
82	3	9	12	-16	54	1	0	0	0	57	5.3

1996-97 statistics:

GP	G	A	TP	+/-	PIM	PP	SH	GW	GT	S	PCT
5	0	0	0	+2	2	0	0	0	0	3	0.0

1997-98 statistics:

GP	G	A	TP	+/-	PIM	PP	SH	GW	GT	S	PCT
60	2	2	4	-14	31	0	0	0	0	43	4.7

1999-2000 statistics:

GP	G	A	TP	+/-	PIM	PP	SH	GW	GT	S	PCT
66	2	8	10	+1	36	0	0	0	0	34	5.9

LAST SEASON

Missed 13 games with knee injury.

THE FINESSE GAME

Neckar understands the position of defenseman but he is fundamentally unsound when it comes time to putting all of the components together. He has to use his body more in addition to learning body position.

Neckar will never put up many points because he doesn't have much offensive sense or very good hands. He has a slow release on his point shot and doesn't do much that's creative, other than put his head down and shoot. He's not a stellar puckhandler or passer.

He is a polished skater, especially backwards. He is not often beaten wide. His forte is his defensive play.

THE PHYSICAL GAME

Neckar is not a good open-ice hitter, but is very strong along the boards and in the corners. Although he will fight if provoked he is not very good at it. He needs to get much stronger. His cardiovascular conditioning is fine, and he can handle a lot of ice time (thrives on it, as a matter of fact, though he averaged 14 minutes last season), but he has to learn to stick and pin his man better. Neckar is a power defenseman, which is valuable.

THE INTANGIBLES

Injuries — including major reconstructive knee surgery and being shuffled through three organizations in a very short time — retarded Neckar's development. Last season was an important step back for him. His confidence has been gradually rebuilt. He wasn't a standout in any way, but he played some very steady, physical defense and should continue to move forward. He finished especially well and had a decent playoffs.

PROJECTION

Neckar should solidify his position in Phoenix's top four and score 10 to 15 points.

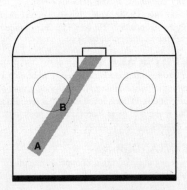

TEPPO NUMMINEN

Yrs. of NHL service: 12
Born: Tampere, Finland; July 3, 1968
Position: left defense
Height: 6-1
Weight: 190
Uniform no.: 27
Shoots: right

Career statistics:

GP	G	A	TP	PIM
872	84	341	425	319

1996-97 statistics:

GP	G	A	TP	+/-	PIM	PP	SH	GW	GT	S	PCT
82	2	25	27	-3	28	0	0	0	0	135	1.5

1997-98 statistics:

GP	G	A	TP	+/-	PIM	PP	SH	GW	GT	S	PCT
82	11	40	51	+25	30	6	0	2	0	126	8.7

1998-99 statistics:

GP	G	A	TP	+/-	PIM	PP	SH	GW	GT	S	PCT
82	10	30	40	+3	30	1	0	0	2	156	6.4

1999-2000 statistics:

GP	G	A	TP	+/-	PIM	PP	SH	GW	GT	S	PCT
79	8	34	42	+21	16	2	0	2	0	126	6.3

LAST SEASON

Led team in plus-minus. Second on team in assists. Led team defensemen in points for third consecutive season. Missed two games with hip flexor, ending consecutive games-played streak at 360 games.

THE FINESSE GAME

Numminen's agility and anticipation make him look much faster than he is. A graceful skater with a smooth change of direction, he never telegraphs what he is about to do. His skating makes him valuable on the first penalty-killing unit. He will not get caught out of position and is seldom bested one-on-one.

If he is under pressure, Numminen is not afraid to give up the puck on a dump-and-chase, rather than force a neutral-zone play. He works best with a partner with some offensive savvy. Otherwise, he takes too much of the offensive game on himself, and his plays look forced. He would rather dish off than rush with the puck, and he is a crisp passer, moving the puck briskly and seldom overhandling it. He is terrific at making the first pass to move the puck out of the zone.

Numminen is not a finisher. He joins the play but doesn't lead it. Most of his offense is generated from point shots or passes in deep. He works the right point on the power play.

He is uncannily adept at keeping the puck in at the point, frustrating opponents who try to clear it out around the boards. He intentionally shoots the puck wide for tip-ins by his surehanded forwards. He is not afraid to pinch, either.

THE PHYSICAL GAME

Numminen plays an acceptable physical game. He can be intimidated and doesn't scare attackers, who will attempt to drive through him to the net. Opponents get a strong forecheck on him to neutralize his smart passing game. He'll employ his body as a last resort, but would rather use his stick and gain the puck. He is even-tempered and not at all nasty. He averaged 23 minutes per game last season and faced other teams' top lines night after night and looked tired down the stretch.

THE INTANGIBLES

Numminen is underrated. He's not a Norris Trophy type, but no NHL team would hesitate to take him and put him on its top pair. That won't happen anytime soon: he signed a long-term contract extension in midseason.

PROJECTION

Numminen is a complete, if not elite, defenseman, and capable of scoring 45 points.

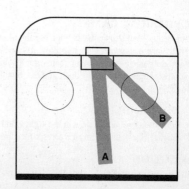

ROBERT REICHEL

Yrs. of NHL service: 9
Born: Litvinov, Czech.; June 25, 1971
Position: centre
Height: 5-10
Weight: 185
Uniform no.: 16
Shoots: left

Career statistics:

GP	G	A	TP	PIM
602	209	298	507	492

1996-97 statistics:

GP	G	A	TP	+/-	PIM	PP	SH	GW	GT	S	PCT
82	21	41	62	+5	26	6	1	3	0	214	9.8

1997-98 statistics:

GP	G	A	TP	+/-	PIM	PP	SH	GW	GT	S	PCT
82	25	40	65	-11	32	8	0	2	2	201	12.4

1998-99 statistics:

GP	G	A	TP	+/-	PIM	PP	SH	GW	GT	S	PCT
83	26	43	69	-13	54	8	1	4	1	236	11.0

1999-2000 statistics:

Did not play in NHL.

LAST SEASON

Did not play in NHL.

THE FINESSE GAME

Reichel's strength in as a playmaker. He thinks "pass" first and needs to play on a line with a pure finisher. He is one of those gifted passers who can make a scoring opportunity materialize when there appears to be no hole; his wingers have to be alert because the puck will find its way to their tape. He has great control of the puck in open ice or in scrums.

Reichel will certainly take the shot when he's got it, but he won't force a pass to someone who is in a worse scoring position than he is. He has an explosive shot with a lot of velocity on it. He pursues loose pucks in front and wheels around to the back of the net to look for an open teammate. He is good in traffic.

At least that's how Reichel plays when things are going well. He's just as likely to go into a slump or a pout, and he doesn't add much to a team when he isn't piling up points.

THE PHYSICAL GAME

Reichel is small but sturdy. He is not a big fan of contact and there are some who question his hockey courage. He's not a player other teams are afraid to play against. He is well-conditioned and can handle a lot of ice time.

THE INTANGIBLES

In the right situation, and if he's in the right frame of mind, Reichel can help a team as a top six forward.

PROJECTION

For the second time, Reichel left the NHL to play a season in Europe. Phoenix will resolve the contract squabble, either with a raise or a trade, and Reichel should return for another half-hearted NHL season of 60 or so points.

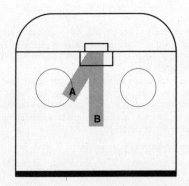

JEREMY ROENICK

Yrs. of NHL service: 11
Born: Boston, Mass.; Jan. 17, 1970
Position: centre
Height: 6-0
Weight: 190
Uniform no.: 97
Shoots: right

Career statistics:

GP	G	A	TP	PIM
828	378	493	871	1020

1996-97 statistics:

GP	G	A	TP	+/-	PIM	PP	SH	GW	GT	S	PCT
72	29	40	69	-7	115	10	3	7	0	228	12.7

1997-98 statistics:

GP	G	A	TP	+/-	PIM	PP	SH	GW	GT	S	PCT
79	24	32	56	+5	103	6	1	3	1	182	13.2

1998-99 statistics:

GP	G	A	TP	+/-	PIM	PP	SH	GW	GT	S	PCT
78	24	48	72	+7	130	4	0	3	0	203	11.8

1999-2000 statistics:

GP	G	A	TP	+/-	PIM	PP	SH	GW	GT	S	PCT
75	34	44	78	+11	102	6	3	12	1	192	17.7

LAST SEASON

Led team in assists and points, both for second consecutive season. Most points since 1993-94. Led team in goals, game-winning goals and shots. Second in NHL in game-winning goals. Tied for first on team in power-play goals. Second on team in shorthanded goals, shots and penalty minutes. Tied for second on team in plus-minus. Missed five games due to suspension.

THE FINESSE GAME

On nights when Roenick is on, he's a force. He skates, he hits, he's mean, he's nasty, he scores. Injuries and age have combined to take some of that famous edge off, but last season was as close Roenick has been to 100 percent in a long time.

He commands a lot of attention on the ice, drawing away defenders to open up ice for his teammates. He has great acceleration and can turn quickly, change directions or burn a defender with outside speed. A defenseman who plays aggressively against him will be left staring at the back of Roenick's jersey as he skips by en route to the net. He has to be forced into the high-traffic areas, where his lack of size and strength are the only things that derail him.

Roenick has great quickness and is tough to handle one-on-one. He won't make the same move or take the same shot twice in a row. He has a variety of shots and can score from almost anywhere on the ice. He can rifle a wrist shot from 30 feet away, or else wait until the goalie is down and lift in a backhand from in tight. He has a drag-and-pull move to his backhand that is highly deceptive, and it also keeps the goalie guessing because he is able to show a backhand but pull it quickly to his forehand once he has frozen the goalie.

THE PHYSICAL GAME

Roenick plays with such a headlong style that injuries are routine. He has trouble keeping weight on, and he tends to wear down late in the season, as he did in the final quarter of last season. He was the Coyotes' leading scorer in their brief playoff appearance.

Roenick takes aggressive penalties — smashing people into the boards, getting his elbows up — and he never backs down. He plays through pain and is highly competitive. His suspension was for a slashing incident.

THE INTANGIBLES

Roenick hasn't been a 50-goal scorer since 1992-93, and no longer belongs among the NHL's goal-scoring elite. It would be interesting to see what happens if the Coyotes get a bona fide number two centre to take some of the checking pressure off him. With one year left on his $5-million deal, will new owner Wayne Gretzky okay a trade? Roenick's trade value may never be this high again, and it would spare the Coyotes the headache of trying to re-sign him or lose him as a free agent in 2001.

PROJECTION

Roenick reclaimed his rank as the team's top clutch player. The Coyotes rarely won when he had a bad game and rarely lost when he had a good one. He's no longer a 100-point player; 75 to 80 is his range.

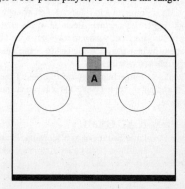

KEITH TKACHUK

Yrs. of NHL service: 8
Born: Melrose, Mass.; Mar. 28, 1972
Position: left wing
Height: 6-2
Weight: 210
Uniform no.: 7
Shoots: left

Career statistics:

GP	G	A	TP	PIM
576	294	258	552	1400

1996-97 statistics:

GP	G	A	TP	+/-	PIM	PP	SH	GW	GT	S	PCT
81	52	34	86	-1	228	9	2	7	1	296	17.6

1997-98 statistics:

GP	G	A	TP	+/-	PIM	PP	SH	GW	GT	S	PCT
69	40	26	66	+9	147	11	0	8	1	232	17.2

1998-99 statistics:

GP	G	A	TP	+/-	PIM	PP	SH	GW	GT	S	PCT
68	36	32	68	+22	151	11	2	7	1	258	14.0

1999-2000 statistics:

GP	G	A	TP	+/-	PIM	PP	SH	GW	GT	S	PCT
50	22	21	43	+7	82	5	1	1	0	183	12.0

LAST SEASON

Missed 23 games with ankle injuries. Missed four games with back spasms. Missed three games with sore neck. Missed two games due to suspension.

THE FINESSE GAME

In front of the net, Tkachuk will bang and crash but he also has soft hands for picking pucks out of skates and flicking strong wrist shots. He can also kick at the puck with his skates without going down. He has a quick release. He looks at the net, not down at the puck on his stick, and finds the openings. He has a great feel for the puck. From the hash marks in, he is one of the most dangerous forwards in the NHL. Eliminating the man-in-the-crease rule has increased his effectiveness and his production, because the trenches are where Tkachuk does his best work. He doesn't just stand in the slot, either, but moves in and out.

Tkachuk has improved his one-step quickness and agility. He is powerful and balanced, and often drives through bigger defensemen. Because of his size and strength, he is frequently used to take draws, and it's a rare face-off where the opposing centre doesn't end up getting smacked by him.

Thanks to numerous nagging injuries, Tkachuk never found his rhythm; 1999-2000 was pretty much a lost season.

THE PHYSICAL GAME

Tkachuk is volatile and mean as a scorpion. He takes bad penalties, and since he has a reputation around the league for getting his stick up and retaliating for hits with a quick rabbit-punch to the head, referees keep a close eye on him. He tried to be more disciplined last season, but still took penalties at the wrong times. He can be tough without buying a time-share in the penalty box.

Tkachuk can dictate the physical tempo of a game with his work in the corners and along the boards. He comes in hard with big-time hits on the forecheck.

THE INTANGIBLES

The Coyotes nearly had him dealt for Keith Primeau. Now, heading into the final year of a contract that will pay him $8.3 million, Phoenix will probably find it impossible to move him, unless the cash-strapped Coyotes pick up part of the contract.

PROJECTION

A healthy Tkachuk is capable of netting 50 goals. Whether he will be able to stay healthy is a huge question mark, given his recent medical history.

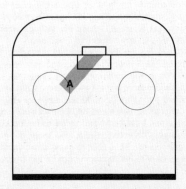

JUHA YLONEN

Yrs. of NHL service: 3
Born: Helsinki, Finland; Feb. 13, 1972
Position: centre
Height: 6-1
Weight: 185
Uniform no.: 36
Shoots: left

Career statistics:

GP	G	A	TP	PIM
192	13	51	64	42

1996-97 statistics:

GP	G	A	TP	+/-	PIM	PP	SH	GW	GT	S	PCT
2	0	0	0	0	0	0	0	0		2	0.0

1997-98 statistics:

GP	G	A	TP	+/-	PIM	PP	SH	GW	GT	S	PCT
55	1	11	12	-3	10	0	1	0	0	60	1.7

1998-99 statistics:

GP	G	A	TP	+/-	PIM	PP	SH	GW	GT	S	PCT
59	6	17	23	+18	20	2	0	1	0	66	9.1

1999-2000 statistics:

GP	G	A	TP	+/-	PIM	PP	SH	GW	GT	S	PCT
76	6	23	29	-6	12	0	1	1	0	82	7.3

of his game is his defense.

LAST SEASON

Career highs in games played, assists and points. Missed four games with hip flexor. Missed one game due to personal reasons.

THE FINESSE GAME

Ylonen earned a job with the Coyotes because of his defense. He may have some offensive upsisde, but it's his aggressive forechecking that keeps him in business.

The Coyotes waited a long time for Ylonen's game to mature. He is very quick, and brings an efficiency to the game. He has excellent hockey sense and thinks the game really well.

His game has some offensive upside. His numbers have been improving gradually season by season, but he has never thought of himself as a big-time scorer and he won't be. He has enough skill level to play alongside a skater like Shane Doan and not look out of place, though Ylonen won't be the finisher. He is not especially creative.

THE PHYSICAL GAME

Ylonen was third among Phoenix forwards in ice time, averaging close to 17 minutes a night. He is an average-sized player who is not very physical, but he plays well positionally and is durable.

THE INTANGIBLES

Ylonen took over as the team's third-line centre and clicked with fellow Finn Mika Alatalo.

PROJECTION

Ylonen can score points in the low 30s, but the beauty

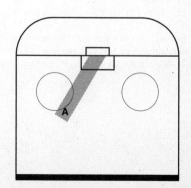

PITTSBURGH PENGUINS

Players' Statistics 1999-2000

POS.	NO.	PLAYER	GP	G	A	PTS	+/-	PIM	PP	SH	GW	GT	S	PCT
R	68	JAROMIR JAGR	63	42	54	96	25	50	10		5	1	290	14.5
C	27	ALEXEI KOVALEV	82	26	40	66	-3	94	9	2	4	1	254	10.2
C	20	ROBERT LANG	78	23	42	65	-9	14	13		5	1	142	16.2
C	82	MARTIN STRAKA	71	20	39	59	24	26	3	1	2		146	13.7
C	38	JAN HRDINA	70	13	33	46	13	43	3		1		84	15.5
R	95	ALEXEI MOROZOV	68	12	19	31	12	14		1			101	11.9
D	71	JIRI SLEGR	74	11	20	31	20	82			2	1	144	7.6
R	14	PAT FALLOON	63	9	22	31	4	14	1				92	9.8
L	18	JOSEF BERANEK	71	13	12	25	-12	57	4		1		139	9.4
R	36	MATTHEW BARNABY	64	12	12	24	3	197			3		80	15.0
R	44	ROB BROWN	50	10	13	23	-13	10	4		3		73	13.7
C	29	TYLER WRIGHT	50	12	10	22	4	45			1		68	17.6
D	28	*MICHAL ROZSIVAL	75	4	17	21	11	48	1		1		73	5.5
D	5	JANNE LAUKKANEN	71	2	18	20	17	67	1				81	2.5
L	9	RENE CORBET	52	5	10	15	-11	60	1				109	4.6
D	11	DARIUS KASPARAITIS	73	3	12	15	-12	146	1		1		76	3.9
D	8	HANS JONSSON	68	3	11	14	-5	12		1	1		49	6.1
D	24	IAN MORAN	73	4	8	12	-10	28					58	6.9
D	6	BOB BOUGHNER	73	3	4	7	-11	166	1		1		40	7.5
C	59	ROBERT DOME	22	2	5	7	1						27	7.4
D	7	*ANDREW FERENCE	30	2	4	6	3	20			1		26	7.7
R	17	TOM CHORSKE	33	1	5	6	-2	2					14	7.1
D	34	PETER POPOVIC	54	1	5	6	-8	30					23	4.3
R	23	STEPHEN LEACH	56	2	3	5	-11	24			1		41	4.9
D	32	JOHN SLANEY	29	1	4	5	-10	10	1				27	3.7
L	12	MARTIN SONNENBERG	14	1	2	3	0		1				19	5.3
D	3	DANIEL TREBIL	3	1		1	2						2	50.0
G	30	*J-SEBASTIEN AUBIN	51		1	1	0	2						
D	22	SVEN BUTENSCHON	3					3					2	
G	1	PETER SKUDRA	20					0						
R	16	DENNIS BONVIE	28				-2	80					6	
G	31	RON TUGNUTT	51					0						

GP = games played; G = goals; A = assists; PTS = points; +/- = goals-for minus goals-against while player is on ice; PIM = penalties in minutes; PP = power-play goals; SH = shorthanded goals; GW = game-winning goals; GT = game-tying goals; S = no. of shots; PCT = percentage of goals to shots; * = rookie

JEAN-SEBASTIEN AUBIN

Yrs. of NHL service: 1
Born: Montreal, Que.; July 19, 1977
Position: goaltender
Height: 5-11
Weight: 183
Uniform no.: 30
Catches: right

Career statistics:

GP	MIN	GA	SO	GAA	A	PIM
68	3545	148	4	2.50	1	2

1998-99 statistics:

GP	MIN	GAA	W	L	T	SO	GA	S	SAPCT	PIM
17	756	2.22	4	3	6	2	28	304	.908	0

1999-2000 statistics:

GP	MIN	GAA	W	L	T	SO	GA	S	SAPCT	PIM
51	2789	2.58	23	21	3	2	120	1392	.914	2

LAST SEASON

First NHL season. Led NHL rookie goalies in wins. Missed two games with shoulder injury. Missed three games with ankle injury.

THE PHYSICAL GAME

Aubin is an average-sized butterfly-style goalie. He relies on his reflexes a lot and needs to develop better fundamentals. He has good balance and lateral movement. He uses his stick and his blocker well.

Aubin isn't a great puckhandler, but he is fairly adept at using his stick to break up plays around his net. He is strong and possesses good stamina. He stops the puck and controls his rebounds well. Pittsburgh has good face-off men, so he is not afraid to pounce on a loose puck for a draw.

Aubin likes to challenge the shooter. He gets in lulls where he stays deep and isn't out on the top of his crease, but he seems to adjust quickly. He will be more steady than spectacular — not a bad trait in a young goalie.

THE MENTAL GAME

Aubin is ready to be a number one goalie. He is very competitive and has the desire to improve and win.

THE INTANGIBLES

Aubin's ankle sprain prevented him from strutting his stuff in the playoffs, but it's clear he is Pittsburgh's goalie of the future, and his future is now. He would benefit greatly from the Penguins adding a veteran backup as a mentor.

PROJECTION

Aubin should get 25 to 28 wins.

MATTHEW BARNABY

Yrs. of NHL service: 7
Born: Ottawa, Ont.; May 4, 1973
Position: right wing
Height: 6-0
Weight: 170
Uniform no.: 36
Shoots: left

Career statistics:

GP	G	A	TP	PIM
399	61	93	154	1479

1996-97 statistics:

GP	G	A	TP	+/-	PIM	PP	SH	GW	GT	S	PCT
68	19	24	43	+16	249	2	0	1	0	121	15.7

1997-98 statistics:

GP	G	A	TP	+/-	PIM	PP	SH	GW	GT	S	PCT
72	5	20	25	+8	289	0	0	2	0	96	5.2

1998-99 statistics:

GP	G	A	TP	+/-	PIM	PP	SH	GW	GT	S	PCT
62	6	16	22	-12	177	1	0	3	0	79	7.6

1999-2000 statistics:

GP	G	A	TP	+/-	PIM	PP	SH	GW	GT	S	PCT
64	12	12	24	+3	197	0	0	3	0	80	15.0

LAST SEASON

Led team and fourth in NHL in penalty minutes. Missed eight games with concussion. Missed five games with strained knee. Missed five games due to suspension.

THE FINESSE GAME

Barnaby's offensive skills are minimal. He gets some room because of his reputation, and that buys him a little time around the net to get a shot away. He is utterly fearless and dives right into the thick of the action going for loose pucks.

But no one hires Barnaby for his scoring touch. His game is marked by his fierce intensity. He hits anyone, but especially loves going after the other teams' big names. He is infuriating.

He skates well enough not to look out of place and is strong and balanced on his feet. He will do anything to win. If he could develop a better scoring touch he would start reminding people of Dale Hunter.

THE PHYSICAL GAME

Barnaby brings a lot of energy to the game; considering his size, it's a wonder he survived the season. He has to do some cheap stuff to survive, which makes him an even more irritating opponent. Big guys especially hate him, because it's a no-win when a Bob Probert or Randy McKay takes on the poor underdog Barnaby. But he's so obnoxious they just can't help it.

THE INTANGIBLES

Barnaby seems like an ill fit among the sleek Penguins, but they need someone with grit and Barnaby is full of it.

PROJECTION

Barnaby would be even more valuable to his team if he ignored some of the nonsense and became a little better player. Expect about 20 points and the requisite 200 penalty minutes.

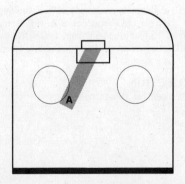

JOSEF BERANEK

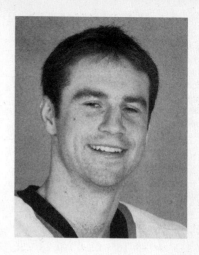

Yrs. of NHL service: 9
Born: Litvinov, Czech.; Oct, 25, 1969
Position: left wing
Height: 6-2
Weight: 195
Uniform no.: 20
Shoots: left

Career statistics:

GP	G	A	TP	PIM
461	109	130	239	355

1996-97 statistics:
Did not play in NHL

1997-98 statistics:

GP	G	A	TP	+/-	PIM	PP	SH	GW	GT	S	PCT
8	3	1	4	-1	4	4	1	0	0	15	20.0

1998-99 statistics:

GP	G	A	TP	+/-	PIM	PP	SH	GW	GT	S	PCT
66	19	30	49	+6	23	7	0	2	0	160	11.9

1999-2000 statistics:

GP	G	A	TP	+/-	PIM	PP	SH	GW	GT	S	PCT
71	13	12	25	-12	57	4	0	1	0	139	9.4

LAST SEASON

Acquired from Edmonton for German Titov, Mar. 14, 2000.

THE FINESSE GAME

Defenders can usually guess "pass" when playing against Beranek. He thinks to make a play first before taking a shot, though he has an accurate shot, especially his wrister. He will often try to force a pass to a teammate instead of taking the shot himself, even when he is in a superior shooting position.

Beranek uses all of the ice, which makes him a natural for the European-style attack used by the Oilers. He can play centre or wing; when on the wing he brings a centre's playmaking ability and vision to the position.

Beranek needs to keep his feet moving. He is a good skater, but not a great one.

THE PHYSICAL GAME

Beranek played in Europe the previous season, and may have hit the wall around midyear in his return to the NHL schedule. His knee surgery is also a concern, though he did return for two games in the playoffs. He doesn't play with much grit.

THE INTANGIBLES

Beranek scored eight points in 13 games with Pittsburgh after the trade, then vanished in the postseason.

PROJECTION

Beranek has never been able to come close to the 28-goal season he had with Philadelphia in 1993-94. He is likely to stay around the 20-goal mark with 40 assists, especially if he gets power-play time with Jaromir Jagr.

BOB BOUGHNER

Yrs. of NHL service: 5
Born: Windsor, Ont.; Mar. 8, 1971
Position: right defense
Height: 6-0
Weight: 206
Uniform no.: 6
Shoots: right

Career statistics:

GP	G	A	TP	PIM
329	8	25	33	797

1996-97 statistics:

GP	G	A	TP	+/-	PIM	PP	SH	GW	GT	S	PCT
77	1	7	8	+12	225	0	0	0	0	34	2.9

1997-98 statistics:

GP	G	A	TP	+/-	PIM	PP	SH	GW	GT	S	PCT
69	1	3	4	+5	165	0	0	0	0	26	3.8

1998-99 statistics:

GP	G	A	TP	+/-	PIM	PP	SH	GW	GT	S	PCT
79	3	10	13	-6	137	0	0	1	0	59	5.1

1999-2000 statistics:

GP	G	A	TP	+/-	PIM	PP	SH	GW	GT	S	PCT
73	3	4	7	-11	166	1	0	1	0	40	7.5

PROJECTION

Boughner will log his 17 to 18 minutes a night and 12 to 13 points a season.

LAST SEASON

Acquired from Nashville for Pavel Skrbek, Mar. 13, 2000.

THE FINESSE GAME

Boughner gets the most out of his talent. For the most part he's a defensive defenseman who plays a conservative game, but who competes hard every night and maxes out his modest skills.

Boughner plays every night against other teams' top lines. He wouldn't be a top two defenseman on many other teams, but the Penguins are bound to ask him to play against other teams' top lines on most nights.

He doesn't have great hands, so he doesn't get involved much in the offense. He doesn't (or shouldn't) try to make the first pass out of the zone. He has to be reminded to keep it simple and just bang the puck off the glass. Playing on a good-skating team will allow Boughner to make more low-risk passes and not try to do too much himself.

THE PHYSICAL GAME

Boughner is very aggressive and loves to hit. His teammates appreciate the way he pays the price and stands up for them. He made a memorable open-ice hit on Keith Primeau that resulted in a concussion for the Flyers centre.

THE INTANGIBLES

Boughner is one of those steady, experienced character guys that always seem in such short supply and high demand. He helped settle the Penguins' defense immediately upon his arrival.

RENE CORBET

Yrs. of NHL service: 5
Born: Victoriaville, Que.; June 25, 1973
Position: left wing
Height: 6-0
Weight: 187
Uniform no.: 20
Shoots: left

Career statistics:

GP	G	A	TP	PIM
319	50	65	115	363

1996-97 statistics:

GP	G	A	TP	+/-	PIM	PP	SH	GW	GT	S	PCT
76	12	15	27	+14	67	1	0	3	1	128	9.4

1997-98 statistics:

GP	G	A	TP	+/-	PIM	PP	SH	GW	GT	S	PCT
68	16	12	28	+8	133	4	0	4	2	117	13.7

1998-99 statistics:

GP	G	A	TP	+/-	PIM	PP	SH	GW	GT	S	PCT
73	13	18	31	+1	68	3	0	1	0	127	10.2

1999-2000 statistics:

GP	G	A	TP	+/-	PIM	PP	SH	GW	GT	S	PCT
52	5	10	15	-11	60	1	0	0	0	109	4.6

PROJECTION

Corbet can score 15 to 20 goals as a role player with the Penguins.

LAST SEASON

Acquired from Calgary with Tyler Moss for Brad Werenka, Mar. 14, 2000. Missed 10 games with bruised shoulder.

THE FINESSE GAME

Corbet has solid NHL credentials as a defensively re-sponsible forward, who also has some offensive up-side. That makes him a good fit in Pittsburgh, which could use some grit up front.

He has a terrific shot with a great release. He was a scoring champion in junior (QMJHL) and tore it up pretty good in the AHL, so he has confidence in his ability to find the net.

Corbet's defensive work has improved, as has his skating. As a young player, he hired Olympic speed skater Gaetan Boucher as a coach. Corbet has quick acceleration, and carrying the puck doesn't slow him down.

THE PHYSICAL GAME

Corbet is of average height but a little on the light side. He actually looks somewhat fragile, since he tends to work in the high-traffic areas and gets bounced around.

THE INTANGIBLES

Not a top-six player, Corbet should work on the third line and get some special teams shifts. He looked like an ideal pickup for a playoff-bound team, but four games into his Penguins career, he suffered a shoulder injury that knocked him out of the rest of the regular season. He returned for seven games in the playoffs and didn't look like his old self.

ROBERT DOME

Yrs. of NHL service: 2
Born: Skalica, Slovakia; Jan. 29, 1979
Position: right wing / centre
Height: 6-0
Weight: 215
Uniform no.: 59
Shoots: left

Career statistics:

GP	G	A	TP	PIM
52	7	7	14	12

1998-99 statistics:

GP	G	A	TP	+/-	PIM	PP	SH	GW	GT	S	PCT
30	5	2	7	-1	12	1	0	0	0	29	17.2

1999-2000 statistics:

GP	G	A	TP	+/-	PIM	PP	SH	GW	GT	S	PCT
22	2	5	7	+1	0	0	0	0	0	27	7.4

LAST SEASON

Appeared in 51 games with Wilkes-Barre (AHL), scoring 12-26 — 38.

THE FINESSE GAME

A first-round draft pick of the Penguins in 1997, Dome is a very good skater with a powerful stride and outside speed. He doesn't have the hand skills or the hockey sense to be a true offensive threat, but he could develop into a nice two-way forward, though the Pens are getting a little tired of waiting for that day to come.

Dome is still a raw talent. He plays a fairly strong game along the boards when he has a mind to, and could become a forechecking force with the right amount of off-ice work and on-ice dedication.

Dome will go through traffic to the net with the puck, but offensively he isn't going to put up great numbers. He is responsible in his own end and will create some things offensively only because of his skating.

THE PHYSICAL GAME

Dome is a bulky player and would probably be more effective if he were to lose 10 or 15 pounds.

THE INTANGIBLES

Maybe new coach Ivan Hlinka will be able to unlock the mystery that is Dome. Dome has to realize the price to pay for a full-time job in the NHL and be willing to pay that price. It's not going to be handed to him, which seems to be his attitude.

PROJECTION

If Dome can snag a full-time role, he could score 15 goals. That might not be enough to keep him from being an ex-Penguin soon.

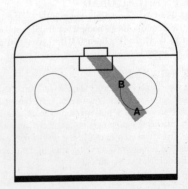

JAN HRDINA

Yrs. of NHL service: 2
Born: Hradec Kralove, Czech.; Feb. 5, 1976
Position: centre
Height: 6-0
Weight: 197
Uniform no.: 38
Shoots: right

Career statistics:

GP	G	A	TP	PIM
152	26	62	88	83

1998-99 statistics:

GP	G	A	TP	+/-	PIM	PP	SH	GW	GT	S	PCT
82	13	29	42	-2	40	3	0	2	0	94	13.8

1999-2000 statistics:

GP	G	A	TP	+/-	PIM	PP	SH	GW	GT	S	PCT
70	13	33	46	+13	43	3	0	1	0	84	15.5

LAST SEASON

Second NHL season. Second on team in shooting percentage. Missed 12 games with sprained ankle.

THE FINESSE GAME

Even taking into account the Jaromir Jagr factor — that anyone playing with the Hart Trophy winner has his status elevated — Hrdina is an impressive specimen.

He is a highly skilled centre whom the Pens have allowed to mature gradually through the minor-league ranks. He does everything well. He is a very good skater with the ability to shift gears and directions effortlessly. He doesn't shoot enough — quite typical of European centres — but he has a terrific wrist shot.

Hrdina is a highly intelligent player in all zones. He is very aware defensively for a young player. Offensively, he is a gifted passer with a sure touch and good vision.

THE PHYSICAL GAME

Hrdina is slightly less than average height but he has a wide body. He fights for the puck and is tough to knock off his feet. He is excellent on draws. Not only does he have quick hands, he is able to tie up the opposing centre's stick, and he uses his feet. He cheats a bit on draws, but usually gets away with it.

THE INTANGIBLES

His injury was a major setback last season, since it seemed to affect his skating, which is such a huge part of his game. Hrdina's major flaw is that he is so intimidated by playing with Jagr that he tries to force passes to him, when Hrdina himself should be taking the shot.

PROJECTION

Hrdina will produce in the 60-point range. With more confidence and consistency, he could get into the 80s, especially if he keeps his job as Jagr's linemate.

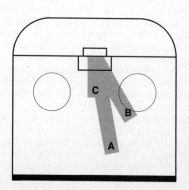

JAROMIR JAGR

Yrs. of NHL service: 10
Born: Kladno, Czech Republic; Feb. 15, 1972
Position: right wing
Height: 6-2
Weight: 216
Uniform no.: 68
Shoots: left

Career statistics:

GP	G	A	TP	PIM
725	387	571	958	551

1996-97 statistics:

GP	G	A	TP	+/-	PIM	PP	SH	GW	GT	S	PCT
63	47	48	95	+22	40	11	2	6	1	234	20.1

1997-98 statistics:

GP	G	A	TP	+/-	PIM	PP	SH	GW	GT	S	PCT
77	35	67	102	+17	64	7	0	8	2	262	13.4

1998-99 statistics:

GP	G	A	TP	+/-	PIM	PP	SH	GW	GT	S	PCT
81	44	83	127	+17	66	10	1	7	2	343	12.8

1999-2000 statistics:

GP	G	A	TP	+/-	PIM	PP	SH	GW	GT	S	PCT
63	42	54	96	+25	50	10	0	5	1	290	14.5

LAST SEASON

Finalist for 2000 Hart Trophy. Won fourth Art Ross Trophy as NHL's leading scorer. Led team and tied for fourth in NHL in goals. Led team and third in NHL in assists. Led team in plus-minus and shots. Fifth in NHL in shots. Tied for team lead in game-winning goals. Second on team in power-play goals. Missed 12 games with pulled hamstring/thigh injury. Missed four games with pulled stomach muscle. Missed two games with bruised upper back. Missed one game with bruised thigh.

THE FINESSE GAME

Opponents know they have one assignment when they play the Penguins: stop Jagr. Few teams can do it. Jagr's exceptional skating and extraordinary ice time make him tough to shadow, even when checkers sag off his less-imposing linemates to key on him.

Jagr is as close to a perfect skater as there is in the NHL. He keeps his body centred over his skates, giving him a low centre of gravity and making it very tough for anyone to knock him off the puck. He has a deep knee bend, for quickness and power. His strokes are long and sure, and he has control over his body and exceptional lateral mobility. He dazzles with his footwork and handles the puck at high tempo. He has been able to maintain his speed and power despite frequent injuries, including a deep thigh bruise from a Michael Peca check last season that eventually required surgery.

Jagr lives and loves to play hockey. He's poetry in motion with his beautifully effortless skating style. And, with his Mario Lemieux-like reach, Jagr can dangle the puck while he's gliding and swooping. He fakes the backhand and goes to his forehand in a flash.

He is also powerful enough to drag a defender with him to the net and push off a strong one-handed shot. He has a big slap shot and can drive it on the fly or fire it with a one-timer off a pass.

THE PHYSICAL GAME

Considering how often he gets pounded and how much ice time he logs, Jagr's durability over the past seven seasons is remarkable. His recurring groin problem resurfaces, but he always seemed to come up with the moves when the team needed him most. Earlier in his career he could be intimidated physically — and he still doesn't like to get hit, but he's not as wimpy as he used to be. He's confident, almost cocky, and tough to catch.

THE INTANGIBLES

Naming Ivan Hlinka as Penguins coach made Jagr happy. He would be even happier if the Pens added some elite level players so he doesn't have to do it all himself. He finished with 30 points more than the next-highest scorer on the Pens, and that's with missing a quarter of the season.

PROJECTION

Jagr failed to break our projected 100-point mark last season, but would have done so easily if he hadn't been injured. Assuming he will have some down time again this season, 100 points and a fifth scoring title are within his grasp.

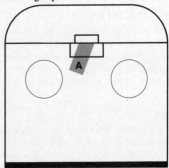

DARIUS KASPARAITIS

Yrs. of NHL service: 8
Born: Elektrenai, Lithuania; Oct. 16, 1972
Position: right defense
Height: 5-10
Weight: 205
Uniform no.: 11
Shoots: left

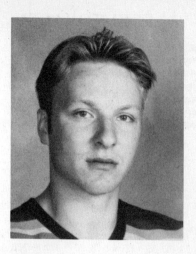

Career statistics:

GP	G	A	TP	PIM
491	16	80	96	866

1996-97 statistics:

GP	G	A	TP	+/-	PIM	PP	SH	GW	GT	S	PCT
75	2	21	23	+17	100	0	0	0	0	58	3.4

1997-98 statistics:

GP	G	A	TP	+/-	PIM	PP	SH	GW	GT	S	PCT
81	4	8	12	+3	127	0	2	0	0	71	5.6

1998-99 statistics:

GP	G	A	TP	+/-	PIM	PP	SH	GW	GT	S	PCT
48	1	4	5	+12	70	0	0	0	0	32	3.1

1999-2000 statistics:

GP	G	A	TP	+/-	PIM	PP	SH	GW	GT	S	PCT
73	3	12	15	-12	146	1	0	1	0	76	3.9

LAST SEASON

Third on team in penalty minutes. Missed four games with knee injury. Missed two games with head injury. Missed three games with two suspensions.

THE FINESSE GAME

Kasparaitis is a strong, powerful skater and he can accelerate in all directions. You can run but you can't hide from this defenseman, who accepts all challenges. He is aggressive in the neutral zone, sometimes overly so, stepping up to break up a team's attack when he would be better off backing off.

Kasparaitis has the skills to occasionally get involved in the offense, although it's not his concern or his strength. He will make a sharp outlet pass and then follow up into the play. He also has good offensive instincts, moves the puck well and, if he plays on his off-side, will open up his forehand for the one-timer. He concentrates heavily on the defensive and physical part of his game, and would be blissfully happy going through the season without a point if he could wreak havoc elsewhere.

Kasparaitis has infectious enthusiasm, which is an inspiration to the rest of his team. There is a purpose to whatever he does. He's highly competitive.

THE PHYSICAL GAME

Kasparaitis is well on his way to succeeding Ulf Samuelsson as the player most NHLers would like to see run over by a bus. It's always borderline interference with Kasparaitis, who uses his stick liberally, waiting three or four seconds after a victim has gotten rid of the puck to apply the lumber. Cross-check, butt-end, high stick — through the course of a season

Kasparaitis will illustrate all of the stick infractions.

His timing isn't always the best, and he has to think about the good of the team rather than indulging in his own vendettas.

Kasparaitis is legitimately tough. It doesn't matter whose name is on back of the jersey — Tkachuk, Modano, Messier — he will goad the stars and the heavyweights equally. He yaps, too, and is as irritating as a car alarm at 3 a.m.

THE INTANGIBLES

Kasparaitis's grit is badly needed in Pittsburgh, which can tend to be a rather fancy team.

PROJECTION

Chalk up another 100 PIM and maybe 20 points, as Kasparaitis will remain one of the Penguins' top four rearguards.

ALEXEI KOVALEV

Yrs. of NHL service: 8
Born: Togliatti, Russia; Feb. 24, 1973
Position: right wing/centre
Height: 6-0
Weight: 205
Uniform no.: 27
Shoots: left

Career statistics:

GP	G	A	TP	PIM
547	165	220	387	590

1996-97 statistics:

GP	G	A	TP	+/-	PIM	PP	SH	GW	GT	S	PCT
45	13	22	35	+11	42	1	0	0	0	110	11.8

1997-98 statistics:

GP	G	A	TP	+/-	PIM	PP	SH	GW	GT	S	PCT
73	23	30	53	-22	44	8	0	3	1	173	13.3

1998-99 statistics:

GP	G	A	TP	+/-	PIM	PP	SH	GW	GT	S	PCT
77	23	30	53	+2	49	6	1	5	0	191	12.0

1999-2000 statistics:

GP	G	A	TP	+/-	PIM	PP	SH	GW	GT	S	PCT
82	26	40	66	-3	94	9	2	4	1	254	10.2

LAST SEASON

Led team in shorthanded goals. Second on team in goals, points and shots. Third on team in assists and power-play goals. Career highs in goals, assists and points. Only Penguin to appear in all 82 games.

THE FINESSE GAME

Kovalev is skilled enough to make breathtaking plays of exquisite grace, and he is stubborn enough to over-handle the puck and manoeuvre himself completely out of the play without the slightest help from an opponent.

You don't often see hands or feet as quick as Kovalev's on a player of his size. He has the dexterity, puck control, strength, balance and speed to beat the first forechecker coming out of the zone or the first line of defense once he crosses the attacking blueline. He is one of the few players in the NHL agile and balanced enough to duck under a check at the side-boards and maintain possession of the puck. Exceptional hands allow him to make remarkable moves, but his hockey thought process doesn't always allow him to finish them off well.

On many occasions, Kovalev's slithery moves don't do enough offensive damage. Sometimes he overhandles, then turns the puck over. Too many times, he fails to get the puck deep. He hates to surrender the puck even when dump-and-chase is the smartest option, and as a result he causes turnovers at the blueline and has to chase any number of opposition breakaways to his team's net.

THE PHYSICAL GAME

The chippier the game, the happier Kovalev is; he'll bring his stick up and wade into the fray. He can be sneaky dirty. He'll run goalies over and try to make it look as if he was pushed into them by a defender. He's so strong and balanced on his skates that when he goes down odds are it's a dive. At the same time, he absorbs all kinds of physical punishment, legal and illegal, and rarely receives the benefit of the doubt from the referees.

Kovalev has very good size and is a willing hitter. He likes to make highlight-reel hits that splatter people. Because he is such a strong skater, he is very hard to knock down unless he's leaning. He makes extensive use of his edges because he combines balance and a long reach to keep the puck well away from his body, and from a defender's. But there are moments when he seems at a 45-degree angle and then he can be nudged over.

THE INTANGIBLES

A happy fit with the EuroPenguins, Kovalev had a surpisingly dull playoffs.

PROJECTION

Given his history of inconsistency, we would hedge our bets on Kovalev matching his career year. He has the ability to score 80 points, but even as the number two winger behind Jaromir Jagr — and thus freed from all that checking attention — Kovalev at 27 isn't likely to surprise.

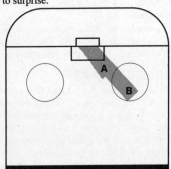

ROBERT LANG

Yrs. of NHL service: 6
Born: Teplice, Czech Republic; Dec. 19, 1970
Position: centre
Height: 6-2
Weight: 216
Uniform no.: 20
Shoots: right

Career statistics:

GP	G	A	TP	PIM
351	72	117	189	80

1996-97 statistics:
Did not play in NHL

1997-98 statistics:
Did not play in NHL

1998-99 statistics:

GP	G	A	TP	+/-	PIM	PP	SH	GW	GT	S	PCT
72	21	23	44	-10	24	7	0	3	3	137	15.3

1999-2000 statistics:

GP	G	A	TP	+/-	PIM	PP	SH	GW	GT	S	PCT
78	23	42	65	-9	14	13	0	5	1	142	16.2

LAST SEASON

Led team in power-play goals and shooting percentage. Tied for team lead in game-winning goals. Second on team in assists. Third on team in points. Career highs in goals, assists and points. Missed two games with mouth injury. Missed one game with back spasms. Missed one game with bruised thumb.

THE FINESSE GAME

Lang has so much talent that he is able to turn a game around with several moves, yet he is so inconsistent that there are nights when he is invisible. Last season he was much better on a nightly basis.

He has deceptive quickness and is very solid on his skates, along with great hands, great hockey sense and the ability to make plays on his forehand or backhand. Players on both wings have to be prepared for a pass that could materialize out of thin air or through a thicket of sticks and skates. He has the presence to draw defenders to him to open up ice for his linemates, and he makes good use of them.

Lang is patient with the puck, in fact, he often holds on too long. He will always pass up a shot if he can make a play instead.

Lang is a smart penalty killer because of his anticipation. He lapses defensively at even strength, however.

THE PHYSICAL GAME

Lang will not take a hit to make a play. He has to show more willingness to hit. He will never trounce anyone, but he has to fight for the puck and fight through his checks.

THE INTANGIBLES

Lang still looks like the player with the best tools to be the centre for Jaromir Jagr, but he frequently played second-line left wing last season.

PROJECTION

Lang took a step forward into the 20-goal range we projected for him. With Ivan Hlinka as new coach, he might get more responsibility, and could improve off last season's totals. He could have an 80-point season ahead.

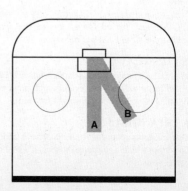

JANNE LAUKKANEN

Yrs. of NHL service: 5
Born: Lahti, Finland; Mar. 19, 1970
Position: left defense
Height: 6-0
Weight: 180
Uniform no.: 27
Shoots: left

Career statistics:

GP	G	A	TP	PIM
291	11	69	80	265

1996-97 statistics:

GP	G	A	TP	+/-	PIM	PP	SH	GW	GT	S	PCT
76	3	18	21	-14	76	2	0	0	0	109	2.8

1997-98 statistics:

GP	G	A	TP	+/-	PIM	PP	SH	GW	GT	S	PCT
60	4	17	21	-15	64	2	0	2	0	69	5.8

1998-99 statistics:

GP	G	A	TP	+/-	PIM	PP	SH	GW	GT	S	PCT
50	1	11	12	+18	40	0	0	0	0	46	2.2

1999-2000 statistics:

GP	G	A	TP	+/-	PIM	PP	SH	GW	GT	S	PCT
71	2	18	20	+17	67	1	0	0	0	81	2.5

LAST SEASON

Acquired from Ottawa with Ron Tugnutt for Tom Barrasso, Mar. 14, 2000. Missed two games with bruised ribs.

THE FINESSE GAME

Laukkanen's hockey sense is about average, but his courage, will to win and character are all very much above average. He is one of the defensemen that his coaches want on the ice in the last minutes of the game, because he will rarely lose a battle. He will do anything to win.

Laukkanen's best physical asset is his skating. He has learned to shift gears smoothly. He will never be a big point producer, though, because he doesn't have a great shot. His hands are pretty good for passing, however. He makes an alert first pass out of the zone and can spot a breaking forward for a home run pass. He earns some power-play time because he is poised with the puck.

Laukkanen kills penalties aggressively and intelligently. He was buried for a time in the strong Colorado system, and is a late bloomer.

THE PHYSICAL GAME

Laukkanen is a brave defenseman who will block shots and battle defensively, even though he is much smaller than most NHL heavyweight forwards.

THE INTANGIBLES

Laukkanen seems recoverd from his serious abdominal surgery of a year ago. He is Pittsburgh's best two-way defenseman.

PROJECTION

Laukkenen can do just a touch more offensively now that he is with Pittsburgh. He scored eight points in 11 games after the trade. He won't maintain that pace, but 30 points isn't too much to ask.

ALEXEI MOROZOV

Yrs. of NHL service: 3
Born: Moscow, Russia; Feb. 16, 1977
Position: right wing
Height: 6-1
Weight: 180
Uniform no.: 95
Shoots: left

Career statistics:

GP	G	A	TP	PIM
211	34	42	76	36

1997-98 statistics:

GP	G	A	TP	+/-	PIM	PP	SH	GW	GT	S	PCT
76	13	13	26	-4	8	2	0	3	0	80	16.3

1998-99 statistics:

GP	G	A	TP	+/-	PIM	PP	SH	GW	GT	S	PCT
67	9	10	19	+5	14	0	0	0	0	75	12.0

1999-2000 statistics:

GP	G	A	TP	+/-	PIM	PP	SH	GW	GT	S	PCT
68	12	19	31	+12	14	0	1	0	0	101	11.9

LAST SEASON

Missed 12 games with charley horse. Missed two games with bruised back.

THE FINESSE GAME

Morozov still has some catching up to do in the coordination department. He can be as awkward as a baby giraffe: all legs, and with a lot of skills that look as if they belong with someone else's body. When the pieces do come together, he looks like he will be a swift skater, able to play the uptempo game that is a Penguins hallmark.

Morozov has a very sneaky, deceptive selection of shots and looks like he will be a big-goal scorer — in terms of importance, if not numbers. He tries to be too cute and make the extra play instead of shooting, but once he learns to use his hard and accurate shot to his advantage, he will be extremely effective. He is a good stickhandler and has a good sense of timing with his passes.

Morozov is still learning the game and will merit more time on the power play once he learns his shot is a bullet that shouldn't be left in the holster.

THE PHYSICAL GAME

Morozov is a little on the stringy side, but he's still growing and will probably fill out into a solid winger. He'll never be confused with a power forward, though.

THE INTANGIBLES

The Penguins keep waiting and waiting and waiting on Morozov. If this isn't his breakthrough year, the Pens will let someone else do the developing.

PROJECTION

Morozov has to post a 20-goal season this year or he will go from prospect to suspect.

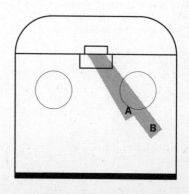

MICHAL ROZSIVAL

Yrs. of NHL service: 1
Born: Vlasim, Czech.; Sept. 3, 1978
Position: right defense
Height: 6-1
Weight: 200
Uniform no.: 28
Shoots: right

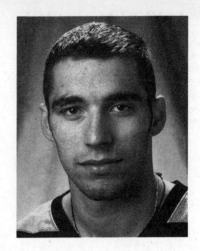

Career statistics:

GP	G	A	TP	PIM
75	4	17	21	48

1999-2000 statistics:

GP	G	A	TP	+/-	PIM	PP	SH	GW	GT	S	PCT
75	4	17	21	+11	48	1	0	1	0	73	5.5

LAST SEASON

First NHL season. Missed two games with hip flexor. Missed five games due to coach's decision.

THE FINESSE GAME

Rozsival has been able to score at the junior- and minor-league levels. He will be more of a two-way defenseman than an offensive defenseman, but he has upside and just needs a little more confidence in his point shot.

Rozsival plays well at both ends of the ice. He has a fairly high panic point. Rozsival is a good passer and playmaker, and is very unselfish. He has built his game from a defensive foundation first, and is tough to beat one-on-one. He is a good skater with speed.

THE PHYSICAL GAME

Rozisval hit the wall down the stretch — he was benched for four of the last seven games — and he needs to improve his conditioning. He's big and strong and plays an abrasive game.

THE INTANGIBLES

Rozsival is yet another one of the Penguins Czech imports who may thrive under new coach Ivan Hlinka.

PROJECTION

Rozsival should be one of Pittsburgh's top four defensemen and should be more productive, with a slight increase to 25 to 30 points.

MARTIN STRAKA

Yrs. of NHL service: 8
Born: Plzen, Czech Republic; Sept. 3, 1972
Position: centre
Height: 5-10
Weight: 178
Uniform no.: 82
Shoots: left

Career statistics:

GP	G	A	TP	PIM
521	132	222	354	202

1996-97 statistics:

GP	G	A	TP	+/-	PIM	PP	SH	GW	GT	S	PCT
55	7	22	29	+9	12	2	0	1	0	94	7.4

1997-98 statistics:

GP	G	A	TP	+/-	PIM	PP	SH	GW	GT	S	PCT
75	19	23	42	-1	28	4	3	4	1	117	16.2

1998-99 statistics:

GP	G	A	TP	+/-	PIM	PP	SH	GW	GT	S	PCT
80	35	48	83	+12	26	5	4	4	1	177	19.8

1999-2000 statistics:

GP	G	A	TP	+/-	PIM	PP	SH	GW	GT	S	PCT
71	20	39	59	+24	26	3	1	2	0	146	13.7

LAST SEASON

Second on team in plus-minus. Third on team in shots. Missed seven games with bruised ribs. Missed three games with knee injuries. Missed one game with bruised shin.

THE FINESSE GAME

Straka can do a lot of things. He is a water bug with imagination. He makes clever passes that always land on the tape and give the recipient time to do something with the puck. He's more of a playmaker than a shooter. He will have to learn to go to the net more to make his game less predictable. He draws people to him and creates open ice for his linemates.

Straka doesn't have the outside speed to burn defenders, but creates space for himself with his wheeling in tight spaces. He has good balance and is tough to knock off his feet, even though he's not big.

Not a great defensive player, Straka is effective in five-on-five situations. He is a perpetual threat.

THE PHYSICAL GAME

Straka has shown little inclination for the typical North American style of play. He is small and avoids corners and walls, and has to be teamed with more physical linemates to give him some room. He needs to learn to protect the puck better with his body and buy some time.

THE INTANGIBLES

Straka is right at home on a team with a European style, though he slipped back into his inconsistent play last season and fell off his point-a-game place. That could have something to do with his shift from centre to left wing. He likes the open ice at centre much better.

PROJECTION

Twenty goals is a minimal output from such a skilled player. He should be in the 35-goal range.

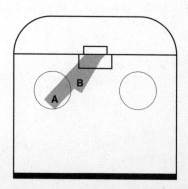

SAN JOSE SHARKS

Players' Statistics 1999-2000

POS.	NO.	PLAYER	GP	G	A	PTS	+/-	PIM	PP	SH	GW	GT	S	PCT
R	11	OWEN NOLAN	78	44	40	84	-1	110	18	4	6	2	261	16.9
C	25	VINCENT DAMPHOUSSE	82	21	49	70	4	58	3	1	1	1	204	10.3
L	39	JEFF FRIESEN	82	26	35	61	-2	47	11	3	7		191	13.6
C	18	MIKE RICCI	82	20	24	44	14	60	10		5		134	14.9
C	14	PATRICK MARLEAU	81	17	23	40	-9	36	3		3		161	10.6
R	24	NIKLAS SUNDSTROM	79	12	25	37	9	22	2	1	2	3	90	13.3
D	7	*BRAD STUART	82	10	26	36	3	32	5	1	3		133	7.5
R	15	ALEXANDER KOROLYUK	57	14	21	35	4	35	3		1	1	124	11.3
D	20	GARY SUTER	76	6	28	34	7	52	2	1			175	3.4
C	19	MARCO STURM	74	12	15	27	4	22	2	4	3		120	10.0
L	32	STEPHANE MATTEAU	69	12	12	24	-3	61			3		73	16.4
D	5	JEFF NORTON	62		20	20	-2	49					45	
R	9	TODD HARVEY	71	11	7	18	-11	140	2				90	12.2
D	10	MARCUS RAGNARSSON	63	3	13	16	13	38					60	5.0
D	40	MIKE RATHJE	66	2	14	16	-2	31					46	4.3
L	21	TONY GRANATO	48	6	7	13	2	39	1				67	9.0
C	12	RON SUTTER	78	5	6	11	-3	34		1	1		68	7.4
R	22	RONNIE STERN	67	4	5	9	-9	151					63	6.3
L	26	DAVE LOWRY	32	1	4	5	1	18					25	4.0
D	27	BRYAN MARCHMENT	49		4	4	3	72					51	
D	43	*SCOTT HANNAN	30	1	2	3	7	10					28	3.6
D	42	ANDY SUTTON	40	1	1	2	-5	80					29	3.4
L	32	MURRAY CRAVEN	19		2	2	-2	4					18	
R	33	BRANTT MYHRES	13		1	1	0	97					2	
D	3	BOB ROUSE	26		1	1	-3	19					20	
G	31	STEVE SHIELDS	67		1	1	0	29						
D	23	*SHAWN HEINS	1				-1	2					1	
G	35	*EVGENI NABOKOV	11				0							

GP = games played; G = goals; A = assists; PTS = points; +/- = goals-for minus goals-against while player is on ice; PIM = penalties in minutes; PP = power-play goals; SH = shorthanded goals; GW = game-winning goals; GT = game-tying goals; S = no. of shots; PCT = percentage of goals to shots; * = rookie

VINCENT DAMPHOUSSE

Yrs. of NHL service: 14
Born: Montreal, Que.; Dec. 17, 1967
Position: left wing
Height: 6-1
Weight: 200
Uniform no.: 25
Shoots: left

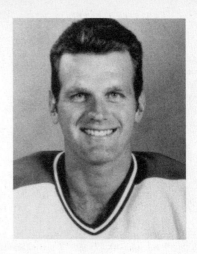

Career statistics:

GP	G	A	TP	PIM
1087	368	631	999	936

1996-97 statistics:

GP	G	A	TP	+/-	PIM	PP	SH	GW	GT	S	PCT
82	27	54	81	-6	82	7	2	3	2	244	11.1

1997-98 statistics:

GP	G	A	TP	+/-	PIM	PP	SH	GW	GT	S	PCT
76	18	41	59	+14	58	2	1	5	0	164	11.0

1998-99 statistics:

GP	G	A	TP	+/-	PIM	PP	SH	GW	GT	S	PCT
77	19	30	49	-4	50	6	2	3	0	190	10.0

1999-2000 statistics:

GP	G	A	TP	+/-	PIM	PP	SH	GW	GT	S	PCT
82	21	49	70	+4	58	3	1	1	1	204	10.3

LAST SEASON

Led team in assists. Third in NHL in power-play assists (27). Second on team in points and shots. Third on team in goals. One of four Sharks to appear in all 82 games.

THE FINESSE GAME

One of the best accolades for a player is that he makes others around him better. Damphousse has done that in San Jose.

Cool in tight, Damphousse has a marvellous backhand shot he can roof; he creates opportunites low by shaking and faking checkers with his skating. He likes to set up from behind the net to make plays. Goalies need to be on the alert when Damphousse is on the attack, because he is unafraid to take shots from absurd angles just to get a shot on net and get the goalie and defense scrambling. It's an effective tactic.

Damphousse shows poise with the puck. Although he is primarily a finisher, he has become less selfish playing with Owen Nolan. His puck control and passing touch are superb. He's a superb player in four-on-four situations. He has sharp offensive instincts and is good in traffic.

Damphousse won't leave any vapour trails with his skating in open ice, but he is quick around the net, especially with the puck. His foot speed isn't as much of a detriment in San Jose because the Sharks have some skaters who can drive the defense back and give Damphousse more time and space for his shot. He has exceptional balance to hop through sticks and checks. In open ice he uses his weight to shift and change direction, making it appear as if he's going faster than he is — and he can juke without losing the puck while

looking for his passing and shooting options.

THE PHYSICAL GAME

Damphousse uses his body to protect the puck, but he is not much of a grinder and loses most of his one-on-one battles. He has to be supported with physical linemates who will get him the puck. He'll expend a great deal of energy in the attacking zone, but little in his own end of the ice, though he is more diligent about this in crunch times.

Damphousse is a well-conditioned athlete who can handle long shifts and lots of ice time. He is not shy about using his stick. He has a pretty high pain threshhold. He has missed only 19 games in 13 NHL seasons.

THE INTANGIBLES

There wasn't a better free agent signing last year. Damphousse could have opted to go anywhere else after being traded to the Sharks in his walk year in 1998-99. He has become an important part of what could be a championship puzzle in San Jose in the next few years. When the intensity of the game steps up, so does he.

PROJECTION

Damphousse fell shy of the 80 points we predicted for him last season, but he should be a point-a-game player.

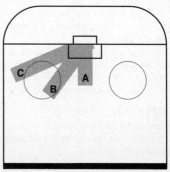

JEFF FRIESEN

Yrs. of NHL service: 6
Born: Meadow Lake, Sask.; Aug. 5, 1976
Position: left wing/centre
Height: 6-0
Weight: 185
Uniform no.: 39
Shoots: left

Career statistics:

GP	G	A	TP	PIM
448	137	177	314	260

1996-97 statistics:

GP	G	A	TP	+/-	PIM	PP	SH	GW	GT	S	PCT
82	28	34	62	-8	75	6	2	5	2	200	14.0

1997-98 statistics:

GP	G	A	TP	+/-	PIM	PP	SH	GW	GT	S	PCT
79	31	32	63	+8	40	7	6	7	0	186	16.7

1998-99 statistics:

GP	G	A	TP	+/-	PIM	PP	SH	GW	GT	S	PCT
78	22	35	57	+3	42	10	1	3	1	215	10.2

1999-2000 statistics:

GP	G	A	TP	+/-	PIM	PP	SH	GW	GT	S	PCT
82	26	35	61	-2	47	11	3	7	0	191	13.6

LAST SEASON

Led team in game-winning goals. Second on team in goals, power-play goals and shorthanded goals. Third on team in assists, points, shots and shooting percentage. One of four Sharks to appear in all 82 games.

THE FINESSE GAME

Friesen is a fast, strong skater, who handles the puck well and has the size to go with those qualities. He is a better finisher than playmaker, and he works well with Vincent Damphousse. Damphousse has a lot of patience and can hold onto the puck for a long time, and Friesen can get into holes with his speed for the pass. Friesen has a quick, strong release on his snap or wrist shot, and is shifty with a smooth change of speed. Carrying the puck doesn't slow him down. He is not a natural goal scorer and probably will never be an elite one, but he works hard for and earns his goals.

Friesen never seems to get rattled or forced into making bad plays. In fact, he's the one who forces opponents into panic moves with his pressure. He draws penalties by keeping his feet moving as he drives to the net or digs for the puck along the boards. He is strong on face-offs.

A pure goal scorer in junior, Friesen developed first as a checking-line winger in his rookie year before becoming a complete player. He deserves a lot of credit for making himself into an all-around player.

THE PHYSICAL GAME

Friesen has dedicated himself to his strength and conditioning. He doesn't have much of a mean streak, but he plays tough and honest.

THE INTANGIBLES

Friesen is a potential future captain of the Sharks. Tabbed with a lazy label in his junior days, he has matured into a hard-working player who cares. He is among the Sharks' impressive corps of young leaders.

PROJECTION

Friesen plays the left side on a line with Damphousse and Owen Nolan, so most of the goal-scoring chances go Nolan's way. Friesen is a good bet for 25 to 30.

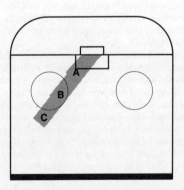

SCOTT HANNAN

Yrs. of NHL service: 1
Born: Richmond, B.C.; Jan. 23, 1979
Position: left defense
Height: 6-2
Weight: 215
Uniform no.: 43
Shoots: left

Career statistics:

GP	G	A	TP	PIM
35	1	4	5	16

1998-99 statistics:

GP	G	A	TP	+/-	PIM	PP	SH	GW	GT	S	PCT
5	0	2	2	0	6	0	0	0	0	4	0.0

1999-2000 statistics:

GP	G	A	TP	+/-	PIM	PP	SH	GW	GT	S	PCT
30	1	2	3	+7	10	0	0	0	0	28	3.6

LAST SEASON

First NHL season. Appeared in 41 games with Kentucky (AHL), scoring 5-12 — 17.

THE FINESSE GAME

Hannan is an intelligent player, which is his best asset. He moves the puck out of his own zone well. He is a smart passer who has his head up looking for the breaking man. He has been an offensive defenseman at the junior and minor-league levels but probably won't be as effective in the NHL.

Hannan is a strong skater and can rush the puck effectively, though he doesn't have dazzling speed. He will develop confidence enough on the rush to try to beat defender wide and take the puck to the net. He has a decent wrist and slap shot, though he does not have elite skills. He is a good penalty killer.

Hannan is a steady player who won't make high-risk plays. He shows signs of developing into a good two-way defenseman, and will become a top four defenseman in the future. He was taken in the same draft as Eric Brewer, but he has moved past Brewer, who was taken 18 slots ahead of Hannan in the first round.

THE PHYSICAL GAME

Hannan is big and strong, with a thick body. He is not overly aggressive but he will get involved. If he develops more of a taste for physical play, he could be a force. He needs to concentrate on some power skating.

THE INTANGIBLES

The Sharks gave Hannan some time to learn his trade in the minors and their patience is paying off. He took a backseat to some older players in the playoffs, as it would have been a risk to have two 20-year-olds in the lineup at the same time, and Stuart was ahead of him in development. But by the second half of this season, Hannan will be a regular.

PROJECTION

Hannan will probably be San Jose's number five defenseman, but his point totals won't be gaudy.

TODD HARVEY

Yrs. of NHL service: 6
Born: Hamilton, Ont.; Feb. 17, 1975
Position: centre/right wing
Height: 6-0
Weight: 195
Uniform no.: 10
Shoots: right

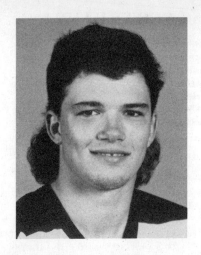

Career statistics:

GP	G	A	TP	PIM
347	60	85	145	661

1996-97 statistics:

GP	G	A	TP	+/-	PIM	PP	SH	GW	GT	S	PCT
71	9	22	31	+19	142	1	0	2	0	99	9.1

1997-98 statistics:

GP	G	A	TP	+/-	PIM	PP	SH	GW	GT	S	PCT
59	9	10	19	+5	104	0	0	1	0	88	10.2

1998-99 statistics:

GP	G	A	TP	+/-	PIM	PP	SH	GW	GT	S	PCT
37	11	17	28	-1	72	6	0	2	1	58	19.0

1999-2000 statistics:

GP	G	A	TP	+/-	PIM	PP	SH	GW	GT	S	PCT
71	11	7	18	-11	140	2	0	0	0	90	12.2

LAST SEASON

Acquired from Florida with fourth-round draft pick in 2001 for Radek Dvorak in three-way deal with N.Y. Rangers, Dec. 30, 1999. Second on Sharks in penalty minutes. Missed one game due to flu.

THE FINESSE GAME

Harvey's skating is rough. In fact, it's pretty choppy, and as a result he lacks speed. To make up for that, he has good anticipation and awareness. He's clever and his hands are very good. When Harvey gets the puck, he has patience and strength with it. He is not a legitimate first-line player, but he can fit in with skilled players if asked because of his effort.

Harvey's goals are ugly ones. He works the front of the net with grit. He goes to the net and follows up shots with second and third effort. He always has his feet moving and he has good hand-eye coordination. He doesn't have the greatest shot, but he battles to get into the prime scoring areas.

Harvey needs to play big every night to maximize his abilities, but he also has to become smarter in picking his spots. It's not going to do his career any good to spend half the season in the trainer's room.

THE PHYSICAL GAME

Harvey's talent level rises when he gets more involved. He's not big enough to be a legitimate NHL heavyweight, but he doesn't back down from challenges. When he's at his best, he gets inside other people's jerseys and heads.

THE INTANGIBLES

Harvey was not in good shape when he reported to the Sharks (this seemed to be a common complaint with former Rangers last season) and needs to hit the bike and the weights more often. The battle for jobs on a deep Sharks team will be ferocious. Harvey can be an effective, chippy third-liner.

PROJECTION

Harvey can play energetic shifts, be annoying, and if he stays in one piece, score 10 to 15 goals.

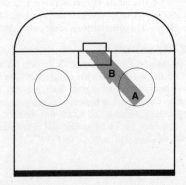

ALEXANDER KOROLYUK

Yrs. of NHL service: 2
Born: Moscow, Russia; Jan. 15, 1976
Position: right wing
Height: 5-9
Weight: 190
Uniform no.: 15
Shoots: left

Career statistics:

GP	G	A	TP	PIM
131	28	42	70	67

1997-98 statistics:

GP	G	A	TP	+/-	PIM	PP	SH	GW	GT	S	PCT
19	2	3	5	-5	6	1	0	0	0	23	8.7

1998-99 statistics:

GP	G	A	TP	+/-	PIM	PP	SH	GW	GT	S	PCT
55	12	18	30	+3	26	2	0	0	1	96	12.5

1999-2000 statistics:

GP	G	A	TP	+/-	PIM	PP	SH	GW	GT	S	PCT
57	14	21	35	+4	35	3	0	1	1	124	11.3

LAST SEASON

Second NHL season. Missed 12 games with back injuries. Missed three games with cut under left eye. Missed 10 games due to coach's decision.

THE FINESSE GAME

Korolyuk is a gifted player whose game is puck possession. Although he is small he's not that easy to get a piece of: he's quick and elusive. He draws a lot of penalties, and, in fact, he's a bit of a diver, but he's good enough to draw the call on most occasions.

Korolyuk makes anyone he plays with better because of his creativity. He is short and stocky and a good playmaker. He needs to shoot more because he has a very good, hard shot.

He adapted quickly to the NHL. Strong along the boards, he's an excellent soccer player, capable of keeping the puck alive with his feet.

THE PHYSICAL GAME

The Sharks would like to think that Korolyuk will develop along Doug Gilmour lines. He certainly has an edge to his game, like Gilmour, but it remains to be seen if he will have that "Killer" instinct that has always fuelled Gilmour to play well above his size. Korolyuk has a wide body and is feisty.

THE INTANGIBLES

Korolyuk was slowed by injuries and might have a hard time fitting in among the team's top six forwards. He is a wonderfully entertaining player to watch. He didn't have a very impressive playoffs and was benched for three games.

PROJECTION

Korolyuk should graduate into the 45-point range if he gets the ice time.

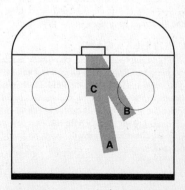

PATRICK MARLEAU

Yrs. of NHL service: 3
Born: Swift Current, Sask.; Sept. 15, 1979
Position: centre
Height: 6-2
Weight: 200
Uniform no.: 14
Shoots: left

Career statistics:

GP	G	A	TP	PIM
236	51	66	117	74

1997-98 statistics:

GP	G	A	TP	+/-	PIM	PP	SH	GW	GT	S	PCT
74	13	19	32	+5	14	1	0	2	0	90	14.4

1998-99 statistics:

GP	G	A	TP	+/-	PIM	PP	SH	GW	GT	S	PCT
81	21	24	45	+10	24	4	0	4	1	134	15.7

1999-2000 statistics:

GP	G	A	TP	+/-	PIM	PP	SH	GW	GT	S	PCT
81	17	23	40	-9	36	3	0	3	0	161	10.6

LAST SEASON

Missed one game due to coach's decision.

THE FINESSE GAME

Because of Marleau's quickness and intelligence, some scouts have described him as a bigger version of Paul Kariya. Marleau has great first- and second-step acceleration, with an extra gear.

Marleau plays an advanced offensive game; his defensive game is developing. He should become a high-level two-way centre. He pounces on a loose puck and is a scoring threat every time he has it. His offensive reads are outstanding. He anticipates plays and has excellent hands. He is a terrific finisher, as well as a fine playmaker. He has to be encouraged to shoot more. He has a quick release with an accurate touch, and will become a valuable power-play weapon.

The only question mark concerning Marleau is his consistency. He had the occasional lulls in the season, but it remains to be seen whether this was simply the natural learning process for a young player, or a defect in his makeup. It is worth remembering that Marleau barely made the cutoff for the 1997 draft. One more day and he would have been in the 1998 draft.

THE PHYSICAL GAME

Marleau is an imposing athlete, physically mature for his age. He skates through his checks and when he hits you, you know it. He has a thick build. He does not go looking to run people, but he will battle to get into traffic for the puck. He will take a check to make a play. He has grown gradually in the past few years; lucky to avoid a sudden growth spurt, he has stayed coordinated.

THE INTANGIBLES

Adding Scott Thornton, who will probably play with Marleau, could make for a breakthrough year for Marleau. He's still very young and is the number two centre behind Vincent Damphousse; Thornton's grit will help him take the next step. Damphousse's arrival not only took pressure off Marleau, but he is showing the younger player how to turn it on night after night, especially at crunch time.

PROJECTION

Marleau needs to be a more consistent scorer, and 20 to 25 goals *is* attainable.

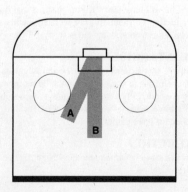

OWEN NOLAN

Yrs. of NHL service: 10
Born: Belfast, N. Ireland; Sept. 22, 1971
Position: right wing
Height: 6-1
Weight: 201
Uniform no.: 11
Shoots: right

Career statistics:

GP	G	A	TP	PIM
637	252	262	524	1210

1996-97 statistics:

GP	G	A	TP	+/-	PIM	PP	SH	GW	GT	S	PCT
72	31	32	63	-19	155	10	0	3	1	225	13.8

1997-98 statistics:

GP	G	A	TP	+/-	PIM	PP	SH	GW	GT	S	PCT
75	14	27	41	-2	144	3	1	1	0	192	7.3

1998-99 statistics:

GP	G	A	TP	+/-	PIM	PP	SH	GW	GT	S	PCT
78	19	26	45	+16	129	6	2	3	1	207	9.2

1999-2000 statistics:

GP	G	A	TP	+/-	PIM	PP	SH	GW	GT	S	PCT
78	44	40	84	-1	110	18	4	6	2	261	16.9

LAST SEASON

Led league in power-play goals. Led team and second in NHL in goals. Led team and tied for fifth in NHL in points. Fourth in NHL in power-play points (33). Led team in shots and shooting percentage. Second on team in assists and game-winning goals. Career highs in goals and points. Missed four games with upper-body soreness.

THE FINESSE GAME

Playing a full season with Vincent Damphousse brought out the best in Nolan. Chris Pronger won the Hart Trophy, but few players were as valuable to their team as Nolan. He made plays, he ran over people, he scored huge goals, he was in great shape.

Nobody knows where Nolan's shot is headed, except Nolan. A pure shooter with good hands, he rips one-timers from the circle with deadly speed and accuracy. Damphousse is so terrific as a set-up man that he had Nolan thinking like a pure finisher. Nolan needs to be selfish.

Nolan has an amazing knack for letting the puck go at just the right moment. He has a little move in tight to the goal with a forehand to backhand, and around the net he is about as good as anyone in the game. On the power play, he is just about unstoppable.

Nolan is a strong skater with good balance and fair agility. He is quick straight ahead but won't split the defense when carrying the puck. He's better without the puck, driving into open ice for the pass and quick shot. Defensively, he has improved tremendously, though it is still not his strong suit.

THE PHYSICAL GAME

His health problems behind him, Nolan was fit and confident. He is a tough customer, but has grasped the fact that he doesn't have to get in a fight every night.

THE INTANGIBLES

Nolan was on fire last season and had an amazing playoffs (eight goals in 10 games) to top it off. The Sharks are only going to get better, and Nolan will be a major part of the reason why. He was a restricted free agent during the off-season. He can name his price.

PROJECTION

Nolan could make the 50-goal breakthrough.

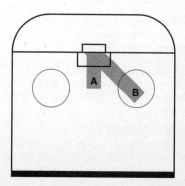

MARCUS RAGNARSSON

Yrs. of NHL service: 5
Born: Ostervala, Sweden; Aug. 13, 1971
Position: left defense
Height: 6-1
Weight: 200
Uniform no.: 10
Shoots: left

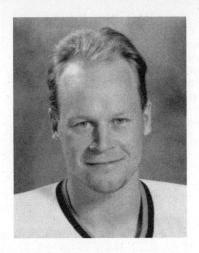

Career statistics:

GP	G	A	TP	PIM
356	19	91	110	274

1996-97 statistics:

GP	G	A	TP	+/-	PIM	PP	SH	GW	GT	S	PCT
69	3	14	17	-18	63	2	0	0	0	57	5.3

1997-98 statistics:

GP	G	A	TP	+/-	PIM	PP	SH	GW	GT	S	PCT
79	5	20	25	-11	65	3	0	2	0	91	5.5

1998-99 statistics:

GP	G	A	TP	+/-	PIM	PP	SH	GW	GT	S	PCT
74	0	13	13	+7	66	0	0	0	0	87	.0

1999-2000 statistics:

GP	G	A	TP	+/-	PIM	PP	SH	GW	GT	S	PCT
63	3	13	16	+13	38	0	0	0	0	60	5.0

He was a restricted free agent during the off-season.

PROJECTION

Ragnarsson's offensive game has more upside but he doesn't want to push the envelope and will probably score 20 or 25 points.

LAST SEASON

Second on team in plus-minus. Missed 16 games with foot contusion. Missed three games with concussion.

THE FINESSE GAME

Ragnarsson has a lot of poise, plus hand skills and skating ability. He has quick feet and he moves the puck well. He makes a good first pass and some good decisions at the blueline to get the puck through.

Ragnarsson controls a lot of the breakout for San Jose and makes smart choices in the neutral zone. He is given a lot of responsibility on the power play, and while he is not in the elite class of quarterbacks, he has a decent, if not outstanding, point shot and is not afraid to shoot. He dropped to the second-unit power play because of the emergence of rookie Brad Stuart.

Defensively, Ragnarsson still has some work to do. He uses his body positionally to take up space, but isn't much of a hitter. He lets his partner Mike Rathje do that. But if opposing forwards don't want to attack Rathje's side, they will attack Ragnarsson's, and he has to be prepared to handle it. He will get the puck out in a hurry when he has time but is vulnerable to a strong forecheck.

THE PHYSICAL GAME

Ragnarsson is built solidly and will play a physical game, though finesse is his forte. He can handle a lot of ice time.

THE INTANGIBLES

Ragnarsson and steady partner Rathje face the opponents' top lines night after night. But Ragnarsson doesn't seem to play as well paired with anyone else.

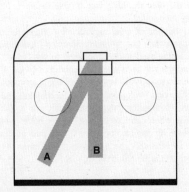

MIKE RATHJE

Yrs. of NHL service: 7
Born: Mannville, Alta.; May 11, 1974
Position: left defense
Height: 6-6
Weight: 220
Uniform no.: 40
Shoots: left

Career statistics:

GP	G	A	TP	PIM
376	13	66	79	249

1996-97 statistics:

GP	G	A	TP	+/-	PIM	PP	SH	GW	GT	S	PCT
31	0	8	8	-1	21	0	0	0	0	22	0.0

1997-98 statistics:

GP	G	A	TP	+/-	PIM	PP	SH	GW	GT	S	PCT
81	3	12	15	-4	59	1	0	0	0	61	4.9

1998-99 statistics:

GP	G	A	TP	+/-	PIM	PP	SH	GW	GT	S	PCT
82	5	9	14	+15	36	2	0	1	0	67	7.5

1999-2000 statistics:

GP	G	A	TP	+/-	PIM	PP	SH	GW	GT	S	PCT
66	2	14	16	-2	31	0	0	0	0	46	4.3

LAST SEASON

Missed 16 games with groin injury.

THE FINESSE GAME

Shhh. Rathje is the best-kept defensive secret in the Western Conference.

A stay-at-home type, Rathje was once again San Jose's best defenseman all season. He has great quickness for a player of his size. He is a lot like Ken Morrow, the kind of player who is so quiet that you have to watch him every game to appreciate how good he is. He is strong enough to play against the league's power forwards and quick enough to deal with faster skilled players. Rathje is routinely matched up against other teams' top lines and just as routinely smothers them.

Rathje has the ability to get involved in the attack, but is prized primarily for his defense. He helps get the puck out of the zone quickly. He can either carry the puck out and make a smart headman pass, then follow the play, or make the safe move and chip the puck out along the wall.

Rathje has great poise and worked well paired with the more offensive-minded Marcus Ragnarsson. He combines his lateral mobility with a good low shot, to get the puck on the net without being blocked.

THE PHYSICAL GAME

Rathje has good size and he's adding more muscle. He has learned to play with controlled aggression. He has a little bit of mean in him, and he likes to hit. He has unbelievable strength and good mobility for his size. His penalty minutes look low because he plays hard without taking bad penalties. Rathje doesn't hit with

Scott Stevens force, but he is well-respected by opponents.

THE INTANGIBLES

Rathje has become a franchise defenseman. He is the cornerstone of the Sharks' blueline.

PROJECTION

Rathje can get 20 points and keep other teams' forward lines off the board.

MIKE RICCI

Yrs. of NHL service: 10
Born: Scarborough, Ont.; Oct. 27, 1971
Position: centre
Height: 6-0
Weight: 190
Uniform no.: 18
Shoots: left

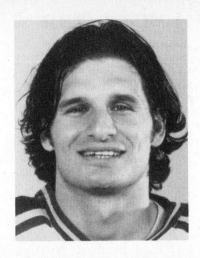

Career statistics:

GP	G	A	TP	PIM
708	174	257	431	704

1996-97 statistics:

GP	G	A	TP	+/-	PIM	PP	SH	GW	GT	S	PCT
63	13	19	32	-3	59	5	0	3	0	74	17.6

1997-98 statistics:

GP	G	A	TP	+/-	PIM	PP	SH	GW	GT	S	PCT
65	9	18	27	-4	32	5	0	2	0	91	9.9

1998-99 statistics:

GP	G	A	TP	+/-	PIM	PP	SH	GW	GT	S	PCT
82	13	26	39	+1	68	2	1	2	1	98	13.3

1999-2000 statistics:

GP	G	A	TP	+/-	PIM	PP	SH	GW	GT	S	PCT
82	20	24	44	+14	60	10	0	5	0	134	14.9

LAST SEASON

Led team in plus-minus. Goals highest total since 1993-94. Second on team in shooting percentage. Third on team in power-play goals and game-winning goals. One of four Sharks to appear in all 82 games. Second among current active ironmen with 229 consecutive games played.

THE FINESSE GAME

Ricci is a known quantity. He has terrific hand skills, combined with hockey sense and an outstanding work ethic. He always seems to be in the right place, ready to make the right play. He sees his passing options well and is patient with the puck. He can rifle it as well. He has a good backhand shot from in deep and scores most of his goals from the slot by picking the top corners. His lone drawback is his speed. He's fast enough to not look out of place and he has good balance and agility, but his lack of quickness prevents him from being more of an offensive force, especially in open ice.

Very slick on face-offs, Ricci has good hand speed and hand-eye coordination for winning draws outright, or he can pick a bouncing puck out of the air. This serves him well in scrambles in front of the net, or he can deflect midair slap shots. He can play wing in addition to his natural position at centre.

Ricci is an effective penalty killer, with poise and a controlled aggression for forcing the play. He blocks shots and aggressively forces the point men.

THE PHYSICAL GAME

Ricci is not big, but he is so strong that it's not unusual to see him skate out from behind the net, dragging along or fending off a checker with one arm while he makes a pass or takes a shot with his other arm. He plays a tough game without being overly chippy. He is also very strong in the corners and in front of the net. He plays bigger than he is.

Ricci will play hurt. He pays attention to conditioning and has a great deal of stamina.

THE INTANGIBLES

Ricci will antagonize and draw penalties. He kills penalties and works the power play, and makes timely plays under pressure. Although not as gifted offensively as Ron Francis, he is similar to Francis in that he is a checking centre who can do so much more than just check.

Ricci's quality, character, leadership and dedication to the game and his teammates are impeccable. He is a throwback, and helps provide some grit in a finesse-laden lineup. His teammates love his upbeat off-ice attitude. Ricci has stepped into the gap between the Sharks' kids and the team's older veterans — he is a great addition to team chemistry.

PROJECTION

Ricci can again produce 40 points over a full season. He gives the Sharks many options in how to best utilize him.

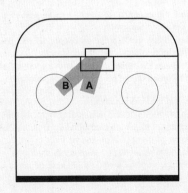

STEVE SHIELDS

Yrs. of NHL service: 2
Born: Toronto, Ont.; July 19, 1972
Position: goaltender
Height: 6-3
Weight: 215
Uniform no.: 31
Catches: left

Career statistics:

GP	MIN	GA	SO	GAA	A	PIM
135	7608	322	8	2.54	2	56

1996-97 statistics:

GP	MIN	GAA	W	L	T	SO	GA	S	SAPCT	PIM
13	789	2.97	3	8	2	0	39	447	.913	4

1997-98 statistics:

GP	MIN	GAA	W	L	T	SO	GA	S	SAPCT	PIM
16	785	2.83	3	6	4	0	37	408	.909	17

1998-99 statistics:

GP	MIN	GAA	W	L	T	SO	GA	S	SAPCT	PIM
37	2162	2.22	15	11	8	4	80	1011	.921	6

1999-2000 statistics:

GP	MIN	GAA	W	L	T	SO	GA	S	SAPCT	PIM
67	3797	2.56	27	30	8	4	162	1826	.911	29

LAST SEASON

Career high in wins.

THE PHYSICAL GAME

Shields has a lot of raw, natural ability, but it's wrapped up at the moment in a slipshod package.

Shields' game has some major hiccups, the primary one of which is: he can't catch the puck. Shields never seems to track the puck coming all the way to his body, which is why he doesn't watch the puck go into his glove. He also loses it after it hits him elsewhere on his body, which is why he is prone to many bad rebounds. This sounds so elementary, but no one seems to have tried to straighten him out, and it's going to be a major trip-up. It may be a habit he picked up from playing with Dominik Hasek in Buffalo. The difference is that Hasek always keeps track of the puck and is able to stop second and third tries.

Shields is mobile and competitive, but he is a big goalie who looks like Darren Pang in the net because of his technical shortcomings.

THE MENTAL GAME

Shields played a huge seventh game against St. Louis in the playoffs after being bombed in the sixth, so he is obviously able to rebound. In his first season as a number one, Shields had some memorable efforts and some forgettable ones. He needs to be consistent on a nightly basis. Shields can win some big games on pure adrenaline when the team doesn't play well in front of him.

THE INTANGIBLES

Is Shields a legitimate number one goalie? We'll find out this season as the Sharks take their game to the next level. This is no longer the little team that could. The Sharks' prospects are all coming of age and San Jose has assembled a terrific defense corps. Shields's teammates like his work ethic and attitude. He is a competitor. The Sharks moved Mike Vernon, a fan favorite in San Jose, to make room for him. We would feel much more confident if he had an elite goalie coach to work with.

PROJECTION

Shields isn't in the top echelon of goaltenders and might not get there. He is a shaky number one, but will have such a high-powered team in front of him that he can win enough 6-3 games for 30 victories.

BRAD STUART

Yrs. of NHL service: 1
Born: Rocky Mountain House, Alta.; Nov. 6, 1979
Position: left defense
Height: 6-2
Weight: 210
Uniform no.: 7
Shoots: left

Career statistics:

GP	G	A	TP	PIM
82	10	26	36	32

1999-2000 statistics:

GP	G	A	TP	+/-	PIM	PP	SH	GW	GT	S	PCT
82	10	26	36	+3	32	5	1	3	0	133	7.5

LAST SEASON

Finalist for 2000 Calder Trophy. Named to NHL All-Rookie Team. Fifth among NHL rookies in assists. Led team defensemen in points. Seventh among NHL rookies in points. One of four Sharks to appear in all 82 games.

THE FINESSE GAME

Stuart is an offensive-minded defenseman. His primary asset is his ability to make a smart first pass. He gets the puck out of the zone intelligently and quickly and opens up the rink for the Sharks. He finds the open man. He plays the point on the first power-play unit (he had 14 power-play points).

Stuart is a powerful skater. He is speedy and mobile and can lead a rush or join the attack as the trailer. He is a good one-on-one defender. Poised and smart, he will soon have the ability to dominate games with his skating and puck possession.

His defensive reads overall are good, though he had nights last season where he was in and out. That will come with experience. He is intelligent and will work to improve his game.

THE PHYSICAL GAME

Stuart played a lot of minutes (he averaged just over 20 per game) and didn't wear down. In fact, he finished strong with 19 points over his last 33 games. He is a willing hitter. Physically fit, Stuart takes to the physical game naturally. He is strong along the wall and in front of the net and doesn't take bad penalties.

THE INTANGIBLES

For a player to step in at age 19, without pro experience, to be a top four defenseman, and to be among the top 10 in freshman scorers, is too much to ask of any kid. The Sharks knew Stuart would be this good. They just didn't know he would be this good this soon. Stuart had a little trouble when play intensified in the playoffs, but for a player of his inexperience, that was to be expected and chalked up as a lesson.

PROJECTION

Stuart will be relied upon to match his freshman numbers and 40 points is not out of the question. He will soon be among the league's defenseman scoring leaders.

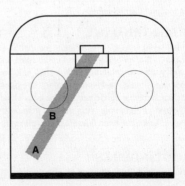

MARCO STURM

Yrs. of NHL service: 3
Born: Dingolfing, Germany; Sept. 8, 1978
Position: centre
Height: 6-0
Weight: 190
Uniform no.: 19
Shoots: left

Career statistics:

GP	G	A	TP	PIM
226	38	57	95	114

1997-98 statistics:

GP	G	A	TP	+/-	PIM	PP	SH	GW	GT	S	PCT
74	10	20	30	-2	40	2	0	3	0	118	8.5

1998-99 statistics:

GP	G	A	TP	+/-	PIM	PP	SH	GW	GT	S	PCT
78	16	22	38	+7	52	3	2	3	2	140	11.4

1999-2000 statistics:

GP	G	A	TP	+/-	PIM	PP	SH	GW	GT	S	PCT
74	12	15	27	+4	22	2	4	3	0	120	10.0

provide an outstanding all-around game.

LAST SEASON

Missed four games with hip pointer. Missed four games with head injury.

THE FINESSE GAME

Sturm may be the best all-around player on the Sharks. A versatile skater who can play all three forward positions, there isn't a lot of maintenance to him. He knows where to be without the puck.

He is also a fine skater with smooth acceleration. He finished second in the fastest skater competition at the NHL All-Star game. And he has good hands for stickhandling and shooting (which, like many Europeans, he needs to do more of). He is a natural scorer, and should gain confidence in his next few seasons in the league.

Sturm is extremely intelligent and hard working. He is not afraid to block shots. He is going to be the kind of player who scores important goals and makes key plays that determine games. He plays on a third line but has the skill to be a top six, and could give the Sharks what Jere Lehtinen gives the Dallas Stars.

THE PHYSICAL GAME

Sturm is not big but he competes every night. He is chippy and feisty, and plays bigger than he is.

THE INTANGIBLES

The most complete, reliable forward on the team, Sturm hasn't produced the way the Sharks had hoped, but he does a lot of little things to help his team win. He was moved around to play several different roles (third-line centre, second-line winger), which may be why his offense hasn't come along more quickly.

PROJECTION

Sturm will probably score in the 20-goal range and

NIKLAS SUNDSTROM

Yrs. of NHL service: 5
Born: Ornskoldsvik, Sweden; June 6, 1975
Position: left wing
Height: 6-0
Weight: 185
Uniform no.: 24
Shoots: left

Career statistics:

GP	G	A	TP	PIM
394	77	123	200	100

1996-97 statistics:

GP	G	A	TP	+/-	PIM	PP	SH	GW	GT	S	PCT
82	24	28	52	+23	20	5	1	4	0	132	18.2

1997-98 statistics:

GP	G	A	TP	+/-	PIM	PP	SH	GW	GT	S	PCT
70	19	28	47	0	24	4	0	1	0	115	16.5

1998-99 statistics:

GP	G	A	TP	+/-	PIM	PP	SH	GW	GT	S	PCT
81	13	30	43	-2	20	1	2	3	0	89	14.6

1999-2000 statistics:

GP	G	A	TP	+/-	PIM	PP	SH	GW	GT	S	PCT
79	12	25	37	+9	22	2	1	2	3	90	13.3

LAST SEASON

Acquired from Tampa Bay with a third-round draft choice in 2000 for Bill Houlder, Andrei Zyuzin, Shawn Burr, and Steve Guolla, Aug. 4, 1999. Second on team in plus-minus. Missed three games due to coach's decision.

THE FINESSE GAME

Sundstrom is a defensive forward who possesses some finishing capabilities. As a scorer, he is opportunistic, but he doesn't have the feel for goal scoring or the drive to pay the price around the net.

A deceptively fast skater with good balance and a strong stride, Sundstrom plays a smart game and does a lot of subtle things well.

A puck magnet, he applies his skills to the defensive game. He reads plays very well, is aware defensively and always makes the safe decision. And when he forechecks, especially when killing penalties, he usually comes up with the puck in a one-on-one battle.

THE PHYSICAL GAME

Sundstrom reported to last year's camp out of shape. He will not get much bigger and has to get stronger, but he is persistent and consistently physical. One of the Swede's talents is lifting an opponent's blade to steal the puck. He absorbs far more punishment than he dishes out, since he doesn't punish anybody, but he's beginning to realize that developing at least a hint of a mean streak is necessary for his survival.

THE INTANGIBLES

Because he doesn't throw big hits or make flashy plays on the ice, and because he is almost constantly smiling off it, Sundstrom gets taken lightly a lot more than he should. He is committed to playing, and playing well. He is also committed to winning, and is enormously respected in the dressing room. Sundstrom was a healthy scratch for three games in Janaury, so the Sharks may question his dedication. He had a goalless stretch of 24 games and did not produce in the playoffs.

PROJECTION

Sundstrom is likely to play on a third line in San Jose, given the team's depth up front. He can score 10 to 15 goals in that role.

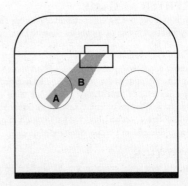

GARY SUTER

Yrs. of NHL service: 15
Born: Madison, Wisc.; June 24, 1964
Position: left defense
Height: 6-0
Weight: 200
Uniform no.: 20
Shoots: left

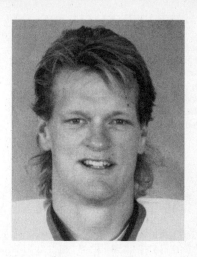

Career statistics:

GP	G	A	TP	PIM
995	187	591	778	1206

1996-97 statistics:

GP	G	A	TP	+/-	PIM	PP	SH	GW	GT	S	PCT
82	7	21	28	-4	70	3	0	0	1	225	3.1

1997-98 statistics:

GP	G	A	TP	+/-	PIM	PP	SH	GW	GT	S	PCT
73	14	28	42	+1	74	5	2	0	0	199	7.0

1998-99 statistics:

GP	G	A	TP	+/-	PIM	PP	SH	GW	GT	S	PCT
1	0	0	0	0	0	0	0	0	0	1	.0

1999-2000 statistics:

GP	G	A	TP	+/-	PIM	PP	SH	GW	GT	S	PCT
76	6	28	34	+7	52	2	1	0	0	175	3.4

LAST SEASON

Missed six games with arthroscopic knee surgery.

THE FINESSE GAME

Suter has great natural skills, starting with his skating. He's secure on his skates with a wide stance for balance. He has all of the components that make a great skater: acceleration, flat-out speed, quickness and mobility. He skates well backwards and can't be bested one-on-one except by the slickest skaters. He loves to jump into the attack, and he'll key a rush with a smooth outlet pass or carry the puck and lead the parade.

Suter has a superb shot. It's not scary-hard, like Al MacInnis's, but he keeps it low. Not a great playmaker, his creativity comes from his speed and dangerous shot. He can handle some penalty-killing time, though it is not his strong suit. He is, however, an excellent shot-blocker.

THE PHYSICAL GAME

Suter may be one of the least-known dirty players in the NHL. Sure, Bryan Marchment gets all the bad press for his kneeto-knee checks, but it was Suter whose hit in the 1991 Canada Cup was the start of Wayne Gretzky's back troubles, and Suter's stick to the head of Paul Kariya threatened that brilliant star's career.

So don't look for his name among the Lady Byng candidates. Suter is a marathon man who can handle 30 minutes of ice time a game and not wear down (he averaged 23 minutes last season). He is exceptionally fit. That is most remarkable since Suter appeared in only one game in 1998-99 because of three elbow surgeries and a heart procedure. He can get carried away with the hitting game and will take himself out of position, even when penalty killing. He doesn't like to be hit; he'll bring his stick up at the last second before contact to protect himself. His defensive reads are average to fair.

THE INTANGIBLES

Suter's healthy return was a huge boost to San Jose's power play and also helped the development of rookie Brad Stuart.

PROJECTION

Suter could flirt with 50 points this season.

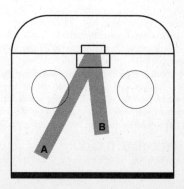

SCOTT THORNTON

Yrs. of NHL service: 10
Born: London, Ont.; Jan. 9, 1971
Position: left wing
Height: 6-3
Weight: 216
Uniform no.: 17
Shoots: left

Career statistics:

GP	G	A	TP	PIM
494	55	62	117	953

1996-97 statistics:

GP	G	A	TP	+/-	PIM	PP	SH	GW	GT	S	PCT
73	10	10	20	-19	128	1	1	1	0	110	9.1

1997-98 statistics:

GP	G	A	TP	+/-	PIM	PP	SH	GW	GT	S	PCT
67	6	9	15	0	158	1	0	1	2	51	11.8

1998-99 statistics:

GP	G	A	TP	+/-	PIM	PP	SH	GW	GT	S	PCT
47	7	4	11	-2	87	1	0	1	1	56	12.5

1999-2000 statistics:

GP	G	A	TP	+/-	PIM	PP	SH	GW	GT	S	PCT
65	8	6	14	-12	108	1	0	1	0	83	9.6

LAST SEASON

Signed as free agent by San Jose from Dallas, July 2, 2000. Acquired by Dallas from Montreal for Juha Lind, Jan. 22, 2000. Led Stars in penalty minutes. Missed three games due to suspension. Missed one game with flu. Missed five games with triceps injury. Missed one game with groin injury.

THE FINESSE GAME

Thornton matches up against just about any forward n the league when it comes to winning puck battles. Although he played wing most of last season and will continue to do so in San Jose, he has also played a great deal at centre and is terrific on face-offs. If Thornton doesn't win a draw outright, he uses his muscle to tie up the opponent and work the puck to a teammate.

He uses his toughness to get rid of a defender, then has good hands when he works in tight to get his scoring chances. Thornton is by no means a sniper, and even though he has concentrated more on the defensive aspects of the game, he is able to convert a scoring chance when it presents itself. He was a scorer at the junior level, although he doesn't have an NHL release.

Thornton is a good skater, not overly fast, but no plodder. He is strong and balanced on his feet and hard to knock off the puck. He is alert positionally. If one of his defensemen goes in deep on the attack, Thornton will be the forward back covering for him.

THE PHYSICAL GAME

Thornton is a big, solid, defensive forward, a young Joel Otto but with better mobility.

THE INTANGIBLES

Thornton will never be a major point producer, but he will fill a steady checking role or act as a safety valve for more offense-minded linemates. He will add toughness to a skilled San Jose lineup.

PROJECTION

Thornton will produce about 10 to 15 goals a season, but provide a bigger payoff in other areas.

ST. LOUIS BLUES

Players' Statistics 1999-2000

POS.	NO.	PLAYER	GP	G	A	PTS	+/-	PIM	PP	SH	GW	GT	S	PCT
R	38	PAVOL DEMITRA	71	28	47	75	34	8	8		4		241	11.6
C	77	PIERRE TURGEON	52	26	40	66	30	8	8		3		139	18.7
D	44	CHRIS PRONGER	79	14	48	62	52	92	8		3	2	192	7.3
C	26	MICHAL HANDZUS	81	25	28	53	19	44	3	4	5	1	166	15.1
R	48	SCOTT YOUNG	75	24	15	39	12	18	6	1	7	1	244	9.8
R	23	LUBOS BARTECKO	67	16	23	39	25	51	3		3		75	21.3
D	2	AL MACINNIS	61	11	28	39	20	34	6		7		245	4.5
R	19	STEPHANE RICHER	56	15	22	37	9	18	5		1		110	13.6
C	32	MIKE EASTWOOD	79	19	15	34	5	32	1	3	3	1	83	22.9
C	17	*JOCHEN HECHT	63	13	21	34	20	28	5		1		140	9.3
C	22	CRAIG CONROY	79	12	15	27	5	36	1	2	3		98	12.2
D	28	TODD REIRDEN	56	4	21	25	18	32			1		77	5.2
C	15	*MARTY REASONER	32	10	14	24	9	20	3				51	19.6
L	33	SCOTT PELLERIN	80	8	15	23	8	48		2	2		120	6.7
C	21	JAMAL MAYERS	79	7	10	17	0	90					99	7.1
L	9	*TYSON NASH	66	4	9	13	6	150		1	1		68	5.9
D	6	DAVE ELLETT	52	2	8	10	-4	12			1		41	4.9
D	37	JEFF FINLEY	74	2	8	10	26	38			2		31	6.5
L	12	DEREK KING	22	2	7	9	-2	8	1				33	6.1
D	4	MARC BERGEVIN	81	1	8	9	27	75					54	1.9
D	7	RICARD PERSSON	41		8	8	-2	38					30	
C	47	*LADISLAV NAGY	11	2	4	6	2	2	1				15	13.3
L	14	GEOFF COURTNALL	6	2	2	4	3	6			1		15	13.3
L	41	BOB BASSEN	27	1	3	4	-3	26					26	3.8
C	25	PASCAL RHEAUME	7	1	1	2	-2	6					5	20.0
D	36	BRYAN HELMER	15	1	1	2	-3	10	1		1		19	5.3
R	39	KELLY CHASE	25		1	1	-5	118					14	
G	1	ROMAN TUREK	67		1	1	0	4						
C	46	*DEREK BEKAR	1				0							
R	10	JIM CAMPBELL	2				0	9					6	
D	20	RUDY POESCHEK	12				-3	24					8	
G	29	JAMIE MCLENNAN	19				0	2						

GP = games played; G = goals; A = assists; PTS = points; +/- = goals-for minus goals-against while player is on ice; PIM = penalties in minutes; PP = power-play goals; SH = shorthanded goals; GW = game-winning goals; GT = game-tying goals; S = no. of shots; PCT = percentage of goals to shots; * = rookie

LUBOS BARTECKO

Yrs. of NHL service: 2
Born: Kezmarok, Czech.; July 14, 1976
Position: left wing
Height: 6-1
Weight: 200
Uniform no.: 56
Shoots: left

Career statistics:

GP	G	A	TP	PIM
99	21	34	55	57

1998-99 statistics:

GP	G	A	TP	+/-	PIM	PP	SH	GW	GT	S	PCT
32	5	11	16	+4	6	0	0	1	0	37	13.5

1999-2000 statistics:

GP	G	A	TP	+/-	PIM	PP	SH	GW	GT	S	PCT
67	16	23	39	+25	51	3	0	3	0	75	21.3

LAST SEASON

Second NHL season. Missed one game due to coach's decision. Appeared in 12 games with Worcester, scoring 4-7 — 11.

THE FINESSE GAME

Bartecko has a stocky build and is quick. Strong on his skates, he has the kinds of skills that stamp him as a pure finisher. Right now, his defensive game is lagging behind his offensive game, but that is hardly unusual for an inexperienced player. He was sometimes a little confused about his job.

He has sure, soft hands and he is very willing to take the puck to the net for a strong wrist shot. He needs to shoot more often.

Bartecko's biggest problem has been his inconsistency. He had to spend a brief stint in the minors last season to wake up.

THE PHYSICAL GAME

Bartecko is solidly built. He won't initiate contact but he won't back down, either.

THE INTANGIBLES

Bartecko is never better than when he plays on the all-Slovak line with Pavol Demitra and Michal Handzus. His game is somewhat diminished away from those two, which is a problem if there are injuries or if the Blues want to mix up their lines. He adds the very important elements of speed and youth to the Blues lineup. He had a good World Championship for Slovakia after the Blues' disappointing first-round playoff exit.

PROJECTION

Bartecko could hit 25 goals this season if he lands a full-time role, as expected.

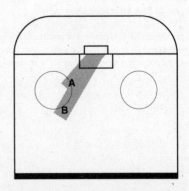

CRAIG CONROY

Yrs. of NHL service: 5
Born: Potsdam, N.Y.; Sept. 4, 1971
Position: centre
Height: 6-2
Weight: 198
Uniform no.: 22
Shoots: right

Career statistics:

GP	G	A	TP	PIM
303	47	80	127	165

1996-97 statistics:

GP	G	A	TP	+/-	PIM	PP	SH	GW	GT	S	PCT
61	6	11	17	0	43	0	0	1	0	74	8.1

1997-98 statistics:

GP	G	A	TP	+/-	PIM	PP	SH	GW	GT	S	PCT
81	14	29	43	+20	46	0	3	1	0	118	11.9

1998-99 statistics:

GP	G	A	TP	+/-	PIM	PP	SH	GW	GT	S	PCT
69	14	25	39	+14	38	0	1	1	0	134	10.4

1999-2000 statistics:

GP	G	A	TP	+/-	PIM	PP	SH	GW	GT	S	PCT
79	12	15	27	+5	36	1	2	3	0	98	12.2

LAST SEASON

Missed three games due to coach's decision.

THE FINESSE GAME

Conroy is a determined player who needs a little more confidence in his game to bring out some assets he has yet to display at the NHL level. A numbers man early in his career, he has worked hard at the defensive aspect of the game to become a more well-rounded player.

Conroy kills penalties well, using his speed, size and anticipation. He is a smart player who can make the little hook or hold to slow down an opponent without getting caught. He has quick hands and is good on draws, taking most of the Blues' key defensive-zone face-offs.

Conroy has been a scorer at the college and minor-league levels (he was leading the AHL in scoring when St. Louis obtained him in 1996) but has never had the same impact at the NHL level. His hands are much better than the average checking centre's. He's reliable in all key situations, defending a lead, in the closing minutes of a period and killing penalties at crucial times.

THE PHYSICAL GAME

Conroy isn't mean, but he is tough in a quiet way. He uses his size well and accepts checking roles against elite players without being intimidated. He is relentless on every shift and has a great work ethic.

THE INTANGIBLES

Conroy is a valuable role player for the Blues. He may be asked to pick up the pace offensively. He sees spot duty on the power play.

PROJECTION

Conroy can score 15 goals and 30 points in a checking role.

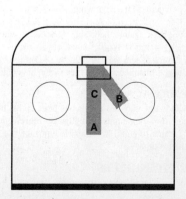

PAVOL DEMITRA

Yrs. of NHL service: 6
Born: Dubnica, Slovakia; Nov. 29, 1974
Position: left wing
Height: 6-0
Weight: 189
Uniform no.: 38
Shoots: left

Career statistics:

GP	G	A	TP	PIM
281	102	143	245	58

1996-97 statistics:

GP	G	A	TP	+/-	PIM	PP	SH	GW	GT	S	PCT
8	3	0	3	0	2	2	0	1	0	15	20.0

1997-98 statistics:

GP	G	A	TP	+/-	PIM	PP	SH	GW	GT	S	PCT
61	22	30	52	+11	22	4	4	6	1	147	15.0

1998-99 statistics:

GP	G	A	TP	+/-	PIM	PP	SH	GW	GT	S	PCT
82	37	52	89	+13	16	14	0	10	1	259	14.3

1999-2000 statistics:

GP	G	A	TP	+/-	PIM	PP	SH	GW	GT	S	PCT
71	28	47	75	+34	8	8	0	4	0	241	11.6

LAST SEASON

Led team in goals and points for second consecutive season. Tied for team lead in power-play goals. Second on team in assists. Second on team and third in NHL in plus-minus. Third on team in shots.

THE FINESSE GAME

Demitra's speed makes things happen. He has great moves one-on-one, and he finds a way to get in the holes. He has good stick skills and loves to shoot. He can really find the top of the net, especially with his one-timer. He is well-versed at picking the top corners and he can do it at speed.

Demitra is a creative and exceptional puckhandler, with a quick, deceptive shot. He's not shy about letting the puck go. He likes to drag the puck into his skates and then shoot it through a defenseman's legs. The move gets the rearguard to move up a little bit, and Demitra gets it by him on net.

Coming in off the right wing, which is his off-side, he will move to the middle on his forehand and throw the puck back against the grain. He needs to work on his puck protection skills. Sometimes he exposes the puck too much and what should be a scoring chance for him gets knocked away. Defensively, he's reliable.

THE PHYSICAL GAME

Demitra is not very big but he has built up his body, adding 10 to 12 pounds of legitimate muscle. He is very competitive and durable. He can take the heat and the ice time.

THE INTANGIBLES

Demitra suffered a season-ending concussion that contributed to the Blues' first-round playoff demise. Demitra has arrived as an NHL star. He wants to succeed and appears to be willing to pay the price to suceed in the NHL. The Blues have added more depth this season, which will help him.

Demitra received a clean bill of health after the playoffs concerning his postconcussion syndrome.

PROJECTION

Demitra can be a 40-goal, 90-point guy.

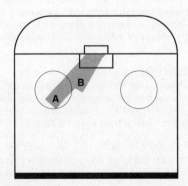

DALLAS DRAKE

Yrs. of NHL service: 8
Born: Trail, B.C.; Feb. 4, 1969
Position: centre
Height: 6-0
Weight: 180
Uniform no.: 11
Shoots: left

Career statistics:

GP	G	A	TP	PIM
501	110	191	301	458

1996-97 statistics:

GP	G	A	TP	+/-	PIM	PP	SH	GW	GT	S	PCT
63	17	19	36	-11	52	5	1	1	0	113	15.0

1997-98 statistics:

GP	G	A	TP	+/-	PIM	PP	SH	GW	GT	S	PCT
60	11	29	40	+17	71	3	0	2	0	112	9.8

1998-99 statistics:

GP	G	A	TP	+/-	PIM	PP	SH	GW	GT	S	PCT
53	9	22	31	+17	65	0	0	3	0	105	8.6

1999-2000 statistics:

GP	G	A	TP	+/-	PIM	PP	SH	GW	GT	S	PCT
79	15	30	45	+11	62	0	2	5	0	127	11.8

LAST SEASON

Signed as free agent from Phoenix, July 1, 2000. Second on Coyotes in game-winning goals. Tied for second on team in plus-minus. Career highs in assists and points. Missed three games with sprained shoulder.

THE FINESSE GAME

Drake is probably best suited to a third-line role, but because he is so involved and so intelligent, he is better than the average grinder. He is an aggressive forechecker, strong along the boards and in front of the net. He's on the small side, so he doesn't stand in and take a bashing, but he'll jump in and out of traffic to fight for the puck or bounce in on rebounds.

Drake is quick and powerful in his skating. He'll get outmuscled but not outhustled. His scoring chances come in deep.

As long as Drake doesn't start thinking like a scorer. He has to keep doing the same dirty things that got him this far, *and* got him a three-year, $9-million free-agent deal with the Blues.

THE PHYSICAL GAME

Drake gets noticed because he runs right over people. He is limited by his size but he will give a team whatever he's got. He's feisty enough to get the other team's attention, and he works to keep himself in scoring position. He has a mean streak. He gave Edmonton's Boyd Devereaux a serious concussion with a hit last season.

THE INTANGIBLES

The Blues were looking for a few missing ingredients after their first-round playoff upset. Drake has a history of strong playoff performances and is just the kind of role player the Blues can use to upgrade their chances.

PROJECTION

Drake exactly hit the goal total we expected for him (15), but by virtue of playing on the top line and staying healthy, for a change, he was far more productive in assists and points. He'll probably play alongside Pierre Turgeon, and could rack up 15 to 20 goals.

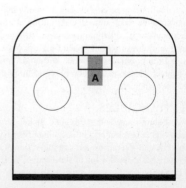

MIKE EASTWOOD

Yrs. of NHL service: 8
Born: Ottawa, Ont.; July 1, 1967
Position: centre
Height: 6-3
Weight: 205
Uniform no.: 32
Shoots: right

Career statistics:

GP	G	A	TP	PIM
483	67	94	161	213

1996-97 statistics:

GP	G	A	TP	+/-	PIM	PP	SH	GW	GT	S	PCT
60	2	10	12	-1	14	0	0	0	0	44	4.5

1997-98 statistics:

GP	G	A	TP	+/-	PIM	PP	SH	GW	GT	S	PCT
58	6	5	11	-2	22	0	0	1	0	38	15.8

1998-99 statistics:

GP	G	A	TP	+/-	PIM	PP	SH	GW	GT	S	PCT
82	9	21	30	+6	36	0	0	0	0	76	11.8

1999-2000 statistics:

GP	G	A	TP	+/-	PIM	PP	SH	GW	GT	S	PCT
79	19	15	34	+5	32	1	3	3	1	83	22.9

PROJECTION

Last season was such a breakout season for Eastwood offensively that we are reluctant to say he can repeat those numbers. It's not as if he's a kid — he's 33 — but he is playing on a strong team that appreciates him and they might just keep dragging him along for the scoring ride. A high end prediction would be 15 goals and 30 points.

LAST SEASON

Led NHL in shooting percentage. Second on team in shorthanded goals.

THE FINESSE GAME

Eastwood put some fire in his game last season and developed into a solid third-line centre for the Blues. His problem has long been a lack of consistency. He is a big player from whom coaches always want more. He has some sparkling games but lacks the confidence and offensive assets — particularly when it comes to the finishing touch — to become an effective everyday player.

Eastwood is sound defensively — alert and aware. He is also deceptively quick as a skater, but doesn't always push himself hard and needs to be urged along by coaches. He kills penalties well and more than holds his own on face-offs.

THE PHYSICAL GAME

Eastwood will never be confused with a body builder. He doesn't have much muscular definition at all and his temperament is equally non-descript. Although he is strong and doesn't get knocked off the puck, he needs to be a presence on the ice and could initiate more contact. He has to work on his conditioning and off-ice strengthening.

THE INTANGIBLES

Eastwood shows size and spunk, and makes himself play at a higher level in bigger spots than his easygoing nature usually requires. He can make things happen but seems to need a lot of prodding. The Blues liked Eastwood enough to re-sign the free agent.

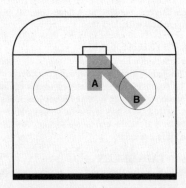

MICHAL HANDZUS

Yrs. of NHL service: 2
Born: Banska Bystrica, Czech Republic; Mar. 11, 1977
Position: centre
Height: 6-3
Weight: 191
Uniform no.: 26
Shoots: left

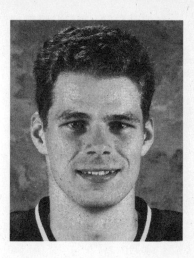

Career statistics:

GP	G	A	TP	PIM
147	29	40	69	74

1998-99 statistics:

GP	G	A	TP	+/-	PIM	PP	SH	GW	GT	S	PCT
66	4	12	16	-9	30	0	0	0	0	78	5.1

1999-2000 statistics:

GP	G	A	TP	+/-	PIM	PP	SH	GW	GT	S	PCT
81	25	28	53	+19	44	3	4	5	1	166	15.1

LAST SEASON

Second NHL season. Led team and tied for third in NHL in shorthanded goals. Third on team in goals, game-winning goals and shooting percentage.

THE FINESSE GAME

Handzus has the brains of a much more experienced player. He is so smart that he is the first forward St. Louis will throw out to kill a penalty when the Blues are two men down. He is very dependable and has a tremendous work ethic.

Handzus has started thinking more offensively, thanks to playing with Pavol Demitra. He has some offensive skill with a big-league shot. Handzus is big (six foot five), though still a little weedy. His skating is the only immediate question mark. It is probably adequate for the NHL, but if he works harder to improve he can become an effective player. He has good balance but needs to add a bit of quickness.

Handzus likes to pass a little too much. He need to take the puck to the net and chase down rebounds. He needs a little more greed in his game.

Handzus's skills and hockey sense allow him to play in all game situations. He can develop into a solid all-around centre, with an emphasis on his offensive skills.

THE PHYSICAL GAME

Handzus needs to fill out just a little, but he has gotten much stronger. He can hold off a defender with one arm and still take a shot or make a pass. He doesn't mind the physical game at all. He has the stamina to handle a lot of ice time, and did last season. The Blues have to be careful not to overuse him since he could be employed in so many situations. He is not very aggressive and will have to decide how badly he wants an NHL job, and be willing to pay a higher price.

THE INTANGIBLES

Handzus has won the number two role behind Pierre Turgeon and has terrific chemistry with Demitra and Lubos Bartecko.

PROJECTION

Handzus improved to the 25 goals we called for him last season. That appears to be his limit, with 30 to 35 assists besides.

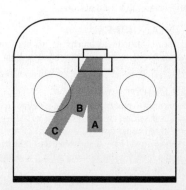

JOCHEN HECHT

Yrs. of NHL service: 1
Born: Mannheim, Germany; June 21, 1977
Position: centre
Height: 6-1
Weight: 180
Uniform no.: 55
Shoots: left

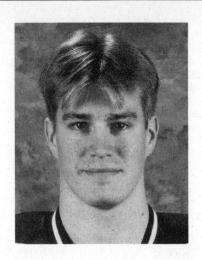

Career statistics:

GP	G	A	TP	PIM
66	13	21	34	28

1998-99 statistics:

GP	G	A	TP	+/-	PIM	PP	SH	GW	GT	S	PCT
3	0	0	0	-2	0	0	0	0	0	4	.0

1999-2000 statistics:

GP	G	A	TP	+/-	PIM	PP	SH	GW	GT	S	PCT
63	13	21	34	+20	28	5	0	1	0	140	9.3

LAST SEASON

First NHL season. Fourth among NHL rookies in shots. Missed 18 games with ankle sprain.

THE FINESSE GAME

Hecht is a rangy forward who can handle all three forward positions. He is a good skater with a good passing touch, and is a playmaker more than a scorer. He plays with a straight-up stance that allows him to see everything. He stickhandles in close, and has a great move walking out from the corner or behind the net.

Hecht has deceptive speed. He is a very smart player. He will probably be a better winger since he isn't strong enough on draws to handle playing centre full time. He is a tough read for opposing defensemen because he doesn't do the same thing every time. He is quite unpredictable: he might try to beat a defender one-on-one on one rush and the next time chip the puck in the corner or work a give-and-go. He uses a lot of play selections. Hecht is far from a reluctant shooter.

THE PHYSICAL GAME

Physical play doesn't bother Hecht but he doesn't initiate it. He has to get a little stronger and learn to play in the dirty areas of the ice. Hecht hit a bit of a wall, but rebounded with a solid playoffs.

THE INTANGIBLES

Hecht wasn't able to break into the top six but showed enough versatility to average 15 minutes a night and earn key second-unit power-play time.

PROJECTION

We are pleased to report that one of our sleeper rookie picks of last season (we pegged him as a 15-goal, 30-point man) came through — or darn close, anyway. And he would have done even better if he hadn't been injured. Hecht did nothing wrong and should keep moving forward.

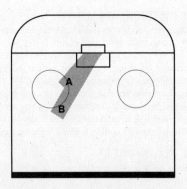

SEAN HILL

Yrs. of NHL service: 8
Born: Duluth, Minn.; Feb. 14, 1970
Position: right defense
Height: 6-0
Weight: 195
Uniform no.: 22
Shoots: right

Career statistics:

GP	G	A	TP	PIM
400	31	101	132	421

1996-97 statistics:

GP	G	A	TP	+/-	PIM	PP	SH	GW	GT	S	PCT
5	0	0	0	+1	4	0	0	0	0	9	0.0

1997-98 statistics:

GP	G	A	TP	+/-	PIM	PP	SH	GW	GT	S	PCT
55	1	6	7	-5	54	0	0	0	0	53	1.9

1998-99 statistics:

GP	G	A	TP	+/-	PIM	PP	SH	GW	GT	S	PCT
54	0	10	10	+9	48	0	0	0	0	44	.0

1999-2000 statistics:

GP	G	A	TP	+/-	PIM	PP	SH	GW	GT	S	PCT
62	13	31	44	+3	59	8	0	2	0	150	8.7

LAST SEASON

Signed by St. Louis as free agent from Carolina, July 1, 2000. Led Hurricanes defensemen in points. Second on team in power-play goals. Career highs in goals, assists and points. Missed 20 games with groin injuries.

THE FINESSE GAME

A good skater, Hill is agile, strong and balanced, if not overly fast. He can skate the puck out of danger or make a smart first pass. He learned defense in the Montreal system but has since evolved into more of a specialty-team player.

Hill has a good point shot and good offensive sense. He likes to carry the puck and start things off a rush or he will jump into the play. He can handle power-play time but is not exceptional. He is more suited to a second-unit role, though that ice time will fall off on an improved team. He has not played for many quality teams in the past few seasons (Anaheim, Ottawa, Carolina). Now we'll see how he fares with a solid defensive team for the first time.

Hill's best quality is his competitiveness. He will hack and whack at puck carriers like an annoying terrier ripping and nipping your socks and ankles.

THE PHYSICAL GAME

For a smallish player, Hill gets his share of points, and he gets them by playing bigger than his size. He has a bit of a mean streak, and though he certainly can't overpower people, he is a solidly built player who doesn't get pushed around easily. Hill is a willing hitter.

THE INTANGIBLES

Hill has had five serious injuries in the last three seasons: major reconstructive knee surgery in October, 1996; a broken leg in 1997-98; a fractured ankle and a fractured face (from a puck) that required reconstructive surgery in 1998-99; and a groin injury that cost him one-quarter of last season.

Despite that, the Blues shelled out $9 million over three years to add Hill to their roster as a number three defenseman behind Chirs Pronger and Al MacInnis.

PROJECTION

A poor man's MacInnis, Hill brings a veteran's composure. He doesn't have elite skills, but at 30 he put together a career year offensively in Carolina. Expectations will be higher from him in St. Louis, but at least he'll have a deeper team and he could match his 40-point effort.

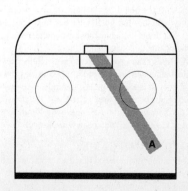

AL MACINNIS

Yrs. of NHL service: 18
Born: Inverness, N.S.; July 11, 1963
Position: right defense
Height: 6-2
Weight: 196
Uniform no.: 2
Shoots: right

Career statistics:

GP	G	A	TP	PIM
1203	301	803	1104	1333

1996-97 statistics:

GP	G	A	TP	+/-	PIM	PP	SH	GW	GT	S	PCT
72	13	30	43	+2	65	6	1	1	0	296	4.4

1997-98 statistics:

GP	G	A	TP	+/-	PIM	PP	SH	GW	GT	S	PCT
71	19	30	49	+6	80	9	1	2	0	227	8.4

1998-99 statistics:

GP	G	A	TP	+/-	PIM	PP	SH	GW	GT	S	PCT
82	20	42	62	+33	70	11	1	2	2	314	6.4

1999-2000 statistics:

GP	G	A	TP	+/-	PIM	PP	SH	GW	GT	S	PCT
61	11	28	39	+20	34	6	0	7	0	245	4.5

LAST SEASON

Led team in shots. Tied for team lead in game-winning goals. Missed 11 games with fractured ankle. Missed six games with chest contusion. Missed three games with back injury.

THE FINESSE GAME

What makes MacInnis's shot so good is that he knows the value of a change-up. If there is traffic in front, he will take a little off his shot to make it more tippable (and so he doesn't break too many teammates' ankles). One-on-one, of course, MacInnis will fire the laser and can just about knock a goalie into the net. And as much as he likes to shoot, he will also fake a big wind-up, which freezes the defenders, then make a quick slap-pass to an open teammate.

MacInnis knows when to jump into the play and when to back off. He can start a rush with a rink-wide pass, then be quick enough to burst up-ice and be in position for a return pass. Even when he merely rings the puck off the boards, he's a threat, since there is so much on the shot the goaltender has to be careful to stop it. MacInnis has a hard shot even when he's moving backwards.

MacInnis skates well with the puck. He is not very mobile, but he gets up to speed in a few strides and can hit his outside speed to beat a defender one-on-one. He will gamble and is best paired with a defensively alert partner, though he has improved his defensive play and is very smart against a two-on-one.

THE PHYSICAL GAME

MacInnis uses his finesse skills in a defensive posture, always looking for the counterattack. He reads de-fenses alertly, and positions himself to tie up attackers rather than try to knock them down. In his own way, he is a tough competitor who will pay the price to win. He was the Blues' top defenseman last season, and was always on the ice late to protect a lead.

THE INTANGIBLES

How many teams can boast two Norris Trophy-winning defensemen on the same unit? MacInnis was fragile last season, which is a concern at his age (37). With the addition of Sean Hill and perhaps rookie Mike Van Ryn, maybe MacInnis won't have to play 26 minutes a night.

PROJECTION

We expected a drop-off in production last season — of course, injuries played a huge part — and would again expect a slgiht decline in points (to around 50 over a full season).

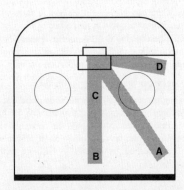

CHRIS PRONGER

Yrs. of NHL service: 7
Born: Dryden, Ont.; Oct. 10, 1974
Position: left defense
Height: 6-5
Weight: 220
Uniform no.: 44
Shoots: left

Career statistics:

GP	G	A	TP	PIM
508	64	185	248	720

1996-97 statistics:

GP	G	A	TP	+/-	PIM	PP	SH	GW	GT	S	PCT
79	11	25	35	+15	143	4	0	0	0	147	7.5

1997-98 statistics:

GP	G	A	TP	+/-	PIM	PP	SH	GW	GT	S	PCT
81	9	27	36	+47	180	1	0	2	0	145	6.2

1998-99 statistics:

GP	G	A	TP	+/-	PIM	PP	SH	GW	GT	S	PCT
67	13	33	46	+3	113	8	0	0	0	172	7.6

1999-2000 statistics:

GP	G	A	TP	+/-	PIM	PP	SH	GW	GT	S	PCT
79	14	48	62	+52	92	8	0	3	2	192	7.3

LAST SEASON

Won 2000 Hart and Norris Trophies. Named to NHL First All-Star Team. Led NHL in plus-minus. Led team in assists with career high. Second among NHL defensemen in points. Tied for first on team in power-play goals. Third on team in points and penalty minutes. Career highs in assists and points. Missed three games due to coach's decision.

THE FINESSE GAME

From the day he was drafted, Pronger has been touted as a young Larry Robinson, and last season he finally achieved his destiny — except for that pesky no-Cup thing. Aside from the lack of a ring, there are certainly similarities in their physique and style. Pronger is lanky with a powerful skating stride for angling his man to the boards for a take-out. He blends his physical play with good offensive instincts and skills. His skating is so fluid and his strides so long and efficient that he looks almost lazy, but he is faster than he looks and covers a lot of ground.

Pronger also handles the puck well when skating and is always alert for passing opportunities. His vision shows in his work on the power play. He patrols the point smartly, using a low, tippable shot. Like many tall defensemen, he doesn't get his slap shot away quickly, but he compensates with a snap shot that he uses liberally. He has good enough hands for a big guy and the Blues occasionally use him up front on the power play.

Pronger not only jumps into the rush, he knows when to, which is an art. He'll back off if the opportunity is not there. Playing with Al MacInnis, one of the game's great offensive defensemen, has helped Pronger in this area. He makes unique plays that make him stand out, great breakout passes and clever feeds through the neutral zone. He is also wise enough to dump-and-chase rather than hold onto the puck and force a low-percentage pass. He focusses more on his defensive role, but there is a considerable upside to his offense.

Disciplined away from the puck and alert defensively, Pronger shows good anticipation — going where the puck is headed before it's shot there. He is very confident with the puck in his own end. His defensive reads are excellent.

THE PHYSICAL GAME

Pronger finishes every check with enthusiasm and shows something of a nasty streak with his stick. He makes his stand between the blueline and the top of the circle, forcing the forward to react. His long reach helps to make that style effective. He also uses his stick and reach when killing penalties. He was the only player in the NHL to average over 30 minutes per game. He still takes some bad penalties.

THE INTANGIBLES

Pronger is among the NHL's elite defensemen and will stay there. Adding Sean Hill and maybe rookie Mike Van Ryn to the defensive mix will take some of the load off of him and MacInnis.

PROJECTION

Pronger is a world-class defenseman who contributes 55 to 60 points a season.

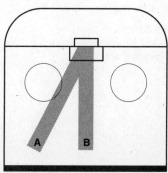

MARTY REASONER

Yrs. of NHL service: 1
Born: Rochester, NY; Feb. 26, 1977
Position: centre
Height: 6-1
Weight: 185
Uniform no.: 15
Shoots: left

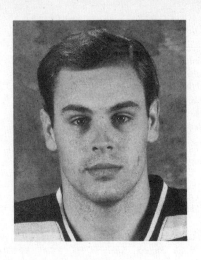

Career statistics:

GP	G	A	TP	PIM
54	13	21	34	28

1998-99 statistics:

GP	G	A	TP	+/-	PIM	PP	SH	GW	GT	S	PCT
22	3	7	10	+2	8	1	0	0	0	33	9.1

1999-2000 statistics:

GP	G	A	TP	+/-	PIM	PP	SH	GW	GT	S	PCT
32	10	14	24	+9	20	3	0	0	0	51	19.6

LAST SEASON

First NHL season. Appeared in 44 games with Worcester (AHL), scoring 23-28 — 51.

THE FINESSE GAME

Reasoner is a playmaker, and most effective when he attacks in straight lines. When he starts to zig-zag, he slows down and loses his speed as a weapon. He has such good hands and vision that he is able to bring the puck in with his deceptive speed and force the defenders to commit.

He has terrific hockey sense. The Blues played him on third- and fourth-lines, and he still managed to pile up some solid numbers, while also seeing some spot duty on the power play.

THE PHYSICAL GAME

Reasoner is average size and hasn't yet shown a knack for the physical part of the game. He can't afford to be a perimeter player. He could afford to work on his upper-body strength and his skating. He had trouble with a shoulder injury that affected his all-around play.

THE INTANGIBLES

Reasoner is stick behind the Blues' two top centres (Pierre Turgeon and Michal Handzus), and that makes it hard for him to find ice time. He is not as effective as a winger. He could be trade bait.

PROJECTION

Reasoner will get another long look in training camp. Most of his points will be assists.

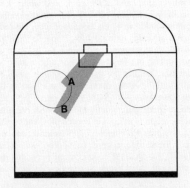

ROMAN TUREK

Yrs. of NHL service: 3
Born: Pisek, Czech.; May 21, 1970
Position: goaltender
Height: 6-3
Weight: 190
Uniform no.: 1
Catches: right

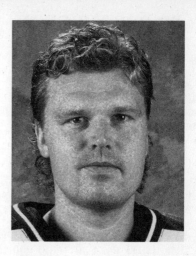

Career statistics:

GP	MIN	GA	SO	GAA	A	PIM
122	6929	235	9	2.04	1	6

1996-97 statistics:

GP	MIN	GAA	W	L	T	SO	GA	S	SAPCT	PIM
6	263	2.05	3	1	0	0	9	129	.930	0

1997-98 statistics:

GP	MIN	GAA	W	L	T	SO	GA	S	SAPCT	PIM
23	1324	2.22	11	10	1	1	49	496	.901	2

1998-99 statistics:

GP	MIN	GAA	W	L	T	SO	GA	S	SAPCT	PIM
26	1382	2.08	16	3	3	1	48	562	.915	0

1999-2000 statistics:

GP	MIN	GAA	W	L	T	SO	GA	S	SAPCT	PIM
67	3960	1.95	42	15	9	7	129	1470	.912	4

LAST SEASON

Led NHL in shutouts. Second in NHL in wins.

THE PHYSICAL GAME

In a word: big. Turek is one of the biggest, widest goalies in the NHL. And that's before he puts his pads on. Turek maximizes his size. He plays a hybird half-butterfly, half-standup style. It's much like Martin Brodeur's, although Turek isn't quite as athletic as Brodeur. He is very good low, flaring out his legs to take away the bottom part of the net. And because he keeps his torso upright, he takes away the top part of the net. Turek doesn't have a go a mile out to cut down the angle on a shooter, and he is always confident he's in the right spot. He can play mind games with shooters as well as any goalie in the NHL.

Turek likes to handle the puck and uses his stick very well. He takes away a shooter's options. He can get across the net quickly and use his flexibility and his big frame.

Turek is sometimes overly aggressive on plays around the net, so that when quick rebounds come, he is not always in position to recover well.

Turek seldom leaves bad rebounds. Pucks just seem to get absorbed in him.

THE MENTAL GAME

Turek spent a long time waiting for a chance to be a number one netminder in this league. Once it happened, he spent the beginning of last season adjusting to that pressure, By midseason, he was far more relaxed. He went into a lot of games knowing that if he allowed a bad goal it would mean a tie or a loss for his team. He played that way as a backup with Dallas, which plays a similar defensive style to the Blues, and adapted easily.

He handled the work load just fine in the regular season, but blew up in the playoffs. He still has something to prove.

THE INTANGIBLES

St. Louis added free agents during the off-season to improve its offense and defense, so Turek will be backstopping an even better team this season. He, as well as the rest of the Blues, learned the hard way that the postseason is totally different from the first 82 games. The Blues were able to keep Turek from over-work by giving Jamie McLennan some starts, but McLennan was lost to Minnesota in the expansion draft.

PROJECTION

Thirty-plus wins appears to be a given.

PIERRE TURGEON

Yrs. of NHL service: 13
Born: Rouyn, Que.; Aug. 28, 1969
Position: centre
Height: 6-1
Weight: 195
Uniform no.: 77
Shoots: left

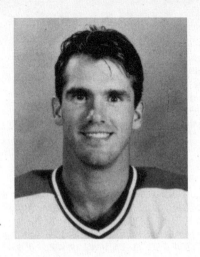

Career statistics:

GP	G	A	TP	PIM
929	423	640	1063	319

1996-97 statistics:

GP	G	A	TP	+/-	PIM	PP	SH	GW	GT	S	PCT
78	26	59	85	+8	14	5	0	7	1	216	12.0

1997-98 statistics:

GP	G	A	TP	+/-	PIM	PP	SH	GW	GT	S	PCT
60	22	46	68	+13	24	6	0	4	0	140	15.7

1998-99 statistics:

GP	G	A	TP	+/-	PIM	PP	SH	GW	GT	S	PCT
67	31	34	65	+4	36	10	0	5	2	193	16.1

1999-2000 statistics:

GP	G	A	TP	+/-	PIM	PP	SH	GW	GT	S	PCT
52	26	40	66	+30	8	8	0	3	0	139	18.7

LAST SEASON

Tied for team lead in power-play goals. Second on team in goals, points and shooting percentage. Third on team in assists and plus-minus. Missed 24 games with torn ligaments in thumb. Missed four games with back injury.

THE FINESSE GAME

Turgeon's skills are amazing. He never seems to be looking at the puck yet he is always in perfect control of it. He has a style unlike just about anyone else in the NHL. He's not a fast skater, but he can deke a defender or make a sneaky-Pete surprise pass. He is tough to defend against, because if you aren't aware of where he is on the ice and don't deny him the pass, he can kill a team with several moves.

Turgeon can slow or speed up the tempo of a game. He lacks breakout speed, but because he is slippery and can change speeds so smoothly, he's deceptive. His control with the puck down low is remarkable. He protects the puck well with the body and has good anticipation, reads plays well and is patient with the puck.

Although best known for his playmaking, Turgeon has an excellent shot. He will curl out from behind the net with a wrist shot, shoot off the fly from the right wing (his preferred side of the ice) or stand off to the side of the net on a power play and reach for a redirection of a point shot. He doesn't have a bazooka shot, but he uses quick, accurate wrist and snap shots. He has to create odd-man rushes. This is when he is at his finest.

THE PHYSICAL GAME

Turgeon battles hard. He isn't very aggressive or big, but he doesn't play a perimiter game and he gets hurt because of it.

THE INTANGIBLES

Turgeon struggled in the playoffs, due to the loss of Pavol Demitra, which left opponents free to key on him, and because of torn ligaments in his thumb.

PROJECTION

Turgeon is a point-a-game player.

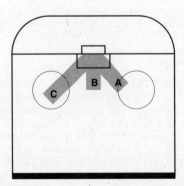

MIKE VAN RYN

Yrs. of NHL service: 0
Born: London, Ont.; May 14, 1979
Position: right defense
Height: 6-1
Weight: 190
Uniform no.: n.a.
Shoots: right

Career junior statistics:

GP	G	A	TP	PIM
61	6	35	41	34

LAST SEASON

Signed as free agent by St. Louis, June 30, 2000. Appeared in 61 games with Sarnia (OHL) scoring 6-35 — 41.

THE FINESSE GAME

Van Ryn is a solid all-around defenseman whose skills will weigh more heavily on the offensive side, though he won't be an elite-level "offenseman."

He is a good skater with strong balance and agility. He is able to pass or skate the puck out of danger. He is poised with the puck.

Van Ryn can play on both special teams. He has a low, hard, accurate shot from the point and mixes things up with some slick passing. He is smart, patient, and reads plays well.

THE PHYSICAL GAME

Van Ryn is still filling out to NHL size. He has an aggressive streak in him. He willingly clears out the front of his net and just has to get a little stronger for those wars. It won't hurt him a bit to play on the same team as Chris Pronger. He's an intense player.

THE INTANGIBLES

Van Ryn became a free agent when an NHL arbitrator ruled that because he left college (University of Michigan) to play junior last season, his draft rights (held by New Jersey) were void. It was a big blow to the Devils, and a huge boon to the Blues. This was the kid the Devils drafted one slot *ahead* of Scott Gomez in 1998. Some scouts believe Van Ryn might have taken a step back in his development by playing junior instead of college last year. He was captain of the Canadian world junior team.

PROJECTION

Van Ryn could be ready to step right into the Blues lineup. If he's not a number four at the start of the year, odds are he will be in the second half of the season.

SCOTT YOUNG

Yrs. of NHL service: 11
Born: Clinton, Mass.; Oct. 1, 1967
Position: right wing
Height: 6-0
Weight: 190
Uniform no.: 48
Shoots: right

Career statistics:

GP	G	A	TP	PIM
822	234	302	536	296

1996-97 statistics:

GP	G	A	TP	+/-	PIM	PP	SH	GW	GT	S	PCT
72	18	19	37	-5	14	7	0	0	0	164	11.0

1997-98 statistics:

GP	G	A	TP	+/-	PIM	PP	SH	GW	GT	S	PCT
73	13	20	33	-13	22	4	2	1	0	187	7.0

1998-99 statistics:

GP	G	A	TP	+/-	PIM	PP	SH	GW	GT	S	PCT
75	24	28	52	+8	27	8	0	4	0	205	11.7

1999-2000 statistics:

GP	G	A	TP	+/-	PIM	PP	SH	GW	GT	S	PCT
75	24	15	39	+12	18	6	1	7	1	244	9.8

LAST SEASON

Tied for team lead in game-winning goals. Missed two games with dislocated right shoulder.

THE FINESSE GAME

Young is a hockey machine. He has a very heavy shot that surprises a lot of goalies, and he loves to fire it off the wing. He can also one-time the puck low on the face-off, or he'll battle for pucks and tips in front of the net. He's keen to score and always goes to the net with his stick down, ready for the puck, though he is not a great finisher. Young has a bit of tunnel vision, and doesn't really see his teammates or use them as well as he might.

With all of that in mind, his defensive awareness is even more impressive, because Young is basically a checking winger. He reads plays in all zones equally well and has good anticipation. He played defense in college, so he is well-schooled.

Young is a fast skater, which, combined with his reads, makes him a sound forechecker. He will often outrace defensemen to get pucks and avoid icings, and his speed allows him to recover when he gets over-zealous in the attacking zone.

THE PHYSICAL GAME

Young's lone drawback is that he is not a physical player. He will do what he has to do in battles along the boards in the defensive zone, but he's more of a defensive force with quickness and hand skills. He's not a pure grinder, but will bump and get in the way.

THE INTANGIBLES

Young stepped up big-time in the playoffs, with six goals in six games. He is a character person as well as an ultrareliable performer. Players with great wheels like Young tend to last a long time, so expect him to display his veteran ability for many more seasons. Just don't expect him to score 50 goals.

PROJECTION

Young will get quality ice time in St. Louis, lots of power-play chances, and 40 points and 20 goals is again likely.

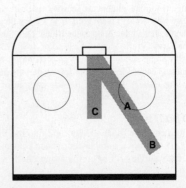

TAMPA BAY LIGHTNING

Players' Statistics 1999-2000

POS.	NO.	PLAYER	GP	G	A	PTS	+/-	PIM	PP	SH	GW	GT	S	PCT
C	4	VINCENT LECAVALIER	80	25	42	67	-25	43	6		3	1	166	15.1
L	33	FREDRIK MODIN	80	22	26	48	-26	18	3		5		167	13.2
R	10	MIKE JOHNSON	80	21	26	47	6	27	6	1	3		132	15.9
R	20	STAN DRULIA	68	11	22	33	-18	24	1	2	1	1	94	11.7
C	9	BRIAN HOLZINGER	73	10	20	30	-3	51	1	2	2		104	9.6
L	8	TODD WARRINER	73	14	14	28	-8	36	3	1			133	10.5
D	13	PAVEL KUBINA	69	8	18	26	-19	93	6		3		128	6.3
D	23	PETR SVOBODA	70	2	23	25	-11	170	2				93	2.2
D	2	*PAUL MARA	54	7	11	18	-27	73	4		1		78	9.0
C	17	*RYAN JOHNSON	80	4	14	18	-8	16					49	8.2
C	14	ROBERT PETROVICKY	43	7	10	17	2	14	1				50	14.0
C	22	WAYNE PRIMEAU	58	7	10	17	-12	63	2		1		75	9.3
R	25	DAN KESA	50	4	10	14	-11	21	1	1	1		55	7.3
L	15	JAROSLAV SVEJKOVSKY	52	6	7	13	-14	30	1				60	10.0
C	19	STEVE MARTINS	59	6	7	13	-12	37		1	1		65	9.2
C	5	BRUCE GARDINER	51	3	9	12	-20	41					48	6.3
D	30	ANDREI ZYUZIN	34	2	9	11	-11	33					47	4.3
D	7	*BEN CLYMER	60	2	6	8	-26	87	2				98	2.0
D	6	BRYAN MUIR	41	3	4	7	-9	45	1				51	5.9
D	21	*CORY SARICH	59		6	6	-6	77					69	
D	3	SERGEY GUSEV	28	2	3	5	-9	6	1				23	8.7
L	28	*NILS EKMAN	28	2	2	4	-8	36	1				42	4.8
L	29	PAVEL TORGAEV	14		4	4	1	6					18	
D	18	*MAREK POSMYK	18	1	2	3	1	20					22	4.5
R	42	*MATT ELICH	8	1	1	2	-1						5	20.0
L	25	*DWAYNE HAY	19	1	1	2	-2	4					14	7.1
D	27	JASSEN CULLIMORE	46	1	1	2	-12	66					23	4.3
L	11	SHAWN BURR	4		2	2	2						6	
L	24	REID SIMPSON	26	1		1	-3	103					13	7.7
R	51	*DALE ROMINSKI	3		1	1	1	2						
D	49	*KASPARS ASTASHENKO	8		1	1	-2	4					3	
G	1	*ZAC BIERK	12		1	1	0							
L	34	*GORDIE DWYER	24		1	1	-6	135					7	
D	46	ANDREI SKOPINTSEV	4				-4	6						
G	93	DAREN PUPPA	5				0	2						
L	9	JEFF SHEVALIER	5				-1	2					2	
G	35	*DIETER KOCHAN	5				0							
L	43	*KYLE FREADRICH	10				-1	39						
G	31	RICH PARENT	14				0	2						
G	35	KEVIN HODSON	24				0	2						
G	39	DAN CLOUTIER	52				0	29						

GP = games played; G = goals; A = assists; PTS = points; +/- = goals-for minus goals-against while player is on ice; PIM = penalties in minutes; PP = power-play goals; SH = shorthanded goals; GW = game-winning goals; GT = game-tying goals; S = no. of shots; PCT = percentage of goals to shots; * = rookie

DMITRI AFANASENKOV

Yrs. of NHL service: 0
Born: Arkhangelsk, Russia; May 12, 1980
Position: left wing
Height: 6-2
Weight: 200
Uniform no.: n.a.
Shoots: right

Career junior statistics:

GP	G	A	TP	PIM
126	84	78	162	104

LAST SEASON

Will be entering first NHL season. Scored 56-43 — 99 in 60 games with Sherbrooke (QMJHL). Eighth in league in goals.

THE FINESSE GAME

Afanasenkov is considered a pure goal scorer. Once he is over the blueline, he wants the puck and he knows what to do with it — he is extremely creative and loves to shoot. He is a right-handed shot, but, like so many Europeans, can play the left wing. This opens up his forehand to the centre of the ice for one-timers. He is also a smart playmaker. He plays a good puck control game.

A powerful skater, Afanasenkov can go end-to-end with the puck. He is deceptively quick and skating with the puck doesn't slow him down. He has excellent vision and good hockey sense.

Afanasenkov should be a natural on the power play. Eighteen of his 56 goals with Sherbrooke were scored with the manpower advantage.

THE PHYSICAL GAME

Afanasenkov has added nearly 20 pounds since his draft year two seasons ago (he was taken 72nd overall by Tampa in the 1998 draft). He is strong along the boards and in front of the net. He doesn't initiate but he doesn't back down, either.

THE INTANGIBLES

Afanasenkov will be given every chance to make the big team's roster in September. Tampa Bay is desperately seeking a sniper to play with Vincent Lecavalier. If the rest of his game is up to NHL calibre, Afanasenkov won't be starting the season in the minors.

PROJECTION

A great sleeper pick if your pool includes rookies.

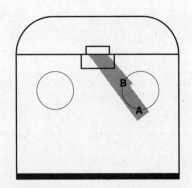

DAN CLOUTIER

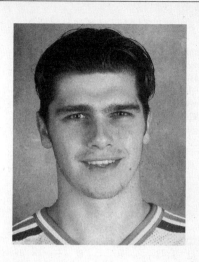

Yrs. of NHL service: 2
Born: Mont-Laurier, Que.; Apr. 22, 1976
Position: goaltender
Height: 6-1
Weight: 182
Uniform no.: 39
Catches: left

Career statistics:

GP	MIN	GA	SO	GAA	A	PIM
86	4140	217	0	3.14	0	50

1997-98 statistics:

GP	MIN	GAA	W	L	T	SO	GA	S	SAPCT	PIM
12	551	2.50	4	5	1	0	23	248	.907	19

1998-99 statistics:

GP	MIN	GAA	W	L	T	SO	GA	S	SAPCT	PIM
22	1097	2.68	6	8	3	0	49	570	.914	2

1999-2000 statistics:

GP	MIN	GAA	W	L	T	SO	GA	S	SAPCT	PIM
52	2492	3.49	9	30	3	0	145	1258	.885	29

PROJECTION

Put Cloutier in Ottawa (a perfect fit, if Marshall Johnston is reading this) and he'll post 30 wins. He'll be lucky to get 15 if he stays in Tampa.

LAST SEASON

Second NHL season. Tied for lead among NHL goalies in penalty minutes. Missed five games with knee injury. Missed four games with neck injury. Missed three games with groin injury. Missed four games due to suspension.

THE PHYSICAL GAME

Cloutier is an athletic, stand-up goalie — surprising in an era of so many Patrick Roy butterfly clones. He doesn't have the reflexes to excel with a less technical style.

He follows the play well and squares his body to the shooter. He will learn to play his angles better with more NHL experience, but he has good size to take away a lot of the net from the shooter.

His skills are still a little raw. He doesn't control his rebounds well off his pads and his stickhandling could use work. But he is an eager student who would benefit from a veteran backup goalie and a goalie coach. Behind a young and inexperienced defense corps last year, Cloutier was frequently left hung out to dry.

THE MENTAL GAME

Cloutier is combative. He earned a four-game suspension due to a fight in Chicago last season. The fight in him extends to his desire to succeed at the NHL level. He is as competitive on the ice as he is easygoing off it, and playing for a losing team night after night can fray on a young goalie's nerves.

THE INTANGIBLES

Cloutier's run-ins with coach Steve Ludzik had the Lightning looking for goaltending help (possibily Nikolai Khabibulin) in the off-season.

SERGEY GUSEV

Yrs. of NHL service: 2
Born: Nizhny Tagil, Russia; July 31, 1975
Position: left defense
Height: 6-1
Weight: 195
Uniform no.: 3
Shoots: left

Career statistics:

GP	G	A	TP	PIM
73	3	10	13	24

1997-98 statistics:

GP	G	A	TP	+/-	PIM	PP	SH	GW	GT	S	PCT
9	0	0	0	-5	2	0	0	0	0	5	0.0

1998-99 statistics:

GP	G	A	TP	+/-	PIM	PP	SH	GW	GT	S	PCT
36	1	7	8	-3	16	0	0	1	0	46	2.2

1999-2000 statistics:

GP	G	A	TP	+/-	PIM	PP	SH	GW	GT	S	PCT
28	2	3	5	-9	6	1	0	0	0	23	8.7

points as a two-way defenseman. He should have a stronger second half than first — not uncommon for players coming back off serious knee injuries.

LAST SEASON
Missed 54 games with knee injury.

THE FINESSE GAME
Gusev has a good offensive upside with considerable skills — all NHL quality. He is an excellent skater, with speed, agility and mobility. He handles the puck well and has a good shot. He has fine offensive instincts, but often looks to get involved in the attack at the wrong times, something he needs to curb. He can work on the power-play point on the first unit.

Gusev has to improve in his defensive positioning and awareness; he is still learning what it takes to be a well-rounded defenseman. He could develop along Darryl Sydor lines.

Gusev was averaging 17 minutes per game when he suffered a season-ending knee injury in December. The Lightning have him pegged as one of their top-four defensemen, but much will depend on his recovery.

THE PHYSICAL GAME
Gusev is not a big banger, and he will have to learn to use his body more consistently to get into the lineup. He still needs to grow and gain some confidence. He can play with a little edge.

THE INTANGIBLES
Gusev was buried in the deep Dallas system, but will become a top-four defenseman and log plenty of ice time with the Lightning. He played well since coming to Tampa, a positive sign. He has had the advantage of learning in a strong defensive system.

PROJECTION
Assuming he is able to rehab completely from his injury in time to start the season, Gusev should score 20

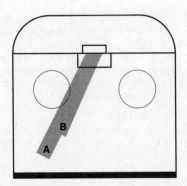

BRIAN HOLZINGER

Yrs. of NHL service: 5
Born: Parma, Ohio; Oct. 10, 1972
Position: centre
Height: 5-11
Weight: 180
Uniform no.: 19
Shoots: right

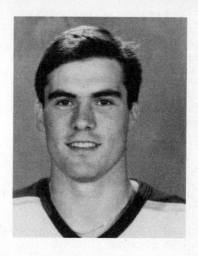

Career statistics:

GP	G	A	TP	PIM
366	73	100	173	223

1996-97 statistics:

GP	G	A	TP	+/-	PIM	PP	SH	GW	GT	S	PCT
81	22	29	51	+9	54	2	2	6	0	142	15.5

1997-98 statistics:

GP	G	A	TP	+/-	PIM	PP	SH	GW	GT	S	PCT
69	14	21	35	-2	36	4	2	1	1	116	12.1

1998-99 statistics:

GP	G	A	TP	+/-	PIM	PP	SH	GW	GT	S	PCT
81	17	17	34	+2	45	5	0	2	0	143	11.9

1999-2000 statistics:

GP	G	A	TP	+/-	PIM	PP	SH	GW	GT	S	PCT
73	10	20	30	-3	51	1	2	2	0	104	9.6

LAST SEASON

Acquired from Buffalo with Wayne Primeau, Cory Sarich and a third-round draft choice in 2000 for Chris Gratton and second-round choice in 2001, Mar. 10, 2000. Tied for first on team in shorthanded goals. Third on team in plus-minus. Missed three games with strained abdomen. Missed three games with separated shoulder.

THE FINESSE GAME

Holzinger has a fine touch down low and patience with the puck to find the open passing lane. He needs to work with a big grinder on one wing, because he is too small to do much work effectively in the corners. He is not as gritty as a number of smaller forwards and plays too much on the perimeter.

Holzinger is not a natural scorer but he has some speed, which he needs to learn to use to his advantage on a more consistent basis. He is crafty and deceptively quick.

The key to Holzinger's development will be adding the little things to his game that make a complete player. He has to ask himself how he can contribute if he's not scoring. He can play, but can he win? He has a lot of raw talent, but at the moment he's an open-ice break player. He has a lot of hockey sense and may be adaptable. His defense has improved.

THE PHYSICAL GAME

Holzinger will have to work for his open ice in the NHL. He is not very big, nor very strong. Strength and conditioning work must figure in his summer vacation plans again, and every season for as long as he wants to stay in the NHL. He has a little bit of an edge to his game, and has to play gritty.

THE INTANGIBLES

Holzinger is the number two centre in Tampa behind Vincent Lecavalier, and he will get his best shot to shine in that role since he is too small to play a third-line checking role. His job could be in trouble if Tampa upgrades the position, though that doesn't seem likely to happen this season.

PROJECTION

Holzinger will probably get enough ice time for 40 points, but he is not an impact player — not even on a team as weak as the Lightning.

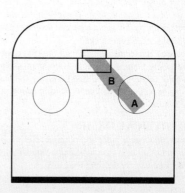

MIKE JOHNSON

Yrs. of NHL service: 3
Born: Scarborough, Ont.; Oct. 3, 1974
Position: right wing
Height: 6-2
Weight: 180
Uniform no.: 20
Shoots: right

Career statistics:

GP	G	A	TP	PIM
254	58	84	142	90

1996-97 statistics:

GP	G	A	TP	+/-	PIM	PP	SH	GW	GT	S	PCT
13	2	2	4	-2	4	0	1	1	0	27	7.4

1997-98 statistics:

GP	G	A	TP	+/-	PIM	PP	SH	GW	GT	S	PCT
82	15	32	47	-4	24	5	0	0	1	143	10.5

1998-99 statistics:

GP	G	A	TP	+/-	PIM	PP	SH	GW	GT	S	PCT
79	20	24	44	+13	35	5	3	2	0	149	13.4

1999-2000 statistics:

GP	G	A	TP	+/-	PIM	PP	SH	GW	GT	S	PCT
80	21	26	47	+6	27	6	1	3	0	132	15.9

LAST SEASON

Acquired from Toronto with Marek Posmyk and Toronto's fifth- and sixth-round draft choices in 2000 for Darcy Tucker and fourth-round draft choice in 2000, Feb. 9, 2000. Led team in shooting percentage and plus-minus. Tied for team lead in power-play goals. Tied for second on team in assists. Third on team in goals and points. Tied career-high in points. Missed one game with facial fracture.

THE FINESSE GAME

Johnson has an amazing, advanced knowledge of how to use the ice — offensively and defensively. He protects the puck on the boards. When he's down low in his own end on defensive-zone coverage, he's strong and supports the puck well.

Offensively, Johnson will take the puck to the net. He knows when to move and doesn't just stand around and stay checked. He moves into scoring positions. His puck movement on the power play is exceptional. He has to get a stronger shot, which should come with physical maturity. He is not a natural scorer and has to work hard for the goals he gets.

Johnson is a terrific skater, with the kind of ability that instantly stamps him as a 10-year pro. He can harry puck carriers when killing penalties and has the one-step breakaway quickness, making him a short-handed threat.

THE PHYSICAL GAME

Johnson has to get bigger and stronger. He is tall and reedy, and if he stands too still near the stick rack he'll get packed away for the next road trip.

THE INTANGIBLES

Johnson became Vincent Lecavalier's right-hand man, possibly the best thing to happen to his career, because Lecavalier is an outstanding playmaker. Johnson doesn't bury nearly enough of the chances he gets from his centre's sweet setups, but he scored 10 goals in 28 games with the Lightning (after scoring 11 in 52 games with the Maple Leafs prior to the trade).

PROJECTION

Johnson's point totals got a big bump from his being teamed with Lecavalier. If Johnson can keep that role this season, he will score in the 60- to 70-point range.

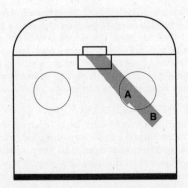

PAVEL KUBINA

Yrs. of NHL service: 2
Born: Vsetin, Czech.; Sept. 10, 1979
Position: right defense
Height: 6-2
Weight: 189
Uniform no.: 13
Shoots: right

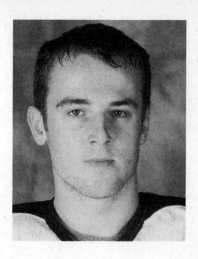

Career statistics:

GP	G	A	TP	PIM
147	18	32	50	195

1997-98 statistics:

GP	G	A	TP	+/-	PIM	PP	SH	GW	GT	S	PCT
10	1	2	3	-1	22	0	0	0	0	8	12.5

1998-99 statistics:

GP	G	A	TP	+/-	PIM	PP	SH	GW	GT	S	PCT
68	9	12	21	-33	80	3	1	1	1	119	7.6

1999-2000 statistics:

GP	G	A	TP	+/-	PIM	PP	SH	GW	GT	S	PCT
69	8	18	26	-19	93	6	0	3	0	128	6.3

LAST SEASON

Second NHL season. Led team defensemen in points. Tied for team lead in power-play goals. Tied for second on team in game-winning goals. Missed nine games with injured heel. Missed two games with rib injury. Missed one game with hand injury. Missed one game due to coach's decision.

THE FINESSE GAME

Kubina is one of the most exciting young defense prospects in the league. Only 22, he is showing continued forward progress off his solid rookie season and Tampa has placed a lot of confidence in him. If he makes a mistake (and he does), the Lightning put him right back out to keep learning. Playing with veteran Petr Svoboda has helped greatly: they speak the same language, and Svoboda is a fundamentally sound NHL defenseman.

Kubina isn't a great skater. He is big and somewhat upright in his stance, and he takes short strides. He lacks lateral quickness, though he has shown improvement. He is very strong on his skates.

The key to his game is his passing. He has fair offensive instincts, though he doesn't have a good shot. And he gets second-unit power-play time. His puck skills and his composure are advanced for such an inexperienced player. He received a lot of ice time (averaging more than 22 minutes for the second consecutive year) and a lot of responsibility, often facing other teams' top lines, and he has grown with the challenges.

THE PHYSICAL GAME

Kubina has good size and he uses it well. He has a bit of an edge to him. All in all, a solid package.

THE INTANGIBLES

Kubina is going to get a heavy workload again this season. He has to be nagged to keep at his conditioning and to work on his off-ice habits.

PROJECTION

In last year's *HSR,* we said: "Kubina has real offensive upside and should lead the Lightning defensemen in scoring with 30 to 35 points." He missed that due to injuries but should attain those numbers if he can stay healthy.

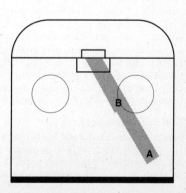

VINCENT LECAVALIER

Yrs. of NHL service: 2
Born: Ile Bizard, Quebec; Apr. 21, 1980
Position: centre
Height: 6-4
Weight: 180
Uniform no.: 8
Shoots: left

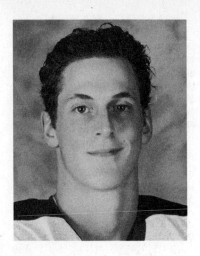

Career statistics:

GP	G	A	TP	PIM
162	38	57	95	66

1998-99 statistics:

GP	G	A	TP	+/-	PIM	PP	SH	GW	GT	S	PCT
82	13	15	28	-19	23	2	0	2	1	125	10.4

1999-2000 statistics:

GP	G	A	TP	+/-	PIM	PP	SH	GW	GT	S	PCT
80	25	42	67	-25	43	6	0	3	1	166	15.1

LAST SEASON

Second NHL season. Led team in goals, assists and points. Tied for first on team in power-play goals. Second on team in shots and shooting perecentage. Tied for second on team in game-winning goals. Missed two games with bruised ankle.

THE FINESSE GAME

Playing in relative hockey obscurity in Tampa, Lecavalier quietly had one of the better sophomore seasons in the league last year.

With the late-season trade of Chris Gratton to Buffalo, he became the team's number one centre, and he is doing the job without the benefit of number one wingers. Lecavalier's puck skills are everything they were advertised to be when the Lightning drafted him first overall in 1998. He is an elite playmaker. His passing skills are world class, and he has gained more confidence in his moves, even daring spin-o-ramas. Like Wayne Gretzky and Mario Lemieux, the two great centres with whom he has been compared, Lecavalier will invent moves lesser players don't even dare dream of. His linemates have to be constantly aware that he can get the puck to them at any time.

Linemates. Now there's a problem. Lecavalier plays with unpolished wingers in Tampa. Any upgrade over Mike Johnson, Todd Warriner or Fredrik Modin will see an upsurge in Lecavalier's point totals.

Like many a young player, Lecavalier will need to focus on his defensive play, but he has a good foundation for that already and should be an apt pupil. He is a shifty skater who can catch a defenseman flat-footed. His speed is major league. He can burst to the outside with the puck and beat a defenseman one-on-one.

THE PHYSICAL GAME

Lecavalier is a tall, skinny kid who has to keep working in the weight room in order to do battle against the league's heavyweights. He has a nasty streak in him, though, and is just as quick to answer a hit with a whack of the stick.

THE INTANGIBLES

At age 20, Lecavalier can be a point-a-game player if he is given any help at all up front. He needed to be the number one centre — now he is, and all of the checking attention will be focussed on him.

PROJECTION

Wow. We thought Lecavalier's progress would be much more gradual. Instead, he more than doubled his rookie point total and is destined for more. If Tampa unearths any kind of winger with any kind of scoring touch — rookie Dimitry Afanashenkov is the great untried hope — Lecavalier could put up 80 points this season.

PAUL MARA

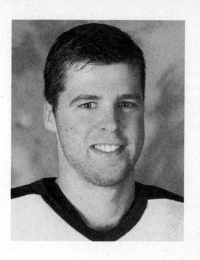

Yrs. of NHL service: 1
Born: Ridgewood, NJ; Sept. 7, 1979
Position: left defense
Height: 6-4
Weight: 202
Uniform no.: 22
Shoots: left

Career statistics:

GP	G	A	TP	PIM
55	8	12	20	73

1998-99 statistics:

GP	G	A	TP	+/-	PIM	PP	SH	GW	GT	S	PCT
1	1	1	2	-3	0	1	0	0	0	1	100.0

1999-2000 statistics:

GP	G	A	TP	+/-	PIM	PP	SH	GW	GT	S	PCT
54	7	11	18	-27	73	4	0	1	0	78	9.0

LAST SEASON

First NHL season. Missed 13 games with broken jaw. Missed one game due to coach's decision. Appeared in 14 games with Detroit (IHL).

THE FINESSE GAME

Mara is primarily an offensive defenseman. His point shot is a weapon not because of its velocity — he is no Al MacInnis — but because he gets it away quickly and keeps it low and on net. He creates chances for tip-ins and scrambles off his rebounds.

Mobile for his size, Mara's skating is quite smooth and powerful. He is also one of those efficient skaters who can stay as strong late in the game as he did on his first few shifts. He logged 31 minutes in one game last season.

He has good vision and is an excellent passer. He is also quick to move the puck out of his zone and will jump up and join the rush.

He is fairly advanced defensively for a young player. He possesses good hockey intelligence.

THE PHYSICAL GAME

Mara makes take-outs, but he is not a punishing hitter. He is tall but lean, and needs to fill out more because he will need more strength to compete in the trenches.

THE INTANGIBLES

The Bolts did the right thing with Mara by starting him off slowly last season. He is ready to take the next step.

PROJECTION

Mara started last season in the minors, and broke his jaw in his NHL debut against Washington. He obviously needs more seasoning. Still, with jobs wide open on the Lightning defense, he could easily step into the top four this season and score 25 points while doing so.

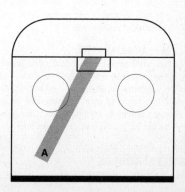

FREDRIK MODIN

Yrs. of NHL service: 4
Born: Sundsvall, Sweden; Oct. 8, 1974
Position: left wing
Height: 6-4
Weight: 220
Uniform no.: 33
Shoots: left

Career statistics:

GP	G	A	TP	PIM
297	60	64	124	109

1996-97 statistics:

GP	G	A	TP	+/-	PIM	PP	SH	GW	GT	S	PCT
76	6	7	13	-14	24	0	0	0	0	85	7.1

1997-98 statistics:

GP	G	A	TP	+/-	PIM	PP	SH	GW	GT	S	PCT
74	16	16	32	-5	32	1	0	4	0	137	11.7

1998-99 statistics:

GP	G	A	TP	+/-	PIM	PP	SH	GW	GT	S	PCT
67	16	15	31	+14	35	1	0	3	1	108	14.8

1999-2000 statistics:

GP	G	A	TP	+/-	PIM	PP	SH	GW	GT	S	PCT
80	22	26	48	-26	18	3	0	5	0	167	13.2

LAST SEASON

Acquired from Toronto for Cory Cross, Oct. 1, 1999. Led team in game-winning goals and shots. Second on team in goals and points with career highs. Tied for second on team in assists with career high. Third on team in shooting percentage.

THE FINESSE GAME

Modin has a heavy cannon shot and a good wrist shot. So why does he pass?

His primary instinct is to set someone else up with a pass, but, especially while playing alongside Vincent Lecavalier, Modin has to pull the trigger more and from more areas of the ice. Throw the puck on net and good things may follow. That message seemed to be sinking in last year, but considering the prime ice time he received with the Lightning, a two-shots-per-game average is not sufficient. He has excellent hands.

Modin has a bit of a knock-kneed skating style, and isn't pretty to watch, but he has NHL-calibre speed and is strong on his skates.

THE PHYSICAL GAME

Modin has a powerful upper body for muscling through plays when he has a notion to, though he remains too much of a perimeter player. On nights when he gets it into his head to play a physical game, he drives to the net with better intent and is far more effective. He has very good size and could be more of a force.

THE INTANGIBLES

Modin got a fresh start in Tampa after being in and out of the Toronto lineup. He enjoyed playing with Lecavalier. (Who wouldn't? The kid is terrific.) But he will need to show more to keep his spot on the top line.

PROJECTION

If Modin can stick on the top line with Lecavalier, he should improve off his totals of last season. A jump to 25 or 30 goals is not illogical.

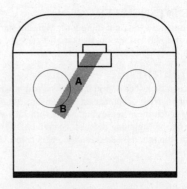

CORY SARICH

Yrs. of NHL service: 1
Born: Saskatoon, Sask.; Aug. 16, 1978
Position: right defense
Height: 6-3
Weight: 193
Uniform no.: 21
Shoots: right

Career statistics:

GP	G	A	TP	PIM
63	0	6	6	77

1998-99 statistics:

GP	G	A	TP	+/-	PIM	PP	SH	GW	GT	S	PCT
4	0	0	0	+3	0	0	0	0	0	2	0.0

1999-2000 statistics:

GP	G	A	TP	+/-	PIM	PP	SH	GW	GT	S	PCT
59	0	6	6	-6	77	0	0	0	0	69	0.0

LAST SEASON

Acquired from Buffalo with Brian Holzinger, Wayne Primeau and a third-round draft choice in 2000 for Chris Gratton and second-round draft choice in 2001, Mar. 10, 2000. First NHL season. Appeared in 15 games with Rochester (AHL), scoring 0-6 — 6.

THE FINESSE GAME

Sarich's game is rough, not polished, and the Lightning will have to live with some of his mistakes as he continues to learn the NHL game.

Sarich is a stay-at-home defenseman who will develop into an extremely steady and reliable bedrock for the Tampa Bay defense. He has NHL skating ability, with decent lateral movement, pivots and balance. He moves the puck very well. Being big and strong and being able to get the puck out of the zone quickly and safely already has Sarich ahead of some NHL veteran defensemen.

Sarich does not get involved in the attack. He knows his game is defense.

THE PHYSICAL GAME

Sarich has pro size and a mean streak. His skating is powerful enough to help him line up opponents for some pretty big hits. He is careful enough not to go running out of position looking for his checks, though. Sarich is a composed and mature player with a high panic point. He competes hard.

THE INTANGIBLES

The Lightning has to do with Sarich what they did with Pavel Kubina: he has to know that when he makes a mistake, they will send him right back out on the next shift to try, try again. Even though he was a minus-8 in his 17 games with the Lightning after the trade, coaches fell in love with his attitude and his physical play.

PROJECTION

Sarich will probably top 100 minutes in penalties, play some solid defense, and not put many more than 15 points on the board.

JAROSLAV SVEJKOVSKY

Yrs. of NHL service: 3
Born: Plzen, Czech Republic; Oct. 1, 1976
Position: left wing
Height: 5-11
Weight: 185
Uniform no.: 34
Shoots: right

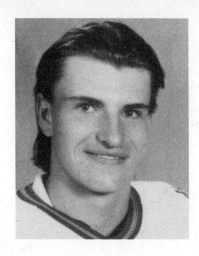

Career statistics:

GP	G	A	TP	PIM
113	23	19	42	56

1996-97 statistics:

GP	G	A	TP	+/-	PIM	PP	SH	GW	GT	S	PCT
19	7	3	10	-1	4	2	0	1	0	30	23.3

1997-98 statistics:

GP	G	A	TP	+/-	PIM	PP	SH	GW	GT	S	PCT
17	4	1	5	-5	10	2	0	1	0	29	13.8

1998-99 statistics:

GP	G	A	TP	+/-	PIM	PP	SH	GW	GT	S	PCT
25	6	8	14	-2	12	4	0	2	0	50	12.0

1999-2000 statistics:

GP	G	A	TP	+/-	PIM	PP	SH	GW	GT	S	PCT
52	6	7	13	-14	30	1	0	0	0	60	10.0

self in training camp in order to win a job. If he does, there is a chance he could put up a 20-goal season that would be a major first step in becoming an NHL regular.

LAST SEASON

Acquired from Washington for a third-round draft choice in 2001 and a seventh-round draft choice in 2000, Jan. 17, 2000. Missed nine games with bruised knee. Missed one game due to coach's decision.

THE FINESSE GAME

Svejkovsky is a pure goal scorer. He will work to get himself in high-percentage zones and is astoundingly accurate with his shot. He has great hands for tipping pucks.

He is a good skater without real breakout speed, but he has a nose for the net and he pays the price. He wants the puck and knows what to do with it. He is a threat every time he's near the puck.

Svejkovsky is hardly a defensive specialist, but his overall game is fairly well developed.

THE PHYSICAL GAME

Svejkovsky is not overly aggressive but he will take hits to make plays. He is an average-sized player and needs to get bigger and stronger. He's tenacious and will take a cross-check or a slash to score goals.

THE INTANGIBLES

Several injuries derailed Svejkovsky's progress with the Caps, who considered him a blue chip prospect until finally giving up. He scored one goal in 23 games with the Caps, and five in 29 after being traded to the Lightning.

PROJECTION

Svejkovsky is definitely on the bubble, even with a weak Tampa team. He needs to mature and prove him-

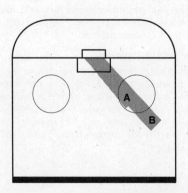

PETR SVOBODA

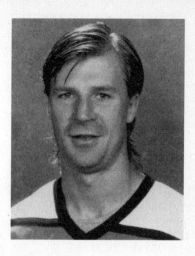

Yrs. of NHL service: 16
Born: Most, Czech Republic; Feb. 14, 1966
Position: left defense
Height: 6-1
Weight: 190
Uniform no.: 23
Shoots: left

Career statistics:

GP	G	A	TP	PIM
1009	57	338	395	1564

1996-97 statistics:

GP	G	A	TP	+/-	PIM	PP	SH	GW	GT	S	PCT
67	2	12	14	+10	94	1	0	0	0	36	5.6

1997-98 statistics:

GP	G	A	TP	+/-	PIM	PP	SH	GW	GT	S	PCT
56	3	15	18	+19	83	2	0	0	0	44	6.8

1998-99 statistics:

GP	G	A	TP	+/-	PIM	PP	SH	GW	GT	S	PCT
59	5	18	23	+1	81	1	1	1	0	83	6.0

1999-2000 statistics:

GP	G	A	TP	+/-	PIM	PP	SH	GW	GT	S	PCT
70	2	23	25	-11	170	2	0	0	0	93	2.2

LAST SEASON

Led team in penalty minutes with career high. Appeared in 1,000th career NHL game. Missed three games with thumb injury. Missed two games with shoulder injury. Missed six games with abdominal injury.

THE FINESSE GAME

Svoboda has very quick feet and is always in motion. He was never strong on his skates, but he has great quickness, balance and agility — you can't hit what you can't catch. He has a long stride. Not a very solid player, he is lean and wiry. His skating is economical.

Svoboda has excellent instincts. He can carry the puck well and join the rush. He has a quick release on his wrist and snap shots, and also a good one-timer that he uses on the power play. He reads plays well, offensively and defensively.

Svoboda is a number four defenseman on his best nights now, but Tampa Bay again asked him to be a number one, which is really too much for him to handle.

THE PHYSICAL GAME

Not one for physical play, Svoboda is still a feisty foe who will take the body, then use his stick to rap a player in the choppers or to pull his skates out from under him. He ticks off a lot of people. He's taken a couple of pretty big hits in recent years, but he keeps bouncing back. His PIM totals come from fighting his own battles — and not with his fists.

Svoboda is lean and isn't going to get much done one-on-one in a close battle. He rides an opponent out of the play well when he can use his skating to gener-

ate some power.

THE INTANGIBLES

Svoboda battles through the excess minutes (he averaged 23 per game last season) against teams' top forward lines, and deserves tremendous credit for trying to rise to the challenge. He has been instrumental in helping the Lightning bring Pavel Kubina along. The two players mesh well together.

PROJECTION

In last year's *HSR,* we said, "Expect about 60 games and 30 points out of Svoboda." There is a lot of wear and tear on him, and the same prediction can be made for this season.

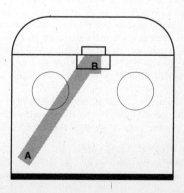

TODD WARRINER

Yrs. of NHL service: 5
Born: Blenheim, Ont.; Jan. 3, 1974
Position: left wing
Height: 6-1
Weight: 200
Uniform no.: 8
Shoots: left

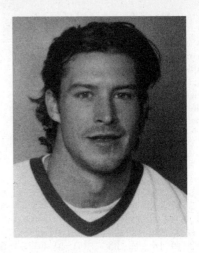

Career statistics:

GP	G	A	TP	PIM
308	47	61	108	125

1996-97 statistics:

GP	G	A	TP	+/-	PIM	PP	SH	GW	GT	S	PCT
75	12	21	33	-3	41	2	2	0	1	146	8.2

1997-98 statistics:

GP	G	A	TP	+/-	PIM	PP	SH	GW	GT	S	PCT
45	5	8	13	+5	20	0	0	1	0	73	6.8

1998-99 statistics:

GP	G	A	TP	+/-	PIM	PP	SH	GW	GT	S	PCT
53	9	10	19	-6	28	1	0	1	0	96	9.4

1999-2000 statistics:

GP	G	A	TP	+/-	PIM	PP	SH	GW	GT	S	PCT
73	14	14	28	-8	36	3	1	0	0	133	10.5

LAST SEASON

Acquired from Toronto for a third-round draft choice in 2000, Nov. 29, 1999. Third on team in shots. Career high in goals. Missed two games with hip injury. Missed one game with groin injury. Missed one game due to coach's decision.

THE FINESSE GAME

Early in his career, Warriner tended to be a streaky/slumpy player. He is very quick, not possessing blazing breakaway speed, but he has the smarts and the first step to jump into holes.

His shot is good, although he needs to make better use of it. He releases his shots quickly from the circles. He has to shoot more off the wing, driving wide on the defenseman, but he might be afraid of getting crunched along the boards, so instead he will try the cutback move into the center of the ice and it doesn't usually work well for him.

Warriner knows the element of surprise in getting his shot away quickly, but on the flip side, he needs to understand his options better and take the time and be patient when he has the time and space. He has a tendency to panic and get rid of the puck well before he must. He also needs to follow up his shot better. Warriner's defensive game has improved. He can be used to kill penalties.

Warriner has relied on his natural ability to get him through the various levels of hockey to the NHL. Now he needs to push himself to stick here.

THE PHYSICAL GAME

Warriner is wiry, a little on the light side, and he needs to maintain regular appointments with the weight room.

THE INTANGIBLES

Warriner has gained a second chance through expansion, and thanks to Tampa Bay's thin ranks up front, could continue in a second-line role this season. He has never shown consistency through a full season. If he does, the job is his. Warriner played his best hockey of the season when jobs were on the line in the closing weeks, which could indicate he is up to the challenge.

PROJECTION

Even if Warriner stays in Tampa Bay's top six, a 20-goal season is his top end.

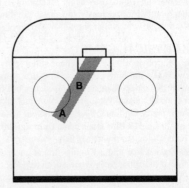

ANDREI ZYUZIN

Yrs. of NHL service: 3
Born: Ufa, Russia; Jan. 21, 1978
Position: left defense
Height: 6-1
Weight: 187
Uniform no.: 20
Shoots: left

Career statistics:

GP	G	A	TP	PIM
115	11	17	28	137

1997-98 statistics:

GP	G	A	TP	+/-	PIM	PP	SH	GW	GT	S	PCT
56	6	7	13	+8	66	2	0	2	0	72	8.3

1998-99 statistics:

GP	G	A	TP	+/-	PIM	PP	SH	GW	GT	S	PCT
25	3	1	4	+5	38	2	0	0	0	44	6.8

1999-2000 statistics:

GP	G	A	TP	+/-	PIM	PP	SH	GW	GT	S	PCT
34	2	9	11	-11	33	0	0	0	0	47	4.3

LAST SEASON

Missed 47 games with shoulder injury and subsequent surgery.

THE FINESSE GAME

Zyuzin is an offensive-minded defenseman, with the kind of speed and anticipation that will prevent him from being too much of a liability on defense (because of his ability to recover and position himself).

He could well prove to be the kind of player who can dictate the tempo of a game, or break it wide open with one end-to-end rush, like Brian Leetch. At the moment, he doesn't seem to possess the exceptional lateral movement along the blueline that sets Leetch apart from most of his NHL brethren, but Zyuzin has a big upside.

He doesn't take his offensive chances blindly; he knows what the score is. He takes a chance when his team needs a goal. And when he needs to stay back on defense, he will. He will also get burned once in awhile, but he makes smart choices.

The young Russian is a fast skater with quick acceleration and balance. He handles the puck well at a high pace and will pass or shoot: a smart playmaker, but one who will not pass up a golden scoring opportunity. He has a hard point shot and will become a good power-play quarterback.

THE PHYSICAL GAME

Zyuzin is not a physical player. He has adequate size but will need a streak of Chris Chelios-like aggressiveness to make the best use of his ability. He does have a desire to excel, and if it means stepping up his game physically he will probably be able to make that transition. He plays with a lot of energy.

THE INTANGIBLES

Zyuzin's progress was put on hold last season due to an October shoulder injury that he tried to play through. He had surgery and should be primed for the start of the season. He needs to work on his strength to become the kind of Ray Bourque, do-it-all defenseman that a lot of scouts believe he can be.

PROJECTION

Zyuzin will be given prime power-play ice time and every chance to produce. He could notch 25 to 30 points over a full season.

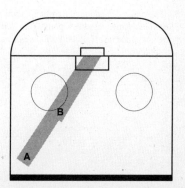

TORONTO MAPLE LEAFS

Players' Statistics 1999-2000

POS.	NO.	PLAYER	GP	G	A	PTS	+/-	PIM	PP	SH	GW	GT	S	PCT
C	13	MATS SUNDIN	73	32	41	73	16	46	10	2	7		184	17.4
L	32	STEVE THOMAS	81	26	37	63	1	68	9		9		151	17.2
R	14	JONAS HOGLUND	82	29	27	56	-2	10	9	1	3		215	13.5
C	16	DARCY TUCKER	77	21	30	51	-12	163	1	2	5		138	15.2
C	22	IGOR KOROLEV	80	20	26	46	12	22	5	3	4	1	101	19.8
C	44	YANIC PERREAULT	58	18	27	45	3	22	5		4		114	15.8
D	15	TOMAS KABERLE	82	7	33	40	3	24	2				82	8.5
L	94	SERGEI BEREZIN	61	26	13	39	8	2	5		4		241	10.8
R	8	DMITRI KHRISTICH	53	12	18	30	8	24	3			1	79	15.2
C	9	*NIK ANTROPOV	66	12	18	30	14	41			2		89	13.5
D	34	BRYAN BERARD	64	3	27	30	11	42	1				98	3.1
D	36	DIMITRI YUSHKEVICH	77	3	24	27	2	55	2	1	1		103	2.9
R	10	GARRY VALK	73	10	14	24	-2	44	1	1	1	1	91	11.0
D	52	ALEXANDER KARPOVTSEV	69	3	14	17	9	54	3				51	5.9
D	4	CORY CROSS	71	4	11	15	13	64			1		60	6.7
R	28	TIE DOMI	70	5	9	14	-5	198			2		64	7.8
C	42	*KEVYN ADAMS	52	5	8	13	-7	39					70	7.1
C	18	ALYN MCCAULEY	45	5	5	10	-6	10	1				41	12.2
D	55	DANNY MARKOV	59		10	10	13	28					38	
L	17	WENDEL CLARK	33	4	2	6	-5	34			1		63	6.3
L	12	KRIS KING	39	2	4	6	4	55					24	8.3
D	2	GERALD DIDUCK	26		3	3	2	33					18	
D	33	CHRIS MCALLISTER	36		3	3	-4	68					12	
L	43	*NATHAN DEMPSEY	6		2	2	2	2					3	
C	21	*ADAM MAIR	8	1		1	-1	6					7	14.3
D	25	GREG ANDRUSAK	9		1	1	1	4					5	
G	30	GLENN HEALY	20		1	1	0	2						
G	31	CURTIS JOSEPH	63		1	1	0	14					1	
D	49	*DMITRIY YAKUSHIN	2				0	2					1	
D	24	*D.J. SMITH	3				-1	5					2	

GP = games played; G = goals; A = assists; PTS = points; +/- = goals-for minus goals-against while player is on ice; PIM = penalties in minutes; PP = power-play goals; SH = shorthanded goals; GW = game-winning goals; GT = game-tying goals; S = no. of shots; PCT = percentage of goals to shots; * = rookie

NIK ANTROPOV

Yrs. of NHL service: 1
Born: Vost, Kazakhstan; Feb. 18, 1980
Position: centre
Height: 6-5
Weight: 203
Uniform no.: 9
Shoots: left

Career statistics:

GP	G	A	TP	PIM
66	12	18	30	41

1999-2000 statistics:

GP	G	A	TP	+/-	PIM	PP	SH	GW	GT	S	PCT
66	12	18	30	+14	41	0	0	2	0	89	13.5

LAST SEASON

First NHL season. Second on team and tied for fourth among NHL rookies in plus-minus. Missed 10 games with concussion/shoulder injury.

THE FINESSE GAME

Antropov is a find — the Leafs made him a first-round draft pick in 1998 — and at a young age he was playing against the best players in Russia before coming to Toronto last season.

Antropov has a long reach and is a smart positional player. Foot speed is a serious problem. He has a long stride but needs to improve his quickness.

Antropov is prone to tunnel vision. He handles the puck well and has a nice passing touch, but doesn't always see his best options.

THE PHYSICAL GAME

Antropov is very tall and not quite yet filled out. He will be adding some pounds — not too many, because of his knee surgery — and strength that will help him in his battles around the net.

THE INTANGIBLES

Antropov suffered a knee injury in the playoffs that required reconstructive surgery. If he hadn't been hurt, it probably would have been a happier playoff result for the Leafs, who need him as a solid number two centre behind Mats Sundin. He might get off to a slow start because of the knee rehab.

PROJECTION

As the second-line centre, Antropov will elude some of the checking pressure. He should improve to 45 points this season.

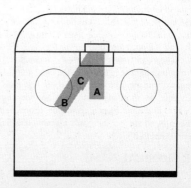

SHAYNE CORSON

Yrs. of NHL service: 14
Born: Barrie, Ont.; Aug. 13, 1966
Position: centre/left wing
Height: 6-1
Weight: 200
Uniform no.: 27
Shoots: left

Career statistics:

GP	G	A	TP	PIM
942	241	368	609	1970

1996-97 statistics:

GP	G	A	TP	+/-	PIM	PP	SH	GW	GT	S	PCT
58	8	16	24	-9	104	3	0	2	0	115	7.0

1997-98 statistics:

GP	G	A	TP	+/-	PIM	PP	SH	GW	GT	S	PCT
62	21	34	55	+2	108	14	1	1	0	142	14.8

1998-99 statistics:

GP	G	A	TP	+/-	PIM	PP	SH	GW	GT	S	PCT
63	12	20	32	-10	147	7	0	4	0	142	8.5

1999-2000 statistics:

GP	G	A	TP	+/-	PIM	PP	SH	GW	GT	S	PCT
70	8	20	28	-2	115	2	0	1	0	121	6.6

LAST SEASON

Led Canadiens in penalty minutes for second consecutive season. Missed 10 games due to colitis. Missed two games with eye injury.

THE FINESSE GAME

Corson makes a lot of things happen by overpowering people around the net. Like Bob Probert in his prime, Corson has surprising scoring ability for a player who is considered a mucker. People give him an extra foot or two because of his muscle, which allows him extra time to pick up loose pucks out of scrums and jam his shots in tight or lift them over a goalie's stick.

Corson scores a lot of rebound goals if he plays on a line with people who throw the puck to the net, because he will go barrelling in for it. He's free to play that style more on left wing than at centre, but he also has some nice playmaking abilities when put in the middle. He won't do anything too fancy, but he is intelligent enough to play a basic short game. He can win draws outright on his backhand.

He is a powerful skater but not very fast or agile. He has good balance for his work along the boards, and has all the attributes of a power forward. He does his dirty work in front of the net for screens and deflections, and has the hands to guide hard point shots. He is wildly inaccurate with any shots that aren't at close range, so on nights when he is not winning the duels around the net he is a nonfactor. From eight to 10 feet around the net, he can't be moved when he puts his mind to it.

THE PHYSICAL GAME

Corson succeeds by fighting for his ice in the slot area.

He takes an absolute beating around the net, but it doesn't show in the stats because the Canadiens were a woeful offensive team last season. No one could get the puck on net while Corson was getting the stuffing beat out of him. He creates second-chance opportunities for himself and his teammates because he is tremendous along the wall. He has grit and plays tough and hard every shift. He is dangerous because of his short fuse. Opponents never know when he will go off; since he's strong and can throw punches, few people want to be around when he does. He inspires fear. He hits to hurt and is so unpredictable he earns himself plenty of room on the ice.

THE INTANGIBLES

Corson signed with Toronto during the off-season and could prove to be the missing piece to the Leafs playoff hopes. He brings fire to every shift.

PROJECTION

At 34, Corson could still have a few productive seasons left, but we doubt 40 goals is in his range. He has become a question mark because of his injuries and illness, yet he is an effective player when healthy. Don't let last year's decline in numbers deceive you. In the right spot, Corson will get his points again.

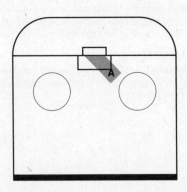

CORY CROSS

Yrs. of NHL service: 6
Born: Lloydminster, Alta.; Jan. 3, 1971
Position: left defense
Height: 6-5
Weight: 212
Uniform no.: 4
Shoots: left

Career statistics:

GP	G	A	TP	PIM
407	16	57	73	441

1996-97 statistics:

GP	G	A	TP	+/-	PIM	PP	SH	GW	GT	S	PCT
72	4	5	9	+6	95	0	0	2	0	75	5.3

1997-98 statistics:

GP	G	A	TP	+/-	PIM	PP	SH	GW	GT	S	PCT
74	3	6	9	-24	77	0	1	0	0	72	4.2

1998-99 statistics:

GP	G	A	TP	+/-	PIM	PP	SH	GW	GT	S	PCT
67	2	16	18	-25	92	0	0	0	0	96	2.1

1999-2000 statistics:

GP	G	A	TP	+/-	PIM	PP	SH	GW	GT	S	PCT
71	4	11	15	+13	64	0	0	1	0	60	6.7

don't expect more than 20 points out of him.

LAST SEASON

Acquired from Tampa Bay with a seventh-round draft choice in 2001 for Fredrik Modin, Oct. 1, 1999. Tied for third on team in plus-minus. Matched career high in goals. Missed five games with shoulder injuries.

THE FINESSE GAME

Cross's most impressive asset is his intelligence. He is smart enough to recognize the mistakes he makes and learn from them. He is also highly skilled: a fine skater who can either lug the puck out of his zone or start things with a pass and then jump up into the play. He has a good shot and will make wise pinches to keep the puck in the zone.

Cross is simply a safe, low-risk defenseman who can be paired with a mobile, offensive type. Nothing about him shouts.

THE PHYSICAL GAME

Cross did not play in a physical environment at the college level, and it took him awhile to learn that it's okay to hit people hard. He has taken a real shine to NHL play, showing a latent aggressive streak. He is a solid skater with good size and is still discovering how truly big and powerful he is. He gets his stick up at times. He could develop even more upper-body strength.

THE INTANGIBLES

Cross is a number five or six defenseman in Toronto and could be on the bubble, and on the move.

PROJECTION

Cross provided a little more offense last season, but

JONAS HOGLUND

Yrs. of NHL service: 4
Born: Hammaro, Sweden; Aug. 29, 1972
Position: left wing
Height: 6-3
Weight: 200
Uniform no.: 44
Shoots: right

Career statistics:

GP	G	A	TP	PIM
302	68	66	134	60

1996-97 statistics:

GP	G	A	TP	+/-	PIM	PP	SH	GW	GT	S	PCT
68	19	16	35	-4	12	3	0	6	1	189	10.1

1997-98 statistics:

GP	G	A	TP	+/-	PIM	PP	SH	GW	GT	S	PCT
78	12	13	25	-7	22	4	0	0	0	186	6.5

1998-99 statistics:

GP	G	A	TP	+/-	PIM	PP	SH	GW	GT	S	PCT
74	8	10	18	-5	16	1	0	0	1	122	6.6

1999-2000 statistics:

GP	G	A	TP	+/-	PIM	PP	SH	GW	GT	S	PCT
82	29	27	56	-2	10	9	1	3	0	215	13.5

still earn a spot in the top six. He was a restricted free agent during the off-season.

PROJECTION

Unless consistency continues to elude Hoglund, he could be sitting on a 30-goal season.

LAST SEASON

Second on team in goals and shots. Tied for second in power-play goals. Third on team in points. Career highs in goals, assists and points. One of two Leafs to appear in all 82 games.

THE FINESSE GAME

Hoglund is a natural goal scorer. Every time he gets the puck he has a chance to score. The trick is to encourage him to shoot more, and instill an intense drive. He lacks a goal scorer's mentality but he has a goal scorer's tools. He has a good, hard slap shot and half-wrister.

Hoglund has adapted well to North American hockey in his defensive and positional play. Play along the boards was a new concept to him, but he was unafraid of getting involved.

Hoglund skates well for a big man. He's no speed skater but his skating is NHL calibre.

THE PHYSICAL GAME

Hoglund is a big guy but doesn't play a physical game. He has a long reach, which he uses instead of his body to try to win control of the puck or slow down an opponent. He's getting used to the idea of hitting. Still, he has to get better at it. When he does his whole game perks up.

THE INTANGIBLES

Hoglund finally came into his own last season. He had a good first round of the playoffs, then vanished in the second. The addition of Shayne Corson and Gary Roberts may affect his power-play time, but Hoglund is 10 years younger than Steve Thomas and should

CURTIS JOSEPH

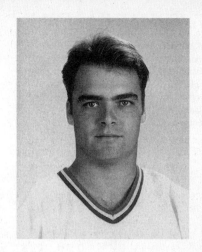

Yrs. of NHL service: 10
Born: Keswick, Ont.; Apr. 29, 1967
Position: goaltender
Height: 5-10
Weight: 182
Uniform no.: 31
Catches: left

Career statistics:

GP	MIN	GA	SO	GAA	A	PIM
587	33957	1631	26	2.88	27	68

1996-97 statistics:

GP	MIN	GAA	W	L	T	SO	GA	S	SAPCT	PIM
72	4089	2.93	32	29	9	6	200	2144	.907	20

1997-98 statistics:

GP	MIN	GAA	W	L	T	SO	GA	S	SAPCT	PIM
71	4132	2.63	29	31	9	8	181	1901	.905	4

1998-99 statistics:

GP	MIN	GAA	W	L	T	SO	GA	S	SAPCT	PIM
67	4001	2.56	35	24	7	3	171	1903	.910	6

1999-2000 statistics:

GP	MIN	GAA	W	L	T	SO	GA	S	SAPCT	PIM
63	3801	2.49	36	20	7	4	158	1854	.915	14

LAST SEASON

Fourth among NHL goalies in wins. Career best goals-against average. Fourth among NHL goalies in shots against. Tied for fifth among NHL goalies in penalty minutes.

THE PHYSICAL GAME

Nothing Joseph does is by the book. He always looks unorthodox and off-balance, but he is one of those hybrid goalies whose success can't be argued with.

Joseph positions himself well, angling out to challenge the shooter. He is one of the best goalies against the breakaway in the NHL. He goes to his knees quickly, but bounces back to his skates fast for the rebound. He tends to keep rebounds in front of him. His glove hand is outstanding.

A strong, if bizarre, stickhandler, Joseph has to move his hands on the stick, putting the butt-end into his catching glove and lowering his blocker. His favourite move is a weird backhand whip off the boards. He is a good skater who moves out of his cage confidently to handle the puck.

He needs to improve his lateral movement. He also uses his stick to harass anyone who dares to camp on his doorstep. He's not Billy Smith, but he's aggressive with his whacks.

Joseph gets into technical slumps, which seem to sprout from fatigue and usually result in his staying too deep in his net.

THE MENTAL GAME

Joseph is accustomed to a lot of work, but cutting back his games by a half-dozen or so would result in a fresher netminder for the playoffs. He is never fazed by facing a ton of shots in a night. But speaking of mental, did you see Joseph go haywire in the playoffs? He somehow managed not to get suspended.

THE INTANGIBLES

The problem with Joseph, as it was with Ed Belfour and is with Dominik Hasek, is that you're never a winner until you win the big prize.

PROJECTION

Joseph will hit the 30-win mark again.

TOMAS KABERLE

Yrs. of NHL service: 2
Born: Rakovnik, Czech.; Mar. 2, 1978
Position: left defense
Height: 6-2
Weight: 200
Uniform no.: 15
Shoots: left

Career statistics:

GP	G	A	TP	PIM
139	11	51	62	36

1998-99 statistics:

GP	G	A	TP	+/-	PIM	PP	SH	GW	GT	S	PCT
57	4	18	22	+3	12	0	0	2	0	71	5.6

1999-2000 statistics:

GP	G	A	TP	+/-	PIM	PP	SH	GW	GT	S	PCT
82	7	33	40	+3	24	2	0	0	0	82	8.5

LAST SEASON

Led team defensemen in points. Third on team in assists. One of two Leafs to appear in all 82 games.

THE FINESSE GAME

Kaberle brings all the skills expected of a good European defenseman and combines them with a taste for the North American style of play. It's an impressive package.

Kaberle is a mobile skater, who makes a smart first pass-he's an excellent puck-moving defenseman. He is always looking to join the rush, and he likes to create offense. He can get too fancy at times when he should be making the simple play instead, and will occasionally get into trouble in his own zone because of that tendency.

Kaberle is still pretty young and has already made great strides. His panic point is a lot higher than it was. In the first half of the season, if his first option was closed to him, he would usually just give the puck away. In the second half and in the playoffs, he showed great poise and seldom coughed up the puck under pressure.

THE PHYSICAL GAME

Kaberle comes to compete hard every night. He needs to get a little bigger and stronger to improve his play around the net, but he's still young and growing and physical maturity will come.

THE INTANGIBLES

Kaberle is a solid top four on anyone's team and he is in the upper tier of the second pairings in the league right now, with the potential to improve that status. He could develop along Scott Niedermayer lines — which is to say, he will never be a star, and should remain just a notch below the league's elite offensive defensemen.

PROJECTION

We're wary of hype coming out of Toronto involving phrases like, "future Norris Trophy contender," but in this case, the praise is not that far off the mark. Kaberle should improve to the 45- to 50-point range.

428

ALEXANDER KARPOVTSEV

Yrs. of NHL service: 7
Born: Moscow, Russia; Feb. 25, 1974
Position: left defense
Height: 6-1
Weight: 200
Uniform no.: 52
Shoots: left

Career statistics:

GP	G	A	TP	PIM
405	27	114	131	317

1996-97 statistics:

GP	G	A	TP	+/-	PIM	PP	SH	GW	GT	S	PCT
77	9	29	28	+1	59	6	1	0	0	84	10.7

1997-98 statistics:

GP	G	A	TP	+/-	PIM	PP	SH	GW	GT	S	PCT
47	3	7	10	-1	38	1	0	1	0	46	6.5

1998-99 statistics:

GP	G	A	TP	+/-	PIM	PP	SH	GW	GT	S	PCT
58	3	25	28	+39	52	1	0	1	0	65	4.6

1999-2000 statistics:

GP	G	A	TP	+/-	PIM	PP	SH	GW	GT	S	PCT
69	3	14	17	+9	54	3	0	0	0	51	5.9

LAST SEASON

Missed six games with shoulder injuries. Missed four ganes with fractured thumb. Missed two games with foot injury.

THE FINESSE GAME

The strength of Karpovtsev's skating game is best reflected in his terrific lateral movement. He covers acres of ground with a huge stride and a long reach, has excellent balance, turns nicely in both directions and boasts a fair amount of quickness and agility. He has a quick first step to the puck.

Karpovtsev has decent puck-carrying skills and the good sense to move the puck quickly, but displays the defensive defenseman's mindset of getting to the redline and dumping the puck into the corner or making a short outlet pass. Under pressure behind his net he tends to whack the puck around the boards, a play that often gets picked off.

Karpovtsev does, at times, show a good instinct for seeing a better passing option than the obvious in the attacking zone. He has an effective, hard shot from the point, and his accuracy has improved.

THE PHYSICAL GAME

Karpovtsev is extremely strong and is not shy about using his strength in front of the net or in the corners. Battling for loose pucks, he will move a player with a forearm shove, then grab the puck while his opponent is recovering from the jolt. He will also throw himself back-first at a player, immobilize the guy against the boards, then recover quickly and grab the puck.

Karpovtsev plays toughest against the toughest players. He does not hesitate to get involved if things turn nasty, and although he is hardly a polished fighter he is a willing one. He likes the big hit but doesn't mind the smaller ones.

A crease clearer and shot-blocker, Karpovtsev is far more comfortable and poised in front of his net than when he chases to the corners or sideboards. Once he gets away from the slot, with or without the puck, he loses either confidence or focus or both, which can lead to unforced errors or turnovers. Still, he is an effective weapon against a power forward. He can tie up the guy in front, lean on him, and hit and skate.

THE INTANGIBLES

Karpovtsev gets hurt. A lot. He is either fearless, unlucky, or fragile. Take your pick. At best, he's a number four defenseman who has frequently been asked to be a top two. Karpovtsev was a retsricted free agent during the off-season.

PROJECTION

A healthy Karpovtsev can score in the 25-point range and log a lot of ice time, but we would bank on him missing about 20 games.

DMITRI KHRISTICH

Yrs. of NHL service: 10
Born: Kiev, Ukraine; July 23, 1969
Position: left wing
Height: 6-2
Weight: 195
Uniform no.: 12
Shoots: right

Career statistics:

GP	G	A	TP	PIM
680	238	300	537	314

1996-97 statistics:

GP	G	A	TP	+/-	PIM	PP	SH	GW	GT	S	PCT
75	19	37	56	+8	38	3	0	2	0	135	14.1

1997-98 statistics:

GP	G	A	TP	+/-	PIM	PP	SH	GW	GT	S	PCT
82	29	37	66	+25	42	13	2	1	0	144	20.1

1998-99 statistics:

GP	G	A	TP	+/-	PIM	PP	SH	GW	GT	S	PCT
79	29	42	71	+11	48	13	1	6	1	144	20.1

1999-2000 statistics:

GP	G	A	TP	+/-	PIM	PP	SH	GW	GT	S	PCT
53	12	18	30	+8	24	3	0	0	1	79	15.2

PROJECTION

If Khristich plays with the same passion and consistency he did last season, he can score 20 goals in his full-time role.

LAST SEASON

Signed as free agent, Oct. 21, 1999. Missed 13 games with groin injury. Missed seven gams with facial injuries.

THE FINESSE GAME

Khristich has good hand-eye coordination for deflections and can even take draws. He is not an especially fast skater, but he has a long, strong stride and very good balance. His hockey sense is excellent, and he is responsible defensively as well.

One weakness is his tendency to put himself in a position where he gets hit, and hurt. Part of that stems from holding onto the puck to make a perfect play.

On the power play, Khristich likes to lurk just off to the goalie's right, with his forehand open and ready for the pass. When the puck reaches his blade, he slams the shot in one quick motion. If the penalty killers are drawn to him, it then opens ice for another forward. Either way, Khristich gets the job done.

THE PHYSICAL GAME

Khristich is a very sturdy skater but lacks physical presence. He will go into the trenches and is tough to knock off the puck. He protects the puck well.

THE INTANGIBLES

Boston walked away after Khristich won a salary arbitration ruling in 1999, and he played as if he had something to prove with the Leafs. Khristich soldiered on through the playoffs despite torn ligaments in his wrist. He will probably play on a third line this season and could provide good numbers while performing his defensive job.

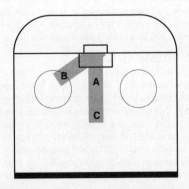

DANIIL MARKOV

Yrs. of NHL service: 3
Born: Moscow, Russia; July 11, 1976
Position: left defense
Height: 6-1
Weight: 196
Uniform no.: 55
Shoots: left

Career statistics:

GP	G	A	TP	PIM
141	6	23	29	103

1997-98 statistics:

GP	G	A	TP	+/-	PIM	PP	SH	GW	GT	S	PCT
25	2	5	7	0	28	1	0	0	0	15	13.3

1998-99 statistics:

GP	G	A	TP	+/-	PIM	PP	SH	GW	GT	S	PCT
57	4	8	12	+5	47	0	0	0	1	34	11.8

1999-2000 statistics:

GP	G	A	TP	+/-	PIM	PP	SH	GW	GT	S	PCT
59	0	10	10	+13	28	0	0	0	0	38	-

LAST SEASON

Second NHL season. Tied for third on team in plus-minus. Missed 10 games with foot injury. Missed eight games with fractured foot. Missed three games with knee injury. Missed one game with headache.

THE FINESSE GAME

Markov is pretty sound positioning-wise, and he is a good skater. Coaches have to constantly keep him in tune with what to do defensively. Markov wants to drift more into an offensive game. He is tempted to make high-risk pinches, and when he gets beat his ice time gets cut. He is just starting to understand that cause-and-effect, and dramatically improved defensively last season.

Markov makes a good first pass. Once he gets the puck he is looking to go up-ice for a play, which not all defensemen do, and a stick-to-stick pass gets him out of trouble. His frequent injuries kept him from getting in a real groove.

THE PHYSICAL GAME

Markov isn't very big but he brings a little edge, and a little chippiness, to his game. He's a bit brash and cocky. He has some grit and steps up his game in big spots, like the playoffs.

THE INTANGIBLES

This is the second straight season that Markov has been bugged by nagging injuries. Still, he's shown enough to be a top four defenseman with the Leafs. He was a restricted free agent during the off-season.

PROJECTION

Markov wants to play like an elite "offenseman," but his skills don't put him in that class. If he plays a smarter defensive game he will get a nice chunk of ice time and score 20 to 25 points.

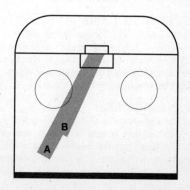

YANIC PERREAULT

Yrs. of NHL service: 6
Born: Sherbrooke, Que.; Apr. 4, 1971
Position: centre
Height: 5-11
Weight: 189
Uniform no.: 44
Shoots: left

Career statistics:

GP	G	A	TP	PIM
371	104	118	222	152

1996-97 statistics:

GP	G	A	TP	+/-	PIM	PP	SH	GW	GT	S	PCT
41	11	14	25	0	20	1	1	0	0	98	11.2

1997-98 statistics:

GP	G	A	TP	+/-	PIM	PP	SH	GW	GT	S	PCT
79	28	20	48	+6	32	3	2	3	0	206	13.6

1998-99 statistics:

GP	G	A	TP	+/-	PIM	PP	SH	GW	GT	S	PCT
76	17	25	42	+7	42	4	3	3	0	141	12.1

1999-2000 statistics:

GP	G	A	TP	+/-	PIM	PP	SH	GW	GT	S	PCT
58	18	27	45	+3	22	5	0	4	0	114	15.8

LAST SEASON

Missed 23 games with fractured arm.

THE FINESSE GAME

Perreault's speed is marginal for the NHL level. He tries to compensate with his intelligence, and that alone will keep earning him NHL jobs on third and fourth lines. He is nifty and shifty in tight quarters, but lacks breakaway speed.

Perreault has very good hands and always has his head up, looking for openings. While he doesn't have open-ice speed, he works hard to put on a quick burst in the offensive zone, to gain a half-step on a defender. Once he is open for the shot he waits for the goalie to commit, or he makes a patient pass.

Tricky and solid on his feet, Perreault works the half-boards on the power play. He has an accurate shot with a quick release, and he slithers around to get in the best position for the shot.

Perreault is exceptional on draws.

THE PHYSICAL GAME

Perreault lacks the size for one-on-one battles in the attacking zone. Defensively, he can't do much except harass a puck carrier with his stick. He is an in-betweener, and if forced to carry the play in any zone his flaws become apparent.

THE INTANGIBLES

Perreault underwent major reconstructive knee surgery for an injury suffered in the first round of the playoffs. It won't help his speed any, and he is likely to miss the start of the season. But somehow Perreault keeps coming back, and we don't expect this season to be any different. The Leafs' improved depth should allow Perreault to drop back into the third-line role. He was frequently pressed into number two duties last season, a real reach for him.

PROJECTION

Perreault works hard and can score 15 to 20 goals as a role player.

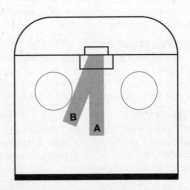

GARY ROBERTS

Yrs. of NHL service: 13
Born: North York, Ont.; May 23, 1966
Position: left wing
Height: 6-1
Weight: 200
Uniform no.: 10
Shoots: left

Career statistics:

GP	G	A	TP	PIM
792	314	335	649	2079

1996-97 statistics:
Did not play in NHL

1997-98 statistics:

GP	G	A	TP	+/-	PIM	PP	SH	GW	GT	S	PCT
61	20	29	49	+3	103	4	0	2	1	106	18.9

1998-99 statistics:

GP	G	A	TP	+/-	PIM	PP	SH	GW	GT	S	PCT
77	14	28	42	+2	178	1	1	4	0	138	10.1

1999-2000 statistics:

GP	G	A	TP	+/-	PIM	PP	SH	GW	GT	S	PCT
69	23	30	53	-10	62	12	0	1	0	150	15.3

LAST SEASON

Signed by Toronto as free agent from Carolina, July 4, 2000. Led team in power-play goals. Tied for second on team in shooting percentage. Third on team in points. Tied for third in team in goals. Missed 11 games with groin injuries. Missed one game with shoulder injury. Missed one game with flu.

THE FINESSE GAME

Roberts has excellent hands and terrific instincts around the net. He works hard for loose pucks and, when he gets control, doesn't waste time trying anything fancy. As soon as the puck is on his blade, it's launched towards the net. He shoots by instinct and is not very creative. His rule is: throw the puck at the front of the net and see what happens.

Roberts is not an agile skater. He can beat the defender one-on-one on the occasional rush, powered by his strong stride and his ability to handle the puck at a fair clip.

He sees the ice well and will spot an open teammate for a smart pass. He forechecks intelligently and creates turnovers with his persistent work. An excellent penalty killer, he anticipates well and turns mistakes into shorthanded scoring chances.

THE PHYSICAL GAME

Despite a neck injury that nearly ended his career, Roberts is still a tough customer around the net. Can there be any better evidence that the Hurricanes are in dire need of an enforcer? A guy who was almost crippled by a neck injury should not be leading a team in penalty minutes.

THE INTANGIBLES

Roberts and Shayne Corson will make everyone in the Toronto lineup play a little bigger.

PROJECTION

With an offense-happy crew in Toronto, Roberts — at age 34 — could return to the 30-goal ranks. He is still among the league's best "garbagemen" around the net, and we mean that as a compliment.

MATS SUNDIN

Yrs. of NHL service: 10
Born: Bromma, Sweden; Feb. 13, 1971
Position: right wing/centre
Height: 6-4
Weight: 215
Uniform no.: 13
Shoots: right

Career statistics:

GP	G	A	TP	PIM
766	328	460	788	591

1996-97 statistics:

GP	G	A	TP	+/-	PIM	PP	SH	GW	GT	S	PCT
82	41	53	94	+6	59	7	4	8	1	281	14.6

1997-98 statistics:

GP	G	A	TP	+/-	PIM	PP	SH	GW	GT	S	PCT
82	33	41	74	-3	49	9	1	5	1	219	15.1

1998-99 statistics:

GP	G	A	TP	+/-	PIM	PP	SH	GW	GT	S	PCT
82	31	52	83	+22	58	4	0	6	0	209	14.8

1999-2000 statistics:

GP	G	A	TP	+/-	PIM	PP	SH	GW	GT	S	PCT
73	32	41	73	+16	46	10	2	7	0	184	17.4

LAST SEASON

Led team in assists and points for second consecutive season. Led team in goals, power-play goals and plus-minus. Second on team in game-winning goals and shooting percentage. Tied for second on team in short-handed goals. Third on team in shots. Missed nine games with fractured ankle.

THE FINESSE GAME

Sundin plays centre but attacks from the off-(left)wing, where he can come off the boards with speed. He protects the puck along the wall and makes it hard for people to reach in without taking him down for a penalty. He gets the puck low in his own end; people can move to him right away, and he has to move the puck. If a checker stays with him Sundin can't get the puck back.

Sundin is a big skater who looks huge, as he uses an ultralong stick that gives him a broad wingspan. For a big man he is an agile skater, and his balance has improved. He has good lower-body strength, supplying drive for battles along the boards. He's evasive, and once he is on the fly he is hard to stop. He is less effective when carrying the puck. His best play is to get up a head of steam, jump into the holes and take a quick shot.

Sundin can take bad passes in stride, either kicking an errant puck up onto his stick or reaching behind to corral it. He isn't a clever stickhandler. His game is power and speed. He doesn't look fast, but he has ground-eating strides that allow him to cover in two strides what other skaters do in three or four. He is quick, too, and can get untracked in a heartbeat.

Sundin's shot is excellent. He can use a slap shot, one-timer, wrister or backhand. The only liability to his reach is that he will dangle the puck well away from his body and he doesn't always control it, which makes him vulnerable to a poke-check when he is in open ice.

THE PHYSICAL GAME

The Devils' ability to shut Sundin down was largely due to his lack of a supporting cast, but the Swede didn't respond as well physically as he should have. Sundin is big and strong. He has shown better attention to off-ice work to improve his strength. His conditioning is excellent — he can skate all night. He has even shown a touch of mean, but mostly with his stick.

THE INTANGIBLES

Adding Gary Roberts as Sundin's likely left winger will add some grit and scoring touch that he so desperately needs. The development of Nik Antropov as a solid number two centre will also help.

PROJECTION

Sundin could be sitting on a career year. He's been able to score 70 to 80 points virtually by himself. Take into account Toronto's wide-open style and new depth up front and make Sundin a high pool pick. This season, look for close to 100 points.

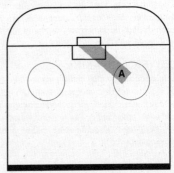

STEVE THOMAS

Yrs. of NHL service: 16
Born: Stockport, England; July 15, 1963
Position: left wing
Height: 5-11
Weight: 185
Uniform no.: 32
Shoots: left

Career statistics:

GP	G	A	TP	PIM
994	378	454	832	1165

1996-97 statistics:

GP	G	A	TP	+/-	PIM	PP	SH	GW	GT	S	PCT
32	15	19	34	+9	46	1	0	2	0	124	12.1

1997-98 statistics:

GP	G	A	TP	+/-	PIM	PP	SH	GW	GT	S	PCT
55	14	10	24	+4	32	3	0	4	1	111	12.6

1998-99 statistics:

GP	G	A	TP	+/-	PIM	PP	SH	GW	GT	S	PCT
78	28	45	73	+26	33	11	0	7	0	209	13.4

1999-2000 statistics:

GP	G	A	TP	+/-	PIM	PP	SH	GW	GT	S	PCT
81	26	37	63	+1	68	9	0	9	0	151	17.2

LAST SEASON

Led team and tied for third in NHL in game-winning goals. Second on team in assists and points. Tied for second on team in power-play goals. Third on team in shooting percentage. Tied for third on team in goals and penalty minutes. Missed one game with toe injury.

THE FINESSE GAME

Thomas has a great shot and loves to fire away. He looks to shoot first instead of pass, sometimes to his detriment, but subtlety is not his forte. Thomas's game is speed and power.

Thomas has a strong wrist shot and a quick one-timer. He likes to win the battle for the puck in deep, feed his centre, then head for the right circle for the return pass. Playing the left side he was not as effective. He has a very short backswing, which allows him to get his shots away quickly.

Thomas is a wildly intense player. His speed is straight ahead, without much deking or trying to put a move on a defender. He works along the boards and in the corners, willing to do the dirty work.

THE PHYSICAL GAME

Thomas is hard-nosed and finishes his checks. He is an effective forechecker because he comes at the puck carrier like a human train. He is not big but he is wide, and tough. He is great along the boards and among the best in the league at keeping the puck alive by using his feet. He is a feisty and fierce competitor and will throw the odd punch.

THE INTANGIBLES

The arrival of Gary Roberts and Shayne Corson, and the fact that Thomas is 37 this season, could mean a loss of ice time, especially on the power-play unit.

PROJECTION

Expect a continuing decline in goal production to the low 20s.

DARCY TUCKER

Yrs. of NHL service: 4
Born: Castor, Alberta; Mar. 15, 1975
Position: centre
Height: 5-11
Weight: 182
Uniform no.: 16
Shoots: left

Career statistics:

GP	G	A	TP	PIM
309	56	78	134	595

1996-97 statistics:

GP	G	A	TP	+/-	PIM	PP	SH	GW	GT	S	PCT
73	7	13	20	-5	110	1	0	3	1	62	11.3

1997-98 statistics:

GP	G	A	TP	+/-	PIM	PP	SH	GW	GT	S	PCT
74	7	13	20	-14	146	1	1	0	0	63	11.1

1998-99 statistics:

GP	G	A	TP	+/-	PIM	PP	SH	GW	GT	S	PCT
82	21	22	43	-34	176	8	2	3	0	178	11.8

1999-2000 statistics:

GP	G	A	TP	+/-	PIM	PP	SH	GW	GT	S	PCT
77	21	30	51	-12	163	1	2	5	0	138	15.2

LAST SEASON

Acquired from Tampa Bay with a fourth-round draft choice in 2000 for Mike Johnson, Marek Posmyk and fifth- and sixth-round draft choices in 2000, Feb. 9, 2000. Second on team in penalty minutes. Tied for second on team in shorthanded goals. Third on team in game-winning goals. Matched career high in goals. Career highs in assists and points.

THE FINESSE GAME

What a treat it was for Tucker to get traded to a team that was a playoff contender. He is the perfect kind of player for the postseason, because every night he brings a level of intensity to his game that supplements — and some might suggest, surpasses — his talent.

Tucker was a scorer in junior (137 points in his last year at Kamloops of the WHL) and the minors (93 points with Fredericton of the AHL in 1995-96), and he brings an offensive awareness that enhances his role as a third-line checking centre. He has decent hands, and a knack for scoring big goals.

Tucker's major drawback is that he lacks big-league speed. He is a good forechecker who will hound the puck carrier, and he can do something with the puck once it's on his stick. He is good on draws and will tie up his opposing centre. He will block shots. He will fill the water bottles. Whatever it takes to win, Tucker is there.

THE PHYSICAL GAME

Tucker is dogged and enjoys the rough going. His is small but highly annoying to play against. He can distract bigger players who just try to squish him. His efforts are pretty consistent — coaches don't have to worry about him getting jazzed up to play a big game.

THE INTANGIBLES

Tucker's got spunk. He cares. He wants to make his team better. Tucker was the only Leafs forward who showed up against the Devils in the playoffs. This trade was an outright steal for Toronto.

PROJECTION

Tucker surpassed our expectations for his production last season. If he continues to get the ice time he did last year, he could top 50 points again. He is a real favourite in these pages.

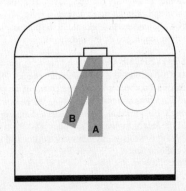

DIMITRI YUSHKEVICH

Yrs. of NHL service: 8
Born: Yaroslavl, USSR; Nov. 19, 1971
Position: right defense
Height: 5-11
Weight: 208
Uniform no.: 36
Shoots: right

Career statistics:

GP	G	A	TP	PIM
567	29	139	168	535

1996-97 statistics:

GP	G	A	TP	+/-	PIM	PP	SH	GW	GT	S	PCT
74	4	10	14	-24	56	1	1	1	0	99	4.0

1997-98 statistics:

GP	G	A	TP	+/-	PIM	PP	SH	GW	GT	S	PCT
72	0	12	12	-13	78	0	0	0	0	92	0.0

1998-99 statistics:

GP	G	A	TP	+/-	PIM	PP	SH	GW	GT	S	PCT
78	6	22	28	+25	88	2	1	0	0	95	6.3

1999-2000 statistics:

GP	G	A	TP	+/-	PIM	PP	SH	GW	GT	S	PCT
77	3	24	27	+2	55	2	1	1	0	103	2.9

LAST SEASON

Missed two games with wrist injury.

THE FINESSE GAME

When Yushkevich pulls everything together mentally and physically, he steps up into a level that isn't elite but is a solid "B" game. His problem in the past was that he did it so infrequently. He has become far more consistent over the past two years.

He is a good skater with a decent shot. It's a real good shot in practice, but in games, he takes too long to unload it. He is strong and well-balanced on his feet. He can move laterally, pivot and put on a short burst of speed, or sustain a rush the length of the rink. Occasionally he can be beaten with outside speed but it takes a pretty good skater to do it.

Yushkevich has improved his defensive reads to where he can be matched against other teams' top lines, and he thrives on the challenge.

THE PHYSICAL GAME

Yushkevich is very fit. He'll grind. He'll hit. He plays with a mean streak. He can hit to hurt and be annoying to play against.

THE INTANGIBLES

Yushkevich isn't the easiest player to deal with, but the Leafs have found the right buttons. He feels wanted here and has responded.

PROJECTION

Yushkevich is losing ice time to some of the younger Toronto defensemen who bring a little more to the rink than he does. He can still score 25 points as a number four or five.

VANCOUVER CANUCKS

Players' Statistics 1999-2000

POS.	NO.	PLAYER	GP	G	A	PTS	+/-	PIM	PP	SH	GW	GT	S	PCT
L	19	MARKUS NASLUND	82	27	38	65	-5	64	6	2	3	1	271	10.0
C	25	ANDREW CASSELS	79	17	45	62	8	16	6		1		109	15.6
C	11	MARK MESSIER	66	17	37	54	-15	30	6		4		131	13.0
L	44	TODD BERTUZZI	80	25	25	50	-2	126	4		2		173	14.5
C	7	BRENDAN MORRISON	56	7	28	35	12	18	2		1		96	7.3
L	72	*PETER SCHAEFER	71	16	15	31	0	20	2	2	4		101	15.8
D	55	ED JOVANOVSKI	75	5	21	26	-3	54	1		1		109	4.6
D	6	ADRIAN AUCOIN	57	10	14	24	7	30	4		1		126	7.9
D	4	GREG HAWGOOD	79	5	17	22	5	26	2				70	7.1
R	26	TRENT KLATT	47	10	10	20	-8	26	8				100	10.0
D	2	MATTIAS OHLUND	42	4	16	20	6	24	2	1	1		63	6.3
L	18	*STEVE KARIYA	45	8	11	19	9	22					41	19.5
C	27	HARRY YORK	54	4	13	17	-4	20	1	1		1	50	8.0
L	9	BRAD MAY	59	9	7	16	-2	90			3		66	13.6
C	15	*HAROLD DRUKEN	33	7	9	16	14	10	2				69	10.1
L	8	DONALD BRASHEAR	60	11	2	13	-9	136	1		3		83	13.3
C	24	MATT COOKE	51	5	7	12	3	39		1	1		58	8.6
D	23	MURRAY BARON	81	2	10	12	8	67					48	4.2
C	20	DENIS PEDERSON	47	6	5	11	-6	18			1		56	10.7
R	17	VADIM SHARIFIJANOV	37	5	5	10	-13	22	1				46	10.9
C	14	DARBY HENDRICKSON	40	5	4	9	-3	14		1	1		39	12.8
C	13	*ARTEM CHUBAROV	49	1	8	9	-4	10			1		53	1.9
D	3	*BRENT SOPEL	18	2	4	6	9	12			1		11	18.2
C	21	JOSH HOLDEN	6	1	5	6	2	2					5	20.0
D	39	CHRIS O'SULLIVAN	11		5	5	2	2					16	
D	34	JASON STRUDWICK	63	1	3	4	-13	64			1		18	5.6
D	5	*ZENITH KOMARNISKI	18	1	1	2	-1	8					21	4.8
G	30	GARTH SNOW	32		2	2	0	8						
G	29	FELIX POTVIN	56		2	2	0	4						
L	37	*JARKKO RUUTU	8		1	1	-1	6					4	
D	3	DOUG BODGER	13		1	1	-6	4					11	
R	38	*BRAD LEEB	2				-2	2					3	
G	33	*ALFIE MICHAUD	2				0							
D	36	*RYAN BONNI	3				-1						1	
C	31	*LUBOMIR VAIC	4				0						2	
G	32	COREY SCHWAB	6				0	2						

GP = games played; G = goals; A = assists; PTS = points; +/- = goals-for minus goals-against while player is on ice; PIM = penalties in minutes; PP = power-play goals; SH = shorthanded goals; GW = game-winning goals; GT = game-tying goals; S = no. of shots; PCT = percentage of goals to shots; * = rookie

ADRIAN AUCOIN

Yrs. of NHL service: 5
Born: Ottawa, Ont.; July 3, 1973
Position: right defenseman
Height: 6-1
Weight: 194
Uniform no.: 6
Shoots: right

Career statistics:

GP	G	A	TP	PIM
294	46	58	104	225

1996-97 statistics:

GP	G	A	TP	+/-	PIM	PP	SH	GW	GT	S	PCT
70	5	16	21	0	63	1	0	0	0	116	4.3

1997-98 statistics:

GP	G	A	TP	+/-	PIM	PP	SH	GW	GT	S	PCT
35	3	3	6	-4	21	1	0	1	0	44	6.8

1998-99 statistics:

GP	G	A	TP	+/-	PIM	PP	SH	GW	GT	S	PCT
82	23	11	34	-14	77	18	2	3	1	174	13.2

1999-2000 statistics:

GP	G	A	TP	+/-	PIM	PP	SH	GW	GT	S	PCT
57	10	14	24	+7	30	4	0	1	0	126	7.9

LAST SEASON

Missed 20 games with finger injury. Missed four games with groin injury.

THE FINESSE GAME

Injuries cost Aucoin a quarter of the season, so he didn't get the chance to prove whether or not his amazing 1998-99 season could be repeated.

He was a low draft pick (117th overall in 1992), but by playing with the Canadian national team and in the 1994 Olympics he has upgraded his offensive skills and developed into an offensive defenseman whose skills are just a notch below the league's elite.

Aucoin is a mobile, agile skater who moves well with the puck. He doesn't have breakaway speed, but he jumps alertly into the play. On the power play, he smartly switches off with a forward to cut in deep, and he has good hands for shots in tight. He also has a good point shot and is very intelligent in his shot selection.

He also kills penalties.

THE PHYSICAL GAME

Aucoin is a strong, good-sized defenseman who often plays smaller. He needs to be more assertive around the net. He has no mean streak to speak of; opponents know he can be pushed around and they take advantage of that. He is more valued for his offensive abilities. He can handle his share of ice time and averaged over 23 minutes per game last season.

THE INTANGIBLES

Aucoin doesn't seem to be a Marc Crawford favourite. Although he scored a mind-boggling 18 power-play goals two seasons ago, he wasn't always on the Canucks' first power-play unit last year.

PROJECTION

Partially because of injuries, Aucoin failed to score even 18 goals — let alone 18 power-play goals — last season. A reasonable prediction is 20 goals with eight on the power play.

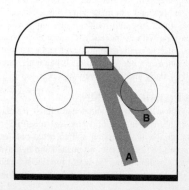

TODD BERTUZZI

Yrs. of NHL service: 5
Born: Sudbury, Ont.; Feb. 2, 1975
Position: left wing
Height: 6-3
Weight: 224
Uniform no.: 44
Shoots: left

Career statistics:

GP	G	A	TP	PIM
323	74	87	161	442

1996-97 statistics:

GP	G	A	TP	+/-	PIM	PP	SH	GW	GT	S	PCT
64	10	13	23	-3	68	3	0	1	0	79	12.7

1997-98 statistics:

GP	G	A	TP	+/-	PIM	PP	SH	GW	GT	S	PCT
74	13	20	33	-17	121	2	1	2	0	102	12.7

1998-99 statistics:

GP	G	A	TP	+/-	PIM	PP	SH	GW	GT	S	PCT
32	8	8	16	-6	44	1	0	3	0	72	11.1

1999-2000 statistics:

GP	G	A	TP	+/-	PIM	PP	SH	GW	GT	S	PCT
80	25	25	50	-2	126	4	0	2	0	173	14.5

LAST SEASON

Second on team in goals, penalty minutes and shots. Third on team in shooting percentage. Career highs in goals, assists and points. Missed one game with concussion. Missed one game due to coach's decision.

THE FINESSE GAME

Bertuzzi could become a poor man's John LeClair. He has physically dominating skills, but he doesn't have great vision. He has a tendency to roam all over the ice and doesn't think the game well. What he won't become is a physical, tough, aggressive fighter — a label the Islanders stuck on him when he began his career with that organization. It's not in his makeup, but he can be an energetic player.

Bertuzzi is instinctive and has great power to his game. For a big man, he's quick for his size and mobile, and he's got a soft pair of hands to complement his skating. With the puck, he can walk over people. He is effective in the slot area, yet he's also creative with the puck and can make some plays. He can find people down low and make things happen on the power play. With the puck, he is powerful and hard to stop, though he needs to improve his game without the puck. When he's not producing, all you notice are the flaws, mentally and defensively.

THE PHYSICAL GAME

Bertuzzi wanders around and doesn't finish his checks with authority. He's a solid physical specimen who shows flashes of aggression and an occasional mean streak, but he really has to be pushed and aggravated to reach a boiling point. He won't run through people or challenge them consistently, and as a result doesn't establish a physical presence. He was much more aggressive last season. Maybe playing with Mark Messier encouraged Bertuzzi to flip that switch on. It doesn't come naturally to him, but he did show a willingness to thump a little more; his game is elevated when he does.

THE INTANGIBLES

Bertuzzi's 1998-99 season was just about a washout due to two serious injuries. He came back very strong last season. He needs to be handled gently by the coaching staff, with an arm around his shoulder and a kick to the butt administered at the right times. He is now a top-line player with the Canucks, and should gain confidence from that. He's a also a fan favourite. It's been a long time since Bertuzzi has felt this good about his game.

PROJECTION

Bertuzzi started slowly (two goals in his first 16 games), as was to be expected from a player coming off knee surgery. He finished well, with nine in his last 12, after a failed experiment at centre. The finish is a good indicator that he will reach the 30-goal category.

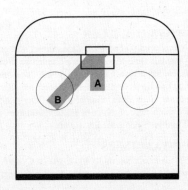

MIKE BROWN

Yrs. of NHL service: 0
Born: Surrey, B.C.; Apr. 27, 1979
Position: left wing
Height: 6-5
Weight: 230
Uniform no.: n.a.
Shoots: left

Career AHL statistics:
GP	G	A	TP	PIM
71	13	18	21	284

LAST SEASON
Will be entering first NHL season. Appeared in 71 games with Syracuse (AHL), scoring 13-18 — 21.

THE FINESSE GAME
Brown was part of the package that came to the Canucks in return for Pavel Bure in 1999. The two players couldn't be more disparate.

Brown is all brawn, but since goons are dinosaurs in today's NHL, Brown has continued to hone the other parts of his game — while getting a good deal of space, we might add. He is an intense competitor, and does what it takes to win, whether it's throw a punch, forecheck like a freight train or score a goal. He has deceptively good hands for a player of his style, and deceptively good moves. In a few years, he may be able to do what Chris Simon is now doing for the Caps: score goals, screen the goalie on the power play *and* protect his linemates.

Of course, he will never be an NHL sniper, and he is going to have to work for his goals. His skating also continues to need work, but he's close.

THE PHYSICAL GAME
Brown has added 45 pounds since his draft year — Florida took him 20th overall in 1997, when he weighed a mere 185 pounds — and it's mostly muscle. He's a mean, nasty hitter who finishes every check and does so with authority.

THE INTANGIBLES
The Canucks were anticipating a lengthy contract battle with restricted free agent (and team penalty leader) Donald Brashear, and here is part of the reason why. Brown is the next big heavyweight in the NHL. He accumulated 284 penalty minutes with the Crunch last season.

PROJECTION
Could stick as a fourth-liner if Brashear and the Canucks can't come to terms. Even if they do, Brown should be on the roster in the second half of the season, with Brashear probably moved.

ANDREW CASSELS

Yrs. of NHL service: 10
Born: Bramalea, Ont.; July 23, 1969
Position: centre
Height: 6-0
Weight: 192
Uniform no.: 21
Shoots: left

Career statistics:

GP	G	A	TP	PIM
728	151	369	520	308

1996-97 statistics:

GP	G	A	TP	+/-	PIM	PP	SH	GW	GT	S	PCT
81	22	44	66	-16	46	8	0	2	0	142	15.5

1997-98 statistics:

GP	G	A	TP	+/-	PIM	PP	SH	GW	GT	S	PCT
81	17	27	44	-7	32	6	1	2	1	138	12.3

1998-99 statistics:

GP	G	A	TP	+/-	PIM	PP	SH	GW	GT	S	PCT
70	12	25	37	-12	18	4	1	3	0	97	12.4

1999-2000 statistics:

GP	G	A	TP	+/-	PIM	PP	SH	GW	GT	S	PCT
79	17	45	62	+8	16	6	0	1	0	109	15.6

LAST SEASON

Led team in assists. Second on team in points and shooting percentage. Tied for second on team in power-play goals. Tied for third on team in goals. Missed three games with sprained thumb.

THE FINESSE GAME

When it comes to hockey smarts, Cassels is a member of Mensa. He is an intelligent player with terrific hockey instincts, who knows when to recognize passing situations, when to move the puck and who to move it to. He has a good backhand pass in traffic and is almost as good on his backhand as his forehand.

Cassels just hates to shoot. He won't do it much, and although he has spent a great deal of time practising it, his release is just not NHL calibre. He has quick hands, though, and can swipe a shot off a bouncing puck in midair. He doesn't always fight through checks to get the kind of shots he should.

A mainstay on both specialty teams, Cassels has improved on draws. He backchecks and blocks shots. He has good speed but lacks one-step quickness. He has improved his puckhandling at a high tempo.

THE PHYSICAL GAME

To complement his brains, Cassels needs brawn. He faces a lot of defensive pressure, especially as a number one centre in Vancouver. He does not force his way through strong forechecks and traffic around the net. He tends to get run down late in the season or during a tough stretch in the schedule, and when he gets fatigued he is not nearly as effective.

THE INTANGIBLES

Cassels signed a three-year, $7.2-million deal in 1999, and is turning out to be a free-agent bargain.

PROJECTION

Cassels exceeded, by far, the 40 points we projected for him last season. As the top centre for the Canucks, he will get a ton of quality ice time and should score in the 60-point range.

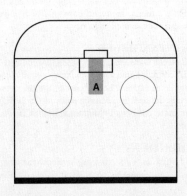

HAROLD DRUKEN

Yrs. of NHL service: 1
Born: St. John's Nfld.; Jan. 26, 1979
Position: centre
Height: 6-0
Weight: 202
Uniform no.: 15
Shoots: left

Career statistics:

GP	G	A	TP	PIM
33	7	9	16	10

1999-2000 statistics:

GP	G	A	TP	+/-	PIM	PP	SH	GW	GT	S	PCT
33	7	9	16	+14	10	2	0	0	0	69	10.1

LAST SEASON

First NHL season. Led team and tied for fourth among NHL rookies in plus-minus. Appeared in 47 games with Syracuse (AHL), scoring 20-25 — 45.

THE FINESSE GAME

A point-a-game player at the minor-league level, Druken is never likely to achieve that level of production in the NHL. He very offensive-minded, however, and has some attractive skills that put him at the head of the Canucks' freshman class last season. In just 33 games, he displayed a nose for the net and earned some power-play time on the second unit. He has excellent offensive instincts and is an opportunistic scorer.

He doesn't have great speed, but Druken doesn't look out of place and can compete. He worked hard on the defensive part of his game, which was considered a major liability. He forechecks diligently and intelligently. He had only three "minus" games, an impressive stat for a 21-year-old.

Druken can play centre or wing and could build a 10-year career if he keeps doing what he did in his brief stint last season. He will not look out of place with the more highly skilled forwards on the Canucks.

THE PHYSICAL GAME

Druken is not very tall but he is solid. He displayed some grit last season, though, an indication to the coaching staff that he wants an NHL job. The Canucks coaching staff want him to improve his conditioning.

THE INTANGIBLES

In 1999, the Canucks nearly lost Druken's rights, signing him just in time before he went back into the entry draft. Druken started the season with the Canucks, was wisely sent to the minors in December, and played well after his February return to the parent club.

PROJECTION

Druken will be penciled in as a third- or fourth-line player, but he is versatile and his skills will allow him to fill in here and there when injuries strike. He could score 25 points in a part-time role.

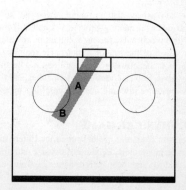

ED JOVANOVSKI

Yrs. of NHL service: 5
Born: Windsor, Ont.; June 26, 1976
Position: left defense
Height: 6-2
Weight: 205
Uniform no.: 55
Shoots: left

Career statistics:

GP	G	A	TP	PIM
359	36	84	120	647

1996-97 statistics:

GP	G	A	TP	+/-	PIM	PP	SH	GW	GT	S	PCT
61	7	16	23	-1	172	3	0	1	0	80	8.8

1997-98 statistics:

GP	G	A	TP	+/-	PIM	PP	SH	GW	GT	S	PCT
81	9	14	23	-12	158	2	1	3	1	142	6.3

1998-99 statistics:

GP	G	A	TP	+/-	PIM	PP	SH	GW	GT	S	PCT
72	5	22	27	-9	126	1	0	1	0	109	4.6

1999-2000 statistics:

GP	G	A	TP	+/-	PIM	PP	SH	GW	GT	S	PCT
75	5	21	26	-3	54	1	0	1	0	109	4.6

LAST SEASON

Led team defensemen in points. Missed six games with groin injury. Missed one game due to coach's decision.

THE FINESSE GAME

Jovanovski started playing hockey later than most NHLers, and his skating, which has improved dramatically, may still be improved a notch. He already streaks through the neutral zone like a freight train. He sure isn't pretty, but he's powerful.

Strong on his feet with a dynamic, quick stride, Jovanovski has more quickness than most big men, perhaps because of early soccer training, and he can use his feet to move the puck if his stick is tied up. His powerful hitting is made more wicked by the fact that he gets so much speed and leg drive. He can make plays, too. He gets a little time because his speed forces the opposition to back off, and he has a nice passing touch.

Jovanovski can also score, but he does not possess a great decision-making process yet and still makes some bad pinches. He has an excellent point shot and good vision of the ice for passing. He may develop along Scott Stevens/Ray Bourque lines and become a defenseman who can dominate in all zones. All of his skills are quite raw and are still catching up to his body.

THE PHYSICAL GAME

Jovanovski is among the best open-ice hitters in the NHL. He hits to hurt. Because of his size and agility, he is able to catch people right where he wants them. They aren't dirty hits, but they are real old-time

hockey throwbacks, administered by a modern-sized defenseman.

The problem is that instead of neutralizing the Brendan Shanahans and the Eric Lindroses, Jovanovski is diverted from his game by smaller, peskier players. He is so easy to distract that this must be at the top of every teams' game plan against the Canucks. He has to play smarter.

THE INTANGIBLES

Jovanovski cut down on bad penalties, quit running around looking for big hits, reduced his errors and tried to make the game more simple. It all worked. Do it again.

PROJECTION

By concentrating on the defensive part of his game, Jovanovski's offense came to him more easily. In the second half of the season, when the Canucks still had a glimmer of a hope of making the playoffs, Jovanovski reverted to his fine rookie form and was one of the club's best players. He can score 30 points.

TRENT KLATT

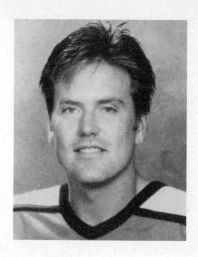

Yrs. of NHL service: 8
Born: Robbinsdale, Minn.; Jan. 30, 1971
Position: right wing
Height: 6-1
Weight: 205
Uniform no.: 26
Shoots: right

Career statistics:

GP	G	A	TP	PIM
507	89	134	223	212

1996-97 statistics:

GP	G	A	TP	+/-	PIM	PP	SH	GW	GT	S	PCT
76	24	21	45	+9	20	5	5	5	0	131	18.3

1997-98 statistics:

GP	G	A	TP	+/-	PIM	PP	SH	GW	GT	S	PCT
82	14	28	42	+2	16	5	0	3	0	143	9.8

1998-99 statistics:

GP	G	A	TP	+/-	PIM	PP	SH	GW	GT	S	PCT
75	4	10	14	-3	12	0	0	0	0	60	6.7

1999-2000 statistics:

GP	G	A	TP	+/-	PIM	PP	SH	GW	GT	S	PCT
47	10	10	20	-8	26	8	0	0	0	100	10.0

LAST SEASON

Led team in power-play goals. Appeared in 24 games with Syracuse (AHL), scoring 13-10 — 23.

THE FINESSE GAME

On a team populated by kids and finesse players, Klatt sticks out like a mule in a Kentucky Derby post parade. But what a hard-working mule he is.

Klatt is something of a choppy skater who doesn't have much use for the fancy stuff. He goes straight ahead — usually until he runs into someone from the other side.

Klatt is a player who can be sent onto the ice for the shift following a goal. In those situations, such players are trusted to continue the momentum if the goal was scored by their team, or reverse the momentum if the goal was scored by the opposition. Deployment at those times is a real compliment; Klatt earns it.

Klatt has a full-bore forechecking style that leads to turnovers. Alas, he doesn't have the hand skills to do much with his chances. But how's this for a stat: eight of his 10 goals came on the power play. Grit happens.

THE PHYSICAL GAME

Klatt looks harmless enough but he is a murderous hitter, thanks to strong leg drive and a powerful upper body. He is 210 densely packed pounds, and his body checks can pack the wallop of a warhead. He may like the regular hits but he will go for the monster hit, the one guys feel for a week, every chance he gets. Those body slams can lift the whole bench. The more Klatt hits, the more the home fans are in the game. Anything else he provides is a bonus.

THE INTANGIBLES

Klatt salvaged his season, and possibly his career, after clearing waivers in a first-half demotion to the minors. He is a third-liner who has enough desire to play on the power play and fill in on the top two lines. And how's this for a bargain: the Flyers are paying his salary as the terms from the 1998 trade that brought him to the Canucks.

PROJECTION

Some checkers remain checkers because there is no pressure to score or do things on the offensive side of the puck; your job is merely to harry your opponent into a turnover or a less dangerous play. It is safe to pencil Klatt in for about 15 goals, and they'll all be honest ones. He is a starter on the NHL's All-Hard-Work Team.

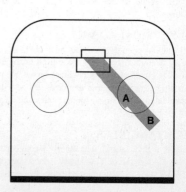

BRENDAN MORRISON

Yrs. of NHL service: 2
Born: North Vancouver, B.C.; Aug. 12, 1975
Position: centre
Height: 5-11
Weight: 180
Uniform no.: 9
Shoots: left

Career statistics:

GP	G	A	TP	PIM
143	25	65	90	36

1997-98 statistics:

GP	G	A	TP	+/-	PIM	PP	SH	GW	GT	S	PCT
11	5	4	9	+3	0	0	0	1	1	19	26.3

1998-99 statistics:

GP	G	A	TP	+/-	PIM	PP	SH	GW	GT	S	PCT
76	13	33	46	-4	18	5	0	2	0	111	11.7

1999-2000 statistics:

GP	G	A	TP	+/-	PIM	PP	SH	GW	GT	S	PCT
56	7	28	35	+12	18	2	0	1	0	96	7.3

LAST SEASON

Acquired from New Jersey with Denis Pederson for Alexander Mogilny, Mar. 14, 2000. Second NHL season. Second on Canucks in plus-minus. Missed eight games in contract dispute with New Jersey.

THE FINESSE GAME

Morrison's hockey sense and vision are outstanding. He works especially well with players of a similar mind, but they are in short supply in Vancouver. He will need to make players who play with him better, a tall task for the third-year centre.

Morrison has a world of confidence in his abilities, almost to the points of cockiness, and he will try some daring and creative moves. He has soft hands for passing and he isn't shy about shooting, using a selection of deceptive and accurate shots. He can work low on the power play or at the point, and he sees all of his options quickly. He doesn't panic and is poised with the puck.

He is a strong skater, with balance, quickness, agility and breakaway speed. Morrison has no trouble with NHL speed, except when it comes to defensive decisions.

THE PHYSICAL GAME

Small but wise enough to stay out of trouble, Morrison has wiry strength for playing in the high traffic areas. He loves to create plays from behind the net. He plays with a little edge to him that demonstrates he will not be intimidated. He is strong on his skates and tough to knock off balance.

THE INTANGIBLES

Morrison, a B.C. native, was clearly happy with the deal that got him out of New Jersey's deep system. He scored 2-7 — 9 in 12 games with the Canucks, and now that Mark Messier is gone, he has every chance to be the number two centre behind Andrew Cassels.

PROJECTION

Morrison will get the kind of quality ice time and special teams play to move him into the 55-point range.

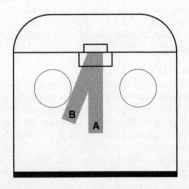

MARKUS NASLUND

Yrs. of NHL service: 7
Born: Bonassund, Sweden; July 30, 1973
Position: left/right wing
Height: 6-0
Weight: 186
Uniform no.: 19
Shoots: left

Career statistics:

GP	G	A	TP	PIM
477	126	150	276	295

1996-97 statistics:

GP	G	A	TP	+/-	PIM	PP	SH	GW	GT	S	PCT
78	21	20	41	-15	30	4	0	4	0	120	17.5

1997-98 statistics:

GP	G	A	TP	+/-	PIM	PP	SH	GW	GT	S	PCT
76	14	20	34	+5	56	2	1	0	0	106	13.2

1998-99 statistics:

GP	G	A	TP	+/-	PIM	PP	SH	GW	GT	S	PCT
80	36	30	66	-13	74	15	2	3	1	205	17.6

1999-2000 statistics:

GP	G	A	TP	+/-	PIM	PP	SH	GW	GT	S	PCT
82	27	38	65	-5	64	6	2	3	1	271	10.0

LAST SEASON

Led team in goals and points for second consecutive season. Led team in shots. Tied for team lead in short-handed goals. Second on team in assists with career high. Tied for second on team in power-play goals. Tied for third on team in game-winning goals. Only Canuck to appear in all 82 games.

THE FINESSE GAME

Naslund is a pure sniper. He has excellent snap and wrist shots and can score in just about every way imaginable, including the backhand in tight. He has quick hands and an accurate touch.

He needs to play with people who will get him the puck. He will not play aggressively and dig in the corners for the puck, and he's a little shy in traffic. But he's a jitterbug on the ice and can keep up with the fastest linemates. He is also confident with the puck, and loves to toast defensemen with an inside-outside move.

Naslund has good hockey sense in the attacking zone, though he does not play well defensively. He loses his assignments and tends to shy away from the boards. He needs to work on his game to become more than a one-way winger.

THE PHYSICAL GAME

Naslund is erratic in his physical play. Some nights he plays a little bigger, and makes something of a pest out of himself; other nights he's invisible. He needs to be involved on a nightly basis.

THE INTANGIBLES

Naslund and Peter Forsberg were born 10 days apart, but they are a world apart in NHL accomplishment. Naslund, a former first-round draft pick (by Pittsburgh in 1991), has never lived up to the hype that surrounded his first few seasons in the NHL. Consistency still eludes him.

PROJECTION

Two seasons ago, Naslund scored a career-high 36 goals. As the number one winger this season, and with a slightly better supporting cast, he is due to return to the 35- to 40-goal range.

MATTIAS OHLUND

Yrs. of NHL service: 3
Born: Pitea, Sweden; Sept. 9, 1976
Position: defense
Height: 6-3
Weight: 209
Uniform no.: 2
Shoots: left

Career statistics:

GP	G	A	TP	PIM
193	20	65	85	183

1997-98 statistics:

GP	G	A	TP	+/-	PIM	PP	SH	GW	GT	S	PCT
77	7	23	30	+3	76	1	0	0	0	172	4.1

1998-99 statistics:

GP	G	A	TP	+/-	PIM	PP	SH	GW	GT	S	PCT
74	9	26	35	-19	83	2	1	1	0	129	7.0

1999-2000 statistics:

GP	G	A	TP	+/-	PIM	PP	SH	GW	GT	S	PCT
42	4	16	20	+6	24	2	1	1	0	63	6.3

LAST SEASON

Missed 38 games with eye injury and surgery.

THE FINESSE GAME

Ohlund has a high skill level and a big body to go with it. He is a lovely, fluid skater with splendid agility for his size. He's very confident with the puck. Because of his skating and his reach, he is difficult to beat one-on-one. He isn't fooled by dekes, either. He plays the crest and maintains his position.

Ohlund is a good power-play player from the right point, and he gets first-unit power-play time. He uses an effective, short backswing on his one-timer. He makes a sharp first pass out of the defensive zone, and gets involved in the attack by moving up into the rush (but he won't get caught deep very often).

Ohlund just keeps growing, but unlike many young skaters who experience sudden growth spurts, he has stayed balanced in his skating.

THE PHYSICAL GAME

Ohlund is big and powerful. He is assertive, won't be intimidated and finishes his checks. He clears out the front of the net and works the boards and corners. For a player considered to be a finesse defenseman, he plays an involved game. He has an iron constitution and averaged 27 minutes of ice time a night last year.

THE INTANGIBLES

How his career-threatening eye injury will affect Ohlund remains to be seen, especially since he faced the possibility of more surgery after last season. At his peak, Ohlund is one of the best young defensemen in the NHL. He has all of the mental and physical tools.

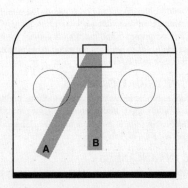

PROJECTION

If healthy, Ohlund is capable of 40 points.

DENIS PEDERSON

Yrs. of NHL service: 4
Born: Prince Albert, Sask.; Sept. 10, 1975
Position: centre/left wing
Height: 6-2
Weight: 190
Uniform no.: 10
Shoots: right

Career statistics:

GP	G	A	TP	PIM
283	47	51	98	243

1996-97 statistics:

GP	G	A	TP	+/-	PIM	PP	SH	GW	GT	S	PCT
70	12	20	32	+7	62	3	0	3	0	106	11.3

1997-98 statistics:

GP	G	A	TP	+/-	PIM	PP	SH	GW	GT	S	PCT
80	15	13	28	-6	97	7	0	1	1	135	11.1

1998-99 statistics:

GP	G	A	TP	+/-	PIM	PP	SH	GW	GT	S	PCT
76	11	12	23	-10	66	3	0	1	0	145	7.6

1999-2000 statistics:

GP	G	A	TP	+/-	PIM	PP	SH	GW	GT	S	PCT
47	6	5	11	-6	18	0	0	1	0	56	10.7

LAST SEASON

Acquired from New Jersey with Brendan Morrison for Alexander Mogilny, Mar. 14, 2000.

THE FINESSE GAME

Pederson's versatility worked against him in New Jersey. He was asked to centre a rough-and-tumble fourth line, work on a checking line, then score as a winger on a top line. He can perform capably in all roles, but needs to find a niche. There seems to be a number two left wing's role ready and waiting for him with the Canucks. Although Pederson would be happier at centre, his natural position, at this stage he'll take the job.

Pederson is an intelligent hockey player who has the potential to develop into a solid two-way forward. His skills aren't elite level, but he makes the most of all of his abilities with his hockey sense. He showed some heady flashes of playmaking and is alert around the net for loose pucks. Most of his goals come from hard work around the cage, not pretty rushing plays. He was a scorer at the junior level and believes he can be at the NHL level as well.

Pederson can work on the power play, where he uses his size down low and crashes the net. He works well in traffic, and has nice hands for picking the puck out of a tangle of skates and sticks. He is a puck magnet because he gives a second and third effort. He has a decent array of shots, including a backhand and a wrist shot, the latter being his best weapon.

THE PHYSICAL GAME

Pederson is strong and competes hard for the puck. He has a little bit of a mean streak in him, enough to keep his opponents on their toes, and he will come unglued once in awhile. But for the most part he is a disciplined player and does not take lazy penalties. He protects the puck well with his body.

Pederson is still gaining size and strength. He should have the goods to compete against any team's power forwards on a nightly basis, though he has been susceptible to nagging injuries.

THE INTANGIBLES

Pederson served as an alternate captain in New Jersey and is a possible future captain. He is a quiet leader whose confidence was damaged by the way he was handled by the Devils, but he was a good soldier throughout his tenure there. He is a very mature player.

PROJECTION

What we like about Pederson is that he's not dainty. He will get down and dirty and earn his ice time honestly. He has a lot to learn yet, but a 20-goal season would not surprise us.

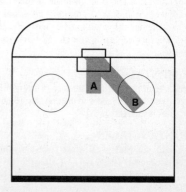

FELIX POTVIN

Yrs. of NHL service: 8
Born: Anjou, Que.; June 23, 1971
Position: goaltender
Height: 6-0
Weight: 190
Uniform no.: 29
Catches: left

Career statistics:

GP	MIN	GA	SO	GAA	A	PIM
414	24033	1148	12	2.87	10	45

1996-97 statistics:

GP	MIN	GAA	W	L	T	SO	GA	S	SAPCT	PIM
74	4271	3.15	27	36	7	0	224	2438	.908	19

1997-98 statistics:

GP	MIN	GAA	W	L	T	SO	GA	S	SAPCT	PIM
67	3864	2.73	26	33	7	5	176	1882	.906	8

1998-99 statistics:

GP	MIN	GAA	W	L	T	SO	GA	S	SAPCT	PIM
11	606	3.66	2	7	1	0	37	345	.893	0

1999-2000 statistics:

GP	MIN	GAA	W	L	T	SO	GA	S	SAPCT	PIM
34	1966	2.59	12	13	7	0	85	906	.906	2

LAST SEASON

Acquired from N.Y. Islanders with two draft choices for Bill Muckalt, Kevin Weekes and Dave Scatchard, Dec. 19, 1999. Missed five games with knee injury.

THE PHYSICAL GAME

Potvin has a habit of playing deep in his net. He prefers to keep his skates in the paint at all times, but seems to be honestly trying to play at the top of his crease instead of back on his goal line. It's a constant battle getting Potvin to leave his comfort zone.

Excellent on low shots, Potvin's style is similar to that of his idol, Patrick Roy: he likes to butterfly and flirt with leaving a five-hole for shooters. The best place to beat Potvin is high, but shooters see that tempting gap between the pads and go for it, and he snaps the pads shut.

Potvin allows very few bad rebounds. He either controls them into the corners or deadens them in front of him. He is a poor stickhandler. He doesn't use his stick well around the net to break up passes and hates to come out of his net to try to move the puck. Potvin prefers to leave the puck work to his defensemen.

THE MENTAL GAME

Players love to play for him because of his unruffled temperament. He is a leader in the dressing room and never alibis his mistakes.

THE INTANGIBLES

Potvin did not play well after first arriving in Vancouver, but he went 11-8 — 4 after the All-Star break. A restricted free agent, the Canucks did not an-ticipate having problems getting him signed in time for training camp.

PROJECTION

Potvin is not an elite goalie, but he's the best the Canucks have and the best they've had in awhile. He'll be playing behind a pretty young team, so 25 wins would be a very good showing.

PETER SCHAEFER

Yrs. of NHL service: 1
Born: Yellow Grass, Sask.; July 12, 1977
Position: left wing
Height: 5-11
Weight: 190
Uniform no.: 29
Shoots: left

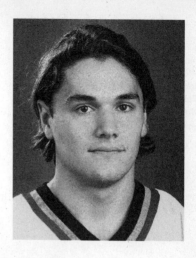

Career statistics:

GP	G	A	TP	PIM
96	20	19	39	28

1998-99 statistics:

GP	G	A	TP	+/-	PIM	PP	SH	GW	GT	S	PCT
25	4	4	8	-1	8	1	0	1	0	24	16.7

1999-2000 statistics:

GP	G	A	TP	+/-	PIM	PP	SH	GW	GT	S	PCT
71	16	15	31	0	20	2	2	4	0	101	15.8

LAST SEASON

First NHL season. Led team and second among NHL rookies in shooting percentage. Tied for team lead in shorthanded goals and game-winning goals. Missed four games with knee injury. Appeared in two games with Syracuse (AHL), scoring 0-0-0. Mised four games due to coach's decision.

THE FINESSE GAME

Schaefer is pure skill. He is a good skater with a fluid style, and he's hard to knock off his skates. He has quick moves and deceptive speed, especially when busting moves to the outside. He also has excellent one-on-one moves.

He has very good hands and is smart around the net. He can shoot the puck well with a quick release, and is also a good passer and playmaker. Schaefer forechecks aggressively and has good hockey sense. He is strong on the puck.

Schaefer likes to cheat a little bit in the defensive zone, but he is aware defensively. He just needs to apply himself a bit more.

THE PHYSICAL GAME

Schaefer has fair size and strength. Not a big hitter, he uses his body to angle the opponent out of the play. He could stand to add some upper-body muscle. He doesn't look for trouble, but won't back down. He competes most nights and is disciplined with a good work ethic.

THE INTANGIBLES

Schaefer's play and his ice time tailed off down the stretch. It's unlikely the Canucks will find room for him on the top two lines, but he could develop into a speedy checking wing with 20-goal potential — a top-notch penalty killer and shorthanded threat, much like Brian Rolston. He doesn't seem to be a favourite with the coaches, and if any of the other kids are standouts in training camp, Schaefer could be on the move.

PROJECTION

Schaefer met our expectations of a 15-goal rookie season. His top end is 20 goals, but that will come only if he gets a regular thir-line role with occasional power-play duty.

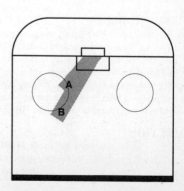

DANIEL SEDIN

Yrs. of NHL service: 0
Born: Ornskoldsvik, Sweden; Sept. 26, 1980
Position: left wing
Height: 6-1
Weight: 200
Uniform no.: n.a.
Shoots: left

Career statistics: (Swedish Elite League)

GP	G	A	TP	PIM
156	52	61	113	74

LAST SEASON

Will be entering first NHL season. Appeared in 61 games with MoDo (Swedish Elite League), scoring 27-32 — 59.

THE FINESSE GAME

Daniel Sedin is considered the finisher; his brother Henrik the playmaker. Daniel has outstanding hockey sense; he is one of those natural goal scorers to whom shooting and shot selection is a reflex. He doesn't have to think about where the puck is going. He knows what he is going to do with it before it's on his stick. He moves the puck quickly.

He has very good hockey vision and intelligence. Primarily an offensive player, it probably won't take him long to learn his defensive duties.

Daniel is fast and strong on his skates. Although he is a shooter first, he also has good playmaking skills.

THE PHYSICAL GAME

Daniel's immediate need will be to beef up. He is barely average size for an NHL forward, and the stats listing his weight seem a little generous. Considering the size of the typical NHL defenseman these days, he needs some upper-body work for the battles in the trenches.

THE INTANGIBLES

Daniel was considered the slightly more talented of the twins, ranked (and drafted) second overall in 1999, while the Canucks made a draft-day deal to love up and take Henrik with the third pick. Since the two have never played apart in Sweden, keeping the duo intact will probably help their development — unless one distances himself from the other at the NHL level.

PROJECTION

Vancouver is anxious to keep the spotlight off the twins, which will be virtually impossible. Expect both to break in on third or fourth lines. And then...not to add to the hype, but a 20-goal rookie season is not out of the question.

HENRIK SEDIN

Yrs. of NHL service: 0
Born: Ornskoldsvik, Sweden; Sept. 26, 1980
Position: centre
Height: 6-2
Weight: 200
Uniform no.: n.a.
Shoots: left

Career statistics: (Swedish Elite League)

GP	G	A	TP	PIM
149	27	73	100	62

LAST SEASON

Will be entering first NHL season. Appeared in 61 games with MoDo (Swedish Elite League), scoring 14-47 — 61.

THE FINESSE GAME

While Henrik is considered the assist man to his twin, Daniel, the scorer, he brings other talents to the table. Henrik may be better suited to the NHL style of play. He's a little bigger than his brother, and a little grittier. He doesn't have a great, soft touch with the puck, but he works hard to complete his plays.

Henrik lacks a finishing shot, so he needs to play with a shooter — like Daniel — to compensate for the fact that he's not gifted. He is a very good, powerful skater, though he doesn't have great acceleration, and he will need to work on his footwork.

HIs defensive game is advanced, but he will need to improve his work on draws. He has very good hockey sense.

THE PHYSICAL GAME

Henrik has NHL size and NHL temperament. Feisty by nature, the physical side of the game comes naturally to him. He is solid on his skates and well-balanced.

THE INTANGIBLES

Along with his twin, Henrik will garner a lot of publicity on his first go-round through the league. He will have to cope with that as well as with the pressure of breaking into the pros on a very young, not very good team.

PROJECTION

Henrik may not be a big point-getter at first, but he is going to become a very good, and very productive, two-way centre in the near future. Since the Canucks are planning to take it slow with both kids, we'll make a conservative 20-point prediction for Henrik's first season.

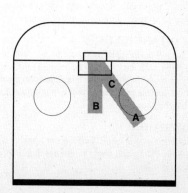

JASON STRUDWICK

Yrs. of NHL service: 3
Born: Edmonton, Alberta; July 17, 1975
Position: left defense
Height: 6-3
Weight: 215
Uniform no.: 34
Shoots: left

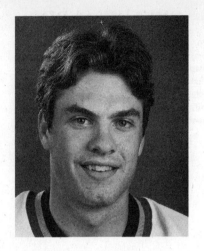

Career statistics:

GP	G	A	TP	PIM
157	1	8	9	250

1996-97 statistics:
Did not play in NHL

1997-98 statistics:

GP	G	A	TP	+/-	PIM	PP	SH	GW	GT	S	PCT
28	0	2	2	-2	65	0	8	0	0	8	0.0

1998-99 statistics:

GP	G	A	TP	+/-	PIM	PP	SH	GW	GT	S	PCT
65	0	3	3	-19	114	0	0	0	0	25	.0

1999-2000 statistics:

GP	G	A	TP	+/-	PIM	PP	SH	GW	GT	S	PCT
63	1	3	4	-13	64	0	0	0	1	18	5.6

LAST SEASON

Missed 10 games with back injury. Missed six games due to coach's decision.

THE FINESSE GAME

Strudwick is strong on his skates, but he lacks the quickness that marks his cousin Scott Niedermayer's game. Strudwick has worked hard to improve his skating, but it remains the weakest part of his game.

Strudwick has to concentrate on his positional play to compensate. He plays a fairly conservative game, won't pinch unwisely and won't step up in the neutral zone. He is learning to let the play come to him. He has a long reach and he uses it well.

Strudwick's game is heavily defense-oriented. His puck skills are okay and he is wise to limit himself. He moves the puck adequately. It would help him to play with a better skater. He is a willing shot-blocker.

THE PHYSICAL GAME

Strudwick plays an energetic and enthusiastic game. He likes to hit and makes good use of his size.

THE INTANGIBLES

Strudwick has struggled adjusting to the pace of the NHL game. If he sticks, it will be because the Canucks like the edge he brings. He will be limited to work on the third defense pair. He is on the bubble and has to play like he knows it.

PROJECTION

Strudwick's point totals will barely approach 10, though his PIM totals could be impressive if he sees enough ice time.

WASHINGTON CAPITALS

Players' Statistics 1999-2000

POS.	NO.	PLAYER	GP	G	A	PTS	+/-	PIM	PP	SH	GW	GT	S	PCT
C	77	ADAM OATES	82	15	56	71	13	14	5		6		93	16.1
D	55	SERGEI GONCHAR	73	18	36	54	26	52	5		3		181	9.9
L	17	CHRIS SIMON	75	29	20	49	11	146	7		5	1	201	14.4
L	22	STEVE KONOWALCHUK	82	16	27	43	19	80	3		1		146	11.0
R	12	PETER BONDRA	62	21	17	38	5	30	5	3	5		187	11.2
R	10	ULF DAHLEN	75	15	23	38	11	8	5		4	1	106	14.2
L	44	RICHARD ZEDNIK	69	19	16	35	6	54	1		2	3	179	10.6
D	6	CALLE JOHANSSON	82	7	25	32	13	24	1		3		138	5.1
C	8	JAN BULIS	56	9	22	31	7	30			1		92	9.8
C	11	*JEFF HALPERN	79	18	11	29	21	39	4	4	1		108	16.7
R	9	JOE MURPHY	55	12	15	27	1	94	4		2	1	118	10.2
C	13	ANDREI NIKOLISHIN	76	11	14	25	6	28		2	2		98	11.2
R	27	TERRY YAKE	61	10	14	24	4	34	3		3		55	18.2
L	14	JOE SACCO	79	7	16	23	7	50			1		117	6.0
D	15	DMITRI MIRONOV	73	3	19	22	7	28	1				99	3.0
D	2	KEN KLEE	80	7	13	20	8	79			2	2	113	6.2
C	20	*GLEN METROPOLIT	30	6	13	19	5	4	1		1		57	10.5
C	28	JAMES BLACK	49	8	9	17	-1	6	1		1		71	11.3
L	33	JIM MCKENZIE	61	4	5	9	-5	64					32	12.5
D	19	BRENDAN WITT	77	1	7	8	5	114					64	1.6
D	29	JOE REEKIE	59		7	7	21	50					32	
L	21	JEFF TOMS	20	1	2	3	-1	4			1		18	5.6
L	36	MIKE EAGLES	25	2		2	-7	15			1		13	15.4
D	4	*ALEXEI TEZIKOV	23	1	1	2	-2	2	1		1		18	5.6
D	24	ROB ZETTLER	12		2	2	-1	19					15	
G	37	OLAF KOLZIG	73		2	2	0	6						
C	23	*MIIKA ELOMO	2		1	1	1	2					3	
D	38	*NOLAN BAUMGARTNER	8		1	1	1	2					6	
L	25	BARRIE MOORE	1					0					2	
L	39	*ALEXANDER VOLCHKOV	3				-2						1	
D	3	JAMIE HUSCROFT	7				-5	11					4	
G	1	CRAIG BILLINGTON	13				0							

GP = games played; G = goals; A = assists; PTS = points; +/- = goals-for minus goals-against while player is on ice; PIM = penalties in minutes; PP = power-play goals; SH = shorthanded goals; GW = game-winning goals; GT = game-tying goals; S = no. of shots; PCT = percentage of goals to shots; * = rookie

KRIS BEECH

Yrs. of NHL service: 0
Born: Salmon Arm, B.C.; Feb. 5, 1981
Position: centre
Height: 6-2
Weight: 180
Uniform no.: n.a.
Shoots: left

Career junior statistics:

GP	G	A	TP	PIM
200	69	121	190	226

LAST SEASON

Will be entering first NHL season. Appeared in 61 games with Calgary (WHL), scoring 28-51 — 79.

THE FINESSE GAME

Beech is a 6-3 centre who can skate (right there, a good formula for future success). Comparisons to Jean Ratelle and maybe even Jean Beliveau will abound because of Beech's size, grace, reach and playmaking ability. He is an excellent skater, widely considered the best skater among the top draft prospects of 1999. He also has good anticipation. Combine that with an explosive first step and you get a hint of what an offensive force Beech could become.

A playmaker first, Beech has a quick release on his wrist shot and a low, hard, accurate slapper. He will need to play with a big winger who likes to drive to the net, so Beech can get the puck through. His defensive game is well developed.

THE PHYSICAL GAME

Beech needs to fill out. He is a little weedy, and while he was able to compete physically in junior, he will have to get a little stronger to do so at the NHL level. Part of that will come as he matures, but he will also need time with a strength coach. He plays with a little edge (he had 92 penalty minutes last year). If you push him, he'll whack you.

THE INTANGIBLES

The Caps will give him a long look in training camp, with plans to start him off on the fourth line as he adapts to the pro game. Beech comes from a successful, professionally run junior program, a good foundation for his pro career.

PROJECTION

Beech will be brought along slowly, so unless he really wows the Caps at the start, his rookie totals may not quite reach the 30-point range. He will be much heavier on assists than goals.

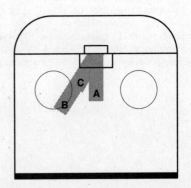

PETER BONDRA

Yrs. of NHL service: 10
Born: Luck, Ukraine; Feb. 7, 1968
Position: right wing
Height: 6-1
Weight: 200
Uniform no.: 12
Shoots: left

Career statistics:

GP	G	A	TP	PIM
672	337	246	583	465

1996-97 statistics:

GP	G	A	TP	+/-	PIM	PP	SH	GW	GT	S	PCT
77	46	31	77	+7	72	10	4	3	2	314	14.6

1997-98 statistics:

GP	G	A	TP	+/-	PIM	PP	SH	GW	GT	S	PCT
76	52	26	78	+14	44	11	5	13	2	284	18.3

1998-99 statistics:

GP	G	A	TP	+/-	PIM	PP	SH	GW	GT	S	PCT
66	31	24	55	-1	56	6	3	5	1	284	10.9

1999-2000 statistics:

GP	G	A	TP	+/-	PIM	PP	SH	GW	GT	S	PCT
62	21	17	38	+5	30	5	3	5	0	187	11.2

LAST SEASON

Second on team in goals, shorthanded goals and shots. Tied for second on team in power-play goals and game-winning goals. Missed 15 games with knee injuries. Missed five games with shoulder injury.

THE FINESSE GAME

At his best, Bondra is in the category of players you would pay to watch play. His speed is exceptional, and he makes intelligent offensive plays. He accelerates quickly and smoothly and drives defenders back because they have to play off his speed. If he gets hooked to the ice he doesn't stay down, but jumps back to his skates and gets involved in the play again, often after the defender has forgotten about him. He has excellent balance and quickness.

Bondra skates as fast with the puck as without it, and he wants the puck early. He cuts in on the off-wing and shoots in stride. He has a very good backhand shot and likes to cut out from behind the net and make things happen in tight. He mixes up his shots. He will fire quickly — not many European players have this good a slap shot — or drive in close and deke and wrist a little shot.

Bondra is a dangerous shorthanded threat with 28 shorthanded goals in the past six seasons. He makes opposing teams' power plays jittery because of his anticipation and breakaway speed, and he follows up his shots to the net and is quick to pounce on rebounds.

THE PHYSICAL GAME

Bondra isn't strong, but he will lean on people.

THE INTANGIBLES

Bondra scored his fewest goals since his rookie season in 1990-91. Two consecutive seasons with serious injuries have taken a toll, but there are other signs that Bondra's days as an elite NHL sniper are over. The Caps were entertaining offers for him last season, so he could be on the way out of Washington.

PROJECTION

Pool players should be wary of Bondra's declining production and his injury woes. Can he be a 50-goal scorer again? Doubtful. Even 40 might be a stretch.

JAN BULIS

Yrs. of NHL service: 3
Born: Paradubicc, Czech Republic; Mar. 18, 1978
Position: centre
Height: 6-0
Weight: 194
Uniform no.: 8
Shoots: left

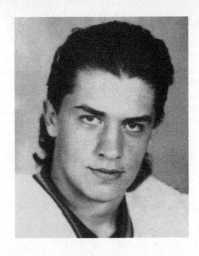

Career statistics:

GP	G	A	TP	PIM
142	21	49	70	54

1997-98 statistics:

GP	G	A	TP	+/-	PIM	PP	SH	GW	GT	S	PCT
48	5	11	16	-5	18	0	0	0	1	37	13.5

1998-99 statistics:

GP	G	A	TP	+/-	PIM	PP	SH	GW	GT	S	PCT
38	7	16	23	+3	6	3	0	3	0	57	12.3

1999-2000 statistics:

GP	G	A	TP	+/-	PIM	PP	SH	GW	GT	S	PCT
56	9	22	31	+7	30	0	0	1	0	92	9.8

LAST SEASON

Missed 20 games with shoulder injury. Missed three games with groin injury. Missed two games with rib injury. Missed one game with trapezius muscle injury.

THE FINESSE GAME

Bulis has decent size and the skating and skills to stamp him as a future top forward. He handles the puck well through traffic or in the open at high tempo. He suffered a broken hand midseason, which set back his development slightly.

More of a playmaker than a scorer, Bulis is not a pure passer. He has a quick release on his wrist shot and will take the shot if that is his better option, rather than try to force the pass. He has a good slap shot, too. His shot was clocked at close to 90 m.p.h. in his first year of junior.

Bulis plays a smart positional game and will not need too much tutoring to learn the defensive aspects of the NHL game. He is a well-conditioned athlete and has a lot of stamina to handle the ice time and travel. He is very good on draws.

THE PHYSICAL GAME

Bulis brings an infectious enthusiasm, whether it's to a game or a practice session. Like Jaromir Jagr, he is one of those players who looks like he is simply having a great time playing hockey, but Bulis is also serious about the sport. He has a work ethic that has earned him the respect of the veterans, and he'll be a quiet leader for his fellow younger players. He isn't aggressive, but he is stocky and strong on his skates. He can compete in a physical game and he likes to hit.

THE INTANGIBLES

The Caps solved nearly all of their health crises last year, except for the gifted Bulis. Hampered by an an-

kle injury in 1998-99, Bulis was just shaking off a slump when he dislocated his left shoulder. He will probably miss training camp recovering from surgery and may not be a factor until the second half of the season. His breakout season is at least a year away.

PROJECTION

The injury makes him a risky pool pick. If he can come back healthy, without missing too much of the season, he will be the number two centre behind Adam Oates. He is capable of scoring 50 points over a full season. Pro-rate accordingly.

SYLVAIN COTE

Yrs. of NHL service: 15
Born: Quebec City, Que.; Jan. 19, 1966
Position: left defense
Height: 6-0
Weight: 190
Uniform no.: 3
Shoots: right

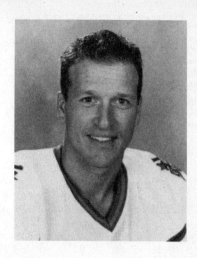

Career statistics:

GP	G	A	TP	PIM
1032	112	291	403	497

1996-97 statistics:

GP	G	A	TP	+/-	PIM	PP	SH	GW	GT	S	PCT
57	6	18	24	+11	28	2	0	0	0	131	4.6

1997-98 statistics:

GP	G	A	TP	+/-	PIM	PP	SH	GW	GT	S	PCT
71	4	21	25	-3	42	1	0	1	0	103	3.9

1998-99 statistics:

GP	G	A	TP	+/-	PIM	PP	SH	GW	GT	S	PCT
79	5	24	29	+22	28	0	0	1	0	119	4.2

1999-2000 statistics:

GP	G	A	TP	+/-	PIM	PP	SH	GW	GT	S	PCT
76	8	27	35	+3	28	5	0	2	0	128	6.3

LAST SEASON

Acquired by Chicago from Toronto for a second-round draft choice in 2001, Oct. 8, 1999. Acquired by Dallas from Chicago with Dave Manson for Kevin Dean, Derek Plante and a second-round draft choice in 2001, Feb. 8, 2000. Missed four games with hamstring injury. Missed one game due to coach's decision.

THE FINESSE GAME

Cote is a solid two-way defenseman. He has good puckhandling skills and can make a pass to his forehand or backhand side with confidence. He overhandles the puck at times, especially in his defensive zone. When he gets into trouble he seems to struggle with his forehand clearances off the left-wing boards.

Cote can do everything in stride. Carrying the puck does not slow him down and he can rush end to end. He is gifted in all skating areas: fine agility, good balance, quick stops and starts. He likes to bring the puck up on the power play. He gets a lot on his shot from the point, which causes rebounds, and it's the source of most of his assists.

Cote has decent hockey sense. He can lead a rush or come into the play as a trailer, but he knows enough not to force and to play more conservatively when the situation dictates. His skating covers up for most of his defensive lapses. His instincts lag well behind his skill level. He can be beaten one-on-one but it takes a good player to do it.

THE PHYSICAL GAME

Cote doesn't have great size, but he is a solid hitter who finishes his checks. He isn't mean, however, and will occasionally fall into the trap of playing the puck instead of the man.

THE INTANGIBLES

Cote's skill levels are beginning to erode slightly with age and wear and tear. He was a good pickup for Dallas, where he is ideally slotted as a number five or six defenseman. An unrestricted free agent, he needs to find another home where he can fulfill the same function.

PROJECTION

If Cote can get the ice time, he can score 25 to 30 points.

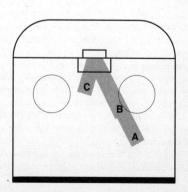

SERGEI GONCHAR

Yrs. of NHL service: 6
Born: Chelyabinsk, Russia; Apr. 13, 1974
Position: left defense
Height: 6-2
Weight: 212
Uniform no.: 55
Shoots: left

Career statistics:

GP	G	A	TP	PIM
364	74	110	184	293

1996-97 statistics:

GP	G	A	TP	+/-	PIM	PP	SH	GW	GT	S	PCT
57	13	17	30	-11	36	3	0	3	0	129	10.1

1997-98 statistics:

GP	G	A	TP	+/-	PIM	PP	SH	GW	GT	S	PCT
72	5	16	21	+2	66	2	0	0	0	134	3.7

1998-99 statistics:

GP	G	A	TP	+/-	PIM	PP	SH	GW	GT	S	PCT
53	21	10	31	+1	57	13	1	3	0	180	11.7

1999-2000 statistics:

GP	G	A	TP	+/-	PIM	PP	SH	GW	GT	S	PCT
73	18	36	54	+26	52	5	0	3	0	181	9.9

LAST SEASON

Led team defensemen in points for second consecutive season. Sixth among NHL defensemen in points. Led team in plus-minus. Second on team in assists and points. Career high in assists. Tied for second on team in power-play goals. Third on team in shots. Missed five games with back injury. Missed four games with neck injuries.

THE FINESSE GAME

It's difficult to believe that Gonchar was known as a defensive defenseman in Russia. He sees the ice well and passes well, but he never put up any big offensive numbers before coming into the NHL. Unlike most young defensemen who have to work in their own end to develop an NHL-calibre game, Gonchar made the quick jump to becoming a complete player by adding offense. He becomes a little too involved with the offensive game, however, and frequently lapses into making high-risk passes. Then when the scoring slumps come, and they do, Gonchar needs to remember to do the other things to help his team win a game.

Gonchar jumps up into the play willingly and intelligently. He has a natural feel for the flow of a game and makes tape-to-tape feeds through people — even under pressure. He sees first-unit power-play time on the point and is maturing into a first-rate quarterback. He plays heads-up. He doesn't have the blazing speed that elite defensemen have when carrying the puck, but he will gain the zone with some speed. He is an excellent passer.

Gonchar's shot is accurate enough but it won't terrorize any goalies. He doesn't push the puck forward and step into it like Al MacInnis. Most of the time he is content with getting it on the net, though he is not reluctant to shoot.

THE PHYSICAL GAME

Gonchar is strong on his skates and has worked hard on his off-ice conditioning. His defense is based more on reads and positional play than on a physical element. He was known as an aggressive player by Russian standards, but he won't run people. Teams like to target him early to scare him off his best effort.

THE INTANGIBLES

Gonchar's 39 goals are the most scored by an NHL defenseman during the past two seasons.

PROJECTION

Just as we expected, Gonchar provided 50 to 55 points last season, and played better defense. He just needs to remain consistent.

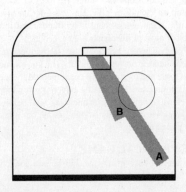

JEFF HALPERN

Yrs. of NHL service: 1
Born: Potomac, MD; May 3, 1976
Position: centre
Height: 6-0
Weight: 195
Uniform no.: 11
Shoots: right

Career statistics:

GP	G	A	TP	PIM
79	18	11	29	39

1999-2000 statistics:

GP	G	A	TP	+/-	PIM	PP	SH	GW	GT	S	PCT
79	18	11	29	+21	39	4	0	2	1	118	10.2

LAST SEASON

First NHL season. Led team in shorthanded goals and shooting percentage. Led NHL rookies in shooting percentage. Tied for first among NHL rookies and second on team in plus-minus. Sixth among NHL rookies in goals. Missed three games with back spasms.

THE FINESSE GAME

Just a local hero? That's what the Caps might have thought when they signed this D.C.-area native out of Princeton in 1999. But Halpern quickly proved he was no novelty act. His training camp showing earned him a job on the fourth line, and by the end of the season he was a mainstay on the third line.

A reliable, low-risk forward, Halpern has even strength, and was rarely on the ice for a goal against last season. But forget about those goals for a minute. Halpern's job as a goal preventer was incredible for so young a player. He can play centre or wing, though is more effective in the middle.

THE PHYSICAL GAME

Halpern isn't big, but he plays with a quiet kind of toughness.

THE INTANGIBLES

Halpern is locked in as the team's third-line centre. He was handled correctly by coach Ron Wilson, who made sure Halpern wasn't overmatched and that each of his "lessons" was gradual. Halpern will continue to upgrade his game as his responsibilities intensify.

PROJECTION

We don't expect a step back for Halpern. He should be in the 15- to 20-goal range as a solid defensive forward.

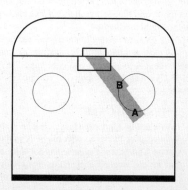

CALLE JOHANSSON

Yrs. of NHL service: 13
Born: Goteborg, Sweden; Feb. 14, 1967
Position: left defense
Height: 5-11
Weight: 200
Uniform no.: 6
Shoots: left

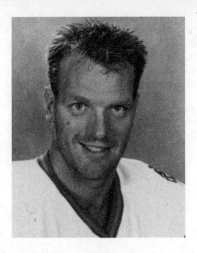

Career statistics:

GP	G	A	TP	PIM
932	107	369	476	463

1996-97 statistics:

GP	G	A	TP	+/-	PIM	PP	SH	GW	GT	S	PCT
65	6	11	17	-2	16	2	0	0	0	133	4.5

1997-98 statistics:

GP	G	A	TP	+/-	PIM	PP	SH	GW	GT	S	PCT
73	15	20	35	-11	30	10	1	1	2	163	9.2

1998-99 statistics:

GP	G	A	TP	+/-	PIM	PP	SH	GW	GT	S	PCT
67	8	21	29	+10	22	2	0	2	1	145	5.5

1999-2000 statistics:

GP	G	A	TP	+/-	PIM	PP	SH	GW	GT	S	PCT
82	7	25	32	+13	24	1	0	3	0	138	5.1

LAST SEASON

One of three Capitals to appear in all 82 games.

THE FINESSE GAME

Johansson has tremendous legs: notably big, strong thighs that generate the power for his shot and his explosive skating. He makes every move look easy. He is agile, mobile and great at moving up-ice with the play. Speed, balance and strength allow him to chase a puck behind the net, pick it up without stopping and make an accurate pass. He is confident, even on the backhand, and likes to have the puck in key spots.

Johansson is also smart offensively. He moves the puck with a good first pass, then has enough speed and instinct to jump up and be ready for a return pass. He keeps the gap tight as the play enters the attacking zone, which opens up more options: he is available to the forwards if they need him for offense, and closer to the puck if it is turned over to the opposition.

Johansson has a low, accurate shot that can be tipped. He is unselfish to a fault, often looking to pass when he should use his shot.

He has good defensive instincts and reads plays well. His skating gives him the confidence (maybe overconfidence) to gamble and challenge the puck carrier. He has a quick stick for poke- and sweep-checks.

THE PHYSICAL GAME

Johansson is not an aggressive player, but he is strong and knows what he has to do with his body in the defensive zone. This part of the game has not come naturally, but he has worked at it. He is not an impact player defensively, though he wins his share of the one-on-one battles because he gets so much power from his legs. He stays in good condition and can (and does) give a team a lot of minutes.

THE INTANGIBLES

Johansson was signed to a contract extension midway through the season. He is a steadying force who will help some of the Caps' younger defensemen, like Alexei Tezikov, develop. He was essential to Brendan Witt's emergence as an NHL force. He is one of the most underrated defensemen in the league.

PROJECTION

Johansson should again produce around 35 points as one of the Caps' top four.

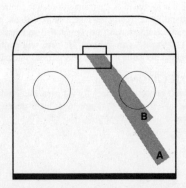

KEN KLEE

Yrs. of NHL service: 5
Born: Indianapolis, IN; Apr. 24, 1971
Position: right wing/defense
Height: 6-1
Weight: 205
Uniform no.: 2
Shoots: right

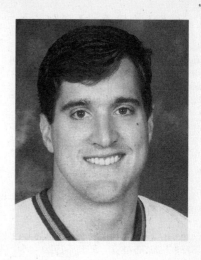

Career statistics:

GP	G	A	TP	PIM
378	32	40	72	421

1996-97 statistics:

GP	G	A	TP	+/-	PIM	PP	SH	GW	GT	S	PCT
80	3	8	11	-5	115	0	0	2	0	108	2.8

1997-98 statistics:

GP	G	A	TP	+/-	PIM	PP	SH	GW	GT	S	PCT
51	4	2	6	-3	46	0	0	1	0	44	9.1

1998-99 statistics:

GP	G	A	TP	+/-	PIM	PP	SH	GW	GT	S	PCT
78	7	13	20	-9	80	0	0	1	0	132	5.3

1999-2000 statistics:

GP	G	A	TP	+/-	PIM	PP	SH	GW	GT	S	PCT
80	7	13	20	+8	79	0	0	2	2	113	6.2

PROJECTION

Klee won't reach double-digits in goals, but he will again provide reliable defense and 15 to 20 points a season.

LAST SEASON

Matched career high in points. Missed one game with foot injury. Missed one game due to coach's decision.

THE FINESSE GAME

The Caps were able to stay healthy enough to keep from doing the forward-defense switch with the malleable Klee, and he was able to be a better defenseman because of it.

Steady and low-risk, Klee is an unsung hero of the Caps' defense. He does nothing fancy. A good skater, he makes the safe plays, acts as a safety valve for his teammates, and does whatever the coaches ask of him. He was able to play a very steady game alongside mistake-happy Dmitri Mironov.

Klee doesn't have great hands. He has a decent shot from the point, so he can handle some point duty on the power play when everyone else is tired. He is not overly creative.

He is one of those players you don't miss until he's out of the lineup. Fortuantely for the Caps, he has proven pretty durable.

THE PHYSICAL GAME

Klee isn't one of the biggest players around but he is solid and uses his body well, either on the forecheck when he is playing wing or in his own zone when he is on defense.

THE INTANGIBLES

Klee will probably be one of the Caps' top five defensemen.

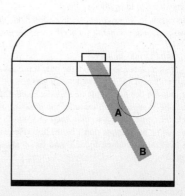

OLAF KOLZIG

Yrs. of NHL service: 5
Born: Johannesburg, South Africa; Apr. 9, 1970
Position: goaltender
Height: 6-3
Weight: 225
Uniform no.: 37
Catches: left

Career statistics:

GP	MIN	GA	SO	GAA	A	PIM
272	15375	637	16	2.49	5	47

1996-97 statistics:

GP	MIN	GAA	W	L	T	SO	GA	S	SAPCT	PIM
29	1644	2.59	8	15	4	2	71	758	.906	4

1997-98 statistics:

GP	MIN	GAA	W	L	T	SO	GA	S	SAPCT	PIM
64	3788	2.20	33	18	10	5	139	1729	.920	12

1998-99 statistics:

GP	MIN	GAA	W	L	T	SO	GA	S	SAPCT	PIM
64	3586	2.58	26	31	3	4	154	1538	.900	19

1999-2000 statistics:

GP	MIN	GAA	W	L	T	SO	GA	S	SAPCT	PIM
73	4371	2.24	41	20	11	5	163	1957	.917	6

LAST SEASON

Career high in wins. Third among NHL goalies in wins. Led NHL goalies in minutes played with career high. Led NHL goalies in shots faced. Fourth among NHL goalies in save percentage. Tied for fourth among NHL goalies in shutouts.

THE PHYSICAL GAME

Kolzig is a big goalie with sharp reflexes and good skating ability for a player of his size. Rather than just lumber around and let the puck hit him, however, he is active and positions himself well to block as much of the net as possible from the shooter.

Kolzig was more aggressive and consistent in his technical play last season than he was in 1998-99, when both he and the Caps suffered through a poor season.

Although still not regarded as an elite NHL goalie, Kolzig is solidly among the second echelon and may soon move up to joining the leaders.

He needs to improve his stickhandling. He could use his stick better to break up plays around the net.

THE MENTAL GAME

Kolzig has matured so much in the past three seasons. He can still be a bit of a hothead in the course of a game, but for the most part he stays relaxed and focussed. He is a good influence in the dressing room and his teammates want to play hard in front of him. Bad goals or bad games don't haunt him. He always gives his team a chance to win, and he steals some games.

THE INTANGIBLES

Adding veteran backup goalie Craig Billington (on Dale Hunter's recommendation) helped Kolzig, and Billington is back for another season. But the biggest credit goes to Kolzig himself.

PROJECTION

Kolzig's equilibrium and playing behind a healthy team should mean another 30-win season. And 40 isn't out of the question.

STEVE KONOWALCHUK

Yrs. of NHL service: 8
Born: Salt Lake City, Utah; Nov. 11, 1972
Position: left wing
Height: 6-1
Weight: 195
Uniform no.: 22
Shoots: left

Career statistics:

GP	G	A	TP	PIM
500	105	145	275	438

1996-97 statistics:

GP	G	A	TP	+/-	PIM	PP	SH	GW	GT	S	PCT
78	17	25	42	-3	67	2	1	3	1	155	11.0

1997-98 statistics:

GP	G	A	TP	+/-	PIM	PP	SH	GW	GT	S	PCT
80	10	24	34	+9	80	2	0	2	0	131	7.6

1998-99 statistics:

GP	G	A	TP	+/-	PIM	PP	SH	GW	GT	S	PCT
45	12	12	24	0	26	4	1	2	0	98	12.2

1999-2000 statistics:

GP	G	A	TP	+/-	PIM	PP	SH	GW	GT	S	PCT
82	16	27	43	+19	80	3	0	1	0	146	11.0

PROJECTION

Konowalchuk is a quality guy to have, on the ice or in the dressing room, and he can score 15 to 20 goals in a third-line role.

LAST SEASON

Third on team in assists with career high. One of three Capitals to appear in all 82 games.

THE FINESSE GAME

Konowalchuk is a willing guy who plays any role asked of him. He's a digger who has to work hard for his goals, and an intelligent and earnest player who uses every ounce of energy on every shift. He is one of the Caps' most eager forecheckers.

There is nothing fancy about his offense. He just lets his shot rip and drives to the net. He doesn't have the moves and hand skills to beat a defender one-on-one, but he doesn't care; he'll go right through him. His release on his shot is improving.

Konowalchuk is reliable and intelligent defensively. On the draw, he ties up the opposing centre if he doesn't win the puck drop outright. He uses his feet along the boards as well as his stick.

THE PHYSICAL GAME

Konowalchuk is very strong. He has some grit in him, too, and will aggravate opponents with his constant effort. He doesn't take bad penalties, but often goads rivals into retaliating. He is very fit and can handle a lot of ice time.

THE INTANGIBLES

Konowalchuk is a heart-and-soul guy. He missed most of the 1998-99 season with injuries, a factor in the Caps missing the playoffs since he is one of the team's gritty leaders. Last year, he didn't miss a shift, and Washington was much better for it.

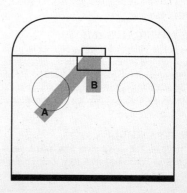

DMITRI MIRONOV

Yrs. of NHL service: 8
Born: Moscow, Russia; Dec. 25, 1965
Position: left defense
Height: 6-3
Weight: 214
Uniform no.: 15
Shoots: right

Career statistics:

GP	G	A	TP	PIM
520	51	201	252	562

1996-97 statistics:

GP	G	A	TP	+/-	PIM	PP	SH	GW	GT	S	PCT
77	13	39	52	+16	101	3	1	2	0	177	7.3

1997-98 statistics:

GP	G	A	TP	+/-	PIM	PP	SH	GW	GT	S	PCT
77	8	35	43	-7	119	3	0	1	0	170	4.7

1998-99 statistics:

GP	G	A	TP	+/-	PIM	PP	SH	GW	GT	S	PCT
46	2	14	16	-5	80	2	0	0	0	86	2.3

1999-2000 statistics:

GP	G	A	TP	+/-	PIM	PP	SH	GW	GT	S	PCT
73	3	19	22	+7	28	1	0	0	0	99	3.0

LAST SEASON

Missed four games with a bruised tailbone. Missed one game with flu. Missed four games due to coach's decision.

THE FINESSE GAME

Mironov likes to get involved in the attack — probably too involved. He can do phenomenal things with the puck. He understands the game well and can shoot bullets, but is often reluctant to let fire. He can work the puck up the ice and handle the point on the power play. He sees the ice well and is a good passer.

Mironov is a major risk factor in his own end. He can be beaten one-on-one and it is imperative that he play with a defensive defenseman. He never plays as hard in his own zone as he likes to do in the attacking zone.

Mironov was one of the few forays into the free-agent market for the Caps in the past three years, and he has likely discouraged the team from trying it again anytime soon.

THE PHYSICAL GAME

Mironov has a long reach and is big, but he plays soft and doesn't use either attribute to his best advantage. He gives up easily on plays in his own end. He likes to step up and challenge in the neutral zone but doesn't take the body well; he often lets the opponent get by him.

THE INTANGIBLES

One of the big free-agent busts from two seasons ago. Coach Ron Wilson played Rob Zettler ahead of Mironov and he is a number six defenseman at best on this squad. The Caps would dearly love to find someone to take him off their hands. If anyone is looking for a high-risk defenseman with a questionable work ethic, call George McPhee.

PROJECTION

Mironov isn't likely to get enough ice time (in Washington or elsewhere) to tally much more than 25 points.

JOE MURPHY

Yrs. of NHL service: 13
Born: London, Ont.; Oct. 16, 1967
Position: right wing
Height: 6-1
Weight: 190
Uniform no.: 17
Shoots: left

Career statistics:

GP	G	A	TP	PIM
765	232	254	486	790

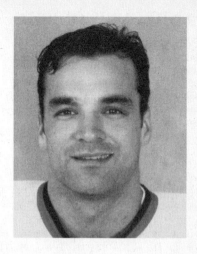

1996-97 statistics:

GP	G	A	TP	+/-	PIM	PP	SH	GW	GT	S	PCT
75	20	25	45	-1	69	4	1	2	1	151	13.2

1997-98 statistics:

GP	G	A	TP	+/-	PIM	PP	SH	GW	GT	S	PCT
37	9	13	22	+9	36	4	0	0	0	81	11.1

1998-99 statistics:

GP	G	A	TP	+/-	PIM	PP	SH	GW	GT	S	PCT
76	25	23	48	+10	73	7	0	2	1	176	14.2

1999-2000 statistics:

GP	G	A	TP	+/-	PIM	PP	SH	GW	GT	S	PCT
55	12	15	27	+1	94	4	0	2	1	118	10.2

LAST SEASON

Acquired from Boston on waivers, Feb. 10, 2000. Signed as free agent by Boston, Nov. 12, 1999. Third on Capitals in penalty minutes. Missed eight games with knee injury. Missed one game with abdominal injury.

THE FINESSE GAME

Murphy can be dangerous as a goal scorer, when he's on his game there aren't many better. He has an explosive burst of speed and can take the puck to the net. He has great hands. He is creative off the forecheck and has confidence with the puck, though he is sometimes too selfish and single-minded when he has made the decision to shoot, even when a better option to pass suddenly presents itself. He needs a pivot who can get him the puck at the right times.

Murphy has a lot of zip on his slap and wrist shots. He gets both away quickly and through a crowd, and he's been a high-percentage shooter through much of his career.

He has streaks where he is brilliant, but consistency has always eluded him, both on and off the ice.

THE PHYSICAL GAME

Murphy makes preemptive hits when going for the puck in the corners — which is a nice way of saying he picks and interferes. He will use his size and strength in front of the net to establish position, and he'll fight along the wall and in the corners. He's not a big banger or crasher, but he does have a nasty streak. Coach Ron Wilson is generally intolerant of players who take bad penalties, so that relationship could be a rocky one.

THE INTANGIBLES

A very strange guy who had a very strange odyssey. After sitting out the first two months without a contract, Murphy was brought East by the Rangers. He worked out with them one day, then signed with the Boston Bruins. The Bruins quickly tired of his act, and the Caps picked him up. Despite a brutal playoffs (no points in five games), Washington signed him to a new contract. He will probably be a top-six forward for the Capitals.

PROJECTION

Assuming he doesn't get lost in the ozone in D.C., Murphy can score 25 goals, with about one-third coming on the power play.

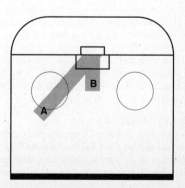

ANDREI NIKOLISHIN

Yrs. of NHL service: 6
Born: Vorkuta, Russia; March 25, 1973
Position: left wing/centre
Height: 5-11
Weight: 180
Uniform no.: 13
Shoots: left

Career statistics:

GP	G	A	TP	PIM
358	56	117	173	146

1996-97 statistics:

GP	G	A	TP	+/-	PIM	PP	SH	GW	GT	S	PCT
71	9	19	28	+3	32	1	0	0	0	98	9.2

1997-98 statistics:

GP	G	A	TP	+/-	PIM	PP	SH	GW	GT	S	PCT
38	6	10	16	+1	14	1	0	1	0	40	15.0

1998-99 statistics:

GP	G	A	TP	+/-	PIM	PP	SH	GW	GT	S	PCT
73	8	27	35	0	28	0	1	1	0	121	6.6

1999-2000 statistics:

GP	G	A	TP	+/-	PIM	PP	SH	GW	GT	S	PCT
76	11	14	25	+6	28	0	2	2	0	98	11.2

LAST SEASON

Missed four games with abdominal injury.

THE FINESSE GAME

Nikolishin is a strong skater with a powerful stride, and he makes some of the tightest turns in the league. His great talent is puckhandling, but like many Europeans he tends to hold onto the puck too long and leave himself open for hits.

He sees the ice well and is a gifted playmaker, but Nikolishin needs to shoot more so his game will be less predictable. He fits best with a finishing winger who can convert his slippery passes. He has become more of a defensive-minded forward, which means it's less likely he will earn a spot on the top two lines. He does a great job on draws — no doubt learning from Adam Oates has helped him. He backchecks, blocks shots and kills penalties.

THE PHYSICAL GAME

Nikolishin is extremely strong on his skates and likes to work in the corners for the puck. He is tough to knock off balance and has a low centre of gravity. He has adapted smoothly to the more physical style of play in the NHL, and although he isn't very big he will plow into heavy going for the puck. When he puts his mind to it, he is one of the tougher defensive forwards in the league.

THE INTANGIBLES

Nikolishin is popular with his teammates, both for his personality and his work habits. With Jan Bulis expected to miss the start of the season rehabbing a shoulder injury, Nikolishin could get some top six ice time, but once the team is healthy, his chief assignment will be as a checker.

PROJECTION

Nikolishin seems content to let his defensive game carry him. He has proven before he can put some numbers up, but it's likely he'll stay in the 30-point range.

ADAM OATES

Yrs. of NHL service: 15
Born: Weston, Ont.; Aug. 27, 1962
Position: centre
Height: 5-11
Weight: 185
Uniform no.: 77
Shoots: right

Career statistics:

GP	G	A	TP	PIM
1049	303	894	1197	335

1996-97 statistics:

GP	G	A	TP	+/-	PIM	PP	SH	GW	GT	S	PCT
80	22	60	82	-5	14	3	2	5	0	160	13.8

1997-98 statistics:

GP	G	A	TP	+/-	PIM	PP	SH	GW	GT	S	PCT
82	18	58	76	+6	36	3	2	3	0	121	14.9

1998-99 statistics:

GP	G	A	TP	+/-	PIM	PP	SH	GW	GT	S	PCT
59	12	42	54	-1	22	3	0	0	0	79	15.2

1999-2000 statistics:

GP	G	A	TP	+/-	PIM	PP	SH	GW	GT	S	PCT
82	15	56	71	+13	14	5	0	6	0	93	16.1

LAST SEASON

Led team in assists for fourth consecutive season. Second in NHL in assists. Led team in points and game-winning goals. Second on team in shooting percentage. Tied for second on team in power-play goals. One of three Caps to appear in all 82 games.

THE FINESSE GAME

Oates remains one of the elite playmakers in the NHL, defying age and battling his way back from injuries. He uses a shorter-than-average stick and a minimal curve on his blade, the result being exceptional control of the puck. Although he's a right-handed shooter, his right wings have always been his preferred receivers. He can pass on the backhand but also carries the puck deep; he shields the puck with his body and turns to make the pass to his right wing.

Use of the backhand gives Oates a tremendous edge against all but the rangiest NHL defensemen. He forces defenders to reach in and frequently draws penalties when he is hooked or tripped. If defenders don't harrass him, he then has carte blanche to work his passing magic.

Passing is Oates' first instinct, though he has a fine shot with a precise touch. Taking more shots makes him a less predictable player, since the defense can't back off and anticipate the pass. He is one of the NHL's best playmakers because of his passing ability and his creativity. He is most effective down low where he can open up more ice, especially on the power play. He has outstanding timing and vision.

Yet, Oates isn't stubborn to a fault. He will also play a dump-and-chase game if he is being shadowed closely, throwing the puck smartly into the opposite corner with just the right velocity to allow his wingers to get in on top of the defense.

He is among the top five in the league on face-offs, which makes him a natural on penalty killing; a successful draw eats up 10 to 15 seconds on the clock, minimum. It seems that every time the Caps have Oates out on the draw, they end up with the puck. That's a huge advantage in a game.

THE PHYSICAL GAME

Oates is not a physical player but he doesn't avoid contact. He's smart enough at this stage of his career to avoid the garbage, and he plays in traffic and will take a hit to make the play. He's an intense player with a wiry strength, but he tends to wear down late in the season as his line receives all the checking attention.

THE INTANGIBLES

Oates will be 38 this year and it could be his last season as a top-line centre.

PROJECTION

Oates barely missed the 80 points we projected for him last season, due to a lack of scoring depth up front. He could produce 70 again this season.

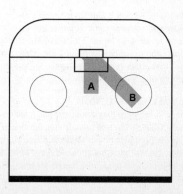

CHRIS SIMON

Yrs. of NHL service: 7
Born: Wawa, Ont.; Jan. 30, 1972
Position: left wing
Height: 6-3
Weight: 219
Uniform no.: 17
Shoots: left

Career statistics:

GP	G	A	TP	PIM
314	72	82	154	952

1996-97 statistics:

GP	G	A	TP	+/-	PIM	PP	SH	GW	GT	S	PCT
42	9	13	22	-1	165	3	0	1	0	89	10.1

1997-98 statistics:

GP	G	A	TP	+/-	PIM	PP	SH	GW	GT	S	PCT
28	7	10	17	-1	38	4	0	1	0	71	9.9

1998-99 statistics:

GP	G	A	TP	+/-	PIM	PP	SH	GW	GT	S	PCT
23	3	7	10	-4	48	0	0	0	0	29	10.3

1999-2000 statistics:

GP	G	A	TP	+/-	PIM	PP	SH	GW	GT	S	PCT
75	29	20	49	+11	146	7	0	5	1	201	14.4

LAST SEASON

Led team in goals with career high. Led team in power-play goals, penalty minutes and shots. Tied for second in team in game-winning goals. Third on team in points and shooting percentage. Career highs in assists and points. Missed seven games with neck injuries.

THE FINESSE GAME

Few players have made such a stunning transition from goon to first-line forward. Like Rick Tocchet and Bob Probert in their prime, Simon has developed into a rare blend of toughness and scoring touch.

Simon made his reputation as a brawler, but he always had some moves where he would deke a defender and score with an honest to goodnees snap shot. Simon always got a lot of room to move, and once he had it, he knew what to do with it. Simon had to improve his skating to earn more ice time, and he has.

Simon has decent hands for a big guy, and most of his successes come in tight. Now he has great confidence in his shot, so he isn't afraid to shoot from almost anywhere. He has improved the release on his shot — that extra room helps again — and he has something of a wicked slapper.

THE PHYSICAL GAME

Simon is as tough as they come and has a wide streak of mean. The difference now is that he doesn't go looking for fights. He doesn't have to prove himself as a battler. He will pick his spots. Players never know when he is going to snap, which is pretty scary. He has already established himself as a player who can throw them when the time comes, but he isn't as easily goaded into going off with another team's fourth-liner. That's beneath him, now. He unleashes some clean, mean shoulder hits on the forecheck.

THE INTANGIBLES

Simon was not only the Caps' comeback kid — his career looked in doubt after playing only 23 games in 1998-99 because of shoulder surgery — but after Olaf Kolzig, Simon was probably the team's most valuable player. Simon is truly an inspiration for players with size and raw skill who want to make themselves into something more. In Simon's case, much more.

PROJECTION

We always knew that Simon had a 20-goal season in him — really, we said it two years ago, you could look it up — but 30? Now that he has raised the bar, why not?

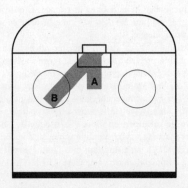

ALEXEI TEZIKOV

Yrs. of NHL service: 1
Born: Togliatti, Russia; June 22, 1978
Position: left defense
Height: 6-1
Weight: 198
Uniform no.: 4
Shoots: left

Career statistics:

GP	G	A	TP	PIM
28	1	1	2	2

1998-99 statistics:

GP	G	A	TP	+/-	PIM	PP	SH	GW	GT	S	PCT
5	0	0	0	-1	0	0	0	0	0	4	.0

1999-2000 statistics:

GP	G	A	TP	+/-	PIM	PP	SH	GW	GT	S	PCT
23	1	1	2	-2	2	1	0	1	0	18	5.6

LAST SEASON

Will be entering first full NHL season. Appeared in 33 games with Portland (AHL), scoring 16-21-37. Missed three games with back injury. Missed two games with flu.

THE FINESSE GAME

Tezikov has more raw talent than the Caps' current top offensive defenseman, Sergei Gonchar, with a little more edge to his game. He can be compared to another teammate, however, since his game is more like Calle Johansson's.

Tezikov is mobile and he can move the puck well. He has great poise. Whether he has to move the puck 10 feet or 40, he finds his target and applies the right touch. That's a real asset when it comes to avoiding the traps run by so many teams in the East.

Tezikov can't run a power play but he will jump into the play. He gets his points, yet won't be known primarily for his scoring. He is a terrific skater who likes to hit; he lines up opponents for rolling hip checks.

THE PHYSICAL GAME

Tezikov dropped the gloves a bit in junior but it's not likely he'll do so at the NHL level. He plays with a bit of a snarl, though, and while he isn't tall, he has a thick body. He brought his playing weight to an ideal 215, and he is very solid. Like Scott Niedermayer, he could develop into a finesse defenseman who will apply the body when necessary.

THE INTANGIBLES

Being on the Portland shuttle (he was recalled five times last season) didn't help Tekizov to feel comfortable. The number five job on the team appears to be his for the taking, and he could work his way up to a number four by the All-Star break.

PROJECTION

Tezikov will likely concentrate on the defensive aspects of his game, but he is capable of putting 20 points up in his first NHL season. He is one of the top rookie defense prospects.

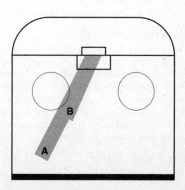

BRENDAN WITT

Yrs. of NHL service: 5
Born: Humboldt, Sask.; Feb. 20, 1975
Position: left defense
Height: 6-1
Weight: 205
Uniform no.: 19
Shoots: left

Career statistics:

GP	G	A	TP	PIM
287	9	24	33	486

1996-97 statistics:

GP	G	A	TP	+/-	PIM	PP	SH	GW	GT	S	PCT
44	3	2	5	-20	88	0	0	0	0	41	7.3

1997-98 statistics:

GP	G	A	TP	+/-	PIM	PP	SH	GW	GT	S	PCT
64	1	7	8	-11	112	0	0	0	0	68	1.5

1998-99 statistics:

GP	G	A	TP	+/-	PIM	PP	SH	GW	GT	S	PCT
54	2	5	7	-6	87	0	0	0	0	51	3.9

1999-2000 statistics:

GP	G	A	TP	+/-	PIM	PP	SH	GW	GT	S	PCT
77	1	7	8	+5	114	0	0	0	0	64	1.6

LAST SEASON

Second on team in penalty minutes. Missed two games with knee injury. Missed one game with back injury. Missed one game with groin injury. Missed one game with bruised thigh.

THE FINESSE GAME

Witt's skill level is high, if not elite, and he applies his abilities in his own zone. His skating is capable: he has worked to improve his agility, though his pivots and passing skills remain a bit rough. Still, he does not overhandle the puck, and by making simple plays he keeps himself out of serious trouble. He skates well backwards and has decent lateral mobility.

Witt gets involved somewhat in the attack, but the extent of his contribution is a hard point shot. He won't gamble low and can't run a power play. He won't ever be an offensive force.

He was one of the steadier, and sometimes scarier, presences on the Caps' blueline last season. He was effective without being flashy. His game is maturing.

THE PHYSICAL GAME

Witt has a strong physical presence on-ice but he can get stronger. He plays at around 220 pounds, though he could still add some muscle and not lose any mobility. He was beaten by some players in one-on-one battles, and a defensive defenseman can't allow that to happen. He blocks shots fearlessly, and is naturally aggressive and intimidating. He is a little too eager to fight and can be goaded into the box.

THE INTANGIBLES

Witt has continued to mature slowly and is one of the

Caps' top three defensemen, and a powerful hitter. He was a plus player for the first time in his career.

PROJECTION

Witt hasn't reached his best level yet, but he's getting closer. One very positive sign is how much he continues to improve each year. Although he won't score a lot of points he will get a lot of ice time. He will also rack up some triple-digit penalty minutes.

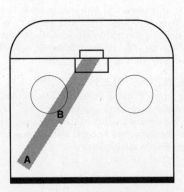

RICHARD ZEDNIK

Yrs. of NHL service: 3
Born: Bystrica, Slovakia; Jan. 6, 1976
Position: right wing
Height: 5-11
Weight: 190
Uniform no.: 44
Shoots: left

Career statistics:

GP	G	A	TP	PIM
195	47	34	81	136

1996-97 statistics:

GP	G	A	TP	+/-	PIM	PP	SH	GW	GT	S	PCT
11	2	1	3	-5	4	1	0	0	0	21	9.5

1997-98 statistics:

GP	G	A	TP	+/-	PIM	PP	SH	GW	GT	S	PCT
65	17	9	26	-2	28	2	0	2	0	148	11.5

1998-99 statistics:

GP	G	A	TP	+/-	PIM	PP	SH	GW	GT	S	PCT
49	9	8	17	-6	50	1	0	2	0	115	7.8

1999-2000 statistics:

GP	G	A	TP	+/-	PIM	PP	SH	GW	GT	S	PCT
69	19	16	35	+6	54	1	0	2	3	179	10.6

PROJECTION
Zednik should score in the range of 20 to 25 goals.

LAST SEASON
Third on team in goals. Career high in goals, assists and points. Missed 13 games with concussion.

THE FINESSE GAME
Zednik has the skating speed and hand skills to mark him as a top six forward — on a team already stocked with gifted players. He has established some nice chemistry with Jan Bulis; those two players can be expected to team in the second line once Bulis returns from his shoulder surgery.

Zednik is very good down low. He can control the game and go to the net, and he has nice hands and is not shy about shooting. He has a very low crouch and gets a lot on his shot. He could be the Caps' left-wing version of Peter Bondra, he is nearly that dynamic. He also prevents other teams from being able to key on Bondra, because Zednik is almost as dangerous.

Zednik was not effective on the power play last season and needs to capitalize more, since he can expect to get a lot of ice time with the man advantage. When his goal slumps occur, he works hard to snap out of his drought.

THE PHYSICAL GAME
Although he is not big, Zednik is strong. Coming off the wing, he just about carries defenders on his back. Solid and sturdy on his skates, he likes to get involved and isn't rattled by physical play, though he does not initiate contact.

THE INTANGIBLES
Injuries have kept Zednik from showing his best game in the past two seasons. He is ready to break out.

PLAYER INDEX